WOMEN and CRIME

To the Division on Women and Crime, in honor of their 30th anniversary (1984–2014).

SM: To my husband, Jeff, for his fierce passion and support, and to my son Keegan,
for all his smiles and laughter.

CI: To Jim, my dearest friend and partner in life; our children, Dane, Drew, & Sarah,
who bring joy to our lives every day; and J.C., who is always there for me.

WOMEN and CRIME

THE ESSENTIALS

STACY L. MALLICOAT
California State University, Fullerton

CONNIE ESTRADA IRELAND
California State University, Long Beach

SAGE

Los Angeles | London | New Delhi
Singapore | Washington DC

Los Angeles | London | New Delhi
Singapore | Washington DC

FOR INFORMATION:

SAGE Publications, Inc.
2455 Teller Road
Thousand Oaks, California 91320
E-mail: order@sagepub.com

SAGE Publications Ltd.
1 Oliver's Yard
55 City Road
London EC1Y 1SP
United Kingdom

SAGE Publications India Pvt. Ltd.
B 1/I 1 Mohan Cooperative Industrial Area
Mathura Road, New Delhi 110 044
India

SAGE Publications Asia-Pacific Pte. Ltd.
3 Church Street
#10-04 Samsung Hub
Singapore 049483

Printed in the United States of America

A catalog record of this book is available from the Library of Congress.

ISBN 978-1-4522-1717-8

Publisher: Jerry Westby
Associate Publisher: MaryAnn Vail
Production Editor: Libby Larson
Copy Editor: Erin Livingston
Typesetter: C&M Digitals (P) Ltd.
Proofreader: Dennis W. Webb
Indexer: Maria Sosnowski
Cover Designer: Edgar Abarca
Marketing Manager: Terra Schultz
Permissions Editor: Jennifer Barron

This book is printed on acid-free paper.

13 14 15 16 10 9 8 7 6 5 4 3 2 1

Contents

Detailed Contents

Preface

The purpose of this book is to introduce readers to the issues that face women as they navigate the criminal justice system. Regardless of the role they play in this participation, women have unique experiences that have significant effects on their perspectives of the system. This book seeks to inform readers on the realities of women's lives as they interact with the criminal justice system. These topics are presented in this book through summary chapters highlighting the key terms and research findings and by incorporating cutting-edge research from scholars whose works have been published in top journals in criminal justice, criminology, and related fields.

⬚ Organization and Contents of the Book

This book is divided into four major parts, each highlighting the role of women in the criminal justice system. Part I explores the foundations of feminist criminology and serves as an orientation and introduction to the study of women and crime. Part II is devoted to a discussion of women as victims, including sexual assault, intimate partner abuse and stalking, and international issues facing women today. Part III highlights issues of women as offenders, with a focus on both victimless and violent crimes committed by women. Part IV focuses on the issues that women face as professionals within the criminal justice system. Within each of these themes, we present individual chapters that highlight the critical issues facing women within each realm of the criminal justice system. Each topic area is designed to introduce students to cutting-edge research, conducted by scholars on women's issues within contemporary criminal justice. Given the interdisciplinary nature of the field of research in criminal justice, we draw on scholars in a variety of academic fields, including sociology, psychology, women's studies, criminology, and political science, to name a few. Each chapter begins with a vignette designed to highlight how several key elements within a given chapter converge in a real-life story. While the specific names in the vignettes are fictional, they weave together examples of actual women's experiences found in the literature, our own early careers as criminal justice practitioners, and our current research. The vignette runs through the entire book, telling a single fictional story constructed entirely from the combined experiences of actual women we have met, interviewed, supervised, and studied. Each chapter concludes with summary points and discussion questions to help guide students' review of the material.

Divided into four general parts, the sections in this book are organized into 14 chapters:

Part I: Foundations of Feminist Criminology

- Women and Crime: Introduction
- Research on Female Offending and Victimization
- Theories of Victimization
- Theories on Female Offending

Part II: Women as Victims

- Women and Victimization: Rape and Sexual Assault
- Women and Victimization: Intimate Partner Abuse and Stalking
- International Issues in the Victimization of Women

Part III: Women as Offenders

- Girls and Juvenile Delinquency
- Female Offenders: Drug, Property, and Victimless Crimes
- Female Offenders: Violent Crimes
- Processing and Sentencing of Female Offenders
- The Supervision and Incarceration of Women

Part IV: Women Professionals and the Criminal Justice System

- Women and Work in the Criminal Justice System: Police, Corrections, and Offender Services
- Women and Work in the Criminal Justice System: Courts and Victim Services

Part I of this book is an overview of women and crime, which has strong roots in feminist criminology. The first chapter provides an introduction and foundation for the book. This section begins with a review of the influence of feminism on the study of crime and introduces the intersections of victimization and offending, a major theme in this text. In Chapter 2, we turn to a review of the current issues that face women as victims, offenders, and workers within the criminal justice system. Chapter 2 concludes with a discussion on the different data sources that present statistics on women as victims and offenders and highlights the strengths and weaknesses of such data and the information that is portrayed regarding the "realities" of crime

Chapter 3 begins with a review of the theories of victimization of women. Gender and victimization are examined through a discussion of victim help-seeking behaviors as well as barriers to obtaining help. The phenomenon of *victim blaming* is also discussed. This chapter turns to a discussion of *fear* of victimization, including a discussion of how fear of victimization is not only predicated on time and place, but largely on gender. This chapter ends with a discussion of salient victimization theories, including the Just World Hypothesis, Routine Activities and Lifestyle Theory, General Strain Theory, and the Feminist Pathways Perspective.

The fourth chapter focuses on the theoretical perspectives of female offending. Chapter 4 begins with a review of historical perspectives of female offending, often discussing traditional theories of criminal behavior and how they have historically failed to adequately explain the unique offending patterns of women. This chapter highlights some of the major criminological theories and their applications (or lack thereof) toward understanding the female offender. We also include a review of research that focuses on the contemporary applications of these theories for a female population. We conclude with a discussion of recent theoretical developments in feminist criminology, highlighting the ways in which these theories not only place women and girls at the center of these perspectives but also address the intersectionality of victimization and offending.

Part II of this book is devoted to a discussion of women as victims. Certainly, victimization is not exclusive to women, as men, women, and transgendered individuals can be victims of crime. However, the literature, criminal justice laws, noteworthy cases, and the media all underscore the issue of women as victims of crime, suggesting an intertwining of culture, gender roles, myths, reality, and our unique focus on women as victims of crime. Part II of this book seeks to unravel some of these issues. Here, we present three chapters that highlight the issues of women as victims: rape and sexual assault (Chapter 5), intimate partner abuse and stalking (Chapter 6), and international perspectives on victimization (Chapter 7).

Chapter 5 of this book explores one of the most intimate and devastating types of female victimization: rape and sexual assault. While notions of rape and sexual assault elicit images of a stranger hiding in the bushes, the reality of sexual assault victimization rarely converges with this myth. Here, we discuss historical perspectives on rape and sexual assault, including laws and the processing of victims both historically and in contemporary times. We attempt to define sexual victimization by considering legal and psychological elements of these offenses. The chapter continues with prevalence rates for sexual victimization and strongly engrained rape myths as well as factors associated with sexual assault that seem to evoke powerful public responses. These include such issues as drug-facilitated sexual assault, spousal rape, and statutory rape. We include a discussion of child rape, often one of the most difficult types of sexual assault to bring to justice, and same-sex rape, a generally underreported type of crime due to social expectations about gender and sexual assault. Racial differences in sexual assault cases as well as policy implications for processing sexual assault cases are also discussed.

Chapter 6 introduces the issues associated with intimate partner abuse (IPA) and stalking. While these are two very different types of crime, there is significant overlap in the types of behaviors and patterns associated with these crimes. This chapter defines and discusses intimate partner abuse, including a discussion of dating violence, children of IPA, same-sex IPA, and issues of race, ethnicity, and immigrant status for IPA victims. Women as both victims and perpetrators of IPA are discussed, and the issue of women who kill their abusers is explored through a case study approach. The cycle of violence as well as barriers to leaving relationships with IPA are also considered. This chapter explores issues of stalking, including the emerging issue of cyberstalking, and examines stalking victims' experiences with police and corrections. Policy issues, including restraining orders, mandatory arrest policies, and treatment for IPA and stalking victims, are also discussed.

Chapter 7 focuses on international issues in the victimization of women. While it is often said that a focus on women in justice is a relatively new phenomenon, the focus on international issues in the victimization of women is an even more recent trend. Only in the last few decades has worldwide attention focused on victimization of groups of women in specific regions of the world. This includes honor-based violence, human trafficking, and crimes against women as a result of war. This chapter includes special discussion of two issues especially salient to U.S. borders: immigration issues related to female victimization and "the dead women of Juarez." Policy implications are also discussed.

Part III of this book explores women as offenders. While men comprise the majority of offenders found within the criminal justice system, the involvement of women as offenders has increased dramatically over the past four decades. As a result, criminologists and policymakers have begun to ask questions: Who are women offenders? How does the system respond to issues of gender? How do women differ from men within the criminal justice system? Part III of this book focuses on each of these issues and highlights some of the major lessons learned about women as offenders. Chapters 8, 9, 10, 11, and 12 each explore a different element of female offending, with earlier chapters (8–10) focusing on different types of female crime and the latter chapters (11 and 12) addressing stages of the criminal justice system and the issues that women face within them.

Chapter 8 examines girls and the juvenile justice system. Beginning with a discussion on patterns of female juvenile delinquency, this section investigates the historical and contemporary standards for young women in society and how the changing definitions of delinquency have disproportionately and negatively affected young girls. Here, we highlight how the sexual double standard has led to the differential treatment of adolescent girls, compared to boys, in juvenile court. We also review how technical violations have become the new way to incarcerate girls for status offenses. In addition, we look at how the decisions by parents, schools, and police have transformed behaviors such as rebellion and defiance into delinquent behaviors. We conclude this section with a discussion of the risk factors for female delinquency and how this information can help inform parents, justice officials, and community providers to meet the needs of delinquent girls.

Together, Chapters 9 and 10 examine women and their crimes, highlighting some of the types of crimes where women are disproportionately represented as offenders. While the text-reader edition on this subject examined all types of female offending in a single chapter, the complexity of issues, distinctions in sentencing, and media focus, as well as the sheer length of this material, led to the separation of drug, property, and victimless crimes in Chapter 9 from violent crimes in Chapter 10. Thus, Chapter 9 begins with a discussion on the most common forms of female offending: nonviolent offenses. Here, we highlight the prevalence and nature of female offending in crimes such as property offenses, white-collar crime, substance abuse, and sex work (e.g., prostitution). In Chapter 10, we shift our discussion to focus on categories of crime that are traditionally represented by male offenders: gangs, rape, and murder. Here, we examine gender differences in gang membership. Cases that make the headlines—female sexual offenders and murderers, including those involved in infanticide and serial killing—are presented here. Beginning with a discussion on violent women, we highlight how cases involving murder are the exception to female offending rather than the rule.

Chapter 11 details the historical and contemporary practices in the processing and sentencing of female offenders. This section highlights research on how factors such as patriarchy, chivalry, and paternalism within the criminal justice system affect women. We reference how the stage of the system, the race of the offender, and legal/extralegal factors can impact whether a female offender receives or is denied chivalrous treatment in the justice system. We conclude this section with a discussion on how gender-neutral practices such as sentencing guidelines and mandatory minimum sentences have had significant negative consequences on the lives of women.

Next, Chapter 12 examines the supervision and incarceration of women. Here, the chapter begins with a focus on the patterns and practices of the incarceration of women. Ranging from historical examples of incarceration to modern-day policies, this section examines how the treatment of women in prison varies from that of their male counterparts and how incarcerated women have unique needs based on their differential pathways to prison. In particular, we highlight how the physical and mental health needs of women differ significantly from the needs of male offenders. Given that the majority of women in prison are mothers to minor children, we focus on how the incarceration of women has a significant impact on the lives of children, the unintentional victims of drugs, crime, and incarceration. We then turn to the concept of gender-responsive programming for women. Here, scholars have argued that the training, supervision, and programmatic options need to consider the differential pathways of women to prison. Gender-responsive programming focuses on how our criminal justice system can effectively respond to these needs, both within the prison walls and outside in the community. This section concludes with a discussion on the complications of reintegration for women following completion of their sentence.

Part IV concludes this text and brings attention to women and work in the criminal justice system, with particular attention to the ways in which gender affects their occupational context. Chapter 13 focuses on women in careers related to policing, corrections, and offender services, while Chapter 14 examines women working in courts and victim services. In each of these chapters, we explore levels of stress and on-the-job demands that women experience in their efforts to work in an environment that has historically been dominated by men. In addition, women face choices and consequences within the context of these career decisions as a result of their gender. Following a discussion of the history of women in these occupations, these chapters discuss the ways in which gender affects the performance of women in these jobs, the proverbial glass ceilings in these careers, and the personal toll that gender has on their lives.

Chapter 13 begins our discussion on women's employment in the criminal justice system with a focus on occupations involving offender services, including police, corrections, and probation/parole. Women in these positions face unique challenges as a result of their gender in these male-dominated fields, and issues of cross-sex supervision are salient. Female probation officers and women in parole face unique challenges within the context of their positions as they balance the role of policing the offender (and maintaining community safety) and advocating for the rehabilitative needs of their clients.

Chapter 14 examines women who work in criminal justice courtrooms as attorneys and judges as well as court-based occupations often affiliated with the criminal justice system: victim services. This chapter outlines the emergence of women in the legal arena and explores contemporary issues for female attorneys and judges. Differential salary, promotion, appointments, and opportunities are discussed, along with some surprising trends which suggest specific settings in which the numbers of female attorneys and judges is near parity with men. The chapter then turns to victim services occupations, which are often dominated by women, as we explore reasons for this trend. Some women are drawn to careers in victim services as a result of their own experiences with victimization, a history that can often place their abilities to serve victims within a unique context. Within this chapter we discuss a few examples of these occupations: rape-crisis workers and domestic violence advocates, including shelter care workers, and victim/witness advocates.

As you can see, this book provides an in-depth examination of the issues facing women in the criminal justice system today. From victimization to incarceration to employment, this book takes a unique approach in its presentation by providing a review of the literature on each of these issues. Each section of this book presents a critical component of the criminal justice system and the role of women in it. As you will soon learn, gender is a pervasive theme that runs deep throughout our system, and how we respond to it has a dramatic effect on the lives of women in society.

Acknowledgments

The authors are indebted to the following individuals who contributed their time, effort, and expertise in the production of this book.

From Stacy Mallicoat: I have to give tremendous thanks to Jerry Westby, publisher of the Criminology and Criminal Justice Division at SAGE Publications. I continue to be indebted to your support and encouragement as an author and for providing me with amazing opportunities to share my passion for all things crime and justice. I also have to give thanks to Craig Hemmens, series editor for the Text/Reader series with SAGE from which the foundations of this text began. Sincere appreciation goes out to all of the scholars who served as reviewers of this text for your constructive commentary. Throughout my career, I have been blessed to be surrounded by amazing scholars, friends, and mentors, including Joanne Belknap, Hillary Potter, Denise Paquette-Boots, Allison Cotton, Criminology Mamas and my peers within the Division on Women and Crime, and my colleagues in the Division of Politics, Administration and Justice at California State University, Fullerton. I have to give a shout-out to Jill Rosenbaum, who provides me with daily doses of perspective and serenity, and to Christine L. Gardiner for her fellowship. Special thanks to my coauthor, Connie Ireland, for her ideas and contributions to this volume and for making this a stronger representation of the multiple issues that impact the relationships between gender and crime. Finally, I would like to acknowledge the love, support, and care by my family, who provide endless encouragement for my adventures in academia and beyond.

From Connie Ireland: I wish to thank my colleagues at California State University, Long Beach (CSULB) for their ongoing support of my work, including Durrell Dew and Joseph Aubele, who keep this place running; Doug Butler and Sue Stanley, for their commitment to service, compassion, professionalism, and excellence, which shows in all they do; my department chairperson, friend, colleague, and mentor, Dr. Henry Fradella, whose dedication, leadership, energy, and vision have both inspired and transformed our department, and whose pithy comebacks never cease to entertain—you are a true genius and visionary, Hank; Drs. Judy Hails, Ryan Fischer, Jim Koval, Aili Malm, Harv Morley, Dina Perrone, Robert Schug, Brenda Vogel, Tracy Tolbert, and John Wang, for their collegiality, professionalism, collaboration, friendship, and for making our department a wonderful place to share one's career; and the late Drs. Bruce Berg and Libby Deschenes, both of whom were extraordinary mentors. I owe special thanks to the following CSULB students, who will undoubtedly continue to make outstanding contributions to the field during their careers: Ms. Becky Marx, who provided research and synopses used in creating many case studies and boxes, and Mr. Kenneth Grundy, who tirelessly searched journal articles and news sources used to develop many of the boxes and tables in this book, energetically edited portions of this text in response to reviewer comments, and authored several boxes included herein. I am grateful for his detailed, insightful, and thought-provoking discussions. Last, and most important, I wish to thank my colleague, friend, and coauthor, Dr. Stacy Mallicoat, whose initial work in this area birthed the current text. You are a superwoman, Stacy, and while our styles may be worlds apart, I am grateful for both our collaboration and friendship.

PART I
Foundations of Feminist Criminology

Women and Crime

Introduction

Karla and Diana were friends since age two, when Karla's family—comprised of an undocumented immigrant mother from Honduras with three children—moved next door to Diana's family. Diana's birth father was in and out of prison most of her life, so the duties of raising her and her three siblings were left to her mother. The two families relied on community support, as both moms worked multiple jobs to put food on the table.

On a typical day, the kids over age 12 watched the younger kids when parents were at work. Sometimes an adult from the community—a parent, grandparent, boyfriend, or cousin—would keep an eye on the kids, but adult supervision was a rarity. Karla and Diana usually went to school, but there was no one to enforce their attendance, as their parents worked long hours and the truant officer avoided their community. There were no formal social arrangements in the projects, but everyone watched out for one another in their shared circumstances of poverty, drugs, guns, crime, and gangs in this urban community.

Karla and Diana liked school, but they liked home better. For now, their moms wanted them to stay home, too, as a neighborhood girl had been shot and killed by a rival gang member on her way to school. Karla and Diana were safe at home; their gang—comprised of older siblings, uncles, and neighbors—made sure that no rival gang could get them. But sometimes, danger wasn't just outside. Diana's mom had a new boyfriend, and he did things that made Karla and Diana feel uncomfortable. . . .

Although their lives took dramatically different paths in their teens, their life paths continued to intersect around their victimization, offending, and careers on the streets and in the courts. You might even say that criminal justice was the common thread for these two women in crime.

Chapter Highlights

- Feminist theory, with a focus on the emergence of feminism in criminology
- Introduction to women as victims, offenders, and workers in the criminal justice system

Since the creation of the American criminal justice system, the experiences of women have been reduced to either a cursory glance or have been completely absent. **Gendered justice**, or rather **injustice**, has prevailed in every aspect of the system. The unique experiences of women have historically been ignored at every turn—for victims, for offenders, and even for women who have worked within its walls. Indeed, the criminal justice system is a gendered experience.

Yet the participation of women in the system is growing in every realm. Women make up a majority of the victims for certain types of crimes, particularly when men are the primary offender. These gendered experiences of victimization in crimes such as **rape**, **sexual assault**, **intimate partner abuse**, and **stalking** demonstrate that women suffer disproportionately from these crimes. Yet their cries for help have traditionally been ignored by a system that many in society believe is designed to help victims. Women's needs as offenders are also ignored, as they face a variety of unique circumstances and experiences that are absent from the male offending population. From classical theories of crime that fail to adequately explain female offending behaviors to the negative treatment women have received by the courts and correctional systems, the conditions of women's lives have gone unnoticed. Historically, most of the understanding about offending was created by male scholars regarding the lives of male offenders. When the discussion turned to the female offender, most perspectives tended to apply these male principles to women without any consideration or adaptation for women's perspectives. This approach has been criticized by feminist scholars for its failure to understand that the lives and experiences of women provide the foundations for their offending (Belknap, 2007). Likewise, the employment of women in the criminal justice system has been limited, as women were traditionally shut out of many of these male-dominated occupations. As women began to enter these occupations, they were faced with a hypermasculine culture that challenged their gender at every turn. While the participation of women in these traditionally male-dominated fields has grown significantly in modern-day times, women continue to struggle for equality in a world where the effects of the **glass ceiling** continue to pervade a system that presents itself as one interested in the notion of justice (Martin, 1991).

The goal of this chapter is to expose students to the foundational issues in the study of gender and crime. In setting the context for the book, you were introduced to two friends at the beginning of this chapter whose lives have been intertwined with the criminal justice system in a variety of ways. Their stories are not unique, as they represent many of the girls and women that the authors of this text have met throughout their own experiences working with juvenile and criminal justice agencies. At the beginning of each chapter, you'll learn more about the lives of Karla and Diana as you gain an understanding for the role that gender plays throughout the criminal justice system. The chapter will then turn to a review of the influence of **feminism** on the study of crime. We also highlight the three major sections of this book: women as victims, female offenders, and women who work in the criminal justice system. Within each of these discussions, gender has a significant impact on the experiences of women and crime.

The Influence of Feminism on Studies of Women and Crime

You may ask yourself, what does feminism have to do with discussions about women and crime? The contribution of feminism plays a central role in identifying and responding to issues of gender throughout the criminal justice system. First, it is important for us to understand what we are talking about when we use the term *women*. Sometimes, people will use the words *sex* and *gender* interchangeably. However, these are two different terms, both of which relate to the study of women and crime. *Sex* refers to the biological or physiological characteristics of what makes someone male or female, a man or a woman. For example, men and women have different genetic profiles, hormonal characteristics, and genitalia. Within the criminal justice system, we might use *sex* to talk about the segregation of men and women in a custody environment, such as jails or prison. In contrast, *gender* refers to the socially defined identities of masculine and feminine. Here, we might reference how social characteristics vary for men and women. For example, historical references to gender dictated that women did not work outside of the home and were expected to remain sexually pure until marriage, whereas these "rules" did not pertain to men. In early theories of criminology, women were often characterized as *masculine*, with the suggestion that female offenders were more like men than women. Despite the fact that sex and gender represent different constructs, the notions of sex and gender are intertwined in the study of women and crime. For example, research on sentencing patterns has indicated that women (sex) are often judged on gendered factors as well as criminal factors. Here, characteristics such as a woman's marital status or if she has minor children may impact the type of sentences she receives. As you will learn throughout this book, sex and gender both play an important role in the lives of women within the criminal justice system.

▲ **Photo 1.1**   The icon of Lady Justice represents many of the ideal goals of the justice system, including fairness, justice, and equality.

The study of women and crime has seen incredible advances in recent history. Many of these advances were related to the social and political efforts of feminism. The 1960s and 1970s shed light on many significant issues for several marginalized groups in society, including women. The momentum of social change as represented by the civil rights and women's movements had significant impacts for society, and the criminal justice system was no stranger in these discussions. Here, the second wave of feminism expanded beyond the focus of the original activists (who were concerned exclusively about women's suffrage and the right to vote) to topics such as sexuality, legal inequalities, and reproductive rights. It was during this time frame that criminology scholars increased their attention on women and offending. Prior to this time, women were largely forgotten in research conversations about crime and criminal behavior. When they were mentioned, they were relegated to a brief footnote or discussed in stereotypical and sexist ways. This is not surprising, given that the majority of scholars within the field were men.

While feminist criminologists during the 1960s and 1970s were the first to break through the glass ceiling of criminological thought, their perspectives were mostly centered on a liberal feminist view, which focused primarily on a search for equality between men and women. Unfortunately, these liberal feminists provided little emphasis on issues of multicultural identities. Their efforts were highly criticized by some for limiting their view, as their understanding of women and crime issues did not accurately represent the realities of women of the women involved in the system. For example,

> by asserting that women universally suffer the effects of patriarchy, the dominance approach rests on the dubious assumption that all women, by virtue of their shared gender, have a common 'experience' in the first place. . . . it assumes that all women are oppressed by all men in exactly the same ways or that there is one unified experience of dominance experienced by women. (Burgess-Proctor, 2006, p. 34)

In response to such concerns, a third wave of feminism was born to acknowledge the multiple diverse perspectives of women as they relate to issues of race, ethnicity, nationality, sexuality, and so on. With the emergence of second-wave and third-wave feminism, scholars began to talk in earnest about the nature of the female offender and began to ask questions about the lives of women involved in the criminal justice system: Who is she? Why does she engage in crime? And, perhaps most importantly, how is she different from the male offender and how should the criminal justice system respond to her?

Changes to paradigms about female offending naturally sparked discussion about female victimization. This second and third wave of feminist theory brought increased attention to women who were victims of crime. How do women experience victimization? How does the system respond to women who have been victims of a crime? How have criminal justice systems and policies responded to the victimization of women?

Feminism also brought a greater participation in the workforce in general, and the field of criminal justice was no exception. Scholars were faced with questions regarding how gender affects the way in which women work within the police department, correctional agencies, and the legal system. What issues do women face within the context of these occupations? How has the participation of women in these fields affected the experiences of women who are victims and offenders?

Today, scholars in criminology, criminal justice, and related fields explore these issues in depth in an attempt to shed light on the population of women in the criminal justice system. Despite all these positive achievements, feminist criminologists continue to face challenges

▲ **Photo 1.2** The image of Rosie the Riveter became an iconic figure of women during World War II. The rise of women in the workplace coincided with the second wave of feminism. As a result, the image of Rosie is often linked to second-wave feminism and the fight for equality for women.

within the criminology and criminal justice literature. Burgess-Proctor (2006) posits that in order for **feminist criminology** to continue to grow, scholars must be willing to investigate not only gender as an isolated construct but gender issues within a multi-identity world of race, ethnicity, class, sexuality, and other identities.

Women and Crime

The influence of gender sheds an interesting light on the criminal justice system. How does the criminal justice system respond to issues of gender? While significant gains have been made in the services to victims; the processing, punishment, and rehabilitation of offenders; and the workplace environment, there is still work to be done in each of these realms.

Women as Victims of Violence

The experience of victimization is something that too many women are intimately familiar with. In 1994, the Bureau of Justice statistics estimated that five million women were victimized by violent crimes (Craven, 1997). By 2010, these numbers had fallen to 1,854,980. In addition, 1,182,340 of these crimes were perpetuated by an intimate partner, other family member, or an acquaintance. While the rates of violent victimization of women had significantly declined from a historical high in 1994 (43.0 per 1,000), women in 2010 continued to experience crimes of violence at a rate of 14.2 per 1,000 persons (Rand, 2008; Truman, 2011).

While men are significantly more likely to be a victim of a crime, women comprise the majority of victims of certain forms of violent crime, particularly intimate partner abuse and sexual assault. In addition, women are most likely to be victimized by someone they know. In many cases, when they do seek help from the criminal justice system, charges are not always filed or are often reduced through plea bargains, resulting in offenders receiving limited (if any) sanctions for their criminal behavior. In many cases, victims find their own lives put on trial to be criticized by the criminal justice system and society as a whole. Based on these circumstances, it is no surprise that many women have little faith in the criminal justice system. Indeed, only 47.3% of women surveyed by the **National Crime Victimization Survey (NCVS)** in 2007 reported their criminal victimization to the police (Rand, 2008).

The needs of women who are victimized are significant, particularly in cases of personal victimization, such as sexual assault and intimate partner abuse. Beyond the physical damage, victims of crimes like these are traumatized emotionally. The experience of being victimized lasts far beyond the event itself and has significant implications not only for the individual but also for her family members and friends. How has the criminal justice system responded to the needs of these victims? While significant gains have been made in the field of victim advocacy, the demand for these services far exceeds the available resources of agencies in this field.

Women Who Offend

What is the nature of offending for women? How does it compare to the offending practices of men? This type of comparison between male and female offending is referred to as the *sex* or *gender* gap in offending. While there are many similarities between male and female offenders, there are also many differences. For example, both men and women tend to engage in high levels of **property crimes** and substance abuse. Men are significantly more likely to be involved in homicide cases. Indeed, men are more likely to engage in most crime categories, with a few exceptions. Generally speaking, research indicates that the sex/**gender gap** in crimes is greater in cases of serious and violent crime and is less likely to be demonstrated in lower-level offenses (Steffensmeier & Allan, 1992).

While men are more likely in general to engage in criminal behavior, certain crimes attract a disproportionate amount of attention when the perpetrator is a woman. For example, **serial killers** (regardless of gender) are rare phenomena. Accounting for less than 1% of all homicide cases, serial killers are also overwhelmingly male (approximately 89% of identified cases of serial killers are male). Therefore, the emergence of a female serial killer leads to a number of different reactions by society. First, these cases garner a significant amount of media attention, which encourages the interest of the public. Second, the hype surrounding these cases tends to invoke gendered discussions about criminal behavior. These discussions often draw on gender-role expectations in the punishment of these behaviors. Gender-role expectations involve societal designations about how women *should* behave. Historical depictions of women involve images of women who are mild mannered, submissive, and serve as homemakers. Women involved in crimes (such as female violent offenders) clearly violate these gender roles. As a result, women may be treated in a harsher manner than men by the legal system for violating not only the law but also their gendered identity of womanhood. In Chapter 11, you'll learn more about how these practices translate into differential treatment by the criminal justice system.

In contrast, other crimes are more likely to be commited by women offenders. One such example of this phenomenon is the crime of prostitution. Often called a "victimless crime," prostitution tends to involve a greater number of women engaging in and being arrested for the act of selling sex. While some jurisdictions around the world have **legalized** or **decriminalized** prostitution, others continue to assert that prostitution is harmful to women. Another crime category that is dominated by girls is **status offenses**. A status offense is an act that is defined as a crime based not only on the actions of the offender but also his or her age. For example, actions such as truancy and consumption of alcohol are only considered illegal for offenders under a designated age (generally 18 or 21, depending on the offense). In comparison, these behaviors are not considered criminal if they involve adults. A review of history shows that status offenses (particularly for crimes like running away from home) are overrepresented by female juveniles. Chapter 8 highlights these type of offenses and highlights how gender plays a key role in how justice officials respond in these cases.

Despite the sensationalism of rare cases or the overrepresentation of women in other crime categories, most female offenders share a common foundation. Many of the women who engage in property crime (the most common crime for women) do so out of either economic need or as a consequence of their addictions. You learn more about these different types of offenders in Chapters 9 and 10 of this book.

Gender impacts not only the types of crimes that women engage in but also the way that the criminal justice system responds to these violations. Shifts from a rehabilitative philosophy to a "tough on crime" retributive model of justice have led to substantial changes to the criminal justice system as a whole and have had important implications for women. The rise in the use of prisons over community corrections for female offenders has not only transformed the way in which women as offenders are punished for violating the law but has also increased the needs of women returning from prison. The collateral consequences for the imprisonment of women are far-reaching. Even beyond her time served, the label of *ex-offender* can threaten her chances for long-term success.

The Intersection of Victimization and Offending

Perhaps one of the greatest contributions of feminist criminology is the acknowledgement of the relationship between victimization and offending. Research has consistently illustrated that a history of victimization of women is a common factor for many women offenders. Indeed, a review of the literature finds that an overwhelming majority of women in prison have experienced some form of abuse—**physical**, psychological, or sexual—and, in many cases, are victims of long-term multiple acts of violence. Moreover, not only is there a strong relationship that leads from victimization to offending, but the relationship between these two variables continues as a vicious cycle. For example, a young girl who is sexually abused by a family member runs away from home. Rather than return to her abusive environment, she ends up selling her body as a way to provide food, clothing, and shelter, as she has few skills to legitimately support herself. As a result of her interactions with potentially dangerous clients and pimps, she continues to endure physical and sexual violence and may turn to substances such as alcohol and drugs to numb the pain of the abuse. When confronted by the criminal justice system, she receives little if any assistance to address the multiple issues that she faces as a result of her life experiences. In addition, her criminal identity now makes it increasingly difficult to find valid employment, receive housing and food benefits, or have access to educational opportunities that could improve her situation. Ultimately, she ends up in a world where finding a healthy and sustainable life on her own is a difficult goal to attain.

Women and Work in the Criminal Justice System

While much of the study of women and crime focuses on issues of victimization and offending, it is important to consider how issues of sex and gender impact the work environment, particularly for those who work within the justice system. Here, the experiences of women as police and correctional officers, **victim advocates**, **probation** and **parole** case managers, and lawyers and judges provide valuable insight on how sex and gender differences affect women. Just as the social movements of the 1960s and 1970s increased the attention on female offenders and victims of crime, the access to opportunities for work within the walls of criminal justice expanded for women. Prior to this era of social change, few women were granted access to work within these occupations. Even when women were present, their duties were significantly limited compared to those of their male counterparts, and their opportunities for advancement were essentially nonexistent. In addition, these primarily male workforces resented the presence of women in "their" world. Gender also has a significant effect for the few "feminine" occupations that are connected to the criminal justice world. For example, the role of victim services, particularly within the realms of rape crisis or domestic violence, has typically been viewed as women's work.

Women continue to face a number of sex- and gender-based challenges directly related to their status as women, such as on-the-job **sexual harassment**, **work-family balance**, and maternity and motherhood. In addition, research reflects on how women manage the roles, duties, and responsibilities of their positions within a historically masculine environment. The experience of womanhood can impact the work environment, both personally and culturally. You'll learn more about these issues in Chapters 13 and 14 of this book.

Conclusion

The feminist movement has had a significant effect on the experience of women in the criminal justice system—from victims to offenders to workers. Today, the efforts of some of the pioneer women of feminist criminology have led to an increased understanding of what leads a woman to engage in crime and the effects of her life experiences on her offending patterns as well as the challenges in her return to the community. In addition, the victim experience has changed for many women in that their voices are beginning to be heard by a system that either blamed them for their victimization or ignored them entirely in years past. The feminist movement has also shed light on what it means to be a woman working within the criminal justice system and the challenges that she faces every day as a woman in this field. While women have experienced significant progress over the last century, there are still many challenges that they continue to face as offenders, victims, and workers within the world of criminal justice.

SUMMARY

- *Sex* refers to the biological characteristics of male and female, while *gender* refers to the socially created identities of masculine and feminine.
- The feminist movement of the 1960s and 1970s (known as second-wave feminism) has had a significant impact on discussions about female participation in crime.
- The emergence of feminist criminology in the 1970s shifted the way in which criminologists think about women and crime. Today, scholars on issues of gender and criminal justice are widely discussed in academic scholarship and have a significant impact on the understandings of women as victims, offenders, and workers in the criminal justice system.
- Women are significantly more likely to be victimized by someone they know and are overrepresented in crimes such as sexual assault and intimate partner abuse.
- Feminist criminology has highlighted a significant link between a history of victimization and patterns of offending.
- Many criminal justice occupations are male dominated and reflect gendered assumptions about women and work within these realms.

KEY TERMS

Decriminalization

Feminism

Feminist criminology

Gender gap

Gendered justice

Glass ceiling

Intimate partner abuse

Legalization

National Crime Victimization Survey (NCVS)

Parole

Physical abuse

Probation

Property crimes

Rape

Serial killer

Sexual assault

Sexual harassment

Stalking

Status offenses

Victim advocate

Work-family balance

DISCUSSION QUESTIONS

1. How has feminism altered how women are viewed within the criminal justice system?

2. Given the relationship between victimization and offending, what are some of the ways that criminal justice policies and practices can alter their response to women?

3. What issues can you identify for the criminal justice system in terms of gender? How do these issues change when you consider additional variables, such as race and class?

REFERENCES

Belknap, J. (2007). *The invisible woman: Gender, crime and justice* (3rd ed.). Belmont, CA: Wadsworth.

Burgess-Proctor, A. (2006). Intersections of race, class, gender and crime: Future directions for feminist criminology. *Feminist Criminology, 1*(1), 27–47.

Craven, D. (1997). Sex differences in violent victimization: 1994. *Bureau of Justice Statistics Special Report.* U.S. Department of Justice, Office of Justice Programs. Retrieved from http://bjs.ojp.usdoj.gov/content/pub/pdf/SDVV.PDF

Martin, L. (1991). *A report on the glass ceiling commission.* Washington, DC: U.S. Department of Labor.

Rand, M. R. (2008). Criminal victimization 2007. *Bureau of Justice Statistics Bulletin.* U.S. Department of Justice, Office of Justice Programs. Retrieved from http://bjs.ojp.usdoj.gov/content/pub/pdf/cv07.pdf

Steffensmeier, D., & Allan, E. (1992). Gender and crime: Toward a gendered theory of female offending. *Annual Review of Sociology, 22,* 459–487.

Truman, J. L. (2011). Criminal Victimization 2010. *Bureau of Justice Statistics.* U.S. Department of Justice, Office of Justice Programs. Retrieved from http://bjs.ojp.usdoj.gov/content/pub/pdf/cv10.pdf

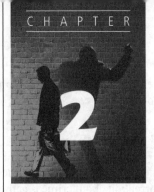

2

Research on Female Offending and Victimization

The police were not welcome in Karla and Diana's neighborhood. The residents didn't want them there, and the police, who didn't want to be there either, usually stayed on the outskirts of the projects. One time, a drunk driver crashed into 12 cars lining the street outside Karla's building, ping-ponging back and forth down the street and around the corner. Several residents called 911, but police didn't respond for nearly four hours. In another incident, an unmarked government vehicle broke down near Diana's apartment. No tow truck driver would come get the car from that part of town, and it took police more than a week to realize their car was still there.

Typically, the police only came to the projects when the media reported gunfire or death. Far, far more crime happened in Karla and Diana's neighborhood than was reported to authorities, but it was a really bad idea to snitch to the cops, as punishment by the gangs was always worse than anything the police might do to help. One time, Karla's mom went to the hospital after a fight with Boyfriend #17, but she didn't tell the cops anything. She lied and said she tripped down the stairs. Karla thought she was rather wise to do so.

Chapter Highlights

- Various data sources that estimate female offending and victimization rates
- The contributions of feminist methodologies in understanding issues about women and crime

How do we learn about crime in society? For each newspaper headline or magazine story about the rise and fall of crime rates, there is a larger story about how these data are collected and their contributions to understanding issues of gender and crime. Like the stories of Karla and Diana throughout this book, findings from the various data sources help provide an understanding on the role of gender and its relationship to crime.

✖ Data Sources on Women as Victims and Offenders

In order to develop an understanding of how often women engage in offending behaviors or the frequency of victimizations of women, it is important to look at how information about crime is gathered. There are several different sources of data involving information about crime. Each of these datasets represents a different point of view. They vary based on the type of information collected (quantitative and/or qualitative) and the purpose for the data collection. Some of these datasets are managed by government agencies, while others involve smaller collectives of university scholars. Finally, each dataset represents a picture of crime for a specific population, region, and timeframe.

Uniform Crime Reports (UCR) represent one of the largest datasets on crime in the United States. The Federal Bureau of Investigations (FBI) is charged with collecting and publishing the arrest data from over 17,000 police agencies in the United States. These statistics are published annually and present the rates and volume of crime by offense type, based on arrests made by police. The dataset includes a number of demographic variables to evaluate these crime statistics, including age, gender, race/ethnicity, location (state), and region (metropolitan, suburban, or rural).[1] UCR data give us a general understanding of the extent of crime in the United States and are often viewed as the most accurate assessment of crime. In addition, the UCR data allow us to compare how crime changes over time, as it allows for the comparison of arrest data for a variety of crimes over a specific time frame (e.g., 1990–2000) or from one year to the next. Generally speaking, it is data from the UCR findings that are typically reported to the greater society through news media outlets and that form the basis for headline stories that proclaim the rising and falling rates of crime.

A review of arrest data from the UCR indicates that the overall levels of crime for women increased 10.5% in 2010, compared to rates in 2001. For the same time period, the number of arrests for men declined 6.8%. A cursory glance at these findings would have us wonder why the crime rates of women skyrocketed while the rates of men fell. A true understanding of this issue requires a deeper look. Table 2.1 illustrates the UCR data on arrest trends for men and women for 2001 and 2010. In 2001, the UCR shows that women made up 22.4% of all arrests (8,468,019 total number of arrests, with women accounting for 1,899,440 arrests). In contrast, 2010 UCR data indicates that 8,221,468 arrests were made, and women

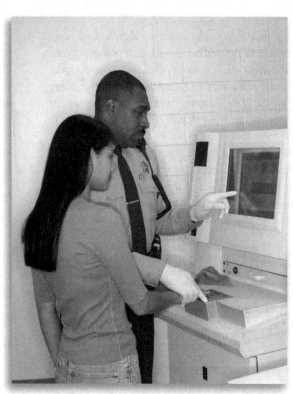

▲ **Photo 2.1** Most official crime statistics are based on arrest data. Here, a woman has her fingerprints entered into a database as part of her arrest process.

Table 2.1	10-Year Uniform Crime Reports Arrest Trends					
	Men			Women		
	2001	**2010**	**% Change**	**2001**	**2010**	**% Change**
All Arrests	6,568,579	6,122,413	−6.8	1,899,440	2,099,055	+10.5
Violent Crime	328,259	289,501	−11.8	69,542	70,019	+0.7
• **Homicide**	7,011	6,276	−10.5	1,060	751	−29.2
• **Forcible Rape**	16,552	12,475	−24.6	193	113	−41.5
• **Robbery**	61,315	62,383	+1.7	6,978	9,010	+29.1
• **Aggravated Assault**	243,381	208,367	−14.4	61,311	60,145	−1.9
Property Crime	707,452	656,367	−7.2	314,149	399,205	+27.1
• **Burglary**	158,422	159,813	+0.9	25,654	30,627	+19.4
• **Larceny-Theft**	468,276	454,079	−3.0	272,887	359,414	+31.7
• **Motor Vehicle Theft**	71,385	36,238	−49.2	13,918	7,887	−43.3
• **Arson**	9,369	6,237	−33.4	1,690	1,277	−24.4

SOURCE: Crime in the United States (CIUS)(2010).

* 8,726 agencies reporting

accounted for 24.6% of these arrests (2,099,055). Numerically, the number of crimes committed by men decreased (comparing 2010 data to 2001 data) while the number of crimes committed by women increased. Since men represent a majority of arrests, any decrease in the number of male arrests results in a small impact to male arrest rates. Likewise, because women represent a minority of arrests, increases in the raw number of incidences have a significantly greater effect on female arrest rates. So an increase of 206,632 arrests of women amounts to an increase of 10.5% in female arrests, comparing 2001 to 2010 data. In comparison, a decrease of 446,166 arrests for men is only a 6.8% reduction. These numbers illustrate the effects of population size in determining the proportion of male and female involvement in arrests. A closer look at the data finds that men make up the majority of all offending types, except for the crimes of embezzlement and prostitution (Crime in the United States [CIUS], 2010).

When assessing overall crime trends, it is important to consider the time period of evaluation. While the 10-year arrest trends demonstrate an increase for women and a decrease for men, the data for 2010 actually represent a decrease from the overall crime rates for both men and women compared to 2009. Table 2.2 demonstrates the arrest trends for these two years. The crime rate for men fell 5.0%, while the crime rate for women decreased 3.1%. In addition, the types of crimes affect how these data are interpreted. A deeper look shows that violent crime fell 5.9% for men and 2.7% for women between 2009 and 2010, while property crime rates declined 5.0% for men and 4.2% for women. A look at the individual crimes presents an interesting lesson about the rise and fall of crime rates. While one violent

Table 2.2 One-Year Uniform Crime Reports Arrest Trends

	Men			Women		
	2009	2010	% Change	2009	2010	% Change
All Arrests	7,546,481	7,157,015	−5.0	2,552,453	2,474,588	−3.1
Violent Crime	346,970	326,440	−5.9	81,143	78,972	−2.7
• **Homicide**	7,771	7,118	−8.4	957	889	−7.1
• **Forcible Rape**	14,970	14,323	−4.3	193	147	−23.8
• **Robbery**	80,327	71,295	−11.2	11,082	10,226	−7.7
• **Aggravated Assault**	243,902	233,704	−4.2	68,911	67,710	−1.7
Property Crime	803,772	763,821	−5.0	483,493	463,371	−4.2
• **Burglary**	188,504	182,762	−3.0	33,813	33,578	−0.7
• **Larceny-Theft**	560,876	532,115	−5.1	437,945	419,326	−4.3
• **Motor Vehicle Theft**	46,752	41,877	−10.4	10,184	8,992	−11.7
• **Arson**	7,640	7,067	−7.5	1,551	1,475	−4.9

SOURCE: Crime in the United States (CIUS) (2010).

* 11,631 agencies reporting

crime showed a significant increase in the percentage of women involved, it is important to look at the raw data (numbers) versus the percentage increase between years. In 2009, 193 women were arrested for the crime of **forcible rape**. In 2010, this number fell to 147, a decrease of 46 cases. Yet when you interpret these numbers as a percentage increase, we find that the arrests of women in cases of forcible rape decreased 23.8% compared to the previous year. Due to the small number of women who engaged in this behavior, any relatively marginal decrease in the number of women arrested has a significant effect on the overall percentage change.

Another example of the effects of small numbers of women's participation in crime and its effects on the year-to-year comparisons can be found by looking at the crime of arson. In 2009, 1,551 women were arrested for arson compared to 1,475 in 2010. This decrease of 27 cases amounts to a decrease of 4.9%. Therefore, when reviewing the increases or decreases of women's (and men's) participation in crime, it is important to note both the raw numbers as well as the percentages of crimes (CIUS, 2010).

UCR data can be also used to provide insight on the victimization of women. For example, the UCR collects data on homicide rates and the Supplemental Homicide Report of the UCR provides data on cases of homicide involving intimate partners. Given that virtually all homicides receive police attention, UCR data are considered a reliable data source on the numbers of homicides. Figure 2.1 highlights the nature of the relationships in cases of homicide involving female victims.

While these data enlighten us about the relationship between offenders and victims for some cases, there are many cases where this information is not reported. This chart represents the 13.2% of victims (both male and female) who were involved in a romantic relationship with the offender (CIUS, 2010). However, what is more startling by this information is what we don't know. These data only tell us about current relationship status. We don't know the extent of how many of cases involved a prior romantic connection (ex-girlfriend or ex-spouse) or how many of the 2,723 cases involving "acquaintances" or 7,452 "nonspecified" or "unknown" cases involved characteristics of intimate partner abuse. Given that many domestic homicides involve intimate partner abuse, these crimes may be under-acknowledged in these official data reports (Gelles, 2000).

While the UCR data can illustrate important trends in arrest rates (and to a certain extent, victimization), the reporting of UCR data as the true extent of crime is flawed for the majority of the crime categories (with the exception of homicide). While the UCR represents crime statistics from almost 95% of the population, it is important to take several issues into consideration. First, the UCR data represent statistics on only those crimes that are reported to the police. Here, the power of police action plays a key role in the collection of data. If the police are not witnesses to a crime or are not called to deal with an

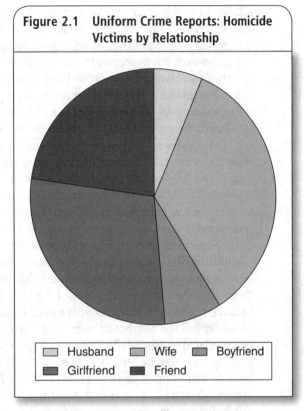

Figure 2.1   Uniform Crime Reports: Homicide Victims by Relationship

Husband   Wife   Boyfriend
Girlfriend   Friend

SOURCE: Crime in the United States (CIUS) (2010).

*Chart represents the 1,732 victims (13.2%) who were killed by a current intimate relationship.

offender, they cannot make an arrest, an action that forms the basis of the UCR data. Thus, unreported crimes are simply not recognized in these statistics. Sadly, many of the victimization experiences of women, such as intimate partner abuse and sexual assault, are significantly underreported and therefore do not appear within the UCR data.

Second, the UCR only collects data on certain types of crime (versus all forms of crime). The classification of crime is organized into two different types of crime: Part 1 offenses and Part 2 offenses. Part 1 offenses, known as *index crimes*, include eight different offenses: aggravated assault, forcible rape, murder, robbery, arson, burglary, larceny-theft, and motor vehicle theft. Historically, the UCR defined forcible rape as "the carnal knowledge of a female forcible and against her will."[2] While the UCR also collects data on attempted rape by force or threat of force within this category, the definition failed to capture the magnitude of sexual assaults. In January 2012, the FBI announced a revised definition for the crime of rape to include "the penetration, no matter how slight, of the vagina or anus with any body part or object, or oral penetration by a sex organ of another person, without the consent of the victim."[3] Not only does the new law allow for both men and women to be identified as victims or offenders, it allows the UCR to include cases where the victim either was unable or unwilling to consent to sexual activity. In addition, the new law removes the requirement that the victim prove that they were forcibly assaulted. The changes to the UCR categorization will capture a greater diversity of sexual assaults, and therefore it is expected that we will see an increase in the UCR for the crime of rape in the following years. However, it is important to keep in mind that changes in the reporting of these data do not reflect an actual increase in the behavior itself, only in the way in which the data are presented. Over time, these changes will help present a more accurate picture of the prevalence of rape and sexual assault, as the new definition is a better reflection of current state laws on these offenses.

Third, the reporting of the crimes to the UCR is incomplete, as only the most serious crime is reported in cases where multiple crimes are committed during a single criminal event. These findings skew the understanding of the prevalence of crime, as several different offenses may occur within the context of a single crime incident. For example, a crime involving **physical battery**, rape, and murder is reported to the UCR by the most serious crime, murder. As a result, the understanding of the prevalence of physical battery and rape is incomplete. Fourth, data are limited by time, as homicides that are committed in one calendar year but may be solved with an arrest and conviction in the following calendar year can initially be read as an "unsolved crime."

Finally, participation by agencies in reporting to the UCR has fluctuated over time and is subject to changing definitions over time. While there are no federal laws requiring agencies to report their crime data, many states today have laws that direct law enforcement agencies to comply with UCR data collection. However, this means that analysis of crime trends over time needs to take into consideration the number of agencies involved in the reporting of crime data, as well as technical issues related to legal definitions and logistical concerns within jurisdictions. For example, some jurisdictions may be slow in adjusting to UCR changes, possibly unaware, for example, of the broader definition of rape as of 2012. Other jurisdictions may have definitional differences that present challenges in accurate reporting. For example, California changed the monetary value which distinguishes petty theft and grand theft, raising the benchmark from $400 to $950 in 2012 (California Penal Code §487 and §488). The UCR, which reports larceny-theft from all jurisdictions, groups all larceny-thefts in a single category but provides distinctions for three distinct property values: under $50, between $50–$200, and over $200. Thus, comparison of UCR larceny-theft data is not likely to provide meaningful comparisons in such jurisdictional distinctions as petty theft versus grand theft. Failure to consider these issues could result in flawed interpretations of reported crime rates over time.

These flaws of UCR data have significant implications for the understanding of crime data by members of society. For the majority of the population, knowledge about crime is gained from news headlines in print, online, and on television media outlets. Few will choose to read the annual reports in their entirety in order to expand their knowledge beyond the 30-second summary of crime rates in society. Indeed, when the UCR was first assigned to the FBI as the home for the collection of data and publication of reports, early scholars commented, "in light of the somewhat questionable source of the data, the Department of Justice might do more harm than good by issuing the Reports" (Robison, 1966). Not only is the average citizen influenced by these statistical moments, but public officials and lawmakers could be swayed by incomplete evidence.

In an effort to develop a better understanding of the extent of offending, the **National Incident Based Reporting System (NIBRS)** was implemented in 1988. Rather than compile monthly summary reports on crime data in their jurisdictions, agencies now forward data to the FBI for every crime incident. The NIBRS catalog involves data on 22 offenses categories and includes 46 specific crimes known as Group A offenses. Data on 11 lesser offenses (Group B offenses) are also collected.[5] In addition, the hierarchy rule of the UCR has been abolished in the NIBRS. This means that criminal events that involve more than one specific offense will see all of those events reported and not just the most serious event. Whereas most categories of the UCR only collect data on completed crime events, NIBRS collects data on both completed as well as attempted crimes.

Overall, NIBRS allows for a more comprehensive understanding of crime in the United States. However, the transition of agencies to the NIBRS has been slow, as only 32 states have been certified by the FBI as of June 2012. The data obtained from these states represent 27% of the reported crime and 43% of all police agencies in the United States, and an additional 8 states are currently testing NIBRS in their jurisdictions, with 7 more states/territories developing plans for NIBRS. Table 2.3 highlights the status of NIBRS agencies and their reporting of criminal statistics. However, this system still carries over a fatal flaw from the UCR in that the NIBRS also only accounts for crimes reported to the police. In spite of this, it is hoped that the improvements in official crime data collection will allow an increased understanding of the extent of female crime and offending patterns in general, compared to the UCR system.

Table 2.3   **National Incident Based Reporting System Certified States and Crime Reporting**

State	Certification Date	Number of Agencies	% of State Population	% of State Crime
Alabama*	9/06	1	2%	1%
Arizona	7/04	7	6%	2%
Arkansas	4/00	295	100%	100%
Colorado	11/97	227	90%	88%
Connecticut	7/99	102	75%	59%
Delaware	7/01	71	100%	100%
District of Columbia*	1/00	1	n/a	5%
Idaho	7/92	142	100%	100%
Illinois*	12/06	1	1%	1%
Iowa	8/92	253	100%	100%
Kansas	2/01	432	90%	73%
Kentucky	1/05	548	83%	63%
Louisiana	1/02	45	16%	12%
Maine	7/03	24	23%	25%
Massachusetts	8/95	309	86%	82%

(Continued)

Table 2.3 (Continued)

State	Certification Date	Number of Agencies	% of State Population	% of State Crime
Michigan	2/96	802	100%	100%
Mississippi*	12/07	1	2%	4%
Missouri	7/05	22	11%	17%
Montana	7/00	121	100%	100%
Nebraska	2/97	116	39%	23%
New Hampshire	5/03	227	100%	100%
North Dakota	2/91	127	100%	100%
Ohio	1/99	704	83%	71%
Oklahoma	10/09	248	28%	11%
Oregon	6/97	87	29%	28%
Rhode Island	5/02	60	100%	100%
South Carolina	1/91	531	100%	100%
South Dakota	2/01	161	100%	100%
Tennessee	7/98	579	100%	100%
Texas	7/98	104	22%	13%
Utah	4/94	91	100%	100%
Vermont	4/94	91	100%	100%
Virginia	11/94	450	100%	100%
Washington	2007	194	45%	34%
West Virginia	9/98	514	100%	100%
Wisconsin	2/97	94	38%	45%

SOURCE: http://www.jrsa.org/ibrrc/background-status/nibrs_states.shtml

*State is not National Incident Based Reporting System-certified by agency; data are individually accepted by FBI.

In contrast to the limitations of the UCR and NIBRS datasets, the National Crime Victimization Survey (NCVS) represents the largest victimization study conducted in the United States. National-level victimization data were first collected in 1971–1972 as part of the Quarterly Household Survey, conducted by the Census Bureau. In 1972, these efforts evolved into the National Crime Survey (NCS), which was designed to supplement the data from UCR and provide data on crime from the perspective of victims. The NCS was transferred to the Bureau of Justice Statistics in 1979, where they began to evaluate the accuracy of the survey instrument and the data collection process. Following an extensive redesign process, the NCS was renamed the National Crime Victimization Survey in 1991. The greatest achievement of the NCVS lies in its attempt to fill the gap between reported and unreported crime, often described as the ***dark figure of crime***. The NCVS gathers additional data about crimes committed and gives criminologists a greater understanding of the types of crimes committed and characteristics of the victims. In 2007, the NCVS interviewed 73,600 individuals age 12 and older in 41,500 households. Based on their survey findings, generalizations are made to the population regarding the prevalence of victimization in the United States.

The redesigned questionnaire of the NCVS was intended to improve the data collection process on criminal victimizations, particularly as it relates to crimes against women. Here, the NCVS employed four key design changes in an effort to provide an increase in the accuracy of reporting of crimes of rape, sexual assault, and other offenses. First, questions were added that allowed respondents to comment on offenses committed by intimates or offenders known to the victim, not just strangers. Second, questions were added that allowed respondents to report on a variety of different incidents, not just those involving weapons or severe violence. Third, interview screeners received additional training and cueing options—in contrast, the prior administration of the NCVS limited many questions to a yes/no response. The redesigned questionnaire allowed for screeners to probe deeper into the different types of victimizations that a victim may have experienced. Finally, traditional criminal justice terms (which may have limited the reporting of behaviors if the victim did not see these events as criminal actions) were replaced by general behavior characterizations. For example, rather than ask a respondent if they have ever been raped, questions were altered to inquire whether they had experienced acts of forced or coerced sexual intercourse (Bachman & Saltzman, 1995).

In 2010, women and girls (age 12 and older) experienced over half a million incidents of violent victimization (nonfatal). Table 2.4 illustrates the types of crimes experienced by women by their intimate partner.[6] In looking at the data, you may be asking yourself, what is a crime rate? A crime rate compares the number of occurrences of a particular crime to the total population. The NCVS presents its findings in relation to how many instances of the crime per 1,000 people. For example, the 551,590 rapes and sexual assaults of women by intimate partners that are indicated by the NCVS

Table 2.4 **National Crime Victimization Survey Violence by Intimate Partners of Female Victims**

	# Women	Rate (per 1,000 households)	# Men	Rate (per 1,000 households)
Overall Violent Crime	551,590	4.3	101,050	0.8
Rape/Sexual Assault	35,690	0.3	8,310	0.1
Robbery	38,820	0.3	*	
Aggravated Assault	70,550	0.5	40,970	0.3
Simple Assault	406,530	3.1	51,770	0.4

SOURCE: Catalano, S., Smith, E., Snyder, H., & Rand, M. (2009).

* Data not available

equals out to 4.3 victimizations per 1,000 persons (Catalano, Smith, Snyder, & Rand, 2009). Crime rates make it easy to understand trends in criminal activity and victimization over time, regardless of changes to the population.

Given that the NCVS documents both reported and unreported crime, the findings generally indicate crime rates that are higher than the rates of crime reported by UCR data. But what does this mean about the true extent of crime? While women comprise a small proportion of most offending categories, are they becoming increasingly more violent? Or have police department arrest policies and practices changed in how women are treated in cases of violent crime offending? A comparison of UCR and NCVS data between 1980 and 2003 finds that the difference between male and female participation in crimes of violence has remained relatively stable. According to UCR data, there has been little change in the gender gap for homicide arrests. Additionally, NCVS data indicate no significant increases in women's participation in assaultive behaviors (Steffensmeier, Zhong, Ackerman, Schwartz, & Agha, 2006). Indeed, women are no more likely today than in the past to seek out participation in violent crimes that have been historically been dominated by men, such as robbery, gangs, and organized crimes (Steffensmeier & Ulmer, 2005). Instead, it appears that policy changes are to blame for much of the "increase" in female crime. For example, crimes that were once dealt with on an informal basis, such as disorderly conduct, minor **harassment**, and resisting arrest, are now considered cases of simple assault. This process of overcharging has created a new category of "violent" women, even though there were limited changes in behavior. This practice of **net widening** has expanded the number of women in the criminal justice system, particularly for low-level cases. Finally, the perception that women are engaging in increasingly higher levels of crime has translated to an increased reporting of female assailants for crimes, even though the rates of victimization by women has remained relatively constant. This trend illustrates a shift in the processing of female offenders and reflects a reduction in the chivalrous treatment of women by the criminal justice system (Steffensmeier et al., 2006).

The comparison of UCR and NCVS data can also provide evidence that the gender gap in offending between men and women is narrowing. Certainly, men engage in crime at a higher rate than women, and men are more likely to be involved in violent crimes than women. A review of data from both the UCR and NCVS between 1973 and 2005 indicates that female rates of violent offending have actually decreased over time, not increased as many might assume. In contrast to research by Steffensmeier et al. (2006) suggesting that the closing of the gender gap was due to changes in police practices (and an increased likelihood to process female offenders using official channels), Lauritsen, Heimer, and Lynch (2009) posit that the reduction in the gender gap is a result of how the rates of both male and female offending decreased. Here, they suggest that the gender gap between male and female offending has narrowed, because the proportion of male offending has decreased at a greater rate than the proportion of female offending.

In an effort to develop a better understanding of how crime affects society beyond official data sources, scholars have created additional ways to gather data on these issues. Self-report studies ask women about their experiences with crime, both as victims and offenders. These can include both quantitative and qualitative measures and have yielded tremendous amounts of data on all aspects of the criminal justice system that are not reflected by official measures of crime. Not only do these data give us an expanded picture about the true extent of crime, we also benefit from the additional details about crime offending and victimization that are provided by these studies and are absent from the UCR and NCVS data. For example, studies on offenders allow us to investigate the lives of women involved in crime. This research is conducted at every stage of the criminal justice process and beyond. Some self-report studies ask women about their participation in crimes in an effort to understand the risk factors for women engaging in criminal behavior. Others seek to understand how incarceration affects the lives of women and their families. These data help inform scholars not only about some of the flaws of criminal justice policies when it comes to women but also about what considerations criminal justice policies should make when it comes to women offenders.

Just as the UCR/NIBRS is not the only data source on offending, the NCVS is not the only data source on victimization. Many research studies address victims of crime and how the justice system responds to their victimization. One example is the **National Violence Against Women Survey (NVAWS).** The NVAWS consists of a random sample of 8,000 women over the age of 18. Data for the NVAWS were first collected between November 1995 and May 1996 by Patricia Tjaden and Nancy Thoennes of the Center for Policy Research and represented one of the first comprehensive data assessments of violence against women by acts of intimate partner abuse, stalking, and sexual assault. Another example is the **National Intimate Partner and Sexual Violence Survey (NISVS),** which is conducted by the Centers for Disease Control and the National Center for Injury Prevention and Control. In 2010, the NISVS included data from 16,507 interviews. Their findings report victimization from a variety of crimes, including sexual assault, intimate partner abuse, and stalking. These findings are then used to create estimates about the extent of crime throughout the United States. Figure 2.2 highlights the lifetime prevalence of rape by race and ethnicity. These results indicate that 1 in 5 White (18.8%) and Black (22%) women and 1 in 7 Latina (14.6%) women in the United States have been raped at some point in their lifetime. While these numbers indicate a high prevalence of rape in their communities, the issue of rape is even more dramatic within the American Indian/Alaska Native population, where 1 in 4 (26.9%) women experience rape in their lifetime. Unfortunately, we don't know much about how race and ethnicity impact rates of male rape

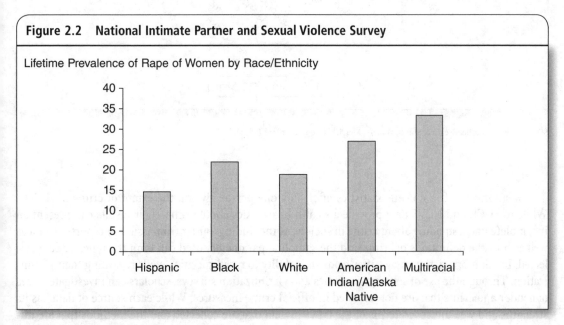

Figure 2.2   National Intimate Partner and Sexual Violence Survey

Lifetime Prevalence of Rape of Women by Race/Ethnicity

SOURCE: Adapted from Black, Basile, Breiding, Smith, Walters, Merrick, Chen, & Stevens. (2011).

from this data, only to say that less than 1 in 50 (2%) White men are impacted by the crime of rape in their lifetime (Black et al., 2011). Figure 2.3 presents the findings from this study for the crime of sexual assault. Here, we can see that not only are these crimes much more prevalent in general, but we are able to see differences for both men and women by race/ethnicity. Studies such as these provide valuable data in understanding the experiences of victims (both men and women) that may not be reflected by the NCVS or UCR data.

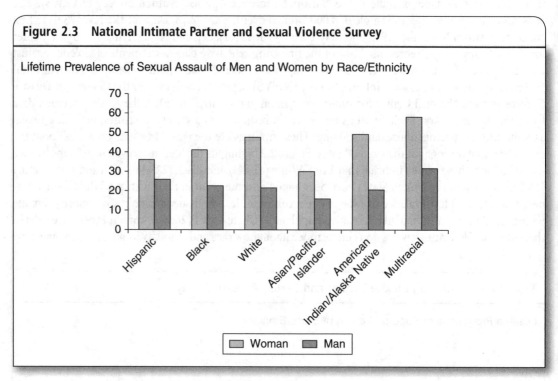

Figure 2.3   National Intimate Partner and Sexual Violence Survey

Lifetime Prevalence of Sexual Assault of Men and Women by Race/Ethnicity

SOURCE: Black, Basile, Breiding, Smith, Walters, Merrick, Chen, & Stevens (2011).

In summary, official crime statistics offer only one perspective on the extent of crime in society. While the UCR and NCVS data provide a wealth of statistics about crime, their results can present an incomplete understanding about crime in society, as the findings suffer from issues in reporting data as well as how the definitions of crime and the sampling parameters used can limit the types of data collected. In addition, victims may suffer from an inability to recall specific details regarding their victimization. Through the use of self-report studies and victimization surveys, scholars can investigate issues of gender and crime that are not reflected in official crime measures. While each source of data has its strengths and weaknesses in terms of the types of data that are collected and the methods that are utilized, together, they provide a wealth of information that is invaluable in understanding the complex nature of gender and crime.

The Contributions of Feminist Methodology to Research on Women and Crime

One of the criticisms of traditional mainstream criminology (and a central theme of feminist criminology) is that traditional perspectives on crime fail to recognize the intricate details of what it means to be a woman in society. The feminist movement has had a significant effect on how we understand women and their relationships with crime by making gender an integral part of the research experience. As a result, the methods by which we conduct research on gender have also evolved. While many scholars who do research on gender engage in quantitative methods of research and analysis, this may not always represent the best approach, particularly when dealing with sensitive issues. Here, the influence of feminist ideals can alter the ways in which we conduct research, evaluate data, and make conclusions based on the findings yielded from the research experience. By incorporating a feminist perspective to the research environment, scholars are able to present a deeper understanding of the realities of women's lives by placing women and women's issues at the center of the research process.

The concept of giving women a voice, particularly in situations where they have been historically silenced, is a strong influence of **feminist research methods**. From the conceptualization of the research question to a discussion of which methods of data collection will be utilized and how the data will be analyzed, feminist methods engage in practices that are contrary to the traditional research paradigms. While the scientific method focuses on objectivity and the collection of data is detached from the human condition, the use of feminist methods requires a paradigm shift from what is traditionally known as research. While many of the researchers who first engaged in research through a feminist lens were women, feminist methodology does not dictate that the gender of the research participant or researcher be a woman. Rather, the philosophy of this method refers to the types of data a researcher is seeking and the process by which data are obtained (Westervelt & Cook, 2007). Feminist methods are largely qualitative in nature and allow for emotions and values to be present as part of the research process. While some feminist methodologists have criticized the process by which data are often quantified, as it does not allow for the intricate nature and quality of women's lives to be easily documented, others argue that quantitative data have a role to play within a feminist context. Regardless of the approach, the influence of feminism allows for researchers to collect data from a subject that are theoretically important for their research versus data that are easily categorized (Hessy-Biber, 2004; Reinharz, 1992).

There is no single method of research that is identified as the *feminist method*. Rather, the concept of feminist methodology refers to *the process by which data are gathered* and *the relationship between the researcher and the subject*. This process involves five basic principles: (1) acknowledging the influence of gender in society as a whole (and inclusive of the research process), (2) challenging the traditional relationship between the researcher and the subject and its link to scientific research and the validity of findings, (3) engaging in consciousness raising about the realities of women's lives as part of the methodological process, (4) empowering women within a patriarchal society through their participation in research, and (5) an awareness by the researcher of the ethical costs of the research process and a need to protect their subjects (Cook & Fonow, 1986).

The traditional relationship between the researcher and subject is one of separation, objectivity, and distance. In contrast, feminist research methodology seeks connectivity between the researcher and the subject. Many feminist researchers discuss the need for a continuum of care for the people who participate in their research. This principle of care involves concern for the person as a whole person and not just as a part of the research process and the information that a subject can provide. This ethic of care involves a greater connectivity between the researchers and the respondent. Indeed, this leads to a pathway of empowerment for those participating in the research studies. As Westervelt and Cook (2007, p. 34) note, "by defining the research as collaborative and the 'subjects' as active participants, the feminist method allows participants agency and an opportunity to own their stories and be heard and accepted in a way often denied to them otherwise." Many feminist researchers discuss the relationships that they develop and maintain with their subjects as a result of the research process.

For many researchers who study women in the criminal justice system, the use of feminist methodologies is particularly beneficial. Not only does it allow for researchers to explore in depth the issues that women face as victims and offenders, it also provides the opportunity for the researcher to delve into their topics in a way that traditional methods fail to explore, such as the context of women's lives and their experiences in offending and victimization. For example, a simple survey question might inquire about whether an incarcerated woman has ever been victimized. We know that scholarship on incarcerated women has consistently documented the relationship between early life victimizations and participation in crime in their adolescent and adult lives. Yet, traditional methods may underestimate the extent and nature of the victimization. Feminist methodologies not only allow for the exploration of these issues at a deeper level, they allow for scholars to develop an understanding of the multifaceted effects of these experiences.

While many feminist researchers largely employ qualitative tactics, it is important to note that the use of feminist methods does not exclude the use of quantitative methods. In fact, quantitative methods can yield valuable data on the experiences of women (Westmarland, 2001). For example, survey data can yield information on the presence of gender discrimination, such as the sexual harassment among women in policing. In addition, the use of quantitative data and statistics is often useful for legislators when developing policies. Reinharz (1992) provides the example of the use of statistics in the development of sexual harassment policies whereby quantitative data "encouraged the establishment of sexual harassment committees in universities and . . . eventually provided legal redress for individuals" (p. 80). Indeed, researchers who study issues of women and crime can benefit from the lessons of feminist methodologies in their use of both quantitative and qualitative methods.

While feminist methods can provide valuable resources for the study of women and crime, feminist methods are not limited to issues of gender. Rather, feminist methodologies employ tools that are applicable across criminological topics.

By recognizing from the outset the class, racial, and gendered structures of oppression that may be at work in women's lives, this method gives voice to the larger structural processes that shape the experiences that often go unseen and unheard by others. Thus this method provides a framework for building trust with those participants who may be unsure about the research process and creates opportunities for understanding individuals and groups who may very well be inaccessible when approached in any other way. (Westervelt & Cook, 2007, p. 35)

SUMMARY

- Data from the Uniform Crime Reports (UCR) and National Incident Based Reporting System (NIBRS) often fail to identify much of female victimization, as crimes of rape, sexual assault, and intimate partner abuse go largely underreported.
- Victimization studies, such as the National Crime Victimization Survey (NCVS), help illuminate the dark figure of crime by collecting data on crimes that are not reported to police.
- A comparison of UCR and NCVS data finds that policy changes are to blame for the perceived increase in female offending.

- Self-report studies, such as the National Intimate Partner and Sexual Violence Survey (NISVS), provide estimates of the prevalence of rape, sexual assault, intimate partner abuse, and stalking in the United States.
- Feminist research methods give women a voice in the research process and influence how data on gender are collected.

KEY TERMS

Dark figure of crime

Feminist research methods

Forcible rape

Harassment

National Incident Based Reporting System (NIBRS)

National Intimate Partner and Sexual Violence Survey (NISVS)

National Violence Against Women Survey (NVAWS)

Physical battery

Uniform Crime Reports (UCR)

DISCUSSION QUESTIONS

1. Discuss how the Uniform Crime Reports (UCR) and the National Incident Based Reporting System (NIBRS) represent the measure of female crime and victimization in society.

2. How does the National Crime Victimization Survey (NCVS) investigate the dark figure of crime?

3. How do other research studies, such as the National Violence Against Women Survey (NVAWS) and National Intimate Partner and Sexual Violence Survey (NISVS), investigate issues of violence against women?

4. How do feminist research methods inform studies on women and crime?

WEB RESOURCES

Centers for Disease Control: http://www.cdc.gov

Crime in the United States 2010: http://www.fbi.gov/about-us/cjis/ucr/crime-in-the-u.s/2010/crime-in-the-u.s.-2010/index-page

National Crime Victimization Survey: http://www.icpsr.umich.edu/icpsrweb/NACJD/NCVS/

National Incident Based Reporting System: http://www.icpsr.umich.edu/icpsrweb/NACJD/NIBRS/

Uniform Crime Reports: http://www.fbi.gov/about-us/cjis/ucr/ucr

REFERENCES

Bachman, R., & Saltzman, L. E. (1995, August). Violence against women: Estimate from the redesigned survey. *National Crime Victimization Survey.* U.S. Department of Justice, Office of Justice Programs. Retrieved from http://bjs.ojp.usdoj.gov/content/pub/pdf/FEMVIED.PDF

Black, M. C., Basile, K. C., Breiding, M. J., Smith, S. G., Walters, M. L., Merrick, M. T., . . . Stevens, M. R. (2011). *The National Intimate Partner and Sexual Violence Survey (NISVS): 2010 summary report, Atlanta, GA.* National Center for Injury Prevention and Control, Centers for Disease Control and Prevention. Retrieved from http://www.cdc.gov/ViolencePrevention/pdf/NISVS_Report2010-a.pdf

Catalano, S., Smith, E., Snyder, H., & Rand, M. (2009). Female victims of violence, 2008. *Bureau of Justice Statistics.* Office of Justice Programs, U.S. Department of Justice. Retrieved from http://bjs.ojp.usdoj.gov/content/pub/pdf/fvv.pdf

Cook, J. A., & Fonow, M. M. (1986). Knowledge and women's interests: Issues of epistemology and methodology in feminist sociological research. *Sociological Inquiry, 56,* 2–29.

Crime in the United States (CIUS). (2010). *Uniform Crime Reports.* U.S. Department of Justice, Federal Bureau of Investigation. Retrieved from http://www.fbi.gov/about-us/cjis/ucr/crime-in-the-u.s/2010/crime-in-the-u.s.-2010/index-page

Gelles, R. J. (2000). Estimating the incidence and prevalence of violence against women: National data systems and sources. *Violence Against Women, 6*(7), 784–804.

Hessy-Biber, S. N. (2004). *Feminist perspectives on social research.* New York, NY: Oxford University Press.

Lauritsen, J. L., Heimer, K., & Lynch, J. P. (2009). Trends in the gender gap in violent offending: New evidence from the National Crime Victimization Survey. *Criminology, 47*(2), 361–399.

Reinharz, S. (1992). *Feminist methods in social research.* New York, NY: Oxford University Press.

Robison, S. M. (1966). A critical review of the Uniform Crime Reports. *Michigan Law Review, 64*(6), 1031–1054.

Steffensmeier, D., & Ulmer, J. (2005). *Confessions of a dying thief: Understanding criminal careers and illegal enterprise.* New York, NY: Aldine Transaction.

Steffensmeier, D., Zhong, H., Ackerman, J., Schwartz, J., & Agha, S. (2006). Gender gap trends for violent crimes: A UCR-NCVS comparison. *Feminist Criminology, 1*(1), 72–98.

Westervelt, S. D., & Cook, K. J. (2007). Feminist research methods in theory and action: Learning from death row exonerees. In S. Miller (Ed.), *Criminal justice research and practice: Diverse voices from the field.* Boston, MA: University Press of New England.

Westmarland, N. (2001). The quantitative/qualitative debate and feminist research: A subjective view of objectivity. *Forum: Qualitative Social Research, 2*(1). Retrieved from http://www.qualitative-research.net/index.php/fqs/article/view/974/2125

NOTES

1. Up-to-date statistical reports on crime data from the Uniform Crime Reports can be accessed at http://www.fbi.gov/ucr/ucr.htm

2. http://www.fbi.gov/about-us/cjis/ucr/crime-in-the-u.s./2010/crime-in-the-u.s.-2010/violent-crime/rape main

3. http://www.fbi.gov/news/pressrel/press-releases/attorney-general-eric-holder-announces-revisions-to-the-uniform-crime-reports-definition-of-rape

4. Part 2 offenses are defined as simple assault, curfew offenses and loitering, embezzlement, forgery and counterfeiting, disorderly conduct, driving under the influence, drug offenses, fraud, gambling, liquor offenses, offenses against the family, prostitution, public drunkenness, runaways, sex offenses, stolen property, vandalism, vagrancy, and weapons offenses.

5. Information on the National Incident Based Reporting System can be found at http://www2.fbi.gov/ucr/faqs.htm

6. The National Crime Victimization Survey categorization of intimate partner abuse includes victimization by spouses, ex-spouses, boy/girlfriends, and ex-boy/girlfriends.

CHAPTER

3

Theories of Victimization

Of course, Karla knew the real reason for her mother's hospitalization; she had been beaten by her boyfriend. Why did both Karla and her mother lie when questioned in the emergency room? They lied for several reasons. First, relationship pressure kept Karla's mom quiet: She was embarrassed about being beaten by her boyfriend, and deep down, she believed she had it coming for making him mad. Karla thought so, too. After all, he had warned her not be such a stupid bitch, and she did make him very angry that night. Second, they both knew he'd beat the shit out of her if she told anyone their personal business. But if they said nothing and just came home, he would be very sorry once he sobered up tomorrow and saw the damage he had done. He was always kind and generous after a really bad fight. Third, they lied about the victimization for fear of gang reprisal. Being a rat or a snitch was a sure way to find oneself badly beaten or dead in the projects. Fourth, whenever the police were involved in their neighborhood, things got worse. The last time the police came to their apartment building—for a fatal shooting the previous summer—the police took three kids into protective custody while their mom was at work, arrested another person on an unrelated warrant, and got into a fight with Billy, who was well known in the neighborhood as a loud but harmless drunk. The police did not understand the way things were, and calling the cops was just a very bad idea.

Karla's mother also worried that if she talked too much to the police, they would find out that she didn't have proper documentation to be in the United States and would deport her, victim or not. So, nine-year-old Karla and her mother sat in the ER, tightlipped. They lied about their names, address, and the cause of the injuries while a hurried medical student wrapped cracked ribs and stitched up her eye and a social work intern read questions from a form.

So when Diana's new stepdad, Gus, started touching Diana and Karla down there, they didn't even think of telling the police. They knew far too well that the best approach was just to avoid Gus whenever possible and avoid the cops at all costs.

Chapter Highlights

- Victims and the criminal justice system
- Gender and fear of victimization
- Theories on victimization

T his chapter is divided into three areas: victims and the criminal justice system, gender and **fear of victimization**, and theories on victimization. The chapter begins with a review of the victim experience in the criminal justice system as well as the experience of help seeking and the phenomenon of **victim blaming**. The discussion on the fear of victimization examines how the fear of being victimized is a gendered experience. The section then turns to the discussion of victimization and how theories seek to understand the victim experience and place it within the larger context of the criminal justice system and society in general.

Victims and the Criminal Justice System

Why do victims seek out elements in the criminal justice system, namely police and courts? Do they desire justice? What does justice mean for victims of crime? Is it retribution? Reparation? Something else? Victims play an important role in the criminal justice process—indeed, without a victim, many cases would fail to progress through the system at all. However, many victims who seek out the criminal justice system for support following their victimization are sadly disappointed in their experiences. In many cases, human victims of crime are reduced to a tool of the justice system or a piece of evidence in a criminal case. As a result, many of these victims express frustration over a system that seems to do little to represent their needs and concerns or even rage over a system that adds to their initial victimization through insensitive processing within the machinations of justice.

As a result of increased pressures to support the needs of victims throughout the criminal justice process, many prosecutors' offices began to establish victim-assistance programs during the mid-1970s to provide support to victims as their cases moved through the criminal justice process. In some jurisdictions, nonprofit agencies for particular crimes, such as domestic violence and rape crisis, as well as specific programs for child victims of sexual assault, also began to provide support for victims during this time (Perona, Bottoms, & Sorenson, 2006; U.S. Department of Justice, 1998). Community agencies, such as rape crisis centers, developed in response to the perceived need for sexual assault prevention efforts, a desire for increased community awareness, and a wish to ameliorate the pain that the victims of crime often experience (Parsons & Bergin, 2010). In response to a backlash against the rights of criminal defendants as guaranteed by the U.S. Constitution, citizens and legislatures increased their efforts toward establishing rights for victims in the criminal justice process.

Several pieces of federal legislation have been passed in reference to victims' rights in general and for particular types of victims (e.g., women, students) and crimes (e.g., sexual assault, domestic violence). For example, in 1992, President Bush signed the Campus Sexual Assault Victims' Bill of Rights as part of a broader umbrella of amendments in higher education. The bill requires colleges and universities to afford rights to sexual assault victims, including notification of outcomes, the right to change academic and housing circumstances in light of a sexual assault, and the right to services including law enforcement and counseling (Pub.L. 102–325, § 486(c)). Initially passed in 1994 and subsequently reauthorized in 2000, 2005 and 2013, the federal **Violence Against Women Act** aimed to provide the coordinated response of law enforcement, courts, and ancillary services for victims of domestic violence, sexual assault, stalking, and **dating violence** (Pub.L. 103–322). Likewise, the Crime Victim's Rights Act of 2004 outlines victim rights, including the right to be informed of hearings and actions (such as parole) as well as the right to be treated "with fairness and with respect for the victim's dignity and privacy" (18 U.S.C. § 3771).

To date, attempts to include an amendment to the U.S. Constitution on victims' rights have been unsuccessful. However, according to the National Center for Victims of Crime (2011), while all state constitutions have a body of victims' rights embedded in existing statues, only 32 state constitutions have been amended to include the rights of victims in criminal cases. While these vary by jurisdiction, Table 3.1 illustrates some of the **core rights of victims** found in many state constitutions.

Much of what we know about victims comes from official crime datasets or research studies on samples of victimized populations. A comparison between official crime data (such as arrest rates) and victimization data indicates that many victims do not report their crime to law enforcement, which affects society's understanding regarding the realities of crime. According to the Bureau of Justice's National Crime Victimization Survey (NCVS), only about half of all victims surveyed report their victimization to law enforcement (Hart & Rennison, 2003), including about 58% of all victims of serious violent crime, 50% of all rape/sexual assault victims, and 39% of all victims of property crime (Truman, 2011). This unfortunate reality of low reporting has been true for decades (Parsons & Bergin, 2010).

There are many reasons why a victim might choose not to report their victimization to the police. Some victims feel embarrassed by the crime. Still others may decide not to report a crime to the police out of the belief that nothing can be done. Most frequently, individuals may not report their victimization to police, because it is a "private or personal matter" or they think it is "not important enough" to report (Hart & Rennison, 2003). Reporting behaviors also vary with the type of offense—robbery was the most likely crime reported (66%), followed by aggravated assault (57%). While women are generally more likely to report crimes to law enforcement than men, cases of personal violence are significantly underreported among female victims (Patterson & Campbell, 2010). For example, the NCVS indicates

---

Table 3.1   **National Center for Victims of Crime, Core Rights of Victims**

The core rights for victims of crime include

- the right to attend criminal justice proceedings;
- the right to apply for compensation;
- the right to be heard and participate in criminal justice proceedings;
- the right to be informed of proceedings and events in the criminal justice process, of legal rights and remedies, and of available services;
- the right to protection from intimidation and harassment;
- the right to restitution from the offender;
- the right to prompt return of personal property seized as evidence;
- the right to a speedy trial; and
- the right to enforcement of these rights.

that only 42% of rapes and sexual assaults are reported, and the Chicago Women's Health Risk Study found that only 43% of women who experience violent acts from a current or former intimate partner contacted the police (Davies, Block, & Campbell, 2007). Certainly, the relationship between the victim and offender is a strong predictor in reporting rates, as women who are victimized by someone known to them are less likely to report than women who are victimized by a stranger (Resnick, Acierno, Holmes, Dammeyer, & Kilpatrick, 2000).

Victim Help-Seeking Behavior

As previously discussed, research suggests that fewer than half of all female victims of violent crime report their victimization to police. However, a failure to report does not mean that women do not seek out assistance for issues related to their victimization experience. Several studies on sexual assault and intimate partner abuse indicate that victims often seek help from resources outside of law enforcement, such as family and friends, and many seek assistance through formal mental health services following a victimization experience (Kaukinen, 2004). While many victims may be reluctant to engage in formal help seeking, research suggests that victims who receive positive support from informal social networks such as friends and family are subsequently more likely to seek out formal services such as law enforcement and therapeutic resources. In these cases, informal networks act as a support system to seek professional help and to make an official crime report (Davies et al., 2007; Starzynski, Ullman, Townsend, Long, & Long, 2007).

The literature on barriers to help seeking indicates that fears of retaliation can affect a victim's decision to make a report to the police. This is particularly true for victims of intimate partner abuse (IPA), who often fear retaliation by violent partners following reporting; research documents that violence can indeed increase following police intervention in IPA (Dugan, Nagin, & Rosenfeld, 2003). The presence of children in domestic violence situations also affects reporting rates, as many victims may incorrectly believe that they will lose their children as a result of intervention from social service agents.

▲ **Photo 3.1** The Clothesline Project is a collection of over 500 projects around the world; it uses t-shirts created by victims and survivors to represent women's stories of abuse and violence. Each shirt color represents a different experience of victimization, ranging from rape to child abuse to domestic violence. The Clothesline Project travels around communities to educate society about violence against women.

Victim Blaming

Reporting and help-seeking behavior are also influenced by the phenomenon of *victim blaming*. Victim blaming is essentially the shifting of responsibility for a crime to the victim instead of the offender. Research has examined various victim attributes related to perceived blame. One such factor includes the victim's engagement in atypical behavior. For example, if a rape victim does not fight back or if the victim of auto theft left their newly acquired vehicle in a rough part of town, an ensuing rape or auto theft might be partially seen as the fault of the victim. Likewise, victim involvement in risky or provocative behavior can also be the crux for victim blaming. For example, a woman walking home from a party while provocatively dressed, alone, and drunk is often seen as somehow responsible for any harm that occurs. As a third factor, perceived victim carelessness in failing to avoid their own criminal victimization can contribute to victim blaming. In this example, college student who provided his credit card number to an e-mail phishing scam might be told "you should have known better" by classmates.

The presence of victim blaming has been linked to the low reporting rates of crime, particularly for cases such as IPA and sexual assault. In many cases like these, victims reach out to law enforcement, community agencies, and family/peer networks in search of support and assistance and are often met with blame and refusals to help. These experiences have a negative effect on the recovery of crime victims.

Research also suggests that victim blaming can and does have an impact on official reporting of victimization. Consider, for example, the rape case against Kobe Bryant in 2003 (see box in Chapter 5). There was widespread discussion about the victim in the media, including headlines reporting that she was sexually promiscuous, mentally unstable, a gold digger, and so on. While most media accounts of sexual assault use the term *victim*, the media overwhelming used the term *accuser* in this particular case, which underscored the popular belief that either no crime occurred or that it was somehow her fault (Franiuk, Seefelt, Cepress, & Vandello, 2008). This certainly may have impacted the individual parties involved in this case, but you may be asking yourself, how does the issue of victim blaming impact crime reporting? According to the Colorado Coalition Against Sexual Assault (2008), the rate of reporting for the crime of forcible rape dropped about 10% in the year following the Kobe Bryant case. As an explanation for the impact of victim blaming, a local spokesperson told reporters, "I talked to specific survivors [of sexual assault] that said, 'I don't want to report this because I saw what happened in the Kobe Bryant case'" (Lopez, 2007).

Victim blaming is not just limited to crimes of sexual assault, although these are probably the most poignant cases to illustrate and are widely discussed in the literature as common phenomena across cultures and jurisdictions (see, for example, a study of victim blaming in Germany by Bieneck & Krahe, 2011). Consider, for example, victim blaming in crimes such as fraud or robbery. We know that fraud often occurs electronically, although the mechanisms change as technology evolves. Telemarketing scams of the 1990s were replaced by e-mail phishing scams in the last decade, which have in turn been dwarfed by concerns over *swiping* scams, which transfer credit and debit card information from the unsuspecting victim. To what extent would we consider the victim somehow blameworthy for his or her victimization? Would we assign greater responsibility to a college student victimized by a swiping scam than an elderly professor? This is victim blaming. It reduces reporting, undermines successful prosecution, and, as a result, leaves more potential victims vulnerable.

As suggested above, victim blaming is most often seen in rape cases, and generally, the blaming comes in the form of media depictions. Victims are not only blamed by the media, they are often blamed by friends and family who suggest the victim "should have known better." The same principle applies in terms of victim blaming and reporting. If one's own friends and family blame the victim, the victim is not likely to report the crime to authorities (Patterson & Campbell, 2010; U.S. Department of Justice, 1998). Further, much research suggests that victims sometimes internalize this, blaming themselves for their own victimization (Arata, 1999; Hall, French, & Marteau, 2003; Littleton & Radecki Breitkopf, 2006; Ullman & Najdowski, 2011).

Consider, for a moment, how the issue of victim blaming might have a disproportionate impact on female victims of crime. Can you make any predictions about the types of crime in which victims are more typically blamed and for which victims are more typically female? Cases of sexual assault and domestic violence are relevant here. Multiple studies have examined the relationship between victim self-blame, reporting, and revictimization. According to Miller, Markman, and Handley (2007), female undergraduate victims of sexual assault who adhere to common **rape myths** are more likely to engage in self-blame and are subsequently at higher risk for revictimization—a second rape—within a short (four-month) period of time.

Secondary Victimization

The concept of **secondary victimization** refers to the practice whereby victims of crime feel traumatized as a result of not only their victimization experience but also by the official criminal justice system's response to their victimization. For those cases that progress beyond the law enforcement investigative process, few are chosen to have charges filed by prosecutors, and only in the rare case is a conviction secured. Indeed, the ideal case for the criminal justice system is one that represents stereotypical notions of what rape looks like, rather than the realities of this crime. The practice of victim blaming through the acceptance of rape myths is an example of secondary victimization. Given the nature of the criminal justice process, the acceptance of rape myths by jurors can ultimately affect the decision-making process.

Historically, sexual assault trials included discussion of victim characteristics and behaviors that closely mirrored rape myths. Such discussions, for example, included information on the victim's sexual history, her attire, and her conduct and mannerisms. Instead of the offender being on trial, many rape victims felt as if they were on trial to defend their sexuality and past choices, and many reported the feeling that they endured a secondary victimization by the courts and the criminal justice system (Call, Nice, & Talarico, 1991; Tamarit, Villacampa, & Fiella, 2010). In an attempt to limit victim blaming in cases of sexual assault, many jurisdictions developed **rape shield laws**, which are used to limit the types of evidence that can be admitted regarding a victim's background and history (Yeum, 2010). Despite their existence, many of these laws allow for judges to make decisions about when and how these laws will be applied. You'll learn more about rape shield laws in Chapter 5. The experience of secondary victimization indicates that many rape victims would not have reported the crime if they had known what was in store for them (Logan, Evans, Stevenson, & Jordan, 2005). The presence of victim/witness assistance programs has helped address this issue, in part by providing coordinated support services such as counseling and advocacy, but the problem of secondary victimization still permeates many victims' experiences today (Campbell, 2005, 2006; Parsons & Bergin, 2010; Patterson & Campbell, 2010; Tamarit et al., 2010).

◤ Fear of Victimization

The majority of Americans have limited direct experience with the criminal justice system. Most are left with images of crime that are generated by the portrayal of victims and offenders in mass media outlets (Dowler, 2003). These images present a distorted view of the criminal justice system with a generalized understanding that "if it bleeds, it leads." This leads to the overexaggeration of violent crime in society (Maguire, 1988; Potter & Kappeler, 2006; Surette, 2003). Research indicates that as individuals increase their consumption of local and national television news, their fears about crime increase, regardless of actual crime rates, gender, or personal history of victimization (Chiricos, Padgett, & Gertz, 2000). In addition to the portrayal of crime within the news, stories of crime, criminals, and criminal justice have been a major staple of television entertainment programming. These images, too, present a distorted view of the reality of crime, as they generally present crime as graphic, random, and violent incidents (Gerbner & Gross, 1980). These elements (including the frequency with which crime is presented in the news and entertainment media, the disproportionate focus on violence when crime is depicted, and the frequency with which these images contain a female victim) must certainly shape the public's view of crime and our relative fear of victimization.

Consider the following scenario:

Imagine yourself walking across a parking lot toward your car. It's late and the parking lot is poorly lit. You are alone. Standing near your car is a man who is watching you. Are you afraid?

When this scenario is presented to groups, scholars find that men and women respond to this situation differently. When asked who is afraid, it is primarily women who raise their hands. Rarely do men respond to this situation with emotions of fear. This simple illustration demonstrates the fear of victimization that women experience in their daily lives. As De Groof (2008) explains, "fear of crime is, in other words, partly a result of feelings of personal discomfort and uncertainty, which are projected onto the threat of crime and victimization" (p. 281). Indeed, research demonstrates that girls are more likely than boys to indicate levels of fear of victimization due to situations such as poorly lit parking lots and sidewalks, overgrown shrubbery, and groups loitering in public spaces (Fisher & May, 2009).

There are two explanations for higher levels of fear among women compared to men. The first is the theory of differential vulnerability (LaGrange & Ferraro, 1989; Maxfield, 1984). The differential vulnerability thesis essentially argues that women's disproportionate fear about crime is related to women's inaccurate perceptions about their own physical vulnerabilities, including such factors as their relative exposure to danger, loss of control, and capacity to resist (Killias, 1990; Killias & Clerici 2000). Other scholars have examined the relative severity of risk, meaning women's fear about specific types of serious crime (e.g., rape; Warr, 1987). It is true that women are victimized by rape far more often than men are; the Centers for Disease Control (CDC) estimates that 1 in 5 women have been raped in their lifetime, compared to 1 in 71 men (Black et al., 2011). However, sexual assault is overwhelmingly perpetrated by persons known to the victim, according to the CDC, which attributes only about 15% of rapes to strangers. Women don't typically report fear of rape by acquaintances but fear of *all* crime types perpetrated by strangers, a relatively rare event for women compared to men. Thus, differential vulnerability may explain some of disparity in fear by gender, but not all.

This explanation ignores an obvious issue: socialization. The way in which women develop a fear of victimization is inherently a gendered experience rooted in how men and women are socialized differently. From a young age, young girls are often taught about fear, as parents are more likely to demonstrate concern for the safety of their daughters, compared to their sons (De Groof, 2008). This fear results in a relative lack of freedom for girls in addition to an increase in the parental supervision of girls. These practices, which are designed to protect young women, can significantly affect their confidence levels regarding the world around them. The worry that parents feel for their daughters continues as they transition from adolescence to adulthood (de Vaus & Wise, 1996). Additionally, this sense of fear can be transferred from the parent to the young female adult as a result of the gendered socialization that she has experienced throughout her life.

Research indicates that the fear of crime for women is not necessarily related to the actual levels of crime that they personally experience. Overall, women are less likely to be victimized than men, yet they report overall higher levels of fear of crime than their male counterparts (Fattah & Sacco, 1989). Snedker (2012) posits that this could be due instead to a "fear of men's violence" (p. 76). Some scholars (Valentine, 1992; Young, 1987) have argued, however, that the gender differences regarding fear of victimization are not based entirely on irrational perceptions or flawed socialization: Women are indeed at greater risk for certain types of crime, namely sexual and interpersonal violence than men. Thus, these high levels of overall fear of victimization may be perpetuated by fear of a specific crime for women—rape and sexual assault. Indeed, rape is the crime that generates the highest levels of fear for women. These levels of fear are somewhat validated by crime statistics, as women make up the majority of victims for sexually based crimes (Warr, 1984, 1985). However, research indicates that this fear of sexual victimization extends beyond fear of rape to fear of all crimes, not just crimes of a sexual nature. The **shadow of sexual assault** thesis suggests that women experience a greater fear of crime in general, because they believe that any crime could ultimately become a sexually based victimization (Fisher & Sloan, 2003). This element—that a simple property crime could devolve into forcible rape by a stranger (**stranger rape**)—may contribute to the fear of crime among women.

For women, fear of victimization is often related to feelings of vulnerability. This is particularly true for women with prior histories of victimization (Young, 1992). Some research suggests that "a loss of control over the situation and a perceived inadequate capacity to resist the direct and indirect consequences of victimization" contribute to women's fears about crime (Cops & Pleysier, 2011, p. 59). Yet even when women engage in measures to keep themselves safe, their fear of sexual assault appears to increase rather than decrease (Lane, Gover, & Dahod, 2009). This sense of vulnerability is portrayed by "movie of the week" outlets that showcase storylines of women being victimized by the *symbolic assailant*—a strange man, often of minority ethnicity, who lurks in dark alleys and behind bushes (Jones-Brown, 2007; Skolnick, 1966; see box on page 37). Unfortunately, these popular culture references toward criminal victimization generally, and rape and sexual assault specifically, paint a false picture of the realities of crime, especially rape. In actuality, most women are victimized not by strangers, as these films would indicate, but instead by people known to them (Black et al., 2011; Rand, 2008).

The fear of crime and victimization has several negative consequences. Women who are fearful of crime, particularly violent or sexual crimes, are more likely to isolate themselves from society in general. This fear reflects not only the concern of potential victimization but also a threat regarding the potential loss of control that a victim experiences as a result of being victimized. Fear of crime can also be damaging toward one's feelings of self-worth and self-esteem. Here, potential victims experience feelings of vulnerability and increased anxiety.

The effects of fear of victimization are reflected both in individual and societal actions (Clear & Frost, 2007). Agents of the criminal justice system can respond to a community's fear of crime by increasing police patrols while district attorneys pursue tough-on-crime stances in their prosecution of criminal cases. Politicians respond to community concerns about violent crime by creating and implementing tough-on-crime legislation, such as habitual sentencing laws such as *three strikes*, and targeting perceived crimes of danger, such as the war on drugs. While the public's concern about crime may be very real, it can also be inflamed by inaccurate data on crime rates or a misunderstanding about the community supervision of offenders and recidivism rates. Unfortunately, as Frost and Phillips (2011) argue, "public policy is influenced more by media misinformation and sensationalized high profile cases than by careful or thoughtful analysis" (p. 88).

Susan Smith: Fear and the Symbolic Assailant

In 1994, a South Carolina child abduction case captured national attention. Susan Smith, single mother of two young boys, 1-year-old Alexander Tyler Smith and 3-year-old Michael Daniel Smith, was the victim of a carjacking and kidnapping when an unidentified Black man took her car while she was stopped at an intersection. Her two young boys were still inside. Smith made impassioned, tearful pleas to local media for the safe return of her precious children. Her heartfelt pleas, as well as the random nature of the crime by the stereotypical offender most frequently feared—an unknown Black man who randomly struck an innocent family—catapulted her case to national attention, and the search for her assailant became a nationwide manhunt.

Within nine days, however, police gained a full confession from an unlikely perpetrator: Susan Smith had killed her children. She let her car roll into the John D. Long lake, with her young boys strapped inside their car seats, which were firmly attached in the backseat of her 1990 Mazda Protégé. Her sons drowned while she watched and waited from the safety of the shore. The motive for her crime appeared to be her desire to capture the love of a wealthy suitor, who had no desire to entangle his life with a "ready-made family."

The issue of mothers who kill their children comes to mind with this case. Certainly, Susan Smith is a painful example of this category. You'll learn more about this phenomenon in Chapter 10. Mental illness and homicide also come to mind, as Susan Smith's defense team argued that her sexual victimization as a child and multiple suicide attempts somehow mitigated her crime.

This crime also illustrates the salience of fear and the symbolic assailant in American media. Smith could have adopted any number of fabrications to explain her sons' disappearance. Why did she pick carjacking and abduction by a young Black man? And why did this case, among nearly 60,000 cases of children abducted by nonfamily members in a given year (Sedlak, Finkelhor, Hammer, & Schultz, 2002), receive such focused national response?

Arguably, two factors converged in this case, launching a national media frenzy (Chermack & Bailey, 2007). The first is the issue of the symbolic assailant, a fictitious perpetrator exemplified by certain behavioral and demographic characteristics (Skolnick, 1966). Most notably, the symbolic assailant in such cases is a young Black man, who hides in dark shadows awaiting the abduction, rape, or murder of unknown innocents. The symbolic assailant attacks at random, is unprovoked, and is difficult to apprehend. As such, the presence of the symbolic assailant is a risk to all, as he could attack anyone at any time. While national crime data overwhelmingly demonstrate that offenders and victims generally know each other (Truman, 2011), the myth of the symbolic assailant undermines this historical reality. The presence of the symbolic assailant is the first salient characteristic of this case that garnered national attention.

The second noteworthy element of this case is the **"missing White woman" syndrome** (Stillman, 2007). True, the missing persons in this case were young White boys, not women, as suggested in the title of this phenomenon. Nevertheless, the compelling media figure central to this case was a young, White, middle-class woman—the boys' mother—who appealed to the nation on behalf of her missing sons.

(Continued)

(Continued)

This evokes a predictable phenomenon wherein the media provide widespread coverage of a criminal event to ensure the safe return of a missing victim who is innocent, vulnerable, and White; this is in contrast to the scant reporting of missing persons of minority race, cases which rarely garner media attention. For example, students are likely to recall the murder of a young pregnant woman, whose badly decomposed body, missing head, and limbs, washed up on the shore of a bay in Northern California in 2002 as that of Laci Peterson; yet the nearly identical story involving Salvadorian immigrant Evelyn Hernandez was scarcely reported in the media and remains unsolved today.

These two factors ensured widespread media coverage, as they played upon widespread fear about criminal perpetration by the symbolic assailant—an unknown young man of color—against innocent, young, White victims of crime.

Theories on Victimization

In an effort to understand the victim experience, social science researchers began to investigate the characteristics of crime victims and the response by society to these victims. While criminology focuses predominantly on the study of crime as a social phenomenon and the nature of offenders, the field of victimology places the victim at the center of the discussion. Early perspectives on victimology focused on how victims, either knowingly or unconsciously, could be at fault for their victim experience, based on their personal life events and decision-making processes.

One of the early scholars in this field, Benjamin Mendelsohn (1963), developed a typology of victimization that distinguished different types of victims based on the relative responsibility of the victim in their own victimization. Embedded in his typology, referred to as *Mendelsohn's six categories of victims,* is the degree to which victims have the power to make decisions that can alter their likelihood of victimization. As a result of his work, the study of victimology began to emerge as its own distinct field of study.

Mendelsohn's theory of victimology is based on six categories of victims. The first category is the *innocent victim*. This distinction is unique in Mendelsohn's typology, as it is the only classification that does not have any responsibility for the crime attributed to the victim. As the name suggests, an innocent victim is someone who is victimized by a random and unprecipitated crime (such as a school shooting) or someone who is victimized by an unforeseen natural disaster (such as victims of Hurricane Katrina). Unlike the remaining types, an innocent victim did nothing to precipitate the criminal event and is seen as having clean hands in their victimization.

Mendelsohn's remaining five categories are victim-precipitated crimes. While not the same as victim blaming, each of these does attribute some degree of responsibility on characteristics of the victim, not the offender. Mendelsohn's second category is the *victim with minor guilt*. In this case, victimization occurs as a result of one's carelessness or ignorance. The victim with minor guilt is someone who, if they had given better thought or care to their safety, would not have been a victim of a crime. For instance, someone who was in the wrong place at the wrong time or one who places oneself in dangerous areas where he or she is at risk for potential victimization is characterized as a victim with minor guilt. An

Table 3.2	Mendelsohn's Categories of Victims	
Category	**Definition**	**Example**
Innocent victim	No responsibility for the crime attributed to victim	Institutionalized victims, the mentally ill, children, or those who are attacked while unconscious
Victim with minor guilt	Victim precipitates crime with carelessness/ignorance	Victim lost in the "wrong part of town"
Voluntary victim	Victim and offender equally responsible for crime	Victim pays prostitute for sex, then prostitute robs victim ("rolling Johns")
Victim who is more guilty than the offender	Victim who provokes or induces another to commit crime	Burning bed syndrome: victim is killed by the domestic partner he abused for years
Victim who alone is guilty	Victim who is solely responsible for their own victimization	An attacker who is killed in self-defense; suicide bomber killed by detonation of explosives
Imaginary victim	Victim mistakenly believes they have been victimized	Mentally ill person who reports imagined victimization as real event

NOTE: Adapted from Sengstock (1976).

example of this is a case of a victim who gets lost in a bad part of town, pulls off the road for directions, and is subsequently robbed. Mendelsohn's third category is a *voluntary victim*, someone who is equally as guilty as the offender. This victim is someone who shares the responsibility of the crime with the offender and deliberately places himself or herself in harm's way. An example of this classification is the individual who seeks out the services of a sex worker, only to contract a sexually transmitted infection as a result of their interaction. As another example, consider the individual who intends to purchase a specific quantity of illegal drugs for a specific price, and the seller takes the money without delivering the drugs. In this case, the victim is defrauded as a result of his or her own illegal drug transaction. The fourth category represents the case whereby the *victim is deemed more guilty than the offender*. This is a victim who is provoked by others to engage in criminal activity. An example of this category is when a victim kills a current or former intimate partner following a history of abuse. The fifth category is a *victim who is solely responsible* for the harm that comes to him or her. These individuals are considered to be the most guilty of victims, as they engaged in an act that was likely to lead to injury on their part. Examples of the most guilty victim include a suicide bomber who engages in an act that results in his or her death or a would-be attacker who is killed by another in an act of self-defense. In this case, the dead attacker becomes the victim, garnering the greatest culpability in Mendelsohn's typology. Mendelsohn's final category the *imaginary victim*. This is an individual who, as a result of some mental disease or defect, believes that he or she has been victimized by someone or something, when in reality this person has not been victimized.

While Mendelsohn focused on the influence of guilt and responsibility of victims, von Hentig's (1948) typology of victims looked at how personal factors, such as biological, psychological, and social factors, influence risk factors for victimization. Von Hentig was acutely interested in the factors that made a victim a victim. This is an important contribution to victimology, as previous criminological theories focused on what made an offender commit crime or assigned various degrees of responsibility on victims, as Mendelsohn's theory did. Table 3.3 lists the **thirteen categories of von Hentig's categories of victims**. The categories in von Hentig's typology of victims include the young; the female; the old; the mentally defective and deranged; immigrants; minorities; dull normals; the depressed; the acquisitive; the wanton; the lonesome or heartbroken; the tormenter; and the blocked, exempted, or fighting.

While the application of Von Hentig's theory helped develop an understanding of victims in general, his typology includes a single category for females. However, given that women can also fit into all of von Hentig's other categories, these can also be applied to explain the victimization of women, who can obviously have multiple traits. For instance, young girls who run away from home are easy targets for pimps who "save" girls from the dangers of the streets and "protect" them from harm. The youth of these girls places them at a higher risk for violence and prostitution activities under the guise of protection. While von Hentig's category of mentally defective was designed to capture the vulnerability of the mentally ill victim, he also referenced the intoxicated individual within this context. Under this category, women who engage in either consensual acts of intoxication or who are subjected to substances unknown to them can be at risk for alcohol- or **drug-facilitated sexual assault**. Likewise, consider von Hentig's category of immigrants and the way in which immigration status can also play a key role for

Table 3.3   Hans von Hentig's Typology of Crime Victims

Category	Description
Young	Youth are seen as vulnerable to victimization as a result of their age.
Female	Women are at risk, as they are physically weaker compared to men.
Old	The old have less physical strength due to age and have greater financial resources.
Mentally defective	Mentally ill or intoxicated individuals are easy prey for attackers.
Immigrants	A new environment (culture, language, acculturation) may place immigrants at risk for victimization.
Minorities	Minorities often face prejudice and discrimination, which can affect the victim experience.
Dull normals	A dull normal is a vulnerable individual who is easily exploited; they typically have lower-than-average IQ scores.
Depressed	Depressed individuals can be more submissive and are less likely to fight off an attacker.
Acquisitive	Acquisitive individuals are at risk for being taken advantage of due to a desire for financial advantage.
Wanton	A wanton individual is particularly vulnerable to stressors at various stages during his or her life cycle.
Lonesome/heartbroken	A lonesome/heartbroken individual may be taken advantage of due to a fear of being alone.
Tormentor	The victim becomes the perpetrator of a crime after years of abuse.
Blocked	One who is unable to help or defend himself or herself out of a negative situation.

SOURCE: Adapted from Von Hentig, H. (1948).

women victims. Many abusers use a woman's immigration status (i.e., undocumented) as a threat to ensure compliance. In these cases, women may be forced to endure violence in their lives or are induced into **sexual slavery** out of fear of deportation or mistreatment by government officials, should their unlawful immigration status become known to authorities. Von Hentig also discusses how race and ethnicity can affect the victim experience, and significant research has demonstrated how these factors affect the criminal justice system at every stage. Clearly, women can have multiple factors identified in von Hentig's typology, such as being young, a minority, an immigrant, and having mental health issues. Imagine for a moment, how a woman with these characteristics might be subject to multiple victimization events over her lifetime.

Just World Hypothesis

This chapter has introduced several recurring themes regarding victimization, particularly the victimization of women. One central theme, both in terms of victim nonreporting and early victimization theorizing, is that, to some extent, these positions place some degree of responsibility for criminal activity on the victim of crime. Why do we blame the victim? At its roots, the process of victim blaming is linked to a belief in a just world. The concept of a just world posits that society has a need to believe that people deserve whatever comes to them. Simply put, bad things happen to bad people, and good things happen to good people (Lerner, 1980). Under these assumptions, if a bad thing happens to someone, then that person must be at fault for their victimization because of who he or she is and what he or she does.

A just world outlook gives a sense of peace to many individuals. Imagining a world where crime victims must have done something foolish, dangerous, or careless allows members of society to distinguish themselves from this identity of victimhood—"I would never do that, so therefore I must be safe from harm." This, in turn, allows individuals to shield themselves from feelings of vulnerability and powerlessness when it comes to potential acts of victimization. However, there are several problematic assumptions surrounding the **just world hypothesis**: Namely, it incorrectly (1) assumes that people are able to change the environment in which they live, (2) implies that only innocent victims are true victims, and (3) creates a false sense of security about the risks of crime and victimization.

Given the nature of victimization patterns in society, few victims of crime meet the criteria for an ideal, innocent victim. Yet, this process of subtle victim blaming inherent in the just world hypothesis allows society to diffuse the responsibility of crime between the victim and the offender. For example, the battered woman is asked, "Why do you stay?" or given the message, "I wouldn't put up with that!" The rape victim is asked, "What were you wearing?" or "Why did you let him come into your apartment if you didn't want sex?" The assault victim is asked, "Why didn't you fight back?" The fraud victim is chastised, "Why did you provide your credit card number online?" The burglary victim is asked, "Why didn't you lock the door?" Essentially, any victim who inadvertently puts themselves in harm's way is asked, "What were you thinking?" Each of these scenarios shifts the blame away from the perpetrator, who, after all, is the person committing the crime, and assigns some degree of responsibility to the victim. Victim blaming enables people to make sense of the victimization and makes them feel somehow different from the person who is victimized. In many cases, the process of victim blaming allows people to separate themselves from those who have been victimized—"I would never have put myself in that situation"—and this belief allows people to feel safe in the world.

The just world hypothesis generally occurs without conscious awareness, and this is problematic for several reasons. Consider, as an example, the application of the just world hypothesis to the crime of sexual assault. First, under the just world hypothesis, the subtle blaming of victims begins to permeate culture, as evidenced by media reporting in high-profile sexual assault cases. These messages may dissuade victims from reporting their victimization, as appears to be the case in Colorado following the Kobe Bryant case (Colorado Coalition Against Sexual Assault, 2008). Second, these messages may increase victim self-blame associated with sexual assault victimization (Arata, 1999; Hall, French, & Marteau, 2003; Littleton & Radecki Breitkopf, 2006; Ullman & Najdowski, 2011). Third, victim self-blame may, in turn, increase the likelihood for revictimization (Miller, Markman, & Handley, 2007). Fourth, these messages may also solidify beliefs that may be associated with increased likelihood of criminal offending. Consider, for example, that college males who were exposed to newspaper articles supporting rape myths were less likely to view nonconsensual sexual acts as criminal and were more likely to support rape myths than either women in general or men who read neutral news accounts of sexual assault (Franiuk, Seefelt, Cepress, & Vandello, 2008). Some studies suggest a strong correlation between men's **rape myth acceptance** and self-reported rape activity (Bohner et al., 1998). Thus, while no longitudinal study has examined these propositions, the application of the just world hypothesis to the crime of rape (and rape myths) could yield reduced reporting, increased repeat victimization, and increased rape offending.

Routine Activities Theory and Lifestyle Theory

While early theories of victimization provided a foundation to understand the victim experience, modern victimization theories expanded from these concepts to investigate the role of society on victimization and to address how personal choices affect the victim experience. One of the most influential perspectives in modern victimology is Cohen and Felson's (1979) **routine activities theory**. Routine activities theory suggests that the likelihood of a criminal act (and, in turn, the likelihood of victimization) occurs with the convergence of three essential components: (1) someone who is interested in pursuing a criminal action (*offender*), (2) a potential victim (*target*) available to be victimized, and (3) the absence of someone or something (*guardian*) that would deter the offender from making contact with the available victim. The name of the theory is derived from a belief that victims and guardians exist within the normal, everyday patterns of life. Cohen and Felson posit that lifestyle changes during the second half of the 20th century created additional opportunities for the victim and offender to come into contact with each other as a result of changes to daily routines and activities. Cohen and Felson's theory was created to discuss the risk of victimization in property crimes. Here, if individuals were at work or out enjoying events in the community, they were less likely to be at home to guard their property against potential victimization, and burglary was more likely to result.

Routine activities theory has been criticized by feminist criminologists, who disagree with the theory's original premise that men are more vulnerable to the risks of victimization than women. Indeed, the guardians that Cohen and Felson suggest protect victims from crime may instead be the ones most likely to victimize women, particularly in cases of IPA and sexual assault. For example, research by Schwartz, DeKeseredy, Tait, and Alvi (2001) indicate that women who engage in recreational substance use (such as alcohol or drugs) are considered to be a suitable target by men who are motivated to engage in certain offending patterns. As another example, consider widespread elements of college safety programs designed to reduce violent crime among student populations.

Attempts by administrators to increase safety on college campuses by implementing protections such as escort patrols, lighted paths, and emergency beacons (modern-day *guardians*) may have little effect on sexual assault rates on campus, given that many of these incidents take place behind closed doors in college dormitories and student apartments. In addition, the concept of self-protective factors (or self-guardians) may not be able to ward off a potential attacker, given that the overwhelming majority of sexual assaults on college campuses are perpetrated by someone known to the victim (Mustaine & Tewksbury, 2002).

Like routine activities theory, **lifestyle theory** seeks to relate the patterns of one's everyday activities to the potential for victimization. While routine activities theory was initially designed to explain victimization from property crimes, lifestyle theory was developed to explore the risks of victimization from personal crimes. Research by Hindelang, Gottfredson, and Garofalo (1978) suggests that people who engage in risky lifestyle choices place themselves at risk for victimization. Based on one's lifestyle, one may increase the risk for criminal opportunity and victimization through both an increased exposure to criminal activity and an increased exposure to motivated offenders.

Given the similarities between the foundations of lifestyle theory and routine activities theory, many researchers today combine the tenets of these two perspectives to investigate victimization risks in general. These perspectives have been used to explain the risks of sexual assault of women on college campuses. Research by Fisher, Daigle, and Cullen (2010) illustrates that young women in the university setting who engage in risky lifestyle decision-making processes (such as the use of alcohol) and have routine activity patterns (such as living alone or frequenting establishments such as bars and clubs where men are present and alcohol is readily available) are at an increased risk for sexual victimization. In addition, women who are at risk for a single incident remain at risk for recurrent victimizations if their behavior patterns remain the same.

General Strain Theory

In 1992, **Robert Agnew** developed a theory of crime called the *general strain theory,* which has evolved and expanded over nearly two decades of empirical study. In this theory, Agnew hypothesized that delinquency and crime occur as a result of strain, which can stem from three factors. The first of these types of strain occurs after a failure to reach positively valued goals. Examples of this first type of strain include failure to reach a desired level of wealth, failure to do well in school, failure to go to college, and so on. The second type of strain in Agnew's theory is the loss of positively valued stimuli. This type of strain includes the death of a parent or loved one, the breakup of a romantic relationship, a job loss, or loss of a scholarship that enables school attendance. The third type of strain is the presence of negative stimuli. Examples of negative stimuli include being bullied, abused, or witnessing or being victimized by crime, especially violent crime.

Most people have an emotional response to strain, and both the type and intensity of the emotional response are predicated on several factors, including individual coping patterns, the presence of delinquent peers, the strength of prosocial bonds, and of course, personal resilience and the magnitude of the strain (Lin, Cochran, & Mieczkowski, 2008). Regardless of the type of strain one experiences (failure to reach positive goals, loss of positive stimuli, presence of negative stimuli), human emotional response to strain occurs within a fairly predictable range. These often include such responses as anger, anxiety, depression, heightened fear response, withdrawal, and so on (Aseltine, Gore, & Gordon, 2000; Broidy, 2001; Manasse & Ganem, 2009; Olweus, 1994).

Nearly two decades of research on general strain theory has examined the impact of strain on crime and delinquency. Instances of property crime are easily explained by general strain theory. For example, if a person is unable to achieve a desired level of wealth or loses a regular source of income and that person is surrounded by delinquent associates (and has few social bonds that would prevent the commission of crime), the person may feel sufficiently angry and justified to commit theft. Early studies examining general strain theory often conceptualized strain in this manner, as a response to a lack of financial resources—the first type of strain—leading to crime for fiscal gain or power.

Many recent studies, however, have examined the complex role of victimization in general strain theory. Agnew (2002) himself identified victimization as a strain likely to cause certain types of delinquency. Early victimization, including such examples as child abuse and vicarious exposure to IPA (such as witnessing violence between one's parents), is a poignant type of strain, one which often leads to negative outcomes for those initially seen as victims. Simply put, child maltreatment is associated with later delinquency (Benda, 2002; Hollist, Hughes, & Schaible, 2009), drug and alcohol abuse (Carson, Sullivan, Cochran, & Lersch, 2009; Lo, Kim, & Church, 2008), running away (Baron, 2003), selection by predators posing as rescuers (Albanese, 2007), and entry into the sex trade (Reid, 2011). For example, Reid (2011) explores the strain of child maltreatment, arguing that it is a path to sexual denigration of self/others and increases vulnerability to commercial sexual exploitation. Simply put, the strain of abuse as a child may put these children at risk of sexual exploitation in adulthood.

Feminist Pathways Perspective

The **feminist pathways perspective** suggests a cycle of criminal justice involvement for women that begins with victimization. Feminist pathways research seeks to use the historical context of women's and girls' lives to relate how life events (and traumas) affect their likelihood to engage in crime. Simply put, this means that female victimization, including such examples as being victimized by child abuse and exposure to IPA between a child's parents, may place a woman on a pathway to criminal offending later in life. Indeed, researchers have identified a **cycle of violence** for female offenders, one that often begins with their own victimization and results with their involvement in offending behavior. While the pathways perspective is discussed at length elsewhere in this book, the topic deserves a brief introduction as we conclude our discussion of theories of victimization.

The feminist pathways approach may provide some of the best understanding about how women find themselves stuck in a cycle that begins with victimization and leads to offending. Research on women's and girls' pathways to offending provides substantial evidence for the link between victimization and offending, as incarcerated girls are three to four times more likely to have been abused than their male counterparts (Belknap & Holsinger, 2006). A review of case files of delinquent girls in California indicates that 92% of delinquent girls in California reported having been subjected to at least one form of abuse, including emotional (88%), physical (81%), or sexual (56%) abuse (Acoca & Dedel, 1998). For female offenders, research indicates that a history of abuse leads to a propensity to engage in certain types of delinquency, most notably offenses such as running away and school failures, rather than acts of violence. The effects of sexual assault are also related to drug and alcohol addiction and mental health traumas, such as **post-traumatic stress disorder** and a negative self-identity (Raphael, 2005). In a cycle from victimization to offending, young girls often run away from home in an attempt to escape from an abusive situation. In many cases, girls were forced to return home by public agencies such as the police, courts, and social services—agencies designed to help victims of abuse. Unfortunately, in their attempt to escape from an abusive situation, girls often fall into criminal behaviors as a mechanism of survival. A discussion of further entry into criminal offending according to the feminist pathways model is included in Chapter 4, including emergence of such criminal offense types as prostitution, robbery, violence, sexual assault, and homicide.

SUMMARY

- Not all victims report their crimes to the police; they may seek out support from other sources.
- Victim-assistance programs have emerged as a key response to the secondary victimization often experienced by victims who come forward to the criminal justice system.
- Federal legislation has outlined key tenets of victim's rights, many of which have been incorporated into state-level constitutional amendments.
- Victim blaming has been linked to low reporting rates.
- Women experience higher rates of fear of crime compared to men.
- Gendered socialization and vulnerability to specific crime types (such as rape) may explain the gendered fear of crime.
- Mendelsohn's typology of victimization distinguishes different categories of victims based on the responsibility of the victim and the degree to which victims have the power to make decisions that can alter their likelihood of victimization.
- Von Hentig's typology of victimization focuses on how personal factors such as biological, social, and psychological characteristics influence risk factors for victimization.
- The just world hypothesis, which holds that people get what they deserve, is a subtle form of victim blaming that implies that there are few truly innocent victims and creates a false sense of security about the risks for victimization.
- Routine activities theory and lifestyle theory have been used to investigate the risk of sexual assault on women.
- Agnew's general strain theory suggests multiple negative consequences for victims, including delinquency, depression, running away, drug and alcohol use, and entry into the sex trade.
- The feminist pathways perspective suggests a cycle of criminal justice involvement for women whereby early victimization is sometimes a precursor to later criminal offending.

KEY TERMS

Agnew, Robert

Core rights of victims

Cycle of violence

Dating violence

Drug-facilitated sexual assault

Fear of victimization

Feminist pathways perspective

General strain theory

Just world hypothesis

Lifestyle theory

Mendelsohn's six categories of victims

Missing White woman syndrome

Post-traumatic stress disorder (PTSD)

Rape myth acceptance	Sexual slavery	Victim blaming
Rape myths	Shadow of sexual assault	Violence Against Women Act (VAWA)
Rape shield law		
Routine activities theory	Stranger rape	von Hentig's 13 categories of victims
Secondary victimization	Symbolic assailant	

DISCUSSION QUESTIONS

1. How do early theories of victimization distinguish between different types of victims? How might the criminal justice system use these typologies in making decisions about which cases to pursue?

2. What type of help-seeking behaviors do female crime victims engage in? How are these practices related to the reporting of crimes to law enforcement?

3. What effects does the practice of victim blaming have for future potential crime victims and the criminal justice system?

4. In what ways do media outlets support or dispel rape myths and victim blaming? How is this related to help-seeking behavior, official reporting, and revictimization?

5. How is fear of crime a gendered experience? What factors contribute to the differences in male versus female fear of crime? Do official crime statistics support or dispel the basis for these fear differences?

6. How might feminist criminologists critique modern-day victimization theories, such as routine activities theory and lifestyle theory?

7. How have historical theories on female offending failed to understand the nature of female offending?

8. How does Agnew's general strain theory explain the relationship between early victimization and later delinquency? How does this theory explain early victimization and later drug use or sexual victimization?

9. What contributions has feminist criminology made in understanding the relationship between gender and offending?

WEB RESOURCES

Bureau of Justice Statistics http://bjs.ojp.usdoj.gov

Feminist Criminology http://fcx.sagepub.com

The National Center for Victims of Crime http://www.ncvc.org

Office for Victims of Crime http://www.ojp.usdoj.gov/ovc/

REFERENCES

18 U.S.C. § 3771 (Crime Victim's Rights Act of 2004)

Acoca, L., & Dedel, K. (1998). *No place to hide: Understanding and meeting the needs of girls in the California juvenile justice system.* San Francisco, CA: National Council on Crime and Delinquency.

Agnew, R. (1992). Foundation for a general strain theory of crime and delinquency. *Criminology 30,* 47–87.

Agnew, R. (2002). Experienced, vicarious, and anticipated strain: An exploratory study on physical victimization and delinquency. *Justice Quarterly, 19,* 603–632.

Albanese, J. (2007). *Commercial sexual exploitation of children: What do we know and what can we do about it?* (NCJ Publication No. 215733). Washington, DC: National Institute of Justice. Retrieved from http://www.ncjrs .gov/pdffiles1/nij/215733.pdf

Arata, C. M. (1999). Coping with rape: The roles of prior sexual abuse and attributions of blame. *Journal of Interpersonal Violence, 14,* 62–78.

Aseltine, R. H., Jr., Gore, S. L., & Gordon, J. (2000). Life stress, anger, anxiety, and delinquency: An empirical test of general strain theory. *Journal of Health and Social Behavior, 41,* 256–275.

Baron, S. W. (2003). Street youth violence and victimization. *Trauma, Violence, & Abuse, 4,* 22–44. doi: 10.1177/1524838002238944

Belknap, J., & Holsinger, K. (2006). The gendered nature of risk factors for delinquency. *Feminist Criminology, 1*(1), 48–71.

Benda, B. (2002). The effect of abuse in childhood and in adolescents on violence among adolescents. *Youth & Society, 33*(3), 339–365.

Bieneck, S., & Krahe, B. (2011). Blaming the victim and exonerating the perpetrator in cases of rape and robbery: Is there a double standard? *Journal of Interpersonal Violence, 26*(9), 1785–1797.

Black, M. C., Basile, K. C., Breiding, M. J., Smith, S. G., Walters, M. L., Merrick, M. T., . . . Stevens, M. R. (2011). *The National Intimate Partner and Sexual Violence Survey (NISVS): 2010 summary report.* Atlanta, GA: National Center for Injury Prevention and Control, Centers for Disease Control and Prevention.

Bohner, G., Reinhard, M., Rutz, S., Sturm, S., Kerschbaum, B., & Effler, D. (1998). Rape myths as neutralizing cognitions: Evidence for a causal impact of anti-victim attitudes on men's self-reported likelihood of raping. *European Journal of Social Psychology, 28*(2), 257–268.

Broidy, L. M. (2001). A test of general strain theory. *Criminology, 39,* 9–35.

Call, J. E., Nice, D., & Talarico, S. M. (1991). An analysis of state rape shield laws. *Social Science Quarterly, 72*(4), 774–788.

Campbell, R. (2005). What really happened? A validation study of rape survivors' help-seeking experiences with the legal and medical systems. *Violence and Victims, 20,* 55–68.

Campbell, R. (2006). Rape survivors' experiences with the legal and medical systems: Do rape victim advocates make a difference? *Violence Against Women, 12,* 30–45.

Carson, D. C., Sullivan, C. J., Cochran, J. K., & Lersch, K. M. (2009). General strain theory and the relationship between early victimization and drug use. *Deviant Behavior, 30*(1), 54–88.

Chermack, S., & Bailey, F. (2007). *Crimes and trials of the century.* Westport, CT: Greenwood Press.

Chiricos, T., Padgett, K., & Gertz, M. (2000). Fear, TV news and the reality of crime. *Criminology, 38*(3), 755–786.

Clear, T., & Frost, N. (2007). Informing public policy. *Criminology & Public Policy, 6*(4), 633–640.

Cohen, L. E., & Felson, M. (1979, August). Social change and crime rate trends: A routine activity approach. *American Sociological Review, 44,* 588–608.

Colorado Coalition Against Sexual Assault. (2008). *2008 Report: Research on rape and violence.* Retrieved from http://www.ccasa.org/research-and-articles/#sarts

Cops, D., & Pleysier, S. (2011). "Doing gender" in fear of crime: The impact of gender identity on reported levels of fear of crime in adolescents and young adults. *British Journal of Criminology, 51*(1), 58–74. doi: 10.1093/bjc/azq065

Davies, K., Block, C. R., & Campbell, J. (2007). Seeking help from the police: Battered women's decisions and experiences. *Criminal Justice Studies, 20*(1), 15–41.

De Groof, S. (2008). And my mama said . . . The (relative) parental influence on fear of crime among adolescent boys and girls. *Youth & Society, 39*(3), 267–293.

de Vaus, D., & Wise, S. (1996). Parent's concern for the safety of their children. *Family Matters, 43,* 34–38.

Dowler, K. (2003). Media consumption and public attitudes toward crime and justice: The relationship between fear of crime, punitive attitudes, and perceived police effectiveness. *Journal of Criminal Justice and Popular Culture, 10*(2), 109–126.

Dugan, L., Nagin, D., & Rosenfeld, R. (2003). Exposure reduction or retaliation: Domestic violence resources on intimate-partner homicide. *Law & Society Review, 37*(1), 169–198.

Fattah, E. A., & Sacco, V. F. (1989). *Crime and victimization of the elderly.* New York, NY: Springer-Verlag.

Fisher, B. S., Daigle, L. E., & Cullen, F. T. (2010). What distinguishes single from recurrent sexual victims? The role of lifestyle-routine activities and first-incident characteristics. *Justice Quarterly, 27*(1), 102–129.

Fisher, B. S., & May, D. (2009). College students' crime-related fears on campus: Are fear-provoking cues gendered? *Journal of Contemporary Criminal Justice, 25*(3), 300–321.

Fisher, B. S., & Sloan, J. J. (2003). Unraveling the fear of sexual victimization among college women: Is the "shadow of sexual assault" hypothesis supported? *Justice Quarterly, 20,* 633–659.

Franiuk, R., Seefelt, J. L., Cepress, S. L., & Vandello, J. A. (2008). Prevalence and effects of rape myths in the media: The Kobe Bryant case. *Violence Against Women, 14,* 287–309.

Frost, N. A., & Phillips, N. D. (2011). Talking heads: Crime reporting on cable news. *Justice Quarterly, 28*(1), 87–112.

Gerbner, G., & Gross, L. (1980). The "mainstreaming" of America: Violence profile no. 11. *Journal of Communication, Summer 1980,* pp. 10–29.

Hall, S., French, D. P., & Marteau, T. M. (2003). Causal attributions following serious unexpected negative events: A systematic review. *Journal of Social and Clinical Psychology, 22,* 515–536.

Hart, T. C., & Rennison, C. M. (2003). National Crime Victimization Survey: Reporting crime to the police. *Bureau of Justice Statistics Special Report.* Retrieved from http://bjs.ojp.usdoj.gov/index.cfm?ty=pbdetail&iid=1142

Hindelang, M. J., Gottfredson, M. R., & Garofalo, J. (1978). *Victims of personal crime: An empirical foundation for a theory of personal victimization.* Cambridge, MA: Ballinger.

Hollist, D. R., Hughes, L. A., & Schaible, L. M. (2009). Adolescent maltreatment, negative emotion and delinquency: An assessment of general strain theory and family-based strain. *Journal of Criminal Justice, 37*(4), 379–387.

Jones-Brown, D. (2007). Forever the symbolic assailant: The more things change, the more they stay the same. *Criminology & Public Policy, 6*(1), 103–121.

Kaukinen, C. (2004). Status compatibility, physical violence, and emotional abuse in intimate relationships. *Journal of Marriage and Family, 66*(2), 452–471.

Killias, M. (1990).Vulnerability: Towards a better understanding of a key variable in the genesis of fear of crime. *Violence and Victims, 5,* 275–295.

Killias, M., & Clerici, C. (2000). Different measures of vulnerability in their relation to different dimensions of fear of crime. *British Journal of Criminology, 40,* 437–450.

LaGrange, R., & Ferraro, K. (1989). Assessing age and gender differences in perceived risk and fear of crime. *Criminology, 27,* 697–719.

Lane, J., Gover, A. R., & Dahod, S. (2009). Fear of violent crime among men and women on campus: The impact of perceived risk and fear of sexual assault. *Violence and Victims, 24*(2), 172–192.

Lerner, M. J. (1980). *The belief in a just world: A fundamental delusion.* New York, NY: Plenum Press.

Lin, W., Cochran, J. K., & Mieczkowski, T. (2008). Direct and vicarious violent victimization and juvenile delinquency: An application of general strain theory. *Sociological Inquiry, 81*(2), 195–222. doi: 10.1111/j.1475 –682X.2011.00368.x

Littleton, H., & Radecki Breitkopf, C. (2006). Coping with the experience of rape. *Psychology of Women Quarterly, 30,* 106–116.

Lo, C., Kim, Y., & Church, W. (2008). The effects of victimization on drug use: A multilevel analysis. *Substance Use & Misuse, 54*(4), 582–613.

Logan, T. K., Evans, L., Stevenson, E., & Jordan, C. E. (2005). Barriers to services for rural and urban survivors of rape. *Journal of Interpersonal Violence, 20*(5), 591–616.

Lopez, A. J. (2007). Expert: Victims' path rockier than celebrities'. *Rocky Mountain News.* Retrieved from http://therocky.com/news/2007/mar/15/expert-victims-path-rockier-than-celebrities/

Maguire, B. (1988). Image vs. reality: An analysis of prime-time television crime and police programs. *Journal of Crime and Justice, 11*(1), 165–188.

Manasse, M. E., & Ganem, N. M. (2009). Victimization as a cause of delinquency: The role of depression and gender. *Journal of Criminal Justice, 37*(4), 371–378.

Maxfield, M. (1984). The limits of vulnerability in explaining fear of crime: A comparative neighborhood analysis. *Journal of Research in Crime and Delinquency, 21,* 233–250.

Mendelsohn, B. (1963). The origin of the doctrine of victimology. *Excerpta Criminologica, 3*(30).

Miller, A. K., Markman, K. D., & Handley, I. A. (2007). Self-blame among sexual assault victims prospectively predicts revictimization: A perceived sociological model of risk. *Basic and Applied Social Psychology, 29*(2), 129–136. doi: 10.1080/01973530701331585

Mustaine, E. E., & Tewksbury, R. (2002). Sexual assault of college women: A feminist interpretation of a routine activities analysis. *Criminal Justice Review, 27*(1), 89–123.

National Center for Victims of Crime. (2011). About victims' rights. *Office of Justice Programs, Victim Law.* Retrieved from http://www.victimlaw.info/victimlaw/pages/victimsRight.jsp

Olweus, D. (1994). Bullying at school: Long-term outcomes for the victims and an effective school-based intervention program. In L. Rowell Huesmann (Ed.), *Aggression behavior: Current perspective* (pp. 97–130). New York, NY: Plenum Press.

Parsons, J., & Bergin, T. (2010). The impact of criminal justice involvement on victims' mental health. *Journal of Traumatic Stress, 23*(2), 182–188. doi: 10.1002/jts.20505

Patterson, D., & Campbell, R. (2010). Why rape survivors participate in the criminal justice system. *Journal of Community Psychology, 38*(2), 191–205, 215. doi: 10.1002/jcop.20359

Perona, A. R., Bottoms, B. L., & Sorenson, E. (2006). Research-based guidelines for child forensic interviews. *Journal of Aggression, Maltreatment & Trauma, 12*(3/4), 81–130. doi: 10.1300/J146v12n03•04

Potter, G., & Kappeler, V. (2006). *Constructing crime: Perspectives on making news and social problems* (2nd ed.). Long Grove, IL: Waveland Press.

Pub.L. 103–322 (Violence Against Women Act of 1994)

Pub.L. 102–325 §486(c) (Campus Sexual Assault Victims' Bill of Rights)

Rand, M. R. (2008). *Criminal Victimization 2007.* Bureau of Justice Statistics, U.S. Department of Justice. Retrieved September 14, 2009, from http://bjs.ojp.usdoj.gov/content/pub/pdf/cv07.pdf.

Raphael, K. G. (2005). Childhood abuse and pain in adulthood: More than a modest relationship?. *The Clinical Journal of Pain, 21*(5), 371–373.

Reid, J. (2011). An exploratory model of girl's vulnerability to commercial sexual exploitation in prostitution. *Child Maltreatment, 16*(2), 146–157.

Resnick, H., Acierno, R., Holmes, M., Dammeyer, M., & Kilpatrick, D. (2000). Emergency evaluation and intervention with female victims of rape and other violence. *Journal of Clinical Psychology, 56*(10), 1317–1333.

Schwartz, M. D., DeKeseredy, W. S., Tait, D., & Alvi, S. (2001). Male peer support and a feminist routing activities theory: Understanding sexual assault on the college campus. *Justice Quarterly, 18*(3), 623–649.

Sedlak, A. J., Finkelhor, D., Hammer, H., & Schultz, D. J. (2002). *National Estimates of Missing Children: An Overview in National Incidence Studies of Missing, Abducted, Runaway, and Thrownaway Children.* Washington, DC: Office of Juvenile Justice and Delinquency Prevention, Office of Justice Programs, U.S. Department of Justice.

Sengstock, M. C. (1976). *Culpable victims in Mendelsohn's typology.* Rockville, MD: National Institute of Justice. Retrieved from https://www.ncjrs.gov/App/publications/Abstract.aspx?id=48998

Skolnick, J. (1966). *Justice without trial.* New York, NY: Wiley.

Snedker, K. A. (2012). Explaining the gender gap in fear of crime: Assessments of risk and vulnerability among New York City residents. *Feminist Criminology, 7*(2), 75–111.

Starzynski, L. L., Ullman, S. E., Townsend, S. M., Long, L. M., & Long, S. M. (2007). What factors predict women's disclosure of sexual assault to mental health professionals? *Journal of Community Psychology, 35*(5), 619–638.

Stillman, S. (2007). The missing white girl syndrome: Disappeared women and media activism. *Gender & Development, 15*(3), 491–502.

Surette, R. (2003). The media, the public, and criminal justice policy. *Journal of the Institute of Justice & International Studies, 2,* 39–52.

Tamarit, J., Villacampa, C., & Fiella, G. (2010). Secondary victimization and victim assistance. *European Journal of Crime, Criminal Law & Criminal Justice, 18*(3), 281–298. doi: 10.1163/157181710X12767720266049

Truman, J. L. (2011). *BJS Bulletin: Criminal Victimization, 2010.* Washington, DC: National Crime Victimization Survey, U.S. Department of Justice.

Ullman, S. E., & Najdowski, C. J. (2011). Prospective changes in attributions of self-blame and social reactions to women's disclosures of adult sexual assault. *Basic & Applied Social Psychology, 26*(10), 1934–1963.

U.S. Department of Justice, Office of Justice Programs. (1998). *New directions from the field: Victims' rights and services for the 21st century.* Washington, DC: U.S. Government Printing Office.

Valentine, G. (1992). Images of danger: Women's sources of information about the spatial distribution of male violence. *Area, 24,* 22–29.

von Hentig, Hans. (1948). *The criminal and his victim.* New Haven, CT: Yale University Press.

Warr, M. (1984). Fear of victimization: Why are women and the elderly more afraid. *Social Science Quarterly, 65*(3), 681–702.

Warr, M. (1985). Fear of rape among urban women. *Social Problems,* 238–250.

Warr, M. (1987). Fear of victimization and sensitivity to risk. *Journal of Quantitative Criminology, 3,* 29–46.

Yeum, E. B. B. (2010). Eleventh annual review of gender and sexuality law: Criminal law, chapter: rape, sexual assault and evidentiary matters. *Geo. J. Gender & L., 11,* 191–869.

Young, J. (1987). The tasks facing a realist criminology. *Crime, Law and Social Change, 11*(4), 337–356.

Young, V. D. (1992). Fear of victimization and victimization rates among women: A paradox? *Justice Quarterly, 9*(3), 419–441.

Theories on Female Offending

Karla was nine years old at her first arrest. Her 16-year-old brother and several other gang members from the neighborhood told her to get some alcohol for a weekend barbeque. When the older kids drank, they would often let Karla have some. They also let her try drugs sometimes, but only the lighter stuff like marijuana and a few other substances that seemed to help her forget all her troubles. So Karla and Diana went to the corner liquor store—which had a new owner they thought wasn't very nice—to steal booze. Diana got out with a big bottle of vodka, some candy, and an air freshener. Karla hid a bottle of wine in her sweatshirt, and filled one pocket with candy and the other with mini liquor bottles. When she tried to slip a second bottle of wine into her sweatshirt, it slipped from her hands, shattering on the floor. She ran, the clerk followed, and she was arrested.

Fearing deportation, Karla's mother did not come to the police station when Karla called. Instead, nine-year-old Karla was booked in juvenile hall, where she spent the weekend. Her case was dismissed the following Monday, despite her young age and the obvious absence of a parent or caretaker at the hearing. To this day, Karla is certain that this was a paperwork error and believes some other poor kid got sent off in her place.

Karla was lauded when she returned home. Her brother and his friends praised her for taking a good rap—doing her time and keeping her mouth shut. However, Karla's mother was very upset about both her criminal activity and also for risking the family's deportation. Boyfriend # 18 beat Karla severely following her return home, and from here on, he alternated his assaults between mother and daughter.

Chapter Highlights

- Feminist criminology
- Critiques of traditional explanations of crime
- The intersections of criminal victimization and offending

T his chapter is devoted to the theoretical explanations of female offending. We begin with a review of the theoretical perspectives on offending and the failures of mainstream criminology to provide adequate explanations for women who offend. In tracing the evolution of a feminist perspective to explain crime, this chapter first examines how traditional theories of crime failed in understanding gender differences in crime and assesses whether modern-day applications of these perspectives can help explain female offending. We then turn to a discussion on how feminist researchers have sought out new perspectives to describe the nature of the female offender and her social world. The chapter concludes with a discussion on feminist criminology and how the offending patterns of women are often intertwined with their experiences of victimization.

Theoretical Perspectives on Female Criminality

Theories on criminality seek to explain why offenders engage in crime and highlight both macro and micro explanations for criminal behavior. Macro theories of criminality explore the large-scale social explanations for crime, while micro theories focus on individual differences between law-abiding and law-violating behaviors. Since the late 19th century, researchers have investigated the relationship between gender, crime, and punishment from macro as well as micro perspectives. As Belknap reflects, "female lawbreakers historically (and to some degree today) have been viewed as abnormal and as worse than male lawbreakers—not only for breaking the law but also for stepping outside of prescribed gender roles of femininity and passivity" (2007, p. 34). Arguments regarding the nature of female criminality have ranged from the aggressive, violent

Figure 4.1   Timeline on Theories of Female Offending

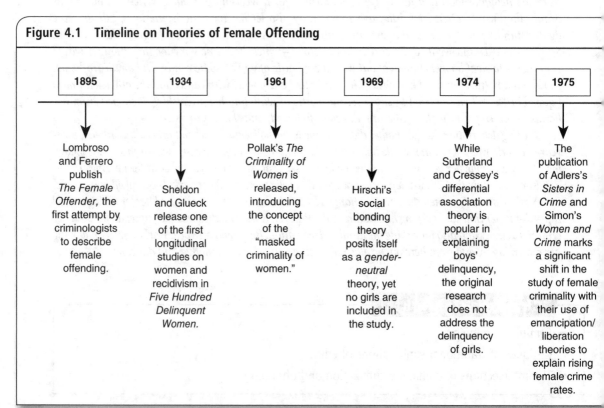

woman to the passive, helpless woman who is in need of protection. Consequently, theories on the etiology of female offending have reflected both of these perspectives. While theories on female crime have grown from their early roots, it is important to debate the tenets of these historical perspectives, as they provide a foundation to build a greater understanding of female offending.

Historical Theories on Female Criminality

Cesare Lombroso and William Ferrero represent the first criminologists to attempt to investigate the nature of the female offender. Expanding on his earlier work, *The Criminal Man,* Lombroso joined with Ferrero in 1895 to publish *The Female Offender.* Lombroso's basic idea was that criminals are biological throwbacks to a primitive breed of man and can be recognized by various "atavistic" degenerative physical characteristics. To test this theory for female offenders, Lombroso and Ferrero went to women's prisons, where they measured body parts and noted physical differences of the incarcerated women. They attributed a number of unique features to the female criminal, including occipital irregularities, narrow foreheads, prominent cheekbones, and a "virile" type of face. While they found that female offenders had fewer degenerative characteristics compared to male offenders, they explained these differences by suggesting that women, in general, are biologically more primitive and less evolved than men. They also suggested that the "evil tendencies" of female offenders "are more numerous and more varied than men's" (Lombroso & Ferrero, 1895, p. 151). Female criminals were believed to be more like men than women, both in terms of their mental and physical qualities, suggesting that female offenders were more likely to experience suppressed "maternal instincts" and "ladylike" qualities. They were convinced that women who engaged in crime would be less sensitive to pain,

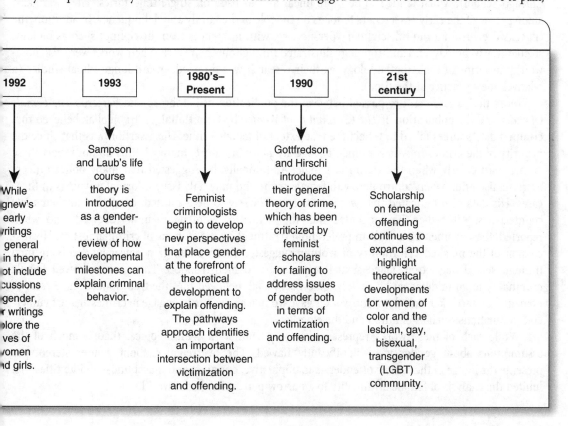

less compassionate, generally jealous, and full of revenge—in short, criminal women possessed all of the worst characteristics of the female gender while embodying the criminal tendencies of the male.

Obviously, the methods and findings of Lombroso and Ferrero have been harshly criticized, mostly due to their small sample size and the lack of heterogeneity of their sample demographics. They also failed to control for additional environmental and structural variables that might explain criminal behavior regardless of gender. Finally, their key assumptions about women had no scientific basis. Their claim that the female offender was more ruthless and less merciful had more to do with the fact that she had violated sex-role and gender-role expectations than the nature of her actual offending behaviors.

The works of Sheldon and Eleanor Glueck represent some of the earliest longitudinal studies on crime and delinquency. Their first book, *Five Hundred Criminal Careers* (1930), documented not only the childhoods and criminal histories of 500 men serving a prison sentence at the Massachusetts Reformatory at Concord but also followed the men for five years after their release from prison. In 1934, the Gluecks followed up this study with similar research on women, titled *Five Hundred Delinquent Women*. In studying 500 women and girls serving their time at the Massachusetts Reformatory of Women, their research not only sought to distinguish female offenders from their male counterparts, but it was also one of the first studies on recidivism amongst female offenders. While *Five Hundred Delinquent Women* was not as well-known as their other works, it was similar in philosophy and methodology to their other publications, as it looked at a variety of different factors to explain criminality. This approach varied dramatically from the perspectives of other researchers at the time (such as the Chicago School), which tended to be more linear and focused on single trajectories. They were also among some of the early researchers to focus on the role of the family and delinquency. In addition, the Gluecks drew from a multidisciplinary perspective, with influences from disciplines such as biology, sociology, psychology, and anthropology illustrated throughout their work. Their works were also noteworthy in terms of their methodology, as their research was directed toward longitudinal studies (a relatively new practice at the time).

More than a half-century passed between the publication of Lombroso and Ferrero's *The Female Offender* and the publication of *The Criminality of Women* by **Otto Pollak** (1961). Pollak believed that criminal data sources failed to reflect the true extent of female crime. His assertion was that since the majority of the crimes in which women engage are petty in nature, many victims do not report these crimes, particularly when the victim is a male. Additionally, he suggested that many police officers exercise discretion when confronted with female crime and may only issue informal warnings in these cases. His data also indicated that women were more likely to be acquitted, compared to their male counterparts. Altogether, he concluded that the crimes of women are underreported, and when reported, these women benefit from preferential treatment by the systems of criminal justice. His discussion of the **masked criminality of women** suggested that women gain power by deceiving men through sexual playacting, faked sexual responses, and menstruation. This power allowed female criminality to go undetected by society. Likewise, Pollak believed that the traditional female roles of homemaker, caretaker, and domestic worker gave women an avenue to engage in crimes against vulnerable populations, such as children and the elderly.

While each of these works represented a new frontier in criminological theory, much of the assumptions about gender were significantly flawed. The overreliance about gender stereotypes presents the image of the female offender as manipulative, cunning, and masculine—all identities that limited the analysis of female criminality to a narrow perception of the world.

Traditional Theories on Crime and Gender

Meanwhile, a number of criminological theories rose to fame during the mid- and late 20th century. The majority of these explanations focused exclusively on male criminality, with little consideration for women's lives. Indeed, the rationale that females represented a small proportion of the offending populations was often used to justify their exclusion from theoretical discussions. Even in cases where theorists presented themselves as gender neutral, they either did not include women in their studies, or they utilized limited samples of girls in testing their gender-neutral approach. As a result, many of these perspectives included gross gendered stereotypes about women and girls. Daly and Chesney-Lind highlight a further argument about the presumed gender neutrality of criminological theories—"what does it mean to develop a gender-neutral theory of crime . . . when neither the social order nor the structure of crime is gender-neutral?" (Daly & Chesney-Lind, 1988, p. 516).

Travis Hirschi's social bond theory (1969) is one such example of a proposed gender-neutral theory that failed to consider the lives of girls and women. While most theories up to this time focused on why offenders engage in crime, Hirschi's work was unique in that it highlighted why people may *not* become involved in criminal activity. His theory focused on four criteria, or *bonds*, that prevent people from acting on potential criminological impulses or desires. He identified these bonds as (1) **attachment**, (2) **commitment**, (3) **involvement**, and (4) **belief**. First, *attachment* refers to the bond that people have with the values of society as a result of their relationships with family, friends, and social institutions (such as government, education, and religion). Here, attachment serves as a form of informal social control. When individuals do not want to disappoint people in their lives, they conform to the legal and normative structures of the community. For example, youth who have positive attachments to parents or peers may inhibit their delinquent behavior out of concern to not disappoint their families and friends. The second concept, *commitment*, refers to the investment that an individual has to the normative values of society. The notion of commitment invokes sentiments of rational choice. For example, if one is committed to obtaining a college degree and a law violation might limit one's ability to achieve that goal, then one might decide not to engage in the illegal behavior out of fear of jeopardizing one's future. Third, *involvement* refers to one's level of participation in conventional activities. For juveniles, this might include studying, playing sports, or participating in other extracurricular activities. Here, Hirschi suggested that youth who are more involved are less likely to engage in delinquent activities. Finally, the concept of *belief* refers to a general acceptance of society's rules in general, as "the less a person believes he should obey the rules, the more likely he is to violate them" (Hirschi, 1969, p. 26).

Throughout Hirschi's work, he illustrated that families can serve as one of the strongest inhibitors of delinquency—"the more strongly a child is attached to his [or her] parents, the more strongly he [or she] is bound to their expectations, and therefore the more strongly he [or she] is bound to conformity with the legal norms of the larger system" (1969, p. 94). Research has indicated that girls are more emotionally attached to their parents, and it is this bond that serves to protect girls from delinquency (Heimer, 1996). Likewise, research by Huebner and Betts (2002) found that a strong attachment bond to parents and other adults serves as a protective factor for girls. However, this may also be related to the increased focus by parents on the lives of their daughters. Additionally, parents are more concerned about girls than boys, and girls are more likely to share the details about their life to their parents, compared to boys. As a result, girls experience higher levels of shaming by their parents compared to their male counterparts when they do deviate from social norms and values (Svensson, 2004).

Ozbay and Ozcan (2008) investigate whether social bond theory can be used to explain the context of male and female delinquency outside of American society. In their research on gender and social bonds among Turkish youth, their results indicate that social bonds have a stronger effect on the lives of female students. Given the heightened status of the family within Turkish culture as well as differences in gender socialization between adolescent boys and girls in this region, it is not surprising that girls would be highly attached to the family unit. For boys, educational bonds, such as an attachment to teachers, is a stronger influence in preventing delinquency. In contrast, studies involving American students indicate that an attachment toward school and educational achievement serves as a protective factor against delinquency for both boys and girls (Lowe, May, & Elrod, 2008). However, girls who are less attached to school are more likely to engage in nonviolent acts of delinquency (Daigle, Cullen, & Wright, 2007).

While Hirschi's social bond theory highlighted the power of positive attachments toward peers as a protective factor against delinquency, **Edwin Sutherland's differential association theory** focused on the influence of these relationships in encouraging delinquent behavior. Differential association theory incorporates characteristics from social learning theory, which suggests that criminality is a learned behavior and not an innate biological or psychological characteristic. Here, delinquency occurs as a result of "an excess of definitions favorable to violations of law over definitions unfavorable to violations of law" (Sutherland & Cressey, 1974, p. 75). Differential association theory posits that definitions are acquired as a result of one's peer associations—people that youth spend time with and therefore influence their knowledge, practices, and judgments on delinquent behavior. The greater the exposure to these delinquent attitudes and behaviors, the more influence they have on the individual. Like many social theories of the 20th century, discussions of gender were absent in differential association theory.

Recent research has provided mixed results in the application of differential association for girls. Race and ethnicity also impact the effects of the peer relationship on delinquent behavior for girls. Silverman and Caldwell (2008) find that peer attitudes have the greatest effect on youth behavior for Hispanic girls. Here, the *strength of the peer relationship* plays a key factor, as rates of violent delinquent behavior increase if the peer group deems that the delinquency is an acceptable behavior. For Caucasian girls, it is *time* that plays the biggest role. Here, the influences of peers on violent delinquent behavior increase with the proportion of time that is spent with the group (Silverman & Caldwell, 2008). However, not all findings demonstrate support for differential association theory for girls, as research by Daigle et al. (2007) and Lowe et al. (2008) indicate that influences from delinquent peers lead to an increase in delinquency for boys, but not for girls. Indeed, it may be that while peer associations can impact delinquency, the effect is stronger for the delinquency of boys than girls (Piquero, Gover, MacDonald, & Piquero, 2005).

Another theory that has frequently been used to explain offending behaviors is *strain theory*. While several theorists have made contributions to the understanding of the role of individual aspirations and social expectations on criminal behaviors, the works of Robert Agnew represent perhaps the most modern of these applications. While traditional theories of strain by scholars such as Merton (1938) and Cohen (1955) emphasized the role of structural limitations in achieving success, Agnew's (1992) general strain theory (GST) expanded into individualized psychological sources of strain. Here, Agnew highlighted three potential sources of strain: (1) failure in achieving positive goals, (2) the loss of positive influences, and (3) the arrival of negative influences.

Since his initial findings, Agnew has continued to develop GST to explain and expand the understanding of not only boys' delinquency but that of girls as well. Research by Broidy and Agnew (1997) argues that GST can be used to explain gender differences in crime. First, males and females experience different types of strain. Here, it is not that male strain is more or less than the strain experienced by females, but it is the *source* of the strain that differs by gender. For example, girls are more likely to experience strain as a result of violence in the home (physical, emotional, and sexual), which in turn leads to delinquent acts such as running away and substance abuse. Second, boys and girls respond to strain differently. Strain can manifest as anger for both boys and girls. Such anger in boys tends to manifest in emotional outbursts while girls are more likely to internalize such emotions, leading to issues such as depression and self-destructive behaviors (Broidy & Agnew, 1997). While boys experience higher levels of traditional strain than girls (defined here as aspirations for higher educational success), girls are more likely to have negative life events and report higher levels of conflict with their parents. It is these issues and not traditional strain that increases involvement in delinquency for girls (Daigle et al., 2007).

While Hirschi's social bond theory approached criminal behavior from a macro-level perspective, his general theory of crime (with Michael Gottfredson) is considered more of a micro-level theory in that it focuses on a single individual-level explanation for criminal behavior—self-control. Gottfredson and Hirschi's argument is that self-control captures all of the reasons behind why someone would engage in or desist from crime. According to the general theory of crime, those individuals with high levels of social control will remain law abiding, while those with low social control will be more likely to engage in deviant and criminal activities. But the question remains: What influences an individual's self-control? Gottfredson and Hirschi posit that the development of self-control is rooted in the family. The more involved parents are in their children's lives, the more likely they are to note challenges to the development of their children's self-control and are more likely to correct these issues at a young age. As a result, Gottfredson and Hirschi's general theory of crime suggests that early intervention efforts are the only effective tool to deter individuals from crime. Variables such as gender, race, and class are irrelevant on their own, as everything comes down to self-control (Gottfredson & Hirschi, 1990).

While Gottfredson and Hirschi did not provide specific definitions for self-control, many researchers have tested the general theory of crime using constructs such as impulsivity, risk taking, and aggression as indicators of self-control. However, results on gender and self-control have been mixed. Some scholars find evidence that weaker family controls for boys lead to increases in impulsive behaviors, which in turn can influence delinquency (Chapple & Johnson, 2007). Here, it seems that the differential socialization of boys and girls during the early years can impact how individuals use self-control toward criminal behavior. Likewise, research by DeLisi et al. (2010) on delinquent youth housed in the California Youth Authority indicate that while self-control measures effectively predict behavioral violations for males, they fail to explain the rates of misconduct for girls. Instead, misconduct in girls is more likely to be explained by other variables, such as age (younger girls are more likely to act out) and the presence of a psychiatric disorder.

Self-control theory also explains higher rates of **white-collar crime** (such as software piracy) offending for males (Higgins, 2006). Self-control can also be used in cases of deviant (but noncriminal) behavior, such as eating disorders and borderline personality characteristics (which are more common among females; Harrison, Jones, & Sullivan, 2008). Yet when measures of opportunity to engage in crime are added to analyses of self-control, research indicates that these two measures together explain higher levels of female property offending than self-control on its own (LaGrange & Silverman, 1999). The effects of low self-control also disappear when measures of social learning theory are introduced (Burton, Cullen, Evans, Alarid, & Dunaway, 1998). On its own, it appears that self-control theory is more effective at explaining male criminality, compared to female criminality.

Feminist critiques of the general theory of crime argue that it may be impossible to effectively investigate whether self-control influences the decision to engage in criminal behavior in women. Scholars have suggested that the concept of self-control is rooted in a masculine identity. As a result, it may be difficult to interpret the meaning of self-control within the context of women's lives (Daly & Chesney-Lind, 1988). Further critiques of self-control theory highlight its ineffectiveness in explaining male criminality in cases of violence against women (Iovanni & Miller, 2008). Intimate partner abuse is not a simple act of losing control—it is a deliberate action of power and control by one individual over another. "When gender relations and differences in power, resources, and opportunities are considered, it becomes clear that the relationship between gender and crime is more complex than the one portrayed by the general theory" (Iovanni & Miller, 2008, p. 140).

While each of these theories offered little evidence or explanation about female criminality in the early stages of their development, later research has investigated whether these traditional theories of crime can explain criminality in women. To date, these conclusions are mixed—while some provide evidence that these theories can make contributions to understanding female crime, others are more suited to explain male criminality, as they were originally conceived.

Modern Theories on Female Offending Behaviors

The emergence of works by **Freda Adler** and **Rita Simon** in the 1970s marked a significant shift in the study of female criminality. The works of Adler and Simon were inspired by the emancipation of women that was occurring during the 1960s and 1970s in the United States and the effects of the second wave of the feminist movement. Both authors highlighted how the liberation of women would lead to an increased participation of women in criminal activities. While Adler (1975) suggested that women's rates of violent crime would increase, Simon (1975) hypothesized that women would commit a greater proportion of property crimes as a result of their liberation from traditional gender roles and restrictions. While both authors broke new ground in the discussion of female crime, their research has also been heavily criticized. Analysis on crime statistics between 1960 and 1975 indicates that while female crime rates for violent crimes skyrocketed during this time period, so did the rates of male violent crime. In addition, one must consider the reference point of these statistics. True, more women engaged in crime. However, given the low number of female offenders in general, small increases in the number of crimes can create a large percentage increase, which can be misinterpreted and overexaggerated. For example, if women are involved in 100 burglaries in one year, and this number increases to 150 burglaries in the next year, this reflects a 50% increase from one year to the next. If, however, men participated in 1,000 burglaries

▲ **Photo 4.1** Throughout the 20th century, the number of arrests involving females has increased dramatically. Feminist criminologists highlight that many of the traditional theories of crime fail to address the unique needs of offending women. In addition, much of these data reflect changes in policies regarding societal perspectives of female offending versus a direct increase in the rates of offending by women.

in one year, and in 1,250 during the next, this is only a 25% increase, even though the actual numerical increase is greater for men than women.

Another criticism of Adler and Simon's works focuses on their overreliance on the effects of the women's liberation movement. While it is true that the emancipation of women created increased opportunities and freedoms to engage in crime, this does not necessarily mean that women were more compelled to engage in crime. Changing policies in policing and the processing of female offenders may reflect an increase of women in the system as a result of changes in the response by the criminal justice system to crimes involving women.

In addition to Adler's and Simon's focus on the emancipation of women as an explanation for increasing crime rates, criminological theory saw an increased interest in developing an understanding of female criminality and in explaining crime in general. Here, theories shifted from a focus on individual pathology to one that referenced social processes and the greater social environment. Drawing influences from social control theory, **power control theory** was one of the few theories to incorporate gender as a central theme in understanding criminal behavior. Developed by **John Hagan** (1989), power control theory looks at the effects of patriarchy within the family unit as a tool of socialization for gender roles. His work begins with the premise that women and girls are socialized in different ways than men and boys. Boys are granted greater freedoms than girls and are encouraged to be more aggressive, ambitious, and outgoing. Here, Hagan suggests that families with patriarchal values are more likely to protect their daughters and restrict freedoms. As a result of such power differentials, the expectation of power control theory is that boys will demonstrate higher rates of delinquency, whereas girls would have fewer opportunities to engage in crime, leading to lower rates of crime. In contrast, families that are structured in a more egalitarian or balanced manner will see fewer differences by gender in the socialization of their children, which in turn leads to fewer gender differences in delinquency.

One of the weaknesses of Hagan's theory lies in its focus of two-parent families. Given the increasing number of children residing in divorced, separated, and non-cohabitating homes, it is important to consider how power control theory might apply in these settings. Research by Bates, Bader, and Mencken (2003) demonstrates that single fathers tend to exert similar levels of parental control over their children as two-parent patriarchal families, while single mothers demonstrate lower levels of patriarchy in the household. In cases of higher levels of parental control, girls are more likely to view deviant behaviors as risky, and they therefore refrain from engagement. Yet the single parent is less likely to be able to monitor youth behaviors outside of the home as compared to a two-parent household. Here, family structure may present an indirect, though important, effect on youth delinquency.

Another modern theory that has been used to investigate the causes of female offending is **Robert Sampson** and **John Laub's** (1993) **life course theory**. Life course theory suggests that the events of one's life (from birth to death) can provide insight as to why one might engage in crime and highlights the importance of adolescence as a crucial time in the development of youthful (and ultimately adult) offending behaviors. Here, ties to conventional adult activities such as family and work can serve as a protective factor in adulthood, even if the individual has engaged in delinquent acts during adolescence. While not specifically a feminist theory of crime, life course theory does allow for a gender-neutral review of how the different developmental milestones in one's life can explain criminal behavior. Recent applications of life course theory have included discussions of gender in their analysis. Research by Thompson and Petrovic (2009) investigated the effects that marriage, education, employment, and children have for women and men on illegal substance use. Their research indicates that social bonds impact men and women differently. While Sampson and Laub suggested that marriage serves to inhibit criminality in men, Thompson and Petrovic (2009) did not find a similar effect for women in terms of illicit drug use. Here, it is not marriage that serves to reduce illicit drug use but rather the strength of the relationship that leads to a reduction of substance abuse for women. Research by Belknap and Holsinger (2006) suggests that while life course theory can have value for understanding the delinquent and criminal behaviors of girls and women, life course theory needs to expand its understanding of what marks a significant life event. In particular, Belknap and Holsinger point to the effects of early childhood abuse traumas, mental health concerns, and sexual identity.

These modern theories made significant improvements in understanding the relationship between gender and crime. Unlike traditional theorists, these modern theories prominently displayed gender within the context of their theoretical development. However, critiques of these theories demonstrate that there is a need for increased discussions about women and crime, particularly given the context of women's lives and the relationship between their lived experiences and their criminality.

Feminist Criminology

The emergence of feminist criminology builds upon the themes of gender roles and socialization to explain patterns of female offending. Here, scholars begin with a discussion of the backgrounds of female offenders in an effort to assess who she is, where she comes from, and why she engages in crime. Feminist criminology reflects several key themes in its development. Frances Heidensohn (1985, p. 61) suggested that "feminist criminology began with the awareness that women were invisible in conventional studies in the discipline. . . . feminist criminology began as a reaction . . . against an old established male chauvinism in the academic discipline." While some criminologists suggested that traditional theories of crime could account for explanations in female offending, others argued that in order to accurately theorize about the criminal actions of women, a new approach to the study of crime needed to be developed.

> Theoretical criminology was constructed by men, about men. It is simply not up to the analytical task of explaining female patterns of crime . . . thus, something quite different will be needed to explain women and crime. . . . existing theories are frequently so inconsistent with female realities that specific explanations of female patterns of crime will probably have to precede the development of an all-inclusive theory. (Leonard, 1982, pp. xi–xii)

While many researchers (both men and women) have provided significant contributions to the field of feminist criminology, the works of Meda Chesney-Lind stand out as some of the most powerful and valuable scholarship in the field. In her article, "Feminist Criminology" (with Kathleen Daly), she highlights how feminist thought can influence the field of criminology. As you learned earlier in this chapter, many of the traditional theories of crime focused only on male criminality. Daly and Chesney-Lind (1988) point out that feminist discussions aren't limited to "women's issues"—rather any discussion of women's lives needs to incorporate conversations on masculinity and the influence of men's lives and issues on women. Given the historical distortions and the casual assumptions that have been made about women's lives in relationship to their criminal behaviors, incorporating feminist perspectives can provide a richer understanding about not only the nature of female offending but also the victimization experiences of women. In addition, feminist perspectives highlight that feminist criminology is not a single identity, but an opportunity to consider multiple influences when understanding issues of gender and crime. Finally, Daly and Chesney-Lind posited that scholars should consider the role of patriarchy in the causes of and responses to female offending.

The use of feminist theory, methodologies, and activism in discussions of criminology has led to a variety of new understandings about gender and crime. Perhaps one of the most influential perspectives to date on female offending is the feminist pathways approach. Feminist pathways research seeks to use the historical context of women's and girls' lives to show how life events (and traumas) affect the likelihood to engage in crime. While the pathways approach has many similarities with other theories such as life course or cycle of violence, these theories do not explain women's criminality from a feminist perspective, while the feminist pathways approach begins with a feminist foundation (Belknap, 2007). Within the feminist pathways approach, researchers have identified a cycle of violence for female offenders that begins with their own victimization and results with their involvement in offending behavior.

For example, Belknap and Holsinger (1998) identify that the entry to delinquency for boys and girls is a gendered experience. Their research suggests that understanding the role of victimization in the histories of incarcerated women may be one of the most significant contributions for feminist criminology, as female offenders report substantially high occurrences of physical, emotional, and sexual abuse throughout their lifetimes. While such an explanation does not fit all female offenders (and also fits some male offenders), the recognition of these risks appears to be essential for understanding the etiology of offending for many girls and women. Yet this link between victimization and offending has largely been invisible or deemed inconsequential by the powers that be in criminology theory building and by those responsible for responding to women's and girls' victimizations and offenses (Belknap & Holsinger, 1998).

Another example of research incorporating a feminist pathways perspective is Wesely's (2006) research on homeless women and exotic dancers. The women in her study experienced levels of abuse and victimization throughout their childhood that were "located within a nexus of powerlessness, gender-specific sexualization and exploitation, economic vulnerability and destitution, and social alienation and exclusion" (Wesley, p. 309). As a result, these victimized women grew up accepting the violence in their lives as an ordinary and normal experience, and this influenced their decision-making practices throughout their lives. For example, these women learned at an early age that their sexuality was a tool that could be used to manipulate and gain control over others. The decision to engage in sex work or to become homeless directly correlated with their decision to leave home at a young age to escape the physical and sexual abuse they experienced by their parents and family members. Ultimately, these decisions contributed to further victimizations in their lives where their "lived experiences contributed to a downward spiral in which the women were preoccupied with daily survival, beaten down, depressed, and unsuccessful at making choices or having opportunities that improved their life conditions" (Wesley, p. 314–315).

Indeed, the feminist pathways approach may provide some of the best information on how women find themselves stuck in a cycle that begins with victimization and leads to offending. Research on women's and girls' pathways to offending provides substantial evidence for the link between victimization and offending, as incarcerated girls are three to four times more likely to be abused than their male counterparts. A review of case files of delinquent girls in California indicates that 92% of delinquent girls in California reported having been subjected to at least one form of abuse (emotional = 88%; physical = 81%; sexual = 56%; Acoca & Dedel, 1997).

For female offenders, research overwhelmingly indicates that a history of abuse leads to a propensity to engage in certain types of delinquency. However, the majority of research points to women committing such offenses as running away and school failure, rather than acts of violence. The effects of sexual assault are also related to drug and alcohol addiction and mental health traumas, such as post-traumatic stress disorder and a negative self-identity (Raphael, 2004). In a **cycle of victimization and offending**, young girls often ran away from home in an attempt to escape from an abusive situation. In many cases, girls were forced to return home by public agencies such as the police, courts, and social services—agencies designed to help victims of abuse. Girls who refused to remain in these abusive situations were often incarcerated and labeled as "out of parental control."

In a review of case files of girls who had been committed to the California Youth Authority during the 1960s, most girls were incarcerated for status offenses (a legal charge during that time frame). Many of these girls were committed to the Youth Authority for running away from home, where significant levels of alcoholism, mental illness, sexual abuse, violence, and other acts of crime were present. Unfortunately, in their attempt to escape from an abusive situation, girls often fell into criminal behaviors as a mechanism of survival. Running away from home placed girls at risk for crimes of survival such as prostitution, where the level of violence they experienced was significant and included behaviors such as robbery, assault, and rape. These early offenses led these girls to spend significant portions of their adolescence behind bars. As adults, these same girls who had committed no crimes in the traditional sense later were convicted for a wide variety of criminal offenses, including serious felonies (Rosenbaum, 1989). Gilfus's (1992) work characterizes the pathway to delinquency as one of "blurred boundaries," as the categories of victim and offender are not separate and distinct. Rather, girls move between the categories throughout their lives, as their victimization does not stop once they become offenders. In addition to the victimization they experienced as a result of their survival strategies, many continued to be victimized by the system through its failure to provide adequate services for girls and women (Gaarder & Belknap, 2002).

Feminist criminologists have also worked at identifying how issues such as race, class, and sexuality impact victimization and offending behaviors (and the system's response to them). This perspective builds upon traditional concepts of feminist criminology by adding an understanding of how women of color experience multiple marginalized identities, which in turn impact the understanding of the trajectories of women and crime. Research by Potter (2006) suggests that combining Black feminist theory and critical race feminist theory with feminist criminology allows for an increased understanding of how Black women experience crime. Black feminist criminology identifies four themes that together alter the experiences for Black women in the criminal justice system: The first of these categories highlights the structural oppression of Black women in society. The second category looks at the unique nature of the Black community and culture. The third category focuses on the intimate and familial relations for Black families. Finally, the fourth category emphasizes the Black woman as an individual (Potter, 2006). Together, these unique dimensions lead to a different experience for Black women within the criminal justice system.

Developments in feminist research have addressed the significant relationship between victimization and offending. A history of abuse is not only highly correlated with the propensity to engage in criminal behaviors, but it often dictates the types of behaviors in which young girls engage. Often, these behaviors are methods of surviving their abuse, yet the criminal nature of these behaviors brings these girls to the attention of the criminal justice system. The success of a feminist perspective is dependent on a theoretical structure that not only has to answer questions about crime and delinquency but also has to address issues such as sex-role expectations and patriarchal structures within society (Chesney-Lind, 2006). The inclusion of feminist criminology has important policy implications for the justice system in the 21st century. As Belknap and Holsinger (2006, pp. 48–49) note,

> the ramifications of the traditionally male-centered approaches to understanding delinquency not only involve ignorance about what causes girls' delinquency but also threaten the appropriateness of systemic intervention with and treatment responses for girls.

As feminist criminology continues to provide both an understanding of the causes of female offending and explanations for the changes in the gender gap of offending, it will also face its share of challenges. Both Chesney-Lind (2006) and Burgess-Proctor (2006) have suggested that the future of feminist criminology centers on exploring the relationship between gender, race, and class. Recent research in these areas highlights how increases in the incarceration of women as a result of the war on drugs has become not only a war on women in general (Bloom, Owen, & Covington, 2004) but specifically a war against women of color (Bush-Baskette, 1998, 1999). In addition, much of the work of feminist scholars has evolved from desire to stimulate change for the lives of women as victims and offenders. Chesney-Lind (2006) advocates that feminist criminologists need to continue to create opportunities to link their research and activism, particularly given some of the recent trends in crime control policies that have both intentional and unintentional consequences for the lives of women, their families, and their communities.

SUMMARY

- Early biological studies of female criminality were based on gross assumptions of femininity and had limited scientific validity.
- Classical theories of crime saw women as doubly deviant—not only did women break the law, but they violated traditional gender role assumptions.
- Applications of social bond theory illustrate that family bonds can reduce female delinquency, while educational bonds have a stronger effect for boys.
- Recent tests of differential association theory indicate that peer associations may have a stronger effect on male delinquency than female delinquency.
- Research on general strain theory illustrates that not only do girls experience different types of strain than boys, but they also respond to experiences of strain differently.
- Life course theory examines how adverse life events impact criminality over time and can provide insight on both female and male offending patterns.
- Theories of female criminality during the 1960s and 1970s focused on the effects of the emancipation of women, gendered assumptions about female offending, and the differential socialization of girls and boys.
- The feminist pathways approach has identified a cycle for women and girls that begins with their own victimization and leads to their offending.

KEY TERMS

Adler, Freda

Attachment

Belief

Commitment

Cycle of victimization and offending

Differential association theory

Emancipation/ liberation theory

Emotional abuse

Hagan, John

Hirschi, Travis

Involvement

Laub, John

Life course theory

Lombroso, Cesare, and William Ferrero

Masked criminality of women

Pollak, Otto

Power control theory

Sampson, Robert

Simon, Rita

Social bond theory

Sutherland, Edwin

White-collar crime

DISCUSSION QUESTIONS

1. How have historical theories on female offending failed to understand the nature of female offending?

2. What has recent research on gender and traditional theories of crime illustrated about the nature of female offending?

3. What contributions has feminist criminology made in understanding the relationship between gender and offending?

WEB RESOURCES

Bureau of Justice Statistics http://bjs.ojp.usdoj.gov

Feminist Criminology http://fcx.sagepub.com

REFERENCES

Acoca, L., & Dedel, K. (1997). *Identifying the needs of young women in the juvenile justice system.* San Francisco, CA: National Council on Crime and Delinquency.

Adler, F. (1975). *Sisters in crime: The rise of the new female criminal.* New York, NY: McGraw-Hill.

Agnew, R. (1992). Foundation for a general strain theory of crime and delinquency. *Criminology, 30,* 47–88.

Bates, K. A., Bader, C. D., & Mencken, F. C. (2003). Family structure, power-control theory and deviance: Extending power-control theory to include alternate family forms. *Western Criminological Review, 4*(3), 170–190.

Belknap, J. (2007). *The invisible woman: Gender, crime and justice* (3rd ed.). Belmont, CA: Wadsworth.

Belknap, J., & Holsinger, K. (1998). An overview of delinquent girls: How theory and practice failed and the need for innovative change. In R. Zaplin (Ed.), *Female crime and delinquency: Critical perspectives and effective interventions* (pp. 21–64). Gaithersburg, MD: Aspen.

Belknap, J., & Holsinger, K. (2006). The gendered nature of risk factors for delinquency. *Feminist Criminology, 1*(1), 48–71.

Bloom, B., Owen, B., & Covington, S. (2004). Women offenders and the gendered effects of public policy. *Review of Policy Research, 21*(1), 31–48.

Broidy, L., & Agnew, R. (1997). Gender and crime: A general strain theory perspective. *Journal of Research in Crime and Delinquency, 34,* 275–306.

Burgess-Proctor, A. (2006). Intersections of race, class, gender and crime: Future directions for feminist criminology. *Feminist Criminology, 1*(1), 27–47.

Burton, V. S., Cullen, F. T., Evans, D., Alarid, L. F., & Dunaway, G. (1998). Gender, self-control and crime. *Journal of Research in Crime and Delinquency, 35*(2), 123–147.

Bush-Baskette, S. (1998). The war on drugs as a war on Black women. In S. L. Miller (Ed.), *Crime control and women* (pp. 113–129). Thousand Oaks, CA: SAGE.

Bush-Baskette, S. (1999). The war on drugs: A war against women? In S. Cook & S. Davies (Eds.), *Harsh punishment: International experiences of women's imprisonment* (pp. 211–229). Boston, MA: Northeastern University Press.

Chapple, C. L., & Johnson, K. A. (2007). Gender differences in impulsivity. *Youth Violence and Juvenile Justice, 5*(3), 221–234.

Chesney-Lind, M. (2006). Patriarchy, crime and justice: Feminist criminology in an era of backlash. *Feminist Criminology, 1*(1), 6–26.

Cohen, A. K. (1955). *Delinquent boys.* Glencoe, IL: Free Press.

Daigle, L. E., Cullen, F. T., & Wright, J. P. (2007). Gender differences in the predictors of juvenile delinquency: Assessing the generality-specificity debate. *Youth Violence and Juvenile Justice, 5*(3), 254–286.

Daly, K., & Chesney-Lind, M. (1988). Feminism and criminology. *Justice Quarterly, 5*(4), 497–538.

DeLisi, M., Beaver, K. M., Vaughn, M. G., Trulson, C. R., Kisloski, A. E., Drury, A. J., & Wright, J. P. (2010). Personality, gender and self-control theory revisited: Results from a sample of institutionalized juvenile delinquents. *Applied Psychology in Criminal Justice, 6*(1), 31–46.

Gaarder, E., & Belknap, J. (2002). Tenuous borders: Girls transferred to adult court. *Criminology, 40*(3), 481–518.

Gilfus, M. E. (1992). From victims to survivors to offenders: Women's routes of entry and immersion into street crime. *Women and Criminal Justice, 4*(1), 63–89.

Glueck, S., & Glueck, E. (1930). *Five hundred criminal careers.* New York, NY: Knopf.

Glueck, S., & Glueck, E. (1935). Five hundred delinquent women. *University of Pennsylvania Law Review,* 551–553.

Gottfredson, M., & Hirschi, T. (1990). *A general theory of crime.* Palo Alto, CA: Stanford University Press.

Hagan, J. (1989). *Structural criminology.* New Brunswick, NJ: Rutgers University Press.

Harrison, M. L., Jones, S., & Sullivan, C. (2008). The gendered expressions of self-control: Manifestations of non-criminal deviance among females. *Deviant Behavior, 29*(1), 18–42.

Heidensohn, F. M. (1985). *Women and crime: The life of the female offender.* New York, NY: New York University Press.

Heimer, K. (1996). Gender, interaction and delinquency: Testing a theory of differential social control. *Social Psychology Quarterly, 59,* 339–361.

Higgins, G. E. (2006). Gender differences in software piracy: The mediating roles of self-control theory and social learning theory. *Journal of Economic Crime Management, 4*(1). Retrieved from http://www.utica.edu/academic/institutes/ecii/publications/jecm.cfm

Hirschi, T. (1969). *Causes of delinquency.* Berkeley, CA: University of California Press.

Huebner, A. J., & Betts, S. C. (2002). Exploring the utility of social control theory for youth development: Issues of attachment, involvement, and gender. *Youth & Society, 34*(2), 123–145.

Iovanni, L., & Miller, S. L. (2008). A feminist consideration of gender and crime. In E. Goode (Ed.), *Out of control: Assessing the general theory of crime* (p. 127–141). Palo Alto, CA: Stanford University Press.

LaGrange, T. C., & Silverman, R. A. (1999). Low self-control and opportunity: Testing the general theory of crime as an explanation of gender differences in delinquency. *Criminology, 37*(1), 41–72.

Leonard, E. B. (1982). *Women, crime, and society.* New York, NY: Longman.

Lombroso, C., & Ferrero, W. (1895). *The female offender.* New York, NY: Barnes and Company.

Lowe, N. C., May, D. C., & Elrod, P. (2008). Theoretical predictors of delinquency among public school students in a mid-southern state: The roles of context and gender. *Youth Violence and Juvenile Justice, 6*(4), 343–362.

Ozbay, O., & Ozcan Y. Z. (2008). A test of Hirschi's social bonding theory: A comparison of male and female delinquency. *Internal Journal of Offender Therapy and Comparative Criminology, 52*(2), 134–157.

Piquero, N. L., Gover, A. R., MacDonald, J. M., & Piquero, A. R. (2005). The influence of delinquent peers on delinquency: Does gender matter? *Youth & Society, 36*(3), 251–275.

Pollak, O. (1961). *The criminality of women.* New York, NY: A. S. Barnes.

Potter, H. (2006). An argument for Black feminist criminology. *Feminist Criminology, 1*(2), 106–124.

Raphael, J. (2004). *Listening to Olivia: Violence, poverty and prostitution.* Boston, MA: Northeastern University Press.

Rosenbaum, J. L. (1989). Family dysfunction and female delinquency. *Crime and Delinquency, 35,* 31–44.

Silverman, J. R., & Caldwell, R. M. (2008). Peer relationships and violence among female juvenile offenders: An exploration of differences among four racial/ethnic populations. *Criminal Justice and Behavior, 35*(3), 333–343.

Sampson, R., & Laub, J. (1993). *Crime in the making: Pathways and turning points through life.* Cambridge, MA: Harvard University Press.

Simon, R. (1975). *Women and crime.* Lexington, MA: D. C. Heath.

Sutherland, E., & Cressey, D. (1974). *Criminology* (9th ed.). Philadelphia, PA: H. B. Lippincott.

Svensson, R. (2004). Shame as a consequence of the parent-child relationship: A study of gender differences in juvenile delinquency. *European Journal of Criminology, 1*(4), 477–504.

Thompson, M., & Petrovic, M. (2009). Gendered transitions: Within-person changes in employment, family and illicit drug use. *Journal of Research in Crime and Delinquency, 46*(3), 377–408.

Wesely, J. K. (2006). Considering the context of women's violence: Gender, lived experiences and cumulative victimization. *Feminist Criminology, 1*(4), 303–328.

PART II

Women as Victims

Women and Victimization

Rape and Sexual Assault

It didn't seem like such a big deal when Karla got pregnant at age 12. She knew her mom's Boyfriend #19 would be angry, and her mom would be disappointed. She could definitely handle that. The big deal was the baby's father: It was her friend Diana's stepdad, Gus. He used to touch them when they were young, but now that Karla was a woman, they did all the things that men and women do together. Of course, they had sex all the time. Karla didn't mind—in fact, she enjoyed it sometimes— and he always brought her presents and treated her really well. He was very nice to her, told her she was beautiful, and even let her sleep over any time things were bad at home with her mother and whatever drunk, angry boyfriend was around at the time. That's when Karla started what she considered her mature, adult relationship with Gus.

Everybody asked who the father was, and Karla always had a smartass comeback, like "your dad!" She didn't tell anyone, not even Diana . . . except as a comeback, which no one believed.

The trouble came when Karla was five months along. Another 12-year-old girl in the neighborhood got pregnant and named Gus the father. What's more, the cops came and arrested him for rape. Soon enough, the authorities were coming down on Karla and her mother, claiming that Karla had been raped, too. Yes, Gus, was the father, but rape? Karla felt like a grown-up woman, but the stupid cops and everyone around her were ruining everything, so she told them so: Gus never raped her; it was consensual. Sure, sometimes he would help her relax with some alcohol, but he never forced her to do it.

It took Karla many years to realize she had been sexually victimized, but she vehemently denied it at the time. As the criminal justice process began to unfold, the associated medical examinations, forensic issues, social work investigation, and court testimony nearly broke her. She felt like a pariah in her own community, which simultaneously blamed her for inviting Gus' sexual interest, snitching to police, and causing trouble for the families involved. The ancillary fallout from this incident, including the birth and adoption of her baby, the loss of her best friend Diana, and her mother's eventual deportation hearings, proved too much for Karla, who turned to the streets as an escape.

```
┌─────────────────────────────────────────────────────────────────┐
│  ┌──────────────────────┐                                         │
│  │  Chapter Highlights  │                                         │
│  └──────────────────────┘                                         │
│                                                                   │
│   •  Historical perspectives on the sexual victimization of women │
│   •  Contemporary paradigms for sexual victimization              │
│   •  Rape myths and rape myth acceptance                          │
│   •  Categories of sexual assault                                 │
│   •  Criminal justice treatment and processing of female sexual   │
│      assault victims                                              │
│   •  Policy implications for female sexual assault victims        │
│                                                                   │
└─────────────────────────────────────────────────────────────────┘
```

W hen is sex a criminal act? Consider the following scenario: An adult male takes a teenage girl to his friend's home as part of a modeling photography session. She is given champagne and Quaaludes. Despite her pleas for him to return her to her family's home, he proceeds to engage in oral, vaginal, and anal intercourse with her against her will. Under most circumstances, most would argue that these circumstances equate to the crimes of rape and sexual assault. However, this was no ordinary case. The year was 1977, and the adult male was famed Hollywood director Roman Polanski. He was 44, while his victim was only 13 years old. Initially charged with multiple crimes, including rape by the use of drugs and lewd and lascivious acts upon a child under 14, Polanski pled guilty to a lesser charge as part of a deal with prosecutors. Prior to his sentencing, Polanski fled the United States and remained a fugitive for 32 years. During this time, he lived as a free man in France, though he never returned to the United States out of fear that he would face the criminal sentencing that he had evaded. Throughout the years, most seemed to forget that he had pled guilty to the crime of unlawful sexual intercourse and instead focused on his artistic accolades, which included an Academy Award for Best Director in 2003. In 2009, he was arrested in Switzerland and faced extradition back to California to be sentenced to a punishment that he had long avoided. While Swiss officials kept Polanski under house arrest for over two months, they eventually denied the U.S. request for extradition. At the time of his arrest, Hollywood debated whether or not Polanski should face punishment for the crimes he committed so many years ago. Even his victim spoke out, arguing that the case against Polanski should be dismissed as she had long moved on from her victimization over 30 years prior. Would the same be said for someone not of his notoriety?

Historical Perspectives

Rape is one of the oldest crimes in society, and it is also one of the most feared (Fattah & Sacco, 1989; Fisher & Sloan, 2003; Lane, Gover, & Dahod, 2009; Valentine, 1992). Rape has existed in every historical and contemporary society around the world. Yet, we are still attempting to understand and respond to this crime. Images of rape have appeared in historical works of art (see Ciofalo, 1995; Hults, 1991), in literature (see Horeck, 2004; Sielke, 2002; Stockton, 2006; Tanner, 1994; Vitz, 1996), in mainstream movies and television (Bufkin, 2000; Eyal, 2007; Jones-Brown, 2007), and throughout advertisements, magazines, and contemporary popular culture (Ward, 2003). Simply put, subtle images of rape permeate our lives.

Laws prohibiting the act of rape have existed for almost four thousand years. One of the first laws prohibiting the crime of rape can be found in the Code of Hammurabi from Babylon in 1900 BCE. Ancient Greek, Roman, and Judaic societies also criminalized the act of rape under various circumstances. Some laws distinguished between the rape of a married versus an unmarried woman, and the punishments for these crimes varied based on the status of the victim (Ewoldt, Monson, & Langhinrichsen-Rohling, 2000). Others viewed rape not as a violent sexual offense but as a property crime, as women were historically viewed as the property of men, and rape of the property (a woman) thus defiled her value (Burgess-Jackson, 1999). At common law, rape of an unmarried woman was a property crime perpetrated against her father, which could be remedied if the rapist married the woman. Likewise, rape against a married woman was a property crime against her husband, punishable by death (Dodderidge, 1632).

Historically, laws have done little to protect women from crimes of sexual violence. At its core, the acknowledgment of a rape is an admission of sexual activity. In many cases of forcible sexual assault, women were historically blamed for tempting offenders into immoral behaviors. During rape trials, a woman's sexual history was often put on display in an attempt to discredit her in front of a jury, and these tactics were often successful in painting female victims of sexual assault as promiscuous or somehow inviting sexual intimacy, which effectively mitigated the perpetrators responsibility or removed it altogether. The courts did not request similar information about a man's sexual history, as it would be considered prejudicial in the eyes of the jury (Odem, 1995). While punishment for sexual offenses ranged from fines to the execution of the offender in early society, women were likely to be deemed sexually immoral in cases of sexual assault. In addition, early laws provided the first distinctions of marital rape as exempt from criminal prosecution and provided class-based definitions of crime and punishment (Burgess-Jackson, 1999).

Until the 20th century, early American statutes on rape limited the definition to a narrow view of sexual assault. Consider the following definition of rape that was included in the Model Penal Code in 1955:

Section 213.1: Rape and Related Offenses

1. Rape. A male who has sexual intercourse with a female not his wife is guilty of rape if:
    a. he compels her to submit by force or by threat of imminent death, serious bodily injury, extreme pain or kidnapping, to be inflicted on anyone; or
    b. he has substantially impaired her power to appraise or control her conduct by administering or employing without her knowledge drugs, intoxicants or other means for the purpose of preventing resistance; or
    c. the female is unconscious; or
    d. the female is less than 10 years old.

What is wrong with this definition? First, it reduces the definition of rape to the act of intercourse, excluding such acts as fondling, oral sex, and sodomy. Second, it limits the victim-offender relationship to a male perpetrator and a female victim. While this is often the case, such a limited scope excludes cases of **same-sex sexual assault** and cases where the victim is male or the offender is female. Third, this definition requires that force, or the threat of force, must be used in order for an act to qualify as rape, and it focuses on violence and brutality as proof of the crime. The requirement of "extreme pain" is noteworthy here. Fourth, this definition suggests that marital status precludes rape: Unwanted sexual activity between a married couple is never rape, even if the offender's actions would meet the criteria for rape if the parties were unmarried. Simply put, it is not a crime for a husband to rape his wife under this definition. Finally, the definition fails to acknowledge attempted rapes as a crime and the traumatic effects of these "near misses" of victimization.

However, two progressive elements from this early definition have affected modern-day laws on rape. First, the Model Penal Code acknowledges that the use of drugs or alcohol to impair the victim, as well as a victim's state of unconsciousness, precludes consent to sexual activity. Second, this definition acknowledges that rape of a child is a crime, even if it limits this definition to the rape of female children under a certain age. In reality, the issues of rape expand far beyond what this early definition provided, as will be discussed in this chapter.

While contemporary definitions of rape vary from state to state, many modern laws include similar provisions. Today, most laws broadly define *sexual victimization* as sexual behaviors that are unwanted and harmful to the victim. Most emphasize the use of force or coercion that is displayed by the offender, rather than focusing on the response or conduct of the victim. This is not to say that the actions of the victim are not offered as mitigation by defense counsel or considered by members of the jury, but the law itself does not require victims to demonstrate physical levels of resistance. In fact, the modern proliferation of rape shield laws exemplifies the growing objection to such considerations in criminal court, even though such extralegal factors as the victim's dress, actions, and previous sexual behavior are hotly debated and discussed ad nauseam in the media, especially in high-profile sexual assault cases.

Another development in contemporary rape laws involves the abolishment of the marital-rape exemption clause, as every state now has laws on the books that identify rape within the context of marriage as a criminal act. In an effort to resolve some of the limitations with the word *rape*, the term *sexual assault* is often used to identify forms of sexual victimization that are not included under the traditionally narrow definition of rape. These laws have expanded the definitions of sexual assault beyond penile-vaginal penetration and include sodomy, forced oral copulation, and unwanted fondling and touching of a sexual nature. Cases of child sexual assault are treated differently in many jurisdictions, and age-of-consent laws have led to the development of statutory rape laws. Finally, sex offender registration laws such as Megan's Law and Jessica's Law require the community notification of sexual offenders and place residential, community, and supervision restrictions on offenders.

The most contemporary change to modern definitions of rape, the revised definition of rape in the Federal Bureau of Investigations (FBI) Uniform Crime Reports (UCR), came in early 2012, in response to nearly a decade of growing concern and criticism among women's rights activists, scholars, and lawmakers (FBI, 2012a; FBI, 2012b; Johnson, 2012; Women's Law Project, 2012). This new definition defines *rape* as "penetration, no matter how slight, of the vagina or anus with any body part or object, or oral penetration by a sex organ of another person, without the consent of the victim" (FBI, 2012b). Note the major changes. First, the term *forcible* has been replaced by "without consent of the victim," which considers instances in which the victim is incapable of consenting because of incapacitation by alcohol or other drugs, mental or physical impairment, or legal age. Second, this revised definition is gender neutral for both victim and offender. For victims, it includes penetration of any orifice—vaginal, anal, or oral—and considers victimization as a gender-neutral event. Further, it includes offender acts involving penetration with any body part or object and oral copulation of the victim, thus including rape by foreign object, female-perpetrated rape, and same-sex rape in the new definition. Under the new U.S. definition, which is more consistent with evolving legal definitions in many states, rape is no longer relegated to the forced penetration of a male perpetrator's penis into a female victim's vagina.

Defining Sexual Victimization

Despite changes to the law, many people who experience acts that are consistent with a legal definition of rape or sexual assault may not label their experience as such. These unacknowledged victims do not see themselves as victims and therefore do not report these crimes to the police nor do they seek out services such as counseling or mental health support. Research indicates that, in many of these cases, women who experience these acts do not define themselves as victims, because their experience differs from their personal definitions of what rape and sexual assault look like: the perpetration by the *symbolic assailant*—a stranger who attacks them in their home or on a dark sidewalk at night. These incidents involve high levels of violence by people unknown to the victim, and they are relatively rare events. In fact, results from the 2010 National Crime Victimization Survey (NCVS) indicate that approximately 75% of rape perpetrators were friends, acquaintances, or intimate partners of the victim (Truman, 2011). This may underestimate rape by known perpetrators, as the Centers for Disease Control (CDC) estimates that stranger rape accounts for only 13.8% of rapes against women and 15.1% of rapes against men (Black et al., 2011). The perpetrator is most commonly an intimate partner (51%), acquaintance (40.8%), family member (12.5%), or person of authority (2.5%) in the overwhelming majority (85%) of rapes against women in the U.S. today (Black et al., 2011).

The lack of an understanding of the definitions of rape and sexual assault affects offenders as well. Many people who engage in behaviors that meet the legal definitions for sexual assault or rape often do not define their own actions as such. One of the most frequently cited studies on rape and sexual assault surveyed 2,971 college men regarding self-reported conduct that met the legal definitions of rape, attempted rape, sexual coercion, and unwanted sexual contact. The results indicated that 1,525 acts of sexual assault had occurred, including 187 acts of rape. Of those whose acts met the legal definition of rape, 84% believed that their acts did not constitute rape (Warshaw, 1994).

Although the FBI has recently updated the definition of rape to be more consistent with modern definitions of rape in many states, there is no single consistent definition for *rape* and *sexual assault*. Legal definitions vary by jurisdiction, and these change over time. Moreover, the statutory elements articulated in a given jurisdiction are not interpreted in a vacuum. In addition to lack of victim awareness (that he or she has been victimized) and the lack of perpetrator awareness that his or her behavior is a crime, the perspectives of the police and prosecuting attorneys in such cases make arrest and filing decisions based on winnable cases. Simply put, some cases that met the legal definitions for rape or sexual assault do not move forward to prosecution due to lack of evidence, which often includes a victim's unwillingness to cooperate with the prosecution. Complicating matters further, elements included in the various legal definitions of rape and sexual assault differ greatly from criteria used by mental health professionals, who seek to provide services and assistance based on the subjective responses of individual victims.

So, where does this leave us in defining these terms? The NCVS (2008; U.S. Department of Justice, 2011) defines rape as "forced sexual intercourse . . . (including) vaginal, oral, or anal penetration by offender(s)" and includes penetration with a foreign object. The U.S. Department of Justice redefined the crime of rape in 2012 to mirror the definitions of many jurisdictions. However, in some jurisdictions, the crime of rape remains narrowly limited to forced vaginal-penile penetration, with all other unwanted sexual contact (including anal sex, oral sex, digital penetration, penetration by a foreign object, and sexual touching) relegated to lesser crimes under the category *sexual assault*. Most jurisdictions have specific legal provisions that address specific types of sexual assault by means of intoxication or drugging a victim, sexual assault against a child or person who is unable to consent, and sexual assault in the context of special relationships, such as in marriage. Again, these vary by jurisdiction, although many are likely to be revised in light of the recent change to the federal definition of rape. (See web resources at the end of this chapter for links to sexual assault information and definitions by state.)

✉ Prevalence of Rape and Sexual Assault

Despite the acknowledgement that rape and sexual assault are the most underreported types of crimes, with fewer than half of all sexual assault victims reporting their crimes to police, the known data indicate that these crimes pervade our society. According to the Rape, Abuse, and Incest National Network, a rape, attempted rape, or sexual assault occurs approximately once every two minutes. This figure represents roughly 213,000 victims of these crimes that are documented by the U.S. Department of Justice's NCVS each year (United States Department of Justice, 2011).[1] While the U.S. Department of Justice in 2003 found that 40% of victims report their crime to the police, other research has placed this number significantly lower, at 16% for adult women (Kilpatrick, Resnick, Ruggiero, Conoscenti, & McCauley, 2007) and only 2% for college women (Fisher et al., 2003). Given the stigmatizing nature of this crime, it is not surprising that rape, attempted rape, and sexual assault are some of the most underreported crimes, making it difficult to determine the extent of this problem. While researchers attempt to estimate the prevalence of sexual assault, they are faced with their own set of challenges, including differences in defining sexual assault, the emphasis on different sample populations (adolescents, college-age adults, adults, etc.), and different forms of data (arrest data vs. surveys). Regardless of these issues and what the data yield, it appears that sexual assault affects most individuals in some way (either personally or through someone they know) at some point in their lifetime.

Prevalence studies report a wide range of data on the pervasiveness of rape and sexual assault in the United States. A national study on rape published in 2007 indicated that 18% of women in America have experienced rape at some point in their lifetime, with an additional 3% of women experiencing an attempted rape (Basile, Chen, Black, & Saltzman, 2007). A comparison of these findings to the National Violence Against Women Survey (NVAWS) in 1996 indicates that little change has occurred in the prevalence of this crime over time (15% of all women; Tjaden & Thoennes, 2000). Indeed, these results demonstrate an increase in the number of rape cases, which is contrary to the belief that rape has declined significantly in recent times. Rates of sexual assault appear to be higher on college campuses, where it is estimated that between 20% and 25% of women will experience a completed or attempted rape at some point during their collegiate career (Fisher, Cullen, & Turner, 2000). The collegiate experience contains many variables that may increase the risk for sexual assault—campus environments that facilitate a party atmosphere, easy access to alcohol and drugs, increases in freedom, and limited supervision by older adults (Sampson, 2003). Findings from studies such as these have led researchers, rape-crisis organizations, and policymakers to posit that one in four American women has or will experience rape or attempted rape during their lifetime.

Rape Myths

Rape myths are defined as "attitudes and beliefs that are generally false but are widely and persistently held, and that serve to deny and justify male sexual aggression against women" (Lonsway & Fitzgerald, 1994, p. 134; Payne, Lonsway, & Fitzgerald, 1999). These include such socially held beliefs as "women incite men to commit rape," "if a woman dresses a certain way she is 'asking for it,'" "men can't be raped," and so on. Table 5.1 highlights some of the most commonly perpetuated myths about rape.

As suggested in Chapter 3, the acceptance of rape myths by society is a contributing factor in the practice of victim blaming. First, the presence of rape myths allows society to shift the blame of rape from the offender to the victim. By doing so, we can avoid confronting the realities of rape and sexual assault in society. This denial serves as a vicious cycle: If we fail to acknowledge the severity of rape and sexual assault, this leads to victims not reporting the crime to authorities, which results in the crime not being taken seriously by society as a whole. Second, the presence of rape myths lends support to the notion of a *just world hypothesis*, which suggests that only good things happen to good people and bad things happen to those who deserve it. Rape myths, such as "she asked for it," serve to perpetuate the notion of the just world in action (Lonsway & Fitzgerald, 1994).

Offenders often use rape myths to excuse or justify their actions. Excuses occur when offenders admit that their behavior was wrong but blame their actions on external circumstances outside of their control. In these instances, offenders deny responsibility for their actions. Statements such as "I was drunk" or "I don't know what came over me" are examples of excuses. In comparison, justifications occur when offenders admit responsibility for their actions but argue that their behavior was acceptable under the circumstances. Examples of justifications include "she asked for it" or "nothing really happened." Miscommunication appears to play a significant role for men as well, who ask, "When does 'no' mean 'no,' and when does 'no' mean 'yes'?" By suggesting that men misunderstand their victim's refusal for sexual activity, the responsibility of rape is transferred from the offender back to the victim.

Table 5.1 Rape Myths
• A woman who gets raped usually deserves it, especially if she has agreed to go to a man's house or to park with him.
• If a woman allows a man to pay for dinner, then it means she owes him sex.
• Acquaintance rape is committed by men who are easy to identify as rapists.
• Only women can be raped or sexually assaulted by men.
• Women who don't fight back haven't been raped.
• Once a man reaches a certain point of arousal, sex is inevitable, and he can't help forcing himself upon a woman.
• Most women lie about acquaintance rape, because they have regrets after consensual sex.
• Women who say "no" really mean "yes."
• Certain behaviors, such as drinking or dressing in a sexually appealing way, make rape a woman's responsibility.
• If a woman has had sex with a man before, she has consented to have sex with him again.
• A man can't rape his wife.
• Only bad women get raped.
• Women secretly enjoy being raped.

SOURCES: Compiled from Payne, D., Lonsway, K., & Fitzgerald, L. (1999) and Franiuk, R., Seefelt, J. L., Cepress, S. L., & Vandello, J. A. (2008).

Some victims accept excuses or justifications for their assault that minimize or deny the responsibility of their offender. In cases where the male offender "got carried away," female victims often accept the actions of the offender as a natural consequence of male sexuality. In these cases, victims feel that they deserve their victimization as a result of their own actions. Many victims argue that "they should have known better" or that "they didn't try hard enough to stop it." In these cases, victims believe that they put themselves at risk as a result of their own decision-making process.

The prevalence and acceptance of rape myths in society does a significant disservice for both victims and society in general in terms of understanding the realities of rape. These myths permit us to believe that *stranger rape* is real or legitimate rape, whereas **acquaintance rape** is less serious, less significant, and less harmful. This mistaken belief permeates culture, despite consistent national data to the contrary: According to the NCVS, approximately 75% of rape victims know their perpetrators, and fewer than 25% of offenders are strangers (Truman, 2011). These figures are relatively stable across the last several decades.

▲ **Photo 5.1**   In response to a Toronto police officer's comment that "women should avoid dressing like sluts in order not to be victimized," over 3,000 people gathered at Queen's Park in Toronto on April 3, 2011, to protest the rape myth that women ask to be sexually assaulted based on their appearance. Since then, "Slut Walks" have been organized around the world to raise awareness about the danger of rape myths and their effects on victims.

Rape myths perpetuate the belief that women should be more fearful of the symbolic assailant—the stranger who lurks in the alley or hides in the bushes and surprises the victim. Rape myths suggest that in order for a woman to be raped, she needs to fight back against her attacker and leave the scene with bruises and injuries related to—and commensurate with—her efforts to thwart the assault. Rape myths also suggest that real rape victims always report their attackers and have evidence collected and that an offender is then identified, arrested, prosecuted, and sentenced to the fullest extent under the law. This is an empirical rarity. In reality, the majority of rapes in society possess few of these characteristics. More commonly, victims know their attacker as an intimate partner, friend, or acquaintance; victims are unlikely to report their sexual assault; and these cases are very difficult to prosecute successfully. In a real rape, the victim is an innocent party who holds no responsibility for causing her own rape, yet the prevalence and power of rape myths serve to narrowly define *rape* within a set of rare circumstances and limit the public's understanding about the realities of rape.

⬛ Acquaintance Versus Stranger Assault

Contrary to the belief perpetuated by popular culture, sexual attacks perpetrated by strangers are not the most prevalent type of rape and sexual assault. Young women are socialized to be wary of walking alone at night, to be afraid that a scary man will jump out of the bushes and attack them. Unfortunately, many prevention efforts that focus on what women can do to keep themselves safe from sexual assault tend to focus on situations involving victimization by strangers. Admonitions such as "lock your doors" and "don't walk alone at night" illustrate this point. While these tools are certainly valuable in enhancing women's safety, they fail to acknowledge the reality of sexual assault, as the majority of rape and sexual assault cases involve a perpetrator known to the victim. Acquaintance rape accounts for 90% of all rapes of college women (Sampson, 2006). Additionally, 60% of all rape and sexual assault incidents occur either at the victim's home or at the home of a friend, neighbor, or relative (Greenfeld, 1997, p. 3). Cases of acquaintance rape and sexual assault tend to entail lesser use of physical force by the offender and involve a lesser degree of resistance by the victim than occurs in cases of stranger sexual assault (Littleton, Breitkopf, & Berenson, 2008).

While the NCVS indicates that fewer than 50% of rape victims report the crime to police and most frequently do so when the offender is a stranger (Truman, 2011), it is often difficult to accurately assess how many sexual assault victims disclose their victimization to police. Research conducted by Millar, Stermac, and Addison (2002) documented that 61% of acquaintance rapes are not reported to the police. In comparison, Rickert, Wiemann, and Vaughan (2005) found that only one of 86 study participants made a report to law enforcement authorities, and an additional four victims sought services from a mental health professional. While these findings demonstrate a dramatic range of reporting rates, it is safe to conclude that acquaintance rape is significantly underreported. Society tends to discount the validity of acquaintance rape, suggesting that it is less serious than stranger rape ("real rape"). Yet research demonstrates that victims of acquaintance rape also suffer significant mental health trauma as a result of their victimization. However, this trauma is often exacerbated by the fact that many victims of acquaintance rape tend to blame themselves for their own victimization. In many cases, these victims are less likely to seek assistance from rape-crisis or counseling services.

Drug-Facilitated Sexual Assault

A *drug-facilitated rape* is defined as an unwanted sexual act following the deliberate intoxication of a victim. In comparison, an **incapacitated rape** is an unwanted sexual act that occurs after a victim voluntarily consumes drugs or alcohol. In both cases, the victim is too intoxicated by drugs and/or alcohol to be aware of her behavior, and she is therefore unable to consent. Kilpatrick et al. (2007) found that 5% of women experience drug-facilitated or incapacitated rape.

Recent research has discussed a rise in incapacitated rapes through the involuntary drugging of victims. The terms *date rape drug* and *drug-facilitated sexual assault* have been used to identify how the involuntary consumption of substances has been used in sexual assault cases. Table 5.2 provides a description of the different types of substances that are commonly used in cases of drug-facilitated sexual assault. In many cases, these substances are generally colorless, odorless, and/or tasteless when dissolved in a drink and result in a rapid intoxication that renders a potential rape victim unconscious and unable to recall events that occurred while she was intoxicated. One research study stated that less than 2% of sexual assault incidents were directly attributed to the deliberate covert drugging of the victim (Scott-Ham & Burton, 2005). However, these findings document reported cases of sexual assault, and it is reasonable to conclude that many cases of drug-facilitated sexual assault go unreported, as victims may be reluctant to report a crime for which they have little recollection. Research indicates that in cases where victims are deliberately intoxicated, they are more likely to be judged as responsible for their victimization than victims who do not voluntarily imbibe (Girard & Senn, 2008).

With the exception of alcohol, the majority of the substances that are used in cases of drug-facilitated sexual assault (such as Gamma-Hydrozybutyric acid [GHB], ketamine, and Rohypnol) are

Table 5.2	Substances Commonly Used in Drug-Facilitated Sexual Assaults

- GHB (Gamma-Hydrozybutyric acid)

  o GHB comes in a few forms—a liquid that contains no odor or color, a white powder, and a pill. GHB has not been approved by the FDA since 1990, so it is considered illegal to possess or sell. GHB can take effect in as little as 15 minutes and can last for 3–4 hours. GHB is considered a Schedule 1 drug under the Controlled Substances Act. GHB leaves the body within 10–12 hours, making it very difficult to detect.

- Ketamine

  o Ketamine is an anesthetic that is generally used to sedate animals in a veterinarian's office. Ketamine can be particularly dangerous when used in combination with other drugs and alcohol. It is very fast-acting and can cause individuals to feel as if they are disassociated from their body and be unaware of their circumstances. It can also cause memory loss, affecting the ability of a victim to recall details of the assault.

- Rohypnol (Flunitrazepam)

  o Rohypnol is a dissolvable pill of various sizes and colors (round, white, oval, green-gray). Rohypnol is not approved for medical use in the United States and much of the supply comes from Mexico. However, the manufacturer of this drug recently changed the chemistry of the pill such that if it is inserted into a clear liquid, it will change the color of the drink to a bright blue color, increasing the chances for potential victims to identify whether their drink has been altered. Rohypnol effects can be noticed within 30 minutes of being ingested; the individual appears overly intoxicated, and the drug affects their balance, stability, and speech patterns. Like many other substances, Rohypnol leaves the body in a rapid fashion, generally between 36–72 hours of ingestion.

- Alcohol

  o Alcohol is one of the most common date rape drugs. Here, victims drink to excess, placing themselves at risk for sexual assault. Not only do victims willingly consume alcohol, it is (generally, based on the age of the individual) legal and easily obtained. The consumption of alcohol impairs judgment, lowers inhibition, and affects a victim's ability to recognize potentially dangerous situations.

SOURCES: Compiled from Hensley (2002), Krajicek (2011), Weir (2001).

labeled as *controlled substances*, and the possession of these drugs is considered a federal offense under the Controlled Substances Act of 1970 (Jones, 2001). In addition, the Drug-Induced Rape Prevention and Punishment Act of 1996 provides penalties for up to 20 years for the voluntary drugging of an individual in cases of violence (Office of the Attorney General, 1997). Many states have enacted laws that provide specific sanctions in cases of drug-facilitated sexual assault. For example, California Penal Code § 261(a)(3) provides the following definition for the crime of rape by intoxication: (1) a male and female engaged in an act of sexual intercourse who are not married; (2) the victim was prevented from resisting by an intoxicating substance; and (3) the victim's condition was known, or reasonably should have been known, by the accused. Here, state law provides an assessment of a victim's ability to consent to sexual relations and holds that the level of intoxication, combined with the resulting mental impairment of the individual, must affect the victim's ability to exercise reasonable judgment. Under this law, convicted offenders can be punished for either three, six, or eight years in state prison. In most cases, offenders are sentenced to six years and can receive a reduced sentence (three years) if mitigating factors are present or an enhanced sentence (eight years) if aggravated factors are present.

Case Study

The People of the State of California vs. Andrew Luster

In 2003, Andrew Luster was put on trial for a series of rapes that took place in Southern California between 1996 and 2000. Luster, the heir to the Max Factor cosmetics fortune, used his $3 million trust fund to support his lifestyle of travel, surfing, and partying in Malibu from the time he reached adulthood until his prosecution for rape began in 2000 (Fischer, 2002).

The prosecution's case against Luster was centered on allegations of rape made by three separate female victims in 1996, 1997, and 2000. All three victims accused Luster of giving them GHB, the "date rape drug," and engaging in multiple acts of rape and sexual assault while they were unconscious and incapacitated. During the execution of a search warrant at Luster's residence for these charges, police found strong evidence against him, including multiple videotapes of Luster engaged in sexual conduct with multiple women who appeared to be unconscious, including the three initial victims. One of the tapes was even titled, "Shauna GHBing" (Krajicek, 2011). The acts depicted in the video resulted in a total of 87 charges filed against Luster, including 20 counts of drug-induced rape, 17 counts of raping unconscious victims, and multiple counts of drug possession, oral copulation, sodomy, and poisoning (Fischer, 2002).

Luster's bail was initially set at $10 million, and he was incarcerated for 5 months pending trial. In 2000, however, the court lowered his bail to $1 million, and, given Luster's substantial resources, he easily made the lower bail and was released from custody in December 2000 (Associated Press, 2009). However, in January 2003, while on trial for these charges, he absconded. While his defense team sought an interruption in proceedings due to Luster's absence, the court proceeded with trial, and Luster was found guilty of 86 of the 87 charges, with the jury deadlocked on a single count of poisoning (Wilson, 2003). Likewise, sentencing ensued during Luster's absence, and he was ultimately sentenced to a total of 124 years in prison for his crimes. Given the violent nature of his offenses, Luster must serve 85% of his sentence, or 105.4 years. This makes Luster eligible for parole in 2108, when Luster will be 145 years old.

Within five months of his sentence, the fugitive Andrew Luster was tracked to Puerto Vallarta, Mexico, by bounty hunter Duane "Dog" Chapman. Chapman and his associates attempted to detain Luster in Puerto Vallarta in June of 2003, an event that resulted in Mexican authorities arresting Chapman for "deprivation of liberty" and returning Luster to the U.S. for imposition of his criminal sentence (CNN Justice, 2003). Charges against "Dog the Bounty Hunter" Chapman were dismissed in 2007, and his A&E reality television series of the same name continues today.

As of November 2011, Andrew Luster is incarcerated as inmate number T97187 at Mule Creek Prison in Ione, California (California Department of Corrections and Rehabilitation, 2011). His appeals have been denied, as the California Court of Appeal ruled that Luster forfeited his right to an appeal under the *fugitive disentitlement doctrine*, which holds that a fugitive from justice cannot seek legal remedy or appeal from the justice system said fugitive is evading. Thus, Luster is not eligible for an appeal on his conviction or sentencing due to his unlawful departure during trial and sentencing (Hernandez, 2009). He has since sold the majority of his assets and has filed bankruptcy in light of mounting legal fees and victim restitution in the amount of $40 million dollars (Krajicek, 2011). In March 2013, Luster's sentence was vacated and a new sentencing hearing is pending (*Los Angeles Times, 2013*).

While there has been increased attention to sexual assault due to involuntary intoxication, this is not the primary form of drug-facilitated sexual assault. Rather, cases where the victim is sexually assaulted following a voluntary intoxication following consumption of alcohol make up the majority of drug-facilitated sexual assaults. In a sample of rape cases among college-age women, alcohol was involved in 79% of cases of nonforcible rape (Kilpatrick et al., 2007). The use of drugs and alcohol places women at a greater risk for sexual assault. Not only may women be less aware of the risk for sexual assault and labeled as a target for potential offenders due to a reduction of their inhibitions, but they may be unable to resist their attackers due to their incapacitated state. Additionally, while voluntarily intoxicated individuals are legally incapable of giving consent for sexual activity (Beynon, McVeigh, McVeigh, Leavey, & Bellis, 2008), these victims are often held as the most responsible of all sexual assault victims, since they chose to use intoxicating substances recreationally. As a result, the actions of perpetrators in these scenarios are most likely to be excused or diminished, given the voluntary intoxication of the female victim (Girard & Senn, 2008).

The Invisible War: Rape in the Military

Rape in the military has, until recently, been swept under the rug. Turchik and Wilson (2010) report that up to one-third of women in the military experience rape or sexual assault during their service. Men are less prone to sexual assault, with rates falling around 1.2% among active service members. However, these numbers are tempered by a staggering nonreported rate of nearly 80%! Translating these numbers leads to a disturbing picture; using conservative sexual assault rates of 10% and 1% for women and men, respectively, and assuming an 80% nonreporting rate, nearly 40 out of 100 women in the military are estimated to be victims of sexual violence, while only 4 out of 100 men fall into this category. Of course, men vastly outweigh women in the military, so the actual prevalence of male victimization is much larger. Clearly, a disparity exists; however, a deeply ingrained sense of loyalty to the military way of life often prevents these crimes from coming to light.

There have also been cases of sexual abuse by military officers against prisoners of war. In 2004, allegations of sexual and other forms of abuse came to light involving members of the U.S. Army and prisoners held at the Abu Ghraib prison in Baghdad, Iraq. The allegations involved significant acts of torture, including being sodomized by a baton, forced oral copulation on another male inmate, forced masturbation, and being doused with chemicals. Several photographs of the abuse were released in conjunction with an article in the *New Yorker* magazine (Hersh, 2004), though officials suggest that there are thousands of photographs depicting acts of abuse. In many of these photographs, military personnel are shown posing with the prisoners, smiling, and giving the "two thumbs up" signal. Drawing from the *Taguba Report*, an internal military document not intended for public release, Hersh detailed the acts of abuse and commented how "the 372nd's abuse of prisoners seemed almost routine—a fact of Army life that the soldiers felt no need to hide" (Hersh, 2004). In an interview on *60 Minutes* with Dan Rather, Former Marine Lt. Col. Bill Cowan said, "We went into Iraq to stop things like this from happening, and indeed, here they are happening under our tutelage" (Leung, 2009). Over the next two years, 11 military personnel were convicted and dishonorably discharged from the army for their involvement in the abuse. Two of the officials depicted in the photographs were

Specialist Charles Granier and Specialist Lynndie England. Much was made of their participation in the acts, as many of the photos released in the *New Yorker* article included Granier and England perpetuating acts of abuse. At the time of her court-martial, England was pregnant with her then-fiancée Granier's child. England's involvement in the acts was particularly condoned by the media as a result of her gender—how could a woman engage in such horrible actions? During her trial, she claimed that she followed the directions of Granier, her lover and superior officer—"I did everything he wanted me to do. I didn't want to lose him" (England, 2008). For their involvement in the Abu Ghraib scandal, Granier was sentenced to 10 years (he served six years) and England received six years (she served three). Despite these punishments, several high-ranking officials continue to suggest that the acts of Abu Ghraib are acceptable techniques of interrogation.

As one of the prestigious Military Academy, the Air Force Academy in Colorado Springs, CO, receives high rankings for their training of pilots (as well as their football team). However, 2003 brought a new level of attention to the Academy, as allegations of sexual abuse amongst the ranks were made public. Not only did victims suggest that rape and sexual assault occurred within the student body on a regular basis, victims suggested that military officials knew of the abuse but did little to stop the systematic assault of female cadets by their male counterparts. Women who came forward with allegations were often punished by their superiors, leading many victims to remain silent about the abuse they endured. While six cadets came forward as part of the allegations, a survey of female graduates in 2003 suggested that the issue of rape, sexual assault, and sexual harassment was much more prevalent than those few cases. Over 88% of the female graduates participated in the survey, and 12% of women acknowledged that they experienced completed or attempted rape at some point during their college career. An additional 70% of women referenced cases of sexual harassment, including pressure to engage in sexual behaviors (Schemo, 2003). Since news of the 2003 scandal broke, more victims have come forward. While the Air Force has identified at least 54 cases of rape and sexual assault, punishment of the offenders is exceedingly rare. Over the past ten years, only two offenders have been court-martialed for their abuse of female cadets. Only one case yielded a conviction, and the offender was sentenced to seven months in custody (Air Force Rape Scandal, 2009).

There are signs that the response by the military toward cases of rape and sexual assault may be shifting. In 2012, filmmaker Kirby Dick presented *The Invisible War* at the Sundance movie festival. Described as heartbreaking and emotionally rending, over 100 interviews with victims of military sexual assault (both men and women) put a face on the taboo topic of rape in the military. Startlingly, utilizing the Department of Defense's own statistics of deaths and sexual assault rates, it was found that female soldiers have a higher probability of being sexually assaulted by a fellow soldier than being killed during combat. Many of those interviewed suffered from post-traumatic stress disorder (PTSD), had their attempts to report their assaults denied or buried in paperwork, or were subjected to harassment and ridicule (Turan, 2012). In response to the sexual assault scandal of 2003, the Air Force Academy established the Sexual Assault Prevention and Response (SARP) team in June 2005. SARP provides a 24/7 hotline for victims and has two victim advocates available to provide services to victims. In addition, SARP delivers approximately 11 hours of training over the cadet's four-year

(Continued)

(Continued)

educational experience on rape and sexual assault prevention. Beginning on Day 2 of basic training, the cadets learn about the various different behaviors that constitute rape and sexual assault. As a result, SARP has seen increased reporting rates of these incidents, with approximately 25% of victims reporting their victimization (T. Beasley, personal communication, September 11, 2012). Despite the implementation of these curricula, rape in the military continues to be a problem. The recent conviction of Air Force Staff Sergeant Luis Walker on seven counts of rape, sexual assault, and aggravated sexual misconduct is a positive step toward fighting against these acts of abuse. Unfortunately, Walker is only one of the 12 boot camp instructors involved in the scandal at Lackland, demonstrating that sexual assault of female military is a pervasive issue (Peterson, 2012). The Department of Defense has implemented policies to reduce its occurrence, but as with all other systemic changes, only time will reveal whether or not change has truly occurred.

✂ Spousal Rape

Throughout history, the rape of a wife by her husband was not considered to be a crime (Hasday, 2000). The *marital rape exception* argues that women automatically consent to sex with their husbands as part of their marriage contract; the exclusion of marital rape under this doctrine dates to 17th-century England, when Chief Justice Hale argued that a husband cannot commit rape against his wife, "for by their mutual matrimonial consent and contract the wife hath given up herself in this kind unto the husband which she cannot retract" (Russell, 1990, p. 17). Historically, women were considered not as equal partners in a marital contract but as an item of property that men were free to do with as they wished. Even once women gained certain legal rights following the suffrage movement, the relationship between a man and wife was viewed as a private manner, and not one for public scrutiny, well into the 1970s. This belief system permitted the criminal justice system to maintain a hands-off policy when it came to **spousal rape**. As existing rape laws began to change throughout the 1970s and 1980s, increased attention was brought to the marital rape exception. In 1978, only five states defined marital rape as a crime. By 1993, all 50 states in the United States of America had either removed the marital exclusion for rape or enacted at least one statute prohibiting rape within the context of marriage. However, many other countries have been reluctant to remove the marital exclusion from rape statutes (Fus, 2006).

Perpetrators use a variety of different tactics to coerce sex from their victims, including victims who are spouses. The majority of cases of marital rape involve cases of emotional coercion, rather than physical force. Examples of emotional coercion include inferences that it is a wife's duty to engage in sex with her husband (referred to as *social coercion*) or the use of power by a husband to exert sexual favors from his wife (referred to as *interpersonal coercion*). A third form of emotional coercion involves cases where a wife engages in sex for fear of unknown threats or damages that may occur if she refuses. Many of these occurrences are related to cases of domestic violence, where the possibility of violence exists. Cases of marital rape by the use of physical force are referred to as *battering rape*. The physical effects of marital rape are generally greater compared to cases of stranger and acquaintance rape. In cases of battering rape, the sexual assault is an extension of the physical and emotional violence that occurs within the context of the relationship (Martin, Taft, & Resick, 2007).

Contrary to popular belief, marital rape is as prevalent as other forms of rape. However, much of this victimization is hidden from public view. Results from randomized studies find that 7%–14% of women experience completed or attempted rape within the context of marriage, cohabitating, or intimate relationship (Bennice & Resick, 2003). Community samples tend to yield significantly higher rates of marital rape—however, they tend to draw from shelters or therapeutic settings, which offer skewed results. These studies find that 10%–34% of women studied experienced rape within the context of marriage (Martin et al., 2007).

Despite the criminalization of spousal rape, the cultural acceptance of marital rape still fails to identify these women as victims. By leaving these victims with the belief that their experiences are not considered "real" rape, these women are less likely to seek assistance for their victimization. Thus, marital rape remains a significant issue in the United States and around the world.

Child Rape

The actual prevalence of **child rape** is difficult to pinpoint, as rape is generally underreported; this underreporting is compounded when the victim is a child, as child sexual assault is often perpetrated by the child's own caretaker (which runs contrary to the myth that children's assailants are strangers; United States Bureau of Justice Statistics, 2000). However, a variety of research studies and national data provide estimates for child sexual assault. According to the Rape, Abuse, & Incest National Network (RAINN), nearly half (44%) of all victims of sexual assault are under the age of 18 (United States Department of Justice, 2004). Given the most recent estimates of 213,000 rape victims in 2010, this suggests that approximately 94,000 children are sexually victimized in the United States each year (Truman & Planty, 2012). This is similar to United States Department of Health and Human Services (2005) data, which reflect 83,600 substantiated cases of child sexual assault in 2005. Of the roughly 90,000 cases of child sexual assault in a given year, most (about 62,000 cases) involve a child between the ages of 12–17, and about one-third (32,000) involve the sexual victimization of a child under the age of 12. This means that roughly 15%–30% of all girls and 5%–8% of all boys are sexually victimized in childhood (Baker & Duncan, 1985; McCauley et al., 1997; Radford et al., 2011a, p. 5; Rind, Tromovitch, & Bauserman, 1998; Whealin, 2007).

The effects of traumatic sexual experiences in childhood are well documented in the literature and include both emotional and physical manifestations as well as short- and long-term impacts. A plethora of research documents the initial effects of child sexual assault, including depression, anxiety, and PTSD (Levitan, Rector, Sheldon, & Goering, 2003; Roosa, Reinholtz, & Angelini, 1999; Widom, 1999). Child sexual assault is associated with a variety of negative outcomes during youth, particularly if the abuse was perpetrated by a parent or caretaker, which is often the case. For example, multiple studies have linked **child sexual abuse** with later delinquency (Benda, 2002; Hollist, Hughes, & Schaible, 2009), drug and alcohol abuse (Carson, Sullivan, Cochran, & Lersch, 2009; Lo, Kim, & Church, 2008), running away from home (Baron, 2003), being selected by predators who pose as rescuers (Albanese, 2007), and entry into the sex trade (Reid, 2010).

Research documents the lasting effects of child rape-related trauma in adult survivors of child sexual assault. These include, for example, PTSD and depression beyond adolescence into adulthood

(Cheasty, Clare, & Collins, 2002; Polusny & Follette, 1995; Saunders, Villeponteaux, Lipovsky, Kilpatrick, & Veronen, 1992). Medical research also documents that adult survivors of childhood sexual assault are more likely to engage in high-risk sexual behaviors (Reid, 2010) and have greater health care needs than women who were not sexually victimized as children (Myskow, 2006). Still other research documents high rates of eating disorders among this population (Messman-Moore & Garrigus, 2007) and increased likelihood for sexual revictimization. In fact, some research suggests that women who are sexually assaulted during childhood are three times more likely to be revictimized in adulthood than women who were not victimized in their youth (Marx, Heidt, & Gold, 2005). According to Schumm, Briggs-Phillips, and Hobfoll (2006), persons who experienced childhood sexual victimization were 17 times more likely to experience PTSD than persons who experienced a single victimization, either in childhood or adulthood.

Statutory Rape

Statutory rape refers to sexual activity that is unlawful because it is prohibited by statute or code—hence the term *statutory* rape. Statutory rape generally does not connote images of forcible, violent sexual assault as is often present with other types of sexual assault; unwanted sexual activity that involves force or use of intoxicants to achieve sexual contact are generally processed under other sexual assault statutes, such as rape, rape by intoxication, forced sodomy, or rape of a child under age 10. Statutory rape generally involves sexual activity with someone who is legally unable to consent, usually due to age. Such cases often involve sex between a female under the age of consent but over the age of puberty and a male over the age of consent. Victims in such cases often assert their willingness to consent, but their age of minority precludes their ability to legally give that consent to their partner. The essential element here is the victim's inability to legally give consent due to age or mental impairment, and the offender's use of coercion to achieve sexual gratification is assumed based on the victim's age or mental state. This bodes the question: When and under what circumstances is one legally able to consent to sexual activity?

Statutes articulating the legal age of consent vary by jurisdiction, and these change over time. In the United States, for example, the age of consent varies from 16 to 18, depending on the state. These statutes often include a variety of exceptions, most notably marital exceptions, age-gap exceptions, and authority exceptions. Marital exceptions allow for consent below the legal age afforded in statute if the victim is married. For example, in a state where the age of consent is 17, a minor who is legally married at the age of 16 can consent to sexual activity with his or her spouse. Likewise, most states have **age-gap exceptions**, sometimes called "**Romeo and Juliet**" **clauses**, which overlook consensual sex between same-age peers. These exceptions prohibit prosecution for statutory rape in cases where the parties' ages are within a specified range, usually 2–5 years, as specified in statute. These exceptions prohibit, for example, the prosecution of an 18-year-old male for engaging in sexual activity with his 16-year-old girlfriend.

In many jurisdictions where the age of consent is under age 18 or when age-gap exceptions apply, there is also a special provision for "position of authority" and "school employee" exceptions. The idea here is that persons under the age of 18 may not truly be able to consent to sex if the potential partner is in a position of authority, such as a teacher or coach. For example, consider the case where a 16-year-old student and 19-year-old assistant coach begin a romantic relationship. In this case, many states would view sexual activity between the two as statutory rape, even if there is a three-year age-gap provision or the age of consent is 16. This exception exists to prevent a person with authority, such as a coach or

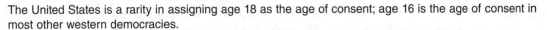

Figure 5.1   International Ages of Consent

The United States is a rarity in assigning age 18 as the age of consent; age 16 is the age of consent in most other western democracies.

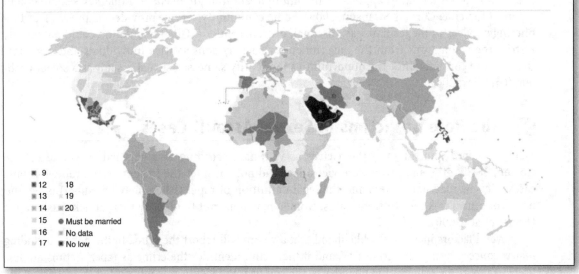

SOURCE: http://www.age-of-consent.info/?page_id=58.

teacher, from using their authority to achieve sex. Thus, many statutes assume coercion if one party is under age 18 and the other is in position of authority, regardless of age-gap exception in that state.

Outside the Unites States, the age of consent varies to as young as 12 and as old as 21. The age of consent is 16 in many Western Democratic countries, including Canada, the United Kingdom, Australia, and the Netherlands. In some countries, consent can be given at marriage and is not based on a year of age.

Same-Sex Sexual Violence

Much of the existing research on rape involves a male offender and a female victim. Many of the theories to explain rape involve the use of violence by men to exert power and control over women. This explanation is rooted in a heterosexist ideology. Indeed, our laws, which in many states identify the crime of rape as the unlawful penetration of a penis into a vagina, do not allow for the legal identification of same-sex cases as rape (though most have additional sexual assault statutes that are inclusive of same-sex acts of sexual violation).

Much of the discussion about same-sex rape is limited to male-on-male sexual assault, and many of these studies are conducted within an incarcerated setting. Research regarding female-on-female sexual violence is limited (Gilroy & Carroll, 2009). One study that compared levels of violence experienced by lesbian and heterosexual women found that women involved in same-sex relationships experienced significantly higher levels of nonsexual physical violence (51%) compared to heterosexual women (33%; Bernhard, 2000).

Women (and men) who report same-sex sexual violence are often confronted with a system where agents of the criminal justice system may reflect homophobic views (Wang, 2011). Such perspectives can potentially silence victims and prevent them from seeking legal remedies and social services. Indeed, advocacy services have been slow in responding to the unique needs of this population, often failing to appreciate the multiple and unique needs of same-sex sexual assault victims (Turrell & Cornell-Swanson, 2005). Some community service providers express a fear that offering services to the lesbian, gay, bisexual, or transgender (LGBT) population could potentially restrict their donations from the government or socially conservative individuals and organizations. These conflicts limit the opportunities to identify same-sex sexual assault as a social problem (Girshick, 2002).

⚅ The Role of Victims in Sexual Assault Cases

Many women do not identify themselves as victims. According to a national survey of college women, 48.8% of women who were victimized did not consider the incident to be rape. In many cases, victims may not understand the legal definition of rape. Others may be embarrassed and not want others to know. In some cases, women may not want to identify their attacker as a rapist (Fisher et al., 2000).

Several factors increase the likelihood that a victim will report the crime to the police, including injury, concern over contracting HIV, and if the victim identifies the crime as rape. Victims are less likely to report the crime if the offender is a friend or if the victim was intoxicated (Kilpatrick et al., 2007). For college-age women, less than 5% of completed and attempted rapes were reported to the police. While women do not report these crimes to law enforcement or school officials, they do not necessarily stay silent, as over two-thirds of victims confided in a friend about their attack. The decision by victims to not report their assault to the police stems from a belief that the incident was not harmful or important enough to report. For these women, it may be that they did not believe that they have been victims of a crime or did not want family members or others to know about the attack. Others had little faith in the criminal justice system, as they were concerned that the criminal justice system would not see the event as a serious incident or that there would be insufficient proof that a crime had occurred (Fisher et al., 2000).

For those victims who decide to report their crime, the most common reason to report was to prevent the crime from happening to others (Kilpatrick et al., 2007). Key findings from the NVAWS documented that only 43% of reported rapes resulted in an arrest of the offender. Of those arrested, only 37% of these cases were prosecuted. Fewer than half (46.2%) of those prosecuted were convicted, and 76% of those convicted were sentenced to jail or prison. Taking unreported rapes into consideration, only 2.2% of all rapists are incarcerated. Of those who reported their rape, less than half of victims indicated that they were satisfied with the way their case was handled by the authorities: 47.7% of victims were satisfied with how their case was handled by the police, while 48.6% of victims were pleased with the outcome of their case by the courts (Tjaden & Thoennes, 2006, p. 46).

Victims who seek out medical treatment are more likely to report their sexual assaults (or attempted assaults) compared to those who do not seek medical treatment, perhaps because medical treatment for their injuries occurs in conjunction with the collection of evidence during a sexual assault examination. In a study of women who sought medical assistance following a sexual assault, 52% had some form of injury to their body, while 20% had direct injuries to their genitals as a result of the sexual assault (Sugar, Fine, & Eckert, 2004). Experiences of rape and sexual assault also place victims at risk for developing long-term mental health concerns. Over half of the victims of sexual assault experience symptoms of PTSD at some point during their lifetime. Symptoms of PTSD can appear months or even years following the assault. The levels of emotional trauma that victims experience lead to significant mental health effects, such as depression, low self-esteem, anxiety, and fear for personal safety. Women with a history of sexual assault are more likely to have seriously considered attempting suicide and are more likely to engage in behaviors that put them at physical, psychological, and emotional risk, including risky sexual behaviors with multiple partners, extreme weight-loss measures, and substance abuse involving alcohol and illegal drugs (Gidycz, Orchowski, King, & Rich, 2008; Kaukinen & DeMaris, 2009). Women who are victimized by strangers may experience anxiety and fear about their surroundings, particularly if the assault occurred in a public setting.

▲ **Photo 5.2** Former child soldier Kristine Abalo sits with her two children outside a hut in Gulu, Uganda, February 27, 2002. Abalo was abducted as a child by the rebel Ugandan group, known as the Lord Resistance Army, and was raped, impregnated, and forced to fight until she was able to escape with her children back to her home.

Victims of rape and sexual assault have both immediate and long-term physical and emotional health needs. Rape-crisis services play an important role in victim advocacy. The current rape crisis movement developed in response to the perceived need for prevention, community awareness, and amelioration of victims' pain. However, even the best community services are limited and lack adequate resources to effectively combat all needs for victims of sexual assault. While attempts to help survivors of sexual assault involve friends, family members, community agencies, and criminal justice personnel, efforts in help seeking may actually enhance the trauma that victims experience due to lack of support, judgment, and blame by support networks. Additionally, victims may experience further trauma by being forced to relive their trauma as part of the official processing of the assault as a crime (Kaukinen & DeMaris, 2009). Due to these negative experiences in disclosure, many victims choose to keep their assault a secret.

Ultimately, cases of rape and sexual assault can be very difficult to prove in a court of law. Convictions are rare, and many cases are plea bargained to a lesser charge, many of which carry little to no jail time. Alas, the acceptance of rape myths by police, prosecutors, judges, and juries limits the punishment of offenders in cases of sexual assault. Figure 5.2 highlights how each stage of the criminal justice system reduces the likelihood that offenders will be arrested, charged, and punished for these cases. The effects of these practices can further discourage victims from reporting these crimes, believing that little can be done by criminal justice officials.

Figure 5.2   Punishment and Rape

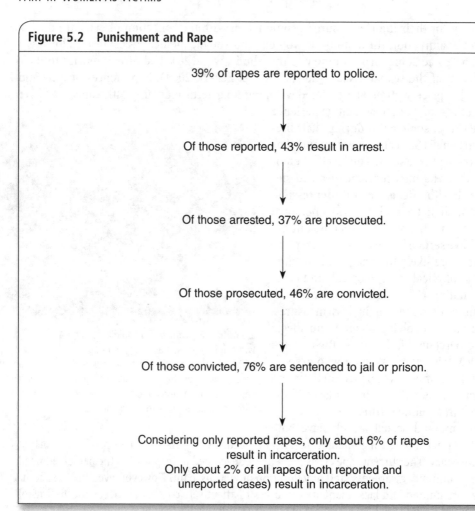

39% of rapes are reported to police.

Of those reported, 43% result in arrest.

Of those arrested, 37% are prosecuted.

Of those prosecuted, 46% are convicted.

Of those convicted, 76% are sentenced to jail or prison.

Considering only reported rapes, only about 6% of rapes
result in incarceration.
Only about 2% of all rapes (both reported and
unreported cases) result in incarceration.

International Perspectives on Sexual Assault: Child Rape in Africa

Students of criminal justice in the United States are often taken aback with the estimates of child rape: Approximately 90,000 cases of child sexual assault occur each year, with one-third against children under age 12, and roughly 25% of all girls in the United States will be sexually assaulted before adulthood (NCVS, 2011; Radford et al., 2011b; United States Department of Health and Human Services, 2005; United States Department of Justice, 2004). Taken in context, these 90,000 child sexual assaults make up approximately 20% of all violent interpersonal crimes during that same year, with property crime occupying an estimated 50% of the remaining violations of law; however, crimes peaked between the years of 2002 and 2003 and have been on a relative decline since (Burger, Gould, & Newham, 2010). While these numbers may be shocking to many, they pale in comparison to the current rates of child rape in Africa, attributed in part to the AIDS epidemic on that continent.

According to Meier (2002), the instances of sexual violence against children in Africa increased 400% between 1992 and 2002, including an increase in violent, high-profile infant rapes, which, in cases where the baby survived, required extensive surgery to repair pelvic, genital, and rectal damage. News media, international organizations, and scholarly research report that South Africa has one of the highest rates of child rape in the world (Epstein, 2006; Jewkes, Sikweyiya, Morrell, & Dunkle, 2009; Meier, 2002). The United Nations (2011) reports that half of all women in South Africa will be raped in their lifetime, which suggests that South African women have a greater likelihood of being raped than learning to read in childhood. The high incidence of child rape in South Africa is due in part to the **virgin rape myth** and also the use of **corrective rape** in that country. Both have particularly harmful implications for girls.

South Africa also has one of the highest HIV rates in the world (Jewkes et al., 2009). Associated with this has been the rise of the *virgin rape myth*, which holds that rape of a virgin cures HIV/AIDS. Unfortunately, virginity is a trait associated with youth: In essence, best way to ensure that one has indeed found a virgin is to select a very young girl. This has led to horrific crimes against female babies, who are very likely to be virgins. The result has been a virtual plague of child rape in South Africa by AIDS-infected men who seek to cure their HIV status through the violent rape of young girls. Officials both in South Africa and worldwide have attempted to address this growing issue through education (both to dispel the myth and to encourage safer sex practices), medical intervention, and other services. But, as Collings (2009) found, child rape victims often experienced secondary victimization with such services; Collings (2011) conducted a recent examination of child rape survivors' perceptions of services and concluded that services currently in place "fail to adequately address the child's basic needs and rights" (p. 5).

The second factor associated with the high rates of child rape in South Africa is the practice of *corrective rape*, which is essentially the rape of a female by a male to correct misbehavior (Di Silvio, 2011). This often involves the rape of a girl by her father or male caretaker as a disciplinary action or the rape of a lesbian by heterosexual males to "cure" her sexual orientation (Bartle, 2000; Hawthorne, 2005).

The child rape epidemic in South Africa has resulted in profound individual harm, including physical trauma of victim. Child rape often results in the need for the child to have reconstructive surgery and sometimes results in death. HIV transmission is also a grave concern. The psychological trauma is well documented in the literature, including increased risk for depression, anxiety, PTSD, and other effects discussed elsewhere in this chapter. In addition to these effects, other research articulates broader sociological implications associated with child rape. According to Jewkes et al. (2009), nearly 25% of South African men self-report the commission of rape, with about 10% of those admitting to the rape of a girl under age 10. Researchers from CIET (Community Information, Empowerment, and Transparency) have examined children's responses and attitudes about sexual assault: In 2007, about 60% of children believed that forcing someone they knew to have sex was not a violent act or a crime.

⊠ Racial Differences in Sexual Assault

Research suggests that women of color have different experiences of sexual assault compared to White women. These differences can be seen in prevalence rates, reporting behaviors, disclosure practices, help-seeking behaviors, and responses by the justice system. For example, research indicates that 18% of White women report a rape or sexual assault during the course of their lifetime, compared to 19% of Black women, 34% of American Indian/Alaska Native women, and 24% of women who identify as mixed race (Tjaden & Thoennes, 2006). Two important issues are raised with these statistics: (1) We already know that rape generally is underreported, so it is possible to assume that the true numbers of rape and sexual assault within different races and ethnicities may be significantly higher than these data indicate; and (2) given the unequal distribution of these statistics by race and ethnicity, compared to their representation in the general population, it is reasonable to conclude that women of color are victimized at a disproportionate rate compared to their White sisters. Despite these issues, the experience of rape and sexual assault within minority communities is significantly understudied in the scholarly research. How do race and ethnicity affect the experience of rape and sexual assault?

While much of the literature on racial differences in rape and sexual assault focuses on the Black female experience, statistics by Tjaden and Thoennes (2006) highlight the extreme rates of rape within the American Indian and Alaska Native population (AIAN). These data are particularly troubling, given that the AIAN population is a small minority in the population, comprising only about 1% of the U.S. population (United States Bureau of the Census, 2000). Research using the NCVS data indicates that compared to other racial and ethnic groups, AIAN women are most likely to experience rape within an intimate partner relationship, versus stranger or acquaintance relationships. Within this context, they were more likely to have a weapon used against them and to be physically assaulted as part of the attack. Alcohol and drugs also play a stronger role in the attacks of AIAN women, with more than two-thirds of offenders under the influence of intoxicants, compared to only one-third of offenders in cases involving White or Black victims. While AIAN victims are more likely to report these crimes to the police, the majority of these reports come from people on behalf of the victim (family, officials, others) rather than the victim herself (Bachman, Zaykowski, Lanier, Poteyeva, & Kallmyer, 2010).

Research by Boykins et al. (2010) investigates the different experiences of sexual assault among Black and White women who sought emergency care following their attack. While no racial and ethnic differences were found between victims in terms of the location of the assault (home, car, outdoors) or whether the offender was known to the victim, Black women were significantly more likely to have a weapon used against them during the attack compared to White women (42% vs. 16.7%). The intoxication of the victim (and offender) also varied by race, as White women were more likely to be under the influence of alcohol (47.2% of White women reported being under the influence, compared to 23.8% of Black women), as were their perpetrators (47.2% of offenders against White women were under the influence, compared to 23.8% of offenders against Black women). In contrast, the use of illicit drugs prior to the assault was more common among Black victims compared to White victims (28.7% vs. 12.5%). However, there were no racial or ethnic differences in the reporting of the assault to police or of the offering or acceptance of counseling resources. Despite the importance of these findings, it is important to keep in mind that few victims seek out emergency services following their assault, which may skew the interpretation of these results.

Not only are women of color less likely to disclose sexual assault, there are a number of factors that vary by race and ethnicity that can affect the disclosure and recovery process. Research by Washington (2001) found that fewer than half of the women interviewed had disclosed their victimization—when they did disclose, they did so to friends or family members within 24 hours of the assault. However, most of these women experienced incidents of victim blaming as a result of their disclosure. As a result of historical, personal, and cultural experiences with law enforcement, the majority of the women did not seek out the police to make an official report of their attack. In addition, many of the Black women talked about not reporting as a cultural expectation of keeping their business to themselves. They also mentioned not wanting to perpetuate additional racist views against members of the Black community, particularly if their assailant was also Black. For example, one woman reported to Washington (2001),

> We have this element in our community that it's the White man or the White race that causes most, if not all, of the problems we have in our communities. If we begin to point out the Black male for specific problems, we tend to get heat . . . even from some women because we as women have been socialized as well. And it's "Don't bring the Black man down. . . . He's already going to jail, dying, rumored to be an endangered species; so why should we as Black women bring our wrath against him? (p. 1269)

Likewise, cultural expectations also can inhibit the official reporting practices of women within the Asian American and Pacific Islander population (AAPI). Like the Black community, there is a high level of distrust of public officials (often due to negative experiences either in the United States or, in the cases of immigrant and refugee individuals, in their home country) as well as a cultural expectation to keep personal issues in the private sphere. In addition, concerns over immigration status, lack of knowledge about the criminal justice system, and language barriers affect both reporting practices as well as the utilization of mental health resources. In addition, research has highlighted that many AAPI women fail to understand the definitions of *rape* and *sexual assault*, which further limits the likelihood that such incidents will be reported (Bryant-Davis, Chung, & Tillman, 2009). The same factors that limit the reporting rates of crimes such as rape and sexual assault also affect the use of therapeutic resources. Indeed, AAPIs have the lowest utilization of mental health services of any racial or ethnic minority group (Abe-Kim et al., 2007).

Within the Hispanic community, Latina women have the highest rates of attempted sexual assault of all ethnic groups. The experience of an attempted rape/sexual assault carries with it many of the same psychological traumas as a completed rape. Stereotypes of Latina women as passionate and sexual women can affect the fears of rape victims that they may have contributed to the assault; this therefore limits the likelihood that they will report (or that their reports will be taken seriously), making it important for agencies in Hispanic/Latino communities to reach out to the population and dismantle some of the stereotypes and attitudes that can inhibit reporting and help-seeking behaviors (Bryant-Davis et al., 2009). Like the AAPI community, some Latina women are confronted by concerns over their immigration status and language barriers that can affect reporting rates of completed and attempted sexual assaults.

Culture shapes the manner in which people represent themselves, make sense of their lives, and relate to others in the social world. Indeed, the experience of trauma is no different, and we find that women of color are less likely than White women to engage in help-seeking behaviors from traditional models of assistance. While many women of color believe that agencies such as rape-crisis centers can provide valuable resources to victims of sexual assault, they may be hesitant to call upon these organizations themselves for fear that these organizations would be unable to understand their experiences as a woman of color. Instead, victims may turn to sympathetic leaders and women within their own communities. In order to increase the accessibility of these services to women of color, victims and scholars argue that services need to be culturally sensitive and address the unique considerations that women of various racial and ethnic identities face as victims of sexual assault (Tillman, Bryant-Davis, Smith, & Marks, 2010).

Policy Implications

Research on rape and sexual assault indicates a number of areas where the criminal justice system and other social institutions can improve prevention and intervention efforts. Given that adolescents and young adults have higher rates of acquaintance rape and sexual assault, much of these prevention efforts have been targeted at college campuses. While college campuses have increased their educational activities aimed toward preventing rape on campuses in recent times, these efforts may still be inadequate, given the number of assaults that occur on campuses around the nation each year. However, the age of victimization appears to be decreasing, indicating a need for education efforts focused on high school students.

Victims indicate that an increase in public education about acquaintance rape and increased services for counseling would encourage more victims to report their crimes (Kilpatrick et al., 2007). Programs focusing on rape and sexual assault prevention should provide accurate definitions of sexual assault behaviors, use realistic examples, discuss alcohol use and the definition of sexual assault, and help individuals understand what it means to consent to sexual activity. By tailoring education efforts toward combating myths about rape, these efforts can help reduce the levels of shame that victims may experience as a result of their victimization and encourage them to seek help following a sexual assault. Services need to be made available and known to students, both in terms of services and outreach on campus and information available online.

Rape Shield Laws

Throughout most of history, rape has been underreported. When it is reported, cases of rape are very difficult to prosecute, often because these cases have erroneously focused on the victim's behavior—her attire, demeanor, and sexual history—instead of the actions of the accused. These practices, which are often grounded in and serve to reinforce rape myths, essentially put the victim on trial.

By the 1970s, feminists and legal scholars began writing to advocate changing these practices, pushing for the passage of rape shield statutes to prevent the undue focus on victims in cases of sexual assault. Generally speaking, *rape shield laws* are various statutes that offer protections to victims in sexual assault cases, with the understanding that female rape victims historically experience secondary victimization during trial (Call, Nice, & Talarico, 1991). While the specific provisions vary by state, they generally include such protections as confidentiality of victim name and limits on defense counsel's ability to cross-examine the victim beyond the specific sexual assault in question. Many states preclude any discussion of the victim's previous sexual history, including, for example, her previous sexual activity with the defendant and prior partners, opinions about the victim's sexual past, or her sexual reputation (National District Attorneys Association, 2011). At the time of this writing, every state and the District of Columbia have some form of rape shield laws for victims in criminal cases, and many also provide similar protections for parties in civil suits (National Center for Victims of Crime, 2011).

Contrary to common belief, rape shield laws do not prohibit the media from publishing the names of rape victims. Most news media voluntarily omit identifying information about the victim during trial, although specific laws to prevent media from disclosing this information have been found unconstitutional (*Florida Star v. B.J.F.,* 1989). Nevertheless, most media outlets voluntarily keep this information from the public. Rape shield laws protect victim identity by referring to the victim as *Jane Doe* in proceedings, which are a matter of public purview.

While the specific provisions of rape shield laws vary by jurisdiction, these overwhelming pertain to admissibility of evidence pertaining to the victim's history. In most cases, this means that the victim's previous sexual history is inadmissible; however, some states have a "catch all" exception that allows the court to decide the admissibility of each piece of evidence in a given case to protect the constitutional rights of the accused (National Center for Victims of Crime, 2011). Thus, victim sexual history has been—and can be—admitted as evidence during rape trials, even in jurisdictions that tout rape shield law protections for victims.

Case Study

The State of Colorado vs. Kobe Bryant

Rape shield laws are only selectively protective of women's accounts of rape. Consider the reporting practices by the news media in cases involving high-profile defendants. In the case of the sexual assault charge against Kobe Bryant, a famous basketball player for the Los Angeles Lakers, hundreds of articles were written about the case in the months before the trial. A review of these articles demonstrates that they included positive statements about the defendant's character as well as his talent as an athlete. In contrast, cases involving an ordinary citizen would be unlikely to receive such treatment. In this case, these articles also contained negative statements about the victim, many of which reflected an acceptance of rape myths such as "she's lying" or "she asked for it" (Franiuk, Seefelt, Cepress, & Vandello, 2008; Lopez, 2007). These themes are reflected in many of the headlines from the time:

"Kobe's Accuser Hospitalized Last Winter as a 'Danger to Herself'"—*Associated Press,* July 24, 2003

"Kobe accuser's credibility under fire"—*Associated Press,* December 17, 2003

Amidst intense public scrutiny, which included the publication of the victim's name, personal details, and sexual history, the victim in this case declined to testify, and the charges against Kobe Bryant were dropped in December of 2003, just five months after the initial charges were filed.

Would this have been the case had Kobe Bryant not been a celebrity? Would rape shield laws have had a larger impact if fame and notoriety had not clouded the public's eye? It is also prudent to wonder how impartial the jury's opinions might have been, especially given the veritable avalanche of media attention this case received.

(Continued)

(Continued)

Based on the experiences of this one victim, it is not surprising that many victims may be fearful of reporting sexual assault if they believe that their experiences will be invalidated and if they are concerned that they will be emotionally attacked by outsiders who blame victims, suggesting she "asked for it," "is lying," or is mentally unstable. In fact, the treatment of this particular Jane Doe may have had an appreciable effect on rape reporting. The Colorado Coalition Against Sexual Assault (2004) reported a nearly 10% drop in rape reporting the year following the Bryant Case. In their 2008 analysis examining the impact of rape myths in the Kobe Bryant case, Franiuk et al. (2008) confirmed most scholars' worst fears: Male subjects exposed to rape myths, such as those contained in the Kobe Bryant rape articles in 2003, were less likely to believe a rape suspect was guilty and more likely to hold rape-supportive attitudes than those reading articles without such rape myths. While the case certainly had a significant impact on the lives of the two parties involved, the media coverage appears to have caused a tremendous setback for rape shield laws and victim's rights.

SUMMARY

- Rape is one of the most underreported crimes of victimization.
- The risk of rape and sexual assault appears to be higher on college campuses.
- The acceptance of rape myths by society contributes to the practice of victim blaming.
- Many victims of rape and sexual assault fail to identify their experiences as a criminal act.
- Excuses and justifications allow perpetrators of rape and sexual assault to deny or minimize levels of blame and injury toward their victims.
- The majority of rapes and sexual assaults involve individuals who are known to the victim prior to the assault.
- The term *date rape drugs* is used to identify a group of drugs (such as GHB, Rohypnol, and Ketamine) that have been used to facilitate a sexual assault.
- Marital (spousal) rape is as prevalent as other forms of rape, though it is significantly underreported and hidden from public view.
- Victims of rape and sexual assault are at risk for long-term physical and emotional health concerns.
- Child sexual assault is the most underreported sexual crime, perhaps because perpetrators are generally close to the child. Child victims of sexual assault have even higher risks of long-term physical and emotional harm than victims of other types of sexually based offenses.
- Statutory rape generally refers to sexual activity between two parties when one is not of legal age to give consent. Age-gap and marital exceptions can prevent overprosecution of these cases between consenting peers, while position of authority exceptions make prosecution more likely in cases where the offender was in a position to unduly influence a minor into sexual activity.

- *Spousal rape*, the forced or coerced sexual activity between a person and his/her spouse, was not recognized as a crime until the late 20th century.
- Rape shield laws, while designed to protect secondary victimization of rape victims at trial, sometimes contain exceptions and loopholes that allow victims' sexual history to be introduced in court.

KEY TERMS

Acquaintance rape	Crimes against Humanity	Same-sex sexual assault
Age-gap exceptions	Extralegal factors	Spousal rape
Child rape	Genocide	Statutory rape
Child sexual abuse	Incapacitated rape	Virgin rape myth
Corrective rape	Romeo and Juliet clauses	

DISCUSSION QUESTIONS

1. How has the definition of rape evolved over time?
2. Why do many victims of rape and sexual assault choose not to report their crimes to the police?
3. What impact do rape myths play in victim blaming and the denial of offender culpability?
4. Why do many victims of rape and sexual assault fail to identify themselves as victims of a crime?
5. Why are acquaintance rape cases not viewed as "real" rape?
6. What tactics do perpetrators use to coerce sex from their victims?
7. In what ways can prevention efforts educate women and men about the realities of rape and sexual assault?
8. Why are child sexual assaults highly underreported? When child rape occurs, who is most likely to be the perpetrator?
9. What are the short- and long-term effects of sexual assault? How might early sexual assault yield a pathway to later victimization? To later delinquency?
10. Is there a standard age of consent in statutory rape cases? What are the exceptions to age of consent, and why were these developed?
11. What factors contribute to the high child-rape rates in South Africa? How might these be combated?
12. What are rape shield laws? Who and what do they shield?

WEB RESOURCES

Bureau of Justice Statistics http://bjs.ojp.usdoj.gov

The National Center for Victims of Crime http://www.ncvc.org

National Clearinghouse on Marital and Date Rape http://ncmdr.org/

Office of Justice Programs http://www.ojp.usdoj.gov/

Rape, Abuse & Incest National Network http://www.rainn.org

Rape, Abuse, & Incest National Network—State Resources http://www.rainn.org/get-help/local-counseling-centers/state-sexual-assault-resources

REFERENCES

Abe-Kim, J., Takeuchi, D. T., Hong, S., Zane, N., Sue, S., Spencer, M. S., . . . Alegría, M. (2007). Use of mental health-related services among immigrant and U.S.-born Asian Americans: Results from the National Latino and Asian American Study. *American Journal of Public Health, 97*(1), 91.

Air Force rape scandal grows. (2009, February 11). *CBS News*. Retrieved from http://www.cbsnews.com/2100–201_162–543490.html

Albanese, J. (2007). A criminal network approach to understanding & measuring trafficking in human beings. *Measuring Human Trafficking*, 55–71.

Associated Press. (2009, January 11). Luster hunter can't cash in. *CBS News*. Retrieved from http://www.cbsnews.com/stories/2003/01/09/national/main535821.shtml

Bachman, R., Zaykowski, H., Lanier, C., Poteyeva, M., & Kallmyer, R. (2010). Estimating the magnitude of rape and sexual assault against American Indian and Alaska Native (AIAN) women. *Australian & New Zealand Journal of Criminology, 43*(2), 199–222.

Baker, A. W., & Duncan, S. P. (1985). Child sexual abuse: A study of prevalence in Great Britain. *Child Abuse and Neglect, 9*(4), 457–467.

Baron, S. W. (2003). Street youth violence and victimization. *Trauma, Violence, & Abuse, 4*(1), 22–44.

Bartle, E. E. (2000). Lesbians and hate crimes. *Journal of Poverty, 4*(4), 23–44. doi: 10.1300/J134v04n04

Basile, K. C., Chen, J., Black, M. C., & Saltzman, L. E. (2007). Prevalence and characteristics of sexual violence victimization among U.S. adults, 2001–2003. *Violence and Victims, 22*(4), 437–448. doi: http://dx.doi.org/10.1891/088667007781553955

Benda, B. B. (2005). Gender differences in life-course theory of recidivism: A survival analysis. *International Journal of Offender Therapy and Comparative Criminology, 49*(3), 325–342.

Bennice, J. A., & Resick, P. A. (2003). Marital rape history, research, and practice. *Trauma, Violence, & Abuse, 4*(3), 228–246.

Bernhard, L. A. (2000). Physical and sexual violence experienced by lesbian and heterosexual women. *Violence Against Women, 6*(1), 68–79.

Beynon, C. M., McVeigh, C., McVeigh, J., Leavey, C., & Bellis, M. A. (2008). The involvement of drugs and alcohol in drug-facilitated sexual assault: A systematic review of the evidence. *Trauma, Violence, & Abuse, 9*(3), 178–188.

Black, M. C., Basile, K. C., Breiding, M. J., Smith, S. G., Walters, M. L., Merrick, M. T., Chen, J., & Stevens, M. R. (2011). *The National Intimate Partner and Sexual Violence Survey (NISVS): 2010 summary report*. Atlanta, GA: National Center for Injury Prevention and Control, Centers for Disease Control and Prevention.

Boykins, A. D., Alvanzo, A. A., Carson, S., Forte, J., Leisey, M., & Plichta, S. B. (2010). Minority women victims of recent sexual violence: Disparities in incident history. *Journal of Women's Health, 19*(3), 453–461.

Bryant-Davis, T., Chung, H., & Tillman, S. (2009). From the margins to the center ethnic minority women and the mental health effects of sexual assault. *Trauma, Violence, & Abuse, 10*(4), 330–357.

Bufkin, J. (2000). Images of sex and rape: A content analysis of popular film. *Violence Against Women, 6*(12), 1317–1344.

Burger, J., Gould, C., & Newham, G. (2010). The state of crime in South Africa. *South Africa Crime Quarterly, 34*, 3–12.

Burgess-Jackson, K. (Ed.). (1999). *A most detestable crime: New philosophical essays on rape.* New York, NY: Oxford University Press.

California Department of Corrections and Rehabilitation. (2011). *Inmate Locator—search for Andrew Luster.* [Website search.] Retrieved from http://inmatelocator.cdcr.ca.gov/search.aspx

California Penal Code § 261(a)(3)

Call, J. E., Nice, D., & Talarico, S. M. (1991). An analysis of state rape shield laws. *Social Science Quarterly, 72*(4), 774–788.

Carson, D. C., Sullivan, C. J., Cochran, J. K., & Lersch, K. M. (2009). General strain theory and the relationship between early victimization and drug use. *Deviant Behavior, 30*(1), 54–88.

Cheasty, M., Clare, A. W., & Collins, C. (2002). Child sexual abuse—A predictor of persistent depression in adult rape and sexual assault victims. *Journal of Mental Health, 11*(1), 79–84.

Ciofalo, J. J. (1995). Unveiling Goya's *Rape of Galatea. Art History, 18*(4), 477–498.

CNN Justice. (2003, June 20). Max Factor heir returns to face prison term. *CNN.com.* Retrieved from http:// http://articles.cnn.com/2003-06-19/justice/max.factor.heir_1_max-factor-heir-andrew-luster-bounty-hunter?_s=PM:LAW

Collings, S. J. (2009). Where the streets have no names: Factors associated with the provision of counselling and social work services for child rape survivors in KwaZulu-Natal, South Africa. *Journal of Child & Adolescent Mental Health, 21*(2), 139–146.

Collings, S. J. (2011). Professional services for child rape survivors: A child-centered perspective on helpful and harmful experiences. *Journal of Child & Adolescent Mental Health, 23*(1), 5–15. doi: 10.2989/17280583.2011.594244

Colorado Coalition Against Sexual Assault. (2004). *CCASA Publications.* Retrieved from http://www.ccasa.org/?page_id=253

Di Silvio, L. (2011). Correcting corrective rape: Carmichele and developing South Africa's affirmative obligations to prevent violence against women. *Georgetown Law Journal, 99*(5), 1469. Retrieved from http://ssrn.com/abstract=1709629

Dodderidge, J. (1632). *The lawes resolutions of women's rights: Or, the law's provision for women.* London, England: John More, Rare Book and Special Collections Division, Library of Congress.

Drug-Induced Rape Prevention and Punishment Act of 1996. 21 U.S.C. Sec. 841(b)(7)

England, L. (2008, March 17). Rumsfeld knew. *Stern Magazine.* Retrieved from http://www.stern.de/politik/ausland/lynndie-england-rumsfeld-knew-614356.html?nv=ct_cb

Epstein, H. (2006). AIDS and Africa's hidden war. *Virginia Quarterly Review, 82*(1), 31–41.

Ewoldt, C. A., Monson, C. M., & Langhinrichsen-Rohling, J. (2000). Attributions about rape in a continuum of dissolving marital relationships. *Journal of Interpersonal Violence, 15*(11), 1175–1183. doi: 10.1177/088626000015011004

Eyal, K. (2007) Sexual socialization messages on television programs most popular among teens. *Journal of Broadcasting & Electronic Media, 51*(2), 316–336.

Fattah, E. A., & Sacco, V. F. (1989). *Crime and victimization of the elderly.* New York, NY: Springer-Verlag.

Federal Bureau of Investigation. (2012a). *Attorney General Eric Holder announces revisions to the Uniform Crime Report's definition of rape: Data reported on rape will better reflect state criminal codes, victim experiences.* [Press Release.] U.S. Department of Justice. Retrieved from http://www.fbi.gov/news/pressrel/press-releases/attorney-general-eric-holder-announces-revisions-to-the-uniform-crime-reports-definition-of-rape

Federal Bureau of Investigation. (2012b). *UCR program changes definition of rape: Includes all victims and omits requirement of physical force.* Criminal Justice Information Service, U.S. Department of Justice. Retrieved from http://www.fbi.gov/about-us/cjis/cjis-link/march-2012/ucr-program-changes-definition-of-rape

Fischer, M. A. (2002, December 1). The thin blurred line. *Los Angeles Times.* Retrieved from http://articles.latimes.com/2002/dec/01/magazine/tm-daterape48

Fisher, B. S., Cullen, F. T., & Turner, M. G. (2000). *The sexual victimization of college women.* [Series: Research Report.] NCJ. Retrieved from http://www.ncjrs.gov/pdffiles1/nij/182369.pdf

Fisher, B. S., Daigle, L. E., Cullen, F. T., & Turner, M. G. (2003). Reporting sexual victimization to the police and others results from a national-level study of college women. *Criminal Justice and Behavior, 30*(1), 6–38.

Fisher, B. S., & Sloan III, J. J. (2003). Unraveling the fear of victimization among college women: Is the "shadow of sexual assault hypothesis" supported? *Justice Quarterly, 20*(3), 633–659.

Florida Star v. B.J.F. (1989). 491 U.S. 524.

Franiuk, R., Seefelt, J. L., Cepress, S. L., & Vandello, J. A. (2008). Prevalence and effects of rape myths in print journalism: The Kobe Bryant case. *Violence Against Women, 14*(3), 287–309.

Fus, T. (2006, March). Criminalizing marital rape: A comparison of judicial and legislative approaches. *Vanderbilt Journal of Transnational Law, 39*(2), 481–517.

Gidycz, C. A., Orchowski, L. M., King, C. R., & Rich, C. L. (2008). Sexual victimization and health-risk behaviors: A prospective analysis of college women. *Journal of Interpersonal Violence, 23*(6), 744–763.

Gilroy, P. J., & Carroll, L. (2009, October). Woman to woman sexual violence. *Women & Therapy, 32*(4), 423–435. doi: 10.1080/02703140903153419

Girard, A. L., & Senn, C. Y. (2008). The role of the new "date rape drugs" in attributions about date rape. *Journal of Interpersonal Violence, 23*(1), 3–20.

Girshick, L. B. (2002). No sugar, no spice: Reflections on research on woman-to-woman sexual violence. *Violence Against Women, 8*(12), 1500–1520.

Greenfeld, L. A. (1997). *Sex offenses and offenders: An analysis of data on rape and sexual assault.* Washington, DC: U.S. Department of Justice, Office of Justice Programs.

Hasday, J. E. (2000, October). Contest and consent: A legal history of marital rape. *California Law Review, 88*(5), 1373–1509.

Hawthorne, S. (2005). Ancient hatred and its contemporary manifestation: The torture of lesbians. *Journal of Hate Studies, 4*(1), 33–58.

Hernandez, R. (2009, November 12). Luster petitions court to free him. *Ventura County Star.* Retrieved from http://www.vcstar.com/news/2009/nov/12/luster-petitions-court-to-free-him/

Hersh, S. M. (2004, May 10). Torture at Abu Ghraib. *New Yorker.* Retrieved from http://www.newyorker.com/archive/2004/05/10/040510fa_fact?currentPage=all

Hollist, D. R., Hughes, L. A., & Schaible, L. M. (2009). Adolescent maltreatment, negative emotion, and delinquency: An assessment of general strain theory and family-based strain. *Journal of Criminal Justice, 37*(4), 379–387.

Horeck, T. (2004). *Public rape: Representing violation in fiction and film.* London, England: Routledge.

Hults, L. C. (1991). Durer's Lucretia: Speaking the silence of women. *Journal of Women in Culture & Society, 16*(2), 205–237.

Jewkes, R., Sikweyiyal, Y., Morrell, R., & Dunkle, K. (2009). *Understanding men's health and use of violence: Interface of rape and HIV in South Africa.* (Report). South African Medical Research Council. Retrieved from http://www.mrc.ac.za/gender/violence_hiv.pdf

Johnson, K. (2012). FBI changes definition of rape to add men as victims. *USA Today.* Retrieved from http://usatoday30.usatoday.com/NEWS/usaedition/2012-01-06-Rape_ST_U.htm

Jones, C. (2001). Suspicious death related to gamma-hydroxybyturate (GHB) toxicity. *Journal of Clinical Forensic Medicine, 8,* 74–76.

Jones-Brown, D. (2007). Forever the symbolic assailant: The more things change, the more they stay the same. *Criminology & Public Policy, 6*(1), 103–121.

Kaukinen, C., & DeMaris, A. (2009). Sexual assault and current mental health: The role of help-seeking and police response. *Violence Against Women, 15*(11), 1331–1357.

Kilpatrick, D. G., Resnick, H. S., Ruggiero, K. J., Conoscenti, L. M., & McCauley, J. (2007). *Drug-facilitated, incapacitated, and forcible rape: A national study.* Charleston, SC: Medical University of South Carolina, National Crime Victims Research & Treatment Center.

Krajicek, D. (2011). *Andrew Luster.* TRU Crime Library, Turner Entertainment Network. Retrieved from http://www.trutv.com/library/crime/criminal_mind/sexual_assault/andrew_luster/1.html

Lane, J., Gover, A. R., & Dahod, S. (2009). Fear of violent crime among men and women on campus: The impact of perceived risk and fear of sexual assault. *Violence and Victims, 24*(2), 172–192.

Leung, R. (2009, February 11). Abuse of Iraqi POWs by GIs probed. *60 Minutes, CBS News.* Retrieved from http://www.cbsnews.com/stories/2004/04/27/60ii/main614063.shtml

Levitan, R. D., Rector, N. A., Sheldon, T., & Goering, P. (2003). Childhood adversities associated with major depression and/or anxiety disorders in a community sample of Ontario: Issues of co-morbidity and specificity. *Depression and Anxiety, 17*(1), 34–42. doi:10.1002/da.10077. PMID 12577276

Littleton, H., Breitkopf, C. R., & Berenson, A. (2008). Beyond the campus unacknowledged rape among low-income women. *Violence Against Women, 14*(3), 269–286.

Lo, C. C., Kim, Y. S., & Church, W. T. (2008). The effects of victimization on drug use: A multilevel analysis. *Substance Use & Misuse, 43*(10), 1340–1361.

Lonsway, K. A., & Fitzgerald, L. F. (1994). Rape myths in review. *Psychology of Women Quarterly, 18*(2), 133–164.

Lopez, A. (2007). Expert: Victims' path rockier than celebrities'. *Rocky Mountain News.* Retrieved from http://therocky.com/news/2007/mar/15/expert-victims-path-rockier-than-celebrities/

Los Angeles Times (March 11, 2013). Convicted rapist Andrew Luster's 124-year sentence vacated. Retrieved at http://latimesblogs.latimes.com/lanow/2013/03/andrew-luster-granted-new-sentencing-hearing.html

Martin, E. K., Taft, C. T., & Resick, P. A. (2007). A review of marital rape. *Aggression and Violent Behavior, 12*(3), 329–347.

Marx, B. P., Heidt, J. M., & Gold, S. D. (2005). Perceived uncontrollability and unpredictability, self-regulation, and sexual revictimization. *Review of General Psychology, 9*, 67–90.

McCauley, J., Kern, D. E., Kolodner, K., Dill, L., Schroeder, A. F., DeChant, H. K., . . . Bass, E. B. (1997). Clinical characteristics of women with a history of childhood abuse. *Journal of the American Medical Association, 7*, 1362–1368.

Meier, E. (2002). Child rape in South Africa. *Pediatric Nursing, 28*(5), 532–536.

Messman-Moore, T. L., & Garrigus, A. S. (2007). The association of child abuse and eating disorder symptomatology: The importance of multiple forms of abuse and revictimization. *Journal of Aggression, Maltreatment & Trauma, 14*(3), 51–72.

Millar, G., Stermac, L., & Addison, M. (2002). Immediate and delayed treatment seeking among adult sexual assault victims. *Women & Health, 35*(1), 53–64.

Myskow, L. (2006). The impact of childhood sexual abuse on women's healthcare. *Cytopathology, 17*, 4–5.

National Center for Victims of Crime. (2011). *Rape shield laws.* Retrieved from http://www.ncvc.org/ncvc/main.aspx?dbID=DB_FAQ:RapeShieldLaws927

National Crime Victimization Survey. (2008). *CAPI interviewing manual for field representatives.* U.S. Census Bureau. Retrieved from http://bjs.ojp.usdoj.gov/content/pub/pdf/manual08.pdf

National District Attorneys Association. (2011). *Rape shield statutes.* Retrieved from http://www.ndaa.org/pdf/NCPCA%20Rape%20Shield%202011.pdf

Odem, M. E. (1995). *Delinquent daughters: Protecting and policing adolescent female sexuality in the United States, 1885–1920.* Chapel Hill, NC: University of North Carolina Press.

Office of the Attorney General. (1997, September 23). *Drug-induced violent crime prosecutions.* [Memorandum for All United States Attorneys.] Washington, DC: Office of the Attorney General. Retrieved from http://www.justice.gov/ag/readingroom/drugcrime.htm

Payne, D., Lonsway, K., & Fitzgerald, L. (1999). Rape myth acceptance: Exploration of its structure and its measurement using the Illinois Rape Myth Acceptance Scale. *Journal of Research in Personality, 33*, 27–68.

Peterson, F. (2012, July 21). Luis Walker, Lackland boot camp instructor, convicted of rape and sexual assault. *Global Post.* Retrieved from http://www.globalpost.com/dispatch/news/regions/americas/united-states/120721/luis-walker-rape-sex-assault-lackland-texas-sexual-air-force-military-boot

Polusny, M. A., & Follette, V. M. (1995). Long-term correlates of child sexual abuse: Theory and review of the empirical literature. *Applied and Preventive Psychology, 4*, 148–166.

Radford, L., Corral, S., Bradley, C., Fisher, H., Bassett, C., Howat, N., & Collishaw, S. (2011a). *Child abuse and neglect in the UK today*. London, England: NSPCC. Retrieved from http://www.nspcc.org.uk/Inform/research/ findings/child_abuse_neglect_research_PDF_wdf84181.pdf

Radford, L., Corral, S., Bradley, C., Fisher, H., Bassett, C., Howat, N., & Collishaw, S. (2011b). *Maltreatment and victimisation of children and young people in the UK*. London, England: NSPCC.

Reid, J. A. (2010). Doors wide shut: Barriers to the successful delivery of victim services for domestically trafficked minors in a southern U.S. metropolitan area. *Women & Criminal Justice, 20*(1–2).

Rickert, V. I., Wiemann, C. M., & Vaughan, R. D. (2005). Disclosure of date/acquaintance rape: Who reports and when. *Journal of Pediatric and Adolescent Gynecology, 18*(1), 17–24.

Rind, B., Tromovitch, P., & Bauserman, R. (1998). A meta-analytic examination of assumed properties of child sexual abuse using college samples. *Psychological Bulletin, 124*(1), 22–53.

Roosa, M. W., Reinholtz, C., & Angelini, P. J. (1999). The relation of child sexual abuse and depression in young women: Comparisons across four ethnic groups. *Journal of Abnormal Child Psychology, 27*(1), 65–76.

Russell, D. E. H. (1990). *Rape in marriage: Expanded and revised edition with a new introduction*. Bloomington, IN: Indiana University Press.

Sampson, R. (2003). Acquaintance rape of college students. *Public Health Resources, 92*.

Sampson, R. (2006). *Acquaintance rape of college students*. Office of Community Oriented Policing Services, U.S. Department of Justice. Retrieved October 1, 2009, from www.cops.usdoj.gov

Saunders, B. E., Villeponteaux, L. A., Lipovsky, J. A., Kilpatrick, D. G., & Veronen, L. J. (1992). Child sexual assault as a risk factor for mental health disorders among women: A community sample. *Journal of Interpersonal Violence, 7*, 189–204.

Scheffer, D. J. (1999). Rape as a war crime. *U.S. State Department*. Retrieved from http://www.converge.org.nz/ pma/arape.htm

Schemo, D. J. (2003, August 29). Rate of rape at Academy is put at 12% in survey. *New York Times*. Retrieved from http://www.nytimes.com/2003/08/29/national/29ACAD.html?th

Schumm, J. A., Briggs-Phillips, M., & Hobfoll, S. E. (2006). Cumulative interpersonal traumas and social support as risk and resiliency factors in predicting PTSD and depression among inner-city women. *Journal of Traumatic Stress, 19*(6), 825–836. doi: 10.1002/jts.20159

Scott-Ham, M., & Burton, F. C. (2005). Toxicological findings in cases of alleged drug-facilitated sexual assault in the United Kingdom over a 3-year period. *Journal of Clinical Forensic Medicine, 12*(4), 175.

Sielke, S. (2002). *Reading rape: The rhetoric of sexual violence in American literature and culture,1790–1990*. Princeton, NJ: Princeton University Press.

Smith, D. (2010, September). UN has failed Congo mass rape victims, says investigator. *The Guardian, 8*.

Smith-Spark, L. (2004, December 8). How did rape become a weapon of war? *BBC News*. Retrieved from http:// news.bbc.co.uk/2/hi/in_depth/4078677.stm

Stockton, S. (2006). *The economics of fantasy: Rape in twentieth-century literature*. Columbus, OH: Ohio State University Press.

Storr, W. (2011, July 17). The rape of men. *The Guardian*. Retrieved from http://www.guardian.co.uk/society/2011/ jul/17/the-rape-of-men

Sugar, N. F., Fine, D. N., & Eckert, L. O. (2004). Physical injury after sexual assault: Findings of a large case series. *American Journal of Obstetrics and Gynecology, 190*(1), 71.

Tanner, L. (1994). *Intimate violence: Reading rape and torture in twentieth-century fiction*. Bloomington, IN: Indiana University Press.

Tillman, S., Bryant-Davis, T., Smith, K., & Marks, A. (2010). Shattering silence: Exploring barriers to disclosure for African American sexual assault survivors. *Trauma, Violence, & Abuse, 11*(2), 59–70.

Tjaden, P., & Thoennes, N. (2000). Full report of the prevalence, incidence, and consequences of violence against women. *National Institute of Justice*. U.S. Department of Justice, Office of Justice Programs. Retrieved from https://www.ncjrs.gov/pdffiles1/nij/183781.pdf

Tjaden, P. G., & Thoennes, N. (2006). Extent, nature, and consequences of rape victimization: Findings from the National Violence Against Women Survey. *National Institute of Justice*. U.S. Department of Justice, Office of Justice Programs.

Truman, J. L. (2011). *BJS bulletin: Criminal victimization, 2010*. Washington, DC: National Crime Victimization Survey, U.S. Department of Justice.

Truman, J. L., & Planty, P. (2012). Criminal victimization, 2011. *Bureau of Justice Statistics*. U.S. Department of Justice, Office of Justice Programs. Retrieved from http://bjs.ojp.usdoj.gov/content/pub/pdf/cv11.pdf

Turan, K. (2012, June 22). Review: 'The invisible war" a heartbreaking look at military rape. *Los Angeles Times*. Retrieved from http://articles.latimes.com/2012/jun/22/entertainment/la-et-invisible-war-20120622

Turchik, J. A., & Wilson, S. M. (2010). Sexual assault in the U.S. military: A review of the literature and recommendations for the future. *Aggression and Violent Behavior, 15*, 267–277. doi:10.1016/j.avb.2010.01.005

Turrell, S. C., & Cornell-Swanson, L. (2005). Not all alike: Within group differences in seeking help for same-sex relationship abuses. *Journal of Gay & Lesbian Social Services, 18*(1), 77–88.

United Nations. (2004). *UNICEF adviser says rape in Darfur, Sudan continues with impunity*. UN News Centre.

United Nations. (2011). *Press Release*. New York, NY: Department of Public Information, News, & Media Division.

United States Bureau of Justice Statistics. (2000). Sexual assault of young children as reported to law enforcement. *Bureau of Justice Statistics*. U.S. Department of Justice, Office of Justice Programs. Retrieved from bjs.ojp.usdoj.gov/content/pub/pdf/saycrle.pdf

United States Bureau of the Census. (2000). *Profiles of general demographic characteristics*. Retrieved from http://www2.census.gov/census_2000/datasets/demographic_profile/0_United_States/2kh00.pdf

United States Department of Health and Human Services. (2005). Child maltreatment 2005. *Administration on Children and Families*. Retrieved from http://www.acf.hhs.gov/programs/cb/pubs/cm05/chapterthree.htm

United States Department of Justice. (2004). Criminal Victimization, 2004. *Bureau of Justice Statistics, National Crime Victimization Survey*. U.S. Department of Justice, Office of Justice Programs. Retrieved from bjs.ojp.usdoj.gov/content/pub/pdf/cv04.pdf

United States Department of Justice. (2007). *National Crime Victimization Survey*.

United States Department of Justice. (2011). *Sexual Assault*. Retrieved from http://www.ovw.usdoj.gov/sexassault.htm

United States War Department. (1899). *The war of the rebellion: A compilation of the official records of the union and confederate armies* (Series 2, Volume 5). Washington, DC: Government Printing Office.

Valentine, G. (1992). Images of danger: Women's sources of information about the spatial distribution of male violence. *Area, 24*, 22–29.

Vitz, E. B. (1996). Rereading rape in medieval literature. *Partisan Review, 63*(2), 280–291.

Wang, Y. (2011). Voices from the margin: A case study of a rural lesbian's experience with woman-to-woman sexual violence. *Journal of Lesbian Studies, 15*(2), 166–175. doi: 10.1080/10894160.2011.521099

Ward, L. (2003). Understanding the role of entertainment media in the sexual socialization of American youth: A review of empirical research. *Developmental Review, 23*(3), 347–388.

Warshaw, R. (1994). *I never called it rape*. New York, NY: Harper Perennial.

Washington, P. A. (2001). Disclosure patterns of Black female sexual assault survivors. *Violence Against Women, 7*(11), 1254–1283.

Whealin, J. (2007). Child sexual abuse. *National Center for Post-Traumatic Stress Disorder, U.S. Department of Veterans Affairs*. Retrieved from http://www.ptsd.va.gov/public/pages/child-sexual-abuse.asp

Widom, C. S. (1999). Posttraumatic stress disorder in abused and neglected children grown up. *The American Journal of Psychiatry, 156*(8), 1223–1229. Retrieved from http://ajp.psychiatryonline.org/cgi/pmidlookup?view=long&pmid=10450264

Wilson, T. (2003, January 22). Max Factor heir guilty of rapes. *Los Angeles Times.* Retrieved from http://articles
.latimes.com/2003/jan/22/local/me-luster22

Women's Law Project. (2012). *Women's Law Project Applauds Attorney General Holder on Changes to UCR
Definition of Rape.* Pittsburgh, PA: Women's Law Project. Retrieved from http://www.womenslawproject.org/
NewPages/wkVAW_SexualAssault_AG2012.html

NOTE

1. The National Crime Victimization Survey does not include victims under the age of 12.

CHAPTER

6

Women and Victimization

Intimate Partner Abuse and Stalking

Diana was 13 years old and reeling from her stepfather's arrest when she met Vance. Their intense relationship lasted about four months, but Vance was fiercely jealous, possessive, and volatile. Diana tried to end the relationship, but he kept showing up uninvited to Diana's school and apartment. One time, she awoke in the middle of the night, certain she saw him in the shadows of her room. He even threatened to kill her uncle, who was helping them with money since Gus was in jail.

With her stepdad Gus' rape case all over local papers and the divorce almost final, Diana and her mother decided to leave their neighborhood. They moved into a garage apartment 15 miles away at the home of her uncle. Vance was not deterred and continued harassing Diana, her friends, and her family. At the advice of her uncle, Diana sought a restraining order, which only seemed to provoke Vance, especially at first. However, with time, distance, and the protection that accompanied Diana's involvement with a new group of associates on the street, his focus waned.

Chapter Highlights

- Historical overview of intimate partner abuse (IPA)
- Contemporary issues in IPA
- Barriers to leaving abusive relationships
- The crime of stalking, its various forms, and its impact on women
- Legal remedies and policy implications for IPA and stalking

Much of history has documented the presence of violence within relationships. Throughout history, women were considered the property of the men in their life. Wife beating was a legal and accepted form of discipline of women by their husbands. During ancient Roman times, men were allowed to beat their wives with "a rod or switch as long as its circumference is no greater than the girth of the base of the man's right thumb" (Stevenson & Love, 1999). The "rule of thumb" continued as a guiding principle of legalized wife beating throughout early European history and appeared in English common-law practices, which influenced the legal structures of the early settlers in America. While small movements against wife beating appear in the United States throughout the 18th and 19th century, it wasn't until 1871 that Alabama and Massachusetts became the first states to take away the legal right of men to beat their wives. However, significant resistance still existed in many states on the grounds that the government should not interfere in the family environment. In 1882, wife beating became a crime in the state of Maryland. While defining wife beating as a crime meant that the act would receive criminal consequences, the enforcement of the act as a crime was limited, and husbands rarely received any significant penalties for their actions.

The rise of the feminist movement in the late 1960s and early 1970s gave a foundation for the **battered women's movement**. Shelters and counseling programs began to appear throughout the United States during the 1970s; however, these efforts were small in scale and the need for assistance significantly outweighed the availability of services. While police officers across the nation began to receive training about domestic violence calls for service, most departments had a no-arrest policy toward cases of domestic violence, as many officers saw their role as a peacemaker or interventionist rather than as an agent of criminal justice. In these cases, homicide rates continued to increase due to the murders of women at the hands of their intimate partners, and more officers were dying in the line of duty responding to domestic violence calls.

The grassroots battered women's movement of the 1970s led to systemic changes in how the police and courts handled cases of domestic violence. The **Minneapolis Domestic Violence Experiment** illustrated that when an arrest was made in a misdemeanor domestic violence incident, recidivism rates were significantly lower compared to cases in which police simply counseled the aggressor (Sherman & Berk, 1984). However, replication studies did not produce similar results and instead indicated that arresting the offender led to increases in violence.

Throughout the 1980s, state and nonprofit task forces assembled to discuss the issues of intimate partner abuse (IPA). By 1989, the United States had over 1,200 programs for battered women and provided shelter housing to over 300,000 women and children each year (Dobash & Dobash, 1992; Stevenson & Love, 1999). In 1994, Congress passed the Violence Against Women Act (VAWA) as part of the federal Crime Victims Act. The VAWA provided funding for battered women's shelters and outreach education as well as funding for domestic violence training for police and court personnel. It also provided the opportunity for victims to sue for civil damages as a result of violent acts perpetrated against them. In 1995, the Office on Violence against Women (OVW) was created within the U.S. Department of Justice and today is charged with administering grant programs aimed at research and community programming that focuses on eradicating intimate domestic abuse and intimate partner abuse in our communities (OVW, n.d.).

While VAWA was reauthorized by Congress in both 2000 and 2005, the current state of the law is in flux. The reauthorization of the VAWA in 2012 became a political debate between Republicans and Democrats within the House and Senate. While the House and Senate versions of the VAWA provide for important resources in fighting against IPA, there are significant differences as well. The bill passed by the Senate is more inclusive and represents the bipartisan philosophy that has typically been present in previous reauthorizations (Poore, 2012). Their version includes protections for unauthorized immigrants, Native Americans, and the lesbian, gay, bisexual, and transgender (LGBT) communities. Not only are these protections absent in the House version of the bill, the House's version further reduces the rights of immigrants by eliminating the current confidentiality protections for abused immigrant women. Republicans within the House have suggested that illegal aliens have fraudulently used claims of IPA to bolster their attempts toward citizenship, a practice that has not been documented by evidence within the system (Grim & Bassett, 2012). Alas, the battle for VAWA carries on. The Senate passed their version of the bill in February 2013, which includes expanded protections for same-sex victims, undocumented immigrants, and Native American victims. The debate now moves on to the House for consideration, and several House Republicans have urged GOP leaders to pass a bipartisan bill that will return protections and funding for victims of IPA (Bendery, 2013).

Defining and Identifying Intimate Partner Abuse

A number of different terms have been used to identify acts of violence against women. Many of these descriptions fall short in capturing the multifaceted nature of these abusive acts. The term *wife battering* fails to identify cases of violence outside of marriage, such as violent relationships between cohabiting individuals, dating violence, or even victims who were previously married to their batterer. Excluding these individuals from the official definition of *battered* often denies these victims any legal protections or services. The most common term used in recent history is *domestic violence*. However, this term combines the crime of woman battering with other contexts of abuse found within a home environment, such as the abuse of children or grandparents. Today, many scholars and community activists prefer the term *intimate partner abuse* (IPA) as it captures any form of abuse between individuals who currently have, or have previously had, an intimate relationship (Belknap, 2007). Definitions of the IPA can vary significantly from study to study, making it difficult to understand the extent of the phenomena. The Centers for Disease Control (CDC) defines IPA as "physical, sexual or psychological harm by a current or former partner or spouse" (CDC, n.d.). The National Violence Against Women Survey (NVAWS) extended this definition to specifically include cases of rape/sexual assault, physical assault, and stalking behaviors (Tjaden & Thoennes, 2000). Other agencies, such as the Bureau of Justice Statistics, include additional crimes within their discussions on IPA, such as homicides and robberies involving intimates (Catalano, 2012).

According to the National Crime Victimization Survey (NCVS), cases of IPA have steadily declined over the past 12 years. However, these rates remain high and indicate that IPA remains a significant issue in society. In the majority of cases, men are the aggressor and women are the victim (85%),[1] with an estimated 1.3 million women physically victimized each year (CDC, 2003). A review of state laws across the nation reveals that most crimes of domestic violence are considered a misdemeanor offense, even for repeat offenders. Most of the time, prosecutors charge offenders with the crime of simple assault (77.9% of cases), which carries with it a penalty of no more than one year in jail (Klein, 2004; Smith & Farole, 2009).

Violence between intimates is often a difficult crime for researchers to measure. Much of the abuse occurs behind closed doors and is not visible to the community. Many victims are reluctant to report cases of abuse to anyone (police, friends, or family members) due to the high levels of shame that they feel as a result of the abuse. Many victims also do not disclose their victimization out of fear that it will happen again or because they believe that the police will not do anything to help. Research demonstrates that women have both positive and negative experiences in reporting crimes of IPA. Some women indicated that the police scolded them for not following through on previous court cases. For others, they were either blamed for causing the violence or were told to fix the relationship with the offender (Fleury-Steiner, Bybee, Sullivan, Belknap, & Melton, 2006).

For a small number of women, physical violence in an intimate relationship escalates to murder. While intimate partner homicide is on the decline, women are more likely to die at the hands of a loved one than a stranger. In 2004, 1,159 women were killed by their partners (Bureau of Justice Statistics, 2006). For these women, death was the culmination of a relationship that had been violent over time, and in many cases, the violence occurred on a frequent basis. The presence of a weapon significantly increases the risk of homicide, as women who are threatened or assaulted with a gun or other weapon

▲ **Photo 6.1**   Intimate partner abuse is comprised of a variety of different behaviors used by an offender to gain power and control over their victim. These include physical, sexual, emotional, and psychological abuse.

are twenty times more likely to be killed (Campbell et al., 2003). Three-fourths of intimate partner homicide victims had tried to leave their abusers, refuting the common question, why doesn't she leave? While many of these women had previously sought help and protection from their batterers, their efforts failed (Block, 2003).

Most people think of physical battering/abuse as the major component of intimate partner abuse. However, abuse between intimates runs much deeper than physical violence. Perhaps one of the most common (and some would argue the most damaging in terms of long-term abuse and healing) is *emotional battering/abuse*. Those who batter their partner emotionally may call them derogatory names, prevent them from working or attending school, or limit access to family members and friends. An abuser may control the finances and limit access and information regarding money, which in turn makes the victim dependent on the perpetrator. Emotional abuse is a way in which perpetrators seek to control their victims, whether it be in telling them what to wear, where to go, or what to do. They may act jealous or possessive of their partner. In many cases, emotional abuse turns violent toward the victim, child(ren), or pet(s). Following acts of physical or sexual violence, the emotional abuse continues when a batterer blames the victim for the violent behavior by suggesting that "she made him do it" or by telling the victim that "you deserve it." Emotional abuse is particularly damaging, because it robs the victim of her self-esteem and self-confidence. In many cases, victims fail to identify that they are victims of IPA if they do not experience physical violence. Yet the scars left by emotional abuse are significant and long lasting. Unfortunately, few laws characterize the acts of emotional abuse as a criminal offense.

Victims of Intimate Partner Abuse

Victims of IPA can include both men and women of any age, race, ethnicity, religion, nationality, and sexual orientation. These acts of violence are committed by spouses, intimates (boyfriend/girlfriend, cohabitating partners), and ex-intimates. This chapter highlights some of the different relationship types and populations where IPA occurs as well as the challenges that victims face in their experiences of violence.

Dating Violence

While initial laws on IPA only recognized physical violence between married couples, recent laws have been changed to reflect the variety of relationship types where IPA can occur. One such example is dating violence. Even though two people are unmarried and not living together, such relationships are not immune from violence. Prevalence rates of dating violence on college campuses indicate that 32% of students report a history of dating violence in a previous relationship, and 21% of students indicate that they currently experience violence in their dating relationship (Sellers & Bromley, 1996). Teens, in particular, are at high risk for dating violence as a result of their inexperience in relationships and their heightened views of "romantic love," combined with a desire to be independent from their parents (Alabama Coalition Against Domestic Violence [ACADV], n.d.). Rates of intimate partner abuse indicate that teens may be at a greater risk for abuse by a significant other, compared to adults (Silverman, Raj, Mucci, & Hathaway, 2001). Given the severity of this issue, it is concerning that few parents believe that dating violence is a significant issue for their children (Women's Health, 2004). Research estimates that one-third of youth experience dating violence during adolescence. Unfortunately, few states allow for legal action, such as protective orders, in teen dating violence. Adolescent girls who experience physical and sexual dating violence are at an increased risk for a variety of health issues, including (1) use of alcohol, tobacco, and cocaine; (2) poor eating habits and dangerous weight management methods; (3) risky sexual health behaviors, including unprotected sex, multiple partners, and risk of pregnancy; and (4) suicidal ideation and suicide attempts. The early onset of violence and abuse in a relationship continues for victims into adulthood, as adolescent victims often find themselves in a pattern of abusive relationships as adults (Silverman et al., 2001).

Children of Intimate Partner Abuse

Intimate partner abuse not only affects the victim but her children as well. Research indicates that 68%–87% of incidents involving IPA occur while children are present (Raphael, 2000). Children are significantly affected by violence within the home environment, even if they are not the direct victims of the abuse. Despite attempts by mothers to hide their abuse from their children, children are affected. One battered woman spoke of the effects this victimization has on children: "Our kids have problems dealing with us. When we argue and fight in front of them, when they see our husbands humiliating, beating, and cursing us, they will get affected. They will learn everything they see" (Sullivan, Senturia, Negash, Shiu-Thornton, & Giday, 2005, p. 928).

Children who reside in a home where violence is present tend to suffer from a variety of negative mental health outcomes, such as feelings of low self-worth, depression, and anxiety. Affected children often suffer in academic settings and have higher rates of aggressive behavior (Goddard & Bedi, 2010). Additionally, many children exposed to violence at a young age continue the cycle of violence into adulthood, as they often find themselves in violent relationships of their own. Research indicates that approximately 30% of young boys who are exposed to a father's violence will engage in violence in their own lives (Boyd, 2001). There are many factors involved in predicting whether children who are exposed to IPA will grow up to offend, including how often they are exposed to violent stimuli and their relationship to the abusive adult (Domestic Violence and Incest Resource Centre, 2005). In an effort to respond to families in need, many agencies that advocate for victims of IPA are connecting with child welfare agencies to provide a continuum of care for children and their families. However, agencies need to be aware of the potential concerns about overemphasizing the relationship between being exposed to violence as a child and perpetuating the abuse as teens and adults, as increased attention on the intergenerational cycle of violence can also label children as potential offenders and victims and lead to a self-fulfilling prophecy (Boyd, 2001).

Same-Sex Intimate Partner Abuse

While the majority of IPA involves a female victim and a male offender, data indicate that battering also occurs in same-sex relationships. The NCVS found that 3% of women who experienced IPA were victimized by another woman, while 16% of male victims were abused by their male counterpart (Catalano, 2007). While these statistics suggest that same-sex IPA is a rare phenomenon compared to heterosexual IPA, other studies indicate that same-sex IPA may be much more common in LGBT relationships than initially believed. Estimates indicate that the rates of IPA in female same-sex relationships are similar to that of heterosexual women (Renzetti, 1992). However, it is difficult for researchers to identify the prevalence of IPA within the LGBT community. Much of the research on this topic is conducted with identified victims (usually who have reached out to community organizations) and not random samples of the population. These methods skew the findings toward cases of victims who report their victimization or seek assistance. Like heterosexual victims of IPA, many same-sex victims are reluctant to report their abuse. The decision to report not only involves the same challenges as a heterosexual battering relationship but includes the additional challenges about exposing their sexual orientation to police, community organizations, peers, and family members (Irwin, 2008).

Research indicates that female victims of same-sex intimate partner abuse face many of the same risk factors for violence as heterosexual battering relationships. Figure 6.1 presents the power and control wheel for the LGBT community. While many of the factors such as economic abuse, emotional abuse, and coercion are similar for both heterosexual and LGBT relationships, this figure highlights the role factors such as heterosexism, external homophobia, and internalized homophobia have on LGBT relationships. For some victims, these factors complicated their efforts to find support within the LGBT community. As one victim notes, "I think that people are very afraid to add to (the stigma of being queer) by saying . . . not only are we queer, but we also have violence in our relationships and in our community" (Bornstein, Fawcett, Sullivan, Senturia, & Shiu-Thornton, 2006, p. 169). Connection to the LGBT community (or lack thereof) also plays a role in the silencing of victims. For women who experienced abuse within the context of their first lesbian relationship, fear about discrimination and a lack of community attachment led to some victims wondering about whether the abuse was a normal component of lesbian relationships. For some of these women, fear of being "outed" led them to stay in the relationship over a longer period of time (Irwin, 2008). In contrast, women who had strong informal networks within the LGBT community were more likely to seek out help when their relationships turned violent (Hardesty, Oswald, Khaw, & Fonseca, 2011).

Gender-role stereotyping has a significant effect on the perceptions of female same-sex intimate partner violence (FSSIPV). Research by Hassouneh and Glass (2008) identified four themes where gender-role stereotypes affect women's experiences of violence within a same-sex battering relationship. Each of these themes has a significant impact on the denial of harm and victimization. The first theme,

Figure 6.1   Lesbian/Gay Power and Control Wheel

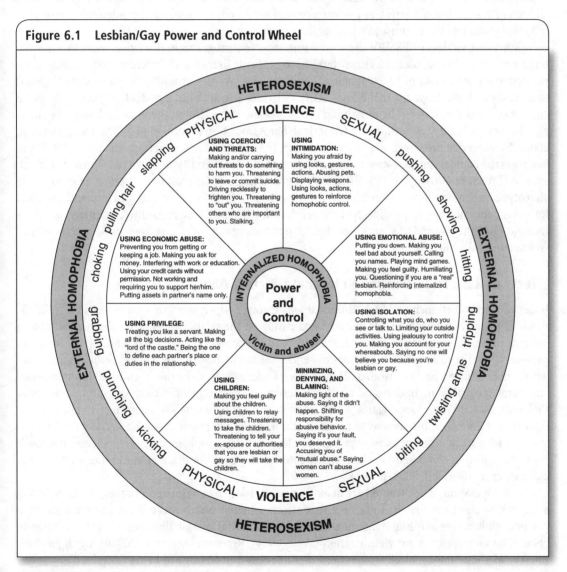

SOURCE: http://www.ncdsv.org/images/TCFV_glbt_wheel.pdf

"girls don't hit other girls," illustrated that many of the women involved in same-sex battering relationships saw their abuse as an indicator of relationship problems where they were to blame rather than a relationship where abuse occurred. The second theme, "the myth of lesbian utopia," suggested that the absence of patriarchy meant that there is no oppression or violence within a lesbian relationship. This theme was echoed in research by Irwin (2008), where many lesbian victims viewed IPA as a heterosexual issue. The third theme, "cat fight," discussed how many women thought that violence within their relationship was less significant than the levels of violence that occur in a male-female domestic violence situation. The fourth theme, "playing the feminine victim," made it difficult for outsiders to identify cases of IPA, particularly when agents of law enforcement were involved. Playing the victim allowed offenders to avoid arrest, as law enforcement would rely on traditional gender-role stereotypes to identify who was the victim and who was the perpetrator.

Given that victims of FSSIPV are in the minority, few programs and services exist to meet the unique needs of this population. Three states have explicitly denied LGBT victims from seeking out a protective order in cases of IPA (Montana, Louisiana, and South Carolina). Only one state (Hawaii) specifically includes language that allows LGBT individuals to seek out a **restraining order** against a current or former intimate. The remaining state-level laws are silent on the issue and leave the interpretation of the law up to the judiciary (American Bar Association Commission on Domestic Violence, 2008). Even service providers often view same-sex IPA incidents as less serious than cases of IPA in heterosexual couples, an assessment that can impact the level and type of services provided by an agency (Brown & Groscup, 2009). Effective programming needs to address the use of gender-role stereotypes when developing education and intervention efforts for the community. In addition, it is important for agencies to provide specific services for the LGBT communities, as many survivors indicate that they would not seek out help from an organization that was not "queer-specific" (Bornstein et al., 2006).

Effects of Race and Ethnicity on Intimate Partner Abuse

Issues of race and ethnicity add an additional lens through which one can view issues of IPA. While much of the early research on IPA focused exclusively on the relationships of gender inequality as a cause of abuse, the inclusion of race and ethnicity (and socioeconomic status) adds additional issues for consideration. For women of color, issues of gender inequality became secondary in the discussion of what it means to be a battered woman. Here, scholars acknowledged the role of cultural differences and structural inequality in understanding the experiences of IPA in ethnically diverse communities (Sokoloff, 2004). When investigating issues of violence among women of color, it is important that scholars not limit their discussions to race and ethnicity. Rather, research needs to reflect on the collision of a number of different factors, as "age, employment status, residence, poverty, social embeddedness, and isolation combine to explain higher rates of abuse within Black communities—not race or culture per se" (Sokoloff, 2004, p. 141).

As a population, Black women are at an increased risk to be victimized in cases of IPA. Scholars are quick to point out that it is not race that affects whether one is more likely to be abused by a partner. Rather, research highlights how economic and social marginalization can place women of color at an increased risk for victimization (West, 2004). Research by Potter (2007b) highlights how interracial abuse among Black women and men is related to feelings of being "devalued" by social stereotypes about "the Black man." Here, victims acknowledged that men of color experience high levels of discrimination by society. This belief system translated into justifying the violent acts by their intimate partner and remaining in the relationship (Nash, 2006).

Racial and ethnic identity also affects how victims deal with the abuse perpetuated by an intimate partner. For some women of color, the decision to not seek out assistance by the criminal justice system was related to not wanting to further criminalize the men in their communities, who are already disproportionately represented within the correctional system (Nash, 2006). Research also highlights how the role of religion and spirituality can serve as a method through which victims are able to cope with the violence in their lives. Many victims of IPA drew upon their spiritual beliefs or connections for support in both enduring the abuse as well as in leaving their batterers. However, many other women who had a relationship with a Christian congregation and sought out religious leaders for advice and support were discouraged by the response they received from their clergy, as they were encouraged to try to stay and work things out. While the women did not generally waiver in their personal faith and spiritual connections with God, these experiences led many to either leave their current congregation or to abandon organized religion in general. In contrast, women who associated with the Islamic (Muslim) faith received greater levels of support from religious leaders and citizens within their community, as these clergy were more likely to condone the violence against women (Potter, 2007a).

Women experiencing IPA may be faced with a multitude of physical and psychological issues, and race and ethnicity can affect whether a victim will seek out support and resources from social service agencies, such as therapeutic and shelter resources. Here, research indicates that Black women were significantly more likely to use emergency hospital services, police assistance, and housing assistance, compared to White and Hispanic/Latina women. For example, 65.4% of Black IPA women indicated that they had used housing assistance during the past year, compared to only 26.9% of White IPA women and 7.7% of Hispanic/Latina IPA women (Lipsky, Caetano, Field, & Larkin, 2006). Women of color also discussed the need for culturally relevant support. Onna, a 54-year-old Black woman who was married to her abuser for 24 years, demonstrated how traditional therapeutic communities were ineffective in her case: "Black folks don't 'do' group. We 'do' church. . . . I will not sit there and [tell] all these White women my business. [Blacks] don't talk about our stuff [in public]—and especially to White folks" (Nash, 2006, p. 1437).

Unique Issues for Immigrant Victims of Intimate Partner Abuse

While IPA is a significant issue for any community, the effects are particularly significant for immigrant communities. Research indicates that men in these communities often batter their partner as a way to regain control and power in their lives, particularly when their immigrant status has deprived them of this social standing. Battering becomes a way in which these men regain their sense of masculinity. For many of these men, the education and training they may have received in their home countries does not easily transfer upon their arrival to the United States. As Bui and Morash (2008) note, "Vietnamese immigrant men have lost power after immigrating to the U.S. Many felt bad because they lack[ed] language and occupational skills and could not support their families" (p. 202).

Faced with their husband's inability to find a job to support the family, many immigrant women are faced with the need to work, which many immigrant men find to be in opposition to traditional cultural roles and a threat to their status within the family. This strain against traditional roles leads to violence. Many men blame the American culture for the gender clash occurring in their relationships.

However, many women accept the violence as part of the relationship, as such behavior is considered normative for their culture. For example, violence is accepted behavior in Vietnamese traditional cultures, wherein men are seen as aggressive warriors and women are seen as passive and meek. Research on IPA in the Vietnamese immigrant community reveals high levels of verbal (75%), physical (63%), and sexual abuse (46%), with 37% of the women reporting experiences with both physical and sexual abuse (Bui & Morash, 2008).

For Ethiopian immigrant women, the violent behavior of men is accepted within the community, making it difficult for women to develop a community understanding that battering is a crime and that they should seek out services. Help seeking is seen as a complaint by women, and in such cases, members of the community turn to support the perpetrator, not the victim (Sullivan et al., 2005). Intimate partner abuse is also discussed as a normal part of relationships for Russian immigrant women. One woman stated that domestic violence "is part of the destiny, and you have to tolerate it" (Crandall, Senturia, Sullivan, & Shiu-Thornton, 2005, p. 945).

Cultural expectations may inhibit women from seeking out assistance, as it would bring shame upon the victim and her family, both immediate and extended. Strict gender-role expectations may lead women to believe that they do not have the right to disobey their partner, which legitimizes the abuse. One woman who emigrated from Russia described the cultural silence that prohibits women from talking of their abuse:

> We were raised differently. I do not know, maybe this is a very developed country, and maybe they think it is best if they tell everyone what is going on in their families, their lives, and everything. We are not used to that. We were ashamed of that. But here it is all different. (Crandall et al., 2005, p. 945)

Latina victims of IPA are less likely to leave an abusive relationship and, in many cases, stay with their batterer. For these women, a desire to maintain the family unit, the fear of losing their children in a custody battle, and a hope that the batterer will change his behavior all contribute to their decision to remain in a violent relationship (Dutton, Orloff, & Hass, 2000).

Many perpetrators use the fear of deportation to prevent victims from leaving an abusive relationship. Indeed, Latina immigrant women are likely to remain in a battering relationship for a longer period of time due to fear surrounding their undocumented immigration status. In addition, Latina immigrants are less likely to seek out help for IPA compared to Latina non-immigrants (Ingram, 2007). While the 2005 reauthorization of the Violence Against Women Act increased the protection of immigrant women who are victims of a crime (including domestic violence), it is unclear how many immigrant women are aware of these protections.

Perpetrators often build upon a negative experience of law enforcement from their home country in an effort to create a sense of distrust of the U.S. legal system. For many Vietnamese women, a call to the police for help was a last resort and often done not to facilitate an arrest, but rather to improve the relationship between the perpetrator and the victim by stopping the violence. Most victims did not want to have their partner arrested or prosecuted for domestic violence but rather wanted to send a message that the abuse was wrong. However, many were reluctant to seek police intervention, as they feared losing control over the process and expressed concern and fear over any civil implications that a criminal record would bring, particularly in jurisdictions with **mandatory arrest** policies (Bui, 2007).

Language barriers may also affect a victim's ability to seek help, as they may not be able to communicate with law enforcement and court personnel, particularly when resources for translators may be significantly limited (National Coalition Against Domestic Violence, n.d.). In an effort to expand access to the courts in domestic violence cases, California amended its domestic violence laws in 2001 to ensure that legal documents in domestic violence cases would be made available in multiple languages. Today, paperwork to request a restraining order and other related documents is available in five different languages: English, Chinese, Spanish, Vietnamese, and Korean.[2] Lack of language skills, combined with a lack of understanding of the American legal system, also can prevent an immigrant/refugee woman from leaving her violent relationship. Not only may a victim not know what services are available, she may not understand how to navigate social systems such as welfare and housing and educational opportunities that are necessary in order to achieve economic independence from her batterer (Sullivan et al., 2005).

Immigrant victims of intimate partner abuse are often unlikely to seek out traditional domestic violence services due to cultural norms. In order to provide assistance to these victims, training and education on IPA should be made available to other service providers likely to come into contact with these women, such as immigration lawyers and health services personnel. Additionally, public service announcements on the laws against IPA and the availability of social services should be made available to all women of an immigrant community, regardless of whether they are a victim. This ensures that even if a victim is unlikely to report her abuse to the police, she may tell a friend or family member who could then direct her to available services (Dutton et al., 2000).

Women as Batterers

While the majority of the research on IPA in heterosexual relationships focuses on women as victims and men as offenders, some scholars have addressed women's experiences with IPA as offenders. The issue of women as batterers first appeared as a result of the work of Richard Gelles and colleagues and their development of the *Conflict Tactics Scale* (CTS). The CTS is a survey comprised of 39 questions on violent and nonviolent behaviors (Gelles, 2000; Gelles & Straus, 1988; Straus, Gelles, & Steinmetz, 1980). Their research has been heavily criticized by feminist scholars for failing to acknowledge the nature and context of the experiences of women who use violence against their intimate partners. In many instances, these "offenders" are simply fighting back against the abuse that they endured within the context of an IPA relationship.

The issue of women as perpetuators of IPA is more complex than Gelles and his colleagues suggested. While research using the CTS focuses on the prevalence of these behaviors, other scholars posit that in order to understand the phenomena of women who batter, research should focus not on the number of IPA incidents by women but the rationale for these actions. For example, information about the instigator of the event, the use of self-defense tactics by the victim, and the resulting injuries for the victim and offender all contribute to the understanding of women as batterers (Miller & Meloy, 2006). Indeed, the majority of published studies on women as perpetuators of violence against their intimate partners cite self-defense as the primary rationale behind the violence. Here, women often engage in acts of violence as a defensive response in situations where either they were actively trying to escape an abusive incident or prevent one from occurring. However, the definition of self-defense can vary and does not necessarily refer to a retaliatory strike following being hit by their partner. In many cases, these preemptive acts of violence served to protect women from potentially increased acts of violence by their partner (Kernsmith, 2005).

While both men and women engage in similar levels of minor abuse (findings that many use to suggest that men and women are mutually combative), the extent of violence perpetuated against an intimate partner varies significantly between men and women. Not only are the levels of violence significantly higher for male offenders, men are also more likely to threaten the lives of a woman and her children compared to female offenders (Feder & Henning, 2005). In addition, the justifications for the violence also differ by gender. While the majority of research illustrates that male offenders blame the victim for their displays of violence, research indicates that women who engage in IPA accept responsibility for their actions and understand the wrongfulness of their actions, despite the fact that many of these violent events stemmed from acts of self-defense. In cases not involving claims of self-defense, women who perpetuate violence against an intimate partner do so to maintain control and power in their own lives, whereas male offenders engage in abuse to maintain power and control over the lives of their victims. Women are also more likely to lash out at their partners as a result of their own feelings of fear and hopelessness (Kernsmith, 2005).

Unfortunately, the response by the criminal justice system toward incidents of IPA often results in the labeling of victims as offenders when they attempt to defend themselves from abuse. It is interesting to note that the rates of violence in events that typically resulted in the women's arrest were often significantly lower compared to the violence that had been perpetrated against them. As a result, most female offenders did not believe that they should be punished by the system for their attempts to defend themselves (Miller & Meloy, 2006).

The Cycle of Violence

In explaining why women stay in abusive relationships, Lenore Walker (1979) conceptualized the cycle of violence to explain how perpetrators maintain control over their victims over time. The cycle of violence is made up of three distinct time frames. The first is referred to as *tension building*, where a batterer increases control over a victim. As anger begins to build for the perpetrator, the victim tries to keep her partner calm. She also minimizes problems in the relationship. During this time, the victim may feel as though she is walking on eggshells, because the tension between her and her partner is high. The tension-building phase is characterized by poor communication skills between the partners. It is during the second time frame, referred to as the *abusive incident*, where the major incident of battering occurs. During this period, the batterer is highly abusive and engages in physical and/or sexual violence to control his victim. This phase, however, is short lived, and the perpetrator moves quickly to stage three, known as the *honeymoon period*. During this stage, the offender is apologetic to the victim for causing harm. He often is loving and attentive and promises to change his behavior. While this stage is filled with manipulation of the victim's feelings by the perpetrator, he is viewed as sincere and, in many cases, is forgiven by the victim. Unfortunately, the honeymoon phase doesn't last forever, and in many cases of IPA, the cycle begins again, tensions increase, and additional acts of violence occur. Over time, the honeymoon stage may disappear entirely.

The cycle of violence was initially designed to provide a framework to understand the cyclical nature of battering and was used in Walker's (1984) introduction of **battered women's syndrome (BWS)**. Battered women's syndrome has become the most recognized explanation of the consequences of IPA and is often introduced as evidence for women on trial for various crimes, including killing their batterers. The goal of introducing evidence of abuse is to provide an understanding to juries regarding why women, in these extreme cases of IPA, believed that their lives were in danger and believed that

Figure 6.2   The Cycle of Violence

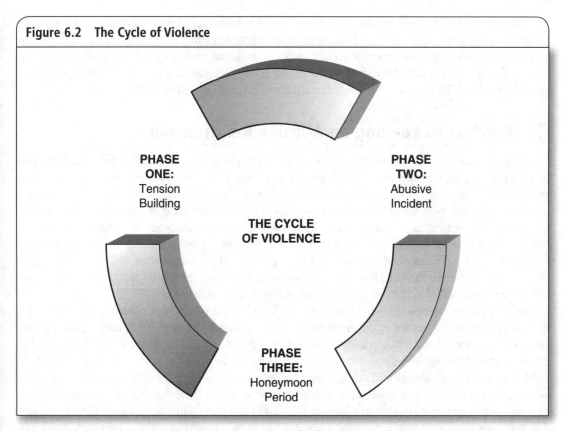

SOURCE: Office of the Kansas Attorney General. http://www.hruth.org/files/library/cycleofviolence.pdf

violence was the only option to ensure their own safety. However, juries and judges generally show little sympathy for women who kill their abusers, and many of these women receive life sentences (Leonard, 2001). Indeed, the use of BWS as a theory of self-defense is often negated by the defendant's own actions to defend herself from her batterer, as research suggests that women who fight back or act aggressively at any time during their relationship are less likely to prove to a jury that killing their abuser was an act of self-defense (Schuller & Rzepa, 2002).

Battered women's syndrome and the cycle of violence have also been used in a number of other arenas, including in custody disputes between parents where IPA is present, in therapeutic resources for survivors of IPA, and in revisions to laws and policy related to IPA. However, the past three decades have given rise to a number of critiques of both BWS and the cycle of violence. Some critiques have suggested that the three stages of the cycle of violence do not effectively capture the context of many battering relationships. For example, research by Copel (2006) found that women with physical disabilities indicated that the *honeymoon* stage was absent from their abusive relationships. Unlike the stages of the cycle of violence, their partners offered no regret for the violence that they caused. Rather than appear apologetic for their behavior, the women described their batterer as *powerful* and *pompous* following the abuse, as if to indicate that they had triumphed over their victim. Other critiques have focused on the lack of a standardized definition of BWS. While scholarship suggests that recent revisions to BWS have been successful in approximating BWS with the characteristics of post-traumatic stress disorder (Roth & Coles, 1995), this may not be enough when using BWS in the legal arena. In addition, the diagnosis of BWS creates an image of a victim who is abnormal or damaged to the public eye. While victims do suffer as a result of the abuse endured, some scholars have argued that BWS can perpetuate stereotypes about IPA that can ultimately cause greater harm to the victim (Dutton, n.d.).

Barriers to Leaving an Abusive Relationship

When hearing of cases of domestic violence, many members of the public ask, why doesn't she just leave? Leaving a relationship where IPA is present is a difficult and complex process. There are many issues that a victim must face, including housing relocation and safety concerns as well as the needs of children and family pets. One of the greatest barriers in leaving a battering relationship is the financial limitations that victims face. Women who lack economic self-sufficiency are less likely to report IPA and less likely to leave the relationship, as they depend on their abuser for financial support. For many victims, support from extended family and friends plays a critical role in their ability to successfully depart from an abusive partner. However, this experience can also increase the practice of victim blaming and a withdrawal of help if the victim returns to the relationship (Moe, 2007).

Inherent in the question of "why doesn't she just leave?" is the question of "why does she stay?" This question places the responsibility on the victim for staying with a violent partner, rather than focusing on why her partner chooses to be violent. The reality is that many women do leave their batterers. The average battered woman leaves seven to eight times before she is successful in leaving for good (ACADV, n.d.). Violence doesn't always end when women report their crimes or leave their abusers. For some women, the levels of violence increase; women who were separated from their batterers reported higher rates of violence compared to women who were married or divorced from their batterer (Catalano, 2007). These acts of violence not only can involve the initial victim but can spread out, placing children, friends, and extended family members of the woman at risk. Concerns regarding these potential increases in violence may influence these women to remain in the relationship out of concern for their loved ones.

For some women, their children become the deciding factor in IPA. Some mothers believe that it is their responsibility to keep the family together, and despite the violence they endure, they do not want to take the children away from their father. While many women are more likely to tolerate the abuse when it only occurs to them, they are less likely to continue the relationship once their children are negatively affected. In these cases, the decision to leave is based on either a child's request for safety from the violent parent or the mother's conclusion that her child's physical and emotional needs overrule any question of remaining in the relationship (Moe, 2009).

In their search for support, some women may turn toward religious institutions for assistance in leaving a relationship characterized by IPA. For many

▲ **Photo 6.2** A domestic violence victim displays her A.W.A.R.E (Abused Women's Active Response Emergency) alarm necklace, which sends out a silent alarm to the police when activated.

women, their faith gives them strength to leave (Wang, Horne, Levitt, & Klesges, 2009). Unfortunately for some of these women, their spirituality may hinder their abilities to leave. Cultural scripts of some religious doctrines may encourage women to try to resolve the struggles of their relationship, as divorce and separation are not viewed as acceptable under the eyes of the church. Here, congregations encourage women to forgive the violence that their partners display (Potter, 2007a). Additionally, clergy may be ill equipped to deal with the issue of IPA within their congregations, due to a lack of understanding of the realities of the problem and limited training on service and support needs (Shannon-Lewy & Dull, 2005).

Many women struggle with their decision to leave an abusive relationship. Some women may still love their partner, despite the violence that exists within the relationship. Others may hope that their partner will change and believe the promises made by their loved one for a different life. In some multicultural communities, there is a greater pressure outside of the family unit to return to one's batterer. Members of these communities often place significant pressures on victims to reunite with their batterer (Sullivan et al., 2005). For many women, they fear what their lives will be like without their partner. These fears may include how they will support themselves (and their children), the possibility that future relationships will have similar results, and even fear of loneliness. A key to successfully leaving an abusive relationship is the victim's belief that she will be better off without her batterer and have the confidence to make a new life free from violence.

Domestic Violence Shelters

As the grassroots efforts of the battered women's movement began to increase the availability of resources and attention on IPA during the 1960s and 1970s, the emergence of shelters represented a valuable resource for women exiting a violent relationship. Designed to provide support and empowerment for victims, shelters provided much-needed services for women. In addition, shelter care also provided women with a safe space to consider options for their future (Bennett, Riger, Schewe, Howard, & Wasco, 2004).

Research by Grossman, Lundy, George, and Crabtree-Nelson (2010) indicates that shelter residences access four different types of services during their stay: (1) legal assistance, (2) counseling services, (3) **wraparound services**, and (4) life-skills assistance. Within the category of legal assistance, 63.3% of residents utilized shelter resources to help file legal protective orders against their abuser. Almost all of the shelter residents received individualized counseling (95.8%), and a majority of residents participated in group therapy sessions (71.9%). Half of the residents (50.8%) utilized wraparound services, which involved collaborative case management with other community agencies such as mental health and substance abuse treatment providers. Fewer residents utilized the life skills resources; just 14.2% received help with finding a job, 11.2% received educational guidance, and 13.9% sought help with economic assistance. In addition to their use of services during their residency, many continued to call on these organizations for assistance even after they departed the shelter.

But what about the women who exit a battering relationship without the assistance of a shelter? How does this affect their utilization of services and resources? Women who did not utilize residential shelter services were more likely to be older, married to their abuser, identify as White or Hispanic (versus Black), and were more likely to receive the majority of their economic support from a job (versus public assistance). Moreover, women who did not utilize onsite shelter options following their first contact with the organization were more likely to be referred to the organization as a result of legal or law enforcement referrals, whereas those who obtained shelter care were referred via a social service agency or hotline contact. Finally, women who did not receive shelter care received fewer services over a shorter time period compared to those who utilized shelter care (and needed a greater number of services over the long term; Grossman & Lundy, 2011).

While shelters represent a key resource for many women who leave an IPA relationship, the demand for these resources significantly outweigh their availability. Indeed, many victims can be denied shelter, either due to a lack of general availability or the lack of specific resources to support victims with children (Moe, 2007). While the typical stay at a shelter is limited to 30–60 days, the needs of women continue even after their departure from the shelter environment (Grossman et al., 2010). Unfortunately, the ability of former residents to access services is significantly limited. In most instances, women relied on only those services that were necessary to help keep themselves safe, such as continued legal support (filing of criminal cases, obtaining protective orders, etc.). Despite the high need for counseling and therapy, many women did not continue their participation following their shelter stay. Here, demands such as time, travel, and access to these resources may limit their participation (Grossman et al., 2010).

As a result of the limited housing options and need for continued services for victims of IPA, organizations have recognized the need for alternative transitional long-term housing programs. Here, residency options are expanded to provide women with stability and sustainability. Transitional housing programs can also expand the abilities of an agency to provide a continuity of care and services for women. Given that many women significantly decrease or eliminate their participation in therapeutic services upon leaving the shelter environment, transitional housing programs can continue to provided needed services and support for women within a safe and accessible location (Baker, Holditch Niolon, & Oliphant, 2009).

While the demand for transitional housing is high, the availability of space for women and families often fails to meet the needs of this community. Much of these limitations are a direct result of reductions of funding. Indeed, the risk of homelessness increases for women in their attempts to leave an IPA relationship, given the limited options of safe housing (Baker et al., 2009).

Given the high demand for services, coupled with budgetary constraints that limit the delivery of services, shelters need to think outside of the box for ways to deliver resources to populations in need, particularly given that many women will continue to rely on assistance and support even after a shelter residency. Here, the use of wraparound services and networking with other community agencies is crucial. While shelters may not be able to provide support for the ongoing, long-term needs of those exiting an abusive relationship, they can provide referrals to related community agencies (Grossman et al., 2010). Options such as these allow communities to continue to serve the victims of IPA in light of the struggles of a tense economic climate.

⬙ Victim Experiences With Police and Corrections

With the rise of criminal justice involvement in cases of IPA, a number of studies have been conducted to investigate the victim's experience with the criminal justice system. Findings of these studies vary— some suggest that victims experience high levels of satisfaction with police and courts, while others highlight areas for significant improvement.

A call to the police represents the first step in seeking protection from violence by an intimate partner. Women who indicated the highest levels of satisfaction felt that the officers actively listened to their concerns and provided information and referrals for help, such as information about shelters and other protection options (Johnson, 2007). Gender of the responding officer also has an impact on victim satisfaction levels, as victims found that female officers were more receptive to their concerns overall and were not just focused on facilitating an arrest (Stalens & Finn, 2000).

Given their experiences with police intervention, would women seek out assistance for future IPA incidents? The answer to this question depends on the type of experience that victims have with the criminal justice system. Women who do not feel that the justice system effectively responded to their needs may be less likely to seek out help in the future. In particular, offenders who are let off with a "slap on the hand" may experience increased risks of violence in the future (Moe, 2007). In contrast, women who had a positive experience with police are more likely to seek out police intervention in the future, compared to those victims who perceived that the officer was not interested in them (Johnson, 2007).

The use of specialized court practices also affects victims' satisfaction levels with the criminal justice system. In their evaluation of a domestic violence court program in South Carolina, research by Gover, Brank, and MacDonald (2007) found that a collaborative courtroom environment between the prosecutor, victim advocate, and judge had a significant effect of victim satisfaction levels. Rather than treat cases in a traditional, adversarial fashion, this program emphasized the therapeutic options designed to treat the offender. As a result, the majority of victims and defendants believed that the outcome of their case was fair, positive, and respectful.

> Even after cases were decided, members of the court team would approach the victims and make sure that they understood the verdict and also understood what was required by both the victim and defendant. If the victim needed any assistance with shelter or legal assistance, the team members were there to help obtain it. (Gover et al., 2007, pp. 621–622)

Case Study

The Decriminalization of Domestic Violence

The month of October is recognized as Domestic Violence Awareness month. So it is somewhat ironic that in October 2011, officials from the city of Topeka, Kansas, voted to decriminalize misdemeanor offenses, including crimes of misdemeanor domestic violence. This drastic move was made in response to budget cuts, which had slashed city resources. While officials argued that cases would still be prosecuted (as acts of violence against intimates and ex-intimates are still considered state crimes), many lacked confidence on whether justice would be served. The district attorney argued that slashes to his own budget would limit his ability to prosecute these crimes, particularly given the demands of a felony caseload. Given the powers of prosecutor discretion, the potential for offenders to go free is high. For example, Topeka police responded to 35 domestic incidents and arrested 18 people over the past month—all of whom were released, because there was no one available to take on these prosecutions. Advocates from around the United States fear that the actions by the city of Topeka send a message that domestic violence is acceptable. In addition, any short-term savings by not prosecuting cases can be lost by the long-term financial effects of domestic violence, where direct and indirect

(Continued)

(Continued)

health costs for victims can exceed 5.8 billion dollars each year. Given the economic challenges that currently face cities and states throughout the country, it remains to be seen whether other jurisdictions will follow Topeka's lead. Ultimately, such economic decisions may increase the risks of harm toward victims of domestic violence (Diamond, 2011; Sulzberger, 2011).

Stalking and Intimate Partner Abuse

According to the NCVS, stalking is defined as "a course of conduct directed at a specific person that would cause a reasonable person to feel fear" (Baum, Catalano, Rand, & Rose, 2009, p. 1). Estimates by the Supplemental Victimization Survey (SVS) indicate that more than 5.9 million adults[3] experience behaviors defined as *stalking*[4] or *harassment*.[5] These data indicate that acts of stalking and harassment occur at a significantly higher rate than the majority of the public believes. In measuring the prevalence of stalking behaviors, the SVS collected data on seven different acts of stalking: (1) making unwanted phone calls; (2) sending unsolicited or unwanted letters or e-mails; (3) following or spying on the victim; (4) showing up at places without a legitimate reason; (5) waiting at places for the victim; (6) leaving unwanted items, presents, or flowers; and (7) posting information or spreading rumors about the victim on the Internet, in a public place, or by word of mouth. In most cases, the acts that constitute stalking, such as sending letters or gifts, making phone calls, and showing up to visit, are not inherently criminal. These acts appear harmless to the ordinary citizen but can inspire significant fear and terror in victims of stalking. Table 6.1 illustrates the prevalence of these behaviors.

Much of what the general public understands about stalking comes from Hollywood, where celebrities have long experienced acts that would be considered stalking according to today's definitions. Consider the actions of John Hinckley Jr., who became infatuated with Jodi Foster when she first appeared as a child prostitute in the film *Taxi Driver*. Hinckley's obsession with Foster continued while she was a student at Yale, but he failed to gain her attention after numerous letters and phone calls. In 1981, Hinckley attempted to assassinate President Ronald Reagan in an effort to impress Foster. He

Table 6.1 Prevalence of Stalking	
experienced at least one unwanted contact per week	46%
were stalked for 5 years or more	11%
experienced forms of cyberstalking	26.1%
received unwanted phone calls or messages	66.2%
received unwanted letters and e-mail	30.6%
had rumors spread about them	35.7%
were followed or spied on	34.3%
experienced fear of bodily harm	30.4%
believed that the behavior would never stop	29.1%

SOURCE: U.S. Department of Justice.

was found not guilty by reason of insanity for his crimes and was committed to St. Elizabeth's Hospital for treatment. Today, he is allowed extended overnight visits outside of the hospital with his family, though he remains in the custody of the facility. Another example of celebrity stalking is Madonna's stalker, Robert Dewey Hoskins. He was convicted in 1996 for making threats against the star—he told the star that he wanted to "slice her throat from ear to ear" ("After Court Order . . .", 1996) and attempted to break into her house on two separate occasions. During one event, he successfully scaled the security wall of her home and was shot by one of her bodyguards. Other Hollywood victims of stalking include David Letterman, Sandra Bullock, Tyra Banks, and Lindsay Lohan, to name a few. Indeed, it seems that a number of Hollywood personalities have been stalked by an obsessed fan at some point during their careers.

While noteworthy events of **Hollywood stalkers** brought significant attention to the crime of stalking, they did so in ways that reduced the social understanding of this crime to one that was limited to celebrities and the Hollywood circuit. Many of these cases involved perpetrators who suffered from mental disease or defect. This narrow definition had significant effects on the legitimization of this crime for ordinary victims of stalking.

For many women, their relationships with their future stalker began in a very ordinary sense. They described these men as attentive, charming, and charismatic. But these endearing qualities soon disappeared, and their interactions became controlling, threatening, and violent. Many women blamed themselves for not recognizing the true colors of their stalker earlier. This pattern of self-blaming affected their ability to trust their own judgment and led these women to be hesitant about their decision-making abilities in future relationships as a result of their victimization.

Like many crimes, victims of stalking often do not report their victimization to police. According to SVS data, more than half of the individuals who were victims of stalking did not report their victimization. For many victims, their decision to not report these crimes stemmed from a fear of intensifying or escalating the stalking behaviors. Others dealt with their victimization in their own way, believing that their experience was a private and personal matter. Additionally, many believed that stalking was not a serious enough offense (or did not believe that a crime had occurred) to warrant intervention from the criminal justice system. Finally, some victims felt that nothing could be done to stop the behavior by their stalkers. For those individuals who did report their crimes, SVS data indicate that charges were filed in only 21% of these cases, further solidifying a belief for many victims that the criminal justice system was unable to effectively punish their stalkers in a court of law.

Victims engaged in several different strategies in an effort to cope with their stalking victimization. Some victims attempted to solve the trauma through self-reflection and sought out therapeutic resources. Women also made significant changes to their behavior patterns. They might avoid community events out of a fear that their stalker would show up at the same function. Other women moved out of the area yet still

▲ **Photo 6.3** Many victims of stalking experience the constant fear of being followed and observed as they attempt to manage their daily lives. In this situation, the psychological terror that victims experience can be just as violent as any physical confrontation.

expressed fear that their stalker would find them. Some victims tried to renegotiate the definitions of their relationship with their offender through bargaining, deception, or deterrence. Finally, some victims moved against their attackers by issuing warnings or pursuing a legal case against them (Cox & Speziale, 2009; Spitzberg & Cupach, 2003).

Laws on Stalking

Despite the number of acts against celebrities and ordinary citizens alike, stalking was not considered to be a crime for the majority of the 21st century. The first law criminalizing the act of stalking was created in 1990 by the State of California, following the murder of actress Rebecca Schaeffer in 1989 by an obsessed fan. Schaeffer had risen to fame as an actress in the popular television show, *My Sister Sam*. Robert Bardo had become obsessed with "Patti," the character played by Schaeffer on the show, and made several attempts to contact her on the set. He sent Schaeffer several letters and had built a shrine to her in his bedroom. However, she did not return his advances. Undeterred, he paid a private investigator $250 to obtain her home address. Bardo became fixated on Schaeffer and told his sister "if [he] couldn't have Rebecca, no one else would." Upon making contact with Schaeffer at her residence, he shot her in the chest. Bardo was convicted of murder and sentenced to life in prison. Since the death of Rebecca Schaeffer and the creation of the first anti-stalking law in California, all 50 states, the District of Columbia, and the federal government have created criminal laws against stalking.

In addition to the general designation of stalking as a criminal offense, several jurisdictions have enacted additional laws that prohibit various forms of stalking behaviors. The U.S. **Federal Interstate Stalking Law** was passed in 1996 (and amended in 2000) and restricts the use of mail or electronic communications for the purposes of stalking and harassment. Other federal laws criminalize the use of wiretaps on telephones and prohibit the display or sale of personal information such as social security numbers to members of the public. Today, the majority of state laws on stalking include details on stalking via electronic methods. Some states include long lists of the types of behaviors covered under these statutes. However, the nature and forms of stalking changes quickly. While intended to provide legal protection to victims of these crimes, these laws are often unable to keep up with the fast-changing evolution of technology.

In order to prosecute someone for stalking, many state laws require victims to indicate that they experienced fear as a result of the offender's actions. While victims of other crimes may experience fear, stalking is unique in that a state of fearfulness is required in order to indicate that a crime occurred. A review of the literature indicates that women are more likely to experience fear as a result of being stalked, and comparisons of male and female victims of stalking find that women are 13 times more likely to indicate that they were "very afraid" of the person stalking them (Davis, Coker, & Sanderson, 2002). Using data from the NVAWS, Dietz and Martin (2007) found that nearly three-fourths of women who were identified as victims of stalking behaviors indicated that they experienced fear as a result of the pursuit by their stalker. The levels of fear depended on the identity of the stalker (women indicated higher levels of fear when they were stalked by a current or former intimate or acquaintance) and how they stalked their victims (physical and communication stalking experiences generated higher levels of fear). But what about women who experienced behaviors consistent with the definition of stalking but who did not feel fearful as a result of these interactions? Are these women not victims of stalking? In many states, they would not be considered victims, and the behaviors perpetrated against them would not be considered a crime.

⋈ Victims and Offenders of Stalking

Who are the victims of stalking? They are men and women, young and old, of every race, ethnicity, and socioeconomic status. Data indicate that there are certain groups who make up the majority of victims of stalking. A meta-analysis of 22 studies on stalking found that female victims made up 74.59% of stalking victims, while 82.15% of the perpetrators were male. In the majority of cases, the perpetrator was someone known to the victim, with 30.3% of all cases occurring as a result of a current or former intimate relationship. Only 9.7% of stalking cases involved someone who was a stranger to the victim (Spitzberg & Cupach, 2003).

Stalking is a common experience for victims of IPA. Indeed, the degree to which victims are stalked is directly related to the levels of physical, emotional, and sexual abuse that they experienced with their intimate partner—the greater the abuse in the relationship, the higher the levels of stalking can be. Several factors appear to influence whether a victim of domestic violence will be stalked. Women who are no longer in a relationship with their abuser are more likely to experience stalking compared to women currently involved in an IPA relationship. Additionally, domestic violence abusers who are more controlling and physically violent toward their victims are more likely to stalk them. Finally, abusers who use drugs and alcohol are more likely to stalk their partners. The experience of stalking appears to intensify when women leave their partners. Research by Melton (2007) indicates that 92.1% of women who had been battered by their intimate partners experienced stalking following the closure of a domestic violence case in criminal court against their batterer. Over time, the prevalence of stalking decreased, with 56.3% of women reporting stalking behaviors after 6 months and 58.1% after 1 year. These data indicate that the prevalence of stalking remains quite high for victims of IPA, as more than half of the women continued to be stalked by their former partners a year after criminal justice system intervention. For most of these women, they indicated that their stalker was checking up on them. The behaviors included unwanted phone calls and being followed or watched by their stalker. For those women who had moved on to new relationships, almost three-fourths of them indicated that their new partner was harassed, threatened, or injured by their stalker.

Economics also impact the stalking experience for victims. Many victims find that they do not have the economic resources of abilities to move out of their communities. Many of these women received government subsidies for housing—to move would mean to give up this assistance, a luxury that the majority of these women could not afford to give up. This lack of mobility made it easier for their perpetrator to continue to stalk and harass their victim. In addition, the close-knit nature of many of these communities led to cases where a batterer's friends and family members were able to help the offender harass and intimidate their victim. Unfortunately, these cases of third-party stalking are not always recognized by the criminal justice system or are not connected to the behaviors of the individual. As a result, many victims believe that an escape from the violence is impossible (Tamborra, 2012).

The experience of stalking has a significant effect on a woman's mental health. Women who experience significant levels of stalking over time are more likely to be at risk for depression and post-traumatic stress disorder (PTSD). These rates of depression and PTSD are significantly higher for women who blame themselves for the behaviors of their perpetrator (Kraaij, Arensman, Garnefski, & Kremers, 2007). Victims indicate feelings of powerlessness, depression, sleep disturbances, and high levels of anxiety (Pathe & Mullen, 1997). They are also likely to develop a chronic disease or other injury since the beginning of their stalking experience (Davis et al., 2002). It is clear that mental health services need to acknowledge how the experience of stalking affects the mental health status of victims and determine how to better provide services to this community.

Cyberstalking

The use of technology has changed the way in which many victims experience stalking. The use of devices such as e-mail, cell phones, and global positioning systems (GPS) by offenders to track and monitor the lives of victims has had a significant effect on the experience of stalking. The term *cyberstalking* was created to address the use of technology as a tool in stalking. Of the 3.2 million victims of stalking identified by the SVS, one out of four individuals reported experiencing acts that are consistent with the definition of cyberstalking. Table 6.2 highlights examples of stalking aided by technology.

Like traditional methods of stalking, cyberstalking involves incidents that create fear in the lives of its victims. Just because cyberstalking does not involve physical contact does not mean that it is less damaging or harmful than physical stalking. Indeed, some might argue that the anonymity under which cyberstalkers can operate creates significant opportunities for offenders to control, dominate, and manipulate their victims, even from a distance, as there are no geographical limits for stalking within the domain of cyberspace. Indeed, someone can be stalked from just about anywhere in the world. For many victims of traditional stalking, cyberstalking presents a new avenue through which victims can be harassed, threatened, and intimidated.

While cyberstalking is a relatively new phenomenon, research indicates that the prevalence of these behaviors is expanding at an astronomical rate. Youth and young adults appear to be particularly at risk for these forms of victimization, given their connections to the electronic world through the use of the Internet, blogs, text messaging, and social networking sites such as Facebook. Research by Lee (1998) indicated that behaviors that can be identified as cyberstalking are rationalized among college-age students as a form of modern-day courtship and were not considered by the majority of the students to be of any particular significance, particularly in cases where the offender is known to the victim. Research by Alexy, Burgess, Baker, and Smoyak (2005) also utilized a sample of college students and found that only 29.9% of students labeled a simulated encounter as cyberstalking, even though 69% indicated that they felt threatened by the behavior. Given the limited understanding of these crimes by victims (and the larger society), it is important that advocates and justice professionals have an understanding about the realities of these crimes in order to provide adequate support for victims.

Table 6.2 Behaviors of Cyberstalking and Technology-Aided Stalking
• monitoring e-mail communications
• sending harassing, disruptive, or threatening e-mails or text messages
• using computer viruses to disrupt e-mail and Internet communications
• fraudulent use of victim's identity online
• use of Internet services to gather and disseminate personal information with the intent of harassing the victim
• use of global positioning devices to track movements of victim
• use of caller identification services to locate whereabouts of victim
• use of listening devices to intercept telephone conversations
• use of spyware and keystroke logging software to monitor computer usage
• use of hidden cameras to observe movement and activities of the victim
• search of online databases and information brokers to obtain personal information about the victim

SOURCE: U.S. Department of Justice.

Policy Implications

Many victims of IPA and cyberstalking did not report their victimization because they didn't believe that what was happening to them was a criminal act, particularly in cases where there was no experience of physical violence. One victim noted that in assessing whether a relationship is healthy, women should look at themselves and any changes in their personal behaviors rather than obsessing on the actions of their stalker. "Think about how you were before this happened and how happy you were, and I think once ladies reminisce on that, I think that's where strength comes from" (Cox & Speziale, 2009, p. 12). Others advised that women should not stay silent on the issues of IPA and stalking in order to protect their own safety, whether that meant filing a police report and obtaining a restraining order or letting friends, family, and coworkers know of their victimization. Here, victims acknowledge an increased need for community awareness about the nature of these victimizations and the resources available to them.

Restraining Orders

With the increased attention on criminal prosecutions of IPA, several jurisdictions began to issue civil protection orders, or *restraining orders,* as a way for victims to receive legal protection from their batterers. Today, civil protection orders are available in every jurisdiction in the United States. Protection orders are designed to provide the victim with the opportunity to separate herself from her abuser and generally prohibit the perpetrator from contacting the victim. As a legal document, violations of the protection order are subject to sanctions by the judiciary. For some victims, the restraining order gives them a sense of safety from the batterer.

In some jurisdictions, temporary restraining orders are issued by a police officer when they are called to a domestic violence incident and an arrest is made. By virtue of their name, temporary restraining orders are indeed temporary and are usually only valid for a specific period of time. In many cases, temporary restraining orders expire within a few days or at the time of the first court appearance by the offender. Following the expiration of a temporary restraining order, victims must apply for an order that will remain in effect for a longer period of time. Not all victims of IPA seek out a restraining order against their batterer. Victims who believe that their partner will change his behavior are less likely to seek out a civil protection order against their loved one. Those who do apply for protective orders generally do so following a long history of violence and abuse. In order for protective orders to be an effective tool in combating IPA, they must be enforced. Federal and state **sentencing guidelines** require punishment for violations of restraining orders. However, a review of these processes in Utah demonstrates that the full enforcement of the law is rarely enacted for restraining order violations. Sentencing guidelines mandate that violators shall be sentenced to batterer intervention programs and jail time and be ordered to pay restitution as punishment for violating a protective order. However, only 24.1% of offenders were sentenced to batterer intervention programming, while 48.9% were sentenced to jail time and 39.1% were ordered to pay a fine. In addition, the surrender of firearms was requested in only 4.5% of cases, even though laws in all 50 states require that offenders in domestic violence cases be required to surrender their guns to the police. This finding is particularly disturbing, given that the leading cause of death in intimate partner homicides involves firearms (Diviney, Parekh, & Olson, 2009). By not sentencing offenders to the fullest extent under the law, we send a message to perpetrators of IPA that following the guidelines of a protective order is optional and that protecting the victim is not a primary concern for the criminal justice system.

While protective orders are used to legally prohibit perpetrators from contacting or harassing their victim, it is unclear how effective such tools are for victims of stalking. Women who are victims of stalking were more likely to report that their perpetrator violated the protective order in their cases. Given the tactics that stalkers use to torment their victims, criminal justice agents may believe that these "minor" or "trivial" acts are not substantive enough to warrant punishment for violating a restraining order. However, criminal justice officials need to understand the context of these incidents related to the larger picture of stalking in order to provide effective services for victims and enforcement of stalking laws against perpetrators (Logan, Shannon, & Cole, 2007).

Mandatory Versus Discretionary Arrest Policies

Drawing from criticisms regarding the **discretionary arrest** policies of many police departments, mandatory arrest or *pro-arrest* policies began to surface in police departments across the nation during the 1980s and 1990s. *Mandatory arrest policies* refer to the legal duty of a police officer to make an arrest if the officer has reason to believe that domestic violence has occurred. The laws vary from state to state, but most state laws recognize both current and previous spouse or cohabitant as protected categories under the law, though not all states cover dating or prior dating relationships. Currently, 22 states have some form of mandatory arrest policy in place. In addition, the laws vary on time limits of when a mandatory arrest can be made. For example, laws in Alaska and Missouri require that a report must be made within 12 hours of the assault, whereas Mississippi and Nevada extend the time frame to the previous 24 hours. Washington state and South Dakota represent some of the most narrowly defined time frames and require that the police make an arrest within 4 hours of the assault. Washington state law is also unique in that it limits cases to individuals who are 16 or older (Hirschel, 2008).

The intent behind these laws was to stop domestic violence by deterring offenders. The movement toward mandatory arrest clarified roles of officers when dealing with domestic violence calls for service. It also removed the responsibility of arrest from the victim's decision and onto the shoulders of police personnel. For many women, they believed that a mandatory arrest policy would make officers understand that domestic violence is a serious issue and that it would legitimize their victimization. Here, women believed that an arrest would decrease levels of violence and send a message to the offender that battering is a crime and he would be punished. However, they acknowledged that the decrease in violence was only a temporary measure and that there existed a possibility of increased violence after an offender returned to the family home following an arrest or court proceedings (Barata & Schneider, 2004; Moe, 2007). In contrast, research by Sokoloff (2004) reflects that many women call the police simply to stop the abuse, not to facilitate an arrest of their partner. Victims can feel disempowered by the mandatory arrest process, as it takes away their decision-making abilities. While one study found that the majority of women supported the application of mandatory arrest policies in a theoretical sense, they did not believe that such laws would benefit them directly (Smith, 2000). This belief that mandatory arrest policies would not be applicable to their lives is an example of Walker's theory of *learned helplessness*, which suggests that a victim may believe that her batterer is exempt from laws against battering and that her status as a victim is unworthy (Walker, 1979). While mandatory arrest policies removed the victim's responsibility for instituting formal charges against an offender, there were some unintentional consequences. In many cases, a victim's call to the police for help resulted in her own arrest, as officers responding to the scene were often unable or unwilling to determine who was the victim and who was the offender. Other victims may be less likely to call for intervention, knowing that their batterer (or themselves) would be arrested (Gormley, 2007; Miller & Peterson, 2007). Many women experiencing IPA supported the concept of mandatory arrest in general and for other victims but were less likely to agree that it was necessary in their own lives (Barata & Schneider, 2004).

The increased attention on IPA has created a higher level of awareness and resources in the community for victims, which in turn has led to a reduction in the number of homicides involving intimate partners over the past two decades. However, this same study found that states with mandatory arrest policies have rates of intimate partner homicides that are 50% higher compared to those states without mandatory arrest policies (Iyengar, 2007). Here, the consequence is that the fear of facilitating an arrest of an intimate partner means that victims don't seek out help . . . until it's too late.

Another issue with mandatory arrest policies is the concern over dual-arrest practices. Dual-arrests are more likely to occur when state laws or policies do not include a primary aggressor designation. Here, laws require officers to make a determination about who the real offender is. Even with a primary aggressor designation, officers may lack the training or experience to make a professional judgment about who to arrest, resulting in both parties being arrested. These dual-arrest practices result in women being arrested for domestic violence with their partner. As a result, many women victims find themselves labeled as offenders of IPA by police and the courts for engaging in acts of self-defense (Miller, 2005). Dual arrest policies also have negative consequences for the LGBT community. Research by Hirschel et al. (2007) found that in cases of IPA, same-sex couples were more likely to be involved in dual arrests (female-to-female = 26.1% and male-to-male = 27.3%) compared to heterosexual couples (3.8%).

The increase in arrests has long-reaching implications for women, including the refusal of help by shelter services and challenges in child custody battles as a result of their "criminal" history (Miller & Meloy, 2006). In addition, gender differences in battering also impact programming options for women who engage in acts of IPA. Here, scholars have noted that traditional batterer intervention programming (which is designed primarily for male offenders) may not be appropriate for women. Instead, therapeutic options should focus on the rationale and factors behind women who engage in IPA (Kernsmith, 2005).

In response to many mandatory arrest policies, many jurisdictions instituted *no-drop policies.* Rather than force a victim to participate against her will, these jurisdictions developed evidence-based practices that would allow the prosecutor to present a case based on the evidence collected at the scene of the crime, regardless of any testimony by the victim (Gormley, 2007). Such policies were developed in response to a victim's lack of participation in the prosecution of her batterer. These policies may actually work against victims. When victims feel that their voice is not being heard by the criminal justice system, they may be less likely to report incidents of IPA. While no-drop policies were designed to prevent victims from dismissing charges against their batterer, they instead led to disempowering victims.

Programming Concerns for Victims of Intimate Partner Abuse

Not only are programs needed to address the needs of victims, but it is important to consider the role of battering prevention programs for men. Over the past three decades, batterer intervention programming has become one of the most popular options when sentencing offenders in cases of IPA. Given the high correlation between substance use and IPA, most programs include substance abuse treatment as a part of their curriculum. The majority of these programs offer group therapy, which is popular not only for its cost effectiveness but also because scholars suggest that the group environment can serve as an opportunity for program participants to support and mentor one another. One criticism of battering intervention programs is that they generally assume that all batterers are alike. This approach does not offer the opportunity for programs to tailor their curriculum to address the differences among men who abuse (Rosenbaum, 2009). In addition, victims of domestic violence voice their dissatisfaction with many of these types of programs, arguing that they are ineffective in dealing with the issues that the men face in their lives (Gillum, 2008).

One of the major themes highlighted by the research findings is the need for services and programming that reflect the unique needs of women. Intimate partner abuse attacks every community, age, religion, race, class, and sexual identity. Like rape crisis, programs that provide services for victims of battering are acknowledging the need for options that are culturally diverse and reflect the unique issues within different racial and ethnic communities. The need for culturally relevant programming also extends to shelter programs for victims of domestic violence. In particular, women noted the absence of women of color (particularly Black women) within the administration and staff, even in environments where the majority of the clientele was Black. Here, the differences stemmed from feelings that the staff (as women of color and IPA survivors themselves) understood what the women were going through and supported them throughout their journey. As one woman noted, "Black womens understand other Black womens. Ain't no way a White woman understands what a Black women going through . . . because. . . . we're different, we are totally different" (Gillum, 2009, p. 67). Additionally, scholars have noted the need for such programs to be based within the targeted community to ensure participation from the community residents—if programs are difficult to access geographically, women are less likely to seek out services as a result of time, money (loss of work hours and cost of child care), and transportation limitations. Research has also highlighted the need for increased public service information in communities, particularly in neighborhoods where women of color and immigrant women reside. Victims of violence also discuss the need to be proactive and engage in prevention efforts with young women and men in the community (Bent-Goodley, 2004).

However, as Sokoloff (2004) points out, culturally diverse programs are not enough to combat issues of violence between intimate partners. Rather, intervention efforts need to attack the systems that create social inequalities—racism, sexism, classism, and so on. In addition, the legal system and program providers need to understand how these issues are interrelated and not dominated by a single demographic factor. Regardless of their individual effects on a single person, many of these interventions have the potential to fail at the macro level as long as the social culture of accepting male violence against women remains (Schwartz & DeKeseredy, 2008).

SUMMARY

- Intimate partner abuse (IPA) is difficult to identify, as much of the abuse occurs behind closed doors and victims are reluctant to report cases of abuse.
- The Violence Against Women Act of 1994 (VAWA) provided funding for battered women's shelters, outreach education, and training on domestic violence for police and court personnel.
- Women are more likely to be killed by someone close to them (compared to a stranger).
- Children who are exposed to violence in the home are at risk for negative mental health outcomes. Additionally, many children continue the cycle of violence as adults.
- Gender-role stereotypes and homophobic views have a significant effect on identifying victims of same-sex IPA and giving them the assistance they need.

- Immigrant victims of domestic violence face a variety of unique issues (such as cultural norms regarding violence, gender-role expectations, and a fear of deportation) that affect their experience with battering.
- Walker's cycle of violence (1979) helps explain how perpetrators maintain control within a battering relationship.
- Women are confronted with a variety of barriers in their attempts to leave a relationship where IPA is present.
- Most women make multiple attempts to leave a violent relationship before they are successful.
- Restraining orders (also known as *protection orders*) are designed to provide victims of IPA the opportunity to separate themselves from their abuser and generally prohibit the perpetrator from contacting the victim.
- For many women, mandatory arrest policies have resulted in only a temporary decrease in the violence in their lives, with the potential of increased violence in the future.
- In response to mandatory arrest policies, many jurisdictions instituted *no-drop policies*, which allow prosecutors to file charges without the consent or participation of the victim.
- *Stalking* is defined as a "course of conduct directed at a specific person that would cause a reasonable person to feel fear" (Baum et al., 2009, p. 1).
- *Cyberstalking* involves the use of technology to track and monitor the lives of victims of stalking.
- Many victims do not report their experiences of being stalked to law enforcement, as they fear that a report will escalate the behavior or do not believe that stalking is a serious matter or that anything can be done to stop the stalking behavior.
- The first criminal law on stalking was enacted in California in 1990, following the murder of Rebecca Schaeffer.
- Stalking is often related to incidents of IPA.
- The experience of stalking generally intensifies when a victim severs her relationship with her stalker.

KEY TERMS

Abusive incident	Hollywood stalkers	Minneapolis Domestic Violence Experiment
Battered women's movement	Honeymoon period	No-drop policies
Battered women's syndrome	Immigrant victims of intimate partner abuse	Restraining order
Cyberstalking		Sentencing guidelines
Discretionary arrest	Learned helplessness	Tension building
Federal Interstate Stalking Law	Mandatory arrest	Wraparound services

DISCUSSION QUESTIONS

1. How have mandatory arrest policies improved the lives of women involved in cases of intimate partner abuse? How have these policies negatively affected victims?

2. What unique issues do immigrant victims of intimate partner abuse face?

3. Describe the different forms of violence that can occur within an intimate partner abusive relationship.

4. Explain how the cycle of violence attempts to explain incidents of intimate partner battering.

5. How has the identification of battered women's syndrome been used in cases of women who kill their batterers?

6. What effects have no-drop policies had for victim rights?

7. What barriers exist for women in their attempts to leave a battering relationship?

8. How has the use of technology changed the way in which victims experience stalking? What challenges do these changes present for law enforcement and the criminal justice system in pursuing cases of cyberstalking?

9. How do victims cope with the experience of being stalked?

WEB RESOURCES

Bureau of Justice Statistics http://bjs.ojp.usdoj.gov

The National Center for Victims of Crime http://www.ncvc.org

National Coalition Against Domestic Violence http://www.ncadv.org/

The National Domestic Violence Hotline http://www.ndvh.org/

Office of Justice Programs http://www.ojp.usdoj.gov/

Office on Violence against Women http://www.ovw.usdoj.gov/

Stalking Victims Sanctuary http://www.stalkingvictims.com

REFERENCES

After court order, Madonna faces accused in stalker case. (1996, January 4). *New York Times*. Retrieved from http://www.nytimes.com/1996/01/04/us/after-court-order-madonna-faces-accused-in-stalker-case.html

Alabama Coalition Against Domestic Violence (ACADV). (n.d.). *Dating violence.* Retrieved from http://www.acadv.org/dating.html

Alexy, E. M., Burgess, A. W., Baker, T., & Smoyak, S. A. (2005). Perceptions of cyberstalking among college students. *Brief Treatment and Crisis Intervention, 5*(3), 279–289.

American Bar Association Commission on Domestic Violence. (2008). *Domestic violence Civil Protection Orders (CPOs) by state.* Retrieved from http://www.americanbar.org/content/dam/aba/migrated/domviol/pdfs/CPO_Protections_for_LGBT_Victims_7_08.authcheckdam.pdf

Baker, C. K., Holditch Niolon, P., & Oliphant, H. (2009). A descriptive analysis of transitional housing programs for survivors of intimate partner violence in the United States. *Violence Against Women, 15*(4), 460–481.

Barata, P. C., & Schneider, F. (2004). Battered women add their voices to the debate about the merits of mandatory arrest. *Women's Studies Quarterly, 32*(3/4), 148–163.

Bassett, L. (2012, May 15). White House threatens to veto House GOP's Violence Against Women Act. *Huffington Post*. Retrieved from http://www.huffingtonpost.com/2012/05/15/violence-against-women-act-white-house-veto-threat_n_1519402.html

Baum, K., Catalano, S., Rand, M., & Rose, K. (2009). National Crime Victimization Survey: Stalking victimization in the United States. *Bureau of Justice Statistics Special Report*. U.S. Department of Justice, Office of Justice Programs. Retrieved from http://www.ovw.usdoj.gov/docs/stalking-victimization.pdf

Belknap, J. (2007). *The invisible woman: Gender, crime and justice*. Belmont, CA: Thomson-Wadsworth.

Bendery, J. (2013, February 11). VAWA reauthorization: House Republicans urge Boehner, Cantor to pass bipartisan bill. *Huffington Post*. Retrieved from http://www.huffingtonpost.com/2013/02/11/vawa-reauthorization_n_2665599.html

Bennett, L., Riger, S., Schewe, P., Howard, A., & Wasco, S. (2004). Effectiveness of hotline, advocacy, counseling, and shelter services for victims of domestic violence: A statewide evaluation. *Journal of Interpersonal Violence, 19*(7), 815–829.

Bent-Goodley, T. B. (2004). Perceptions of domestic violence: A dialogue with African American women. *Health and Social Work, 29*(4), 307–316.

Block, C. R. (2003). How can practitioners help an abused woman lower her risk of death? *NIJ Journal, 250*, 4–7. Retrieved from http://www.ncjrs.gov/pdffiles1/jr000250c.pdf

Bornstein, D. R., Fawcett, J., Sullivan, M., Senturia, K. D., & Shiu-Thornton, S. (2006). Understanding the experiences of lesbian, bisexual and trans survivors of domestic violence. *Journal of Homosexuality, 51*(1), 159–181.

Boyd, C. (2001). The implications and effects of theories of intergenerational transmission of violence for boys who live with domestic violence. *Australian Domestic & Family Violence Clearinghouse Newsletter, 6*, 6–8.

Brown, M. J., & Groscup, J. (2009). Perceptions of same-sex domestic violence among crisis center staff. *Journal of Family Violence, 24*, 87–93.

Bui, H. (2007). The limitations of current approaches to domestic violence. In R. Muraskin (Ed.), *It's a crime* (4th ed.). Upper Saddle River, NJ: Pearson Prentice Hall.

Bui, H., & Morash, M. (2008). Immigration, masculinity and intimate partner violence from the standpoint of domestic violence service providers and Vietnamese-origin women. *Feminist Criminology, 3*(3), 191–215.

Bureau of Justice Statistics. (2006). Intimate partner violence. *Office of Justice Programs*. Retrieved from http://bjs.ojp.usdoj.gov/content/pub/press/ipvpr.cfm

Campbell, J. C., Webster, D., Koziol-McLain, J., Block, C. R., Campbell, D., Curry, M. A., Gary, F., . . . Wilt, S. (2003). Assessing risk factors for intimate partner homicide. *NIJ Journal, 250*, 14–19. Retrieved from http://www.ncjrs.gov/pdffiles1/jr000250e.pdf

Catalano, S. (2007). Intimate partner violence in the United States. *Bureau of Justice Statistics*. Washington, DC: U.S. Department of Justice. Retrieved from http://bjs.ojp.usdoj.gov/content/pub/pdf/IPAus.pdf

Catalano, S. (2012). Intimate partner violence in the United States. *Bureau of Justice Statistics*. Washington, DC: U.S. Department of Justice. Retrieved from http://bjs.ojp.usdoj.gov/content/intimate/ipv.cfm

Centers for Disease Control and Prevention (CDC). (2003). *Costs of intimate partner violence against women in the United States: 2003*. Atlanta, GA: National Centers for Injury Prevention and Control.

Centers for Disease Control and Prevention (CDC). (n.d.). *Intimate partner violence*. Retrieved from http://www.cdc.gov/ViolencePrevention/intimatepartnerviolence/definitions.html

Copel, L. C. (2006). Partner abuse in physically disabled women: A proposed model for understanding intimate partner violence. *Perspectives in Psychiatric Care, 42*(2), 114–129.

Cox, L., & Speziale, B. (2009). Survivors of stalking: Their voices and lived experiences. *Affilia: Journal of Women and Social Work, 24*(1), 5–18.

Crandall, M., Senturia, K., Sullivan, M., & Shiu-Thornton, S. (2005). No way out: Russian-speaking women's experiences with domestic violence. *Journal of Interpersonal Violence, 20*(8), 941–958.

Davis, K. E., Coker, A. L., & Sanderson, M. (2002). Physical and mental health effects of being stalked for men and women. *Violence and Victims, 17*(4), 429–443.

Diamond, M. (2011, October 6). Topeka, Kansas, city council considers decriminalizing domestic violence to save money. *Think Progress.* Retrieved from http://thinkprogress.org/justice/2011/10/06/338461/topeka-kansas-city-council-considers-decriminalizing-domestic-violence-to-save-money/

Dietz, N. A., & Martin, P. Y. (2007). Women who are stalked: Questioning the fear standard. *Violence Against Women, 13*(7), 750–776.

Diviney, C. L., Parekh, A., & Olson, L. M. (2009). Outcomes of civil protective orders: Results from one state. *Journal of Interpersonal Violence, 24*(7), 1209–1221.

Dobash, R., & Dobash, R. E. (1992). *Women, violence and social change.* New York, NY: Routledge.

Domestic Violence and Incest Resource Centre. (2005). *Young people and domestic violence fact sheet.* Retrieved from http://www.burstingthebubble.com/YoungPeopleDV%20FactSheet.pdf

Dutton, M. (n.d.). Critique of the "battered women syndrome" model. *American Academy of Experts in Traumatic Stress.* Retrieved from http://www.aaets.org/article138.htm

Dutton, M. A., Orloff, L. E., & Hass, G. A. (2000). Characteristics of help seeking behaviors, resources and service needs of battered immigrant Latinas: Legal and policy implications. *Georgetown Journal on Poverty, Law and Policy, 7,* 245–305.

Feder, L., & Henning, K. (2005). A comparison of male and female dually arrested domestic violence offenders. *Violence and Victims, 20*(2), 153–171.

Fleury-Steiner, R., Bybee, D., Sullivan, C. M., Belknap, J., & Melton, H. C. (2006). Contextual factors impacting battered women's intentions to reuse the criminal legal system. *Journal of Community Psychology, 34*(3), 327–342.

Gelles, R. (2000). Domestic violence: Not an even playing field. *The Safety Zone.* Retrieved from http://www.Serve.com/zone/everyone/gelles/html

Gelles, R., & Straus, M. A. (1988). *Intimate violence: The causes and consequences of abuse in the American family.* New York, NY: Touchstone.

Gillum, T. L. (2008). Community response and needs of African American female survivors of domestic violence. *Journal of Interpersonal Violence, 23*(1), 39–57.

Gillum, T. L. (2009). Improving services to African American survivors of IPV: From the voices of recipients of culturally specific services. *Violence Against Women, 15*(1), 57–80.

Goddard, C., & Bedi, G. (2010). Intimate partner violence and child abuse: A child-centered perspective. *Child Abuse Review, 19,* 5–20.

Gormley, P. (2007). The historical role and views towards victims and the evolution of prosecution policies in domestic violence. In R. Muraskin (Ed.), *It's a crime* (4th ed.). Upper Saddle River, NJ: Pearson Prentice Hall.

Gover, A. R., Brank, E. M., & MacDonald, J. M. (2007). A specialized domestic violence court in South Carolina: An example of procedural justice for victims and defendants. *Violence Against Women, 13*(6), 603–626.

Grim, R., & Bassett, L. (2012, May 16). House VAWA bill picks up unhelpful ally: National Coalition for Men. *Huffington Post.* Retrieved from http://www.huffingtonpost.com/2012/05/16/vawa-house-bill-national-coalition-for-men_n_1521762.html

Grossman, S. F., & Lundy, M. (2011). Characteristics of women who do and do not receive onsite shelter services from domestic violence programs. *Violence Against Women, 17*(8), 1024–1045.

Grossman, S. F., Lundy, M., George, C. C., & Crabtree-Nelson, S. (2010). Shelter and service receipt for victims of domestic violence in Illinois. *Journal of Interpersonal Violence, 25*(11), 2077–2093.

Hardesty, J. L., Oswald, R. F., Khaw, L., & Fonseca, C. (2011). Lesbian/bisexual mothers and intimate partner violence: Help seeking in the context of social and legal vulnerability. *Violence Against Women, 17*(1), 28–46.

Hassouneh, D., & Glass, N. (2008). The influence of gender-role stereotyping on female same-sex intimate partner violence. *Violence Against Women, 14*(3), 310–325.

Hirschel, D. (2008). Domestic violence cases: What research show about arrest and dual arrest rates. *National Institute of Justice.* Retrieved from http://www.nij.gov/nij/publications/dv-dual-arrest-222679/dv-dual-arrest.pdf

Hirschel, D., Buzawa, E., Pattavina, A., Faggiani, D., & Reuland, M. (2007). Explaining the prevalence, context and consequences of dual arrest in intimate partner cases. *U.S. Department of Justice.* Retrieved from https://www.ncjrs.gov/pdffiles1/nij/grants/218355.pdf

Ingram, E. M. (2007). A comparison of help seeking between Latino and non-Latino victims of intimate partner violence. *Violence Against Women, 12*(2), 159–171.

Irwin, J. (2008). (Dis)counted stories: Domestic violence and lesbians. *Qualitative Social Work, 7*(2), 199–215.

Iyengar, R. (2007). The protection battered spouses don't need. *New York Times.* Retrieved from http://www.nytimes.com/2007/08/07/opinion/07iyengar.html

Johnson, I. M. (2007). Victims' perceptions of police response to domestic violence incidents. *Journal of Criminal Justice, 35*, 498–510.

Kernsmith, P. (2005). Exerting power or striking back: A gendered comparison of motivations for domestic violence perpetration. *Violence and Victims, 20*, 173–185.

Klein, A. R. (2004). *The criminal justice response to domestic violence.* Belmont, CA: Wadsworth Thomson Learning.

Kraaij, V., Arensman, E., Garnefski, N., & Kremers, I. (2007). The role of cognitive coping in female victims of stalking. *Journal of Interpersonal Violence, 22*(12), 1603–1612.

Lee, R. K. (1998). Romantic and electronic stalking in a college context. *William and Mary Journal of Women and the Law, 4,* 373–466.

Leonard, E. D. (2001). Convicted survivors: Comparing and describing California's battered women inmates. *The Prison Journal, 81*(1), 73–86.

Lipsky, S., Caetano, R., Field, C. A., & Larkin, G. L. (2006). The role of intimate partner violence, race and ethnicity in help-seeking behaviors. *Ethnicity and Health, 11*(1), 81–100.

Logan, T. K., Shannon, L., & Cole, J. (2007). Stalking victimization in the context of intimate partner violence. *Violence and Victims, 22*(6), 669–683.

Melton, H. C. (2007). Predicting the occurrence of stalking in relationships characterized by domestic violence. *Journal of Interpersonal Violence, 22*(1), 3–25.

Miller, S. (2005). *Victims as offenders: The paradox of women's violence in relationships.* New Brunswick, NJ: Rutgers University Press.

Miller, S. L., & Meloy, M. L. (2006). Women's use of force: Voices of women arrested for domestic violence. *Violence Against Women, 12*(1), 89–115.

Miller, S. L., & Peterson, E. S. L. (2007). The impact of law enforcement policies on victims of intimate partner violence. In R. Muraskin (Ed.), *It's a crime* (4th ed.). Upper Saddle River, NJ: Pearson Prentice Hall.

Moe, A. M. (2007). Silenced voices and structured survival: Battered women's help seeking. *Violence Against Women, 13*(7), 676–699.

Moe, A. M. (2009). Battered women, children, and the end of abusive relationships. *Afilia: Journal of Women and Social Work, 24*(3), 244–256.

Nash, S. T. (2006). Through Black eyes: African American women's constructions of their experiences with intimate male partner violence. *Violence Against Women, 11*(11), 1420–1440.

National Coalition Against Domestic Violence. (n.d.). [Website.] Retrieved from www.ncadv.org

National Task Force to End Sexual and Domestic Violence Against Women. (n.d.). [Website.] Retrieved from http://4vawa.org/

Office on Violence against Women (OVW). (n.d.). [Website.] U.S. Department of Justice. Retrieved from http://www.ovw.usdoj.gov

Pathe, M., & Mullen, P. E. (1997). The impact of stalkers on their victims. *British Journal of Psychiatry, 170*, 12–17.

Poore, T. (2012, July 12). Gridlock must end for VAWA. *The Hill's Congress Blog.* Retrieved from http://thehill.com/blogs/congress-blog/judicial/237537-gridlock-must-end-for-vawa

Potter, H. (2007a). Battered Black women's use of religious services and spirituality for assistance in leaving abusive relationships. *Violence Against Women, 13*(3), 262–284.

Potter, H. (2007b). *Battle cries: Understanding and confronting intimate partner abuse against African-American women.* New York, NY: New York University Press.

Raphael, J. (2000). *Saving Bernice: Battered women, welfare and poverty.* Boston, MA: Northeastern University Press.

Renzetti, C. M. (1992). *Violent betrayal: Partner abuse in lesbian relationships.* London, England: SAGE.

Rosenbaum, A. (2009). Batterer intervention programs: A report from the field. *Violence and Victims, 24*(6), 757–770.

Roth, D. L., & Coles, E. M. (1995). Battered women syndrome: A conceptual analysis of its status vis-à-vis DSM IV mental disorders. *Med Law, 14*(7–8), 641–658.

Schuller, R. A., & Rzepa, S. (2002). Expert testimony pertaining to battered woman syndrome: Its impact on jurors' decisions. *Law and Human Behavior, 26*(6), 655–673.

Schwartz, M. D., & DeKeseredy, W. S. (2008). Interpersonal violence against women: The role of men. *Journal of Contemporary Criminal Justice, 24*(2), 178–185.

Sellers, C., & Bromley, M. (1996). Violent behavior in college student dating relationships. *Journal of Contemporary Criminal Justice, 12*(1), 1–27.

Shannon-Lewy, C., & Dull, V. T. (2005). The response of Christian clergy to domestic violence: Help or hindrance? *Aggression and Violent Behavior, 10*(6), 647–659.

Sherman, L. W., & Berk, R. A. (1984). The Minneapolis Domestic Violence Experiment. *Police Foundation Reports.* Retrieved from http://www.policefoundation.org/pdf/minneapolisdve.pdf

Silverman, J. G., Raj, A., Mucci, L. A., & Hathaway, J. E. (2001). Dating violence against adolescent girls and associated substance use, unhealthy weight control, sexual risk behavior, pregnancy and suicidality. *Journal of American Medical Association, 285*(5), 572–579.

Smith, A. (2000). It's my decision, isn't it? A research note on battered women's perceptions of mandatory intervention laws. *Violence Against Women, 6*(12), 1384–1402.

Smith, E. L., & Farole, D. J., Jr. (2009). Profile of intimate partner violence cases in large urban counties. *Bureau of Justice Statistics Special Report.* U.S. Department of Justice, Office of Justice Programs. Retrieved from http://bjs.ojp.usdoj.gov/content/pub/pdf/pipvcluc.pdf

Sokoloff, N. J. (2004). Domestic violence at the crossroads: Violence against poor women and women of color. *Women Studies Quarterly, 32*(3/4), 139–147.

Spitzberg, B. H., & Cupach, W. R. (2003). What mad pursuit? Obsessive relational intrusion and stalking related phenomena. *Aggression and Violent Behavior, 8*, 345–375.

Stalens, L. J., & Finn, M. A. (2000). Gender differences in officers' perceptions and decisions about domestic violence cases. *Women and Criminal Justice, 11*(3), 1–24.

Stevenson, T., & Love, C. (1999). *Her story of domestic violence: A timeline of the battered women's movement.* Safework, CA: California's Domestic Violence Resource. Retrieved from http://www.mincava.umn.edu/documents/herstory/herstory.html

Straus, M. A., Gelles, R., & Steinmetz, S. (1980). *Behind closed doors: Violence in the American family.* Newbury Park, CA: SAGE.

Sullivan, M., Senturia, K., Negash, T., Shiu-Thornton, S., & Giday, B. (2005). For us it's like living in the dark: Ethiopian women's experiences with domestic violence. *Journal of Interpersonal Violence, 20*(8), 922–940.

Sulzberger, A. G. (2011, October 11). Facing cuts, a city repeals its domestic violence law. *New York Times*. Retrieved from http://www.nytimes.com/2011/10/12/us/topeka-moves-to-decriminalize-domestic-violence.html

Tamborra, T. L. (2012). Poor, urban, battered women who are stalked: How can we include their experiences. *Feminist Criminology, 7*(2), 112–129.

Tjaden, P., & Thoennes, N. (2000). Extent, nature and consequence of intimate partner violence. *National Institute of Justice*. U.S. Department of Justice, Office of Justice Programs. Retrieved from https://www.ncjrs.gov/pdf files1/nij/181867.pdf

Walker, L. E. (1979). *The battered woman*. New York, NY: Harper and Row.

Walker, L. (1984). *The battered woman syndrome*. New York, NY: Springer Publishing.

Wang, M. C., Horne, S. G., Levitt, H. M., & Klesges, L. M. (2009). Christian women in IPV relationships: An exploratory study of religious factors. *Journal of Psychology and Christianity, 28*(3), 224–235.

West, C. M. (2004). Black women and intimate partner violence: New directions for research. *Journal of Interpersonal Violence, 19*(12), 1487–1493.

Women's Health. (2004). *UMHS Women's Health Program*. [Website.] Retrieved from http://www.med.umich.edu/whp/newsletters/summer04/p03-dating.html

NOTES

1. Given that the majority of data finds men as the perpetrator and women as the victim, this text generally uses the term *he* to refer to the abuser and *she* to refer to the victim. The use of these terms is not meant to ignore male victims of violence or abuse within same-sex relationships but only to characterize the majority of cases of IPA.

2. Each state has different policies on the availability of legal documents in languages other than English. Forms for the State of California are located at http://www.courts.ca.gov/formsrules.htm

3. The SVS only includes data on respondents age 18 and older who participated in the National Crime Victimization Survey during January–June 2006. The data assess victimization incidents that occurred during the 12 months prior to the interview.

4. According to these data, 3.4 million people are victims of stalking each year.

5. *Harassment* is defined by the SVS as acts that are indicative of stalking behaviors but do not incite feelings of fear in the victim.

International Issues in the Victimization of Women

Things were hard for Karla as Gus' trial approached. Four days after her 13th birthday, Karla gave birth to a daughter, who she gave up for adoption, but not before the authorities took blood samples and confirmed that Angel (as Karla planned to name her daughter) had indeed been fathered by Gus when Karla was just 12 years old. Karla didn't know the authorities could make her give blood, but it happened. She also didn't expect to lose her friend Diana, but that happened, too, when Diana moved away to live with an uncle.

Another unexpected event happened with the rape trial: Karla and her mother were reported to immigration authorities. The two came to the U.S. when Karla was just a baby, and neither had proper documentation. It looked as if she and her mother would be deported. However, the district attorney told them there might be a way to stay. The U.S. Citizenship and Immigration Service implemented a new program for a special visa that protected crime victims who were also undocumented immigrants. So long as Karla agreed to cooperate with authorities—to talk about her relationship with Gus truthfully on the witness stand—the D.A. would provide the certification necessary to obtain the visas. Facing certain deportation, Karla and her mother reluctantly agreed.

As Gus' trial came to a close, Karla learned she indeed qualified for the rare visa the D.A. had promised. However, her mother did not and would face deportation, as the protection applied to undocumented immigrants who were victims of crime in the U.S., not necessarily their parents.

Karla didn't wait for the verdict on either Gus' trial or her mother's immigration hearing. She sought escape, and finding the numb of heroin a welcome reprieve, she turned to the streets.

> ## Chapter Highlights
>
> - International human rights for women
> - International examination of the sexual assault and murder of women
> - Honor-based violence
> - Human trafficking of women
> - The Dead Women of Juárez
> - Sexual assault as a crime of war

While there are a number of concerns involving the human rights of women around the world, this section highlights three examples of victimizations of women: the practice of **honor-based violence** against women, the issue of **human trafficking** and female slavery, and the issue of sexual assault as a crime of war. Each of these crimes is related to the status of women within their communities, and suggestions for change are rooted within a shift of gendered normative values and the treatment of women in these societies. Each discussion focuses on the nature of the crime, the implications for women involved, and the role of these issues in discussions about criminal justice policies in an international context.

As you read through the experiences of the women and their victimizations, it is important to consider how the cultural context of their lives affects their victimization experience. The effects of culture are significant, as they can alter not only how these crimes are viewed by agents of social control (police, legal systems) but also how the community interprets these experiences. These definitions play a significant role in determining how these crimes are reported (or if reports are made) as well as any response that may arise from these offenses. It can be dangerous to apply a White, middle-class lens or an *Americanized identity* to these issues—what we might do as individuals may not necessarily reflect the social norms and values of other cultures.

Honor-Based Violence

The category of honor-based violence (HBV) includes practices such as honor killings, bride burnings, customary killings, and dowry deaths. Each of these crimes involves the murder of a woman by a male family member, usually a father, brother, or male cousin. These women are killed in response to a belief that the women have offended a family's honor and have brought shame to the family unit. The notion of *honor* is one of the most important cultural values for members of these communities. "Honor is the reason for our living now . . . without honor, life has no meaning. . . . It is okay if you don't have money, but you must have dignity" (Kardam, 2005).

At the heart of the practice of HBV is a double standard rooted in patriarchy, which dictates that women should be modest, meek, pure, and innocent. Women are expected to follow the rules of their fathers and, later, their husbands. In some cases, honor killings have been carried out in cases of adultery or even perceived infidelity. Hina Jilani, a lawyer and human rights activist, suggests that in some cultures, the "right to life of women . . . is conditional on their obeying social norms and traditions"

(Amnesty International, 1999). Women are viewed as a piece of property that holds value. Her value is based on her purity, which can be tainted by acts that many Western cultures would consider to be normal, everyday occurrences, such as requesting a love song on the radio or strolling through the park (Arin, 2001). For many women, their crime is that they wanted to become **Westernized** or participate in modern-day activities such as wearing jeans, listening to music, and developing friendships. For other women, their shame is rooted in a sexual double standard where a woman is expected to maintain her purity for her husband. To taint the purity of a woman is to taint her honor, and thereby the honor of her family. The concept of honor controls every part of a woman's identity. As Kardam (2005) explains, "when honor is constructed through a woman's body, it entails her daily life activities, education, work, marriage, the importance of virginity [and] faithfulness" (p. 61). Unfortunately, despite the fact that a simple Internet search will bring up dozens of media reports of this issue worldwide, recent academic literature on this topic has been sparse.

Even women who have been victimized through rape and sexual assault are at risk of death via an honor killing, as their victimization is considered shameful for the family. In many cases, the simple perception of impropriety is enough to warrant an honor killing. Women who are accused of bringing negative attention and dishonor to their families are rarely afforded the opportunity to defend their actions (Mayell, 2002). Amnesty International (1999) explains the central role of *perception* of honor in Pakistan:

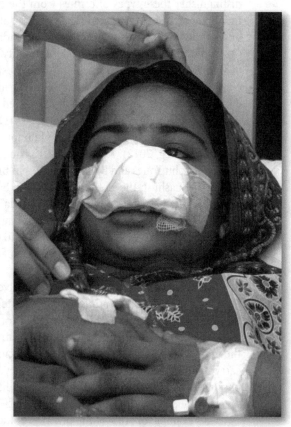

> The distinction between a woman being guilty and a woman being alleged to be guilty of illicit sex is irrelevant. What impacts the man's honour is the public perception, the belief of her infidelity. It is this which blackens honour and for which she is killed. To talk of "alleged kari" or "alleged siahkari" [alleged acts of immoral behavior such as alleged marital infidelity, refusal to submit to an arranged marriage, or requesting a divorce from a husband] makes no sense in this system nor does your demand that a woman should be heard. It is not the truth that honour is about, but public perception of honour.

The practice of honor and customary killings are typically carried out with a high degree of violence. Women are subjected to acts of torture, and their deaths are often slow and violent. They may be shot, stabbed, strangled, electrocuted, set on fire, or run over by a vehicle. In fact, doing so is expected in certain cases, as "a man's ability to protect his honour is judged by his

▲ **Photo 7.1** A young woman is treated for injuries that she received in an attempted honor attack in rural Pakistan. While she was lucky to survive the attack, hundreds of women die each year in these honor attacks, which are generally committed by male relatives (husband, father, brother, etc.) for bringing shame on to the family.

family and neighbors. He must publicly demonstrate his power to safeguard his honour by killing those who damaged it and thereby restore it" (Amnesty International, 1999). One would assume that the women in these countries would silently shame these acts of violence. Contrary to this belief, however, research indicates that the women in the family support these acts of violence against their daughters and sisters as part of the shared community understanding about honor (Mayell, 2002).

While the United Nations (2000, 2010) estimates that there are more than 5,000 honor killings each year around the world, researchers and activists indicate that the true numbers of these crimes are significantly greater. Estimates indicate that tens of thousands of women are killed each year in the practice of HBV. Yet many of these crimes go unreported, making it difficult to develop an understanding of the true extent of the issue. According to research by Chesler (2010), which reviewed 230 cases of news-reported honor killings worldwide, the majority (95%) of the victims are young women (mean age of 23). In 42% of cases, there were multiple perpetrators involved in the killing, a characteristic that distinguishes these types of crimes from the types of single-perpetrator **femicide** that are most commonly reported in Western countries. Over half of these women were tortured to death and were killed by methods such as stoning, burning, beheading, strangulation, or stabbing/bludgeoning. Nearly half (42%) of these cases involved acts of infidelity or alleged sexual impropriety, while the remaining 58% of women were murdered for being "too Western" and defying the expectations that are set through cultural and religious normative values. Yet men are never criticized for their acceptance of Western culture. Women in such cultures "are expected to bear the burden of upholding these ancient and allegedly religious customs of gender apartheid" (Chesler, 2010).

Western cultures see incidences of honor killings as well, largely through their immigrant populations (Korteweg, 2012). Korteweg (2012) outlines several high-profile murders in Western countries, such as "Heshu Yones and Banaz Mahmod in Britain; Fadime Sahindal in Sweden; Mrs. Güll, Zarife, and Schijman Kuashi in the Netherlands; Hatun Sürücü in Germany; and Amandeep Atwal, Aqsa Parvez, and the Shafia sisters and their aunt in Canada" (p. 136). Less recently, the *New York Times* reported that Brazil has also seen incidences of honor killings, enough so to require a Supreme Court order banning the practice (Brooke, 1991). Countries around the world are increasingly adopting statutes banning the practice, but completely stemming the tide of cultural mores leading to its occurrence is a significant roadblock to achieving this goal.

Even if justice officials do become involved in these cases, perpetrators are rarely identified, and even more rarely are they punished to any extent. When human rights organizations and activists identify these incidents as HBV, family members of the victim are quick to dismiss the deaths of their sisters and daughters as "accidents." In Turkish communities, if a woman has fractured the honor of her family, the male members of her family meet to decide her fate. In the case of customary killings, the task of carrying out the murder is often given to the youngest male member of the family. In many cases, these boys are under the age of criminal responsibility, which further reduces the likelihood that any punishments will be handed down in the name of the victim (Arin, 2001).

One example of HBV is the practice of **karo-kari** murder in Pakistan. Karo-kari is a form of premeditated killing and is part of the cultural traditions of the community. The terms "karo" and "kari" literally translate to "Black male" and "Black female" and are used in reference to someone who is an adulterer or adulteress. In the majority of karo-kari cases, women are killed for engaging in acts of immoral behavior. These acts can include alleged marital infidelity, refusal to submit to an arranged marriage, or requesting a divorce from a husband (even in cases where abuse is present). In 2003, an estimated 1,261 women were killed in the name of karo-kari in Pakistan. More recently, a 2010 State

Department report on Pakistan indicated that over 40 women and men in Kandahar Province alone became victims of this practice (U.S. Department of State, 2011a). Unofficial statistics place this number as significantly higher, given that many of these crimes occur within the family and may not be reported to the authorities. The practice of karo-kari in Pakistan is unique compared to honor killings in many other countries, as men can also be victims under karo-kari traditions. Generally speaking, cultural norms require the killing of both the man and woman involved in the infidelity in order to restore honor. This distinction is unique to karo-kari, whereas most other forms of customary killings involve only the woman. However, in some cases, the karo (man) is able to negotiate with the tribal counsel for the community to pay money or offer other forms of settlement (property of another woman) to compensate the victim (Amnesty International, 1999). Few such alternatives exist for women in these instances, which overwhelmingly result in the woman's death.

Honor-based violence is a violation of many international treaties and acts. As United Nations Secretary General Ban Ki-moon (United Nations, 2010) argues,

> honour killings are . . . not something that can be simply brushed aside as some bizarre and retrograde atrocity that happens somewhere else. . . . They are an extreme symptom of discrimination against women, which—including other forms of domestic violence—is a plague that affects every country.

Yet, the problem remains today. In fact, the laws in many countries contain provisions that permit acts of HBV, including Syria, Morocco, Jordan, and Haiti. The practice of honor killings was condoned under the Taliban, and data indicate that since the fall of the Taliban regime, there has been an increase in reporting acts of violence against women (Esfandiari, 2006). Even in cases where there is no legal legitimization of the practice, cultural traditions and tribal justice sanction these crimes of violence and often shield offenders from punishment, and offenders continue the practice with impunity (Patel & Gadit, 2008). Some countries may offer lesser penalties to men who murder female relatives. Other countries have laws on the books that identify customary killings as a criminal act, yet offer opportunities for the offender to escape punishment. One such example is Pakistan. While the Pakistani Parliament passed legislation in 2004 that punished honor killings with a seven-year sentence and would allow for the death penalty for the worst cases, many activists question whether such a punishment will ever be carried out. In addition, the law contains a provision where the offender could negotiate a pardon with the victim's family members. Given that many of the offenders are indeed members of the victim's family, many believe that the retention of this provision will enable the offenders of these crimes to escape punishment altogether (Felix, 2005).

There are few options for escape for women in these countries where HBV prevails. International support for women at risk of becoming a victim of an honor killing is limited. There are few shelters for women seeking to escape their families. Any attempt to contact the police or other agents not only sends a woman back to the arms of her family, where she is at greatest risk, but her actions in seeking help create shame and dishonor for the family by exposing their private life to public and community scrutiny. The only customary option for these women is to escape to the tribal leader of the community (*sadar*), who can provide shelter while they negotiate a safe return of the woman to her home or to another community far from her family. However, this option is limited, as it still requires women to abide by traditional community standards and is not an option for women who are interested in asserting their rights or improving their status as women outside of their cultural norms (Amnesty International, 1999).

In their quest to improve the lives of women who may be victims of the practice of honor killings, Amnesty International (1999) outlines three general areas for reform:

1. *Legal Measures.* The current legal system in many of these countries does little to protect victims from potential violence under the normative structures that condone the practice of honor killings. Women have few, if any, legal rights that protect them from these harms. Legal reforms must address the status of women and provide them with opportunities for equal protection under the law. In cases where women survive an attempted honor killing, they need access to remedies that address the damages they experienced. In addition, the perpetrators of these crimes are rarely subjected to punishment for their actions. Indeed, the first step toward reform includes recognizing that violence against women is a crime, and such abuses need to be enforced by the legal communities. International law also needs to recognize these crimes and enforce sanctions against governments that fail to act against these offenders. However, it is unclear how effective these legal measures will be for individual communities. In their discussions of what can be done to stop the practice of honor killings, Turkish activists did not feel that increasing the punishments for HBV would serve as an effective deterrent, particularly in regions where the practice is more common and accepted within the community, as "punishments would not change the social necessity to kill and [spending] long years in jail can be seen as less important than [a] lifelong loss of honor" (Kardam, 2005, p. 51).

2. *Preventive Measures.* Education and public awareness is the first step toward reducing HBV toward women. These practices are rooted in culture and history. Attempts to change these deeply held attitudes will require time and resources aimed at opening communication on these beliefs. This is no easy task, given the normative cultural values that perpetuate these crimes. One of the first tasks may be to adopt sensitivity-training programming for judicial and legal personnel so that they may be able to respond to these acts of violence in an impartial manner. In addition, it is important to develop a sense of the extent of the problem in order to provide effective remedies. Here, an enhanced understanding of data on these crimes will help shed light on the pervasiveness of HBV as a first step toward addressing this problem.

3. *Protective Measures.* Given the limited options for women seeking to escape HBV, additional resources for victim services need to be made available. These include shelters, resources for women fleeing violence, legal aid to represent victims of crime, provisions for the protection of children, and training to increase the economic self-sustainability for women. In addition, the agencies that offer refuge for these women need to be protected from instances of backlash and harassment.

While these suggestions offer opportunities for change, many agents working in the regions most affected by honor-based killings indicate feelings of hopelessness that such changes are even possible. Certainly, the road toward reform is a long one, as it is rooted in cultural traditions that present significant challenges for change. "When an honor killing . . . starts to disturb everybody . . . and when nobody wants to carry this shame anymore, then finding solutions will become easier" (Kardam, 2005, p. 66). Indeed, the first step in reform involves creating the belief that success is possible.

The Women of Juárez.

The Mexican city of Ciudad Juárez sits across the Rio Grande from El Paso, Texas. A fast-growing industrial area, the region is known as a major manufacturing center for many American companies. With more than three hundred assembly plants (known as *maquiladoras*) in the region, Ciudad Juárez is a booming area for production. Since the 1994 passing of NAFTA (North American Free Trade Agreement), U.S. Corporations such as Ford, General Electric, and DuPont (to name a few) have established manufacturing centers in a region where labor costs are cheap and taxes are low, which results in high profits for companies. With four separate border access points, the region is a major center for exporting goods and transportation between Central Northern Mexico and the United States (Chamberlain, 2007). Awarded the "City of the Future" designation by *fDi Intelligence Magazine* and the Financial Times Group in 2008, Ciudad Juárez represents a region of opportunity and development:

> It appears to be a win-win situation for the United States. Americans enjoy relatively inexpensive consumer goods, and American-owned corporations enjoy the free aspect of the free trade zone: it is free of unions, minimum wages and largely free of enforceable regulations. (Spencer, 2004, p. 505)

However, this "City of the Future" is also filled with extreme poverty. Drawn to the region by the promise of a better life, Mexican citizens arrive from rural towns only to discover a new form of economic disparity in border towns such as Ciudad Juárez. While filled with factories, the city receives few benefits to stimulate its economy. The *maquiladoras* generated over $10 billion of profit for U.S. companies in 2000, yet the city of Ciudad Juárez received less than $1.5 million in taxes to provide a sustainable community structure for residents. Shantytowns surround the *maquiladoras*, as there are few options for housing for the workers. There is no money to build schools or provide services to the residents of the city (Spencer, 2004). The high profit margins for companies come at a price for the *maquiladoras'* workforce, where women make up more than 80% of the workforce and where cases of poor working conditions, low wages ($60 a week for their labor), and traumatic work environments have been documented.

Mexican border towns are also known for their high levels of violence and narcotics trafficking (Amnesty International, 2003; Pantin, 2001). Today, Ciudad Juárez is considered one of the most dangerous cities in the world due to violent feuds between the drug cartels and police. Ciudad Juárez is also dangerous for one particular population: young women. Since 1993, estimates suggest that over 400 women have been murdered in and around the city. While some of these girls are students who disappeared as they traveled to and from school, the majority of femicides in this region involve young women between the ages of 11 and 24 who traveled from their villages to Ciudad Juárez looking for work in the *maquiladoras*. Their bodies are discovered days, weeks, and months following their disappearances and are typically abandoned in vacant lots in Ciudad Juárez and the surrounding areas; some women are never found. Many of these cases involve significant acts of sexual

▲ **Photo 7.2** A field of crosses stand today in the deserts of Ciudad Juárez, Mexico, where hundreds of bodies of women have been found. Local and international organizations estimate that thousands of other women have gone missing and have yet to be found.

torture, including rape and the slashing of the breasts and genitals of the victims (Newton, 1999, 2003). The women who are killed and tortured in this fashion become members of a club known as *las muertas de Juárez,* or *the Dead Women of Juárez.*

In describing the murders of these women, several commentaries have pointed toward a clash among the traditional roles for women, a *machista* (chauvinistic) culture, and the rise of women's independence as an explanation for the violence. One author suggests that "these crimes are more murderous than murder, if such a thing is possible—they are crimes of such intense hatred that they seek to destroy the personhood of the women, negating their humanity and erasing their existence" ("The Disappearing Women of Juárez," 2002). According to a 2003 report by the Inter-American Commission on Human Rights (IACHR), the crimes against women in Ciudad Juárez have received international attention due to the extreme levels of violence in the murders and the belief that these killings may have been the result of a serial killer. However, their research indicates that these cases of femicide are not the result of a single serial killer but are part of a larger social issue related to a pattern of gender-based discrimination, where the violence against women is not considered to be a serious issue. Given the relationship with gender in these cases, any official response to address these crimes must consider the larger social context of crimes against women and the accessibility of justice for women in these cases (see also Ensalaco, 2006).

In attempting to solve these crimes, police have jailed dozens of suspects for the murders throughout the years. Some of these presumed offenders were railroaded by a system desperate to quash an inquisition into police practices. Many of these alleged perpetrators had their confessions coerced from them. Some argue that the authorities have shown little concern for these crimes and their victims, sending a message that these women are unworthy victims. Indeed, victim-blaming tactics have often been used to explain the murders, suggesting that these women wore revealing clothing, frequented bars and dance clubs, and were prostitutes. The National Human Rights Commission has found that the "judicial, state and municipal authorities were guilty of negligence and dereliction of duty" (Agosin, 2006, p. 16).

The quest for justice by journalists, social activists, and the families of these young women has been a challenging road, as many of them have been threatened with violence if they continue their investigations (Valdez, 2002). Others have been silenced due to the inaction by authorities. Given the poor treatment of victims' family members by the authorities, recent improvements have been made in the areas of legal, psychological, and social services. However, there is concern that there are limited funds allocated to meet the demands for these services (Inter-American Commission on Human Rights, 2003). The Mexican government has also created a victims services fund designed to provide monetary compensation to the families of the women and girls who have been murdered in Ciudad Juárez. However, the program is poorly organized, and few families have been able to access the funds (Calderon Gamboa, 2007).

While the creation of a special prosecutor's office in 1998 did little to end the killings in Ciudad Juárez, improvements have been made in recent times regarding the organization of evidence, the tracking of case details, and the streamlining of investigations and assignment of personnel. While Mexican authorities claim they have resolved the majority of the murders, their definition of *resolved* is based on a presumption of motive and the identification of a perpetrator and does not require that an offender be charged, tried, or convicted of the crime (Dillon, 1998). Understandably, many families are dissatisfied by this definition of *resolved*. As of 2003, only three convictions have been handed down, and the community has little faith in the validity of these convictions (Castillo, 2003; Simmons, 2006).

Many human rights and activist groups have blamed the Mexican government for the inadequate investigation of these crimes and the lack of accountability by police agents (Herrick, 1998; Moore, 2000). Indeed, Mexico's failure to act in these cases constitutes a violation of international laws such as the American Convention of Human Rights and the Inter-American Convention on the Prevention, Punishment, and Eradication of Violence Against Women (Calderon Gamboa, 2007).

While it is unclear whether the victims' families will ever receive closure in the deaths of their loved ones, human rights organizations have called for a systematic reform of conditions to ensure the future safety of women in Ciudad Juárez. Their suggestions are presented within a framework designed to mend the cultural systems that historically have minimized the traumas of female victimizations. A key component of reform includes addressing the root causes of these murders by eliminating the *machista* culture that is prevalent in these communities. Suggestions include increasing employment opportunities for males in the *maquiladoras'* labor force, providing gender-sensitivity training for the workplace, and creating safe public spaces for women to gather in and travel to, from, and within the city of Ciudad Juárez (Calderon Gamboa, 2007).

Human Trafficking

The following scenarios, recorded by the U.S. Department of State through 2011, represent the experiences of actual trafficking victims: Rathana was born to a very poor family in Cambodia.

> When Rathana was 11 years old, her mother sold her to a woman in a neighboring province who sold ice in a small shop. Rathana worked for this woman and her husband for several months. She was beaten almost every day, and the shop owner never gave her much to eat. One day, a man came to the shop and bought Rathana from the ice seller. He then took her to a faraway province. When they arrived at his home, he showed Rathana a pornographic movie and then forced her to act out the movie by raping her. The man kept Rathana for more than eight months, raping her sometimes two or three times a day. One day, the man got sick and went to a hospital. He brought Rathana with him and raped her in the hospital bathroom. Another patient reported what was happening to the police. Rathana was rescued from this man and sent to live in a shelter for trafficking survivors.

> Salima was recruited in Kenya to work as a maid in Saudi Arabia. She was promised enough money to support herself and her two children. But when she arrived in Jeddah, she was forced to work 22 hours a day, cleaning 16 rooms daily for several months. She was never let out of the house and was given food only when her employers had leftovers. When there were no leftovers, Salima turned to dog food for sustenance. She suffered verbal and sexual abuse from her employers and their children. One day, while Salima was hanging clothes on the line, her employer pushed her out the window, telling her, "You are better off dead." Salina plunged into a swimming pool three floors down and was rescued by police. After a week in the hospital, she returned to Kenya with broken legs and hands.

> Katya, a student athlete in an Eastern European capital city, dreamed of learning English and visiting the United States. Her opportunity came in the form of a student visa program, through which international students can work temporarily in the United States. But when she got to America, rather than being taken to a job at a beach resort, the people who met her put her on a bus to Detroit, Michigan. They took her passport away and forced her and her friends to dance in strip clubs for the traffickers' profit. They controlled the girls' movement and

travel, kept keys to the girls' apartment, and listened in on phone calls the girls made to their parents. After a year of enslavement, Katya and her friend were able to reach federal authorities with the help of a patron of the strip club in whom they had confided. Due to their bravery, six other victims were identified and rescued. Katya now has immigration status under U.S. trafficking law (U.S. Department of State, 2011b).

Each of these scenarios represents a common story for female victims of human trafficking, many of whom are manipulated, abused, and exploited. These are but a few examples of the crimes that make up the category of human trafficking.

According to the U.S. **Trafficking Victims Protection Act** (TVPA), which was passed by Congress in 2000, human trafficking involves

> sex trafficking in which a commercial act is induced by force, fraud or coercion, or in which the person induced to perform such an act has not attained 18 years of age; or the recruitment, harboring, transportation provision, or obtaining a person for labor or services through the use of force, fraud or coercion for the purpose of subjection to involuntary servitude, peonage, debt bondage, or slavery. (U.S. Department of State, 2009, p. 7)

Human trafficking is the second-largest criminal activity and the fastest-growing criminal enterprise in the world. Estimates by the United Nations (2008) suggest that approximately 2.5 million people from 127 countries are victims of trafficking. Due to the nature of these crimes, it is difficult to determine a precise number of human trafficking victims worldwide. According to data provided by the U.S. State Department, between 600,000 and 820,000 men, women, and children are trafficked across international borders every year. These numbers do not include the thousands, and potentially millions, of individuals who are trafficked within the boundaries of their homelands (U.S. Department of State, 2011b).

Trafficking can involve cases within the borders of one's country as well as transport across international boundaries. Thailand is a well-known location for the sexual trafficking of women and girls who migrate from other Southeast Asian countries such as Cambodia, Laos, Myanmar (Burma), and Vietnam as well as other Asian countries such as China and Hong Kong. Other victims find their way to Thailand from the United Kingdom, South Africa, Czech Republic, Australia, and the United States (Rafferty, 2007). However, examples of trafficking are not limited to countries from the Southeast Asian region. The sexual trafficking of women and children is an international phenomenon and can be found in many regions around the world, even in the United States. Between January 2007 and September 2008, there were 1,229 documented incidents[1] of human trafficking in the United States. An astounding 83% of these cases were defined as alleged incidents of sex trafficking (such as forced prostitution and other sex crimes), of which 32% involved child sex trafficking and 62% involved adults (Kyckelhahn, Beck, & Cohen, 2009).

Traffickers use several methods to manipulate women and girls into the sex trade and prey on their poor economic standing and desires for improving their financial status. These enticements include offers of employment, marriage, and travel. Each of these opportunities is a ruse to trap women into sexual slavery. In some cases, women may be kidnapped or abducted, although these tactics are rare compared to the majority of cases, which involve lies, deceit, and trickery to collect victims (Simkhada,

2008). In some cases, young children are recruited by family friends or community members or may even be intentionally sold into servitude by their own parents. According to Rafferty (2007),

> traffickers use a number of coercive methods and psychological manipulations to maintain control over their victims and deprive them of their free will, to render them subservient and dependent by destroying their sense of self and connection to others, and to make their escape virtually impossible by destroying their physical and psychological defenses. The emotional and physical trauma, as well as the degradation associated with being subjected to humiliation and violence, treatment as a commodity, and unrelenting abuse and fear, presents a grave risk to the physical, psychological and social-emotional development of trafficking victims. (p. 410)

Victims are dependent on their traffickers for food, shelter, clothing, and safety. They may be trafficked to a region where they do not speak the language, which limits opportunities to seek assistance. They may be concerned for the safety of their family members, as many traffickers use threats against loved ones to ensure cooperation (Rafferty, 2007). Girls who are imprisoned in a **brothel** are often beaten and threatened in order to obtain compliance. They are reminded of their "debts," which they are forced to work off through the sale of their bodies. Most girls have little contact with the world outside the brothel and are unable to see or communicate with the family members that are left behind.

While some girls are able to escape the brothel life on their own, most require the intervention of police or social workers. Girls receive services from rehabilitation centers, which provide health care and social welfare assistance to victims of trafficking. The intent of these agencies is to return girls to their homes; however, many of these girls indicate they experience significant challenges upon return to their communities. Many of these girls are not looked upon as victims but rather as damaged goods when they return home. As such, they are shunned and stigmatized not only by society at large but also by their family members (Simkhada, 2008).

Despite being aware of trafficking as a social issue, many jurisdictions have failed to effectively address the problem in their communities. Much of the intervention efforts against trafficking involve nongovernmental organizations (NGOs), national and international anti-trafficking agencies, and local grassroots organizations. While several countries have adopted legislation that criminalizes the sale and exploitation of human beings, many have yet to enact anti-trafficking laws. In some cases, countries may have laws on the books but have limited resources or priorities for enforcing such laws. Still other countries punish the victims of these crimes, often charging them with crimes such as prostitution when they seek out assistance from the police. While grassroots and anti-trafficking organizations have developed policies and practices designed to punish traffickers and provide assistance to the victims, few of these recommendations have been implemented effectively or on a worldwide scale.

Defining Human Trafficking

Various terms are used to define *human trafficking*, sometimes called *trafficking in persons*. In the literature and official reports, *human trafficking* is the umbrella term used to describe several distinct types of forced human service. There are several types of trafficking in persons studied worldwide, including forced labor or involuntary servitude; debt bondage, particularly for migrant laborers; and sex trafficking. In addition, child victims of human trafficking often experience specific forms of exploitation given their age, including child soldiering, child sex trafficking, and child labor (Belser, 2005; Kara, 2009; United Nations, 2000; U.S. Department of State, 2011b). These are discussed below.

Forced labor is the coercion or exploitation of workers, especially persons who are vulnerable due to extreme poverty or unemployment or who are marginalized because of civil, racial, or political conflict. Such conditions often bring together vulnerable, disadvantaged people who have few resources and parties eager to exploit them. Immigrant populations, especially migrant workers, undocumented immigrants, and refugees, are particularly vulnerable to this type of human trafficking. In such cases, victims of forced labor trafficking are forced into labor as a type of involuntary servitude, where victims are forced to work against their will, often in the face of threatened or actual violence. In many of these cases, persons exploiting such victims make ownership claims, and victims have restricted freedom to leave, or they stay for fear of violence against themselves or a loved one. The International Labour Organization (2005) estimates that forced labor generates more than $30 billion worldwide every year. Women are disproportionately victimized in forced labor, often exploited in domestic servitude, forced factory labor, or various forms of sexual slavery, such as forced prostitution or pornography (U.S. Department of State, 2011b).

Debt bondage, or *bonded labor*, relies on the victim's belief in a debt owed, and the payment of debt is demanded as labor. Sometimes, the debt is inherited, leading to generations of debt bondage in some cases. In other cases, the debt is acquired as a condition of employment, and the employee essentially finds him or herself unable to leave exploitive employment because of the debt. Immigrants are particularly vulnerable to this type of human trafficking, especially when the debt is in the form of transportation costs, immigration fees, visas, or other documentation associated with immigration to, and gaining employment in, the country of employment. Unscrupulous employers capitalize on these costs, leaving the laborer with insurmountable debt they believe can only be repaid with continued forced labor (U.S. Department of Health and Human Services, 2011). In some cases, the risk of deportation facilitates debt bondage, as the worker's status in a foreign country (e.g., work permit, visas, or employment card, etc.) is tied to the employer (U.S. Department of State, 2011b). Thus, migrant laborers who cross borders in search of economic freedom often find themselves trapped in bonded labor indefinitely.

Sex trafficking is the form of human trafficking that is most widely discussed, and it generates great public fear and concern. Sex trafficking is the enslavement and transportation of a human for the purposes of sexual exploitation (Siddharth, 2009). This includes trafficking for sexual exploitation in strip clubs, pornographic film, prostitution, and other forced sexual servitude. Economically deprived and politically marginalized women are vulnerable to sex trafficking, as traffickers play on these vulnerabilities, often by advertising marriage (mail-order brides), education, or employment opportunities (Orlova, 2004). Women answering these ads often hope for a new start in a country with greater opportunities and freedoms yet find themselves in involuntary sexual servitude. However, sex trafficking is not limited to transportation of women from an economically disadvantaged country to another. Other vulnerable groups include runaways, drug addicts, and refugees as targets for sex trafficking (Hodge, 2008; Reid, 2011; U.S. Department of State, 2011b). In such cases, the trafficker is a pimp or madam who appears as a rescuer, promising protection and care, given the woman's disadvantaged situation. Instead of a better life, however, these women find themselves forced to perform in strip clubs, pornographic films, or as prostitutes (U.S. Department of State, 2011b).

Sex trafficking is not limited to international exploitation of disadvantaged women or the exploitation of immigrants, runaways, and drug addicts within a single country. Children are often at substantial risk for domestic sex trafficking within their own country. According to Kyckelhahn et al.'s (2009) analysis of official investigations of reported sex trafficking cases, nearly two-thirds of sex trafficking victims in the United States are U.S. citizens, and nearly one-third are under the age of 18. These are known, investigated cases. Other research estimates at least 100,000 victims of domestic sex trafficking in the United States, with another 325,000 youth at risk (Estes & Weiner, 2002; Hughes, 2007; U.S. Department of Justice, 2007b), leading Kotrla (2010) to suggest that youth are the group most vulnerable to sex trafficking in the United States.

Children are not only at increased risk for sex trafficking, they are also at risk for slavery and forced labor, child soldiering, and drug trafficking, particularly when they live in economically disadvantaged regions (Noguchi, 2002). Forced child labor is considered by the International Labour Organization as one of the worst forms of child labor and also one of the most difficult to eradicate (International Labour Organization, 2005). In instances of regional economic issues, children are essentially sold into slavery when a caregiver sends their child to another region for work, with the promise that the child will be able to earn enough money for a better life (U.S. Department of State, 2011b). Sometimes, these are cultural expectations codified by policymakers as "children's rights" or in support of "street families" (Droz, 2006). Once in the hand of a third party, however, the child has little recourse, and physical confinement, severe abuse, and near-starvation compel them to continue. These are difficult cases in which to intervene in some cases, as forced child laborers are often confined together outside the public view or they may appear to be under the care of a parent.

Likewise, *child soldiering* is a particularly egregious form of human trafficking. Child soldiering involves the acquisition of children for warfare, often in regions fraught with civil war. In the last century, government forces, rebels, and warring civil factions have taken children in war-torn areas, trained them to kill, and used them to achieve military ends (Singer, 2006; U.S. Department of State, 2011b). While all forms of human trafficking can involve male or female victims, this is the rare type that predominantly involves exploitation of boys. Both the Geneva Convention (1949) and the United Nations Convention on the Rights of the Child (1989) state that parties in a conflict "shall take all feasible measures" to avoid the use of soldiers under the age of 15. There is no U.N. provision for soldiering above age 15, and different countries permit armed services at ages 16 and above. However, the use of young child soldiers has been widespread in recent conflicts, most notably in Africa, where the United Nations (2003) reports an estimated 100,000 child soldiers. These include documented use of child soldiers, sometimes as young as seven years old, in armed conflicts in Chad, Congo, Rwanda, Sierra Leone, Somalia, Sudan, and Uganda, to name a few (Child Soldiers International, 2004). The issue of child soldiers is especially problematic when warlords use child soldiers for extreme acts of violence during conflict, such as mass murder and rape. For child soldiers who commit such acts, which would otherwise be considered war crimes, the *Paris Principles* (United Nations, 1991) apply, which, in essence, assures the treatment of child soldiers under age 15 as victims, not as war criminals.

Various forms of national legislation and international policy outline efforts to address human trafficking worldwide. While there is no uniform standard across jurisdictions, these generally include three basic themes involving the prosecution of traffickers, protection of victims, and prevention of human trafficking.

Case Study

Female Child Soldiers

Furaa, Girl Soldier

The genocide in Rwanda is known for many things, some previously discussed in this text; however, one of the most tragic is the use of female child soldiers. *Reuters* (Congo Case Study: Furaa, Girl Soldier, 2006) interviewed Furaa, a teenage girl and survivor of the Rwandan nightmare. She was pregnant for part of the time she spent fighting. Entered into the conflict because of an abusive father, Furaa spent three years on the front lines of the conflict fighting for the *Interahamwe*, a militant group of Hutu extremists:

> One day my father took the money that we had in the house and gave that money to a prostitute. Then he said that he would kill me, accusing me of taking the money he had given away. He took a machete and he wanted to kill me, but then some people came and tried to stop him.

> I entered the armed forces because of the situation with my father. I fought for the Interahamwe. I spent three years with my unit. We fought because we have to return to Rwanda through our own strength.

> Sometimes we carried many things—weapons, bullets, and if you had a child, you needed to carry the child as well.

> A spell was cast over me while I was with them, and I became ill for a year. They have no medicines there—only local medicinal herbs and plants. There was great suffering.

> The fighting was brutal, with very little protection given to the children. Terror ran rampant throughout the ranks.

> It was strong war—a terrible war. The higher officers were scared of the war. As I was a sub-officer, when they gave me orders to go in front, I couldn't ignore the orders. In one battle, I fought against some Tutsis and was harmed. They shot me. Happily I was wearing new boots and the bullet didn't enter into my leg.

Furaa was also forced to take a husband; she was not yet 13 years old Though she did not enter into marriage by choice, her husband acted as a protector and guardian, as many in the Interahamwe tended to do. When he was caught and imprisoned for pillaging a home, she was forced, all by herself, to subsist among thieves and plunderers. Many of those in her "armed group," as she calls it, stole others' belongings in the course of their attacks:

> In general, as we were in a forest, the men looked after and stayed with their women. When the men were pillaging people's villages, they would rape women. But at that time they wouldn't take us with them.

Furaa has since found freedom, and she was reunited with her husband at a transit center some years later. But not all are so lucky. Nagle (2011) highlights the fact that many children are coerced into soldiering through drugs and brainwashing. Further, of those who survive, many are socially ostracized and cast out of society, leading lives of crime, murder, and hopelessness (p. 3). It is further noted that while girls face unique problems as children of combat (through rape, pregnancy, and a multitude of patriarchal practices), both boys and girls are recruited equally to be thrown onto the front lines of often-bloody conflicts (Lara, 2011).

Human Trafficking in the United States

In the United States, legislation known as the Trafficking Victims Protection Act (TVPA)[2] is designed to punish traffickers, protect victims, and facilitate prevention efforts in the community to fight against human trafficking. Enacted by Congress in 2000, the law provides that traffickers can be sent to prison for up to 20 years for each victim. In 2008, the U.S. Department of Justice obtained 77 convictions in 40 cases of human trafficking, with an average sentence of 112 months (9.3 years). Over two-thirds of these cases involved acts of sex trafficking. At the state level, 42 states currently have anti-trafficking legislation in their jurisdictions and are active in identifying offenders and victims of these crimes (U.S. Department of State, 2008).

While the TVPA includes protection and assistance for victims, these provisions are limited. For example, victims of trafficking are eligible for a **T-visa**, which provides a temporary visa. However, there are only 5,000 T-visas available (regardless of the numbers of demand for these visas), and issuance of this type of visa is limited to "severe forms of trafficking [such as those] involving force, fraud or coercion or any trafficking involving a minor" (Haynes, 2004, p. 241). In addition, applications for permanent residency are conditional on a victim's participation as a potential witness in a trafficking prosecution. In the two years following the implementation of the T-visa program, only 23 visas had been granted, a far cry from the demand, given that over 50,000 people are trafficked into the United States alone each year (Oxman-Martinez & Hanley, 2003).

Global Response to Human Trafficking

In 2000, the United Nations proposed the ***Protocol to Prevent, Suppress and Punish Trafficking in Persons, especially Women and Children***. This multinational legal agreement was developed in an effort to facilitate international cooperation in detecting and prosecuting persons responsible for human trafficking. It also aimed to articulate basic human rights and protect human trafficking victims worldwide. However, resulting changes have been slow in coming. Although in effect since 2003, it only applies to countries that have agreed to comply with the Protocol. As of 2011, 147 countries have accepted, approved, or ratified the Protocol; however, many of these countries have raised procedural and jurisdictional objections to the Protocol and have carved out jurisdictional exceptions. Specifically, 28 nations submitted declarations and reservations pursuant to the ratification of the Protocol, including the United States. Most commonly, countries have objected to the provision for third-party arbitration in the event of a conflict involving another country. This is a rather ironic and unfortunate exception, given that some of the most egregious human trafficking cases are, by their very definition, transnational crimes. Yet, many countries that have agreed to the Protocol will not accept arbitration in transnational human trafficking cases. Thus, while successful in articulating worldwide concern over the problem of human trafficking, the Protocol has not been successful in coordinating or facilitating action. Simply put, it has no teeth.

A U.N. resolution is not the only transnational solution to human trafficking. Many nations have established policies and laws that articulate international protocols with neighboring nations and set priorities in human trafficking cases. In fact, one beneficial ancillary to the Protocol is the creation of a "3P anti-trafficking policy index," which essentially evaluates the anti-trafficking policies and laws in a given country and allows for ranking of a country according to its anti-trafficking policies (Cho, Dreher, & Neumayer, 2011). The index considers three elements of anti-trafficking policy: *prosecution* of traffickers, *protection* for trafficking victims, and *prevention* of trafficking crimes. In the last decade, anti-trafficking policies have improved globally, especially prosecution policy. However, protection policy has decline slightly in the same period, suggesting that in the decade since the U.N. Protocol was written, policies protecting human trafficking victims have actually eroded. Despite this, the 2009 ranking identified seven countries with high scores (5 out of 5) on each of the three policy areas. These countries were Australia, Belgium, Germany, Italy, Netherlands, Sweden, and the United States. While an encouraging start, the scores for these countries indicate the extent to which they have established policies for prosecuting trafficking offenders, protecting trafficking victims, and preventing cases of human trafficking; they do not indicate the extent to which a given country has decreased the prevalence of human trafficking in their jurisdiction.

Similar to the TVPA in the United States and as suggested by Cho et al. (2011), the European Union (EU) policies on trafficking prioritize the prosecution of offenders over the needs of victims, and visas are granted only for the purposes of pursuing charges against the traffickers. In addition, there is no encouragement or pressure by the EU for states to develop programs to address the needs of trafficked victims (Haynes, 2004). While the push to jail the offender of these crimes appears positive, the reality is that few prosecutions have succeeded in achieving this task. Even in cases where prosecutions are successful and traffickers are held accountable for their crimes, their convictions result in short sentences and small fines, the effect of which does little to deter individuals from participating in these offenses in the future.

In contrast to the prosecution-oriented approach, several international organizations have developed models to fight trafficking that focus on the needs of the victim. These approaches focus on the security and safety of the victim, allowing them to regain control over their lives and empowering them to make positive choices for their future while receiving housing and employment assistance. While this approach provides valuable resources for victims, it does little to control and stop the practice of trafficking from continuing.

Promising Solutions to End Human Trafficking

Given the limitations of the *jail the offender* and *protect the victim* models, research by Haynes (2004) provides several policy recommendations that would combine the best aspects of these two approaches. These recommendations include the following actions:

1. Protect, don't prosecute, the victim—As indicated earlier, many victims find themselves charged with prostitution and other crimes in their attempts to seek help. Not only does this process punish the victim, but it serves to inhibit additional victims from coming forward out of fear that they too might be subjected to criminal punishments. Anti-trafficking legislation needs to ensure that victims will not be prosecuted for the actions in which they engaged as a part of their trafficked status. In addition, victims need to be provided with shelter and care to meet their immediate needs following an escape from their trafficker.

2. Develop community awareness and educational public service campaigns—Many victims of trafficking do not know where to turn for help. An effective media campaign could provide victims with information on how to recognize if they are in an exploitative situation, avenues for assistance such as shelters and safety options, and long-term planning support such as information on immigration. Media campaigns can also help educate the general public on the ways in which traffickers entice their victims and provide information on reporting potential victims to local agencies. Recent examples of prevention efforts in fighting trafficking have included raising public awareness through billboard campaigns; the development of a national hotline to report

possible human trafficking cases; and public service announcements in several languages, including English, Spanish, Russian, Korean, and Arabic, to name a few (U.S. Department of State, 2009). These efforts help increase public knowledge about the realities of human trafficking within the community.

3. Address the social and economic reasons for vulnerability to trafficking—The road to trafficking begins with poverty. Economic instability creates vulnerability for women as they migrate from their communities in search of a better life. For many, the migration from their homes to the city places them at risk for traffickers, who seek out these women and promise them employment opportunities, only to hold them against their will for the purposes of forced labor and slavery. Certainly, the road to eradicating poverty around the world is an insurmountable task, but an increased understanding of how and why women leave could inform educational campaigns, which could relay information about the risks and dangers of trafficking and provide viable options for legitimate employment and immigration.

4. Prosecute traffickers and those who aid and abet traffickers—Unfortunately, in many of these jurisdictions, law enforcement and legal agents are subjected to bribery and corruption, which limits the assistance that victims of trafficking may receive.

   Police are known to tip off club workers suspected of harboring trafficked women in order to give owners time to hide women or supply false working papers [and] are also known to accept bribes, supply false papers or to turn a blind eye to the presence of undocumented foreigners. (Haynes, 2004, p. 257)

   In order to effectively address this issue, police and courts need to eliminate corruption from their ranks. In addition, agents of justice need to pursue cases in earnest and address the flaws that exist within the system in order to effectively identify, pursue, and punish the offenders of these crimes.

5. Create immigration solutions for trafficked persons—An effective immigration policy for victims of trafficking serves two purposes: Not only does it provide victims with legal residency rights and protections but it also helps pursue criminal prosecutions against traffickers, especially since the few effective prosecutions have relied heavily on victim cooperation and testimony. At its most fundamental position, victims who are unable to obtain even temporary visas will be unable to legally remain in the country and assist the courts in bringing perpetrators to justice. In addition, victims who are offered immigration visas contingent upon their participation in a prosecution run the risk of jeopardizing potential convictions, as defense attorneys may argue that the promise of residency could encourage an alleged victim to perjure his or her testimony. Finally, the limited opportunities to obtain permanent visa status amount to winning the immigration lottery in many cases, as these opportunities are few and far between and often involve complex applications and long waiting periods.

6. Implement the laws—At the end of the day, policy recommendations and legislation does little good if such laws are not vigorously pursued and enforced against individuals and groups participating in the trafficking of humans. In addition, such convictions need to carry stern and significant financial and incarceration punishments if they hope to be an effective tool in solving the problem of human trafficking.

While efforts to prioritize the implementation of anti-trafficking laws may slow the progress of these crimes against humanity, the best efforts toward prevention focus on eliminating the need for people to migrate in search of opportunities to improve their economic condition. An ecological perspective suggests that the cause of trafficking lies within issues such as poverty, economic inequality, dysfunction within the family, gender inequality, discrimination, and the demand for victims for prostitution and cheap labor. At its heart, human trafficking "is a crime that deprives people of their human rights and freedoms, increases global health risks, fuels growing networks of organized crime and can sustain levels of poverty and impede development in certain areas" (U.S. Department of State, 2009, p. 5). Until these large-scale systemic issues are addressed, the presence of trafficking will endure within our global society.

Immigration Issues in the United States

According to the U.S. Office of Immigration Statistics, the United States has an estimated 31,950,000 foreign-born immigrants. This includes roughly 21 million foreign-born legal residents and another 10.8 million who are undocumented immigrants (Hoefer, Rytina, & Baker, 2011). More than half of these are from Central America, and Mexico (60%). The rise in numbers of immigrants, combined with racial/ethnic tension enticed by terrorism fears and the perceived economic impact of undocumented immigrants, makes this population ripe for victimization.

The Illegal Immigration Reform and Immigrant Responsibility Act (1996) has led to increased deportations in the United States, yet there remain more than 10 million undocumented persons in the United States, including 6 to 7 million undocumented migrant workers from Mexico (Hoefer, Rytina, & Baker, 2009, 2011; Passel, 2006). While many U.S. citizens fear crime perpetrated by Mexican immigrants, fewer than 3% of immigrants are involved in crime. Criminal convictions of undocumented persons are, in more than 81% of cases, due to their unlawful entrance into the United States. Some research suggests that, aside from the crime of unlawful entry, immigrants are less likely to commit crime, especially violent crime, than native-born persons. As but one example, Sorenson and Lew (2000) report that native persons are 1.3 times more likely to commit homicide as immigrants, based on a sample from Los Angeles, California.

Rather than being the source of crime, undocumented immigrants are more often the object of it. Velazquez and Kempf-Leonard (2010) suggest that 11% of immigrants to the U.S. are victimized by crime, often because of "the obviousness of their vulnerabilities" and due to hostilities about immigration status, which leads to at-risk situations (p. 145). Fussell (2011) argues that this undocumented status results in a near-constant threat of deportation. This creates a *deportation threat dynamic*, whereby undocumented workers seek (and find) work with unscrupulous employers who prey on this vulnerability. The undocumented status of workers allows employers to withhold earned wages (*wage theft*) and commit other abuses, as they count on **deportation fear** to limit reporting of crimes to authorities. The fear of deportation may leave undocumented immigrants vulnerable to the kinds of human trafficking, such as forced labor, sexual exploitation, and bond labor, discussed in this chapter.

Research also documents the increased risk of economic, sexual, and violent victimization for undocumented immigrants beyond the obvious risk posed by unscrupulous employers. Peguero (2009), for example, reports that children of immigrants are more fearful at school than children of native-born parents, and they have good reason to be: Children of immigrant parents are at increased risk of violent victimization such as assault, especially at school, than children of native-born parents. Likewise, Decker, Raj, and Silverman (2007) found that immigrant girls are not only at higher risk of sexual assault, they are at higher risk of *recurring* sexual victimization than native-born girls in the United States. Increased risk is not limited to economic, physical, and sexual victimization; it also extends to homicide. Some research suggests immigrants are at higher risk of being murdered than native-born persons, yet native-born persons are 1.3 times more likely to commit homicide than immigrants (Sorenson & Lew, 2000).

Given the high risk for victimization and high rates of actual victimization for immigrants in the United States, efforts have been made to provide appropriate resources. The Trafficking Victims Protection Act (TVPA) authorizes the issuance of not only T-visas for trafficking victims but also **U-visas** to crime victims who are noncitizens, including undocumented immigrants. The U.S. Citizenship and Immigration Service (2010a) advertises U-visas to provide protection for undocumented immigrants who are victims of crime. Victims who wish to obtain a U-visa must obtain certification from a law enforcement agency and meet the following criteria: (1) be a crime victim who has suffered "substantial physical or mental abuse" from the crime; (2) possess substantial information about the crime; (3) be willing to assist in prosecution; and (4) be a victim of crime that violated U.S. law.

While this is a good start, legal scholars have articulated many concerns with the U-visa and note the low rates of U-visas issued in the years following inception. In fact, not a single U-visa was issued between the time the U-visa was authorized (2000) and 2007, the year a class-action lawsuit was filed against the government for failing to issue regulations on the U-visa (Bernstein, 2007). Congress subsequently published specific rules governing the U-visa. During this interim seven-year period, temporary remedies were sometimes granted in lieu of the visas in certain cases, but these were the exception (Dinnerstein, 2008). There is also an equal protection controversy with the U-visa, which essentially provides rights to noncitizen victims not afforded citizen victims, particularly in regards to the protections afforded indirect victims of crime. As McCormick (2011) argues, "since the statute required that the crime victim be an alien, it seemed to exclude from protection the non-citizen family members of U.S. citizen victims" (p. 590). This is of particular concern when one considers that citizen child victims are given neither the protections of adult citizens, who can petition for citizenship of noncitizen family members, or the protections of noncitizen crime victims, whose family members can apply for the U-visa. Nevertheless, the U.S. Citizenship and Immigration Services began issuing U-visas in 2007 and, in 2010, reached the statutory maximum of 10,000 U-visas for that year. These are important steps in combating victimization of immigrants in the United States, but we have yet to address the primary barrier that keeps immigrant victims from seeking help—fear of deportation.

Rape as a War Crime

Is rape an element of war? Reports of rape as a consequence of war date as far back as human history. In the Bible, for example, Isaiah's account of the war in Babylon reads, "Anyone who is captured will be cut down—run through with a sword. Their little children will be dashed to death before their eyes. Their homes will be sacked, and their wives will be raped" (Isaiah 13:15–16). Likewise, Homer's *Iliad* documents war rape in his account of the rape (abduction) of Helen, with themes echoed by the Thebian poet Colluthus in *The Rape of Helen,* written in the early 6th century. Gengis Khan is believed to have regularly perpetrated rape against conquered people, possibly as an element of psychological warfare, in 12th-century Mongolia (Man, 2004). Japanese commanders were faulted for failing to prevent war rape in the Nanking Massacre in the Second Sino-Japanese War. Reports of rape in World War II abound, including rape of Jewish women by Nazis and rape of Japanese women by troops (Levene & Roberts, 1999; Lilly, 2007). Given the centuries-old practice of rape during war, is rape simply an unfortunate element of human warfare?

Arguably, the rape of women subsequent to war may be a reflection of traditional views of women as property. Thus, the rape of a woman during war was a property crime against the man who rightfully owned her. However engrained this idea has been throughout history, modern scholars, leaders, and humanitarians consider rape as an act of war a crime against humanity.

War rape typically involves the sexual assault of women by invading male soldiers. War rape is unlawful under the Fourth Geneva Convention (1949) as well as Protocol 1 relating to the Protection of Victims of International Armed Conflicts (1977), ratified by 170 countries. Rape was certainly involved in military actions following the Fourth Geneva Convention in 1949: Conflicts in the former Yugoslavia in the 1990s resulted in atrocious treatment of women (including mass gang rape, sexual torture, and sexual enslavement) perpetrated by soldiers, officials, and men in authority. Rape during warfare was first declared a "crime against humanity" given the egregious and widespread sexual violence in this conflict, by the International Criminal Tribunal for the former Yugoslavia, with estimates that as many as 50,000 women were raped during this time. What is particularly troubling is not only the number of women who were sexually brutalized but the circumstances under which these crimes occurred. Most reports suggest that mass rape was often part of a larger effort toward **ethnic cleansing**. For example, many of these reports involved rape of Croatian and Muslim women by Serbian men for the purpose of intentional impregnation. In many other reports, women were raped by multiple men, with many witnesses present. These violent attacks were arguably designed to make the targeted victims—Croatians—flee, resulting in ethnic cleansing of the region (de Brouwer, 2005; Human Rights Watch, 2001).

Likewise, armed conflict in Rwanda in 1994 led to the mass rape of perhaps 500,000 Tutsi girls and women, resulting in 3,000–5,000 pregnancies (de Brouwer, 2005). Given the cultural expectation that children are the ethnicity of their father, the magnitude of these war-based sexual assaults constitutes **genocide**, according to the International Criminal Tribunal for Rwanda (1999), which argued that war-based rape was an intentional and systematic effort to destroy a specific ethnic group, thereby constituting the crime of genocide. Similar atrocities involving sexual violence during war have been well documented in recent conflicts in Sri Lanka, Sudan, Iraq, Colombia, Chad, and Afghanistan, to name a few.

Most recently, conflict in the Republic of Congo has garnered worldwide attention. In 2008, the United Nations recorded more than 16,000 cases of war rape in a single year, which leaves current estimates at around 200,000 people, most commonly girls and women, as the victims of sexual assault perpetrated during war in that region (Peterman, Palermo, & Bredenkamp, 2011). The International Criminal Court is currently prosecuting Congan officials for crimes against humanity, including rape and sexual slavery during the military conflict in that region (International Criminal Court, 2011). In 2011, allegations of war rape in Libya captured the media. In fact, at the time of this writing, the International Criminal Court is considering charges against Libyan officials for hundreds of sexual assaults perpetrated as a war tactic during an eight-month conflict ("ICC Prosecutor May Bring Libya Rape Charges," 2011).

Case Study
Female Genital Mutilation

Mariam Jelle was taken from her Bristol home to Somalia in the school holidays when she was nine. There she underwent female genital mutilation. She says: "I remember my mother holding me between my legs and the woman cutting me. I was told not to scream or I would not get any presents." (Learner, 2012, p. 1)

In a short but poignant article, Sue Learner (2012) broaches the topic of female genital mutilation (also known as *female genital cutting* or *female circumcision*) through a heartbreakingly human lens. Detailing the stories of several British girls, she recounts their experiences of being taken from their homes, flown to various locations in Africa, and held down while women removed their external sexual organs. Often undergone without anesthetic, these procedures are done to purify and cleanse the girls in order to make them more appealing as marriage prospects. In some cases, the vaginal lips are sewn shut, ensuring men's ability to determine whether or not their betrothed still retains her virginity. Yirga, Kassa, Gebremichael, and Aro (2012) list the four types of female genital mutilation:

Type 1, partial or total removal of the clitoris and/or the prepuce (clitoridectomy); type 2, partial or total removal of the clitoris and labia minora, with or without excision of the labia majora (excision); type 3, narrowing of the vaginal orifice with creation of a covering seal by cutting and appositioning the labia minora and/or the labia majora, with or without excision of the clitoris (infibulation); and type 4, all other harmful procedures to the female genitalia for nonmedical purposes, e.g., pricking, piercing, incising, scraping, and cauterization. (p. 46)

(Continued)

(Continued)

Tragically, despite regulatory efforts, this is not a problem that is going away. FORWARD—the Foundation for Women's Health Research and Development—(2012) reports that between 100 and 140 million African women annually are genitally mutilated. A 2012 study by the World Health Organization revealed that Sierra Leone and Gambia, both countries in Africa, retained staggering percentages of individuals continuing this practice (Sipsma et al., 2012). In Sierra Leone, for instance, 94% of women had been circumcised, while nearly 79% of women in Gambia faced the same issue. Further, approximately 88% and 77%, respectively, believed that the practice should continue. Yirga et al. (2012) further contribute that in eastern Ethiopia, as many as 94% of adult women have undergone this procedure. Studies have shown that this belief is related to lack of education; however, outreach efforts are currently being conducted in an attempt to decrease its prevalence (Simister, 2010).

The health effects suffered because of this practice are debilitating. FORWARD (2012) reports that infection and sterilization are major concerns; many of the individuals carrying out the procedures have no medical training. "Basic tools such as knives, scissors, scalpels, pieces of glass and razor blades" (FORWARD, 2012, para. 3) are used in conjunction with iodine and herbal remedies to both tighten the wound and staunch any bleeding. Long-term effects include damage to the reproductive system, cysts, neuromas, pregnancy complications, sexual and menstrual dysfunctions and difficulties, as well as a variety of psychological ailments (FORWARD, 2012, "Consequences").

As mentioned, several regulatory efforts have been implemented. The World Health Organization conducts extensive research and public awareness campaigns in hopes of educating African women about the detrimental effects of genital mutilation (World Health Organization, 2012). FORWARD similarly conducts outreach in the United Kingdom among African and Malaysian families (Learner, 2012).

SUMMARY

- Honor-based violence involves the murder of women for violating gendered cultural norms. Death is required in order to restore the honor of a woman's family in the community.
- Women who have been killed in the name of honor are typically killed for acts of sexual impropriety, alleged infidelity, or for becoming too Westernized.
- Most incidents of honor-based violence are committed by a male family member, such as a father, husband, brother, or cousin.
- Even though some jurisdictions have laws against the practice, offenders of honor-based violence are rarely punished, as the killings are an accepted practice within the communities.
- Efforts toward reducing or eliminating honor-based violence include legal reform, education and public awareness, and additional resources for victim services.
- Human trafficking involves the exploitation of individuals for the purposes of forced labor or involuntary servitude, debt bondage, and sexual exploitation. The majority of these cases involve sexual exploitation and abuse, and human trafficking disproportionately affects women.

- Children are at risk for specific types of human trafficking, including child labor, child sex trafficking, and child soldiering.
- Human trafficking is an international phenomenon, with hundreds of thousands of victims trafficked within and across borders every year.
- Traffickers prey on women from poor communities and appeal to their interests in improving their economic standing as a method of enticing them into exploitative and manipulative work environments.
- Many countries have failed to effectively address the problem of trafficking in their communities, where the majority of offenders go undetected. In the rare cases where a trafficker is brought to justice, their punishments rarely involve significant incarceration or financial penalties.
- International efforts to combat human trafficking have focused on "3Ps": *prosecution* of traffickers, *protection* of victims, and *prevention* of trafficking cases, but there has been little international progress to reduce the prevalence of human trafficking worldwide.
- Recommendations for best practices against trafficking involve combining features from *jail the offender* and *protect the victim* models, and seek to improve victim services, increase public awareness about trafficking, and implement and enforce stricter laws against the practice.
- The pattern of femicides in Ciudad Juárez, Mexico, involves the violent rape and torture of hundreds of women and girls who travel from their homes in search of work in factories, where they endure poor working conditions and are paid little for their labor.
- There have been few convictions for trafficking crimes, and most of the cases are unresolved. Victim blaming is a common practice, and many families and victim-rights groups have protested over the lack of attention paid to these incidents.
- Some scholars point toward the clash between the traditional roles of women, the *machista* culture, and the rise of women's independence as an explanation for the violence in Ciudad Juárez.
- *War rape* refers to the sexual assault of citizens by soldiers and officials during war and conflict.
- War rape has been common in human history and was criminalized in the Fourth Geneva Convention (1949).
- Worldwide accounts of war rape today have been reported in many countries, with the sexual atrocities amounting to crimes against humanity, ethnic cleansing, and genocide.
- The United States now issues two special visa for victims: the T-visa for human trafficking victims and the U-visa for noncitizen victims of crime.
- Immigrant populations are at greater risk of victimization than native-born groups, often due to deportation fear.

KEY TERMS

Brothel	*Jail the offender* and *protect the victim* models	Protocol to Prevent, Suppress and Punish Trafficking in Persons, especially Women and Children
Deportation fear		
Ethnic cleansing	Karo-kari	
Femicide	Las muertas de Juárez/Dead women of Juárez	Trafficking Victims Protection Act
Genocide		
Honor-based violence	Machista	T-visa and U-visa
Human trafficking	Maquiladoras	Westernized

DISCUSSION QUESTIONS

1. How is the pattern of femicides in Ciudad Juárez linked to larger social issues such as patriarchy, masculine identity, and the entry of women into the workforce?

2. What steps have local and national agencies in Mexico taken to solve the cases of *las muertas de Juárez*? How have these efforts failed the families of the victims?

3. How is the concept of shame created in cultures where honor-based violence is prevalent?

4. To what extent are offenders in honor-based violence cases punished? What measures need to be implemented to protect women from these crimes?

5. How do women enter and exit the experience of sexual trafficking?

6. Compare and contrast the *jail the offender* and the *protect the victim* models of trafficking enforcement. What are the best practices that can be implemented from these two models to address the needs of trafficking victims?

7. Why have international efforts to combat human trafficking been unsuccessful to date? In what ways can nations facilitate the international efforts to prosecute traffickers, protect victims, and prevent trafficking?

8. What distinguishes war rape from other kinds of rape? What characteristics of war rape have led to the assertion of war rape as a crime against humanity? How is war rape used in the process of ethnic cleansing? In what way might war rape be consider genocide?

9. What caused the delay in issuing T-visas and U-visas to crime victims in the United States? What solutions might facilitate issuance of these visas in the future?

WEB RESOURCES

HumanTrafficking.org http://www.humantrafficking.org

Not for Sale http://www.notforsalecampaign.org/about/slavery/

Polaris Project http://www.polarisproject.org/

U.S. Department of State: Trafficking in Persons Report 2011 http://www.state.gov/g/tip/rls/tiprpt/2011/index.htm

Women of Juárez http://womenofJuárez.egenerica.com/

Women on the Border http://womenontheborder.org/

REFERENCES

Agosin, M. (2006). *Secrets in the sand: The young women of Juárez*. New York, NY: White Pine Press.
Amnesty International. (1999). *Document—Pakistan: Violence against women in the name of honour*. Retrieved from http://amnesty.org/en/library/asset/ASA33/017/1999/en/53f9cc64-e0f2-11dd-be39-2d4003be4450/asa330171999en.html

Amnesty International. (2003). *Intolerable killings: 10 years of abductions and murders of women in Ciudad Juárez and Chihuahua.* New York, NY: Author.

Arin, C. (2001). Femicide in the name of honor in Turkey. *Violence Against Women, 7*(7), 821–825.

Belser, P. (2005, March). Forced labor and human trafficking: Estimating the profits. *Declaration on Fundamental Principles and Rights at Work and International Labour Office.* Paper 17. Retrieved from http://digitalcom mons.ilr.cornell.edu/forcedlabor/17

Bernstein, N. (2007, March 7). Special visas for victims remain elusive despite a law. *New York Times.* Retrieved from http://www.nytimes.com/2007/03/07/nyregion/07visas.html?pagewanted=all&_r=0

Brooke, J. (1991, March 29). 'Honor' killing of wives is outlawed in Brazil. *New York Times.* Retrieved from http://www.nytimes.com/1991/03/29/us/honor-killing-of-wives-is-outlawed-in-brazil.html.

Calderon Gamboa, J. (2007, Winter). Seeking integral reparations for the murders and disappearances of women in Ciudad Juárez: A gender and cultural perspective. *Human Rights Brief, 14*(2), 31–35. Retrieved from http://www.wcl.american.edu/hrbrief/14/2calderon.pdf

Castillo, E. E. (2003, May 6). Federal Mexican authorities accuse state prosecutors of blocking investigation in border slayings. *Atlanta Journal Constitution.* Retrieved from http://takenbythesky.net/Juárez/may6_2003.html

Chamberlain, L. (2007). 2 cities and 4 bridges where commerce flows. *New York Times,* p. 28.

Chesler, P. (2010, Spring). Worldwide trends in honor killings. *Middle East Quarterly,* pp. 3–11.

Child Soldiers International. (2004). *Child soldier global report 2004: Africa regional overview.* London, England: Coalition to Stop the Use of Child Soldiers. Retrieved from http://www.child-soldiers.org/user_uploads/pdf/globalreporttextweb7361911.pdf

Cho, S.-Y., Dreher, A., & Neumayer, E. (2011). The spread of anti-trafficking policies—Evidence from a new index. Discussion Paper Series No. 119. Georg-August- Universität Göttingen, Germany. (Also IZA Discussion paper No. 5559 and CESifo Working Paper 3376)

Congo case study: Furaa, girl soldier. (2006, July 7). *Reuters.* Retrieved from http://www.trust.org/alertnet/news/congo-case-study-furaa-girl-soldier/

de Brouwer, A.-M. (2005). *Supranational criminal prosecution of sexual violence.* Oxford, England: Intersentia. Retrieved from www.gbv.de/dms/spk/sbb/toc/505732521.pdf

Decker, M. R., Raj, A., & Silverman, J. G. (2007). Sexual violence against adolescent girls. *Violence Against Women, 13*(5), 498–513.

Dillon, S. (1998). 70 deaths unsolved in Juárez. *New York Times.* Retrieved from http://takenbythesky.net/Juárez/feb_1999.html

Dinnerstein, J. E. (2008). The "new" and exciting U: No longer just my imaginary friend. *Immigration & Nationality Law Handbook, 2008–2009.* Washington, DC: American Immigration Lawyers Association.

The disappearing women of Juárez. (2002). *Revolutionary Worker #1166.* Retrieved from http://revcom.us/a/v24/1161-1170/1166/Juárez.htm

Droz, Y. (2006). Street children and the work ethic: New policy for an old moral, Nairobi (Kenya). *Childhood, 13*(2), 349–363.

Ensalaco, M. (2006). Murder in Ciudad Juárez: A parable of women's struggle for human rights. *Violence Against Women, 12*(5), 417–449.

Esfandiari, G. (2006). Afghanistan: Rights watchdog alarmed at continuing "honor killings." *Women's United Nations Report Network.* Retrieved from http://www.wunrn.com/news/2006/09_25_06/100106_afghanistan_violence.htm

Estes, R. J., & Weiner, N. A. (2002). *The commercial sexual exploitation of children in the U.S., Canada and Mexico.* Philadelphia: University of Pennsylvania, School of Social Work, Center for the Study of Youth Policy. Retrieved from http://www.sp2.upenn.edu/restes/CSEC_Files/Exec_Sum_020220.pdf

Felix, Q. (2005). Human rights in Pakistan: Violence and misery for children and women. *Asia News.* Retrieved from http://www.asianews.it/news-en/Human-rights-in-Pakistan:-violence-and-misery-for-children-and-women-2554.html

Foundation for Women's Health, Research and Development (FORWARD). (2012). *Female genital mutilation.* Retrieved from http://www.forwarduk.org.uk/key-issues/fgm

Fussell, E. (2011). The deportation threat dynamic and victimization of Latino migrants: Wage theft and robbery. *Sociological Quarterly, 52*(4), 593–615.

Haynes, D. F. (2004). Used, abused, arrested and deported: Extending immigration benefits to protect the victims of trafficking and to secure the prosecution of traffickers. *Human Rights Quarterly, 26*(2), 221–272.

Haynes, D. (2007). (Not) found chained to a bed in a brothel: Conceptual, legal, and procedural failures to fulfill the promise of the Trafficking Victims Protection Act. *Georgetown Immigration Law Journal, 21*(3), 337–381.

Herrick, T. (1998, May 10). *Feminists decry police handling of murders in border city.* Retrieved from http://taken bythesky.net/Juárez/may10_1998.htm

Hodge, D. R. (2008). Sexual trafficking in the United States: A domestic problem with transnational dimensions. *Social Work, 52,* 143–152.

Hoefer, M., Rytina, N., & Baker, B. C. (2009). *Estimates of the unauthorized immigrant population residing in the United States: January 2008.* Washington, DC: Office of Immigration Statistics, Policy Directorate, U.S. Department of Homeland Security. Retrieved from http://www.dhs.gov/xlibrary/assets/statistics/publica tions/ois_ill_pe 2008.pdf

Hoefer, M., Rytina, N., & Baker, B. C. (2011). *Estimates of the unauthorized immigrant population residing in the United States: January 2010.* Washington, DC: Office of Immigration Statistics. Retrieved from http://www .dhs.gov/xlibrary/assets/statistics/publications/ois_ill_pe_2010.pdf

Hughes, D. (2007, July 30). Enslaved in the U.S.A. *National Review Online.* Retrieved from http://www .nationalreview.com/articles/221700/enslaved-u-s/donna-m-hughes

Human Rights Watch. (2001). Bosnia: Landmark verdicts for rape, torture and sexual enslavement. *Human Rights Watch.* Retrieved from http://www.hrw.org/news/2001/02/22/bosnia-landmark-verdicts-rape-torture-and-sexual-enslavement

ICC prosecutor may bring Libya rape charges. (2011). *Reuters.* Retrieved from http://af.reuters.com/article/topNews/idAFJOE7A80CK20111109

Inter-American Commission on Human Rights. (2003). *The situation of the rights of women in Ciudad Juárez, Mexico: The right to be free from violence and discrimination.* Retrieved from http://www.cidh.org/annualrep/2002eng/chap.vi.Juárez.htm

International Criminal Court. (2011). *Situation in the Democratic Republic of the Congo.* Retrieved from http://www2.icc-cpi.int/Menus/ICC/Situations+and+Cases/Situations/Situation+ICC+0104/

International Criminal Tribunal for Rwanda. (1999). *Fourth annual report of the International Criminal Tribunal for Rwanda to the general assembly.* Retrieved from http://www.unictr.org/

International Labour Organization. (2005). *A global alliance against forced labour.* Geneva, Switzerland: United Nations.

Kara, S. (2009). *Sex trafficking: Inside the business of modern slavery.* New York, NY: Columbia University Press.

Kardam, N. (2005). Gender and institutions: Creating an enabling environment. *United Nations Division for the Advancement of Women.* Retrieved from http://www.un.org/womenwatch/daw/egm/enabling-environ ment2005/docs/EGM-WPD-EE-2005-EP.9.pdf

Korteweg, A. C. (2012). Understanding honour killing and honour-related violence in the immigration context: Implications for the legal profession and beyond. *Canadian Criminal Law Review, 16,* 135–160.

Kotrla, K. (2010). Domestic minor sex trafficking in the United States. *Social Work, 55*(2), 181–187.

Kyckelhahn, T., Beck, A. J., & Cohen, T. H. (2009). Characteristics of suspected human trafficking incidents. *Bureau of Justice Statistics Special Report.* U.S. Department of Justice, Office of Justice Programs. Retrieved from http://www.ojp.usdoj.gov/bjs/abstract/cshti08.htm

Lara, C. E. (2011). Child soldier testimony used in prosecuting war crimes in the International Criminal Court: Preventing further victimization. *Southwestern Journal of International Law, 17,* 309–329.

Learner, S. (2012). Scarred for life. *Nursing Standard, 26*(18), 20–21.

Levene, M., & Roberts, P. (1999). *The massacre in history.* New York, NY: Oxford.

Lilly, J. R. (2007). *Taken by force: Rape and American GIs in Europe during WWII.* Hampshire, UK: Palgrave Macmillan.

Man, J. (2004). *Genghis Khan: Life, death and resurrection.* New York, NY: Bantam Press.

Mayell, H. (2002, February 12). Thousands of women killed for family "honor." *National Geographic News.* Retrieved from http://news.nationalgeographic.com/news/2002/02/0212_020212_honorkilling.html

McCormick, E. M. (2011). Rethinking indirect victim eligibility for U non-immigrant visa status to better protect immigrant families and communities. *Stanford Law & Policy Review, 22*(2) 587–632.

Moore, M. (2000, June 26). Justice elusive for slain women. *Washington Post.* Retrieved from http://takenbythesky.net/Juárez/june26_2000.html

Nagle, L. E. (2011). Child soldiers and the duty of nations to protect children from participation in armed conflict. *Cardozo Journal of International and Comparative Law, 19,* 1–58.

Newton, M. (1999). *Ciudad Juárez: The serial killer's playground.* Retrieved from http:///www.crimelibrary.com

Newton, M. (2003). *Ciudad Juárez: The serial killer's playground.* Retrieved from http://www.trutv.com/library/crime/serial_killers/predators/ciudad_Juárez/11.html

Noguchi, Y. (2002). International Labor Organization Convention No. 182 on the worst forms of child labour and the Convention on the Rights of the Child. *International Journal of Children's Rights, 10*(4), 355–369.

Orlova, A. V. (2004). From social dislocation to human trafficking. *Problems of Post-Communism, 51*(6) 14–22.

Oxman-Martinez, J., & Hanley, J. (2003, February 20). Human smuggling and trafficking: Achieving the goals of the UN Protocols? *Cross Border Perspectives: Human Trafficking.* Retrieved from http://www.maxwell.syr.edu/uploadedFiles/campbell/events/OxmanMartinez%20oped.pdf

Pantin, L. (2001). 250 murders prompt Mexico anti-violence campaign. *Women's E-news.* Retrieved from http://takenbythesky.net/Juárez/dec21_2001.html

Passel, J. S. (2006, March 7). Size and characteristics of the unauthorized migrant population in the U.S.: Estimates based on the March 2005 current population survey. *Pew Hispanic Center.* Retrieved from http://pewhispanic.org/reports/report.php?ReportID=61

Patel, S., & Gadit, A. M. (2008). Karo-kari: A form of honour killing in Pakistan. *Transcultural Psychiatry, 45*(4), 683–694.

Peguero, A. (2009). Victimizing the children of immigrants: Latino and Asian American student victimization. *Youth & Society, 41*(2), 186–208.

Peterman, A., Palermo, T., & Bredenkamp, C. (2011). Estimates and determinants of sexual violence against women in the Democratic Republic of Congo. *American Public Health Association, 101*(6), 1060–1067. doi: 10.2105/AJPH.2010.300070

Rafferty, Y. (2007). Children for sale: Child trafficking in Southeast Asia. *Child Abuse Review, 16*(6), 401–422.

Rape: It's a war crime. (2009). *Los Angeles Times.* Retrieved from http://articles.latimes.com/2009/aug/13/opinion/ed-rape13

Reid, J. A. (2011). An exploratory model of girls' vulnerability to commercial sexual exploitation in prostitution. *Child Maltreatment, 16*(2), 146–157.

Reparations proposed in Mexican killings. (2003, November 13). *The New York Times,* p. 11.

Siddharth, K. (2009). *Sex trafficking: Inside the business of modern slavery.* New York, NY: Columbia University Press.

Simister, J. G. (2010). Domestic violence and female genital mutilation in Kenya: Effects of ethnicity and education. *Journal of Family Violence, 25,* 247–257. doi: 10.1007/s10896-009-9288-6

Simkhada, P. (2008). Life histories and survival strategies amongst sexually trafficked girls in Nepal. *Children and Society, 22,* 235–248.

Simmons, W. P. (2006, Spring). Remedies for the women of Ciudad Juárez through the Inter-American Court of Human Rights. *Northwestern Journal of International Human Rights, 4*(3). Retrieved from http://www.law.northwestern.edu/journals/jihr/v4/n3/2/Simmons.pdf

Singer, P. W. (2006). Child soldiers: The new faces of war. *American Educator, 29*(4), 28–37.

Sipsma, H. L., Chen, P. G., Ofori-Atta, A., Ilozumba, U. O., Karfo, K., & Bradley, E. H. (2012). Female genital cutting: Current practices and beliefs in western Africa. *Bulletin of the World Health Organization, 90,* 120–127. doi: 10.2471/11.090886

Sorenson, S. B., & Lew, V. (2000). Homicide and nativity: A look at victimization and offending in Los Angeles County. *Homicide Studies, 4*(2), 162–185.

Spencer, G. C. (2004/2005). Her body is a battlefield: The applicability of the Alien Tort Statute to corporate human rights abuses in Juárez, Mexico. *Gonzaga Law Review, 40,* 503.

United Nations. (1949). *Fourth Geneva Convention.* Retrieved from http://www.icrc.org/ihl.nsf/full/380

United Nations. (1977). *Protocol 1, addendum to Geneva Convention.* Retrieved from http://www.icrc.org/ihl.nsf/full/470?opendocument

United Nations. (1989). *Convention on the Rights of the Child, Article 38.* Retrieved from http://www2.ohchr.org/english/law/crc.htm#art38

United Nations. (1991). *Paris Principles.* Retrieved from http://www2.ohchr.org/english/law/parisprinciples.htm

United Nations. (2000). *Protocol to prevent, suppress and punish trafficking in persons, especially women and children.* United Nations, Geneva. Retrieved from http://www2.ohchr.org/english/law/protocoltraffic.htm

United Nations. (2003). Africa: Too small to be fighting in anyone's way. *Humanitarian News and Analysis: Office for the Coordination of Humanitarian Affairs.* Retrieved from http://www.irinnews.org/Report/66280/www.irinnews.org/www.irinnews.org/Asia.xml

United Nations. (2008). UN-backed container exhibit spotlights plight of sex trafficking victims. *UN News Centre.* Retrieved from http://www.un.org/apps/news/story.asp?NewsID=25524&Cr=trafficking&Cr1

United Nations. (2010). Impunity for domestic violence, 'honor killings' cannot continue. *UN News Centre.* Retrieved from http://www.un.org/apps/news/story.asp?NewsID=33971&Cr=violence+against+women&Cr1

U.S. Citizenship and Immigration Service. (2010a). *Immigration Options for Victims of Crime: Information for Law Enforcement, Healthcare Providers, and Others.* Retrieved from http://www.uscis.gov/USCIS/Humanitarian/Battered%20Spouse,%20Children%20&%20Parents/Immigration%20Options%20for%20Victims%20of%20Crimes.pdf

U.S. Citizenship and Immigration Service. (2010b). *USCIS reaches milestone: 10,000 U visas approved in fiscal year 2010.* Retrieved from http://www.uscis.gov/portal/site/uscis/menuitem.5af9bb95919f35e66f614176543f6d1a/?vgnextoid=749a58a734cd9210VgnVCM100000082ca60aRCRD&vgnextchannel=68439c7755cb9010VgnVCM10000045f3d6a1RCRD

U.S. Department of Health and Human Services. (2011). National human trafficking resource center fact sheet. *Office of Refugee Resettlement, U.S. Department of Health and Human Services.* Retrieved from http://www.acf.hhs.gov/programs/orr/resource/fact-sheet-national-human-trafficking-resource-center

U.S. Department of Justice. (2007a). *Child exploitation and obscenity section: Child prostitution.* Retrieved from http://www.usdoj.gov/criminal/ceos/prostitution.html

U.S. Department of Justice. (2007b). *Child exploitation and obscenity section: Trafficking and sex tourism.* Retrieved from http://www.usdoj.gov/criminal/ceos/trafficking.html

U.S. Department of State. (2008). *Trafficking in persons report.* Washington, DC: U.S. Department of State.

U.S. Department of State. (2009). *Trafficking in persons report.* Washington, DC: U.S. Department of State.

U.S. Department of State. (2011a). *2010 Human Rights Report: Pakistan.* Washington, DC: U.S. Department of State. Retrieved from http://www.state.gov/j/drl/rls/hrrpt/2010/sca/154485.htm

U.S. Department of State. (2011b). *Trafficking in persons report.* Washington, DC: U.S. Department of State.

Valdez, D. W. (2002, June 23). Families, officials claim cover-ups keeping killings from being solved. *El Paso Times.* Retrieved from http://takenbythesky.net/Juárez/june23_2002.html

Velazquez, A. M., & Kempf-Leonard, K. (2010). Mexican immigration: Insiders' views on crime, risks, and victimization. *Journal of Ethnicity in Criminal Justice, 8*(2), 127–149.

Victims of Trafficking and Violence Protection Act of 2000. (2000). P.L. 106–386, 114 Stat. 1464

World Health Organization. (2012). *Sexual and reproductive health.* Retrieved from http://www.who.int/reproduc-tivehealth/about_us/en/index.html.

Yirga, W. S., Kassa, N. A., Gebremichael, M. W., & Aro, A. R. (2012). Female genital mutilation: Prevalence, per-ceptions, and effect on women's health in Kersa district of Ethiopia. *International Journal of Women's Health, 2*(4), 45–54.

NOTES

1. The Human Trafficking Reporting System (HTRS) is part of the U.S. Department of Justice and tracks incidents of suspected human trafficking for which an investigation, arrest, prosecution, or incarceration occurred as a result of a charge related to human trafficking.

2. Reauthorized by Congress in December 2008.

PART III

Women as Offenders

Girls and Juvenile Delinquency

Diana adjusted quickly in her new neighborhood. Her family connections facilitated her transition to the east side; it would have been far more difficult for a south-side girl to thrive here without such strong family ties. The gang became Diana's primary support; they even kept Diana's ex-boyfriend Vance away when he showed up every few months. One night, however, things went bad. Diana's cousin, a local gang member, confronted Vance in the neighborhood, and Vance killed him. The incident happened about 10 yards from the front doors of a state parole office, which garnered tremendous media attention about rampant gangs and crime in the inner city. Vance was eventually apprehended. Even thought he was only 16 years old, he was tried and convicted as an adult and sentenced to 25 years in prison.

Around this time, a local community organization opened a gang intervention program in the neighborhood. A female gang worker there took Diana under her wing and showed her a way out of the cycle of drugs, gangs, and violence all around her. With a dedicated mentor and new possibilities, Diana plotted a new course for her life. She graduated high school and started community college. She was involved in a police explorer program, and worked part-time as a tutor and child care worker in the housing projects to pay bills. In two years she earned her Associate of Arts degree from a local community college and transferred to a four-year university. She interned at the same police department where she had served in the police explorer program, and she earned her BS degree in just three years. She was hired as a sworn officer one month after her 22nd birthday.

Things weren't going as well for Karla, who became immersed in the streets. Her gang protected and provided for her at first, but her erratic behavior led to frequent in-fighting, and her continual drive for her next high led her away from her gang and deeper into the streets. She was arrested for a myriad of crimes before her 21st birthday, including petty theft, assault, possession of a controlled substance, disturbing the peace, and solicitation.

Chapter Highlights

- The rise of the juvenile court
- The double standard for girls in the juvenile justice system
- The violent girl
- Contemporary risk factors associated with girls and delinquency
- Gender-specific needs of young female offenders

While the majority of this book focuses on the needs of women and girls generally, this chapter highlights some of the specific issues facing girls within the juvenile justice system. Beginning with a discussion on the rise of the juvenile courts, this chapter highlights the historical and contemporary standards for young women in society and how the changing definitions of delinquency have disproportionately and negatively affected young girls. We then look at how these practices have manifested into today's standards to address cases of female delinquents. This chapter concludes with a discussion of reforms designed to respond to the unique needs of girls within the juvenile justice system.

The Rise of the Juvenile Court and the Sexual Double Standard

The understanding of adolescence within the justice system is a relatively new phenomenon, historically speaking. Originally, the development of the term *juvenile delinquent* reflected the idea that youths were "malleable" and could be shaped into law-abiding citizens (Bernard, 1992). A key factor in this process was the doctrine of **parens patriae**. *Parens patriae* began in the English Chancery Courts during the 15th century and evolved into the practice whereby the state could assume custody of children for cases where the child had no parents or the parents were deemed unfit care providers. As time passed, *parens patriae* became the government's justification for regulating adolescents and their behaviors under the mantra "in the best interests of the child" (Sutton, 1988).

Prior to the development of the juvenile court, the majority of cases of youthful offending were handled on an informal basis. However, the dramatic population growth, combined with the rise of industrialization, made it increasingly difficult for families and communities to control wayward youth. The doctrine of *parens patriae* led to the development of a separate system within the justice system, designed to oversee the rehabilitation of youth who were deemed out of control.

Developed in 1825, the New York House of Refuge was one of the first **reformatories** for juvenile delinquents and was designed to keep youth offenders separate from the adult population. Unlike adults, youths were not sentenced to terms proportionate to their offenses in these early juvenile institutions. Instead, juveniles were committed to the institutions for long periods of time, often until their 21st birthday. Here, the doctrine of *parens patriae* was often used to discriminate against children of the poor, as the youth who were sent to the House of Refuge had not necessarily committed a criminal offense. Rather, these youth were more likely to be described as "coming from an unfit home" or displaying "incorrigible behaviors" (Bernard, 1992). The practices at the House of Refuge during the 19th century were based less on controlling criminal behaviors and more on preventing future pauperism, which the reformers believed led to delinquency and crime (Sutton, 1988). Rather than address the conditions facing poor parents and children, reformers chose to respond to what they viewed as the "peculiar weaknesses of the children's moral natures" and "weak and criminal parents" (Bernard, 1992, p. 76).

The Progressive Era of the late 19th and early 20th century in the United States led to the *child-saving movement*, which was comprised of middle- and upper-class White citizens who "regarded their cause as a matter of conscience and morality [and] viewed themselves as altruists and humanitarians dedicated to rescuing those who were less fortunately placed in the social order" (Platt, 1969, p. 3). The efforts of the child-savers movement led to the creation of the first juvenile court in Chicago in 1899. The jurisdiction of the juvenile court presided over three youth populations: (1) children who committed adult criminal offenses, (2) children who committed status offenses, and (3) children who were abused or neglected by their parents (Chesney-Lind & Shelden, 2004).

Parens patriae significantly affected the treatment of girls who were identified as delinquent. During the late 19th and early 20th centuries, moral reformers embarked on an **age-of-consent campaign**, which was designed to protect young women from "vicious men" who preyed on the innocence of girls. Prior to the age-of-consent campaign, the legal age of sexual consent in 1885 ranged between 10 and 12 for most states. As a result of the efforts by moral reformers, all states raised the age of consent to 16 or 18 by 1920. While their attempt to guard the chastity of young women from exploitation was rooted in a desire to protect girls, these practices also denied young women an avenue for healthy sexual expression and identity. The laws that resulted from this movement were often used to punish young women's displays of sexuality by placing them in detention centers or reformatories for moral violations with the intent to incarcerate them throughout their adolescence. These actions held women to a high standard of sexual purity, while the sexual nature of men was dismissed by society as normal and pardonable behavior. In addition, the reformers developed their policies based on a White, middle-class ideal of purity and modesty—anyone who did not conform to these ideals was viewed as out of control and in need of intervention by the juvenile court (Chesney-Lind & Shelden, 2004). This exclusive focus by moral reformers on the sexual exploitation of White, working-class women led to the racist implication that only the virtues of White women needed to be saved. While reformers in the Black community were equally interested in the moral education of young women and men, they were unsupportive of the campaign to impose criminal sanctions on offenders for sexual crimes, as they were concerned that such laws would unfairly target men of color (Odem, 1995).

Age-of-consent campaigners viewed the delinquent acts of young women as inherently more dangerous than the acts of their male counterparts. Due to the emphasis on sexual purity as the pathway toward healthy adulthood and stability for the future, the juvenile reformatory became a place to shift the focus away from their sexual desire and train young girls for marriage. Unfortunately, this increased focus on the use of the reformatory for moral offenses allowed for the practice of net-widening to occur, and more offenders were placed under the supervision of the juvenile courts. *Net-widening* refers to the practice whereby more offenders become involved in the justice system through programs such as early interventions for at-risk youth. One example of this is diversion. Diversion programs allow for the juvenile court to intervene in minor cases of delinquency without a formal adjudication. While these programs provide limited interventions, such as educational classes aimed at preventing future problem behaviors and service to the community, these practices often expanded the reach to offenses and populations that previously were outside the reach of the juvenile justice system. The effects of this practice actually increased the number of offenders under the general reach of the system, whether informally or formally.

Beyond the age-of-consent campaign, the control of girls' sexuality extended to all girls involved in the juvenile court, regardless of offense. A review of juvenile court cases between 1929 and 1964 found that girls who were arrested for status offenses were forced to have gynecological exams to determine whether or not they had engaged in sexual intercourse and if they had contracted any sexually transmitted diseases. Not only were these girls more likely to be sent to juvenile detention than their male counterparts, they spent three times as long in detention for their "crimes" (Chesney-Lind, 1973). Indeed, throughout the early 20th century, the focus on female sexuality and sexually transmitted infections reached epic proportions, and any woman who was suspected to be infected with a sexually transmitted infection was arrested, examined, and quarantined (Odem, 1995).

In addition to being placed in detention centers for engaging in consensual sex, young women were often blamed for "tempting defendants into immoral behavior" (Odem, 1995, p. 68) in cases where they were victims of forcible sexual assault. Other historical accounts confirm how sexual victimization cases were often treated by the juvenile court in the same manner as consensual sex cases—in both situations, the girl was labeled as delinquent for having sex (Shelden, 1981). These girls were doubly victimized, first by the assault and then by the system. During these court hearings, a woman's sexual history was put on display in an attempt to discredit her in front of a jury, yet the courts did not request similar information about a man's sexual history, as it would "unfairly prejudice the jury against him" (Odem, 1995, p. 70). These historical accounts emphasized that any nonmarital sexual experience, even forcible rape, typically resulted in girls being treated as offenders.

The trend of using sexuality as a form of delinquent behavior for female offenders continued throughout the 20th and into the 21st century. The court system has become a mechanism through which control of female sexuality is enforced. Males enjoy a sense of sexual freedom that is denied to girls. In regards to male sexuality, the only concern generally raised by the court is centered on abusive and predatory behaviors toward others, particularly younger children. Here, probation officer narratives indicate that court officials think about sexuality in different ways for male and female juvenile offenders. For boys, no reference is made regarding noncriminalized sexual behaviors. Yet for girls, the risk of victimization becomes a way to deny female sexual agency. Here, probation officers comment in official court reports about violations of moral rules regarding sexuality and displays of sexual behavior. In many cases, these officers express concern for the levels of sexual activity in which the girls are engaging. In many cases, such professional concerns are used as grounds for identifying youth as out of control and therefore in need of services by the juvenile court (Mallicoat, 2007). The consequence of this desire to protect young girls results in their learning about sexuality in terms of disease and victimization, not in terms of pleasure and agency—"speak very often not of the power of desire but of how their desire may get them in trouble" (Tolman, 1994, p. 338). Regardless of the nature of offending for a woman, it is often interpreted as sexual in nature or is accompanied by a disturbance or unfavorable behavior that involves her sexuality (Triplett & Myers, 1995). Some researchers have argued that the continued control of female sexuality is related to the general control of women in society. For example, Alder notes,

> Any discourse which legitimizes [a young woman's pleasure], acknowledges her sexual knowledge, values her performance and places it under her control is potentially threatening to his masculinity. . . . Without a discourse of desire, but within discourses of victimization, we deny the female sexual subject, we deny girls sexual agency, they cannot speak about and we do not hear them speak about their sexuality or their sexual experience, both desired and imposed. (Alder, 1998, pp. 86–87)

⬚ The Nature and Extent of Female Delinquency

Girls are the fastest-growing population within the juvenile justice system. Not only has the number of arrests involving girls increased, but the volume of cases in the juvenile court involving girls has also expanded at a dramatic rate. Despite the increased attention on women by the agents of the juvenile justice system and the public in general, it is important to remember that girls continue to represent a small proportion of all delinquency cases, as boys' offending continues to dominate the juvenile justice system.

As discussed in Chapter 1, the Uniform Crime Reports (UCR) reflect the arrest data from across the nation. This resource also includes information on juvenile offenders. Given that law enforcement officials represent the most common method through which juvenile offenders enter the system, arrest data provide a first look at the official processing of juvenile cases. Here, we can assess the number of crimes reported to law enforcement involving youth offenders, the most serious charge within these arrests, and the disposition of the police in these cases. In Chapter 2, you learned that the UCR data are not without their flaws. Given that juveniles are often involved in acts that are not serious and are non-violent in nature, these practices of crime reporting and how the data are compiled can have a significant effect on the understanding of **juvenile delinquency** by society. Despite these flaws, the UCR remains the best resource for investigating arrest rates for crime (Snyder & Sickmund, 2006).

UCR data on juvenile offenders indicate that in 1980, girls represented 20% of juvenile arrests. By 2003, girls' participation in crimes increased to 29%, where it remains today. A comparison of 1980 to 2003 data indicates that the female proportion of violent crime index offenses increased from 10% to 18%, while property offenses increased from 19% to 32%. These shifts in girls' arrests have certainly increased the attention of parents, juvenile court officials, and scholars (Knoll & Sickmund, 2010; Snyder & Sickmund, 2006). However, it appears that the majority of this increase occurred during the late 1980s to early 1990s, when the rise of "tough on crime" philosophies spilled over into the juvenile arena. Chart 8.1 illustrates data on the estimates of juvenile arrests and the percentages of women involved in crimes for 2001 and 2010. Here, arrest data indicate that girls in 2010 represented the same proportion of juvenile offenses as they did in 2001.

Despite the fact that women continue to represent a smaller proportion of the offending population compared to males, the hype of the female delinquent continues to dominate discussions about juvenile delinquency. The increased attention on female delinquency by law enforcement has, in turn, affected the handling of these cases by the juvenile courts. In 2007, the U.S. juvenile courts were dealing with an estimated 1.7 million cases each year. Since the early 1990s, girls have represented a growing proportion of cases in the juvenile courts. In 1991, girls made up 19% of delinquency cases, 26% in 2002, and 27% in 2007. By 2007, the juvenile courts were dealing with 448,900 cases with female defendants, which is more than twice the number of female juvenile court cases in 1985 (Knoll & Sickmund, 2010; Snyder & Sickmund, 2006). In addition to the increase in the number of cases referred to the juvenile court, cases today are more likely to be processed formally by the court instead of informally. **Informal processing** involves sanctions in which youth participate on a voluntary basis. Rather than file formal charges, informal processing allows youth to participate in community service, victim restitution, and mediation and voluntary supervision. If they complete these arrangements successfully, the case is closed without the **formal processing**, and youth are diverted from the system. In cases handled formally by the court, a petition is filed requesting a court hearing, which can result in the youth being labeled a delinquent. In 1985, only 35% of girls' cases (and 48% of boys') were processed in a formal manner. In

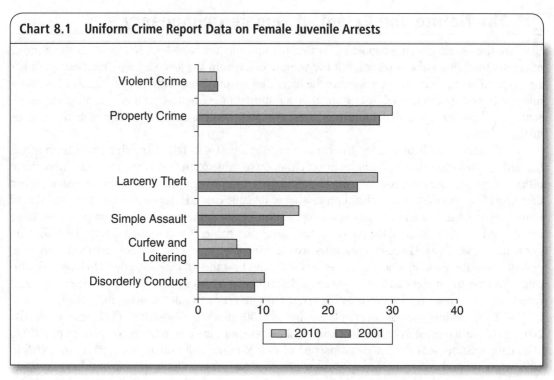

Chart 8.1 Uniform Crime Report Data on Female Juvenile Arrests

SOURCE: Crime in the United States. (2010). Retrieved from http://www.fbi.gov/about-us/cjis/ucr/crime-in-the-u.s/2010/crime-in-the-u.s.-2010

comparison, 50% of girls' cases (and 61% of boys') were handled formally by juvenile court authorities in 2007, signaling an end to informal sanctions by the court. While girls were slightly less likely to be adjudicated as delinquent (64% compared to 67% of boys), this difference is negligible (Knoll & Sickmund, 2010; Snyder & Sickmund, 2006). Research by Steffensmeier, Schwartz, Zhong, and Ackerman (2005) found the increase in arrests and formal processing of juvenile cases has disproportionately impacted girls through the practice of *up-charging* by prosecutors, whereby less serious forms of conduct are processed as assault cases, and a decrease in tolerance for girls who act out. Generally speaking, it appears that the juvenile justice system is less tolerant of girls who break the socially proscribed norms of gendered behavior and are punished by officials for acting out, while boys benefit from a greater acceptance of these "unacceptable" behaviors (Carr, Hudson, Hanks, & Hunt, 2008).

Given the increase in the number of female cases that are formally processed and adjudicated delinquent, it is no surprise that punishments have also increased for girls. While boys are more likely to be detained for their cases (22% of cases, compared to 17% of girls' cases), girls who are denied release generally spend significantly greater amounts of time in detention compared to boys (Belknap, Dunn, & Holsinger, 1997; Snyder & Sickmund, 2006). In addition, girls are subjected to longer periods of supervision, a practice that appears to increase the delinquency in girls due to excessive and aggressive monitoring techniques (Carr et al., 2008). Finally, the number of residential placements or sentences to formal probation terms has also increased for girls. For both boys and girls, the number of cases involving residential out-of-home placement between 1985 and 2002 increased 44%, though boys were more likely to be placed out of the home than girls (Snyder & Sickmund, 2006). Girls of color appear to be disproportionately affected by the shift to formal processing of delinquency cases, as Black and Hispanic girls are more likely to receive detention, whereas White girls are more likely to be referred to a residential treatment facility (Miller, 1994).

Technical Violations: The New Status Offense

Like the historical and contemporary control of female sexuality, status offenses are another realm where doctrines such as *parens patriae* allow for the juvenile court to intervene in the lives of adolescents. *Status offenses* are acts that are only illegal if committed by juveniles. Examples of status offenses include the underage consumption of alcohol, running away from home, truancy, and curfew violations. While the juvenile court was founded with the idea of dealing with both delinquency and status offenses, today's courts have attempted to differentiate between the two offense categories due to constitutional challenges on status offenses (Bernard, 1992). One of the elements of the **Juvenile Justice and Delinquency Prevention (JJDP) Act of 1974** called for the decriminalization of status offenses in any state that received federal funds. Prior to its enactment, young women were much more likely to be incarcerated for status offenses compared to their male counterparts (Chesney-Lind & Shelden, 2004). While the institutionalization of sexually wayward girls officially ended with the JJDP Act of 1974, funds were not made available to provide resources to address the needs of these girls. "Status offenders are not a unique or discrete category of juveniles, and they share many of the same characteristics and behavioral versatility as other delinquent offenders" (Feld, 2009, p. 245). Given that status offense charges were frequently used as the basis to incarcerate girls, many assumed that the presence of girls in the juvenile justice system would decrease following the decriminalization of status offenses. However, this decline did not last long. While youth can no longer be incarcerated specifically for status offenses, researchers contend that the practice of institutionalizing girls who are deemed out of control continues today (Acoca & Dedel, 1998; Chesney-Lind & Shelden, 2004). The modern-day practice of institutionalizing girls for status offenses is known as ***bootstrapping***. The process of bootstrapping involves cases where a girl currently on probation or parole for a criminal offense is then prosecuted formally for a probation violation as a result of committing a status offense such as running away from home or truancy (Owen & Bloom, 1998). While provisions of the 1992 revision of the JJDP Act attempted to make the practice of bootstrapping more difficult for courts, evidence indicates that the practice continues in an inequitable fashion against girls. Research by Feld (2009) suggests that acts that were once treated as status offenses are now processed as minor acts of delinquency due to the expansion of the discretionary powers available to schools, police, and juvenile justice officials. The replacement of status offenses by probation violations has allowed justice officials to recommit girls to these residential facilities. While a commitment to a state institution or detention center for these type of status offenses is prohibited by the original authorization of the JJDP Act in 1974, it appears that these community-based residential facilities serve as a way to alternatively incarcerate young girls deemed out of control by the courts (Carr et al., 2008). Feld notes this practice:

> The failure to provide alternatives to institutional confinement for "troublesome girls" creates substantial pressures within the juvenile justice system to circumvent DSO (deinstitutionalization of status offenders) restrictions by the simple expedient of relabeling them as delinquents by charging them with assault. (2009, p. 261)

The increase of female delinquency and the changes in the processing of offenders have brought new concerns for the juvenile justice system. The majority of female offending is nonviolent in nature and often results from technical violations of probation (Owen & Bloom, 1998). Caseloads for girls are more likely to reflect offenses like simple assault and larceny theft and are less likely to involve cases of robbery, burglary, vandalism, and drugs, compared to boys (Snyder & Sickmund, 2006). The increase in penalties for girls is also reflected in the limited availability for community-based and rehabilitative programming options. Some scholars suggest that it is the failure of other social systems (such as schools, child welfare, and mental health programs) that indicates that these resources fail at the early stages of prevention and intervention and set the stage for future delinquency (Goodkind, 2005). The lack of resources both within and outside the juvenile justice system, combined with the "get tough on youth crime" agenda, has led to the increased institutionalization of girls, many of whom are charged with less severe crimes and who are not a risk to public safety (Beger & Hoffman, 1998). This practice of net-widening ensures that once in the system, girls find it difficult to escape the watchful eye of the juvenile justice system (Chesney-Lind, 1997).

Case Study

The Sexual Abuse of Girls in Confinement

While historical discussions on facilities for delinquent girls have highlighted the practices of physical and sexual abuse by both guards and other inmates, the majority of the public assumes that these practices are a thing of the past. Unfortunately, these abuses still continue at many juvenile institutions.

The Prison Rape Elimination Act of 2003 (PREA) requires that the Bureau of Justice Statistics (BJS) collect and analyze data on sexual abuse within confinement facilities such as prisons, jails, and juvenile facilities. As part of this mandate, the BJS collected data from 166 state and 29 local/private juvenile facilities. As one of the first comprehensive studies of its kind, the National Survey of Youth in Custody involved 9,198 adjudicated youth housed in juvenile facilities across the United States (Beck, Harrison, & Guerino, 2010). Their findings indicate that the abuse of youth in confinement is not an issue of the past. While 2.6% of the youth indicated that they had been victimized by another youth, the findings indicate that the majority of these assaults are perpetuated by staff (10.3% or 2,730 youth). Within these cases, 4.3% of the youth indicated that the sexual abuse occurred through the use of force by the officer, while the remaining 6.4% indicated that the sexual relationship was consensual (even though state law would disagree with this definition of *consensual*, given the context of the relationship). Additionally, the majority of the abuse was perpetuated by opposite-gendered staff (male victims were more likely to be abused by female staff, while female victims were more likely to be abused by male staff members). While males were more likely to be victimized by facility staff members compared to girls (10.8% of boys versus 4.7% of girls), girls were significantly more likely to engage in sexual activity with other youth (9.1% of girls compared to 2.0% of boys). Youth who identified as homosexual or bisexual were more likely to indicate that they had been victimized (12.1%)

compared to heterosexual youth (1.3%). The risk of trauma for transgendered youth was particularly high. Transgendered girls found themselves victims of sexual harassment and physical and sexual abuse, as they were housed in male facilities in accordance with their birth gender (Just Detention International, 2009). In many cases, staff members not only failed to protect transgendered youth in custody but often joined in on the abuse (Fellner, 2010). In addition, female-only facilities had the highest rates of youth-on-youth sexual abuse, while male-only facilities recorded the highest rates of staff-on-youth assaults. While the National Survey of Youth in Custody yielded valuable information about the nature of abuse within juvenile facilities, the data were collected anonymously, making it difficult for facility and state officials to follow up on these cases of abuse. In addition, few of these assaults were ever reported to officials. Youth are hesitant about talking about the abuse, particularly when it involves other staff members, out of fear of increased victimization (Human Rights Watch, 2006). Factors such as these may skew the findings of research on the extent of staff sexual assault on incarcerated youth and indicate that the actual extent of this problem is significantly higher than initially believed.

As a result of the high rates of assault within detention centers, the Justice Department is tracking the implementation of recommendations by the National Prison Rape Elimination Commissions. Many of these reforms are costly and out of reach, such as building new facilities that would allow for increased supervision of inmates and staff. In addition, public officials have argued that conducting annual reviews of abuse within juvenile facilities would be too costly. However, allowing such abuse to continue is also an expensive burden, both emotionally for the youth who are victimized as well as for the facilities that are later sued by youth and their families for failing to keep youth safe. In 2007, Alabama paid $12.7 million to settle a case brought by 48 girls at the state youth correctional facility based on charges of significant abuse over time involving over 15 staff members.[1] However, such cases are not limited to juvenile facilities. In 2009, Michigan agreed to pay 100 million dollars in a class-action lawsuit for cases of sexual abuse of over 800 women by prison staff (Fellner, 2010). While international standards under the United Nations prohibit the supervision of female offenders by male staff (a policy that could potentially limit the cases of abuse of female youth by male guards), many facilities continue to allow cross-gender supervision (Human Rights Watch, 2006).

Table 8.1 Prevalence of Sexual Victimization by Gender Facilities

Gender Housed at Facility	Youth Reporting Any Sexual Victimization	Youth Reporting Sexual Victimization by Another Youth	Youth Reporting Sexual Victimization by Facility Staff
Males only	12.6%	2.0%	11.3%
Females only	14.0%	11.0%	5.0%
Males and females	9.6%	3.0%	7.6%

◸ The Violent Girl

Over the past two decades, media reports have alluded to the rise of the violent juvenile offender. This portrayal of "bad girls" by the media has been linked to data that reflected a significant increase in the number of arrests for crimes of violence involving girls. Here the question is, are girls really becoming more violent or have parents, schools, and police changed the way in which they respond to incidents of girls who are deemed to be out of control? While official crime rates appear to indicate that the rate of violence among juvenile girls is increasing, such data only reflect the rise in arrest rates, not the actual prevalence of violence in the community. Indeed, self-report studies do not confirm this position and demonstrate that the levels of violence have actually decreased for both boys and girls. Given the contradiction between self-report and arrest data, scholars have concluded that the levels of violence amongst girls have not changed. Rather, it is the response by agents of social control that has shifted, leading to an increase in the arrest and formal processing of cases involving adolescent girls. A review of these cases indicates an overrepresentation of incidents of school- and family-based violence, cases that historically were handled on an informal basis (Brown, Chesney-Lind, & Stein, 2007).

How do scholars explain the rise in school- and family-based assault cases among juvenile girls? Adolescence represents a time of inquiry and growth in the lives of adolescents. Alas, this new discovery for freedom collides with challenges in parental control and authority. In an attempt to regain control over their daughters, many parents turn to the police and the juvenile court for help. Juvenile authorities may talk to or threaten the youth, using fear as a tool to gain compliance from the youth (Davis, 2007). Due to the high degree of discretion granted to police, officers have the ability to deal with these cases in an informal matter. In the majority of cases, the police treat these interventions as a social service rather than a criminal matter. However, repeated contacts under these circumstances can try the patience of law enforcement. In turn, their discretionary power can be used to bring youth to the attention of juvenile court authorities in cases of minor disputes within the family. Typically, these cases are examples of the symbolic struggles of adolescence, whereby youth battle their parents for power, control, and freedom.

In addition to the shift from informal to formal processing, research indicates that many cases that represent the rise in violence for girls stem from changes in the handling of domestic disputes between parents and children. While many of these cases were traditionally treated on an informal basis, recent shifts have resulted in the official handling of these cases. Indeed, these family struggles have become the new road to the juvenile justice system, whereby youth are arrested in cases of domestic dispute and minor assault against siblings, parents, and other family members

▲ **Photo 8.1**   Recent years have seen an increase in the reporting of cases involving violent girls. Are girls really becoming more violent or have parents, schools, and police changed the way in which they respond to incidents of girls who are deemed to be out of control?

(Brown et al., 2007; Feld, 2009). Here, the struggle for parental control culminates in a physical event, which in turn invites official action by the police and courts system:

> Many of these family assault charges seem to have one theme in common. They appear to almost always involve a parent's attempting to physically block the daughter from taking some kind of action, such as leaving the house, and a daughter's subsequent push to resist the parent's restraining action results in the parent's alleging assault. (Davis, 2007, p. 422)

Many parents believe that once their kids are involved in the juvenile justice system, increased opportunities for therapeutic resources become available. Research demonstrates that parents seek out the police because they don't know what else to do (Sharpe, 2009). While the formal processing of these cases becomes the basis to place a child under probation supervision, any subsequent power struggles between the parent and child become the grounds for a technical violation of probation. Here, the court becomes a new and powerful method for enforcing parental authority. Indeed, it is not uncommon during juvenile court proceedings for a judge to consult with a parent when determining an outcome of a case. If a parent agrees that a child can come home (under the order of obeying house rules), the court may be more likely to return the youth home. If however a parent does not want physical custody of the child, a judge may decide to institutionalize the youth (Davis, 2007). In addition, the threat of reporting any infractions or disciplinary problems to the juvenile court becomes a new bargaining tool for parents. Ultimately, this attempt to reinstate and reinforce parental authority only increases the punitive consequences for youth who are labeled by the system as out of control.

In addition to shifts in the handling of domestic cases, changes in dealing with incidents of school-based violence have also contributed to the rise of girls' delinquency. As a result of **zero-tolerance policies**, cases that were once handled internally with punishments such as detention or suspension are now dealt with by local police agencies, who utilize officers on school grounds (often called *school resource officers*) to officially handle such events. Given that girls are more likely to engage in acts of violence against family members or peers (whereas boys are more likely to commit acts of violence against distant acquaintances or strangers), such policies may be more likely to unfairly target girls' delinquency (Feld, 2009).

Risk Factors for Female Delinquency

Earlier chapters of this text have highlighted the historical failures of criminology to address the unique causes of women's and girls' offending. The theoretical inattention to these issues has significantly affected the identification and delivery of services for women and girls. It is a failure for policymakers and practitioners to assume that just because girls typically engage in nonviolent or nonserious acts of crime and delinquency, their needs are insignificant (Chesney-Lind & Shelden, 2004). Indeed, a historical review of the juvenile justice system finds that programs and facilities are ill equipped to deal with the needs of girls. While boys and girls can exhibit many of the same risk factors for delinquency (family dysfunction, school failures, peer relationships, and substance abuse), the effects of these risk factors may resonate stronger for girls than they do for boys (Moffitt, Caspi, Rutter, & Silva, 2001). In addition, research indicates that girls possess significantly higher risk factors toward delinquency than boys. It is interesting to note that while White girls tend to exhibit significantly higher levels of risk for certain categories (such as substance abuse), female youth of color, particularly Black youth, are significantly overrepresented in the juvenile court (Gavazzi, Yarcheck, & Lim, 2005). Given these failures of the juvenile courts, it is important to understand the **risk factors for female delinquency** in an effort to develop recommendations for best practices for adolescent delinquent and at-risk girls. For juvenile girls, the most significant risk factors for delinquency include a poor family relationship, a history of abuse, poor school performance, negative peer relationships, and a history of substance abuse. In addition, these risk factors are significantly interrelated.

The influence of the family unit is one of the most commonly cited references in the study of delinquency. The family represents the primary mechanism for the internalization and socialization of social norms and values (Hirschi, 1969), and social control theorists have illustrated that a positive attachment to the family acts as a key tool in the prevention of delinquency. Yet research indicates that girls may have stronger attachments to the family compared to boys, which can serve as a protective factor against delinquency. However, families can only serve as a protective factor when they exist in a positive, prosocial environment. Research indicates that girls benefit from positive communication, structure, and support in the family environment (Bloom, Owen, Deschenes, & Rosenbaum, 2002b). Just as the family unit can protect girls from delinquency, it can also lead girls into delinquency at a young age. Youth may turn to delinquency to enhance their self-esteem or to overcome feelings of rejection by their families (Matsueda, 1992). Research has indicated that negative family issues constitute a greater problem for girls than boys. Family fragmentation due to divorce, family criminality, and foster care placements and family violence and negative family attachment have been identified as family risk factors for female delinquents. Families with high levels of conflict and poor communication skills, combined with parents who struggle with their own personal issues, place girls at risk for delinquency (Bloom et al., 2002b). Research involving incarcerated girls in California indicated that several of the girls had experienced the loss of or witnessed the death of one or both of their parents, and half of their mothers and/or fathers had been incarcerated at some point in their lives (Acoca & Dedel, 1998). Regardless of the reason behind the loss of a parent in their life, girls who are raised in a single-parent home have a greater risk for delinquency involvement compared to girls raised in a two-parent household (McKnight & Loper, 2002). In addition, once a girl becomes immersed in the juvenile justice system, her delinquency can serve to increase the detachment between her and her family (Girls Incorporated, 1996).

Sexual, physical, and emotional abuse has long been documented as significant risk factors for female offenders. The impact of abuse is intensified when it occurs within the family. Such abuse can be detrimental to the positive development of the adolescent girl and can result in behaviors such as running away, trust issues, emotional maladjustment, and future sexual risk behaviors. Girls are 3–4 times more likely to be abused than their male counterparts, and 92% of incarcerated girls in a California study reported having been subject to at least one form of abuse (emotional 88%, physical 81%, sexual 56%; Acoca & Dedel, 1998). Similar results are echoed in research by Belknap and Holsinger (2006), where 58.9% of girls (versus 18.5% of boys) indicated that they had been sexually abused either by a family member or other individual in their life. While sexual abuse is the most studied form of abuse for girls, other forms of maltreatment can have a significant effect on the development of girls. Girls experience higher rates of abuse than their male counterparts—62.9% of girls (compared to 42.8% of boys) indicated a history of long-term physical abuse (Belknap & Holsinger, 2006). Longitudinal research studies conducted by Cathy Spatz Widom (1989, 1991) indicate that youth (boys and girls) who experience abuse and neglect throughout childhood are at significant risk for delinquent behaviors and juvenile court intervention. In many cases, girls who experience violence as victims later engage in acts of violence toward others. While girls tend to engage in minor acts of delinquency, these violations are often the tip of the iceberg for the issues that affect preteen and adolescent girls. In many cases, status offenses such as running away from home reflect an attempt to escape from a violent or abusive home environment. Unfortunately, in their attempt to escape from an abusive situation, girls often fall into criminal behaviors as a mechanism of survival. Widom (1989) found that childhood victimization increases the risk that a youth will run away from home and that childhood victimization and running away increase the likelihood of engaging in delinquent behaviors. A history of sexual abuse also affects the future risk for victimization, as girls who are sexually abused during their childhood are significantly more likely to find themselves in a domestically violent relationship in the future (McCartan & Gunnison, 2010).

Research has also focused extensively on the role of peer relationships in adolescent offending. The presence of delinquent peers presents the greatest risk for youth to engage in their own acts of delinquency. While much of the research suggests that girls are more likely to associate with other girls (and girls are less likely to be delinquent than boys), research by Miller, Loeber, and Hipwell (2009) indicates that girls generally have at least one friend involved in delinquent behaviors. While girls in this study indicated that they associated with peers of both genders, it is not the gender of the peers that can predict delinquency. Rather, it is the number of delinquent peers that determines whether a youth engages in problem behaviors. Here, the effects of peer pressure and the desire for acceptance often lead youth into delinquency, particularly if the majority of the group is involved in law-violating behaviors.

Several factors can affect one's association with delinquent peers. First, scholars indicate the shift toward unsupervised free time among youth as a potential gateway to delinquency, as youth who are involved in after-school structured activities are less likely to engage in delinquency (Mahoney, Cairns, & Farmer, 2003). Given the slashing of school-based and community programs due to budgetary funds, there are fewer opportunities to provide a safe and positive outlet for youth in the hours between the end of the school day for youth and the end of the work day for parents. Second, age can also affect the delinquent peer relationship. For girls, peer associations with older adolescents of the opposite sex have an impact on their likelihood to engage in delinquent acts if the older male is involved in crime-related behaviors (Stattin & Magnusson, 1990). Finally, negative family attachment also affects the presence of delinquent peers, as girls whose parents are less involved in their daily lives and activities are more likely to engage in problem behaviors (such as substance abuse) with delinquent peers (Svensson, 2003).

School failures have also been identified as an indicator of concern for youth at risk. Truancy is a concern for educational professionals, as it can be an indication of other school failures such as suspension, expulsion, or being held back. In research by Acoca and Dedel (1998), 85% of incarcerated girls in their study compared their experience in school to a war zone, where issues such as racism, sexual harassment, peer violence, and disinterested school personnel increased the likelihood of dropping out. For girls, success at school is tied to feelings of self-worth—the more students feel attached to the school environment and the learning process and develop a connection to their teachers, the less likely they are to be at risk for delinquency (Crosnoe, Erickson, & Dornbusch, 2002). Additionally, the slashing of prosocial extracurricular activities has also negatively affected girls. Here, activities that involve creativity, build relationships, and enhance personal safety help to build **resiliency** in young women and guard against delinquent behaviors (Acoca & Dedel, 1998). Finally, the involvement of a parent in the daughter's school progress can help build resiliency for girls (Bloom et al., 2002b).

Several risks have been identified for adolescent girls' involvement in alcohol and drug use: early experimentation and use, parental use of drugs and alcohol, histories of victimization, poor school and family attachments, numerous social opportunities for drug and alcohol use, poor self-concept, difficulties in coping with life events, and involvement with other problem behaviors. Often, substance abuse highlights the presence of other risk factors for delinquency (Bloom et al., 2002b). Substance abuse affects female delinquency in two ways. First, girls who experience substance abuse in their families may turn to behaviors such as running away to escape the violence that occurs in the home as a result of parental drug and alcohol use. Second, girls themselves may engage in substance abuse as a mechanism of self-medication to escape from abuse (Chesney-Lind & Shelden, 2004). In addition, research indicates that the use of substances can be a gendered experience. While boys tend to limit their drug use to marijuana, girls experiment with and abuse a variety of substances, including methamphetamines, cocaine, acid, crack, and huffing chemicals. Not only did their poly-drug use indicate significant addiction issues, their substance abuse altered their decision-making abilities, influenced their criminal behaviors, and placed them at risk for danger (Mallicoat, 2007). While substance abuse increases the risk for delinquency for girls, the absence of substance abuse serves as a protective factor against delinquency (McKnight & Loper, 2002).

Over the past decade, issues of emotional and mental health have exploded in the juvenile justice system. Youth in custody have experienced high rates of trauma throughout the course of their lives. Examples of traumatic exposure include not only experiencing life-threatening harm but also witnessing events of victimization and harm toward others. As a result of exposures to these traumatic life events, youth are at risk for developing mental health challenges, such as post-traumatic stress disorder (PTSD; Shufelt & Cocozza, 2006). However, girls suffer from significantly higher rates of emotional trauma than boys. (See Hennessey, Ford, Mahoney, Ko, & Siegfried, 2004, for a review of the literature.) Not only do a majority of girls in detention experience suicidal thoughts (52%), 45% of girls indicated that they had attempted suicide at some point in their lives (Belknap & Holsinger, 2006).

Research indicates that over 70% of youth in custody meet the criteria for at least one mental health diagnosis. Girls are more likely to suffer from anxiety-related disorders than boys, and these disorders often stem from their experiences with abuse and victimization in early childhood. In many instances, these disorders co-occur with issues of substance abuse, creating unique challenges for programming and treatment (Shufelt & Cocozza, 2006). Given that many girls suffer from emotional and mental stress as a result of their experiences with trauma, it is important for the juvenile justice system to note and respond to these issues accordingly. Many detention facilities are ill equipped to deal with the mental health needs of youth in custody. A failure by the system to effectively recognize these needs risks placing girls not only at future risk for harm but also at risk for increased involvement with the system (Hennessey et al., 2004). This perpetuates an unfortunate cycle, where,

> in many cases, involvement in the juvenile justice system exacerbates the difficulties they face as adolescent girls. The characteristics of the detention environment (e.g., seclusion, staff insensitivity, loss of privacy) can add to the negative feelings and loss of control girls feel, resulting in suicide attempts and self-mutilation. (National Mental Health Association, 2004, p. 10)

⊠ Meeting the Unique Needs of Delinquent Girls

While girls may make up a minority of offenders in the juvenile justice system, their needs should not be absent from juvenile justice policies. As indicated earlier, girls have a number of different and inter-related issues that historically have been ignored by the system. The **1992 reauthorization of the JJDP**

Act acknowledged the need to provide gender-specific services to address the unique needs of female offenders. The allocation of funds by Congress to investigate **gender-specific programming** provides that each state should

> (1) conduct an analysis of the need for an assessment of existing treatment and services for delinquent girls; (2) develop a plan to provide needed gender-specific services for the prevention and treatment of juvenile delinquency; and (3) provide assurance that youth in the juvenile system are treated fairly regarding their mental, physical and emotional capabilities, as well as on the basis of their gender, race and family income. (Belknap & Holsinger, 1998, p. 55)

Over the past two decades, research has highlighted the factors that may affect a young woman's road to delinquency, and the reauthorization of the JJDP Act mandates that states incorporate this understanding into the assessment tools and programming options for girls.

In an effort to respond to the declaration for gender-specific services, many states have embarked on systematic evaluations designed to investigate the needs of girls in their facilities and develop recommendations of best practices for girls. Here, the goal is that information will be used by program providers in developing and implementing prevention and intervention strategies for girls. In a report on gender-specific services for adolescent girls, Belknap et al. (1997) write,

> When examining gender-specific programming, it is important to recognize [that] equality does not mean sameness. Equality is not about providing the same program, treatment and opportunities for girls and boys. . . . Equality is about providing opportunities that mean the same to each gender. The new definition legitimizes the differences between boys and girls. Programs for boys are more successful when they focus on rules and offer ways to advance within a structured environment, while programs for girls are more successful when they focus on relationships with other people and offer ways to master their lives while keeping these relationships intact. (p. 23)

What should gender-specific programming look like? Programs must be able to address the wide variety of needs of the delinquent girl—given that many of the risk factors for delinquency involve a web of interrelated issues, programs need to be able to address this tangled web of needs rather than attempt to deal with issues on an individual and isolated basis. Research identifies that a history of victimization represents one of the most significant foundational issues facing at-risk and delinquent girls. The prevalent nature of a victimization history in adolescent girls raises this issue to one of central importance in gender-specific programming. Indeed, 55.8% of girls and 40.1% of boys believe that their experiences with abuse throughout their childhood had an effect on their offending behaviors (Belknap & Holsinger, 2006). Not only do programs need to provide counseling services for both boys and girls that focus on the trauma in their lives, but placement services for youth need to be expanded. Given that many girls run away from home to escape an abusive environment, punishment in detention is not an appropriate place for girls. Because early childhood victimization often leads to risky sexual behaviors with the conclusion of teenage pregnancy and parenthood, education should be offered to these girls as a preventive measure for pregnancy and sexually transmitted diseases.

Multicultural Issues in Programming for Girls

Research has indicated that race and ethnicity impact the pathways of girls to the juvenile justice system. A review of characteristics among delinquent girls in Ohio demonstrate that White girls experience higher levels of physical and sexual abuse and substance abuse compared to Black girls. However, the abuse of girls of color remains high, with 70% of Black girls indicating a history of physical abuse (compared to 90% of White girls), and 46% of Black girls have been sexually abused in their lifetime (compared to 62% of White girls; Holsinger & Holsinger, 2005). In contrast, factors such as lack of parental monitoring, antisocial attitudes, lack of school commitment, and peer pressure were more likely to explain delinquency for girls in the Hmong community (Ciong & Huang, 2011).

Not only do we see differences by race and ethnicity in the pathways to delinquency, but we also can observe that these factors can alter the way in which girls respond to these experiences. Research by Holsinger and Holsinger (2005) references that the experience of abuse is more common among Black girls who engage in acts of serious violence, yet similar patterns are not demonstrated for White girls. This finding indicates that girls of color may respond differently to the experience of abuse than White girls. Additional analyses indicate a strong relationship between a history of abuse and mental health, as Black girls are less likely to engage in self-injurious behaviors or display thoughts of suicidal ideation than White girls. Here, it appears that White girls are more likely to respond to the abuse experience through internally harming behaviors, while girls of color are more likely to engage in outward displays of violence (Holsinger & Holsinger, 2005).

Juvenile justice facilities are often ill equipped to deal with the physical and mental health needs of incarcerated girls. Girls who cycle in and out of the juvenile justice system throughout their adolescence indicate high levels of behavioral and mental health issues. Unfortunately, these needs are not adequately met by the limited therapeutic resources that are available in most juvenile facilities (Tille & Rose, 2007). The emotional needs of developing teenagers, combined with the increase in the prevalence of mental health disorders of incarcerated females makes this an important component for gender-specific programming for female populations. Physical and mental health complaints by youth need to be interpreted by staff and facilities as a need, not as a complaining or manipulating behavior. Additionally, such interventions must be established on an ongoing basis for continual care versus limited to an episodic basis (Acoca & Dedel, 1998).

The greatest long-term successes come from programs that provide support not just for the individual girl but for her extended family as well. Unfortunately, many family members resist being involved in programming, as they fail to accept responsibility for the role that they may have played in the development of their daughter's delinquency (Bloom et al., 2002a). This lack of involvement raises significant concerns for the family environment of these girls. Although more than one-half of girls reported that they did not get along with their parents (51%) and viewed their relationship with their parents as contributing to their delinquency (59%), 66% of the girls stated that they would return to live with their parents following their release from custody. This is particularly concerning, given that 58% of the girls surveyed reported experiencing some form of violence in the home. It is impossible to develop programs for incarcerated females without reevaluating policies that contribute to the destruction of the family.

Gender-specific programming for adolescent girls needs to focus on rebuilding the family unit and developing positive role modeling. Here, programs such as family counseling and family substance abuse treatment models can positively affect troubled families.

Listening to Girls' Voices

As you learned in in earlier chapters, listening to the stories of women and girls is one of the key strengths of feminist research methods. From this type of research, we learn that girls have a lot to share about their lives and their experiences with the juvenile justice and criminal justice systems and have ideas about what they need to improve their lives. Research indicates that girls benefit from a structured environment, particularly given that many of the girls come from chaotic environments. Here, tools such as effective discipline, expectations for behavior, and guidance provide valuable support for girls (Garcia & Lane, 2010). In addition, girls discuss the power that a positive role model has for their lives. Here, strong female staff within the juvenile justice system (and related ancillary organizations) can provide valuable mentorship support and guidance for girls (Bright, Ward, & Negi, 2011). In addition to therapeutic resources to address drug addiction and victimization histories, girls argue that training in independent life skills and **reentry** programming is essential in preventing recidivism as a girl transitions into adulthood (Garcia & Lane, 2010).

Beyond discussions about the types of programming and the role of mentors in their lives, this research provides a vivid picture of the environments that these girls come from—and ultimately will return to. Many of the girls referenced the inadequacy of the services provided by social service agencies, whose mission is to help families at risk. In many cases, they were either denied services due to term limits on assistance or offered limited resources that failed to meet the needs of the family. As a result, many youth turn to delinquency in an effort to cry out for help. One girl, Camille, describes how her family struggled financially:

The welfare system would have been a little bit better for my mom because she couldn't afford to survive. . . . She couldn't get section 8. . . . If the welfare system would have offered a lot more help, it would have been a lot easier. . . . [Also] child support would've helped an awesome amount. . . . [My father has] been ordered to pay child support for me for twenty-five years and he's never paid a dime. (Bright et al., 2011, p. 40)

The economic marginality that surrounds the lives of girls impacts their future outlooks for success. For many of the girls, what they see within their own families and communities is all they know. To hope and aspire for a better life simply seems like a dream that is out of reach. As a result, many young girls submit themselves to a life filled with violence:

I came from the ghetto. And people didn't go to college. They barely made it out of high school, if they made it out of high school. So it's not normal for us to think, you know it's just not something that crosses our minds. (Garcia & Lane, 2010, p. 237)

(Continued)

(Continued)

Regardless of the successes that girls may experience within the juvenile justice system, the reality is that these girls will most likely return to the chaotic environments of their families and communities. While some girls fight to maintain the positive changes in their lives by working toward goals for their future, others reference that these will be an uphill battle based on the environments in which they reside. As these girls note,

> It was just harsh, hard. You had to be a rough kid. . . . It was a place that should have been condemned a long time ago. Every day people getting shot. You stand on the sidewalk, you know, somebody running by with a gun, kids getting ran over, people sneaking in people's windows, raping people. (Bright et al., 2011, p. 40)

> Hey, I'm going back to the same environment, the same people . . . my friends, my same family who didn't help me. (Garcia & Lane, 2010, p. 237)

For other girls, returning to the juvenile system represents perhaps the safest place for them. Given the economic marginality, violence, and chaos that encompasses their lives, it is no surprise that a structured orderly environment that provides food, clothing, and shelter is viewed as a favorable option, even if it means being incarcerated.

> Here I am back on the streets and if I do this again and get into trouble them I'm just gonna go back to a place where they are gonna feed me and I don't have to worry about somebody beatin' me there. I don't have to worry about somebody molestin' me there, you know? (Garcia & Lane, 2010, p. 235)

Although traditional research on female offenders has focused on the risk factors that lead to negative behaviors, recent research has shifted to include resiliency or protective factors to fight against the risks of delinquent behavior. These factors include intelligence; brilliance; courage; creativity; tenacity; compassion; humor; insightfulness; social competence; problem-solving abilities; autonomy; potential with leadership; engagement in family, community, and religious activities; and a sense of purpose and belief in the future. While these resiliency factors typically develop within the context of the family, the support for such a curriculum needs to come from somewhere else, since many delinquent girls often come from families in crisis (Acoca & Dedel, 1998).

While the intent to provide gender-specific services indicated a potential to address the unique needs of girls, not all scholars are convinced that girls will be able to receive the treatment and programs that are so desperately needed. While many states embarked on data-heavy assessments reflecting the needs of girls, few of these assessments have translated into effective programmatic changes (Chesney-Lind & Shelden, 2004). Funding remains the most significant barrier in providing effective services for girls. Even when gender-specific programming options exist, the need for these services can outweigh the available options. The limited number of placements, combined with long waiting lists for such services, often makes treatment options unavailable for most girls (Bloom et al., 2002a).

However, several individual and community factors also affect program delivery, including lack of information or difficulties in accessing services, resistance toward programming by girls and their families, and distrust of service providers. In addition, racial, economic, and cultural issues can affect whether communities will seek out assistance and the degree to which these services will reflect culturally relevant issues (Bloom et al., 2002b). In order to develop effective and available programming, the system needs to place the allocation of resources as a priority in identifying and addressing the needs of girls in the juvenile justice system.

SUMMARY

- The age-of-consent campaign raised the age of sexual consent to 16 or 18 in all states by 1920.
- Historically, women have been denied an avenue for healthy expression of sexuality.
- Female victims were blamed for tempting men into immoral acts in cases of forcible sexual assault.
- Arrest data and self-report data present contradictory images on the nature and prevalence of female violence.
- While arrests for violent offenses involving girls have increased, self-report data amongst girls indicates a decrease in the levels of violence.
- Scholars suggest that agents of social control have altered the way in which they respond to cases of female delinquency, particularly in cases of family or school violence.
- Many incidents of family violence stem from symbolic struggles for adolescent freedom between girls and their parents.
- For juvenile girls, the most significant risk factors for delinquency include a poor family relationship, a history of abuse, poor school performance, negative peer relationships, and issues with substance abuse.
- Issues of emotional and mental health are a high area of need for delinquent girls.
- Effective gender-specific programming needs to provide long-term programming for girls and their social support network and address the causes of delinquency in girls' lives.
- Programming that includes resiliency or protective factors plays a significant role in gender-specific programming.
- Programs face significant barriers in implementing services for girls.

KEY TERMS

1992 Reauthorization of the Juvenile Justice and Delinquency Prevention (JJDP) Act

Age-of-consent campaign

Bootstrapping

Formal processing

Gender-specific programming

Informal processing

Juvenile delinquency

Juvenile Justice and Delinquency Prevention (JJDP) Act of 1974

Parens patriae

Reentry

Reformatory

Resiliency

Risk factors for female delinquency

Zero-tolerance policies

DISCUSSION QUESTIONS

1. How did the age-of-consent campaign punish girls and deny healthy expressions of sexuality? What effects of this movement remain today?

2. How have girls continued to be punished for status offenses, despite the enactment of the Juvenile Justice and Delinquency Prevention Act of 1974?

3. What risk factors for delinquency exist for girls?

4. How has the treatment of girls by the juvenile justice system altered society's understanding of violence amongst girls?

5. What should gender-specific programming look like? What challenges do states face in implementing these programs?

WEB RESOURCES

Girls Study Group http://girlsstudygroup.rti.org/

National Center for Juvenile Justice http://www.ncjj.org

Office of Juvenile Justice and Delinquency Prevention http://www.ojjdp.gov

REFERENCES

Acoca, L., & Dedel, K. (1998). *Identifying the needs of young women in the juvenile justice system.* San Francisco, CA: National Council on Crime and Delinquency.

Alder, C. M. (1998). Passionate and willful girls: Confronting practices. *Women and Criminal Justice, 9*(4), 81–101.

Beck, A. J., Harrison, P. M., & Guerino, P. (2010). *Sexual victimization in juvenile facilities reported by youth, 2008–2009.* U.S. Department of Justice, Bureau of Justice Statistics. Retrieved from http://bjs.ojp.usdoj.gov/content/pub/pdf/svjfry09.pdf

Beger, R. R., & Hoffman, H. (1998). Role of gender of detention dispositioning of juvenile probation violators. *Journal of Crime and Justice, 21,* 173–188.

Belknap, J., Dunn, M., & Holsinger, K. (1997). *Moving toward juvenile justice and youth serving systems that address the distinct experience of the adolescent female.* (Report to the Governor). Columbus, OH: Office of Criminal Justice Services.

Belknap, J., & Holsinger, K. (2006). The gendered nature of risk factors for delinquency. *Feminist Criminology, 1*(1), 48–71.

Belknap, J., & Holsinger, K. (1998). An overview of delinquent girls: How theory and practice failed and the need for innovative change. In R. Zaplin (Ed.), *Female crime and delinquency: Critical perspectives and effective interventions* (pp. 31–64). Gaithersburg, MD: Aspen Publishers.

Bernard, T. J. (1992). *The cycle of juvenile justice.* New York, NY: Oxford University Press.

Bloom, B., Owen, B., Deschenes, E. P., & Rosenbaum, J. (2002a). Improving juvenile justice for females: A statewide assessment in California. *Crime and Delinquency, 48*(4), 526–552.

Bloom, B., Owen, B., Deschenes, E. P., & Rosenbaum, J. (2002b). Moving toward justice for female offenders in the new millennium: Modeling gender-specific policies and programs. *Journal of Contemporary Criminal Justice, 18*(1), 37–56.

Bright, C. L., Ward, S. K., & Negi, N. J. (2011). "The chain has to be broken": A qualitative investigation of the experiences of young women following juvenile court involvement. *Feminist Criminology, 6*(1), 32–53.

Brown, L. M., Chesney-Lind, M., & Stein, N. (2007). Patriarchy matters: Towards a gendered theory of teen violence and victimization. *Violence Against Women, 13*(12), 1249–1273.

Carr, N. T., Hudson, K., Hanks, R. S., & Hunt, A. N. (2008). Gender effects along the juvenile justice system: Evidence of a gendered organization. *Feminist Criminology, 3*(1), 25–43.

Chesney-Lind, M. (1973). Judicial enforcement of the female sex role. *Issues in Criminology, 8,* 51–70.

Chesney-Lind, M. (1997). *The female offender: Girls, women, and crime.* Thousand Oaks, CA: SAGE.

Chesney-Lind, M., & Shelden, R. G. (2004). *Girls, delinquency and juvenile justice.* Belmont, CA: West/Wadsworth.

Ciong, Z. B., & Huang, J. (2011). Predicting Hmong male and female youth's delinquent behavior: An exploratory study. *Hmong Studies Journal, 12,* 1–34. Retrieved from http://www.hmongstudies.org/XiongandHuangHSJ 12.pdf

Crosnoe, R., Erickson, K. G., & Dornbusch, S. M. (2002). Protective functions of family relationships and school factors on the deviant behavior of adolescent boys and girls. *Youth and Society, 33*(4), 515–544.

Davis, C. P. (2007). At risk girls and delinquency: Career pathways. *Crime and Delinquency, 53*(3), 408–435.

Feld, B. C. (2009). Violent girls or relabeled status offenders? An alternative interpretation of the data. *Crime and Delinquency, 55*(2), 241–265.

Fellner, J. (2010). Sexually abused: The nightmare of juveniles in confinement. *Huffington Post.* Retrieved from http://www.huffingtonpost.com/jamie-fellner/sexually-abused-the-night_b_444240.html

Garcia, C. A., & Lane, J. (2010). Looking in the rearview mirror: What incarcerated women think girls need from the system. *Feminist Criminology, 5*(3), 227–243.

Gavazzi, S. M., Yarcheck, C. M., & Lim, J.-Y. (2005). Ethnicity, gender, and global risk indicators in the lives of status offenders coming to the attention of the juvenile court. *International Journal of Offender Therapy and Comparative Criminology, 49*(6), 696–710.

Girls Incorporated. (1996). *Prevention and parity: Girls in juvenile justice.* Indianapolis, IN: Girls Incorporated National Resource Center & Office of Juvenile Justice and Delinquency Prevention.

Goodkind, S. (2005). Gender specific services in the juvenile justice system: A critical examination. *Affilia, 20*(1), 52–70.

Hennessey, M., Ford, J. D., Mahoney, K., Ko, S. J., & Siegfried, C. B. (2004). Trauma among girls in the juvenile justice system. *National Child Traumatic Stress Network Juvenile Justice Working Group.* Retrieved from http://www.nctsn.org/nctsn_assets/pdfs/edu_materials/trauma_among_girls_in_jjsys.pdf

Hirschi, T. (1969). *Causes of delinquency.* Berkeley, CA: University of California Press.

Holsinger, K., & Holsinger, A. M. (2005). Differential pathways to violence and self-injurious behavior: African American and White girls in the juvenile justice system. *Journal of Research in Crime & Delinquency, 42*(2), 211–242.

Human Rights Watch. (2006). Custody and control: Conditions of confinement in New York's juvenile prisons for girls. *ACLU.* Retrieved from http://www.hrw.org/sites/default/files/reports/us0906webwcover.pdf

Just Detention International. (2009). *Incarcerated youth at extreme risk of sexual abuse.* Retrieved from http://www.justdetention.org/en/factsheets/jdifactsheetyouth.pdf

Knoll, C., & Sickmund, M. (2010). Delinquency cases in juvenile court, 2007. *Office of Juvenile Justice and Delinquency Prevention.* U.S. Department of Justice, Office of Justice Programs. Retrieved from http://www.ncjrs.gov/pdffiles1/ojjdp/230168.pdf

Mahoney, J. L., Cairns, B. D., & Farmer, T. W. (2003). Promoting interpersonal competence and educational success through extracurricular activity participation. *Journal of Educational Psychology, 95*(2), 409–418.

Mallicoat, S. L. (2007). Gendered justice: Attributional differences between males and females in the juvenile courts. *Feminist Criminology, 2*(1), 4–30.

Matsueda, R. (1992). Reflected appraisals, parental labeling and delinquency: Specifying a symbolic interactionist theory. *American Journal of Sociology, 97*(6), 1577–1611.

McCartan, L. M., & Gunnison, E. (2010). Individual and relationship factors that differentiate female offenders with and without a sexual abuse history. *Journal of Interpersonal Violence, 25*(8), 1449–1469.

McKnight, L. R., & Loper, A. B. (2002). The effect of risk and resilience factors on the prediction of delinquency in adolescent girls. *School Psychology International, 23*(2), 186–198.

Miller, J. (1994). Race, gender and juvenile justice: An examination of disposition decision-making for delinquent girls. In M. Schwartz & D. Milovanivoc (Eds.), *Race, gender and class in criminology: The intersection* (pp. 219–246). New York, NY: Garland.

Miller, S., Loeber, R., & Hipwell, A. (2009). Peer deviance, parenting and disruptive behavior among young girls. *Journal of Abnormal Child Psychology, 37*(2), 139–152.

Moffitt, T. E., Caspi, A., Rutter, M., & Silva, P. A. (2001). *Sex differences in antisocial behavior: Conduct disorder, delinquency and violence in the Denedin Longitudinal Study.* New York, NY: Cambridge University Press.

National Mental Health Association. (2004). *Mental health treatment for youth in the juvenile justice system: A compendium of promising practices.* Retrieved from https://www.nttac.org/views/docs/jabg/mhcurriculum/mh_mht.pdf

Odem, M. E. (1995). *Delinquent daughters: Protecting and policing adolescent female sexuality in the United States: 1885–1920.* Chapel Hill, NC: University of North Carolina Press.

Owen, B., & Bloom B. (1998). *Modeling gender-specific services in juvenile justice: Final report to the office of criminal justice planning.* Sacramento CA: OCJP.

Platt, A. M. (1969). *The child savers.* Chicago, IL: University of Chicago Press.

Sharpe, G. (2009). The trouble with girls today: Professional perspectives on young women's offending. *Youth Justice, 9*(3), 254–269.

Shelden, R. G. (1981). Sex discrimination in the juvenile justice system: Memphis, Tennessee, 1900–1917. In M. Q. Warren (Ed.), *Comparing Male and Female Offenders* (pp. 55–72). Beverly Hills, CA: SAGE.

Shufelt, J. L., & Cocozza, J. J. (2006, June). Youth with mental health disorders in the juvenile justice system: Results from a multi-state prevalence study. *Research and Project Briefs.* National Center for Mental Health and Juvenile Justice. Retrieved from http://www.ncmhjj.com/pdfs/publications/PrevalenceRPB.pdf

Snyder, H. N., & Sickmund, M. (2006). Juvenile offenders and victims: 2006 national report. *National Center for Juvenile Justice, Office of Juvenile Justice and Delinquency Prevention.* Retrieved from http://www.ojjdp.gov/ojstatbb/nr2006/

Stattin, H., & Magnusson, D. (1990). *Pubertal maturation in female development, vol. 2.* Hillsdale, NJ: Erlbaum.

Steffensmeier, D., Schwartz, J., Zhong, H., & Ackerman, J. (2005). An assessment of recent trends in girls' violence using diverse longitudinal sources: Is the gender gap closing? *Criminology, 43,* 355–405.

Sutton, J. R. (1988). *Stubborn children: Controlling delinquency in the United States, 1640–1981.* Berkeley, CA: University of California Press.

Svensson, R. (2003). Gender differences in adolescent drug use. *Youth and Society, 34,* 300–329.

Tille, J. E., & Rose, J. C. (2007). Emotional and behavioral problems of 13- to 18-year-old incarcerated female first-time offenders and recidivists. *Youth Violence and Juvenile Justice, 5*(4), 426–435.

Tolman, D. L. (1994). Doing desire: Adolescent girls' struggles for/with sexuality. *Gender and Society, 8*(3), 324–342.

Triplett, R., & Myers, L. B. (1995). Evaluating contextual patterns of delinquency: Gender based differences. *Justice Quarterly, 12*(1), 59–84.

Widom, C. S. (1989). The cycle of violence. *Science, 244,* 160–166.

Widom, C. S. (1991). Childhood victimization: Risk factor for delinquency. In M. E. Colten & S. Gore (Eds.), *Adolescent stress: Causes and consequences* (pp. 201–221). New York, NY: Aldine De Gruyter.

NOTE

1. For a state-by-state review of systematic maltreatment within juvenile facilities, go to http://www.aecf.org/OurWork/JuvenileJustice/~/media/Pubs/Topics/Juvenile%20Justice/Detention%20Reform/NoPlaceForKids/SystemicorRecurringMaltreatmentinJuvenileCorrectionsFacilities.pdf

9

Female Offenders

Drug, Property, and Victimless Crimes

Over the next several years, Diana worked patrol and was eventually promoted to vice. She was a good officer, but she didn't get kudos for her police skill. Instead, she heard rumors that she was promoted to vice because she would look hot as a decoy prostitute. She pretended she didn't know what the male officers said about her, and she did her best to do good police work and make solid arrests.

By this time, Karla had spent more than a decade on the streets, ensnared with drug use, prostitution, and property theft. Like Diana, Karla was also promoted: from sex work to "rolling Johns"—pretending to be a prostitute, then robbing the would-be client. She had multiple arrests and convictions on solicitation and drug charges, but these never amounted to much time. Because of overcrowding in the local jails, a 30-day sentence would often result in one or two days in custody.

Karla and Diana met again one day in March, when 29-year-old Diana was working vice and 28-year-old Karla was rolling Johns. Karla was in motel with her client, who was told to pay first. Karla then slipped into the bathroom and called her pimp/boyfriend, who "broke in" and robbed the pair. The pimp took the customer's wallet, watch, cell phone, and car keys. A wedding ring suggested the victim was married, and the pair was confident the victim would not call the police from a motel room with a prostitute. So they drove his car to an ATM to withdraw cash and used his credit cards before they were reported stolen.

In this instance, their plan didn't work. The victim called police from the motel lobby, saying he was carjacked by a Bonnie-and-Clyde pair at the intersection adjacent to the motel. He also had Karla's street name, Angel Baby, a nickname she had taken in honor of her daughter. This moniker was linked to Karla in a gang database, and she was arrested later that same night—in the same motel room with a new John. Diana, who was working vice less than two miles away, was with the team that responded and arrested Karla.

Chapter Highlights

- Women and drugs
- White-collar and property crimes by women offenders
- Female offenders and their male codefendants
- Prostitution and sex work

W omen engage in every type of criminal activity. Much like their male counterparts, women are involved in a variety of crime types, including nonviolent crimes such as white-collar crimes and property offenses; drug offenses, including the manufacture, sale, and use of controlled substances; sex offenses, including prostitution, rape, and child molestation; and violent crimes ranging from simple assault and robbery to first-degree murder. This chapter focuses on the types of crime most often associated with female offending, which are overwhelmingly nonviolent in nature: drug crimes, **property crimes**, and sex work. Chapter 10 examines issues of violent and sexual offending by women, which are far less common than the crimes presented here, yet they receive far more media attention.

While men have always engaged in greater numbers of criminal acts than their female counterparts, the representation of women among the ranks of criminal offenders is increasing. Research over the past several decades has focused on the narrowing of the gender gap, which refers to the differences between male and female offending for different types of offenses. But what does this really mean? Are women becoming more violent than they were in the past, as media reports have suggested? Is the rise in the number of women incarcerated a result of more women engaging in serious criminal acts? What factors contribute to these changes? How do we investigate these questions?

In Chapter 2, you learned about the changes in male and female crime participation over a one-year and 10-year period, using arrest data from the Uniform Crime Reports (UCR). Using these same data, we can investigate the gender gap in offending. Table 9.1 compares the percentage of males and females in different offense types. These data illustrate that the proportion of violent crime cases is far greater for males than females. In contrast, the proportion of property crimes is greater for females than males, as property crimes comprise 18.73% of all female arrests, compared to 10.66% of male arrests. While these data illustrate that the gender gap may be narrowing in terms of gender proportions of crime, it is important to note that the number of male arrests is almost three times greater than the number of arrests of women for all crimes.

Arrest trends over time also demonstrate an overall decrease in crimes for both men and women, although there are certain crimes that have demonstrated significant increases for women. Table 9.2 demonstrates the five-year trends in male and female arrests from 2006 to 2010. For example, between 2006 and 2010, women's arrests in property-related crimes increased 27.9%. Much of this increase comes from a 34.7% increase in larceny-theft crimes. While the participation of women in offending behaviors has increased throughout the 20th and 21st century, they remain a small proportion of offending.

While statistics from the UCR provide valuable insight into the status of female offending today, research by Steffensmeier and Allan (1996) examines the proportion of male and female arrests for three separate years over the 20th century: 1960, 1975, and 1990. Their findings indicate that females made up 15% (or less) of arrestees for most types of major crimes (such as crimes against persons and major property crimes) across all time periods. For minor property offenses, the greatest increases are noted between 1960 and 1975, according to arrest data. Here, the female percentage of arrests increased from 17% in 1960 to 30% in both 1975 and 1990. The only exception where women make up the majority of arrests is for the crime of prostitution (where women make up between two-thirds and three-fourths of all arrests across all three time periods).

What has happened with female offenders since Steffensmeier and Allan's comparison of female arrests in the late 20th century? Research by Rennison (2009) compared offending data from the National Crime Victimization Survey (NCVS) for the nine years, between 1992 and 2001, and indicated that there had been negligible differences in the gender gap between male and female offending behaviors. Their use of the NCVS presents a different view of offending behaviors, as it includes data on crimes that were not reported to the police and those crimes where an arrest was not made. Their findings note that any differences in the gender gap result not from the increases of female offending but rather the decreases in male offending rates for particular offenses, which fell at a greater rate than the decreases in female offending rates.

While women participate in many different types of crimes, the remaining focus of this chapter highlights four general categories of crime, all of which are embedded with gendered expectations about offenders. The first category focuses on a topic that is at the heart of the dramatic rise of female participation in the criminal justice system: drug addiction. The second topic addresses the most common crime type amongst female offenders in official data: property crime. While property crimes are committed by both men and women, this section explores gendered expectations for property crimes offenses, including female white-collar offenders. The third section highlights the phenomena of women who engage in criminal activity in conjunction with the men in their lives. The fourth section in this chapter focuses on prostitution, a crime that is often suggested to be a victimless crime. However, a deeper look at the lives of women involved in this lifestyle shows that these women face significantly higher levels of victimization compared to other women.

Table 9.1	2010 Uniform Crime Reports Arrest Data: Males Versus Females	
	Percentage of Offense Type Within Gender (%)	
	Males	**Females**
Violent crime	4.55	3.19
Homicide	.10	.04
Forcible rape	.20	.006
Robbery	.99	.41
Aggravated assault	3.26	2.74
Property crime	10.66	18.73
Burglary	2.55	1.34
Larceny-theft	7.42	16.95
Motor vehicle theft	.58	.36
Arson	.10	.06

SOURCE: FBI-Uniform Crime Report (UCR).

NOTE: Total male arrests = 7,167,015; total female arrests = 2,474,588.

Table 9.2	Five-Year Arrest Trends, 2006–2010: Uniform Crime Reports Arrest Data: Males Versus Females	
	Percentage Change Within Gender Between 2006 and 2010	
	Males	**Females**
Violent crime	−11.3	−3.2
Homicide	−14.8	−16.7
Forcible rape	−12.8	−29.6
Robbery	−11.7	−2.8
Aggravated assault	−11.0	−2.9
Property crime	−2.9	+27.6
Burglary	−4.4	+3.3
Larceny-theft	+5.1	+34.7
Motor vehicle theft	−45.5	−45.8
Arson	−30.1	−27.6

SOURCE: FBI-Uniform Crime Report (UCR).

NOTE: Overall crime percent change for men was −11.1%; overall crime percent change for women was −2.0%.

The Media and the Female Offender: Lindsay Lohan

Celebrities live their lives in the public eye, a fact most evident when a celebrity gets in trouble with the law. Lindsay Lohan, teen film star of *The Parent Trap, Mean Girls,* and *Herbie: Fully Loaded,* discovered this firsthand when she was arrested in 2007 for driving under the influence (DUI) of alcohol.

In May of 2007, Lohan crashed her Mercedes-Benz on a curb and was arrested for DUI. Within two months, Lohan was arrested for a second DUI and charged with possession of cocaine. In August of 2007, she plead guilty to drunk driving and misdemeanor cocaine use and was sentenced to one day in jail, ten days of community service, fines, completion of a substance abuse education program, and three years of probation. Due to overcrowding, she was in custody for a total of 84 minutes.

This was just the beginning of Lohan's dealings with the criminal justice system. In October of 2009, her probation was extended, because she failed to attend a court-ordered drug program. In May of 2010, she failed to appear for a court progress report, claiming she was in France and unable to return to the United States because someone stole her passport.

In July of 2010, Lohan's probation was revoked and she was ordered to serve 90 days in jail followed by a 90-day inpatient rehabilitation facility. She served just 14 of 90 days in jail due to overcrowding and just 23 of 90 days in rehab, as her physician stated she had completed all inpatient drug treatment requirements. Within two months, however, she failed a drug test and her probation was revoked yet again. She was returned to custody for a few hours before being released again on bail. She was ordered by court to the Betty Ford Center, where she remained until January 11, 2011. Within one month of her release, Lohan was arrested for theft of a $2,500 necklace from a Venice jewelry store and sentenced to 120 days in jail, which she served on 35 days of house arrest. In October of 2011, Lohan's probation was once again revoked, and she was ordered back to jail, where she spent just a few hours before posting bail. At her hearing in November of 2011, she was sentenced yet again to a 30-day jail term, serving less than five hours behind bars. In June of 2012, Lohan allegedly crashed her Porsche into a truck in Santa Monica, California, leading to charges of reckless driving (for the crash) and lying to the police (for denying she was behind the wheel). In March of 2013, she accepted a plea deal in which she was sentenced to another 90-day drug rehab for the incident.

In all, Lohan was sentenced to over 250 days of jail time, but she spent less than 15 days in custody. Did her status as a celebrity help her case or invite intense scrutiny, leading to her many violations? Is this an example of the media focusing undue attention on a relatively minor crime at the exclusion of more common malfeasances? Or did her celebrity status attract attention to recurring criminal justice themes of addiction, relapse, and overcrowding among the women (and men) who enter the justice system today?

Without a doubt, Lohan's resources helped her secure posh, if not top-of-the-line, treatment that most offenders simply cannot afford. She also avoided jail time through house arrest/electronic monitoring, another pricey option that exceeds the resources of most offenders. On one hand, this is certainly an example of the media's heightened focus on celebrity debacles. On the other hand, however, it illustrates the most common pattern for female offenders: a cycle of substance use, failed treatment episodes, property offending, and a prolonged, costly yet unproductive period of court supervision. The astute criminal justice agent should pause for a moment and ask: Is jail the most effective criminal justice response for those accused of a DUI, drug possession, or other crimes rooted in underlying substance abuse issues?

Typical female offenders have neither the fiscal nor media resources afforded celebrity offenders like Lindsay Lohan; most instances of female crime reported in the media involve celebrities like Lohan or rare cases of heinous violence, such as those committed by serial killer Aileen Wuornos or Andrea Yates, a mother who drowned her five children in the bathtub. However, the issues raised in the Lohan case reflect a far more frequent pattern for women in criminal justice—involving addiction, treatment, relapse, and recidivism—than typically portrayed in the media.

✂ Women and Drugs

Throughout the majority of the 20th century, women were not identified as the typical addict or drug abuser; this label was overwhelmingly reserved for men, particularly men of color, those who lived in immigrant communities, and the homeless. The American public was primarily concerned with substances associated with marginalized populations, such as alcohol consumed by the homeless town drunk, opium dens found in Chinese labor communities, and marijuana smoked by Mexican immigrants. In many cases, the use of prescription and illegal substances by women, particularly White women, was normalized, as society often viewed such drug use as a response to the pressures of gender-role expectations. For example, cocaine and opiates were legally sold in pharmacies and were frequently prescribed by doctors for a variety of ailments. When purchased and consumed by middle-class housewives, it was not cause for concern; in contrast, the consumption of the same opiates in immigrant labor communities was vilified.

Historically speaking, "women's addiction [was] constructed as the product of individual women's inability to cope with changing versions of normative femininity" (Campbell, 2000, p. 30). Examples of this can be found in advertisements depicting the use of anti-anxiety medications to calm the frenzied housewife who was overwhelmed with her duties as a wife and mother. Remnants of this phenomenon for White women can still be seen in modern times. For example, drug use was sometimes promoted as desirable with the image of the heroin chic fashionista of the 1990s, personified by supermodel Kate Moss. More commonly, however, the high moral and behavioral standards often associated with women can lead to greater stigma for female addicts than in the past (Cohen, 2002). This has led to increased negative attitudes about female addicts, especially substance-abusing women who are also mothers.

Without question, the War on Drugs has had a singular impact on addicted women: It targets them for incarceration. In the last few decades, female incarceration rates grew 108%, but raw numbers grew eightfold (Beck & Harrison, 2001; Harrison & Beck, 2006). These incarcerated women are overwhelmingly female drug offenders, ensnared for both drug charges as well as property crimes related to drug use (Beck & Harrison, 2004; Bloom, Chesney-Lind, & Owen, 1994, p. 12; Bloom, Owen, & Covington, 2004; Bush-Baskette, 1999, 2000; Owen, 1998). In the United States today, the War on Drugs has effectively been a war on women (Bloom et al., 1994; Chesney-Lind, 1997), leading to an explosion in the number of addicted, incarcerated women (Bush-Baskette, 2000; Chesney-Lind, 2000; Radosh, 2008; Reynolds, 2008). For examples of the many U.S. drug laws passed in the last 100 years, see Table 9.3 on page 197 below.

For many women, the addiction of substance abuse is inextricably intertwined with property crimes and sex work, namely prostitution. Radosh (2008) and others argue that addicted women engage in drug crimes, but they also disproportionately commit crimes of prostitution and property

▲ **Photo 9.1** Research highlights that women and men vary in their drug use, both in terms of their drug of choice as well as their motivations for use. Here, a woman is shown using drugs intravenously. The cycle of drug addiction for women is heavily related to issues of economics and abuse.

offenses to support their addiction. Deschenes, Owen, and Crow (2007) call these "survival crimes . . . tied to economic and emotional struggles" (2007, p. 58). Female addicts are often under the influence of alcohol or other substances when they commit their offenses, whether these be drug offenses, sex work, or property crimes. This constellation of offenses—drugs, property, and prostitution crimes—is an undercurrent through all discussions of female addiction.

Much has been written about addiction, but as many feminist scholars have noted, these are often based on the experiences of male addicts and don't adequately or accurately reflect that of women (Chesney-Lind, 1997). However, there are some broad similarities in addiction between the sexes. Both male and female addicts experience an intense compulsion to use the object of their addiction, whether it is alcohol or other drugs. For many addicts, drug using leads to arrest for possession of a controlled substance, drug paraphernalia, disorderly conduct/disturbing the peace, DUI, or other crimes directly related to substance use and abuse. For both men and women, addiction can also lead to secondary criminality, as the compulsion to use alcohol and other drugs can be a precursor to property offending. For example, addicts often engage in a variety of larceny-theft, burglary, and other property crimes to obtain resources to support their drug use. The large numbers of addicted offenders in prison today and over the last 20 years suggests that the social problem of drug addiction, manifested in both drug and property crimes, is addressed primarily through incarceration. A sobering fact to this discussion is that some research suggests that the course of substance abuse among addicts lasts nearly three decades before a year of sobriety is achieved for many addicts (Dennis, Scott, Funk, & Foss, 2005). In sum, our incarceration rates have exploded with untreated addicts, sentenced for both drug and property crime in pursuit of addiction, which is often a lifetime battle.

While there are similarities, however, addiction is also very different for women than men in many ways, including onset/entry, secondary crimes, incarceration, and treatment. These differences are underscored by marked physical, emotional, physiological, and social differences between the sexes, as seen in arrest, incarceration, supervision, and treatment data (Covington, 2008; Glaze & Maruschak, 2008; Gray & Saum, 2005; Kassebaum, 1999; Palm, 2007; Wells & Bright, 2005). Further, addicted female offenders often have very severe drug and alcohol problems compared to male offenders, and they experience a constellation of high-risk factors associated with continued criminality and relapse (Substance Abuse and Mental Health Services Administration [SAMHSA], 2009).

There is an endless number of pathways to the onset of drug addiction and offending. However, the literature consistently illustrates similar pathways of drug use for women, regardless of race, ethnicity, or drug of choice. Whether the discussion focuses on women addicted to crack cocaine in lower-income communities or middle-class women who abuse alcohol or prescription drugs, women often share

Table 9.3	United States Drug Policy Timeline

United States Drug Policy 100-Year Timeline		
1906	Pure Food & Drug Act	Forms Food & Drug Administration (FDA). Labeling of drugs is now required over concerns of unlabeled use of animal products and addictive or harmful substances. Drugs can contain these so long as they are labeled. Results in appreciable drop in addiction in the U.S.
1909	Opium Exclusion Act	Bans imported, nonmedicinal opium smoking
1914	Harrison Tax Act	Opium and cocaine distributors must register and pay tax. Act is a tax only—opiates and narcotics still available through prescriptions. Views addiction as a medical issue, not a criminal justice issue
1920	18th Amendment (Volstead Act)	Prohibition of alcohol in the U.S.
1922	Narcotic Drug Import & Export Act	Limits use of narcotics to medical use
1924	Heroin Act	Makes heroin manufacture illegal
1926	Rolleston Committee in UK	Establishes medical response, not criminal justice response, to addiction in UK. Prompts court cases in U.S., in which medical authority loses to criminal justice interest on issues of addiction
1933	21st Amendment	Overturns 18th Amendment
1936	Film *Reefer Madness*	Propaganda film depicts dangers of addiction, is released in the U.S.
1937	Marijuana Tax Act	Control of marijuana similar to narcotics: taxes grower, distributor, seller, buyer. Superseded by Controlled Substance Act of 1970
1938	Food, Drug, and Cosmetic Act	Establishes FDA authority over drug safety, extended beyond mere labeling. Defines drugs, establishes drugs administered by prescription versus nonprescription drugs
1942	Opium Poppy Control Act	Establishes that growers must have license to grow opium poppies
1942	Methadone patented	Patents long-acting, low-cost analgesic, distributes for medicinal use
1951	Durham-Humphrey Amendment	Establishes guidelines for prescription drugs
1951	Boggs Amendment to Harrison Narcotic Act	Establishes first mandatory sentences for narcotics violations
1956	Narcotics Control Act	Imposes severe penalties for drug violation
1962	Kafauver-Harris Amendments	Essentially establishes the FDA as agency responsible for testing and approving drugs. Drugs must be effective and approved before human trials can begin.
1963	Methadone maintenance	Introduces Methadone in U.S. as alternative to heroin for heroin addicts

(Continued)

Table 9.3 (Continued)

United States Drug Policy 100-Year Timeline		
1965	Drug Abuse Control Amendments	Regulates amphetamines and barbiturates as "dangerous drugs," establishes ongoing regulation of other drugs in future, is first federal prohibition of particular substances
1966	Narcotic Addict Rehabilitation Act	Allows treatment in lieu of jail for drug offenders
1968	DACA Amendments	Allows suspended sentence & expungement for offenders with no repeat drug violation within one year
1969	Operation Intercept	Inspects every vehicle crossing U.S.-Mexico border for 20 days. Results in impact on drug trade, which is costly on both sides of border. According to G. Gordon Liddy, the impetus for the operation was not an actual effort to reduce drug trafficking: "The Mexicans, using diplomatic language of course, told us to go piss up a rope. The Nixon administration didn't believe in the U.S. taking crap from any foreign government. Its reply was Operation Intercept."
1969–1970	Methadone treatment becomes standard practice in Washington DC	Methadone treatment for heroin addicts begins in Washington DC jails. As Nixon expands funding throughout Washington DC, burglaries decrease 41%
1970	Comprehensive Drug Abuse Prevention and Control Act (Controlled Substances Act)	Updates all narcotic laws in U.S, is first effort to control all drugs through enforcement (Department of Justice), not through just taxation (Treasury). Establishes Department of Justice control over most controlled substances, separate commission to study marijuana
1971	Nixon declares War on Drugs	Nixon declares War on Drugs in June 1971 speech, declaring drugs "public enemy number 1." Despite tough rhetoric, Nixon spends more money on treatment than enforcement.
1972	Drug Abuse Office and Treatment Act	Establishes federal funds for drug prevention and treatment
1973	Methadone Control Act	Establishes the regulations for methadone dispensation and licensing
1973	Heroin Trafficking Act	Increases penalties for heroin
1973	Alcohol, Drug Abuse and Mental Health Administration (ADAMHA) established	Consolidates former agencies: National Institute of Mental Health (NIMH), National Institute on Drug Addiction (NIDA), and National Institute on Alcohol Abuse and Alcoholism (NIAAA)
1973	Drug Enforcement Administration (DEA)	Reorganizes Bureau of Narcotics and Dangerous Drugs into DEA, the "super-agency" handling all aspects of illegal drug issues in U.S., including enforcement, customs, and school education. U.S. policy is criticized internationally for demonization of addiction over harm reduction
1976	Carter moves to decriminalize cannabis	Candidate Jimmy Carter campaigns for President on decriminalization of cannabis campaign.

United States Drug Policy 100-Year Timeline		
1978	Alcohol and Drug Abuse Education Amendments	Responsibility for drug education becomes part of Department of Education
1980	Drug Abuse, Prevention, Treatment and Rehabilitation Amendments	Extends prevention, education, and treatment efforts for drug abuse and addiction.
1984	Just Say No	First Lady Nancy Reagan introduces "Just Say No" campaign. Birth of Drug Abuse Resistance Education (DARE), which Lindesmith Center chastises as "indoctrination, not education."
1984	Drug Analogue (Designer Drug) Act	Makes designer drugs with similar effects & structure subject to same law as existing drug
1985	Crack Epidemic	Crack epidemic starts in early 1980s, especially in New York.
1986	Anti-Drug Abuse Act	Increases penalties for drug trafficking, establishes mandatory minimums for drugs. 100:1 sentence disparity between powdered/crack cocaine, leading to racial disparities in sentencing
1988	Senator John Kerry, U.S. Senate Committee on Foreign Relations	Senate report alleges CIA involved with cocaine sales, using proceeds to fund arms purchases
1988	Anti-Drug Abuse Act	Establishes office of National Drug Control Policy
1988	Omnibus Drug Act (Chemical Diversion and Trafficking Act)	Increases penalties for drug users and traffickers; addresses money laundering and weapons in drug markets; allows seizure of vehicles and assets used in drug trade
1990	Bush escalates War on Drugs	President Bush administration approves 50% spending increase for War on Drugs. Spending increase earmarked for enforcement, not prevention or treatment.
1992	Clinton on cannabis	President Clinton admits to smoking cannabis but not inhaling
1992	ADAMHA reorganized	ADAMHA reorganizes: NIDA, NIMH, and NIAAA moved to National Institute of Health; programs moved to Substance Abuse and Mental Health Services Administration (SAMHSA)
1994	Violent Crime Control and Law Enforcement Act	Largest crime bill in U.S. history. In addition to weapon and violent crime provisions, mandates drug testing for federal parolees
1995	U.S. Sentencing Commission recommends revisions on mandatory minimum sentences	U.S. Sentencing Commission seeks to address sentencing disparity in federal sentencing guidelines. Congress rejects recommendations of the very commission charged with making specific recommendations to Congress.
1996	Comprehensive Methamphetamine Control Act	Limits access to equipment and chemicals used in production of methamphetamines
2005	Combat Methamphetamine Act	Classifies Pseudophedrine (active ingredient in Sudafed) as Schedule V substance; requires ID for purchase. Methamphetamine production drops in U.S.
2010	Fair Sentencing Act	Reduces sentencing disparity between crack and powdered cocaine from 100:1 to 18:1

experiences that lead them toward substance use and abuse as a method of coping with their lives (Inciardi, Lockwood, & Pottiger, 1993). For women, the primary **pathways to addiction** tend to revolve around early exposure to alcohol and other drugs, early victimization and recurring trauma, social marginalization and economic pressures, and mental health needs (Bloom, Owen, & Covington, 2003).

For some women, entry into addiction begins with early exposure to drugs and alcohol, often in the home by family members, typically older male relatives. This is an important pathway to note, as both early onset of drug use and addiction in the family predict longevity of substance abuse. Dennis et al. (2005) suggest that addicts whose onset of drug use began prior to age 15 continue in addiction about 10 years longer than those who began using drugs after age 15. Other research suggests that addiction is more common among children of addicts, either due to environment, genetics, access to drugs and alcohol, or a combination of these factors. Regardless of the reasons, women who are exposed to drugs and alcohol at an early age, particularly in homes ripe with drug and alcohol abuse, often begin their own path of addiction that can last for decades.

Victimization and Trauma

A second, and tragically common, pathway to addiction for women is related to strained family relationships, victimization, and trauma (Covington, 2008; Nijhawan, Salloway, Nunn, Poshkus, & Clarke, 2010; Poehlmann, 2005). Women with histories of violence and abuse in their early years are more likely to abuse alcohol and other drugs than women without such victimization (Covington, 2008; Covington & Cohen, 1984; Green, Miranda, & Daroowalla, 2005; SAMHSA, 2009). An overwhelming body of literature demonstrates high rates of early trauma for adult female addicts (Fischer & Kopf, 2005; Harlow, 1999; Hequembourg, Mancuso, & Miller, 2006; Herman, 1992; Prescott, Soares, Konnath, & Bassuk, 2008). Some studies assert that the majority of substance-abusing women have traumatic histories, with estimates ranging from 52%–74% (Covington & Cohen, 1984) to 48%–90% of addicted women experiencing physical or sexual victimization (Kassebaum, 1999; SAMHSA, 2009).

Victimization and trauma are primary entry mechanisms for women in multiple studies of incarcerated women, women in treatment, and relapse prevention programs. Some girls who experience the traumas of physical and sexual abuse in their families of origin, enduring repeated abuse in their early years, leave home to seek safety in late childhood or early adolescence. For many, the streets offer relative safety compared to certain abuse at home. Once on the streets, however, these vulnerable girls are often targeted by pimps, who find runaways easy prey when offered such basic necessities as food and shelter. Pimps, as well as other socially marginalized people with whom runaways associate on the streets, also offer the escape afforded by drugs and alcohol. This sets the stage for one of the most common pathways to addiction, as drugs are a primary mechanism to escape untreated trauma.

Once the abused teenage runaway is indoctrinated on the streets and becomes dependent on drugs for escape (if not dependent on a pimp for basic human needs like food and shelter), she is often exploited for sex. Many addicted young women turn to prostitution to earn money for their survival as well as to continue their drug supply. Not surprisingly, female addicts are more likely to be engaged in sex work (prostitution) than women who are not addicted; and thus employed on the streets, prostitution leads to further trauma (Burnette, Schneider, Timko, & Ilgen, 2009). For example, sex work under these conditions further marginalizes women, exposing them to the repeated trauma of physical and sexual violence by both customers and pimps. This begets a cycle of victimization, where initial trauma leads to addiction, which leads to an ongoing lifestyle in which trauma and victimization are regularly experienced.

Economic/Material Needs

Not surprisingly, many addicted women find themselves unable to meet economic and material needs as a result of their addiction. According to O'Brien (2001) addicted women have a variety of related issues that may exacerbate addiction or at least present barriers to recovery. These include unemployment, lack of basic job skills, illiteracy, low educational attainment, homelessness, domestic violence, mental health issues, and limited social networks (Durose et al., 2005; Flower, 2010; Glaze & Maruschak, 2008; Harlow, 2003; James & Glaze, 2006; Morash, Bynum, & Koons, 1998; Mumola & Karberg, 2006). This is especially true for younger female addicts, who are less educated, have lower levels of monthly income, and have greater social deficits than older female addicts (Reisig, Holtfreter, & Morash, 2002). For many of these women, addiction leads to further marginalization through property offending. Lacking the educational or job skills necessary to succeed in legitimate employment, addicted women enter prostitution and/or property offending to provide for basic needs, including food, shelter, clothing, and so on.

Mental Health Needs

For many women, co-occurring mental health issues exacerbate addiction and provide additional barriers to recovery (Fendrich, Hubbell, & Lurigio, 2006; James & Glaze, 2006; Zilberman, Tavares, Blume, & El-Guebaly, 2003). Research suggests that female addicts experience more frequent and severe mental health issues than male addicts (Gray & Saum, 2005). Left untreated, mental illness can extend the period of active substance abuse, as addicted women may self-medicate using alcohol and other drugs in lieu of psychological treatment, which may not be readily accessible to addicted women during active episodes of mental illness. Thus, many women with co-occurring disorders (simultaneous mental illness and addiction) remain on the streets, engaged in sex work and property crimes for economic survival, experiencing trauma and violence as a result of their circumstances. While the plight of addicted women with mental illness on the streets is dire, psychological intervention can help both conditions. In one drug court study, for example, being prescribed psychotropic medication was a significant predictor of success among female addicts; this also increased their quality of life (Gray & Saum, 2005; Kleinpeter, Deschenes, Blanks, Lepage, & Knox, 2006).

Other Pathways to Addiction

For some, using drugs is a way to bring excitement to a life that may be described as depressing or boring. Yet the excitement often fades as women express a desire to leave the drug lifestyle; many addicted women feel they have few options available to improve their life. Despite the struggles within the lifestyle, some addicted women believe that the realities of sobriety would be too painful and challenging to deal with. Here, addiction remains a way to escape life, if only on a temporary basis (Roberts, 1999).

Regardless of pathway, an increasing number of women began using drugs, and the marginalization of addicts and especially addicted women fed the War on Drugs. As the behaviors of addicted women shifted toward criminal activity in an effort to support their drug habit, the perception that drug addiction is dangerous spread among the general public. Drug use became something to fear by members of society, particularly as drug use became increasingly associated with other forms of crime, including property offenses and prostitution. Indeed, the images of the pregnant addicted mother and crack babies of the 1980s and 1990s represented the greatest form of evil found in the drug-abusing women. Chapters 10 and 11 detail ways in which the criminal justice system responds to drug-involved women, both in the United States and abroad.

⬙ Property Crime

Property crime refers to a relatively broad category of crime that involves the illegal acquisition of money, goods, or valuables without the use of force or fear to obtain the property. Property crime includes different specific crime types, depending on the agency or jurisdiction reporting it. For example, the NCVS includes burglary, motor vehicle theft, and theft (larceny) in its definition of property crime, while the UCR considers arson, burglary, larceny-theft, and motor vehicle theft in defining property crime. The National Incident Based Reporting System (NIBRS) includes many more types of property offenses than the UCR or NCVS, including, for example: arson, bribery, burglary, vandalism, embezzlement, blackmail, fraud, larceny-theft, motor vehicle theft, stolen property offenses, and bad checks.

According to the Bureau of Justice Statistics, the U.S. property crime victimization rate (property crime per 1,000 households) has seen a steady decline since 1993. The 2010 property crime victimization rate (about 120 victimizations per 1,000 households) dropped 5% from the 2009 rate. The 2010 U.S. property crime victimization rate is roughly one-third of the 1993 victimization rate, which was about 320 victimizations per 1,000 households (Truman, 2011).

While female offenders are more common in property offenses than other types of crimes, men commit the overwhelming majority of property crimes; about 62% of all property crimes were committed by men in 2010. However, the rates of female property offending vary considerably when one considers the specific property crime type. So, while women commit about 38% of all property crimes in the U.S., female offenders commit 42% of all fraud offenses and about 51% of all reported embezzlement crimes in the United States (Federal Bureau of Investigation, 2011).

As you learned in the previous section of this chapter, the changing practices around the use and sale of controlled substances has had a profound effect for women. Here, the role of drugs is significantly related to the offending behaviors of women, particularly in cases involving property crimes. Research overwhelming suggests that female property offending is typically rooted in substance abuse and secondarily in subsistence living—which is often necessary due to substance abuse. Simply put, many female property offenders engage in property crime to obtain money to get drugs, or they commit property crimes while under the influence of a controlled substance. This is especially true for the types of property crimes typically committed on the streets, such as larceny-theft, shoplifting, burglary, and dealing in stolen goods.

Denton and O'Malley (2001) observed non-incarcerated female drug dealers over a four-year period who successfully engaged in drug dealing. Researchers noted the growing use of property crimes as a regular activity among this group of drug-dealing, drug-using women, including crimes of shoplifting, theft, burglary, fraud, forgery, and trafficking in stolen goods. The authors conclude that such property crimes were "tightly integrated," a key part of the drug trade. Thus, for some women in engaged in the drug trade, property crime may simply be a regular part of doing business.

Similarly, Johnson (2004) surveyed 470 incarcerated women in Australia and found that the most common reason these women were reported for committing property crimes involved drugs, including obtaining money for drugs (52%) or being drunk or high at the time of the crime (44%). For many female offenders, property crime is rooted in drugs and addiction. Consider that incarcerated female property offenders reference illegal drugs as a primary factor in their crimes (42%) far more often than female violent offenders, who only report drugs as a primary factor in about one-quarter (28%) of their crimes.

Drugs are the most common factor in female property offending, and addicted women commit more crimes overall than their nonaddicted counterparts. Drug-dependent women report higher levels of "regular offending," meaning two or more crimes per week, than female offenders who are not drug-dependent. Johnson (2004) suggests that drug-dependent females report ongoing patterns of offending about twice as often as women who are not drug dependent. Specifically, about half (49%) of nondependent women engage in crimes twice weekly, while an astonishing 95% of drug-dependent women report committing crimes twice weekly. When asked specifically about property crimes, nearly half (44%) of drug-dependent women engaged in such crimes twice weekly, while fewer than one-quarter of women who were not drug-dependent reported such rates.

Bonnie Without Clyde: Bank Robbery Is Not Just a Man's World

Historically, bank robberies have been a man's crime. While women commit far less crime than men overall, women's participation in bank robbery has been negligible, comprising between 3% and 5% of all crimes in this category, compared to men, who have historically committed more than 95% of all bank robberies in the United States. But times are changing.

The percentage of bank robberies committed by women has nearly doubled in the last decade. In 2002, the Federal Bureau of Investigation (FBI) attributed 4.9% of all bank robberies to women. By 2006, that figure increased significantly, with women responsible for 6.2% of bank robberies nationwide. In 2011, the FBI attributed nearly 9% of all bank robberies to women (see table below). This trend has been so pronounced in the last few years, the media have dubbed this phenomenon "Bonnie without Clyde" (Barnett, 2001; Federal Bureau of Investigation, 2012).

Race, Ethnicity, and Sex of U.S. Bank Robbery Offenders, 2011					
	White	Black	Hispanic	Other	Unknown
Male	2,478	2,378	415	73	229
Female	220	166	26	4	13

SOURCE: Federal Bureau of Investigation. (2011). *Bank crime statistics, 2011 final report.*

What's more, this new breed of bank robber is not just female; she is most often White and often from suburban, middle-class backgrounds. Women arrested for bank robbery in the last few years have included the "Church Lady Bandit" in Ohio, dubbed so because witnesses said she looked like a lady who just came from church; the "Barbie Bandits" in Georgia, so named because these strippers-turned-felons were just plain hot; and the "Mad Hatters," a bank robbing mob composed of six little old ladies. The new breed of bank robbers have been college students in their 20s, mothers in their 30s and 40s, and even grandmothers. Some committed more than a dozen bank robberies before arrest, as was the case with the 18-bank tally of Washington's "Bad Hair Bandit." Still others remain at large.

(Continued)

(Continued)

Why has there been an increase in the number of robberies committed by women? Some attribute it to economic need, arguing that this phenomenon is, in part, a reflection of the nation's poor economy combined with an increased number of financially self-supporting women today compared to the past. During previous economic downturns, the number of bank robberies committed by men increased as men sought to provide for their family. Today, women fill this role. Others suggest that bank robbery is a relatively safe crime, as the rates of injury and death are quite low for robbery compared to other forms of property crime. In bank robbery, one needs only to pass a note to a teller to receive cash. And certainly, a team of little old ladies donning hats can stand in line at the bank, holding a small piece of paper and large satchels, without attracting too much attention today.

A second but related factor in female property offending is survival. Nearly one-third of all female property-offenders indicate that they committed their property crime out of economic need (Johnson, 2004). Roughly 32% of female property offenders report that they committed property crimes to get money to support themselves or their family, while 31% attributed their property crimes to necessity following unemployment. This is consistent with national data on incarcerated persons in the United States, which suggests that only about 40% of female inmates in state prisons were gainfully employed prior to arrest, compared to about 60% of male inmates. When one considers that about two-thirds of women in state prisons lived with minor children prior to incarceration, compared to about 40% of male inmates, the implications are clear: Lack of resources due to unemployment, combined with the need to provide for families, leads some women to commit property crime. This pattern may be more poignant for female than male offenders.

Although the obvious conclusion to be drawn from the data above is that poverty and family needs lead to property offending, this is a simplistic link that requires additional investigation. Most unemployed women with children do not commit property crime to support their families, which suggests that something else may be going on here. In some cases, a lack of financial resources may be a secondary consequence of addiction. Arguably, substance abuse interferes with many aspects of economic survival, including the ability to maintain employment and effectively manage fiscal resources. Addicts are often unable to maintain employment, because the use of controlled substances interferes with regular sleep cycles and the ability to be on time, complete tasks, remain focused, and so on; the need for an addict to find their next high often becomes a stronger need than reporting for work on time. Even when an addict maintains employment or secures a regular source of legitimate income, an addict's money is often redirected from household bills to the purchase of drugs to maintain the addict's high. Thus, addiction may also manifest as a need for financial resources to support one's basic needs, as an addict's fiscal resources are often diverted to alcohol and other drugs.

While the roots of street level property offending may involve substance abuse and economic disadvantage, addiction certainly does not explain all types of property crimes committed by women today. There is a dearth in the literature about white-collar crime by women, including forgery, fraud, and embezzlement. Decades ago, scholars argued that growth in female property crime was explained in part by the "increased participation of women in activities outside the home" (Shelley, 1981). Others argued that the rise in female white-collar crimes in response to the women's movement, an oft-held societal perception, was a myth (Steffensmeier, 1978). While female white-collar offending is more common today than in prior decades (due in large part to women's increased presence in the workplace), current studies suggest that women and men report different, and often gendered, motivations for their offending (Klenowski, Copes, & Mullins, 2011). Haantz (2002), for example, suggests that women's increasing representation as white-collar offenders is not due to greater numbers of women being present in boardrooms—it represents women's increasing role as the primary wage earner and largely represents opportunities to turn to embezzlement and forgery to provide for their family's needs. While these theories abounded in the late 20th and early 21st century, recent statistics do not support this trend.

According to the Bureau of Justice Statistics (2002, 2004, 2006b, 2008, 2010), the number of arrests for white-collar crimes in the United States (including forgery/counterfeiting, fraud, and embezzlement) dropped from 284,996 in 2002 to 208,826 in 2010. While women comprised an astonishing 44% of white-collar arrestees in the last decade of the 20th century, both the number of white-collar crimes and proportion of white-collar crimes committed by women has dropped in recent years. Specifically, the number of female white-collar arrests dropped from a high of 137,658 in 2003 to a low of 86,598 in 2010; male arrests dropped from 165,169 to 122,228 over the same period. Thus while both male and female property offending dropped in this period, the decline was greater for women, with the proportion of white-collar arrests by women dropping from nearly 46% in 2003 to about 41% in 2010.

Recent cases of white-collar crime by female executives, including CEOs, board members, and corporate officers, have garnered media attention (Cerone, 2012). One such example is the federal case against Martha Stewart, detailed in the box below.

White Collar Crime and the Case of Martha Stewart

In 2001, Martha Stewart was an icon in American culture, building a billion-dollar empire of books, magazines, products, and media specials on social entertaining. In 1995, *New York Magazine* dubbed Stewart "the definitive American woman of our time," and in 1999, her brand, Martha Stewart Living Omnimedia, went public on the New York Stock Exchange. All appeared congruous with her perfect image, until she was accused of committing a handful of acts that are commonly identified as *white-collar crimes*.

In late December of 2001, Stewart allegedly received insider information from her stockbroker, Peter Bacanovic, who reportedly advised Stewart to sell her stock in ImClone (Securities Exchange Commission, 2003; *Securities Exchange Commission v. Stewart and Bacanovic*). The Food and Drug Administration did not approve a new ImClone drug, and this news, once released, was expected to reduce the price of the stock. Stewart sold her shares, valued at $230,000, on December 27, 2001; the FDA decision was announced the following day, and the value of the stock dropped 16%. Her timely sale of ImClone saved Stewart roughly $45,000.

In the early months of 2002, officials began investigating the timely rash of ImClone sales among ImClone insiders just days before the unfavorable FDA announcement. Several ImClone insiders and family members were investigated, and broker Peter Bacanovic's assistant, Doug Faneuil, became a

(Continued)

(Continued)

whistleblower. Faneuil reportedly told officials of Bacanovic's tip to Stewart and her subsequent sale of ImClone stock. Rumors hounded Stewart through 2003, when Stewart was indicted on nine counts of securities fraud, obstruction of justice, and conspiracy. She resigned shortly thereafter (Ulick, 2003).

Although she staunchly maintained her innocence in the debacle, taking out a full-page ad in *USA Today* to this effect, Stewart was convicted of four federal charges in 2004: conspiracy, obstruction of justice, and making false statements to federal investigators (two counts). She was sentenced to five months in federal prison, serving her time at the Alderson Federal Prison Camp in West Virginia. She also received two years of probation and was ordered to pay a $30,000 fine in conjunction with her federal criminal conviction. In 2006, the civil suit levied against her by the Securities and Exchange Commission (SEC) was settled for $195,081, with total criminal and civil fines of nearly a quarter of a million dollars, plus legal fees.

At the time of these legal troubles, many people argued that Stewart was unfairly targeted for prosecution because of her celebrity status or her reputation as an aggressive, arguably harsh business woman. Others felt she was given an unfairly light sentence because of her fame. Many speculated that her media empire would crumble with her conviction, as the mogul of elegant dining and entertaining certainly could not withstand such a well-publicized fall from grace. However, her post-incarceration career appears to have surpassed her earlier achievements; *Forbes* (Goldman & Blakeley, 2007) reported her net worth at $638 million in 2008, making her the third-richest woman in entertainment (behind Oprah Winfrey and J. K. Rowling).

While this case certainly does not exemplify the typical female property offender, it illustrates several important themes for women and crime. First, the case illustrates the media's propensity toward the female offender. Stewart, the rare female accused of insider trading (but convicted of obstruction, not insider trading), garnered exponentially more media coverage for her $45,000 malfeasance than did ImClone founder, Samuel Waksal, whose insider information led to the illegal sale of stock approaching $18,000,000, including stock sales by his father, Jack (who sold $8.1 million in shares, including $1 million in shares from Jack's daughter [Sam's sister Patty]); Sam's daughter Aliza (who sold $2.5 million in shares); ImClone general counsel, John Landes (who sold $2.5 million in shares); ImClone vice president, Ronald Martell (who sold $2.1 million in shares); and friends (Zvi Fuks [who sold $5 million in shares] and Sabina Ben-Yehuda [who sold $73,000 in shares]). In all, prison terms resulted for Stewart (five months), Peter Bacanovic (five months), and Sam Waksal (seven years); no other prison terms were given, despite several parties with individual sales far exceeding Stewart's $45,000 transaction (*Securities Exchange Commission v. Samuel Waksal, Jack Waksal, & Patti Waksal*). In the ensuing civil suits, fines and penalties amounted to more than $3 million (Sam and Jack Waksal), $2.6 million (Fuks), $240,000 (Stewart), $110,000 (Ben-Yehuda), and $75,000 (Bacanovic) (Securities and Exchange Commission, 2006; Securities and Exchange Commission Litigation Release No. 19128, 19456, 19794).

Second, this case illustrates the societal view of female offenders as somehow different from male offenders; our culture indulges in the exploration of these gendered and sexual differences. The singular media focus on Stewart illustrates the extent to which gendered expectations garner our attention, especially when those gender roles are not played out as expected. Certainly, Stewart is an extreme example of the tensions we have about appropriate female roles. On the one hand, Stewart's fame and fortune initially hinged on her ability to "sell" quintessential feminine traits to the public, exemplified by her cooking, hosting, and entertaining empire. Once accused, however, the media reported extensively on personality traits that did not suit this female image, including reports of her management style as a bully and a very aggressive business woman; TV specials produced around this time capitalized on these non-feminine traits. This focus is completely unrelated to charges against her, but it reflects society's general discomfort for women who behave outside typical gender roles. Aggressiveness in business is typically seen as a male trait, with such depictions generally viewed as a compliment when used to describe men. Although other parties' stock sales far exceeded Stewart's, the media provided no similar coverage of the other parties involved as sinister or aggressive. Certainly, no such coverage existed for the other women involved, including Sam Waksal's sister Patty and daughter Aliza. While each woman's sales dwarfed Stewart's, they were depicted as naïve instruments of their brother/father's crime, while Stewart's moniker as bitch reigned supreme.

Female Offenders and Their Male Codefendants

Since the days of Bonnie and Clyde, society has been fascinated by the actions of women who become entangled with the criminal activities of the men in their lives. Consider Bonnie Elizabeth Parker (1910–1934), who became romantically involved with Clyde Chestnut Barrow (1909–1934), a local criminal. While urban legend suggests that Bonnie was an equal participant in the robberies and murders committed by Clyde and his gang, Bonnie never actually killed a single victim. Together with Clyde, she was killed in a shootout with law enforcement in Louisiana on May 23, 1934. (See Table 10.3, Femme Fatales: Notorious Female Murderers, page 239.)

Such cases of criminal women and their male codefendants become newsworthy and capture the attention of the media and the public alike. Much of this fascination centers around the degree to which women were involved in these crimes—was she an innocent bystander who got sucked into illicit activities as a result of her relationship, or was she more involved as a coconspirator or even an instigator of the criminal event? Here, the concept of *gender entrapment* illustrates how women can be led into criminal activities as a result of "culturally expected gender roles, the violence in their intimate relationships, and their social position in the broader society" (Ritchie, 1996, p. 133). In his review of fifty cases of co-offending women in England, Jones (2008) found that over one-third of the cases involved a violent intimate partner relationship between the offenders. Within these relationships, men are generally older than their female counterparts, a factor that may impact the nature of these relationships. The majority of cases (40%) involved women engaging in crimes such as burglary and theft to support their drug habits. In most cases, these women committed their crimes in response to the expectations of their male partners. In only a small proportion of cases (12%) did a woman's intimate partner threaten or coerce them into criminal activity. Finally, a third of these cases involved women who considered themselves as equal partners in the crime. While many of these women accepted responsibility for their actions, they also admitted that their involvement was related to their emotional bond with their codefendant.

However, other cases find women as not only an equal but as a leading member of the crime group. Consider the case of Lee Grace Dougherty, who together with her brother Ryan Dougherty and stepbrother Dylan Dougherty Stanley found themselves on a crime spree that led them from Florida to Colorado in August of 2011. Dubbed the *Dougherty Gang*, their crimes included firing at police officers in both Florida and Colorado and robbing a local bank in Georgia. They were captured in Colorado and were sentenced for their Colorado-based crimes in April of 2012. While all three had previous brushes with the law, it was Lee Grace's comments that garnered the attention of the media. In an online profile, she stated "I love to farm, shoot guys and wreck cars" and "I like causing mayhem with my siblings." As a result of her involvement in these crimes, she was sentenced to 24 years in prison, while her brothers received 18 and 32 years respectively. They also faced additional charges in federal court related to the bank robbery in Georgia (Coffman, 2012; Gast, 2011; MacIntosh, 2011).

Prostitution

Hollywood images of prostitution depict a lifestyle that is rarely found in the real world. Movies such as *Pretty Woman, Leaving Las Vegas,* and *Taxi Driver* paint a picture of the young, beautiful prostitute who is saved from her life on the streets. In reality, there are few Prince Charmings available to rescue these women. The reality that awaits most of these women is one filled with violence, abuse, and addiction—deep scars that are challenging to overcome.

▲ **Photo 9.2**   While street prostitution comprises a small proportion of sex work, it is one of the most visible forms. It is also one of the most dangerous forms of sex work. Many women who work the streets risk significant victimization from their clients. Unfortunately, many victims do not report these crimes to the police out of concern that their cases will not be treated seriously by the justice system.

Prostitution involves the act of selling or trading sex for money. Prostitution can take a variety of forms, including escort services; Craigslist; or work in brothels, bars, truck stops, and street corners. Some sources estimate that approximately 15% of women in prostitution find themselves working in street-level sex work, with the remainder in brothels, escort services, massage parlors, and the like; other sources estimate that the majority of prostitutes are employed in street-level sex work, which is the most visible venue and the one in which most sex workers are arrested (Moses, 2006; Raphael & Shapiro, 2002; Sweet, 2006). The FBI reports roughly 75,000 arrests for prostitution offenses in the United States annually; these typically represent arrests of women working as street-level prostitutes as opposed to the traffickers often involved in sex trafficking, pimps, and customers associated with sex work (FBI, 2010). For these women, money may not be the only commodity available in exchange for their bodies, as they also trade sex for drugs or other tangibles such as food, clothing, and shelter (Williamson & Folaron, 2003). While these women do not make up the majority of women in prostitution, they do experience the greatest levels of risk for violence and victimization (Williamson & Cluse-Tolar, 2002).

The journey into prostitution is not a solitary road. Rather, it involves a variety of individual, contextual, and environmental factors. Trends in the literature have acknowledged a variety of risk factors for women in prostitution, including abandonment, abuse, addiction, and poverty. A history of abuse is one of the most commonly referenced risk factors for prostitution, and research by Dalla (2000) indicates that drug addiction almost always paves the way for work in prostitution.

Another common pathway for women in prostitution is the experience of early childhood sexual victimization. While there is no direct link that indicates that the experience of incest is predictive of selling one's body, research indicates that there is a strong correlation between the two (Nokomis Foundation, 2002), and one **prostitution recovery program** indicates that 87% of their participants experienced abuse throughout their early childhood, often at the hands of a family member. For these women, incest became the way in which they learned about their sexuality as a commodity that could be sold and traded, and some suggest that this process of bargaining became a way in which these victims could once again feel powerful about their lives (Mallicoat, 2006).

A history of child abuse is also highly correlated with running away from home during the teen years. Once on the streets, victimized girls turn to prostitution and pimps in an effort to survive (Chesney-Lind & Shelden, 1998). However, some suggest this is a path for predation by pimps and sex traffickers, who target not only women abroad but also marginalized girls from within the United States (U.S. Department of State, 2012). In this tragic path to prostitution, rational choice and assertion of individual power are not considerations for victimized, runaway, underage girls, who find themselves trapped as slaves in the sex trade within their own communities. For many of these women, ample threats hold them relative or literal slaves in the sex trade, including extreme poverty and economic dependence, physical and sexual violence, and fear of legal sanction, including arrest and deportation; for them, there is no escape.

Women in prostitution experience high levels of violence during their careers. Female sex workers witness and experience daily violence on the streets. More than 90% of women engaged as **street prostitutes** are brutally victimized (Romero-Daza, Weeks, & Singer, 2003). They are robbed, raped, and assaulted by their customers and pimps alike (Raphael & Shapiro, 2004). Many do not report these incidents out of fear that they will be arrested for engaging in prostitution, coupled with a belief that the police will do little to respond to these crimes (Sanders & Campbell, 2007). Indeed, women often return to the streets immediately following their victimization. Any temporary intervention (recovering from attack, seeking medical treatment, or making a report to police) is viewed as a delay in work, rather than an opportunity to search for an exit strategy. One woman characterized her experience as normal—"society and law enforcement consider a prostitute getting raped or beat as something she deserves. It goes along with your lifestyle. There's nothing that you can do" (Dalla, 2000, p. 381).

Female sex workers also witness significant acts of violence perpetuated against their peers, an experience that often leads to significant mental health issues. Drug use becomes a way to cope with the violence in their daily lives. As the pressure to make money increases in order to sustain their addictions or to provide a roof over their head at night, women may place themselves in increasingly risky situations with their customers (Norton-Hawk, 2004). In an effort to protect against potential harms, women rely on their intuition to avoid potentially violent situations. Many girls indicate that they won't leave a designated area with a client and generally refuse to get into a car with a client. Others carry a weapon such as a knife. Despite the risks, some women reference the thrill and power they experience when they are able to survive a violent incident (Dalla, Xia, & Kennedy, 2003). Many women are surprised when they reflect on the levels of violence that they experienced on the streets. Some may dissociate themselves from the realities of this journey and believe that the experience was not as traumatic as they originally believed. However, the battle scars from their time on the streets provide the evidence for the trauma they endured, both physically and mentally.

Sex Work: A Victimless Crime?

What is sex work? Who are sex workers? The term *sex worker* was coined by Carol Leigh in 1978 to include all people who work in the sex industry, including those engaged in delivery of sexual services (such as exotic dancers, strippers, adult film stars, prostitutes, etc.) as well as those ancillary to it (including film and camera crew, phone sex operators, etc.). Although the term is quite broad, it is often used to mean those employed in the world's oldest profession: prostitutes.

Most of the general public begrudgingly views prostitution as a "victimless" crime insofar as neither the sex act itself nor evidence of sex contaminates the senses of those not so engaged and so long as it involves consenting adults (West & Orr, 2007). In other words, most people call prostitution a victimless crime so long as they don't find a condom on their lawn or see a prostitute and client coupling in public. But is the perspective of a would-be observer all that matters in determining whether or not a crime is victimless? Does the experience of the sex worker matter?

In practice, most prostitution laws in the United States today marginalize sex workers. The business of sex work must be unseen, lest it be punishable by arrest and prosecution. Thus, most sex workers remain in the periphery, taking their "Johns" to secluded areas to avoid detection. However, engaging in sexual activity in remote locations exposes many sex workers to physical and sexual violence at the hands of customers, pimps, and sometimes even the police.

Sex workers overwhelmingly report that the biggest threat to their safety is their inability to seek help by reporting victimization to police. Sex workers rarely report the sexual or physical victimization they may experience, as in doing so they admit to prostitution, a crime. As a result, sex workers, especially those who work in outdoor venues (street prostitutes), experience high rates of victimization and see few viable options for legal protection. On the other hand, sex workers who work in legal venues, such as legal brothels in Nevada or adult film studios, report significantly reduced victimization rates, primarily because they can call police for assistance when needed.

Some suggest that the criminalization of sex work essentially creates a class of victims by transforming a bona fide service (sex for money, which some argue could be taxed for state revenue) into marginalized one. Indeed, interviews of sex workers overwhelming suggest that the harm they experience is not a direct function of sex work itself; harm is attributed to the marginalization of sex work, which relegates them to a subpopulation of persons from deviant subcultures engaged in illegal activity.

Although controversial, some suggest decriminalization and regulation of sex work as one solution (Sanchez, 2001; Scoular, 2004; Scoular & O'Neil, 2007; Weitzer, 2005). Arguably, this would reduce the victimization of sex workers by allowing them access to legal protections as well as generate tax revenue that far exceeds the current fiscal drain associated with ineffective crackdowns of the world's oldest profession. Is decriminalization a viable solution? Do you think it would reduce victimization among sex workers? Would the public support such an approach? Are there other solutions to this problem? Do you think sex work is indeed a victimless crime?

The role of substance abuse is central to the discussion of risk for prostituting women. About 70% of women in prostitution have issues with drug addiction. Some women begin their substance use prior to their entry in prostitution to cope with the pain associated with past or current sexual violence in their lives. They then resort to prostitution to fund their drug habits (Raphael, 2004). For others, entry into substance abuse comes later in an effort to self-medicate against the fear, stress, and low self-esteem resulting from the selling of sex (Nixon, Tutty, Downe, Gorkoff, & Ursel, 2002). As their time on the streets increases, so does their substance abuse. Indeed, the relationship between drug use and prostitution may be a self-perpetuating circle in which they feed off one another. A sample of women in jail for prostitution had significantly higher rates of drug use compared to women arrested for non-prostitution-related offenses (Yacoubian, Urbach, Larsen, Johnson, & Peters, 2000).

In recent years, media accounts have focused significant attention on the use of crack cocaine by street prostitutes. Research has linked the presence of crack to an increased number of individuals working on the street, which in turn decreases the amount of money that women receive for their services. Addiction to drugs such as crack has created an economy where money is no longer traded for sex. Rather, sexual acts become a commodity to be exchanged for drugs. The levels of violence associated with the practice of selling sex increases in this drug-fueled economy (Maher, 1996).

While drug addiction presents a significant health concern for women in prostitution, additional issues exist for women in terms of long-term physical health. Women engaged in sex work are at risk for issues related to HIV, hepatitis, and other chronic health concerns, including dental, vision, neurological, respiratory, and gynecological problems (Farley & Barkin, 1998). Finally, the death rate of women in prostitution is an astonishing 40 times higher than the death rate of the overall population (Nokomis Foundation, 2002).

Mental health concerns are also a significant issue for women engaged in the sex trade. Cases of post-traumatic stress disorder (PTSD) are directly related to the levels of violence that women experience on the streets, and an estimated two-thirds of prostituted women experience symptoms of PTSD (Schoot & Goswami, 2001). Prostitutes suffering from PTSD may be unable to accurately assess the levels of threat and violence that surround their lives, which in turn places them at increased risk for ongoing physical and sexual victimization (Valera, Sawyer, & Schiraldi, 2000).

The Legalization Debate

The question of whether prostitution should be considered a criminal activity is one of considerable debate. In Nevada, legal prostitution is limited to counties with a population under 400,000, excluding high-traffic areas such as Reno and Las Vegas from offering legalized brothels.[1] The laws within Nevada focus almost exclusively on the minimization of risk and reduction of violence for women in prostitution. Since 1986, Nevada has required that prostitutes who work in brothels must submit to weekly exams to assess for any sexually transmitted infections or the presence of HIV. Brothels also implement a variety of regulations to ensure the safety and security of the brothel and the women who work there. Technology helps in these efforts, including audio monitoring and call buttons in the rooms to ensure safety of sex workers during transactions. Most brothels limit services outside of the brothel environment to control any potentially negative behaviors of clients. Research indicates that women who work in brothel settings feel safe and rarely experienced acts of violence while working as a prostitute. Indeed, it is these safety mechanisms that lead women to believe that brothel sex work is by far the safest environment in which to engage in prostitution, compared to the violence and danger that street prostitutes regularly experience (Brents & Hausbeck, 2005).

In the Netherlands, the legalization of brothels in 2000 created a new way to govern the sex trade. While the act of prostitution has been legalized since the early 20th century, it was the brothel environment (popularized by the red light district and "window" shopping in the city of Amsterdam and other cities) that was illegal. At the time of brothel legalization, the practice of prostitution in the Netherlands was not an uncommon phenomenon, and estimates suggest that over 6,000 women per day were working in prostitution-related activities (Wagenaar, 2006). The effects of the legislation lifted the formal prohibition of the brothel, even though many municipalities had tolerated their presence, and agents of social control such as law enforcement and the courts had largely refrained from prosecuting cases. By creating a system whereby brothels had to be licensed, authorities were able to gain control over the industry by mandating public health and safety screenings for sex workers. As part of the decriminalization of prostitution, the state created the opportunity for brothel owners to have a legal site of business. Labor laws regarding the working conditions for prostitutes were put into effect. In addition, it created a tax base through which revenue could be generated (Pakes, 2005). The goals of decriminalization allowed the Dutch government to improve the lives of women in prostitution by creating safe working conditions; creating a system of monitoring of the sex trade; and regulating illegal activities that might be associated with the selling of sexuality, such as streets crimes associated with prostitution, the exploitation of juveniles, or the trafficking of women into the sex industry (Wagenaar, 2006).

By creating a sustainable economy of prostitution, some critics suggest that not only are the needs of the customer met but that these regions create an economic strategy for women, particularly women within challenged economic situations. However, creating a system of legislation is no guarantee that laws will be followed; even with the legalization of prostitution in New South Wales, Australia, the majority of brothels fail to register their businesses and pay little attention to the regulatory rules for operation. In addition, illegal sexual practices have continued to flourish—the Netherlands is identified as a leading destination for pedophiles and child pornographers, many of whom may operate under the belief that the promotion of legalized prostitution has created opportunities for illegal prostitution in these regions as well (Raymond, 2004).

Other legislation focuses on the criminalization of the demand for sexual services. In addressing the issue of prostitution in Sweden, legislatures have focused on making the purchasing of sex from women a criminal act. The belief here is that by criminalizing the male demand for sex, it may significantly decrease the supply of women who engage in these acts. By criminalizing the "Johns," Sweden has taken a stand against a practice that it feels constitutes an act of violence against women (Raymond, 2004). In the passing of these laws, the parliament indicated, "it is not reasonable to punish the person who sells a sexual service. In the majority of cases . . . this person is a weaker partner who is exploited" (Ministry of Labour, Sweden, 1998, p. 4).

In the United States, even in an environment where both the purchaser and seller of sex can be subjected to criminal prosecution, the data indicate that women are significantly more likely to face sanctions for selling sex compared to men who seek to purchase it (Farley & Kelly, 2000). While the focus on demand is an important characteristic in the selling of sex, it is not the only variable. Indeed, larger issues such as economics, globalization, poverty, and inequality all contribute to a system where women fall victim to the practices of sexual exploitation.

Farley and Kelly (2000) suggest that even with the legalization of the brothel environment, prostitution remains a significant way in which women are brutalized and harmed. The social stigma of women who engage in the selling of sex does not decrease simply because the act of prostitution becomes legal. Indeed, the restriction of brothels to specific regions only further isolates women from mainstream society and magnifies the stigma they may experience (Farley, 2004). In cases of victimization, women employed in sex work continue to experience significant levels of victim blaming when they are victimized, even if prostitution is decriminalized. The system of public health, which is promoted as a way to keep both the prostitute and her client safe, fails to meet some of the most critical needs of women in this arena, as these efforts toward promoting safety are limited exclusively to physical health, and little to no attention is paid to the mental health needs of women engaged in prostitution (Farley, 2004).

Research indicates that women involved in street prostitution often want to leave the lifestyle, but they express concern over how their multiple needs (including housing, employment, and drug treatment) may limit their abilities to do so. There are few programs that provide adequate levels of services to address the multiple needs of women during this transition. A review of one prostitution recovery program found that affordable safe housing is the greatest immediate need for women in their transition from the streets (Mallicoat, 2011). Homelessness puts women at risk for relapse, and, as Yahne and colleagues note, "without reliable housing, it is challenging to escape the cycle of prostituting" (Yahne, Miller, Irvin-Vitela, & Tonigan, 2002, p. 52).

In addition, women must possess necessary skills and have access to support in order to facilitate this process. Women exiting the streets indicate a variety of therapeutic needs, including life skills, addiction recovery programming, and mental health services designed to address the traumas they experienced. An exit strategy needs to acknowledge the barriers to success and continuing struggles that women will experience as a result of these traumas.

SUMMARY

- Women engage in every category of crime, yet their rates of offending are significantly lower than male offending practices.
- Regardless of race, ethnicity, or class, women have similar pathways to addiction: depression, abuse, and social and economic pressures.
- For many women, entry into addiction is rooted in early trauma: Drugs are used for escape, and prostitution and property crime are then committed for survival.
- Female patterns of offending often include recurring instances of drug crimes, prostitution offenses, and property offenses, all connected to life on the streets.
- The War on Drugs has led to increased incarceration rates for both men and women but has had particularly damaging effects for women.
- Approximately 15% of women in prostitution work on the streets.
- Street prostitutes face the highest levels of risk for violence and victimization.
- Women in prostitution face significant mental and physical health issues as a result of their time on the streets. These issues lead to significant challenges as they try to exit prostitution and make a new life off the streets.

KEY TERMS

Gender entrapment

Pathways to addiction

Property crimes

Prostitution recovery program

Street prostitution

DISCUSSION QUESTIONS

1. Why are the media obsessed with the image of the female offender? What implications does this have on understanding the realities of female offending?

2. What does research say about the gender gap in offending?

3. How have drug addiction and the War on Drugs become a gendered experience?

4. How are drugs, property crimes, and prostitution connected for many female offenders on the streets?

5. What does the drug-theft-prostitution connection suggest for gender-responsive treatment strategies?

6. What are the risk factors for prostitution? How do these issues affect a woman's ability to exit the streets?

7. Why are jurisdictions reluctant to legalize or decriminalize prostitution?

8. Why do women engage in property offenses?

9. What factors might explain the rising rates of female robberies?

WEB RESOURCES

Children of the Night http://www.childrenofthenight.org

National Gang Center http://www.nationalgangcenter.gov/

National Incident Based Reporting System http://www.fbi.gov/about-us/cjis/ucr/frequently-asked-questions/nibrs_faqs#offenseinfo

Prostitutes Education Network http://www.bayswan.org

Prostitution Research and Education http://www.prostitutionresearch.com

SAMHSA Center for Substance Abuse Treatment http://www.samhsa.gov/about/csat.aspx

SAMHSA Nation Center for Trauma Informed care http://www.samhsa.gov/nctic/

The Sentencing Project http://www.sentencingproject.org

Women and Gender in the Drug War http://www.drugpolicy.org/communities/women

REFERENCES

Barnett, C. (2001). *The measurement of white-collar crime using Uniform Crime Reporting data.* Washington, DC: U.S. Department of Justice. Retrieved from http://www.fbi.gov/about-us/cjis/ucr/nibrs/nibrs_wcc.pdf

Beck, A. J., & Harrison, P.M. (2001). *Prisoners in 2000.* Washington, DC: Bureau of Justice Statistics. http://bjs.ojp.usdoj.gov/content/pub/pdf/p00.pdf

Beck, A. J., & Harrison, P. M. (2004). *Prisoners in 2003.* Washington, DC: Bureau of Justice Statistics. Retrieved from http://bjs.ojp.usdoj.gov/content/pub/pdf/p03.pdf

Bloom, B., Chesney-Lind, M., & Owen, B. (1994). *Women in California prisons: Hidden victims of the war on drugs.* San Francisco, CA: Center on Juvenile and Criminal Justice.

Bloom, B., Owen, B., & Covington, S. (2003). *Gender-responsive strategies: Research, practice, and guiding principles for women offenders.* Washington DC: National Institute of Corrections.

Bloom, B., Owen, B., & Covington, S. (2004). Women offenders and the gendered effects of public policy 1. *Review of Policy Research, 21*(1), 31–48.

Brents, B. G., & Hausbeck, K. (2005). Violence and legalized brothel prostitution in Nevada: Examining safety, risk and prostitution policy. *Journal of Interpersonal Violence, 20*(3), 270–295.

Brody, L. M., & Cauffman, E. E. (2006). *Understanding the female offender.* Washington, DC: U.S. Department of Justice. Retrieved from https://www.ncjrs.gov/pdffiles1/nij/grants/216615.pdf

Bureau of Justice Statistics. (2002). Table 4.9: Arrests by offense charged, sex and age group, United States. *Sourcebook of Criminal Justice Statistics Online.*

Bureau of Justice Statistics. (2004). Table 4.9: Arrests by offense charged, sex and age group, United States. *Sourcebook of Criminal Justice Statistics Online.*

Bureau of Justice Statistics. (2006a). Crime and victim statistics. *Bureau of Justice Statistics.* Washington, DC: U.S. Department of Justice, Office of Justice Programs. Retrieved from http://www.ojp.usdoj.gov/bjs/cvict.htm

Bureau of Justice Statistics. (2006b). Table 4.9: Arrests by offense charged, sex and age group, United States. *Sourcebook of Criminal Justice Statistics Online.*

Bureau of Justice Statistics. (2008). Table 4.9: Arrests by offense charged, sex and age group, United States. *Sourcebook of Criminal Justice Statistics Online.*

Bureau of Justice Statistics. (2010). Table 4.9: Arrests by offense charged, sex and age group, United States. *Sourcebook of Criminal Justice Statistics Online.*

Burnette, M. L., Schneider, R., Timko, C., & Ilgen, M. A. (2009). Impact of substance-use disorder treatment on women involved in prostitution: Substance use, mental health, and prostitution one year after treatment. *Journal of Studies on Alcohol and Drugs, 70*(1), 32.

Bush-Baskette, S. R. (1999). Women, drugs and prison in the United States. In S. Cook & S. Davies (Eds.), *Harsh punishment: International experiences of women's imprisonment* (pp. 211–229). Boston, MA: Northeastern University Press.

Bush-Baskette, S. R. (2000, December). The War on Drugs and the incarceration of mothers. *Journal of Drug Issues, 30*(4), 919–928.

Campbell, N. D. (2000). *Using women: Gender, drug policy and social justice.* New York, NY: Routledge.

Cerone, J. (2012). Women and white collar crime. *Jill Online.* Retrieved from http://www.jillmagonline.com/index.php?option=com_content&task=view&id=521

Chesney-Lind, M. (1997). *The female offender: Girls, women and crime.* Thousand Oaks, CA: SAGE.

Chesney-Lind, M. (2000). Women and the criminal justice system: Gender matters. *Topics in Community Corrections, 5,* 7–10.

Chesney-Lind, M., & Shelden, R. G. (1998). *Girls, delinquency and juvenile justice.* Belmont, CA: West/Wadsworth.

Coffman, K. (2012, April 30). Dougherty gang sentenced in Colorado for police shootout. *Reuters.* Retrieved from http://news.yahoo.com/dougherty-gang-sentenced-colorado-police-shootout-230049502.html

Cohen, M. (2002). *Counseling addicted women: A practical guide.* Thousand Oaks, CA: SAGE.

Covington, S. (2008, November). Women and addiction: A trauma-informed approach. *Journal of Psychoactive Drugs,* SARC Supplement 5. Retrieved from http://www.stephaniecovington.com/pdfs/CovingtonSARC5.pdf

Covington, S., & Cohen, J. (1984). Women, alcohol, and sexuality. *Advances in Alcohol and Substance Abuse, 4*(1), 41–56.

Dalla, R. L. (2000). Exposing the "pretty woman" myth: A qualitative examination of the lives of female streetwalking prostitutes. *Journal of Sex Research, 37*(4), 344–353.

Dalla, R. L., Xia, Y., & Kennedy, H. (2003). "You just give them what they want and pray they don't kill you": Street-level workers' reports of victimization, personal resources and coping strategies. *Violence Against Women, 9*(11), 1367–1394.

Dennis, M. L., Scott, C. K., Funk, R., & Foss, M. A. (2005). The duration and correlates of addiction and treatment careers. *Journal of Substance Abuse Treatment, 28*(2), S51–S62.

Denton, B., & O'Malley, P. (2001). Property crime and women drug dealers in Australia. *Journal of Drug Issues, 31*(2), 454–486.

Deschenes, E. P., Owen, B., & Crow, J. (2007). *Recidivism among female prisoners: Secondary analysis of the 1994 BJS Recidivism data set.* Retrieved from www.ncjrs.gov/App/ Publications/abstract.aspx?ID=238573

Durose, M. R., Harlow, C. W., Langan, P. A., Motivans, M., Rantala, R. R., & Smith, E. L. (2005). Family violence statistics including statistics on strangers and acquaintances. *Bureau of Justice Statistics*. Washington DC: U.S. Department of Justice, Office of Justice Programs. NCJ 207846.

Farley, M. (2004). "Bad for the body, bad for the heart": Prostitution harms women even if legalized or decriminalized. *Violence Against Women, 10*(10), 1087–1125.

Farley, M., & Barkin, H. (1998). Prostitution, violence and post-traumatic stress disorder. *Women and Health, 27*(3), 37–49.

Farley, M., & Kelly, V. (2000). Prostitution: A critical review of the medical and social sciences literature. *Women and Criminal Justice, 11*(4), 29–64.

Federal Bureau of Investigation (FBI). (2006). *Crime in the United States, 2005: Uniform Crime Reports.* Washington, DC: U.S. Department of Justice, Federal Bureau of Investigation.

Federal Bureau of Investigation (FBI). (2010). *Crime in the United States, 2010: Uniform Crime Reports.* Washington, DC: U.S. Department of Justice, Federal Bureau of Investigation.

Federal Bureau of Investigation (FBI). (2011). *Crime in the United States, 2010: Uniform Crime Reports.* Washington, DC: U.S. Department of Justice, Federal Bureau of Investigation. Retrieved from http://www.fbi. gov/about-us/cjis/ucr/crime-in-the-u.s/2010/crime-in-the-u.s.-2010

Federal Bureau of Investigation (FBI). (2012). *Bank crime statistics, 2011, final report.* Washington, DC: U.S. Department of Justice, Federal Bureau of Investigation. Retrieved from http://www.fbi.gov/stats-services/publications/bank-crime-statistics-2011/bank-crime-statistics-2011

Fendrich, M., Hubbell, A., & Lurigio, A. J. (2006). Providers' perceptions of gender-specific drug treatment. *Journal of Drug Issues, 36*(3), 667–686.

Flower, S. M. (November 2010). *Employment and female offenders: An update of the empirical research.* Washington, DC: U.S. Department of Justice, National Institute of Corrections.

Gast, P. (2011, August 10). Siblings wanted in bank robbery, shootout arrested after chase. *CNN.* Retrieved from http://www.cnn.com/2011/CRIME/08/11/georgia.three.siblings.manhunt.archives/index.html?iref=allsearch

Glaze, L. E., & Maruschak, L. M. (2008). *Bureau of Justice Statistics special report: Parents in prison and their minor children.* Washington, DC: U.S. Department of Justice, Office of Justice Programs. NCJ 222984.

Goldman, L., & Blakeley, K. (2007). The 20 richest women in entertainment. *Forbes.* Retrieved from http://www.forbes.com/2007/01/17/richest-women-entertainment-tech-media-cz_lg_richwomen07_0118womenstars_lander.html

Gray, A. R., & Saum. C. A. (2005). Mental health, gender, and drug court completion. *American Journal of Criminal Justice, 30*(1), 55–69.

Green, B. L., Miranda, J., & Daroowalla, A. (2005). Trauma exposure, mental health functioning, and program needs of women in jail. *Crime & Delinquency, 51*(1), 133–151.

Greenfeld, L., & Snell, T. L. (2000). *Women offenders: Bureau of Justice Statistics special report*. Retrieved from http://bjs.ojp.usdoj.gov/content/pub/pdf/wo.pdf

Haantz, S. (2002). *Women and white collar crime*. Fairmont, WV: National White Collar Crime Research Center.

Harlow, C. W. (1999). Prior abuse reported by inmates and probationers. *Bureau of Justice Statistics Selected Findings*. Retrieved from http://www.wcl.american.edu/faculty/smith/0303conf/article2.pdf

Harlow, C. W. (2003). *Bureau of Justice Statistics special report: Education and correctional populations*. Washington, DC: U.S. Department of Justice, Office of Justice Programs. NCJ 195670.

Harrison, P. M., & Beck, A. J. (2006). Prisoners in 2005. *Bureau of Justice Statistics Bulletin*. Washington, DC: U.S. Department of Justice. Retrieved from http://www.ojp.usdoj.gov/bjs/pub/pdf/p05.pdf

Harrison, P. M., & Beck, A. J. (2006). Prison and jail inmates at midyear 2005. *Bureau of Justice Statistics Bulletin*. Washington, DC: U.S. Department of Justice. Retrieved from http://bjs.ojp.usdoj.gov/content/pub/pdf/pjim05.pdf

Hequembourg, A., Mancuso, R., & Miller, B. (2006). A comparative study examining associations between women's drug-related lifestyle factors and victimization within the family. *Violence and Victims, 21*(2), 231–246.

Herman, J. (1992). *Trauma and recovery*. New York, NY: Basic Books.

Inciardi, J. A., Lockwood, D., & Pottiger, A. E. (1993). *Women and crack-cocaine*. Toronto, Canada: Maxwell Macmillian.

James, D. J., & Glaze, L. E. (2006). *Bureau of Justice Statistics special report: Mental health problems of prison and jail inmates*. Washington, DC: U.S. Department of Justice, Office of Justice Programs. NCJ 213600.

Johnson, H. (2004). Drugs and crime: A study of incarcerated female offenders. *Australian Institute of Criminology, 63*. Retrieved from http://www.aic.gov.au/documents/E/B/8/%7BEB8A400C-E611-42BF-9B9F-B58E7C5A0694%7DRPP63.pdf

Jones, S. (2008). Partners in crime: A study of the relationship between female offenders and their co-defendants. *Criminology and Criminal Justice, 8*(2), 147–164.

Kassebaum, P. A. (1999). *Substance abuse treatment for women offenders: Guide to promising practices*. Washington, DC: U.S. Department of Health and Human Services. SAMHSA. TAP 23.

Kleinpeter, C., Deschenes, E., Blanks, J., Lepage, C., & Knox, M. (2006). Providing recovery services for offenders with co-occurring disorders. *Journal of Dual Diagnosis, 3*(1), 59–85.

Klenowski, P., Copes, H., & Mullins, C. (2011). Gender, identity and accounts: How white-collar offenders do gender when making sense of their crimes. *Justice Quarterly, 28*(1), 46–69.

MacIntosh, J. (2011, August 9). "Rack" and ruin: Stripper goes on "crime spree" with brothers. *New York Post*. Retrieved from http://www.nypost.com/p/news/national/vixen_faces_rack_ruin_q5hnBQ1AlZJrIImUY4CHCP

Maher, L. (1996). Hidden in the light: Occupational norms among crack-using street level sex workers. *Journal of Drug Issues, 26*, 143–173.

Mallicoat, S. L. (2006). *Mary Magdalene project: Kester program evaluation*. Presented to the Program Committee of the Mary Magdalene Project, Van Nuys, CA, in August 2006.

Mallicoat, S. L. (2011). Lives in transition: A needs assessment of women exiting from prostitution. In R. Muraskin (Ed.), *It's a crime: Women and justice* (4th ed., pp. 241–255). Upper Saddle River, NJ: Prentice Hall.

Ministry of Labour in cooperation with the Ministry of Justice and the Ministry of Health and Social Affairs, Government of Sweden. (1998). *Fact sheet*. Secretariat for Information and Communication, Ministry of Labour.

Morash, M., Bynum, T., & Koons, B. (1998). *Women offenders: Programming needs and promising approaches*. Washington, DC: National Institute of Justice.

Mumola, C. J., & Karberg, J. C. (2006). Drug use and dependence, state and federal prisoners, 2004. *Bureau of Justice Statistics Special Report*. Washington, DC: U.S. Department of Justice, Office of Justice Programs. NCJ213530.

Moore, L. D., & Elkavich, A. (2008).Who's using and who's doing time: Incarceration, the war on drugs, and public health. *American Journal of Public Health, 98*, 782–786.

Moses, M. C. (2006). Understanding and applying research on prostitution. *National Institute of Justice, 255*. Retrieved from http://www.nij.gov/journals/255/prostitution_research.html

Nijhawan, A. E., Salloway, R., Nunn, A. S., Poshkus, M., & Clarke, J. G. (2010). Preventive healthcare for underserved women: Results of a prison survey. *Journal of Women's Health, 19*(1), 17–22.

Nixon, K., Tutty, L., Downe, P., Gorkoff, K., & Ursel, J. (2002).The everyday occurrence: Violence in the lives of girls exploited through prostitution. *Violence Against Women, 8*(9), 1016–1043.

Nokomis Foundation. (2002). *We can do better: Helping prostituted women and girls in Grand Rapids make healthy choices: A prostitution round table report to the community.* Retrieved from http://www.nokomisfoundation .org/documents/WeCanDoBetter.pdf

Norton-Hawk, M. (2004). A comparison of pimp and non-pimp controlled women. *Violence Against Women, 10*(2), 189–194.

O'Brien, P. (2001). *Making it in the "free world": Women in transition from prison.* Albany, NY: SUNY Press.

Owen, B. (1998). *In the mix: Struggle and survival in a woman's prison.* New York, NY: State University of New York Press.

Pakes, F. (2005). Penalization and retreat: The changing face of Dutch criminal justice. *Criminal Justice, 5*(2), 145–161.

Palm, J. (2007). Women and men—same problems, different treatment. *International Journal of Social Welfare, 16*(1), 18–31.

Poehlmann, J. (2005). Representations of attachment relationships in children of incarcerated mothers. *Child Development, 76*(3), 679–696.

Prescott, L., Soares, P., Konnath, K., & Bassuk, E. (2008). A long journey home. *National Center on Family Homelessness.* Rockville, MD: Center for Mental Health Services, Substance Abuse and Mental Health Services Administration; and the Daniels Fund; National Child Traumatic Stress Network; and the W.K. Kellogg Foundation. Retrieved from http://www.familyhomelessness.org/media/89.pdf

Radosh, P. F. (2008). War on drugs: Gender and race inequities in crime control strategies. *Criminal Justice Studies, 21*(2), 167–178.

Raphael, J. (2004). *Listening to Olivia: Violence, poverty and prostitution.* Boston, MA: Northeastern University Press.

Raphael, J., & Shapiro, D. (2002). *Sisters speak out: The lives and needs of prostituted women in Chicago.* Retrieved from http://www.impactresearch.org

Raphael, J., & Shapiro, D. L. (2004). Violence in indoor and outdoor venues. *Violence Against Women, 10*(2), 126–139.

Raymond, J. G. (2004). Prostitution on demand: Legalizing the buyers as sexual consumers. *Violence Against Women, 10*(10), 1156–1186.

Reisig, M. D., Holtfreter, K., & Morash, M. (2002). Social capital among women offenders. *Journal of Contemporary Criminal Justice, 18*(2), 167–187.

Rennison, C. M. (2009). A new look at the gender gap in offending. *Women and Criminal Justice, 19,* 171–190.

Reynolds, M. (2008). The war on drugs, prison building, and globalization: Catalysts for the global incarceration of women. *NWSA Journal, 20*(2), 72–95.

Ritchie, B. (1996). *Compelled to crime: The gender entrapment of battered Black women.* New York, NY: Routledge.

Roberts, C. A. (1999). Drug use among inner-city African American women: The process of managing loss. *Qualitative Health Research, 9*(5), 620–638.

Romero-Daza, N., Weeks, M., & Singer, M. (2003). "Nobody gives a damn if I live or die": Violence, drugs, and street-level prostitution in inner city Hartford, Connecticut. *Medical Anthropology, 22,* 233–259.

Sanchez, L. (2001). Gender troubles: The entanglement of agency, violence, and law in the lives of women in prostitution. In C. M. Renzetti & L. Goodstein (Eds.), *Women, crime, and criminal justice* (pp. 60–76). Los Angeles, CA: Roxbury Publishing Company.

Sanders, T., & Campbell, R. (2007). Designing out vulnerability, building respect: Violence, safety and sex work policy. *The British Journal of Sociology, 58*(1), 1–19.

Schoot, E., & Goswami, S. (2001). *Prostitution: A violent reality of homelessness.* Chicago, IL: Chicago Coalition for the Homeless.

Scoular, J. (2004). The "subject" of prostitution: Interpreting the discursive, symbolic and material position of sex/work in feminist theory. *Feminist Theory, 5(3),* 343–355.

Scoular, J., & O'Neill, M. (2007). Regulating prostitution: Social inclusion, responsibilization and the politics of prostitution reform. *British Journal of Criminology, 47*, 764–778.

Securities and Exchange Commission. (2003). *SEC Charges Martha Stewart, broker Peter Bacanovic with illegal insider trading.* Retrieved from http://www.sec.gov/news/press/2003-69.htm

Securities and Exchange Commission. (2006). *Martha Stewart and Peter Bacanovic settle SEC's insider trading charges.* Retrieved from http://www.sec.gov/news/press/2006/2006-134.htm

Securities and Exchange Commission Litigation Release No. 18408. Retrieved from http://www.sec.gov/litigation/litreleases/lr18408.htm

Securities and Exchange Commission Litigation Release No. 19128. Retrieved from http://www.sec.gov/litigation/litreleases/lr19128.htm

Securities and Exchange Commission Litigation Release No. 19456. Retrieved from http://www.sec.gov/litigation/litreleases/lr19456.htm

Securities and Exchange Commission Litigation Release No. 19794. Retrieved from http://www.sec.gov/litigation/litreleases/2006/lr19794.htm

Securities and Exchange Commission v. Samuel Waksal, Jack Waksal, and Patti Waksal. Retrieved from http://www.sec.gov/litigation/complaints/comp18408.htm

Securities and Exchange Commission v. Stewart and Bacanovic. Retrieved from http://www.sec.gov/litigation/complaints/comp18169.htm

Shelley, L. (1981). *Crime and modernization—The impact of industrialization and urbanization on crime.* Carbondale, IL: Southern Illinois University Press.

Steffensmeier, D. (1978). Crime and the contemporary woman: An analysis of changing levels of female property crime, 1960–1975. *Social Forces, 57*(2), 566–584.

Steffensmeier, D., & Allan, E. (1996). Gender and crime: Toward a gendered theory of female offending. *American Review of Sociology, 22*, 459–487.

Substance Abuse and Mental Health Services Administration (SAMHSA). (2009). Substance abuse treatment: Addressing the specific needs of women. A treatment improvement protocol TIP 51. *Center for Substance Abuse Treatment.* Retrieved from http://mentalhealth.samhsa.gov/cmhs/CommunitySupport/women_violence/ default.asp

Sweet, E. M. (2006). *The intersystem assessment on prostitution in Chicago.* Chicago, IL: City of Chicago, Mayor's Office on Domestic Violence. Retrieved from https://www.cityofchicago.org/content/dam/city/depts/fss/supp_info/DV/ProstitutionSystemAssmtChicago.pdf

Truman, J. L. (2011). Criminal victimization, 2010. *Bureau of Justice Statistics.* Washington, DC: U.S. Department of Justice, Office of Justice Programs. Retrieved from http://bjs.ojp.usdoj.gov/content/pub/pdf/cv10.pdf

Ulick, J. (2003). Martha indicted, resigns: Stewart exits as CEO after pleading not guilty to charges related to her sale of ImClone stock. *CNN Money.* Retrieved from http://money.cnn.com/2003/06/04/news/martha_indict/index.htm

U.S. Department of State. (2012). *Trafficking in persons report, 2011.* Retrieved from http://www.state.gov/j/tip/

Valera, R. J., Sawyer, R. G., & Schiraldi, G. R. (2000). Violence and post-traumatic stress disorder in a sample of inner city street prostitutes. *American Journal of Health Studies, 16*(3), 149–155.

Wagenaar, H. (2006). Democracy and prostitution: Deliberating the legalization of brothels in the Netherlands. *Administration and Society, 38*(2), 198–235.

Weitzer, R. (2005). New directions in research on prostitution. *Crime, Law & Social Change, 43*, 211–235.

Wells, D., & Bright, L. (2005). Drug treatment and reentry for incarcerated women. *Corrections Today, 62*(7), 98–99.

West, D. M., & Orr, M. (2007). Morality and economics: Public assessments of the adult entertainment industry. *Economic Development Quarterly, 21*(4), 315–324.

Williamson, C., & Cluse-Tolar, T. (2002). Pimp-controlled prostitution: Still an integral part of street life. *Violence Against Women, 8*(9), 1074–1092.

Williamson, C., & Folaron, G. (2003). Understanding the experiences of street level prostitution. *Qualitative Social Work, 2*(3), 271–287.

Yacoubian, G. S., Urbach, B. J., Larsen, K. L., Johnson, R. J., & Peters, R. J. (2000). A comparison of drug use between prostitutes and other female arrestees. *Journal of Alcohol and Drug Education, 46*(2), 12–26.

Yahne, C. E., Miller, W. R., Irvin-Vitela, L., & Tonigan, J. S. (2002). Magdalena Pilot Project: Motivational outreach to substance abusing women street sex workers. *Journal of Substance Abuse Treatment, 23*(1), 49–53.

Zilberman, M. L., Tavares, H., Blume, S. B., & El-Guebaly, N. (2003). Substance use disorders: Sex differences and psychiatric comorbidities. *Canadian Journal of Psychiatry, 48(1),* 5–13.

NOTE

1. However, evidence exists that street prostitution and escort services are still prevalent within these regions.

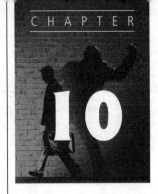

Female Offenders

Violent Crimes

After six years in vice, Diana was promoted to the rank of detective in the robbery homicide unit. At first, she believed she had finally made it to the ranks of real police work. Teams of officers were on a rotation such that the team at the top of the list got the next robbery or homicide call, then moved to the bottom of the list as they worked their case. It only took Diana a few weeks to notice that she and her partner, who was despised for his testimony against a fellow officer in a neighboring jurisdiction, seemed to get trivial cases or ones needing a female touch. They handled a mercy killing, drug overdoses, major crimes with prostitute victims, and an infanticide while other teams responded to multiple shooter events, gang retaliation, and harder crime in the community. Diana was certain that dispatch was keeping them out of the rotation, but there was not much she could do about it.

In her first year of robbery homicide, Diana handled one of the most intense cases of her entire career when she responded to a crime scene of infanticide/suicide involving a single mom, her two-year-old son, and her twin infant girls. The scene was gruesome and the tragedy heart wrenching, but what struck Diana was the media frenzy. Although she was in the initial responding team, two news vans had arrived at the location first. And what troubled her even more deeply was that no such response came with the weekly victim toll from street violence, gang activity, and drug addiction nor the plight of female sex workers abused by pimps, Johns, and the system that arrested them for moments at a time before sending them back to the horrors of the streets. These features plagued the inner city and were painful reminders of her own childhood experience—yet the media ignored the harsh daily realities of an impoverished urban community and instead sensationalized the tragic but rare case of a mother who took her own life and the lives of her three children.

<hr>

Chapter Highlights

- Girls and gangs
- Women's crimes against children
- Female-perpetrated sex crimes against children
- Mothers who kill their children
- Female violent offenders
- Female sex offending
- Female serial killing

<hr>

As discussed in Chapter 9, female offenders commit all types of crime. While their involvement in property crimes, drug offenses, and sex work represents the most common types of crime committed by women (often due in large part to untreated addictions and poverty), these are not crimes for which the general public expresses worry or fear—unless, of course, these women offenders are visible on street corners in the community. For the most part, the public is content to ignore the devastating issues associated with female addiction and sex work, including the extreme physical and sexual victimization of these women and the economic and legal disenfranchisement that keeps them as virtual or literal slaves.

More commonly, the media focus a disproportionate amount of attention on the relatively rare woman who commits crimes of a sexual (but not consensual) or violent nature. If one used the media as a primary source, one could reasonably assume women are becoming more violent than ever before, with an increasing number of women committing serious, egregious acts of violence. This is not based in reality.

The image of the female offender has become a sensationalized topic as a result of the increased media attention on female offending. True crime documentaries and fictionalized television dramas that highlight women's participation in criminal activity give the perception that the rates of female offending, particularly in cases involving violence, have increased dramatically in recent years. The cable television show *Snapped* (Oxygen network) focuses on true crime cases of women who kill and their motivations for crime, citing that approximately 7% of all U.S. murders are committed by women. Yet, rates of crime for women in these types of cases have actually decreased since 2000, with homicide offending rates for females declining from 3.1 offenders per 100,000 in 1980 to 1.6 offenders per 100,000 in 2008. These findings are contrary to the increased attention by the media on female offenders, which often suggests that female violent offending has seen a dramatic rise in recent years.

As seen in Table 10.1, men commit far more violent crimes than women. With almost 10 million arrests in 2010, women represent a smaller percentage in offending for all categories compared to men with the exception of prostitution and commercialized vice, where women accounted for 71% of all arrests in 2010. This pattern is not uncommon, as we see that the gender differences in offending persist over time (Table 10.2). For example, women's participation in crimes of homicide accounts for less than half of the arrests for homicide for men. Despite the increased media attention on the growth of violent female offending, women's participation in crimes of aggravated assault represent less than 3% of all female arrests. Additionally, trends over the past five years indicate that female arrest for violent crime have decreased 3.2%, not increased as the popular media outlets would like the public to believe. Simply put, women's involvement in crime is miniscule compared to that of men.

This chapter highlights sexually based and violent crimes committed by women. Although by no means the typical female offense, these crimes do occur. The representation of these cases highlights two tensions in the field of women and crime: On the one hand, violent crimes involving women are widely discussed in the media and foremost on students' minds; on the other hand, the few examples of these cases form the basis for the perpetuation of these myths about female offending that are overexaggerated compared to their presence in reality.

This chapter begins with a discussion of girls and gangs, addressing the role of gender within the gang culture. The case of female sex offenders, a category of offending that is laden with gender roles and myths, is also discussed here. Within this topic, we also explore female perpetration in crimes typically seen as male dominated, such as child sexual victimization and forcible rape. The third category of rare but salient female crime deals with crimes that are committed by women that are typically dominated by men; these crimes also receive the greatest public outcry: **violent offenses**. Here, the section investigates the crimes of assault and robbery committed by women as well as a very rare category of offender: the female serial killer. We also highlight a category of crime that garners significant media attention: mothers who kill their children.

Girls and Gangs

While girls comprise a small proportion of gang members, there has been significant media attention on the rise of violent girls and gang girls throughout the late 20th century.

It is difficult to determine the extent of female gang membership. Surveys conducted by law enforcement agencies in the 1990s estimated that between 8% and 11% of gang members were female (Moore & Terrett, 1998). These rates remained consistent throughout 2007 and reflect little change in rates of female gang

Table 10.1 **2010 Uniform Crime Reports Arrest Data: Males Versus Females**

	Percentage of Offense Type Within Gender (%)	
	Males	Females
Violent crime	4.55	3.19
Homicide	.10	.04
Forcible rape	.20	.006
Robbery	.99	.41
Aggravated assault	3.26	2.74
Property crime	10.66	18.73
Burglary	2.55	1.34
Larceny-theft	7.42	16.95
Motor vehicle theft	.58	.36
Arson	.10	.06

SOURCE: FBI Uniform Crime Report (UCR).

NOTE: Total male arrests = 7,167,015; total female arrests = 2,474,588.

Table 10.2 **Five-Year Arrest Trends 2006–2010: Uniform Crime Reports Arrest Data: Males Versus Females**

	Percentage Change Within Gender Between 2006 and 2010	
	Males	Females
Violent crime	−11.3	−3.2
Homicide	−14.8	−16.7
Forcible rape	−12.8	−29.6
Robbery	−11.7	−2.8
Aggravated assault	−11.0	−2.9
Property crime	−2.9	+27.6
Burglary	−4.4	+3.3
Larceny-theft	+5.1	+34.7
Motor vehicle theft	−45.5	−45.8
Arson	−30.1	−27.6

SOURCE: FBI Uniform Crime Report (UCR).

NOTE: Overall crime percent change for men = −11.1%; overall crime percent change for women = −2.0%.

participation, contrary to the image that is perpetuated by the media (National Youth Gang Center, 2009). However, not all law enforcement jurisdictions include girls in their counts of gang members, a practice that can skew data about the number of girls involved in gangs (Curry, Ball, & Fox, 1994). Self-report studies during this same time frame reflect a higher percentage of female gang participation compared to law enforcement data and suggest that 38% of the self-identified gang members between the ages of 13 and 15 were girls (Esbensen, Deschenes, & Winfree, 1999).

Who are female gang members? Much of the early literature on girls and gangs looked at female gang members as secondary to issues surrounding male gangs. Classic studies by Campbell (1984) and Moore (1991) illustrated that girls entered the gang lifestyle as a result of a brother or boyfriend's affiliation. Here, the men in their lives paved the way for girls to engage in gang-affiliated crimes and activities. Girls in the gang were often distinguished from their male counterparts by their sexuality. This sexualization manifested in several ways: (1) as a girlfriend to a male gang member, (2) as one who engages in sex with male gang members, and (3) as one who uses her sexuality in order to avoid detection by rival gang members and law enforcement (Campbell, 1995). Modern research builds upon this early work, suggesting that female gangs are not only increasing their membership ranks but also expanding their function and role as an **independent female gang**, an entity separate from the male gang. Girls in the gang are no longer the sexual toys of the male gang but have become active participants in crimes of drugs and violence.

Recent literature draws upon two theoretical perspectives to explain the nature and roles of girls within the gang. The *liberation hypothesis,* influenced by the emancipation/liberation theories of the 1970s (Adler, 1975; Simon, 1975), suggests that the increase of female participation in gangs is related to an increase in opportunities to participate in other traditionally male domains of crime. Another interpretation suggests that girls may experience autonomy and feelings of empowerment as a result of their gang activities (Nurge, 2003). However, research by Joe and Chesney-Lind (1995) counters the position that gang life is liberating for girls. Their work suggests that gang participation is not about adolescent rebellion but rather provides a peer-support network to help both girls and boys cope with the violence and disorder that runs throughout their families and community. The second theme is known as the *social injury hypothesis*, which posits that girls in gangs experience higher levels of risk, danger, and injury compared to their male counterparts (Moore, 1991). Here, girls in the gang experience greater levels of risk compared to any benefits that gang membership may provide. While these two perspectives independently contribute to our understanding of female gang members, they offer greater explanatory power when considered together. While girls involved in the gang lifestyle may experience a new sense of freedom and thrill in their lives, their membership also places them at increased risk for violence and victimization (Nurge, 2003).

The lives of girls in gangs tell a story filled with violence, poverty, racism, disenfranchisement, and limited resources. They come from families who struggle to make ends meet in economically depressed areas. In these communities, opportunities for positive, prosocial activities are significantly limited, and the pressure to join a gang runs rampant. Many of the girls have limited achievements in the classroom, and their educational experience has little to do with books or teachers. Instead, they share stories of disorder, threats, and crime (Molidor, 1996). The majority of their parents never married, and the presence of intimate partner abuse within their childhood home was not uncommon. Many of the girls had a parent or other family members who were involved in the criminal justice system and were either currently incarcerated or had been incarcerated during some part of their lives.

For some girls, membership in a gang is a family affair, with parents, siblings, and extended family members involved in the gang lifestyle. Research by Miller (2000) indicates that 79% of girls who were involved in a gang had a family member who was a gang member, and 60% of the girls had multiple family members in gangs. For these girls, gang affiliation comes at an early age. During the childhood and preteen years, their gang activities may consist of limited acts of delinquency and drug experimentation. During junior high, girls exhibit several risk factors for delinquency, including risky sexual behavior, school failures, and truancy. By the time these girls become teenagers, they are committed to the gang and criminal activity and participate in a range of delinquent acts, including property crimes, weapons offenses, and violent crimes against persons. The later adolescent years (age 15–18) represent the most intense years of gang activity (Eghigian & Kirby, 2006).

While the gang is a way of life for some girls, many others find their way to the gang in search of a new family. Many girls involved in gangs have histories of extensive physical and sexual abuse by family members during early childhood. Many of the girls run away from the family residence in an attempt to escape the violence and abuse in their lives. In an attempt to survive on the streets, the gang becomes an attractive option for meeting one's immediate and long-term needs such as shelter, food, and protection. Not only does the gang provide refuge from these abusive home environments, but it provides a sense of family that was lacking in their families of origin (Joe & Chesney-Lind, 1995). Research by Miller (2000) indicates that it is not so much a specific risk factor that propels girls into the gang but rather the relationship among several factors, such as a neighborhood exposure to gangs, a family involvement in the lifestyle, and the presence of problems in the family, that illustrates the trajectory of girls into the gang lifestyle.

The literature on female gangs indicates that the lifestyle, structure, and characteristics of female gangs and their members are as diverse as male gangs. Some girls hang out in gangs to search for a social life and peer relationships but typically do not consider themselves as members of the gang. The structure of the girl gang ranges from being a **mixed-gender gang** to functioning as an independent unit. For girls involved in mixed-gender gangs, their roles range from being an **affiliate** of the male gang unit to, in some cases, having a separate but equal relationship to their male counterparts (Schalet, Hunt, & Joe-Laidler, 2003).

One historical example of a female auxiliary gang is the **Vice Queens**, which was an affiliate of the Vice Lords, a Black conflict gang in Chicago during the 1960s. Unlike the Lords, the Queens lacked cohesion within the group and had no formalized leadership structure. Much of their connection to the Lords was through their relationships, and significant portions of their time were spent hanging out with the boys and encouraging the boys to engage in sexual acts with them. While there were few examples of formal dating between the members, there was a sense of temporary monogamy. In most of the relationships, sex was a common tool used by the girls. Rarely did the girls view these relationships as something that had promise for long-term romance and stability. However, the Queens also participated in activities independent of their male counterparts. Their involvement in delinquency ranged from running away, truancy, and shoplifting to the occasional foray into more masculine crimes such as auto theft and grand larceny. Most of their delinquent activity with the Lords involved instigating fights with rival gang members. Their experience with fighting and hustling provided the girls with a unique skill set, which allowed them to survive the violence and trauma that existed in their neighborhood (Fishman, 1995).

The initiation process for girls ranged from being *jumped in* or *walking the line*, whereby the girls were subjected to assault by their fellow gang members, to being *sexed in* or *pulling a train*, an experience that involved having sex with multiple individuals, often the male gang members. However, not all of these initiation rites came with a high degree of status within the gang, as those girls who were sexed in generally experienced lower levels of respect by fellow gang members (Miller, 2000). Girls who had been sexed into the gang were subjected to continued victimization from within the gang. While not all girls were admitted to the gang in this manner, this image negatively affected all of the girls:

> The fact that there was such an option as "sexing in" served to keep girls disempowered, because they always faced the question of how they got in and of whether they were "true" members. In addition, it contributed to a milieu in which young women's sexuality was seen as exploitable. (Miller, 1998, p. 444)

Recent media attention has targeted gang girls and the perception that violence by these girls is increasing. Research by Fleisher and Krienert (2004) indicated that among girls who described themselves as active members of a gang, almost all (94%) had engaged in a violent crime during the previous six months, and two-thirds (67%) had sold drugs during the past two months. More than half (55%) had participated in property crimes such as graffiti or destruction to property, while two-thirds (67%) engaged in economic crimes such as prostitution, burglary, robbery, or theft in the previous six months. However, research indicates that this increased attention is less about the crimes that girls commit and more about their violations of gender-role expectations. The negotiation of the *bad girl* identity allows for girls to appear tough, command respect, and legitimize their independence and power within the gang. However, the terms *tough*, *respect*, and *power* take on a very different meaning for girls compared to boys. Traditional notions of femininity, such as appearance and restrained sexuality, are inherent in commanding respect within the gang (Joe-Laidler & Hunt, 2001). At the same time, respect is about making sure that no one takes advantage of you and that you stand up for yourself. For example, much of the assaultive behavior in which gang girls participate involves fights with members of rival female gangs.

▲ **Photo 10.1** The issue of gender and gangs has highlighted the roles of girls and women within the gang. Here, a group of young women hang out on a corner in their neighborhood drinking malt liquor while one girl shows off the razor blade that she hides in her mouth.

For girls in the gang lifestyle, violence is more than just engaging in criminal offenses. Indeed, the participation in a delinquent lifestyle that is associated with gang membership places girls at risk for significant victimization. Girls who are independent of a male gang hierarchy tend to experience high levels of violence as a result of their drug selling and interactions on the streets with other girls. These independent girls are aware of the potential risks they face and take a number of precautionary measures to enhance their safety, such as possessing a weapon, staying off the streets at night, and traveling in groups. While the close relationship with a male gang can often serve as a protective factor, it can also place girls at risk of rape and sexual assault by their "homeboys" (Hunt & Joe-Laidler, 2001). In addition, girls whose gang membership is connected to a male gang unit tend to experience higher levels of violence on the streets compared to girls who operate in independent cliques. These girls are at a higher risk of victimization due to the levels of violence that they are exposed to from assaults and drive-by shootings involving the male gang members. Indeed, many of these crimes (and potential risks of victimization) would not be present if they were not involved in the gang lifestyle (Miller, 1998).

The exit from the gang lifestyle for girls can occur in several ways. For most girls, this exit coincides with the end of adolescence. They may withdraw from the lifestyle, often as a result of pregnancy and the need to care for their young children. For others, their exit is facilitated by an entry into legitimate employment or advanced education. Others will be removed from their gangs as a result of incarceration in a juvenile or adult correctional facility. While some may choose to be *jumped out*, most will simply diminish their involvement over time rather than be perceived as betraying or deliberately going against their gang peers (Campbell, 1995). The few women who choose to remain in the gang have several pathways from which to choose. They may continue their gang participation as active members and expand their criminal résumé. Their relationships with male gang members may continue with their choice of marriage partners, which allows them to continue their affiliation in either a direct or indirect role (Eghigian & Kirby, 2006).

Sexually Based Offenses by Females

The public is increasingly concerned with sex offenses committed by female offenders, most likely in light of noteworthy cases of female sex crimes that make media headlines. Cases like that of Mary Kay Letourneau, the 30-something schoolteacher convicted of raping a 13-year-old student, make headlines and cause public outcry. To date, however, there is far less research on female sex offenders than male sex offenders, leaving this body of literature in its infancy. This should not imply we know nothing or very little about sex crimes perpetrated by female offenders. On the contrary, official reports estimate the prevalence of female sex offending and outline various categories of female sex crimes as well as different typologies of female offenders. The literature also outlines the treatment and supervision approaches that are most effective for this special population.

What is the prevalence and nature of female sex offending? Certainly women are a rare type of offender in these types of male-dominated crimes, and such offenses comprise a miniscule proportion of female offenders in general. However, it is the power of the media that makes these cases noteworthy. Female sex offending encompasses a broad array of sex offenses, including forcible rape, statutory rape, and child sexual abuse. The National Crime Victimization Survey (NCVS) estimates that sex crimes are one of the most significantly underreported crime types, so we can assume the problem is greater than official statistics report. Nonetheless, female offenders account for about 10% of all sex crime perpetrated in the United States (Federal Bureau of Investigation [FBI], 2010).

Sex offenses fell dramatically in the United States between 2001 and 2010. Men committed 24.6% fewer forcible rapes in 2010 than in 2001, and the drop in forcible rape by women dropped 41.5% during the same period. In 2010, women were arrested for 113 forcible rapes, compared to 12,475 male arrests for the same crime, accounting for fewer than 1% (0.89%) of all rape arrests in the United States (FBI, 2010). Of course, forcible rape is but one category of sex offending monitored by the FBI. All other sex offenses (aside from forcible rape and prostitution) are included in the broad category *Sex Offenses*. In this category, male offending dropped 18.9% between 2001 and 2010, while female offending dropped 26.8% during the same period. Thus, in 2010, females represented only 7% (3,256) of the 46,089 arrests for sex offenses that year.

Most official sources agree that official data on female sex offending underestimate female perpetration of sex crimes. Although somewhat dated, Schwartz and Cellini (1995) suggest that approximately two-thirds of female victims and one-third of male victims of sexual assault are victimized by a woman. Sexual victimization by women is underreported for a variety of reasons. One factor may be sociocultural expectations and norms (Denov, 2004; Frey, 2006; Hislop, 2001). Society expects sex offenders to be men, and thus sexual offending by women is often interpreted (by victims, offenders, and broader society) as misguided nurturing or within the context of a nontraditional relationship (e.g., a 30-year-old teacher and 13-year-old student). Society permits no similar justification for male sexual offending. This translates into the misperception that sexual victimization by female offenders is somehow less harmful than sexual victimization by male offenders (Denov, 2004; Hislop, 2001). Also, particularly in cases where there is no pretext of a relationship, victims, the media, and justice professionals often question a female's ability to commit sex crimes (Hislop, 2001). After all, consummation of intercourse is contingent on an erect penis, and a female rapist would thus be unable to rape an unwilling man. This notion is problematic, as it ignores the physiological response to genital stimulation in female-perpetrated rape of men, same-sex rape, and rape by foreign object. These biases transcend public perception and also influence professional decision making among medical professionals, law enforcement, and justice personnel, further limiting the recognition, reporting, treatment, and legal options for justice for victims of female sex offenders (Becker, Hall, & Stinson, 2001; Denov & Cortoni, 2006).

Scholars have developed typologies for female sex offending (Mathews, Matthews, & Speltz, 1989; Nathan & Ward, 2002; Vandiver & Kercher, 2004). The first is male-coerced female involvement in the sexual assault of her own children (Mathews et al., 1989; Vandiver, 2006). In this typology, the female sex offender is a passive participant, often coerced by a male lover into shared sexual abuse of the woman's children. In this typology, a male predator often seeks a weak female partner with children for the purpose of sexual exploitation. A second typology is the predisposed female sex offender, whose sexual offenses are a function of psychological issues often triggered by their own sexual abuse in childhood. Like the male-coerced female sex offender, predisposed female sex offenders often perpetrate their crimes against their own children or children in their family, but this is not always the case. Aileen Wuornos (see Table 10.3) is an example of this type. A third type posited by Mathews et al. (1989) and supported in subsequent research includes the teacher/lover offender, who often establishes a "consensual relationship" with an underage victim who is willing but who cannot legally consent (Vandiver & Kercher, 2004). In such cases, female sex offenders minimize their responsibility by describing the sexual victimization in the context of a loving and nurturing romantic relationship. Although most such offenders do not marry their victims, Mary Kay Letourneau is an example of this type (see case study on page 230).

Forcible Rape Perpetrated by Female Offenders

As the FBI data suggest, forcible rape by women is a relatively rare phenomenon, accounting for less than 1% of all forcible rape cases in the United States. According to the Bureau of Justice Statistics ([BJS], 2006b), these statistics may underestimate female involvement in sex offending, particularly sex offenses involving multiple perpetrators. In many such cases, men may complete the forcible sex act with the assistance of female accomplices (Nathan & Ward, 2001; Vandiver, 2006). Thus, female involvement in perpetrating forcible rape is underreported when a man commits the primary sex act.

The BJS (2006b) estimates that women are involved in an estimated 40% of forcible rapes involving multiple offenders.

Other research suggests that when women are the sole or primary perpetrator in crimes of forcible rape, the victims are most likely to be women, not men (Center for Sex Offender Management, 2007, Vandiver, 2006). Such female-on-female rape cases are underreported, because many such victims don't recognize their victimization as rape. When they do, they often fail to report for fear they won't be taken seriously or will be laughed out of the system. Unfortunately, these fears are often realized. Of the victims who do attempt to file police reports, few are successful in having formal charges brought against the perpetrator. Again, societal myths about what rape really is—a man forcing a woman into unwanted intercourse—may limit the awareness of medical and criminal justice professionals who fail to take such crimes seriously.

Female-Perpetrated Sex Crimes Against Children

Probably the most troubling crime for our culture to accept is the female-perpetrated sexual violation of children. As discussed throughout this book, societal expectations of women are, and have historically been, rooted in a motherly, nurturing persona. Women are seen as unfortunate victims of crime, but their victimization is almost expected, given the relative lack of assertion, strength, and autonomy expected of women compared to men. Criminal victimization perpetrated by women turns these notions upside-down, which explains, in part, the extensive media coverage surrounding female offenders. This is doubly so when those crimes are sexual in nature. And of all the sexual offenses, none raises public fury more than sexual offenses committed against children. Thus, female-perpetrated sex crimes against children represent the most heinous types of crimes committed by the most vulnerable of populations by the most unexpected of offenders.

Although rare, female sex crimes against children do occur. The BJS (2006b) estimates that when women do sexually offend against children, they most often do so in conjunction with a male co-offender. Considering the typology developed by Mathews et al. (1989), such crimes often involve a woman coerced into sexually abusing her own children by a male lover she fears losing. In such scenarios, the woman assists in grooming the child for sexual abuse and is often present during the sex act to "protect" the victim from undue harm. For example, in 1990, Karla Homolko assisted in the drugging and rape of her 15-year-old sister by her then-fiancée Paul Bernardo in order to reduce risk of harm and "keep it in the family" (Williams, 1996). In Homolko's case, she observed the rape committed by Paul, and eventually, Homolko herself committed rape against her teenage sister. Likewise, the case of Rose West in the United Kingdom illustrates the pairing of male-female perpetrators in the sexual victimization of children (Carter, 2011). West, along with her husband, Fred, is believed to have sexually assaulted several girls in the1970s, including Fred's daughter and stepdaughter from a previous marriage and at least one of the couple's own biological daughters. After nearly a decade of increasingly heinous rapes, sexual torture, and murder, the couple was convicted of rape and murder.

But not all female perpetrators of sexual crimes against children act in conjunction with male offenders. In some cases, women act alone. According to Dube et al. (2005), child victims of sex crimes report a female-only perpetrator in 23% of cases, compared to 22% who were victimized by both a male and a female offender. Likewise, Boroughs (2004) estimated that nearly one-quarter of all child victims of sexual assault are victimized by a woman, with their mother being the most common offender.

In some cases, a woman commits sex crimes against a vulnerable victim within the context of a relationship, but the victim is not legally able to consent. These cases don't blur the lines of *Romeo and Juliet laws*, which often curtail prosecution when the age of two sex partners is within a few years but one or more is not yet of age to legally consent (e.g., a 16- and 18-year-old pair). This category often involves sexual activity of a much older female offender with an underage male victim, as in the case of 34-year-old Mary Kay Letourneau and a 13-year-old student. In such cases, the victim does not recognize the activity as a crime, and societal response to such situations often minimizes the seriousness of these acts. Instead, our culture often gives kudos to the victims of such crimes, implying that they "got lucky." In contrast, most media outlets would report sex between a 34-year-old male teacher and 13-year-old female student with vehemence. Unfortunately, this type of female-perpetrated sex offending against children is rarely detected and when detected, it is rarely seen as a crime. The case of Mary Kay Letourneau, detailed below, provides a clear example of gendered expectations for sex crimes by females against children.

Case Study

Mary Kay Letourneau

Most of the time when people think about sex offenders, they think of the creepy guy that lives down the street or the male relative that always seemed a bit odd. It's not unusual to jump to these conclusions—after all, the majority of child sex assaults are perpetrated by someone known to the victim, and many of the high-profile child abductions and murders (Polly Klass, Samantha Runnion, and Danielle van Dam are a few examples of these phenomena) involve cases of men who lived in the victims' neighborhoods. Few immediately think of the female sex offender who engages in sexual contact with young men. These types of behaviors are often excused or justified, suggesting that sexual relations between a young boy and an older female are acceptable. Consider how these stories are played in the media—in songs like "Hot for Teacher" and "Mrs. Robinson" and in films such as *The Graduate*.

However, sex crimes involving women are criminal acts and involve real victims. Perhaps one of the most well-known stories of a female sex offender involves the case of Mary Kay Letourneau. She was 34, married, a mother of four, and a schoolteacher from Washington state. Her victim was 13-year-old Vili Fualaau, a young boy that she had first met when he was in the second grade at Shorewood Elementary School, her first teaching job. Mary Kay was promoted in 1995 and was assigned to teach fifth and sixth graders, where she once again came into contact with Vili. Mary Kay began to spend significant amounts of time with the young Vili, inviting him to her home after school and during the summers. She even included him on a family vacation to Alaska. The high levels of attention that Mary Kay paid to Vili caused a rift in the relationship with her husband, which was already strained by their financial troubles and his extramarital affairs. Mary Kay and Vili's relationship soon turned sexual and she discovered that she was pregnant. Knowing that the child was not his, Steve Letourneau made an anonymous phone call to the Department of Social Services and the school administration, where he reported the relationship between his wife and the young child to the authorities. Mary Kay was arrested on the charge of statutory rape. Despite Vili's (and his mother's) cries that he was not a victim, the law identified him as one due to his age and the nature of their relationship.

Letourneau gave birth to their daughter (Audrey Lokelani Fualaau) in May 1997 while she was awaiting trial. As part of a plea-bargain agreement, she pled guilty to the charge of child rape, served three months in jail, and was released on probation. In addition, Mary Kay was to give up custody of Audrey to Vili's mother and obey a no-contact order with Vili. Within one month of her release from prison, Vili and Mary Kay were caught in a "compromising" position in a parked car. Letourneau was arrested for violating her probation and sentenced to 7.5 years in prison, the maximum sentence under the law. Yet, this steamy encounter had led to another pregnancy, a girl named Georgia, who was born while Mary Kay was incarcerated in October 1998.

Mary Kay was able to visit with her children throughout her incarceration, as Washington state has a program that promotes mother-child bonding opportunities for women during their incarceration. While both she and Vili maintained that they would "be together forever," their relationship did struggle. Vili was a young boy forced to grow up quickly as a result of his interactions with Mary Kay and the birth of their daughters. He had some minor infractions with the law, including a case of auto theft, where he received probation.

Letourneau was released from prison in August 2004. She was required to register as a sex offender for the rest of her life. Because of the nature of the case, the court had mandated a no-contact order between Mary Kay and Vili for the rest of their lives—however, they returned to court and successfully had the court order lifted in order to make their co-parenting practices easier. Following the removal of the no-contact order, Vili and Mary Kay resumed their relationship and married in May 2005.

While not a typical case of female sex offenders, this sensationalized case highlights one example of this crime. However, many media reports have questioned whether this case should have been considered a crime and whether Vili was indeed a victim. In the eyes of the laws as they currently stand, the answer to both questions is yes.

Violent Female Offenders

Much has been written about violence by female offenders in the last two decades. If one relied on media reports, the perception of female violent offending is that female violent crime has risen in the last two decades, with an increase in all types of female violence, including assault, murder, **filicide** (killing one's child), and serial killing perpetrated by women (Michels, 2009). The research does not support these media assertions.

According to the BJS (2002, 2010), female violence has actually declined in the last 20 years. This includes rates of female assault, gang violence, homicide, and serial killing, as discussed herein. Female violence does happen, but it is a relatively rare event compared to violent offending by men, which accounts for about nine times more violent crime than female offending (BJS, 2009; Cooper & Smith, 2011). Current research has also provided some insight as to the context for female violent offending. Again and again, research studies and official data link female offending to substance use, addiction, trauma and abuse, mental health issues, and economic deprivation (James & Glaze, 2006; Proctor, 2009; Sentencing Project, 2007; United Nations Office on Drugs and Crime, 2008).

Homicide

Homicide offenders are overwhelmingly male. Between 1980 and 2008, the male homicide offending rate was about nine times higher (15 per 100,000) than the female homicide offending rate (1.7 per 100,000; Cooper & Smith, 2011). Data on 2008 homicides report a slightly narrowed gap in homicide offending by gender, with men committing about seven times as many homicides as women. While this might appear to mean that female homicide offending has risen, this is not the case. Homicide offending for both men and women declined markedly between 1980 and 2008, but the decline in male homicide is more robust, given the far higher rate of male offending to begin with. Specifically, male homicide offending rate dropped from about 20.8 per 100,000 in 1991 to 11.3 per 100,000 in 2008, while the female homicide offending rate dropped from 3.1 per 100,000 in 1991 to 1.6 per 100,000 in 2008. Thus, while it is true that men commit seven times more homicides than women today (as opposed to nine times more homicides than women two decades ago), this reflects a significant drop in homicide rates for both genders, but especially male murderers (see Table 10.2).

Manson Women

In the late 1960s, the charismatic Charles Manson lived with a few dozen followers on an abandoned ranch/movie lot near Topanga Canyon in L.A. County, engaging in free love and drug experimentation. He called these followers his family. Among his more radical ideas, Manson believed a race war, called "Helter Skelter," was coming, and he developed a plan to initiate this inevitable race war. He convinced several of his followers to commit murder, thereby testing their loyalty and sparking Helter Skelter. Several members of his "family" followed his request, including the "Manson Women": Susan Atkins, Leslie Van Houten, and Patricia Krenwinkle.

Susan Atkins and Patricia Krenwinkle participated in the now-infamous murder of the pregnant actress Sharon Tate and her houseguests on August 8, 1969. They, along with another follower of Manson, Charles "Tex" Watson, stabbed the five victims at Tate's house over 100 times, smearing blood on the walls of the home. Atkins reportedly wanted to cut out Sharon Tate's unborn baby, but there wasn't time. Two days later, Van Houten joined in as Atkins, Krenwinkle, and Watson stabbed a wealthy grocer, Leno LaBianca, and his wife, Rosemary, leaving another gruesome crime scene in their wake.

During their arrest, trial, and initial incarceration, the Manson Women remained loyal to Manson and appeared the monsters depicted in the media, often chanting and behaving in a bizarre fashion, presumably at Manson's instruction. The Manson Women were convicted and sentenced to death for committing murder, and although he did not commit murder himself, Manson was sentenced to death for his role in initiating this conspiracy to commit murder.

The Manson Women began serving their sentence in 1971. In 1972, however, their death sentences were commuted when state and federal courts declared capital punishment, as administered, unconstitutional. Overnight, the sentences for Manson and his followers were commuted to life in prison, with the possibility of parole. The public was outraged that these violent female murderers would not face execution and might someday be released to commit more murders.

After they began serving their time in prison, however, Manson's alleged control over them began to wane. The women realized they had been under Manson's influence and control, and they denounced Manson and his beliefs. They disclosed that they were also under the influence of LSD, a powerful hallucinogenic drug, and that the LSD altered their mental functioning, allowing them to accept Manson's views on the world and follow his instruction without question (A&E Networks, n.d.).

A psychiatrist who performed a psychiatric evaluation of Susan Atkins shortly after she entered prison expressed his belief that Atkins would eventually change her worldview in opposition to Manson's, suggesting she would no longer be a danger to society. As early as her first parole hearing in 1975, doctors recommended Atkins for release. It was never granted. For the next 30 years, her parole petitions were denied. She was a model prisoner who got along well with the other inmates and the correctional staff throughout her imprisonment; she participated in many prison programs and even started a prison choir. When she was diagnosed with brain cancer in March of 2008, her husband, James Whitehouse, petitioned for a compassionate medical release; his petition was denied (Whitehouse, 2010). In September of 2009, the Parole Board once again held a hearing on whether or not to grant Atkins parole. The Board denied parole for the 13th time, stating that Atkins was still a danger to society. At this time, Atkins was living in a skilled nursing facility inside a prison compound, near death from terminal brain cancer. She died three weeks later on September 24, 2009, as an inmate in the California prison system ("Ex-Manson Follower Susan Atkins Dies," 2009).

Leslie Van Houten has also been described as a model prisoner. She denounced her ties with Manson months before being sent to death row. She is currently working toward a master's degree and is very active in the Prison Pups program, which allows inmates to train services dog for the disabled. Van Houten was denied parole for the 17th time in July 2010 (Montaldo, "Leslie Van Houten," n.d.; Netter, 2010).

Patricia Krenwinkle was very involved in taking care of the Manson-family children before she committed murder. She has also been described by prison staff as a model inmate. In January of 2011, Krenwinkle was denied parole for the 13th time, at the age of 63. The Parole Board set her next hearing date for 2018 (Deutsch, 2011; Lopez, 2011; Montaldo, "Patricia "Katie" Krenwinkel," n.d.).

All three of these women were described by the prison staff at the California Institute of Women, where they served most of their sentence, as model prisoners. They have perfect prison records, never having been written up for any disciplinary reason. All three earned college degrees while serving their time. They were each in different prison programs: Krenwinkle helped other inmates learn to read, Van Houten worked as a college tutor for other inmates, and Atkins taught classes in prison.

The prison staff continually recommends to the parole board that these women be released, and the Parole Board continues to deny their requests, saying these female murderers remain a danger to society nearly half a century after their murderous summer in 1969.

The Manson Women have served well over 40 years for violent crimes they committed in their 20s and while under the influence of drugs. This is much longer than most murderers spend incarcerated for their crimes and well past the age of desistance for most offenders. Yet they remain examples of the rare but sensational female homicide offender whose gruesome offenses targeted strangers as victims.

When they kill, women are four times more likely to kill a male victim than a female victim (Cooper & Smith, 2011). Female murderers are about twice as likely to know their victims as male murderers. Kellermann and Mercy (1992) found that female homicide offenders knew their victim in 60% of female-perpetrated murders, while 40% of victims were unknown to female homicide offenders. In contrast, male murderers knew their victim in only about 20% of all male-perpetrated homicide, with 80% male-perpetrated homicide victims being strangers. Most commonly, female-perpetrated homicide involves women killing their spouses, boyfriends/paramours, and children. As you learned in earlier chapters, many of these female-perpetrated homicide cases involve years of abuse at the hands of the intimate partner, and many of the women who commit homicide in these instances kill their batterers.

Women are disproportionately represented in child homicide. Official statistics indicate that women commit nearly 40% of all homicides against a child under the age of five. While the majority of perpetrators arrested for child murder (about 60%) are men, child murder is one of the few crime types where women's rate of offending approaches that of men. Again, context is key here: Roughly 30% of all homicides victims under the age of five in the United States were murdered by their mothers, a topic discussed in greater detail later in this chapter. Of young children killed by someone other than a parent, 20% are killed by a woman, most commonly a family member, friend, or acquaintance, not a stranger (Cooper & Smith, 2011).

Mothers Who Kill Their Children

While the crime of filicide is a rare occurrence, it raises significant attention in the media. The case of Andrea Yates is one of the most identifiable cases of filicide in the 21st century. After her husband left for work on June 20, 2001, Yates proceeded to drown each of her five children one at a time in the bathtub of the family home. Her case illustrates several factors that are common to incidents of maternal filicide. Yates had a history of mental health issues, including bipolar disorder, and she had been hospitalized in the past for major depression. She was the primary caretaker for her children and was responsible for homeschooling the older children. She and her husband were devout evangelical Methodists. Yates indicated that she felt inadequate as a mother and wife, believed that her children were spiritually damaged, and stated that she was directed by the voice of Satan to kill her children (Spinelli, 2001, 2004).

The case involving the children of Andrea Yates is just one tragic example of a mother engaging in *filicide*, or the killing of her children. There are several different categories of filicide. *Neonaticide* refers to an act of homicide during the first 24 hours after birth, compared to cases of *infanticide*, which includes acts whereby a parent kills his or her child within the first year of life. Here, the age of the child distinguishes these cases from general acts of filicide, which include the homicide of children older than one year of age by their parent. While the practice of filicide does not exclude the murder of a child by its father, mothers make up the majority of offenders in cases of infanticide and neonaticide.

What leads a woman to kill her child? There are several different explanations for this behavior. Research by Resnick (1970) distinguishes five different categories of infanticide. The first category represents cases where the infant was killed for altruistic reasons. In these incidents, the mother believes that it is in the best interests of the child to be dead and that the mother is doing a good thing by killing the child. The mother believes (whether real or imagined) that the child is suffering in some way and that the child's pain should end. Based on Resnick's (1970) typology, Yates would be identified as a mother who kills her children out of altruistic reasons. A review of Yates's case indicates two themes common to **altruistic filicide**. The first theme reflects the pressure that exists in society for women to be good mothers. For Yates, this pressure was influenced by her religious fundamentalism, which placed the importance of the spiritual life of her children under her responsibility. The pressure to be a perfect mother was exacerbated by her history of mental illness. The second theme reflected the pressure of bearing the sole responsibility of caring for the children. Here, Yates expressed feeling overwhelmed by the demands of their children's personal, academic, and spiritual needs in addition to the responsibilities of caring for the family home. She also lacked any support from outside of the family, which further contributed to her feelings of being overburdened (West & Lichtenstein, 2006).

The second category in Resnick's typology refers to the killing of a child by an acutely psychotic woman. These cases are closely linked with explanations of postpartum psychosis, where the mother suffers from a severe case of mental illness and may be unaware of her action or be unable to appreciate the wrongfulness of her behaviors (Bienstock, 2003). Examples of this type of filicide may involve a woman who hears voices that tell her that she needs to harm her child. The third category represents the killing of an unwanted infant. In many cases, these are cases of neonaticide. Research indicates that there are similar characteristics within the cases of mothers who kill their children with their first day of life. These women tend to be unmarried, under the age of 25, and generally concealed their pregnancy from friends and family. Some women may acknowledge that they are pregnant, but their lack of actions toward preparing for the birth of the child indicate that they may be in denial that they may soon give birth. Others fail to acknowledge that they are pregnant and explain away the symptoms of pregnancy (Miller, 2003). They typically give birth without medical intervention and generally do not receive any form of prenatal care. The majority of these women do not suffer from any form of mental illness that would help to explain the death of their children. Instead, most of the cases of homicide of the infant are simply a result of an unwanted pregnancy. In these instances, the children are typically killed by strangulation, drowning, or suffocation (Meyer & Oberman, 2001). The fourth category involves the "accidental" death of a child following incidents of significant child abuse and maltreatment. Often, the death of a child occurs after a long period of abuse. The fifth category represents cases where the death of a child is used as an act of ultimate revenge against another. In many cases, these vengeful acts are against the spouse and father of the child (Resnick, 1970).

Mothers who kill their children present a significant challenge to the cultural ideals of femininity and motherhood. Society dictates that mothers should love and care for their children, behave in a loving and nurturing manner, and not cause them harm or place their lives in danger. In many cases, the presence of a psychological disorder makes it easier for society to understand that a mother could hurt her child. Information on **postpartum syndromes** is used at a variety of different stages of the criminal justice process. Evidence of psychosis may be used to determine whether a defendant is legally competent to participate in the criminal proceedings against her. However, this stage is temporary, as the woman would be placed in a treatment facility until such a time that she is competent to stand trial. Given that postpartum syndromes are generally limited to a short period of time (compared to other forms of psychiatric diagnoses), these court proceedings would only be delayed temporarily.

More often, information about postpartum syndromes is used as evidence to exclude the culpability of the woman during a trial proceeding. In some states, this evidence forms the basis of a verdict of "not guilty by reason of insanity." Here, the courts assess whether the defendant knew that what she was doing at the time of the crime was wrong. "The insanity defense enables female violence to coexist comfortably with traditional notions of femininity. It also promotes empathy toward violent women, whose aberrance becomes a result of external factors rather than conscious choice" (Stangle, 2008, p. 709). In cases where an insanity defense is either not available or is unsuccessful, evidence of postpartum syndromes can be used to argue for the diminished capacity of the offender.

A third option allows for courts to find someone guilty but mentally ill (GBMI). Here, the defendant is found guilty of the crime, but the court may mitigate the criminal sentence to acknowledge the woman's mental health status. For many offenders, this distinction can allow them to serve a portion of their sentence in a treatment hospital or related facility (Proano-Raps & Meyer, 2003). While Andrea Yates was convicted of murder and sentenced to 40 years to life by the State of Texas in 2002, her conviction was later overturned. In her second trial, she was found not guilty by reason of insanity and was committed to a state mental health facility for treatment (Keram, 2002).

Female Serial Killing

Serial killing is an extremely rare phenomenon. Although different definitions abound, *serial killing* is defined by the U.S. Code as

> a series of three or more killings, not less than one of which was committed within the United States, having common characteristics such as to suggest the reasonable possibility that the crimes were committed by the same actor or actors. (18, USC, Chapter 51, Section 1111)

Overall, serial killers are responsible for an estimated 100 of the roughly 13,000 U.S. homicides annually, so the likelihood that a murder victim was killed by a serial killer is about 1 in 130, or .769%. Considering the 12,996 people who were murdered in 2010 and the total U.S. population of 308,745,538 that same year, the risk of being a homicide victim was .0000421%, or 1 in roughly 24,000 people (Farrell, Keppel, & Titterington, 2011; FBI, 2010; U.S. Census, 2010).

The risk of being killed by a serial killer in 2010 was thus .000000324%, or about 1 in 3 million people. Official statistics do not report homicides by serial killing, but consider that about 89% of homicide overall is perpetrated by men. Thus, a gross overestimate of the risk of being murdered by a female serial killer is about 1 in 30 million people in the United States, assuming similar gender rates in serial killing as exists in homicide generally. But of course, we know that male murderers are twice as likely to kill unknown persons (unknown victims in 80% of male homicide cases) as female murderers (unknown victims in 40% of female homicide cases), so the risk of being murdered by a female serial killer could be as low as 1 in 90 million people in the United States. Some sources suggest that female serial killers are more likely than male serial killers to know their victims (Kelleher & Kelleher, 1998), so perhaps 1 in 30 million is the more accurate estimate of victimization risk—but in either case, this estimate represents a tiny risk, perhaps only 3–30 of the 13,000 murders that occur in the United States each year.

Research suggests that when female serial killing does occur, it often involves a special subset of offenders: health care workers. In fact, serial killing by health care workers is one subtype of serial killing wherein female offenders outnumber male offenders (Brantley & Kosky, 2004). Perhaps this is due in part to the large overrepresentation of women in health care professions, or perhaps this is due to the gendered power differential between male and female health care workers, with overwhelming numbers of nurses being women. One recent example of such a case is Genene Jones, a Texas nurse believed to have killed between 15 to 50 pediatric patients under her care. Jones is believed to have intentionally injected her patients with lethal medication to stop their breathing/heartbeat then attempted to revive them and be seen as a hero. She was convicted and sentenced to 99 years in prison.

One of the most notorious female serial killers in recent times is Aileen Wuornos (see case study box below). Wuornos was a Florida prostitute believed to have killed eight men in the 1990s (*Wuornos v. State*, 1996). At the time of her arrest, she claimed that the men she murdered were a small subset of clients who had threatened her with sexual or physical violence, and she killed them in self-defense. Subsequent to her conviction, she claimed to have murdered the men in cold blood, although at least one had a history of violence against women consistent with Wuornos's initial claim that she killed in self-defense (Wuornos & Berry-Dee, 2004; "Wuornos' Last Words," 2004). To some, this case illustrates a common characteristic associated with female serial killing: mental illness. Nevertheless, she was convicted of six counts of first-degree murder and was executed by lethal injection by the state of Florida in 2002.

Case Study

Aileen Wuornos

It sounds like a story straight out of a Hollywood movie: A female prostitute robs and murders men along rural highways to make enough money to keep her girlfriend. This story was depicted in the 2003 movie *Monster*, starring Charlize Theron, who won a Best Actress Oscar for her role as the murderous femme fatale in the film. But *Monster* was not a fictional Hollywood tale; it was based on the true story of one of America's most notorious female serial killers: Aileen Wuornos.

Wuornos was born on February 29, 1956, in Rochester, Michigan, to a teenage mother. Her mother abandoned her and her brother when she was very young, leaving them with their grandparents. Wuornos's early life was tumultuous. Her grandfather was an angry and violent man who beat Wuornos throughout her childhood. By the time Wuornos was 11, she was trading sex for money and cigarettes with boys in the neighborhood. At age 14, she became pregnant and was sent to a group home to have the baby, a son she was forced to give up for adoption. Wuornos was 15 when her grandmother died in 1971, and her grandfather subsequently kicked her out of the house. Wuornos spent the next 20 years wandering the country, engaging in prostitution to make a living.

In 1976, 20-year-old Wuornos settled in Florida and was briefly married to a 69-year-old man. The marriage lasted less than three months, due in part to Wuornos's unchecked rage; she reportedly beat her elderly husband with his cane. Her violent tendencies often escalated to arrests for assault and disturbing the peace. Her grandfather's suicide and brother's death from throat cancer that same year led to her further decline, and in 1978, Wuornos tried to commit suicide by shooting herself in the stomach. Wuornos received very little psychological counseling in response to her suicide attempt.

Wuornos's criminal propensity went unchecked for the next decade, and her pattern of assaults escalated to robbery. In 1981, Wuornos robbed a mini-mart at gunpoint and was sentenced to three years in prison. She served 18 months and returned to her former life of crime and prostitution upon her release.

After more than a decade of unsuccessful relationships with men, Wuornos met her girlfriend, Tyria Moore, at a biker bar in 1986. Moore would become the most successful long-term romantic relationship Wuornos would ever have, lasting only 4 years. In the fall of 1989, Wuornos and Moore's

(Continued)

(Continued)

relationship was on the rocks. Money was a constant stressor, and Wuornos believed she was going to lose Moore if she could not find a way to provide for them. On November 30, 1989, Wuornos once again went out to a Florida highway to sell her body for money. A man named Richard Mallory—who had a criminal history of violence against women—stopped to pick up Wuornos; she shot him, left his naked body in the woods, took his money, stole his car, went home, and bragged to her girlfriend about what she had done. Moore was not sure whether Wuornos actually committed murder, so she did not go to the police.

By the mid-1990s, Wuornos had robbed and murdered at least three other men in the same manner (Macleod, 2002). When Wuornos tried to tell Moore what she had done, Moore told Wuornos that she did not want to hear about it. Moore would later claim that fear of Wuornos kept her from reporting Wuornos's crimes to the police. Police finally put out a description of the two women they believed were involved with the murders, but it was Wuornos's thumbprint that would become her undoing. Wuornos had pawned several of the items that belonged to her first victim, Richard Mallory, and she was required to leave a thumbprint on the pawn card. Investigators were able to match this thumbprint with a warrant for arrest on one of Wuornos's aliases.

On January 9, 1991, Wuornos was arrested outside of a biker bar in Florida. Police tracked down Moore, who had fled to Pennsylvania to get away from Wuornos. Moore agreed to come to Florida to speak with Wuornos in hopes of obtaining a confession. Moore told Wuornos that the police were after her and her family and that she was afraid she was going to be arrested also. Although Wuornos suspected Moore of working with the police, she assured Moore that she would confess to the crimes. On January 16, 1991, Wuornos confessed to murdering her victims in self-defense (A&E Networks, 2008).

Wuornos went to trial for the murder of Richard Mallory in early 1992. Wuornos insisted on taking the stand in her own defense, claiming that she shot Mallory in self-defense when he tried to rape her. However, Wuornos appeared a very angry woman and was not a sympathetic defendant. The jury found her guilty and recommended she be put to death. Over the next 18 months, Wuornos pled no contest or guilty to five additional murder cases, resulting in five additional death sentences.

Wuornos remained on death row in Florida for 11 years while her mandatory appeals ran their course. Wuornos eventually requested that the appeals be stopped. Psychiatric examination determined that she understood what was happening to her, and she was deemed fit to be executed. She was executed by lethal injection on October 9, 2002 (Koch, 2002).

There is no doubt that Wuornos had endured a painful childhood. Was this traumatic childhood responsible for her growing up to become the "Damsel of Death"? Wuornos was described as a very angry person. Psychiatrists who examined her as an adult claimed that she suffered from borderline personality disorder. The symptoms of this disorder could certainly have been exacerbated by the circumstances of her early life, which may have also contributed to the anger she exhibited at trial and throughout her adulthood. But Wuornos's diagnosis of borderline personality disorder was not a severe mental illness that would keep her from being executed. Wuornos's case illustrates the possible impact of early trauma and mental health issues in criminal offending, and it raises questions about how the criminal justice system struggles to balance offender mental health issues and due process with the public's demand for justice in extremely violent cases such as this.

While the prevalence of female perpetrated homicide is rare, it garners attention like few other crimes. Table 10.3 highlights notorious female killers, including serial killers with possible mental illness, health care workers who killed patients in their care, sexual-sadistic female serial killers who raped and murdered their victims with a male codefendant, and black-widow murderers who killed several husbands for insurance money. The infamous Bonnie Parker, who is often depicted as a female serial killer but who in fact is believed to have not killed a single victim, is also included, as are mothers who kill their children, a category discussed in detail earlier in this chapter.

Table 10.3	Femme Fatales: Notorious Female Murderers					
Name	**Occupation**	**Jurisdiction & Year**	**Murder Victims**	**Victim Characteristics**	**Crime/Method**	**Case Outcome**
Countess Elizabeth Bathory de Ecsed (Erzsebet) (1560–1614)	Aristocrat	Hungary (Slovakia) ~1600–1610	~600+	Young women	Tortured and murdered women and bathed in their blood	Arrested and placed under house arrest, with trial suspended indefinitely. Servants who assisted her were convicted of 90 murders and sentenced to death.
Jane Toppan (1857–1938)	Nurse	Massachusetts, 1885	31	Patients	Drugging patients to brink of death and then reviving them, raping victims on brink of death	Not guilty by reason of insanity, sent to Taunton Insane Asylum
Lizzie Andrew Borden (1860–1927)	Social activist with Christian Women's Temperance Union	Massachusetts, 1892	2	Father & stepmother	Murder by axe	Acquitted at trial, public perception of her guilt plagued her until her death from pneumonia in 1927
Mary Ann (Robson) Cotton (1832–1873)	Nurse and dressmaker	England, 1850–1873	21	3 husbands, 2 lovers, her mother, 12 children	Murder by arsenic poisoning	Convicted of one murder (Charles Edward Cotton), executed by hanging
Belle Sorenson Gunness (1859–1908)	Housemaid until 1884, lived on insurance money until 1908	Illinois, 1884–1908	~15–42	Husbands, boyfriends, biological children	Murder for profit (insurance)	Murdered by unknown assailant, body beheaded and burned beyond recognition. Some believe the body was not hers but that she staged her own murder to evade capture.

(Continued)

Table 10.3 (Continued)

Name	Occupation	Jurisdiction & Year	Murder Victims	Victim Characteristics	Crime/Method	Case Outcome
Bonnie Elizabeth Parker (1910–1934)	Waitress, bank robber after 1930	Texas, Oklahoma, Iowa, Illinois, Louisiana, Missouri, Indiana, Minnesota, 1930–1934	0	Although present during more than 100 felonies, including bank robbery and murder committed by associates, and despite public belief to the contrary, Bonnie Parker did not kill anyone.	N/A	Ambushed and killed by posse of Texas and Louisiana law enforcement officers
Rosemary Pauline "Rose" (Letts) West (1953–)	Prostitute	England, 1972–1978	10–30	Teenage girls, including stepdaughters and biological daughter	Torture and murder of 10–30 women with husband, Fred	Convicted of rape and murder, sentenced to life in prison without parole
Genene Anne Jones (1950–)	Pediatric nurse	Texas, 1970s–1984	~15–50	Infants and children under her care in the hospital	Murder by lethal injection of medications, often attempted to revive victims	Convicted, sentenced to 99 years in prison, mandatory parole anticipated in 2017
Marybeth Tinning (1942–)	Nurse's aide	New York, 1971–1985	9	Eight biological children, one adopted child	Murder by smothering children; believed to be a case of Munchausen syndrome by proxy	Convicted of one murder (Tami Lynne), sentenced to 20 years. Denied parole in 2007, 2009, 2011, and 2013. Next parole eligibility date: 2015
Karla Leanne (Teale) Homolka (1970–)	Veterinary assistant	Ontario, Canada, 1990–1992	3	Sister (Tammy), 2 other teenagers	Drugged, raped, tortured, and murdered victims with husband, Paul Bernardo	Manslaughter plea-bargain, served 12 years, released from prison in 2005. Husband/codefendant, Paul Bernardo, sentenced to life in prison, eligible for parole in 2020

Name	Occupation	Jurisdiction & Year	Murder Victims	Victim Characteristics	Crime/Method	Case Outcome
Aileen Wuornos (1956–2002)	Prostitute	Florida, 1989–1990	6–8	Men she met on the streets	Robbery and murder by shooting; Wuornos claimed all men attempted to rape her, and she killed in self-defense; later admitted to robbery and murder	Convicted of six counts of murder, sentenced to death. Executed by lethal injection
Susan Leigh Vaughan Smith (1971–)	Student/unemployed	South Carolina, 1994	2	Her biological children	Murder by drowning; rolled her car into a lake, with sons strapped into their car seats, reportedly to win the love of a boyfriend who did not want a ready-made family	Convicted of two counts of murder, sentenced to life, eligible for parole in 2024
Andrea Pia (Kennedy) Yates (1964–)	Nurse, primary caretaker to 5 children	Texas, 2001	5	Her biological children	Drowned victims in bathtub; believed to have suffered postpartum psychosis	Convicted in 2002 of murder, sentenced to life in prison; overturned on appeal. In 2006, found not guilty by reason of insanity, committed to state mental hospital

SUMMARY

- Women engage in every category of crime, yet their rates of offending are significantly lower than male offending practices.
- Violent and sexual offending by women is relatively rare, yet the media focus overwhelmingly on such crimes by women at the exclusion of more common types of female offending.
- Evidence of postpartum syndrome is often used in criminal cases of women who kill their children.
- There are several different reasons why mothers may kill their children, but not all reasons involve issues of mental illness.
- There are several different types of girl gangs, including mixed-gender gangs, affiliate or auxiliary gangs, and independent girl gangs.
- Sexuality can be a component of the gang life for some girls, but it is not necessarily the experience for all girls involved in gangs.

- Although female-perpetrated homicide is rare, it is sensationalized in the media when it occurs.
- Female murderers are far more likely than men to know their victim (often a family member).
- The rate of female-perpetrated homicide is about 1.6 per 100,000; male-perpetrated homicide occurs about seven times more often.
- Female-perpetrated sexual offending is rare, but it is generally sensationalized in the media when it occurs.

KEY TERMS

Affiliate	Jumped in (walking the line)	Pulling a train (sexed in)
Altruistic filicide	Liberation hypothesis	Social injury hypothesis
Filicide	Mixed-gender gangs	Vice Queens
Independent female gang	Neonaticide	Violent offenses
Infanticide	Postpartum syndrome	

DISCUSSION QUESTIONS

1. Why are the media obsessed with the images of the female offender? What implications does this have on understanding the realities of female offending?

2. What does research say about the gender gap in offending?

3. What role does mental illness play in cases of women who kill their children?

4. How do girls use their gender within the gang context?

5. Discuss the exit strategies for girls in gangs.

6. Discuss the types of violent crimes in which women most typically engage. What approaches might address this problem?

WEB RESOURCES

National Crime Victimization Survey http://www.icpsr.umich.edu/icpsrweb/ICPSR/series/95

National Gang Center http://www.nationalgangcenter.gov/

National Incident Based Reporting System http://www.fbi.gov/about-us/cjis/ucr/frequently-asked-questions/nibrs_faqs#offenseinfo

The Sentencing Project http://www.sentencingproject.org

Uniform Crime Reports http://www.fbi.gov/about-us/cjis/ucr/ucr#cius

REFERENCES

18, USC, Chapter 51, Section 1111. (*serial killing* as defined by U.S. Code)

A&E Networks. (Producer). (2008). *Biography—Biography Aileen Wuornos.* Retrieved from http://www.biography.com/people/aileen-wuornos-11735792

A&E Networks. (n.d.). *Biography—The Manson Women.* Retrieved from http://www.biography.com/people/Charles-manson-9397912/videos/the-manson-women-full-episode-207340838/

Adler, F. (1975). *Sisters in crime: The rise of the new female criminal.* New York, NY: McGraw-Hill.

Becker, J., Hall, S., & Stinson, J. (2001). Female sexual offenders: Clinical, legal and policy issues. *Journal of Forensic Psychology Practice, 1,* 29–50.

Bienstock, S. L. (2003). Mothers who kill their children and postpartum psychosis. *Southwestern University Law Review, 32*(3), 451.

Boroughs, D. S. (2004). Female sexual abusers of children. *Children and Youth Services Review, 26*(5), 481–487.

Brantley, A. C., & Kosky, R. H. (2004). Serial murder in the Netherlands: A look at motivation, behavior, and characteristics. *FBI Law Enforcement Bulletin, 74*(1), 27–29.

Bureau of Justice Statistics (BJS). (2002). Table 4.9: Arrests by offense charged, sex and age group, United States. *Sourcebook of Criminal Justice Statistics Online.*

Bureau of Justice Statistics (BJS). (2006a). Crime and victim statistics. *Bureau of Justice Statistics.* Washington, DC: U.S. Department of Justice, Office of Justice Programs. Retrieved fromhttp://www.ojp.usdoj.gov/bjs/cvict.htm.

Bureau of Justice Statistics (BJS). (2006b). Table 4.9: Arrests by offense charged, sex and age group, United States. Sourcebook of criminal justice statistics online.

Bureau of Justice Statistics (BJS). (2009). Table 4.9: Arrests by offense charged, sex and age group, United States. *Sourcebook of Criminal Justice Statistics Online.*

Bureau of Justice Statistics (BJS). (2010). Table 4.9: Arrests by offense charged, sex and age group, United States. *Sourcebook of Criminal Justice Statistics Online.*

Campbell, A. (1984). *The girls in the gang.* New Brunswick, NJ: Rutgers University Press.

Campbell, A. (1995). Female participation in gangs. In M. W. Klein, C. L. Maxson, & J. Miller (Eds.), *The modern gang reader* (pp. 70–77). Los Angeles, CA: Roxbury.

Carter, W. J. (2011). *Rose West: The making of a monster.* London, England: Hodder & Stoughton.

Center for Sex Offender Management. (2007). *Female sex offenders.* Washington, DC: Office of Justice Programs, U.S. Department of Justice. Retrieved from http://www.csom.org/pubs/female_sex_offenders_brief.pdf

Cooper, A., & Smith, E. L. (2011). *Homicide trends in the United States: Annual rates for 2009 and 2010.* U.S. Department of Justice. Retrieved from http://bjs.ojp.usdoj.gov/content/pub/pdf/htus8008.pdf

Curry, G. D., Ball, R. A., & Fox, R. J. (1994). *Gang crime and law enforcement record keeping. Research in brief.* Washington, DC: U.S. Department of Justice, Office of Justice Programs, National Institute of Justice. Retrieved from http://www.ncjrs.gov/txtfiles/gcrime.txt

Denov, M. (2004). *Perspectives on female sex offending: A culture of denial.* Hampshire, England: Ashgate Publishing.

Denov, M., & Cortoni, F. (2006). Women who sexually abuse children. In C. Hilarski & J. S. Wodarski (Eds.), *Comprehensive mental health practice with sex offenders and their families* (pp. 71–99). Binghamton, NY: The Haworth Press.

Deutsch, L. (2011, January 21). No parole for Manson follower Patricia Krenwinkel. *AOLNews.* Retrieved from http://www.aolnews.com/2011/01/21/no-parole-for-manson-follower-patricia-krenwinkel/

Dube, S. R., Anda, R. F., Whitfield, C. L., Brown, D. W., Felitti, V. J., Dong, M., & Giles, W. H. (2005). Long-term consequences of childhood sexual abuse by gender of victim. *American Journal of Preventative Medicine, 28*(5), 430–438.

Eghigian, M., & Kirby, K. (2006). Girls in gangs: On the rise in America. *Corrections Today, 68*(2), 48–50.

Esbensen, F.-A., Deschenes, E. P., & Winfree, L. T., Jr. (1999). Differences between gang girls and gang boys: Results from a multisite survey. *Youth and Society, 31*(1), 27–53.

Ex-Manson follower Susan Atkins dies. (2009, September 25). *CNN.com.* Retrieved from http://articles.cnn.com/2009–09–25/justice/California.manson.atkins_1_pregnant-actress-Sharon-tate-manson-family-parole-hearings?_s=PM:CRIME

Farrell, A. L., Keppel, R. D., & Titterington, V. B. (2011, August). Lethal ladies: Revisiting what we know about female serial murderers. *Homicide Studies, 15*(3), 228–252. doi: 10.1177/1088767911415938

Federal Bureau of Investigation (FBI). (2010). *Crime in the U.S. 2010: Uniform Crime Reports.* Washington, DC: U.S. Department of Justice, Federal Bureau of Investigation. Retrieved from http://www.fbi.gov/about-us/cjis/ucr/ucr

Fishman, L. (1995). The Vice Queens: An ethnographic study of Black female gang behavior. In M. W. Klein, C. L. Maxon, & J. Miller (Eds.), *The modern gang reader* (pp. 83–91). Los Angeles, CA: Roxbury.

Fleisher, M. S., & Krienert, J. L. (2004). Life-course events, social networks, and the emergence of violence among female gang members. *Journal of Community Psychology, 32*(5), 607–622.

Frey, L. L. (2006). Girls don't do that, do they? Adolescent females who sexually abuse. In R. E. Longo & D. S. Prescott (Eds.), *Current perspectives: Working with sexually aggressive youth and youth with sexual behavior problems* (pp. 255–272). Holyoke, MA: NEARI Press.

Hislop, J. (2001). *Female sex offenders: What therapists, law enforcement and child protective services need to know.* Ravensdale, WA: Issues Press/Idyll Arbor.

Hunt, G., & Joe-Laidler, K. (2001). Situations of violence in the lives of girl gang members. *Health Care for Women International, 22,* 363–384.

James, D. J., & Glaze, L. E. (2006). Mental health problems of prison and jail inmates. *Bureau of Justice Statistics.* Retrieved from http://bjs.ojp.usdoj.gov/content/pub/pdf/mhppji.pdf

Joe, K., & Chesney-Lind, M. (1995). Just every mother's angel: An analysis of gender and ethnic variation in youth gang membership. *Gender and Society, 9*(4), 408–430.

Joe-Laidler, K., & Hunt, G. (2001). Accomplishing femininity among girls in the gang. *British Journal of Criminology, 41,* 656–678.

Kelleher, M. D., & Kelleher, C. (1998). *Murder most rare: The female serial killer.* New York, NY: Random House.

Kellermann, A. L., & Mercy, J. A. (1992). Men, women, and murder: Gender-specific differences in rates of fatal violence and victimization. *The Journal of Trauma, 33*(1), 1–5.

Keram, E. A. (2002). The insanity defense and game theory: Reflections on *Texas v. Yates. Journal of the American Academy of Psychiatry and the Law, 30*(4), 470.

Koch, J. (2002, October 9). Serial killer Aileen Wuornos executed. *United Press International.* Retrieved from http://www.upi.com/Top_News/2002/10/09/Serial-Killer-Aileen-Wuornos-executed/UPI-91991034175817

Lopez, R. (2011, January 20). Manson follower Patricia Krenwinkel denied parole. *Los Angeles Times.* Retrieved from http://latimesblogs.latimes.com/lanow/2011/01/manson-follower-patricia-krenwinkel-denied-parole.html

Macleod, M. (2002). Aileen Wuornos: Killer who preyed on truck drivers. *truTV Crime Library: Criminal Minds and Methods, Notorious Murders, Women Who Kill.* Retrieved from http://www.trutv.com/library/crime/notorious_murders/women/wuornos/1.html

Mathews, R., Matthews, J., & Speltz, K. (1989). *Female sexual offenders: An exploratory study.* Brandon, VT: The Safer Society Press.

Meyer, C. L., & Oberman, M. (2001). *Mothers who kill their children: Understanding the acts of moms from Susan Smith to the "Prom Mom."* New York, NY: New York University Press.

Michels, S. (2009). Why do some women kill? *ABC News.* Retrieved from http://abcnews.go.com/US/story?id=7326555

Miller, J. (1998). Gender and victimization risk among young women in gangs. *Journal of Research in Crime and Delinquency, 35,* 429–453.

Miller, J. (2000). *One of the guys: Girls, gangs and gender.* Oxford, UK: Oxford University Press.

Miller, L. J. (2003). Denial of pregnancy. In M. G. Spinelli (Ed.), *Infanticide: Psychosocial and legal perspectives on mothers who kill* (pp. 81–104). Washington, DC: American Psychiatric Publishing.

Molidor, C. E. (1996). Female gang members: A profile of aggression and victimization. *Social Work, 41*(3), 251–257.

Montaldo, C. (n.d.). Leslie Van Houten. *About.com Crime/Punishment.* Retrieved from http://crime.about.com/od/murder/p/leslievanhouten.htm

Montaldo, C. (n.d). Patricia "Katie" Krenwinkel. *About.com Crime/Punishment.* Retrieved from http://crime.about.com/od/history/p/krnwkl.htm

Moore, J. W. (1991). *Going down to the barrio: Homeboys and homegirls in change.* Philadelphia, PA: Temple University Press.

Moore, J., & Terrett, C. P. (1998). *Highlights of the 1996 National Youth Gang Survey. Fact sheet.* Washington, DC: U.S. Department of Justice, Office of Justice Programs, Office of Juvenile Justice and Delinquency Prevention.

Nathan, P., & Ward, T. (2001). Females who sexually abuse children: Assessment and treatment issues. *Psychiatry, Psychology, and Law, 8,* 44–55.

Nathan, P., & Ward, T. (2002). Female sex offenders: Clinical and demographic features. *The Journal of Sexual Aggression, 8,* 5–21.

National Youth Gang Center. (2009). *National Youth Gang Survey analysis.* Retrieved from http://www.national-gangcenter.gov/Survey-Analysis

Netter, S. (2010, July 6). Leslie Van Houten denied parole for role in Manson murders. *ABCNews.* Retrieved from http://abcnews.go.com/US/Charles-manson-follower-leslie-van-houten-parole/story?id=11075382

Nurge, D. (2003). Liberating yet limiting: The paradox of female gang membership. In L. Kontos, D. Brotherton, & L. Barrios (Eds.), *Gangs and society: Alternative perspectives* (pp. 161–182). New York, NY: Columbia University Press.

Proano-Raps, T. C., & Meyer, C. L. (2003). Postpartum syndrome and the legal system. In R. Muraskin (Ed.), *It's a crime: Women and justice* (3rd ed., pp. 53–76). Upper Saddle River, NJ: Prentice Hall.

Proctor, J. (2009). The imprisonment insights of female inmates: Identity & cognitive shifts for exiting a criminal lifestyle. *Justice Policy Journal, 6*(1). Retrieved from http://www.cjcj.org/files/the_imprisonment.pdf

Pron, N. (2005). *Lethal marriage: The uncensored truth behind the crimes of Paul Bernardo and Karla Homolka.* Toronto, Canada: Seal Books.

Resnick, P. J. (1970). Murder of the newborn: A psychiatric review of neonaticide. *American Journal of Psychiatry, 126,* 1414–1420.

Schalet, A., Hunt, G., & Joe-Laidler, K. (2003). Respectability and autonomy: The articulation and meaning of sexuality among girls in the gang. *Journal of Contemporary Ethnography, 32*(1), 108–143.

Schwartz, B., & Cellini, H. (1995). Female sex offenders. In B. Schwartz & H. Cellini (Eds.), *The sex offender: Corrections, treatment and legal practice* (pp. 5-1–5-2). Kingston, NJ: Civic Research Institute.

Simon, R. (1975). *Women and crime.* Lexington, MA: D.C. Heath.

Sounes, S. H. (1995). *Fred and Rose: The full story of Fred and Rose West and the Gloucester house of horrors.* London, England: Warner Books.

Spinelli, M. G. (2001). A systematic investigation of 16 cases of neonaticide. *American Journal of Psychiatry, 158,* 811–813.

Spinelli, M. G. (2004). Maternal infanticide associated with mental illness: Prevention and the promise of saved lives. *American Journal of Psychology, 161,* 1548–1557.

Stangle, H. L. (2008). Murderous Madonna: Femininity, violence, and the myth of postpartum mental disorder in cases of maternal infanticide and filicide. *William and Mary Law Review, 50,* 700–734.

The Sentencing Project. (2007). *Women in the criminal justice system.* National Criminal Justice Reference Service. Retrieved from https://www.ncjrs.gov/spotlight/wgcjs/publications.html#ResearchonFemaleOffenders

United Nations Office on Drugs and Crime. (2008). *Handbook for prison managers and policymakers on women and imprisonment.* Retrieved from http://www.unodc.org/documents/justice-and-prison-reform/women-and-imprisonment.pdf

U.S. Census. (2010). *U.S. Census Population Counts, 2010*. Retrieved from http://www.census.gov/2010census/

U.S. Department of Justice. (2012). *Crime in the United States, 2010: Expanded Homicide Table 3*. Retrieved from http://www.fbi.gov/about-us/cjis/ucr/crime-in-the-u.s/2010/crime-in-the-u.s.-2010/tables/10shrtb103.xls

Vandiver, D. (2006). Female sex offenders: A comparison of solo offenders and co-offenders. *Violence and Victims, 21*, 339–354.

Vandiver, D., & Kercher, G. (2004). Offender and victim characteristics of registered female sexual offenders in Texas: A proposed typology of female sexual offenders. *Sexual Abuse: A Journal of Research and Treatment, 16*, 121–137.

West, D. A., & Lichtenstein, B. (2006). Andrea Yates and the criminalization of the filicidal maternal body. *Feminist Criminology, 1*(3), 173–187.

Whitehouse, J. (2010). *Susan Atkins-Whitehouse*. [Website.] Retrieved from http://www.susanatkins.org

Williams, S. (1996). *Invisible darkness*. New York, NY: Little, Brown and Company.

Williams, S. (2004). *Karla: A pact with the devil*. Berkeley, CA: Seal Press.

Wuornos v. State. (1996). 676 So. 2d 972 Fla.

Wuornos, A., & Berry-Dee, C. (2004). *Monster: My true story*. London, England: John Blake.

Wuornos' last words: "I'll be back." (2004). *CNN.com*. Retrieved from http://www.webcitation.org/5bGafqK0R

Processing and Sentencing of Female Offenders

Karla's court experience went as expected. She was charged with robbery, auto theft, and solicitation, but her public defender got her an incredible deal. Due to state budget cuts and prison overcrowding, she was given a three-year suspended sentence: She was free on probation. So long as she sought drug treatment and engaged in no further criminal activity, that sentence would not be imposed.

Karla began attending court-ordered drug treatment meetings—the first few, at least. With cutbacks in the county budget, no probation officer was tracking her progress, and she didn't have to report. Since no one was following up, it was only too easy to skip meetings and continue her criminal lifestyle.

Within six months of her suspended prison sentence, Karla was arrested in a sting operation for soliciting an undercover officer. She was arrested and charged with one count of solicitation, where she expected to be released as usual. However, there was a warrant out for her arrest for a previous violation. . . . She recalled a recent arrest in the neighboring county, but the details were fuzzy because of her copious consumption of drugs and alcohol. The judge imposed the previously suspended three-year sentence, and Karla was sent to state prison to begin serving her first of many prison terms.

Chapter Highlights

- Processing and sentencing of female offenders
- Treatment of female offenders
- The role of patriarchy, chivalry, and paternalism in processing and sentencing female offenders

As you learned in Chapter 2, the gender gap in crime has remained consistent since 1990, contrary to the perceptions that dominate media representation of crime. For most crime types, the increase in female arrests reflects not an increase in offending rates of women but rather a shift in policies to formally arrest and process cases within the criminal justice system that historically had been treated on an informal basis (Rennison, 2009; Steffensmeier & Allan, 1996; Steffensmeier, Zhong, Ackerman, Schwartz, & Agha, 2006). This chapter highlights the different ways in which gender bias occurs in the processing and sentencing of female offenders.

How might we explain the presence of gender bias in the processing of female offenders? Research highlights that women and girls can be treated differently than their male counterparts by agents of social control, such as police, prosecutors, and judges, as a result of their gender. Gender bias can occur in two different ways: (1) women can receive lenient treatment as a result of their gender, or (2) women may be treated harsher as a result of their gender. These two competing perspectives are known as the **chivalry** *hypothesis* and the **evil woman hypothesis**. The *chivalry hypothesis* suggests that women receive preferential treatment by the justice system. As one of the first scholars on this issue, Otto Pollak (1950) noted that agents of the criminal justice system are reluctant to criminalize women, even though their behaviors may be just as criminal as their male counterparts. However, this leniency can be costly, as it reinforces a system whereby women are denied an equal status with men in society (Belknap, 2007). While most research indicates the presence of chivalrous practices toward women, the potential for sex discrimination against women also exists when they are treated more harshly than their male counterparts, even when they are charged with the same offense. Here, the *evil woman hypothesis* suggests that women are punished not only for violating the law but also for breaking the socialized norms of gender-role expectations (Nagel & Hagan, 1983). Finally, a third hypothesis suggests that women receive equal treatment, regardless of their gender.

Throughout the past forty years, research has been inconclusive about whether or not girls receive chivalrous treatment. While the majority of studies indicate that girls do receive leniency in the criminal justice system, the presence of chivalry is dependent on several factors. This chapter focuses on five general themes in assessing the effects of chivalry on the processing and treatment of female offenders: (1) the stage of the criminal system, (2) the race and ethnicity of the offender, (3) the War on Drugs and its effects on women, (4) the effect of legal and extralegal factors, and (5) the effects of sentencing guidelines on judicial decision making. We conclude this discussion with a look at international examples in the processing of female offenders.

▧ Stages of the Criminal Justice System

Chivalry can occur at different stages of the criminal justice system. Much of the research on whether women benefit from chivalrous treatment looks only at one stage of the criminal justice process. As a result, it is difficult to determine how chivalry is displayed for a particular case, region, or time throughout the entire criminal justice process.

While arrests mark the entry into the criminal justice system, the extension of chivalry can begin much earlier in the process, as there are many actions by police officers that involve the use of discretion but do not necessarily end in an arrest. Research has highlighted how stops and searches by the police may also provide examples of chivalrous treatment. Research by Brunson and Miller (2006) with Black youth noted that boys appeared to receive greater levels of attention by police officers compared to girls:

> The police will mess with the males quicker than the females. If it's a group of girls standing across the street and it's a group of dudes standing across the street, [the police] fina [getting ready to] shine they lights on the dudes and they ain't fina mess with the girls. (p. 539)

While all of the girls in this study indicated that they were involved in some form of delinquent behavior, the harassment that they experienced by the police generally involved low-level violations, such as truancy or curfew violations. In contrast, the boys were more likely to be approached on more serious issues, such as drug possession or distribution.

Women have also generally experienced preferential treatment by officers during traffic stops. However, it's not just the sex of the driver that impacts whether preferential treatment is given. A review of traffic stops across Rhode Island during 2005 finds that agencies with a higher proportion of female officers are more likely to issue citations against female drivers during traffic stops. Here, it appears that men are the beneficiaries of chivalrous treatment, as they are less likely to receive a ticket from agencies with a larger number of women among the police ranks (Farrell, 2011).

While cultural assumptions have suggested that women benefit from chivalrous treatment, research findings on the arrest experiences of women call such beliefs into question. In one of the earliest studies on gender, chivalry, and arrest practices, Visher (1983) found that age, race, and behavior had a strong effect on whether police excused the offending behaviors of women. For example, older Caucasian women were most likely to benefit from preferential treatment by the police, while younger women were more likely to be arrested. In addition, women of color experienced significantly higher levels of arrest compared to White women, even in cases of similar offending behaviors.

As you learned in Chapter 8, shifts in the handling of family and school violence cases have had a significant impact on the arrest rates of juveniles, particularly for girls. Changes in mandatory arrests policies for cases of intimate partner abuse across the United States have also introduced a ripple effect as well. While both male and female juvenile arrest rates in cases of family violence have increased since the implementation of these pro-arrest policies, girls are more likely to be arrested in these cases, lending further support to the claims that police practices toward girls in cases of simple assault have changed. Here we see that girls who engage in behaviors that are outside of traditional gender-norm expectations (such as violence) are treated more harshly by police (Strom, Warner, Tichavsky, & Zahn, 2010).

At the pretrial stage, research indicates that women are more likely to be treated leniently than men. Here, the power of discretion is held by the prosecutor, who determines the charges that will be filed against an offender and whether charge-reduction strategies will be employed in order to secure a guilty plea. Charge-reduction strategies involve instances where an offender agrees to plead guilty in exchange for a lesser charge and a reduction in sentence. Some research indicates that women are less likely to have charges filed against them or are more likely to receive charge reductions compared to their male counterparts (Albonetti, 1986; Saulters-Tubbs, 1993). Research by Spohn, Gruhl, and Welch (1987) found that women of all ethnic groups were more likely to benefit from a charge reduction compared with men of all ethnic groups. Given the shift toward determinant sentencing structures and the reduction of judicial discretion, the power of the prosecutor in this practice increases. While research by Woodridge and Griffin (2005) indicated an increase in the practice of charge reductions under state sentencing guidelines in Ohio, their results indicated that women did not benefit from this practice any more or less than male offenders. While seriousness of crime and criminal history remain the best predictors of receiving a charge reduction, research is inconclusive on the issue of the effect of gender on this process.

Of all the stages of the criminal justice system, the likelihood of pretrial release is the least studied; given that this stage has one of the highest potentials for discretion by prosecutors and the judiciary, it is important to assess whether gender plays a role in the decision to detain someone prior to trial. Research by Demuth and Steffensmeier (2004) found that women are less likely to be detained at the pretrial stage than men, controlling for factors such as offense severity and criminal history. Several factors can influence the presence of chivalrous treatment for women at this stage. Offense type affects this process, as female offenders who were charged with property-based offenses were less likely to receive pretrial detention compared to men with similar offenses (Ball & Bostaph, 2009). Generally speaking, women are typically viewed as less dangerous than their male counterparts, which results in the lenient treatment of women and makes them less likely to be detained during the pretrial process (Leiber, Brubaker, & Fox, 2009). Women are also more likely to have significant ties to the community, such as family and childrearing duties, which make it less likely that they will fail to appear for future court proceedings (Steffensmeier, Kramer, & Streifel, 1993). Women who are charged with drug or property crimes are significantly less likely to be detained prior to trial compared to women who engage in crimes against persons (Freiburger & Hilinski, 2010). Indeed, this bias appears throughout the pretrial process, as women are 30% less likely than men to be detained prior to trial and also receive lower bail amounts than men (and therefore run less risk of being forced to remain in custody due to an inability to make bail). While this preferential treatment exists for women compared to men regardless of race/ethnicity, White women do receive the greatest leniency compared to Hispanic and Black women. Here, research indicates that women of color are less likely to be able to post bond, resulting in their detention at the pretrial stage.

The appearance of preferential or chivalrous treatment in the early stages of criminal justice processing also affects how women and girls will be treated in later stages, as females who already receive more favorable treatment by prosecutors continue to receive such chivalrous treatment as their cases progress. The majority of research indicates that women are more likely to receive chivalrous treatment at sentencing. At this stage of the criminal justice process, women are less likely to be viewed as dangerous (Freiburger & Hilinski, 2009) and are less likely to recidivate (Daly, 1994). Women without a prior criminal record, and who receive a reduction in charges, are more likely to receive leniency at sentencing, as they were less likely to receive a jail sentence and more likely to be sentenced to probationary supervision (Farnworth & Teske, 1995). Indeed, women are viewed as better candidates for probationary supervision compared to male offenders (Freiburger & Hilinski, 2009). Research on the decision to incarcerate reflects that women are less likely to be sent to jail or prison for their crimes compared to men (Spohn & Beichner, 2000). However, research on the length of sentences for women who are incarcerated is a bit mixed. While most research indicates that women receive shorter sentences of incarceration, a deeper look reveals that women are more likely to receive shorter sentences to jail, but no gender differences exist for length of prison sentences (Freiburger & Hilinski, 2009). Offense type also affects the relationship between gender and sentencing, as women are less likely to receive prison sentences for property and drug cases than their male counterparts. In those cases where women are incarcerated for these crimes, their sentence length is significantly shorter compared to the sentence length for men's property and drug offenders. Here, the disparity in sentencing can be attributed to the levels of discretion exercised by judges in making sentencing decisions (Rodriguez, Curry, & Lee, 2006).

⧄ Race Effects and the Processing of Female Offenders

Historically, Black women have been punished more harshly than White women. This punishment reflected not only a racial bias but a pattern consistent with their levels of offending, as women of color engaged in higher levels of crimes than White women and the types of offenses they engaged in had more in common with male offenders than female offenders. Over time, research indicated that the offending patterns of White women shifted such that women, regardless of race or ethnic status, engaged in similar levels of offending.

Significant bodies of research address concerns over the differential processing of male offenders on the basis of race and ethnicity. Here, research consistently agrees that men of color are overrepresented at every stage of the criminal justice system. Given these findings, what effect does discrimination have for female offenders? Several scholars have suggested that chivalry is selective and is more likely to advantage White females over women of color. "As a rule, women of color, poor women, younger women, women immigrants, and lesbians are afforded less leniency or are processed more prejudicially than other females" (Belknap, 2007, p. 154). While White women made up the majority of the prison population in 2008 (45.9%), Black women constituted 25.4% of incarcerated women, and Hispanic/Latina women made up 17.8% of the prison population (Guerino, Harrison, & Sabol, 2011). Given that U.S. Census data for 2009 indicate that Black women make up 13.3% of the population and women of Hispanic origin make up 15.0%, these statistics reflect a practice of overrepresentation of ethnic minorities among incarcerated women (U.S. Census Bureau, 2010). In addition, women incarcerated at the federal level for drug offenses are predominantly Black. Given these findings, some researchers have questions on whether discriminatory views about women offenders, and particularly women of color, may negatively influence prosecutorial and judicial decision-making processes (Gilbert, 2001). Given the significant powers of prosecutors in making charge decisions, offering plea agreements and charge reductions, and making sentence recommendations, the potential effects of racial and ethnic bias can be significant. However, research also indicates that women in general (regardless of race) receive preferential treatment compared to Black and Hispanic men. Here, scholars suggest that women of color may be more "salvageable" than male offenders of color (Spohn & Brennan, 2011).

In the early stages of crime processing, the interactions between gender and race can give the impression that women of color are treated more harshly by the criminal justice system. However, research findings indicate that the bias may be one of economics rather than race. Katz and Spohn (1995) found that White women are more likely to be released from custody during the pretrial stages (compared to Black women) as a result of the ability to fulfill demands for bail. When defendants cannot make bail, there may be incentives for them to accept a plea deal that would limit the time spent in custody. Yet this "freedom" comes at a cost, as the label of *ex-felon* can affect them and limit the available options for the future for the rest of their lives.

Race can also serve as an indirect effect on sentencing practices. **Legal factors** (such as prior record and charge severity) and **extralegal factors** (such as class, employment status, educational status, and ties to the community) do impact sentence outcomes. For example, research by Brennan (2006) indicates that it is racial differences between these legal and extralegal factors that ultimately impact the sentence outcomes for female misdemeanor cases. Her findings show that Black women were more likely to have prior convictions compared to White and Hispanic women, which in turn led to an increased likelihood of incarceration. Black and Hispanic women were also less likely to be able to demonstrate strong positive ties to their community, a factor that also increased the likelihood of incarceration.

Adding to the question of chivalry and race, some research indicates the presence of leniency at sentencing for girls and women of color. Here, scholars suggest that the preferential treatment of Black girls by judges is seen as an attempt to remedy the biased decision making of criminal justice actors during earlier stages of the criminal justice process, which may have led to harsher attention (lack of pretrial release and bail options, less likely to receive charge reductions, etc.; Leiber et al., 2009). Research indicates that race can have an effect on the sentencing practices for both adult and juvenile offenders. In one study on sentencing outcomes for juveniles, Guevara, Herz, and Spohn (2008) indicated that race effects did not always mean that girls of color were treated more harshly than White girls. Their results indicate that White females were more likely to receive an out-of-home placement. While many would suggest that an out-of-home placement is a more significant sanction, their research indicates that juvenile court officials may be engaging in child-saving tactics in an effort to rehabilitate young offenders. Because girls of color were less likely to receive this sentencing option, juvenile justice officials might be suggesting that White girls were more likely to receive help from an out-of-home placement.

Perceptions about race are also influenced by the skin tone of offender. Research by Viglione, Hannon, and DeFina (2011) notes that Black women who are characterized as light skinned receive less prison time at sentencing and ultimately end up serving less time in prison, controlling for parole status, habitual offender status, and offense type (homicide and burglary). Here, women of lighter complexions see their sentences reduced by 12%, compared to those offenders considered to have darker skin. Their research supports similar findings within the Black male community whereby darker-skinned men tend to receive harsher punishments from the criminal justice system compared to lighter-skinned Black men (Gyimah-Brempong & Price, 2006). These conclusions rely heavily on racialized stereotypes about both the severity of the offender and their likelihood to rehabilitate and create a bias in the treatment of offenders.

It is important to note that while the literature on the effects of race and ethnicity demonstrates some important findings for female offenders of color, these results are significantly limited. The majority of studies and race and gender effects involve either a comparison between White and Black women or incorporate the variable of ethnicity with the inclusion of data on Hispanic women. However, few studies investigate the effects of processing for other racial/ethnic groups such as Asian Americans, Native Americans, or Pacific Islanders. In addition, while recent census data have added the category of "one race or more" to acknowledge that many women of color identify as biracial or multiracial, many studies on the processing of female offenders have been slow to include this variable in their research. One explanation for this stems from the sources of data used in many research studies, as many scholars rely on official data statistics for their research. Unfortunately, many states only collect race data for a single category or make their assessments on race not from the self-identification of the offender but rather from the perceptions of police, intake workers, and correctional personnel.

◨ The War on Drugs and Its Effects for Women

The heightened frenzy about the dangerousness of drugs has fueled the War on Drugs into an epidemic. The War on Drugs first appeared as an issue of public policy in 1971, when President Richard Nixon called for a national drug policy in response to the rise of drug-related juvenile violence. Over the next decade, controlled substances such as cocaine were illegally smuggled into the United States by drug kingpins and cartels throughout Mexico and South America (National Public Radio, 2007).

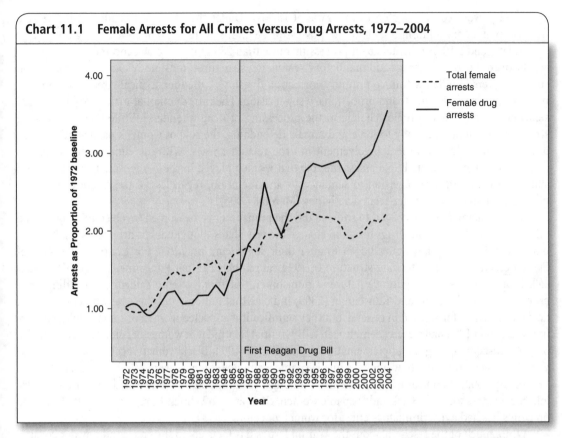

Chart 11.1   Female Arrests for All Crimes Versus Drug Arrests, 1972–2004

SOURCE: Merolla, D. (2008). The war on drugs and the gender gap in arrests: A critical perspective. *Critical Sociology, 34*(2), 355–370.

Since the 1980s and the passage of the Anti-Drug Abuse Act, the incarceration rates for both men and women have skyrocketed. Chart 11.1 demonstrates how these new laws impacted the arrest rates for women. Using 1972 data as a baseline, the passage of the first drug bill by President Ronald Reagan caused the arrest rates for drug cases to skyrocket (Merolla, 2008). Yet the majority of persons imprisoned on these charges are not dangerous traffickers who bring drugs into neighborhoods and place families and children at risk. Rather, it is the drug user who is at the greatest risk for arrest and imprisonment. In response to the social fears about crack cocaine in the inner city, lawmakers developed tough-on-crime sentencing structures designed to increase the punishments for crack cocaine. Sentencing disparities between powder and crack cocaine created a system whereby drug users were treated the same as mid-level dealers. In 1995, the U.S. Sentencing Commission released a report highlighting the racial effects of the crack and powder cocaine sentencing practices and advised Congress to make changes to the mandatory sentencing practices to reduce the discrepancies. Their suggestions fell on deaf ears among congressional members, who did nothing to change these laws. For the next 15 years, cases of crack and powder cocaine perpetuated a 100-to-1 sentencing ratio, whereby offenders in possession of five grams of crack cocaine were treated the same as dealers in possession of 500 grams of powder cocaine. In 2010, President Obama signed the Fair Sentencing Act, which reduced the disparity between crack and powder cocaine sentences to a ratio of 18-to-1. Under the new law, offenders will receive a five-year mandatory minimum sentence for possessing 28 grams of crack (compared to five grams under the old law) and a 10-year sentence for possessing more than 280 grams of crack cocaine.

Prior to the War on Drugs and mandatory sentencing structures, most nonviolent drug conviction sentences were handled within community correction divisions. Offenders typically received community service, drug treatment, and probationary supervision. The introduction of mandatory minimum sentencing represented a major change in the processing of drug offenders. While these sentencing structures are applied equally to male and female defendants, the role of women's participation often differs substantially from men's involvement in drug-related crimes. With the elimination of judicial discretion, judges were unable to assess the role that women played in these offenses. The result was a shift from community supervision to sentences of incarceration, regardless of the extent of women's participation in criminal drug-related activities (Merolla, 2008).

As sentencing practices began to shift, so did the punishments for women involved in drug-related offenses. While the War on Drugs began to change the way states thought about drug offenses, it wasn't until the 1990s that many states began to alter their sentencing practices. For example, the State of Florida created a new sentencing structure in 1994 called the Criminal Punishment Code (CPC) that called for increases in the punitive nature of punishment for many offense categories including drug crimes. Research by Crow and Kunselman (2009) indicate that not only did these new practices have a detrimental effect for women in general, but they significantly impacted women of color. While sentencing practices in 1994 had already demonstrated differential treatment of women of color, these disparities only increased following the implementation of the CPC. In 1994, Black women received sentences that were 27% longer than White women's, while Hispanic women's sentences were 24% longer than those of Whites. By 2003, the racial gap in sentencing amongst drug offending women had increased to 38% longer sentences for both Black and Hispanic women, compared to Whites. Here, it appears that the War on Drugs has had a discriminatory effect for women of color.

While much of the research about the War on Drugs has focused on the crack and powder cocaine disparities, drug trends have changed such that it is no longer these substances that are most popular with women. The rise of methamphetamine use, particularly among women, has led to the label of meth as the "pink collar crack" (Campbell, 2000). Like the shifting of laws in the 1990s for crack and powder cocaine, methamphetamine laws also saw significant changes that increased both the likelihood of incarceration as well as the length of time sentenced. Consequently, the proportion of women sentenced for a meth-related drug conviction increased from 10.3% in 1996 to 23.0% in 2006, making it the second-most-popular drug amongst female drug convictions (behind marijuana; Bush-Baskette, 2010). In addition, the sentences for methamphetamine for women increased 300% between 1996 and 2006 (Bush-Baskette & Smith, 2012). While the majority of women convicted and sentenced for meth-related offenses are overwhelmingly White (99.5% in 1996), the representation of women of color in these cases is increasing (27% in 2006).

The shift to incarceration from community supervision had a detrimental effect on women. Between 1986 and 1991, the incarceration rates of women for drug-related offenses increased 433%, compared to a 283% increase for men (Bush-Baskette, 2000). Drug-convicted women make up 72% of the incarcerated population at the federal level (Greenfeld & Snell, 2000). Most of these cases involve women as users of illegal substances. Even in the small proportion of cases where women are involved in the sale of drugs, they rarely participate in mid- or high-level management in the illegal drug market, often due to sexism within the drug economy (Maher, 2004). In addition, the presence of crack shifted the culture of the street economy, particularly for women involved in acts of prostitution. The highly addictive nature of crack led more women to the streets in an effort to find a way to get their next high. At the same time, the flood of women in search of sex work created an economy whereby the value of sexual services significantly decreased.

While recent changes in federal drug sentencing laws have reduced the disparities in sentencing, the damage has already been done. The effects of these laws created a new system of criminal justice where the courts are overloaded with drug possession and distribution cases, and the growth of the prison economy has reached epic proportions. Yet these efforts appear to have done little to stem the use and sale of such controlled substances. Indeed, the overall rates of crimes other than drug-related cases have changed little during the last 40 years. The effects of these policies have produced significant consequences for families and communities, particularly given the increase in the incarceration rates of women. Chapter 12 explores in depth the consequences in the incarceration of the individual woman, for herself, her family, and her community. It is these consequences that have led some scholars to suggest that the War on Drugs has, in effect, become a war on women (Chesney-Lind, 1997).

The Effects of Legal and Extralegal Factors on Sentencing Women

The assessment of whether women benefit from chivalrous treatment by the criminal justice system is not as simple as comparing the sentences granted to men and women in general. Many factors must be considered, including the severity of the offense, the criminal record of the offender, the levels of injury experienced by the victim, and the culpability or blameworthiness of the offender. For example, women generally have a shorter criminal history than men and are less likely to engage in violent offenses or play a major role in criminal offenses.

In assessing whether women receive chivalrous treatment, it is important to control for these legal and extralegal factors. Research indicates that legal factors do affect the decision-making process for both men and women, albeit in different ways. In addition, the effects of gender vary with each stage of the criminal justice system. For example, offense type influences whether a defendant will be detained during the pretrial stages. Here, women who were charged with a property crime were less likely to be detained or denied bail compared to women charged with a drug offense. In comparison, men charged with a property crime were more likely to be detained compared to those charged with a drug offense (Ball & Bostaph, 2009). Second, the presence of a prior record or being under the supervision of the criminal justice system significantly increased the likelihood of being detained at the pretrial stage for both men and women; however, the effect of these variables had a stronger effect for female offenders than male offenders (Freiburger & Hilinski, 2010). Finally, women who were convicted of a lesser offense had significantly lower odds of receiving an incarceration sentence compared to men who were convicted of the same charge (Spohn & Beichner, 2000).

Research by Spohn and Beichner (2000) indicated that not only do legal factors affect sentencing decisions, but the gender effect of these indicators can also vary by jurisdiction. For example, female offenders from Kansas City were more likely than men to be incarcerated if they were currently on probation at the time of the current offense. In comparison, the presence of a prior record of incarceration had a greater effect for men than women in Chicago.

Not only do legal factors such as criminal history and offense severity appear to affect the pretrial decision process for women; extralegal factors, such as the type of attorney, also affect the likelihood of pretrial release for women. Women who were able to hire a private attorney were 2.5 times more likely to make bail compared to those women who were reliant on the services of a public defender. Clearly, the ability to hire (and financially afford) a private attorney is linked to the ability to satisfy the financial demands of bail as set by the court. In comparison, women who were represented by a public defender were twice as likely to be detained at the pretrial stage (Ball & Bostaph, 2009).

Ties to the community (such as family life) can also serve as an extralegal factors that can mediate sentencing practices. For example, motherhood appears to mitigate a sentence of incarceration, as women with dependent children are less likely to be incarcerated compared to women who do not have children. In these cases, judges appear to consider the social costs of imprisoning mothers and the effects of incarceration on children, particularly in cases of nonviolent or drug offenses (Spohn & Beichner, 2000). In a review of departures from strict sentencing guidelines, research by Raeder (1995) indicates that single parenthood and pregnancy may be used as rationale for granting women a reduced sentence. Here, it is not gender specifically that accounts for mitigation but rather concern for the family (as women without children do not receive similar instances of leniency in sentencing). These departures have been confirmed by the courts in cases such as *U.S. v. Johnson*. Indeed, such departures are not reserved exclusively for women but can also benefit male defendants who are the primary caregiver for minor children (see *U.S. v. Cabell*), which granted a departure from the sentencing guidelines for a male offender who was the primary caregiver for the children of his deceased sister.

The Effects of Sentencing Guidelines on Judicial Decision Making

Throughout most of history, judges have had high levels of discretion in handing out sentences to offenders. In most cases, judges were free to impose just about any terms and conditions at sentencing, from probation to incarceration. Essentially, the only guidance for decision making came from the judge's own value system and belief in justice. This created a process whereby there was no consistency in sentencing, and offenders received dramatically different sentences for the same offenses, whereby the outcome depended on which judge heard their case. While this practice allowed for individualized justice based on the needs of offenders and their potential for rehabilitation, it also left the door open for the potential of bias based on the age, race, ethnicity, and gender of the offender.

During the 1970s, the faith in rehabilitation for corrections began to wane and was replaced with the *theory of just deserts,* a retributive philosophy that aimed to increase the punishment of offenders for their crimes against society. In an effort to reform sentencing practices and reduce the levels of discretion within the judiciary, many jurisdictions developed sentencing guidelines to create systems by which offenders would receive similar sentences for similar crimes. At the heart of this campaign was an attempt to regulate sentencing practices and eliminate racial, gender, and class-based discrimination in courts. As part of the Sentencing Reform Act of 1984, the U.S. Sentencing Commission was tasked with crafting sentencing guidelines at the federal level. Since their implementation in November 1987, these guidelines have been criticized for being too rigid and unnecessarily harsh. In many cases, these criticisms reflect a growing concern that judges are now unable to consider the unique circumstances of the crime or characteristics of the offender. Indeed, the only standardized factors that are to be considered under the federal sentencing guidelines are the offense committed, the presence of aggravating or mitigating circumstances, and the criminal history of the offender.

Prior to sentencing reform at the federal level, the majority of female offenders were sentenced to community-based programs, such as probation. Under federal sentencing guidelines, not only are the numbers of incarcerated women expanding but the length of time that they will spend in custody has increased as well. In addition, these changes in sentencing practices also led to the abolition of parole at the federal level and in many states—meaning that women have few options to reduce their sentences due to their rehabilitative efforts. While the federal sentencing guidelines were implemented to control for disparities in sentencing practices, research indicates that such differences continue to exist, particularly for offenders of color. Female offenders receive more lenient sentences compared to male offenders, regardless of race. Here, evidence indicates that the sentences for women are 25% shorter than their male counterparts. Race and ethnic identity serve to increase the gender gap in sentencing between men and women, as women of color are 50% less likely be sentenced to jail or prison compared to men of color. A similar pattern emerges in looking at the gender gap for length of time sentenced for offenders sent to jail or prison. Black women receive sentences that are 36% shorter than those of Black men, while the sentences of White women are 20% shorter than those of their White male counterparts (Doerner & Demuth, 2010).

Research by Koons-Witt (2006) investigates the effects of gender in sentencing in Minnesota. Minnesota first implemented sentencing guidelines in 1980. Like the federal sentencing guidelines, Minnesota founded their guidelines on a retributive philosophy focused on punishment for the offender. The guidelines were designed to be neutral on race, gender, class, and social factors. However, the courts could consider aggravating and mitigating factors such as the offender's role in the crime if they made a decision outside of the sentencing guidelines. Koons-Witt (2006) investigated the influence of gender at three distinct points in time: prior to the adoption of sentencing guidelines in Minnesota; following their introduction (early implementation, 1981–1984); and in 1994, 14 years after the sentencing guidelines were implemented (late implementation). Her research indicated that female offenders were more likely to be older than their male counterparts and have a greater number of dependent children. In contrast, men were faced with more serious crimes, were more likely to be under community supervision at the time of the current offense, and had greater criminal histories. Prior to the implementation of sentencing guidelines, gender did not appear to have an effect on sentencing guidelines. This finding contradicted the findings of other research, which illustrated that judges did treat female offenders in a chivalrous fashion. The one exception for Koons-Witt's findings was that sentences were reduced for women who had dependent children. Following the early implementation of sentencing guidelines (1981–1984), several legal outcomes increased the potential for incarceration, regardless of gender. These legal factors include prior criminal history and pretrial detention. This pattern was repeated during the late implementation time period (1994). However, the influence of extra-legal factors reappeared during this time period, whereby women with dependent children were more likely to receive community correctional sentences compared to women who did not have children. In these cases, Koons-Witt suggests that the courts may be using the presence of dependent children as a mitigating factor in their decision to depart from the sentencing guidelines, producing an indirect effect for the preferential treatment of women.

Like Minnesota, Ohio also employs sentencing guidelines. However, Ohio's structure allows for increased judicial discretion. Felony crimes are organized into five basic categories. For the top two categories, the presumed sentence is one of incarceration, while the bottom two categories demonstrate support for a community-based sentence. In addition, each category has a broad sentencing range, creating an increase of opportunities for judicial discretion, particularly compared to other structured sentencing schemes. While most states saw increases both in the number of offenders sent to prison and increases in the length of prison sentences, Ohio actually saw decreases in both of these categories for both women and men and in the majority of offense categories (with drug cases as the exception). In addition, the implementation of these guidelines decreased the racial disparities in sentences for Black female offenders (Griffin & Wooldredge, 2006).

While the sentencing guidelines in states such as Minnesota mirror many of the same characteristics found at the federal level, not all states approach directive sentencing in the same fashion. Consider the guidelines in Pennsylvania. Unlike Minnesota, whose sentencing guidelines reflect a retributive philosophy, Pennsylvania's sentencing guidelines allow for the inclusion of other sentencing philosophies, such as rehabilitation, deterrence, and incapacitation in addition to retribution. Here, the effect is that judges may be allowed increased opportunities for judicial discretion. First developed in 1982, the Pennsylvania guidelines were suspended in 1987 and reinstated with alterations in 1988. Research by Blackwell, Holleran, and Finn (2008) reviewed the impact of gender on sentencing both during the time frames when the sentencing guidelines were in effect (1986–1987 and 1988–1990) and during the suspension (1987–1988). Their findings indicate that while women were less likely than men to receive a sentence of probation compared to either jail or prison during the pre-suspension and post-suspension time frames, a similar pattern emerged during the suspension period. These findings led the authors to conclude that sentencing guidelines, at least within the state of Pennsylvania, do not have an effect on reducing the levels of gender disparity in sentencing. However, these findings may be influenced by the increased level of judicial discretion within the guidelines as compared to other states.

Some critics of **gender-neutral laws** argue that directed sentencing structures such as the federal sentencing guidelines have affected women in a negative fashion. These sentence structures assume that men and women have an equal position in society, and therefore, the unique needs of women do not need to be considered when making sentencing decisions. While the intent behind the creation of sentencing guidelines and mandatory minimums was to standardize sentencing practices so that offenders with similar legal factors received similar sentences, the effect has been an increased length of incarceration sentences for both men and women. Given the inability of judicial officials to consider extralegal factors in making sentencing decisions, these efforts to equalize sentencing practices have significantly affected women.

International Perspectives on the Processing of Female Offenders

While the United States has made significant gains in equality for women over the past century, it is clear that women continue to either benefit from chivalrous treatment by the criminal justice system or suffer at the hands of paternalistic attitudes, which can often yield harsher punishments for women who violate both the law as well as proscribed gender roles. What is the case for women in other countries who violate the law? How do women fare under criminal justice systems in countries where paternalistic attitudes may be stronger toward women?

Like many other countries of the Eastern World, China has been a long-standing champion of paternalism toward women in general. Women are viewed as subordinate members of society compared to their male counterparts. This status often translates to disparities in the treatment of women under the law. The need to protect women is part of their cultural identity, which in turn could lead to reductions in punishment. In China, officials have seen a significant increase in recent years of women involved in drug possession and trafficking cases. As a result, court officials have been faced with how to deal with these cases. Research by Liang, Lu, and Taylor (2009) found that in cases of drug trafficking, female drug traffickers received significantly more lenient punishments compared to their male counterparts. For lesser offenses, this practice of chivalrous treatment benefited women even when their crimes and criminal history were similar to male drug traffickers. Here, the most important variable in sentencing is a woman's behavior before the court, as the demonstration of behaviors such as contrition and respect to the court benefited women's sentences. However, this gendered treatment extended only to cases of lower-level offenders, as cases involving a potential death sentence did not indicate any preferential treatment by gender. In these cases, the practice of patriarchy toward women is overpowered by the desire for equality within the Chinese legal tradition.

Likewise, women in South Korea also benefit from some levels of chivalry in sentencing. Male offenders are more likely to be sent to prison and receive significantly longer sentences than female offenders in South Korea. Offenders who had a prior criminal history and were detained at the pretrial stage received significantly harsher punishments. Given that more men fell into these categories, it is not surprising that these men received longer sentences than their female counterparts. In addition, drug of choice has a significant impact as well. While cases involving methamphetamines received harsher punishments compared to marijuana cases (a likely response, given stricter legal directives), women in these cases benefited from reduced punishments compared to male offenders. Here, the chivalrous treatment toward women does not impact the decision to incarcerate, but it does affect the length of sentence handed down.

While the research from both China and South Korea yields similar results for drug offenders, a study conducted by Hsu and Wu (2011) investigates the role of gender for South Taiwanese women. Their work provides a unique insight into the ways in which gender can alter the practices of the courtroom, ultimately influencing punishment practices. Hsu and Wu (2011) found that female defendants are expected to demonstrate a submissive and apologetic demeanor toward the judge. In return, they benefit from leniency in their punishment. The resulting effect is that the persona of the defendant acts much like a legal factor, such as type of offense or criminal history. Given the emphasis that demeanor plays on sentencing outcomes, it appears that the court is more concerned with the violations of gender-normative values than the law in and of itself.

Whereas the United States demonstrates evidence of chivalrous treatment in certain cases, women in Finland do not benefit from preferential treatment by justice officials. As a society, Finnish policies and practices indicate a greater level of gender equality between men and women throughout the workplace and home. Much of this equality stems from family-leave policies that are more generous than those in the United States, which has created increased opportunities for mothers to participate in the workforce. Women are also more likely to be active in the political realm in Finland compared to women in the United States. As a result of the reductions of gender inequality throughout other realms of society, the practices of equal treatment have carried into the criminal justice system. In Finland, gender appears to have no significant effect on sentencing decisions, controlling for legal factors (such as criminal history and crime severity) and social factors (such as employment and family status; Kruttschnitt & Savolainen, 2009).

Research on sentencing practices in Australia looks at whether indigenous women receive preferential treatment by the courts. The term *indigenous* refers to a minority group that typifies the early inhabitants of a region. For example, we would identify Native Americans as an indigenous group in the United States. In Australia, a person who identifies as indigenous is of either aboriginal or Torres Strait Islander origin. Research finds that offenders of indigenous status, regardless of gender, receive preferential treatment by justice officials. In addition, the effects of this chivalry is stronger for women than for men (Bond & Jeffries, 2012). These findings suggest that judicial officials weigh the risk that indigenous offenders pose to the community in comparison to the potential consequences that incarcerating indigenous persons for a significant period of time can have for these communities. Specifically, the courts take into account the context of an offender's life, such as the presence of trauma in early childhood and the marginalization of their cultural identity. These traits appear to reduce the assignment of blame in these offenders' cases. These findings demonstrate that justice officials consider unique extralegal factors such as history and politics in their decision-making process. However, once the decision was made to send an offender to prison, indigenous offenders received longer sentences compared to their non-indigenous counterparts (Bond & Jeffries, 2009, 2012).

Conclusion

This chapter reviewed how and when preferential treatment is extended to female offenders. Whether chivalry exists within the criminal justice system in not an easy question to answer, as it is dependent on the stage of the criminal justice system, the intersections of race and ethnicity, legal and extralegal factors, and the implementation of determinate sentencing structures. Even in cases where research suggests that chivalrous treatment serves women through shorter sentences and an increased likelihood to be sentenced to community-based sanctions over incarceration, not all scholars see this preferential treatment as a positive asset for women. For many, the presence of chivalry is also linked to these gender-role expectations whereby "preferential or punitive treatment is meted out based on the degree to which court actors perceive a female defendant as fitting the stereotype of either a good or bad woman" (Griffin & Wooldredge, 2006, p. 896). Not only does the potential for women to be punished for breaking gender role expectations exist (i.e., the evil woman hypothesis) but there exists a double-edged sword in fighting for special treatment models. *Gender equality* does not necessarily mean *sameness*. Rather, this perspective suggests that women possess cultural and biological differences that should be considered in determining the effects of justice. However, there is a potential danger in treating women differently as a result of these cultural and biological indicators. Given that the law affords reductions in sentencing based on mental capacity and age (juvenile offenders), to extend this treatment toward women can suggest that women "cannot be expected to conform their behavior to the norms of the law. . . . Thus when women are granted special treatment, they are reduced to the moral status of infants" (Nagel & Johnson, 2004, p. 208).

SUMMARY

- Chivalry can occur at different stages of the system. Women who receive preferential treatment in the early stages of processing may continue to benefit from chivalry in the later stages.
- Generally speaking, women are more likely to be released during pretrial stages, receive charge reductions, and receive a jail or probationary supervision sentence.
- When women are incarcerated, they typically receive shorter sentences compared to men.

- While research generally finds that men of color are treated more harshly than White men, research on race and gender is mixed, with some studies indicating that women of color are treated more harshly than Whites, and other researchers finding that women of color are treated in a more lenient fashion compared to White women.
- Legal factors such as criminal history and offense type affect the processing of women.
- Extralegal factors such as the type of attorney can affect the likelihood of pretrial release for women.
- Women who are responsible for the care of young children are more likely to be afforded chivalrous treatment by the courts at the time of sentencing.
- Gender-neutral laws, such as sentencing guidelines, have significantly increased the number of women serving time in U.S. prisons.

KEY TERMS

Chivalry

Gender-neutral laws

Evil woman hypothesis

Legal factors

DISCUSSION QUESTIONS

1. Why is it important to study the processing of female offenders at each stage of the criminal justice system versus only during the final disposition?

2. How do prosecutors and judges use their discretion to give preferential or chivalrous treatment toward women?

3. Which legal and extralegal factors appear to have the greatest impact on the processing of women? Which variables indicate preferential treatment of women in unexpected ways?

4. How do women in foreign countries benefit from chivalrous treatment?

REFERENCES

Albonetti, C. A. (1986). Criminality, prosecutorial screening, and uncertainty: Toward a theory of discretionary decision making in felony case processing. *Criminology, 24*(4), 623–645.

Ball, J. D., & Bostaph, L. G. (2009). He versus she: A gender-specific analysis of legal and extralegal effects on pretrial release for felony defendants. *Women and Criminal Justice, 19*(2), 95–119.

Belknap, J. (2007). *The invisible woman: Gender, crime and justice* (3rd ed.). Belmont, CA: Thomson Wadsworth Publishing Company.

Blackwell, B. S., Holleran, D., & Finn, M. A. (2008). The impact of the Pennsylvania sentencing guidelines on sex differences in sentencing. *Journal of Contemporary Criminal Justice, 24*(4), 399–418.

Bond, C., & Jeffries, S. (2009). Does indigeneity matter? Sentencing indigenous offenders in South Australia's higher courts. *Australian & New Zealand Journal of Criminology, 42*, 47–71.

Bond, C. E. W., & Jeffries, S. (2012). Harsher sentences? Indigeneity and prison sentence length in Western Australia's higher courts. *Journal of Sociology, 48*(3), 266–286.

Brennan, P. K. (2006). Sentencing female misdemeanants: An examination of the direct and indirect effects of race/ethnicity. *Justice Quarterly, 23*(1), 60–95.

Brunson, R., & Miller, J. (2006). Gender, race and urban policing: The experience of African American youths. *Gender & Society, 20,* 531–552.

Bush-Baskette, S. R. (2000). The war on drugs and the incarceration of mothers. *Journal of Drug Issues, 30,* 919–928.

Bush-Baskette, S. R. (2010). *Misguided justice: The war on drugs and the incarceration of Black women.* New York, NY: iUniverse.

Bush-Baskette, S. R., & Smith, V. C. (2012). Is meth the new crack for women in the War on Drugs? Factors affecting sentencing outcomes for women and parallels between meth and crack. *Feminist Criminology, 7*(1), 48–69.

Campbell, N. D. (2000). *Using women: Gender, drug policy and social justice.* New York, NY: Routledge.

Chesney-Lind, M. (1997). *The female offender.* Thousand Oaks, CA: SAGE.

Crow, M. S., & Kunselman, J. C. (2009). Sentencing female drug offenders: Reexamining racial and ethnic disparities. *Women & Criminal Justice, 19*(3), 191–216.

Daly, K. (1994). *Gender, crime and punishment.* New Haven, CT: Yale University Press.

Demuth, S., & Steffensmeier, D. (2004). The impact of gender and race-ethnicity in the pretrial release process. *Social Problems, 51*(2), 222–242.

Doerner, J. K., & Demuth, S. (2010). The independent and joint effects of race/ethnicity, gender, and age on sentencing outcomes in U.S. federal courts. *Justice Quarterly, 27*(1), 1–27.

Farnworth, M., & Teske, R. H. C. (1995). Gender differences in felony court processing. *Women and Criminal Justice, 6,* 23–44.

Farrell, A. (2011, November 8). Explaining leniency: Organizational predictors of the differential treatment of men and women in traffic stops. *Crime & Delinquency.* doi: 10.1177/0011128711420108

Freiburger, T. L., & Hilinski, C. M. (2010). The impact of race, gender and age on the pretrial decision. *Criminal Justice Review, 35*(3), 318–334.

Gilbert, E. (2001). Women, race and criminal justice processing. In C. Renzetti & L. Goodstein (Eds.), *Women, crime and criminal justice: Original feminist readings* (pp. 222–231). Los Angeles, CA: Roxbury.

Greenfeld, L. A., & Snell, T. L. (2000). *Women offenders.* Washington, DC: Bureau of Justice Statistics. Retrieved from http://bjs.ojp.usdoj.gov/content/pub/pdf/wo.pdf

Griffin, T., & Wooldredge, J. (2006). Sex-based disparities in felony dispositions before versus after sentencing reform in Ohio. *Criminology, 44*(4), 893–923.

Guerino, P., Harrison, P. M., & Sabol, W. J. (2011). Prisoners in 2010. *Bureau of Justice Statistics.* U.S. Department of Justice, Office of Justice Programs. Retrieved at http://bjs.ojp.usdoj.gov/content/pub/pdf/p10.pdf

Guevara, L., Herz, D., & Spohn, C. (2008). Race, gender and legal counsel: Differential outcomes in two juvenile courts. *Youth Violence and Juvenile Justice, 6*(1), 83–104.

Gyimah-Brempong, K., & Price, G. N. (2006). Crime and punishment: And skin hue too? *American Economic Association, 96*(2), 246–250.

Hsu, H., & Wu, B. (2011). Female defendants and criminal courts in Taiwan: An observation study. *Asian Criminology, 6,* 1–14.

Katz, C. M., & Spohn, C. (1995). The effect of race and gender and bail outcomes: A test of an interactive model. *American Journal of Criminal Justice, 19,* 161–184.

Koons-Witt, B. (2006). Decision to incarcerate before and after the introduction of sentencing guidelines. *Criminology, 40*(2), 297–328.

Kruttschnitt, C., & Savolainen, J. (2009). Ages of chivalry, places of paternalism: Gender and criminal sentencing in Finland. *European Journal of Criminology, 6*(3), 225–247.

Leiber, M., Brubaker, S., & Fox, K. (2009). A closer look at the individual and joint effects of gender and race in juvenile justice decision making. *Feminist Criminology, 4,* 333–358.

Liang, B., Lu, H., & Taylor, M. (2009). Female drug abusers, narcotic offenders and legal punishment in China. *Journal of Criminal Justice, 37,* 133–141.

Maher, L. (2004). A reserve army: Women and the drug market. In B. Price & N. Sokoloff (Eds.), *The criminal justice system and women: Offenders, prisoners, victims and workers* (3rd ed., pp. 127–146). New York, NY: McGraw-Hill.

Merolla, D. (2008). The war on drugs and the gender gap in arrests: A critical perspective. *Critical Sociology, 34*(2), 355–370.

Nagel, I., & Hagan, J. (1983). Gender and crime: Offense patterns and criminal court sanctions. In N. Morris & M. Tonry (Eds.), *Crime and justice* (Vol. 4, pp. 91–144). Chicago, IL: University of Chicago Press.

Nagel, I. H., & Johnson, B. L. (2004). The role of gender in a structured sentencing system: Equal treatment, policy choices and the sentencing of female offenders. In P. Schram & B. Koons-Witt (Eds.), *Gendered (in)justice: Theory and practice in feminist criminology* (pp. 198–235). Long Grove, IL: Waveland Press.

National Public Radio. (2007). *Timeline: America's war on drugs.* Retrieved from http://www.npr.org/templates/story/story.php?storyId=9252490

Pollak, O. (1950). *Criminality of women.* Baltimore, MD: University of Pennsylvania Press.

Raeder, M. S. (1995). *The forgotten offender: The effect of the sentencing guidelines and mandatory minimums on women and their children.* 8 Fed. Sent. R. 157.

Rennison, C. M. (2009). A new look at the gender gap in offending. *Women & Criminal Justice 19*(3), 171–190.

Rodriguez, S. F., Curry, T. R., & Lee, G. (2006). Gender differences in criminal sentencing: Do effects vary across violent, property and drug offenses. *Social Science Quarterly, 87*(2), 318–339.

Saulters-Tubbs, C. (1993). Prosecutorial and judicial treatment of female offenders. *Federal Probation, 57*(2), 37–42.

Spohn, C., & Beichner, D. (2000). Is preferential treatment of female offenders a thing of the past? A multisite study of gender, race, and imprisonment. *Criminal Justice Policy Review, 11*(2), 149–184.

Spohn, C., & Brennan, P. K. (2011). The joint effects of offender race/ethnicity and gender on substantial assistance departures in federal courts. *Race and Justice, 1*(1), 49–78.

Spohn, C., Gruhl, J., & Welch, S. (1987). The impact of the ethnicity and gender of defendants on the decision to reject or dismiss felony charges. *Criminology, 25*(1), 175–192.

Spohn, C., Welch, S., & Gruhl, J. (1985). Women defendants in court: The interaction between sex and race in convicting and sentencing. *Social Science Quarterly, 66,* 178–185.

Steffensmeier, D., & Allan, E. (1996). Gender and crime: Toward a gendered theory of female offending. *Annual Review of Sociology, 22,* 459–487.

Steffensmeier, D., Kramer, J., & Streifel, C. (1993). Gender and imprisonment decisions. *Criminology, 31,* 411–446.

Steffensmeier, D., Zhong, H., Ackerman, J., Schwartz, J., & Agha, S. (2006). Gender gap trends for violent crimes, 1980 to 2003: A UCR-NCVS comparison. *Feminist Criminology, 1*(1), 72–98.

Strom, K. J., Warner, T. D., Tichavsky, L., & Zahn, M. A. (2010, September 8). Policing juveniles: Domestic violence arrest policies, gender and police response to child-parent violence. *Crime & Delinquency.* doi: 10.1177/0011128710376293

U.S. Census Bureau, Population Division. (2010). *Table 3. Annual estimates of the resident population by sex, race and Hispanic origin for the United States: April 1, 2000, to April 1, 2009.* Retrieved from http://www.census.gov/compendia/statab/2012/tables/12s0006.pdf

U.S. v. Cabell. (1995). 890 F. Supp. 13, 19 [D.D.C.]

U.S. v. Johnson. (1992). 964 F.2d 124 [2d Cir.]

Viglione, J., Hannon, L., & DeFina, R. (2011). The impact of light skin on prison time for Black female offenders. *The Social Science Journal, 48,* 250–258.

Visher, C. A. (1983). Gender, police arrest decisions, and notions of chivalry. *Criminology, 21,* 5–28.

Woodridge, J., & Griffin, T. (2005). Displaced discretion under Ohio sentencing guidelines. *Journal of Criminal Justice, 33,* 301–316.

The Supervision and Incarceration of Women

Karla's prison experience was like that of many other women. She was sent to a women's facility where drugs and sex were readily available. Other inmates in her dorm became her pseudo-family, and she began a relationship with another inmate. Karla didn't consider herself a lesbian, but the narrow pool of romantic partners transformed many heterosexual inmates to same-sex consumers. While Karla was one of the lucky few to receive treatment for her substance abuse issues while in prison, she found the experience a waste of time, as the program seemed to be out of touch with the experiences of her life. After release, Karla was placed on parole, which she inevitably and repeatedly violated for possession of drug paraphernalia or solicitation for prostitution. Once, she was returned to prison on a technical violation for having a small pocketknife in her pocket.

After nearly a decade in and out of prison, Karla was finally sent to a facility for nonviolent inmates with drug problems. After nine months, she was paroled to a coed drug treatment program in the community that had a reputation as a flop house. This was why she had requested this particular placement.

Despite its designation as a drug treatment program, the facility was rife with drugs and sex. Karla found it easy to continue using heroin, and she began trading sex for favors with a guard. Their trade was as follows: She would give him oral sex in exchange for clean urine samples, which enabled her to remain in the drug treatment program and continue using drugs. Fortunately for Karla, an unrelated sex scandal—involving a female administrator suspected of engaging in sex with at least five different male inmates—suspended the program's state contract, and she was transferred to another drug treatment program.

At the new, female-only facility, Karla became sober for the first time since she was 13 years old. Although she had been ordered by court to drug treatment at least four other times (during which time she absconded, forged signatures, or used drugs throughout treatment), this was the first time she actively participated in actual drug treatment.

Sobriety following more than two decades of addiction was almost more than Karla could bear. While her drug treatment program included education, relapse prevention, and job skills, her greatest challenge involved two particularly difficult therapy groups: Overcoming Trauma and Guilt & Loss. Karla began to address her early sexual victimization as well as the birth and adoption of her first child when she was only 13 years old. Traumas that had been stuffed down for years begin to emerge, including physical abuse by pimps and sexual torture by customers. However, one of the deepest sources of pain for Karla came from remembering her mother, who faced deportation because of Karla's actions. Karla had had no contact with her mother or older brothers for more than 20 years, and she was overwhelmed with guilt, not knowing if her mother was in the United States, back in Honduras, or even alive. The second unbearable trauma for Karla came when recounting the birth of a child she had delivered eight years earlier. She was working the streets while pregnant and went into labor after an encounter with a particularly violent customer. At the time, her heroin use numbed both the physical pain and emotional trauma, and she collapsed on the street two months before she was due. Her pimp/boyfriend found her in a pool of blood and dropped her off at the ER, where she delivered the tiny baby 45 minutes later. The pimp snuck her out of hospital about three hours after delivery.

Karla relapsed the night following these disclosures, and she left the program. She was in and out of treatment for the next six months, but she finally got sober again. But this time, Karla expressed her certainty that she could remain sober.

Chapter Highlights

- Historical trends in the incarceration of women
- Contemporary issues in the incarceration of women
- Gender-responsive treatment and programming for incarcerated women
- Supervision of women in the community
- Barriers to reentry for incarcerated women

This chapter focuses on issues related to the supervision and incarceration of women. Drawing from historical examples of incarceration and modern-day policies, this chapter examines the treatment of women in prison and the challenges that women face. Following this discussion, this chapter highlights how the differential pathways of female offending affect the unique needs for women in the correctional system and presents a review of the tenets of **gender-responsive programming**. We investigate how issues such as motherhood and physical/mental health needs dominate the lives of women in the correctional system. We also discuss how these issues affect women on probation and the role of risk-assessment tools in making decisions about the supervision of women. This chapter concludes with a conversation about the lives of women following incarceration and how policy decisions about offending have often succeeded in the "jailing" of women, even after their release from prison.

Historical Context of Female Prisons

Prior to the development of the all-female institution, women were housed in a separate unit within the male prison. Generally speaking, the conditions for women in these units were horrendous and were characterized by an excessive use of solitary confinement and significant acts of physical and sexual abuse by both the male inmates and the male guards. Women in these facilities received few, if any, services (Freedman, 1981). At Auburn State Prison in New York, women were housed together in an attic space where they were unmonitored and received their meals from male inmates. In many cases, these men would stay longer than necessary to complete their job duties. To no surprise, there were many prison-related pregnancies that resulted from these interactions. The death of a pregnant woman named Rachel Welch in 1825 as a result of a beating by a male guard led to significant changes in the housing of incarcerated women. In 1839, the first facility for women opened its doors. The Mount Pleasant Prison Annex was located on the grounds of Sing Sing, a male penitentiary located in Ossining, New York. While Mount Pleasant had a female warden at the facility, the oversight of the prison remained in the control of the administrators of Sing Sing, who were male and had little understanding about the nature of female criminality. Despite the intent by administrators to eliminate the abuse of women within the prison setting, the women incarcerated at Mount Pleasant continued to experience high levels of corporal punishment and abuse at the hands of the male guards.

Conditions of squalor and high levels of abuse and neglect prompted moral reformers in England and the United States to work toward improving the conditions of incarcerated women. A key figure in this crusade in the United Kingdom was **Elizabeth Fry** (1780–1845). Her work with the Newgate Prison in London during the early 19th century served as the inspiration for the American women's prison reform movement. Fry argued that women offenders were capable of being reformed and that it was the responsibility of women in the community to assist those who had fallen victim to a lifestyle of crime. Like Fry, many of the reformers in America throughout the 1820s and 1830s came from upper- and middle-class communities with liberal religious backgrounds (Freedman, 1981). The efforts of these reformers led to significant changes in the incarceration of women, including the development of separate institutions for women.

The Indiana Women's Prison (IWP) is identified as the first stand-alone female prison in the United States. It was also the first maximum-security prison for women. At the time of its opening in 1873, IWP housed 16 women (Schadee, 2003). By 1940, 23 states had facilities designed to exclusively house female inmates.

A review of facilities across the United States reveals two different models of institutions for women throughout the 20th century: **custodial institutions** and reformatories. Custodial institutions were similar in design and philosophy to male institutions. Women were simply warehoused, and little programming or treatment was offered to inmates. Women in custodial institutions were typically convicted on felony- and property-related crimes, with a third of women convicted of violent crimes. The custodial institution was more popular with Southern states. In cases where a state had both a reformatory and a custodial institution, the distribution of inmates was made along racial lines—custodial institutions were more likely to house women of color who were determined to have little rehabilitative potential, while reformatories housed primarily White women (Freedman, 1984). Black women were also sent to work on state-owned penal plantations under conditions that mimicked the days of slavery in the south. Women of color generally had committed less serious offenses compared to White women, yet they were incarcerated for longer periods of time. It was rare to see women of color convicted of

Figure 12.1 Timeline on the Development of Women's Prisons

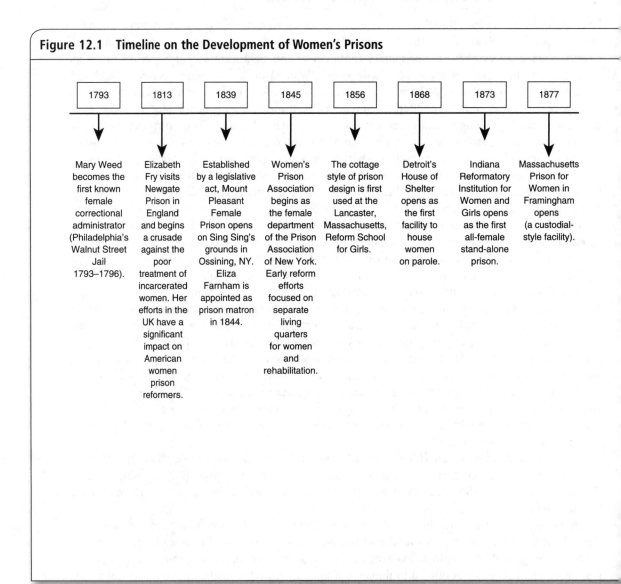

1793	1813	1839	1845	1856	1868	1873	1877
Mary Weed becomes the first known female correctional administrator (Philadelphia's Walnut Street Jail 1793–1796).	Elizabeth Fry visits Newgate Prison in England and begins a crusade against the poor treatment of incarcerated women. Her efforts in the UK have a significant impact on American women prison reformers.	Established by a legislative act, Mount Pleasant Female Prison opens on Sing Sing's grounds in Ossining, NY. Eliza Farnham is appointed as prison matron in 1844.	Women's Prison Association begins as the female department of the Prison Association of New York. Early reform efforts focused on separate living quarters for women and rehabilitation.	The cottage style of prison design is first used at the Lancaster, Massachusetts, Reform School for Girls.	Detroit's House of Shelter opens as the first facility to house women on parole.	Indiana Reformatory Institution for Women and Girls opens as the first all-female stand-alone prison.	Massachusetts Prison for Women in Framingham opens (a custodial-style facility).

SOURCES: Freedman, E. B. (1984); Rafter, N. H. (1990); Watterson, K. (1996); Women's Prison Association (2004).

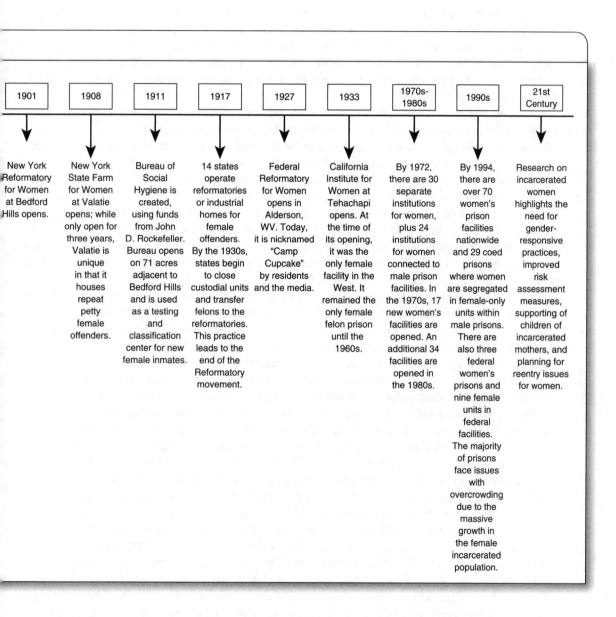

1901	1908	1911	1917	1927	1933	1970s–1980s	1990s	21st Century
New York Reformatory for Women at Bedford Hills opens.	New York State Farm for Women at Valatie opens; while only open for three years, Valatie is unique in that it houses repeat petty female offenders.	Bureau of Social Hygiene is created, using funds from John D. Rockefeller. Bureau opens on 71 acres adjacent to Bedford Hills and is used as a testing and classification center for new female inmates.	14 states operate reformatories or industrial homes for female offenders. By the 1930s, states begin to close custodial units and transfer felons to the reformatories. This practice leads to the end of the Reformatory movement.	Federal Reformatory for Women opens in Alderson, WV. Today, it is nicknamed "Camp Cupcake" by residents and the media.	California Institute for Women at Tehachapi opens. At the time of its opening, it was the only female facility in the West. It remained the only female felon prison until the 1960s.	By 1972, there are 30 separate institutions for women, plus 24 institutions for women connected to male prison facilities. In the 1970s, 17 new women's facilities are opened. An additional 34 facilities are opened in the 1980s.	By 1994, there are over 70 women's prison facilities nationwide and 29 coed prisons where women are segregated in female-only units within male prisons. There are also three federal women's prisons and nine female units in federal facilities. The majority of prisons face issues with overcrowding due to the massive growth in the female incarcerated population.	Research on incarcerated women highlights the need for gender-responsive practices, improved risk assessment measures, supporting of children of incarcerated mothers, and planning for reentry issues for women.

moral offenses—since Black women were not held to the same standards of what was considered acceptable behavior for a lady, they were not deemed as in need of the rehabilitative tools that characterized the environments found at the reformatory (Rafter, 1990). Prison conditions for women at the custodial institution were characterized by unsanitary living environments, with inadequate sewage and bathing systems, work conditions that were dominated by physical labor and corporal punishment, a lack of medical treatment for offenders, and the use of solitary confinement for women with mental health issues (Kurshan, 2000).

In comparison to the custodial institution, the reformatory was a new concept in incarceration, as it was a facility designed with the intent to rehabilitate women. Here, women did not receive a fixed sentence length. Rather, they were sent to the reformatory for an indeterminate period of time—essentially until they were deemed to have been reformed. Women sent to the reformatories were most likely to be White, working-class women. Based on the philosophy that the reformatory was designed to improve the moral character of women, women were sentenced for a variety of "crimes," including "lewd and lascivious conduct, fornication, serial premarital pregnancies, adultery [and] venereal disease" (Anderson, 2006, pp. 203–204). These public-order offenses were based on the premise that such behaviors were "unladylike." Generally speaking, the conditions at the reformatory were superior to those found at the custodial institution. By staffing the reformatory with women guards and female administrators, the reformatory was effective in responding to abuse of women inmates by male guards. While they were the first to provide treatment for female offenders, their rehabilitative efforts have been criticized by feminist scholars as an example of patriarchy at its finest, as women were punished for violating the socially prescribed norms of femininity. The reformatory became a place that embodied an attempt by society to control the autonomy of women—to punish wayward behaviors and instill women with the appropriate morals and values of society (Kurshan, 2000).

One of the most successful reformatories during this time frame was the Massachusetts Correctional Institution (MCI) in Framingham. Opened in 1877, MCI possessed a number of unique characteristics, including an all-female staff, an inmate nursery that allowed incarcerated women to remain with their infants while they served their sentence, and an on-site hospital to address the inmates' health care needs. Several activities were provided to give women opportunities to increase their self-esteem, gain an education, and develop a positive quality of life during their sentence. While MCI is the oldest running prison still in use today, it bears little resemblance to its original mission and design; the modern-day institution bears the scars of the tough-on-crime movement. Today's version of the institution has lost some of the characteristics that made MCI a unique example of the reformatory movement and now mimics the structure and design of the male prisons located throughout the state (Rathbone, 2005).

Like the early days of MCI, the 1960s at the California Institution for Women also embraced a philosophy of rehabilitation. Prisoners were generally sentenced to indeterminate terms of incarceration, and decisions for parole were based not only on the offense committed by the woman but also on her behavior and participation in various programs during her sentence. The majority of these programs were very gendered: "Like the ideal mother, each WCS [women's correctional supervisor] also supervised prisoners' training in homemaking, deportment, dress and grooming, and was expected to participate in the moral regulation of prisoners, particularly as this related to their sexuality" (Gartner & Kruttschnitt, 2004, p. 279). By the mid-1970s, the pendulum on punishment had swung in the opposite direction. The passage of California's Uniform Determinate Sentencing Act in 1976 aligned the mission of the state prisons with a retributive philosophy. As a result, group and individualized counseling was no longer a mandatory offering for the inmates and only a few options for rehabilitation were made available. For the few programs that did exist, they were either run by volunteers from community agencies or by the inmates themselves:

> Work, educational, vocational and volunteer programs were offered as way for women to empower themselves, boost their self-esteem, and accept personal responsibility for their lives in order to change them. The prisoner was no longer expected to rely on clinical experts to design her route to rehabilitation but had become a rational actor. (Gartner & Kruttschnitt, 2004, p. 282–283)

Today, most states have at least one facility dedicated to a growing population of female offenders. As a result, women's prisons will house offenders of all security levels, whereas the number of men's prisons allows for different facilities to house offenders of a specific classification. In many cases, these facilities for women are located in remote areas of the state, far from the cities where most of the women were arrested and where their families reside. The distance between an incarcerated woman and her family plays a significant role in the ways in which she copes with her incarceration and can affect her progress toward rehabilitation and a successful reintegration. In contrast, the sheer number of male facilities increases the probability that these men might reside in a facility closer to their home, which allows for an increased frequency in visitations by family members.

Contemporary Issues for Incarcerated Women

Since the 1980s, the number of women incarcerated in the United States has multiplied at a dramatic rate. As discussed in Chapter 11, sentencing policies such as mandatory minimum sentences and the War on Drugs have had a dramatic effect on the numbers of women in prison. These structured sentencing formats, whose intents were to reduce the levels of sentencing disparities, have only led to an increase in the numbers of women in custody. At the end of 2010, there were 112,822 women incarcerated in prisons in the United States (Guerino, Harrison, & Sabol, 2011). Table 12.1 illustrates a profile of women found in the criminal justice system today. Much of the rise in female criminality is the result of minor property crimes, which reflect the economic vulnerability that women experience in society, or cases involving drug-related crimes, which reflect the addiction issues facing women.

Table 12.1 Profile of Women in the Criminal Justice System

- disproportionately women of color
- in their early to mid-thirties
- most likely to have been convicted of a drug-related offense
- fragmented family histories, with other family members also involved with the criminal justice system
- survivors of physical and/or sexual abuse as children and adults
- significant substance abuse problems
- multiple physical and mental health problems
- unmarried mothers of minor children
- high school degree/GED, but limited vocational training and sporadic work histories

Table 12.2	Rate of Incarceration of Women by Race/Ethnicity	
Race/Ethnicity of Women	**Rate of Incarceration per 100,000**
All women	67
White	47
Black	133
Hispanic	77

SOURCE: U.S. Department of Justice (n.d.).

While Blacks and Hispanics make up only 24% of the U.S. population, 63% of women in state prisons and 67% of women in federal prisons are Black or Hispanic, a practice that indicates that women of color are significantly overrepresented behind bars. Indeed, research indicates that Black women today are being incarcerated at a greater rate than both White women and Black men (Bush-Baskette, 1998). This is highlighted by higher rates of incarceration for women of color. Table 12.2 highlights the rates of incarceration of White, Black, and Hispanic women. As you can see, women of color have rates that are often three times greater than the rate of incarceration of White women. Women of color are also more likely to be incarcerated for violent and drug-related offenses, while White women are more likely to be incarcerated for property offenses (Guerino et al., 2011). Poverty is also an important demographic of incarcerated women, as many women (48%) are unemployed at the time of their arrest, which affects their ability to provide a sustainable environment for themselves and their children. In addition, incarcerated women tend to come from impoverished areas, which may help explain why women are typically involved in economically driven crimes such as property crimes, prostitution, and drug-related offenses. These women also struggle with limited education and a lack of vocational training, which places them at risk for criminal behavior. The majority of women in state prisons across the United States have not completed high school and struggle with learning disabilities and literacy challenges. For example, 29% of women in custody in New York have less than a fifth-grade reading ability. Yet many prison facilities provide limited educational and vocational training, leaving women ill prepared to successfully transition to the community following their release. For example, of the 64% of women who enter prison without a high school diploma, only 16% receive their GED and only 29% participate in any form of vocational training while they are incarcerated (Women's Prison Association [WPA], 2003, 2009a).

The rise in the incarceration rates for women means that many facilities operate beyond their design capacity. Overcrowding in prison facilities not only creates a strain on basic resources within the facility, but it can impact the delivery of services of women and increase the levels of stress and anxiety for women in prison. Research by Sharkey (2010) highlights that overcrowding can also contribute to negative mental health issues for incarcerated women, including suicidal ideation. Such feelings of depression and thoughts of self-harm can potentially increase when staff members are overwhelmed with their basic job duties and are unable to provide emotional support for the inmates. Sharing a cell due to overcrowding also increased the levels of stress for the women, which can lead to feelings of self-harm. Here, the link between suicide risk and overcrowding suggests that as resources are stretched too thin, staff may be unable to effectively recognize the signs of suicide risk and other psychological needs among the prison population.

Given the deprivations associated with the prison environment, woman in prison develop internal support structures for emotional support. How do inmates develop these social support networks behind bars? For some women, their connections were based on prior experiences, such as being in county jail together or being from the same neighborhood. For others, the dormitory-style housing environments provided an opportunity for women to develop relationships. As one incarcerated woman notes, "Well, you have people that you live with every day, and you start getting attached to them. You start being real good friends with them" (Severance, 2005, p. 352). However, building trust with other inmates can be a challenging process. Several of the women indicated frustration about the lack of privacy and the high levels of gossip that exist in the facility. For example, according to one inmate, "It's important to have somebody you can talk to and not spread your business around to everybody. Not having privacy since I've been here and having to work for it has made it more important to me" (Severance, 2005, p. 354).

Research by Severance (2005) illustrates that inmate relationships fall into four different categories: acquaintances, friends, family, and girlfriends. *Acquaintances* are people with whom the relationship is temporary, superficial, and involves low levels of trust. *Friends* are a less common type of relationship, but these are more meaningful, as they involve an increased level of trust between the women. In addition, these relationships have the potential to continue beyond the prison experience. Research by Kruttschnitt, Gartner, and Miller (2000) echoes the importance of these relationships, as "the friendships inmates established with each other were a critical component of the way they did their time" (p. 703). *Family* relationships, or **pseudo-families**, can provide supportive networks to help with the pains of imprisonment. However, these family relationships aren't always seen as a positive asset due to the limited respect that can occur between members of the family unit. Finally, *girlfriends* are a romantic relationship that develops between inmates. What makes romantic relation-

▲ **Photo 12.1** A woman spends time with a family member during a no-contact visit. A no-contact visit means that the inmate cannot touch or hug her family and friends when they come to visit. For many women, the lack of physical contact with their loved ones can contribute to the stress and loneliness of incarceration.

ships behind the prison walls unique is that the majority of women identify as heterosexual, not homosexual. Contrary to popular belief, very few of these relationships involve intimate contact and instead focus on emotional support and companionship.

 ## Physical and Mental Health Needs of Incarcerated Women

Women in custody face a variety of physical and mental health issues. In many cases, the criminal justice system is ill equipped to deal with these issues. Given the high rates of abuse and victimization these women experience throughout their lives, it is not surprising that the incarcerated female population has a high demand for mental health services. Women in prison have significantly higher rates of mental illness compared to women in the general population. Official data indicate that 13% of women in federal facilities and 24% of women in state prisons have been diagnosed with a mental disorder (General Accounting Office, 1999). Meanwhile, other data suggest that 68% of incarcerated women possess the factors of post-traumatic stress disorder (PTSD; Zlotnick, 1997).

The pains of imprisonment, including the separation from family and adapting to the prison environment, can exacerbate mental health conditions. Alas, the response by many facilities is to provide prescription psychotropic medications in excess. In addition, many facilities fail to provide therapeutic resources as part of their treatment to address the mental health needs of inmates. Research by Kitty (2012) found that 21 of the 22 participants in her study were given the prescription Seroquel,[1] even though only one of the women was officially diagnosed with bipolar disorder. In addition, the majority of the participants indicated that they failed to receive any sort of follow-up or reassessment by treatment staff as recommended by the manufacturer. Even though many of the incarcerated women in this study could obtain easily certain prescription drugs, other drugs appeared to be unavailable for the women, despite positive results in the community. One woman noted that

> prison doctors just do whatever they want; the opposite of what you were getting before you went in so that they can show you who's boss. It's just a way for them to show you how much control they have. (Kitty, 2012, p. 171)

Failure to comply with a prescribed medication protocol can be grounds not only for the denial of privileges and other disciplinary actions while in prison but can also be used against an offender during a parole hearing.

Unfortunately, prescription medications appear to be the primary form of psychiatric treatment behind bars, and offenders have limited access to therapeutic interventions. When therapeutic interventions are available, scholars recommend that programs need to emphasize the importance of trust and support in order to build a positive therapeutic relationship. Without this context, such interventions are largely ineffective. In the words of one inmate: "Prison doctors. Psychologists. They all work for the system. They aren't there for me and my best interests. . . . I'm just being told to do something or think some way that the prison wants you to" (Kitty, 2012, p. 174).

As you learned earlier in this chapter, issues such as prison overcrowding can contribute to increased risks for suicidal ideation. Factors such as psychological distress, unemployment, and length of sentence can also increase suicidal ideation. In response to these risks, prisons need to provide adequate resources not only to screen for potential self-harming behaviors but also to develop therapeutic resources to address these issues within the incarcerated female population (Clements-Nolle, Wolden, & Bargmann-Losche, 2009).

Women also face a variety of physical health needs. Women in prison are more likely to be HIV positive compared to women in the community, presenting a unique challenge for the prison health care system. While women in the general United States population have an HIV infection rate of 0.3%, the rate of infection for women in state and federal facilities is 3.6%, a tenfold increase. In New York state, this statistic rises to an alarming 18%, a rate 60 times that of the national infection rate. These rates are significantly higher than the rates of HIV-positive incarcerated men. Why is HIV an issue for women in prison? When we consider the lives of women prior to their incarceration, we find that these pathways are filled with experiences of abuse, which in turn place women at risk for unsafe sexual behaviors and drug use, factors that increase the potential for infection.

For example, women who are HIV positive are more likely to have a history of sexual abuse compared to women who are HIV negative (WPA, 2003). While the rates of HIV-positive women have declined since an all-time high in 1999, the rate of hepatitis C infections has increased dramatically within the incarcerated female population. Estimates indicate that between 20% and 50% of women in jails and prisons are affected by this disease. Hepatitis C is a disease that is transmitted via bodily fluids such as blood and can lead to liver damage if not diagnosed or treated. Offending women are at a high risk to contract hepatitis C, given their involvement in sex crimes and drug crimes. Few prison facilities routinely test for hepatitis C, and treatment can be expensive due to the high cost of prescriptions (Van Wormer & Bartollas, 2010).

Given the high rates of substance abuse for incarcerated women (and the differences in their motivations to use), drug treatment programming is a high need for women's prison facilities. Traditionally, drug treatment programs in prison have been based on therapeutic community (TC) models, which focus on living a drug-free lifestyle. One of the criticisms about TC models of drug treatment is that they were designed for male populations and may not address the unique needs of female drug users. Research by Messina, Grella, Cartier, and Torres (2010) compared the outcomes for women in a TC drug program with a gender-specific drug treatment program at Valley State Prison, a women's prison facility in California. Their results indicate that women in the gender-specific drug treatment program were more successful on parole, stayed away from drugs longer, and remained in an aftercare treatment program following their release for a greater period of time compared to those who participated in a TC treatment program. These findings indicate the importance in offering programs designed with the unique needs of women in mind. In addition, women who participate in prison-based treatment programs have higher rates of success in community-based treatment and have lower rates of recidivism over the long term (Grella & Rodriguez, 2011).

While female inmates have a higher need for treatment compared to male inmates (both in terms of prevalence as well as severity of conditions), the prison system is limited in its resources and abilities to address these issues. For example, most facilities are inadequately staffed or lack the diagnostic tools needed to address women's gynecological issues. Women also have higher rates of chronic illnesses than the male population (Anderson, 2006). However, the demands for these services significantly outweigh their availability. While states such as New York indicate that more than 25% of women receive mental health treatment while they are incarcerated, the lack of accessible services ranks high on the list of inmate complaints regarding quality-of-life issues in prison (WPA, 2003).

While the decision in *Todaro v. Ward* (1977) mandated reforms to health care in prisons, women continue to receive fewer resources compared to the male incarcerated population (Anderson, 2006). Elaine Lord, the former superintendent of Bedford Hills Correctional Facility (a maximum-security prison for women in New York State) told of the challenges that face a facility wherein a large percentage of the women suffer from mental health issues. She highlighted how facilities struggled to provide adequate resources to address these issues, and she stated that in these instances, challenges to the court are not necessarily a bad thing, as they can force states to provide additional funds to expand the options and availability for management and treatment of these issues (Lord, 2008).

▧ Children of Incarcerated Mothers: The Unintended Victims

Another key issue for women in prison involves the effects of incarceration on children. Children of **incarcerated mothers** (and fathers) deal with a variety of issues that stem from the loss of a parent, including grief, loss, sadness, detachment, and aggressive or at-risk behaviors for delinquency.

▲ **Photo 12.2**   The rise of female incarceration has had significant impacts on the lives of children who are left to grow up without their mothers. Here, children visit with their mothers at Rikers Island Prison in New York.

Additionally, these children are at high risk for ending up in prison themselves as adults. The location of many prisons makes it difficult for many children to retain physical ties with their mother throughout her incarceration. While more than two-thirds of incarcerated mothers have children under the age of 18, only 9% of these women will ever get to be visited by their children while they are incarcerated (Van Wormer & Bartollas, 2010).

For the 5%–10% of women who enter prison while pregnant, the majority will return to prison without their children within a few days after giving birth. This experience can have significant implications for the mental health of the mother. Pregnant women in custody also have concerns about how their incarceration might impact the well-being of their child. One primary concern centers on the quality of prenatal care for women within the prison. These women are worried about the potential health concerns of their unborn child as they consider both the quality of their health prior to being incarcerated (presence of sexually transmitted diseases and substance abuse) as well as the stressors they experience within the prison. Much of this stress is related to questions regarding who will care for their baby following its birth as well as concerns about losing the physical and emotional connection with their child as a result of their separation (Wismont, 2000).

The delivery experience for pregnant incarcerated women can be a traumatizing experience. As of 2011, 36 states had policies that permitted women to be shackled both during the transportation to the hospital as well as throughout the labor and delivery of their child. The argument by these states was that prisoners needed to be restrained due to safety and security concerns. Several professional organizations, including the American Congress of Obstetricians and Gynecologists and the American Medical Association have issued criticisms of this practice, citing concerns about the health risks to both the mother and her baby (Berg, 2011). For example, shackles can make it difficult for medical personnel to assist a woman during normal childbirth practices and can significantly complicate the delivery during emergencies. This has potentially disastrous effects for women and children, as one source notes, "if the fetal heartbeat slows, and an immediate Caesarian-section is required, the time lost to fumbling with shackle locks could cause brain damage and even death" (WPA, n.d.).

Recent years have seen a number of states enact legislation that forbids the practice of shackling inmates during delivery. For example, Florida recently abolished the use of shackling of any pregnant woman during labor and delivery, the first such law in a southern state. In addition, the bill sets forth policy on the treatment of all pregnant inmates who are in custody (Lopez, 2012). However, the practices in some jurisdictions have been slow to respond to policy changes. Despite their outlawing of the practice in 1999, inmates at the Cook County Jail in Chicago, Illinois, continued to be shackled during labor until 2010. In May 2012, a federal judge awarded $4.1 million dollars in damages as part of a class-action suit to inmates who had been shackled during labor (Mastony, 2012).

In an effort to improve both the emotional well-being of the mother and encourage mother-child attachment and bonding, nine states (New York, California, Illinois, Indiana, Ohio, Nebraska, South

Dakota, Washington, and West Virginia) have integrated prison nurseries into their facilities, which allows women to remain with their infant children for at least part of their sentence (WPA, 2009b). The oldest prison nursery program is located at Bedford Hills Correctional Facility in New York. Founded in 1901, this program is the largest in the country and allows for 29 mothers to reside with their infant children. Women who participate in the prison nursery program take classes on infant development and participate in support groups with other mothers. While most programs limit the time that a child can reside with his or her mother (generally 12–18 months), the Washington Correctional Center for Women is unique in that their prison nursery program allows for children born to incarcerated women to remain with their mothers for up to 3 years (WPA, 2009b). Other states allow for overnight visits with children, either in special family units on the prison grounds or in specialized cells within the facility. At Bedford Hills, older children can participate in programs at the facility with their mothers (Van Wormer & Bartollas, 2010). These programs help families repair and maintain ties between a mother and her child(ren) throughout her incarceration.

While some have suggested that prison is not an appropriate place for children, studies show that children who are removed from their mother's care as a result of incarceration are more likely to have

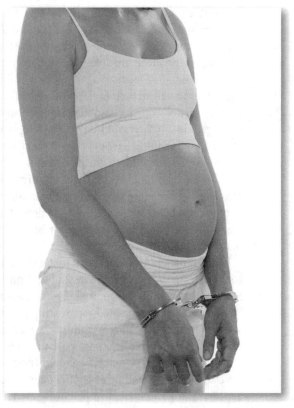

▲ **Photo 12.3**   While many states have outlawed the practice of shackling women during childbirth, the use of restraints on pregnant women continues to present a number of health risks for both the mother and the child.

educational challenges and limited emotional attachments as well as an increased risk for delinquency and criminality. Not only do these program help end the cycle of incarceration for both the mother and child, but they also assist in the reduction of recidivism once a woman is released from custody (WPA, 2009b).

While the concept of the prison nursery and programming for children of incarcerated mothers helps promote the bond between parent and child, what about those states where these types of programs are not available? What happens to these children? The majority of women in the criminal justice system are the primary custodial parents for their young children, and these women must face the issue of who will care for their children while they are incarcerated. Some may have husbands and fathers to turn to for assistance, though many will seek out extended family members, including grandparents, who will be charged with the task of raising their children. Seventy-nine percent of children who have an incarcerated parent are raised by an extended family member (WPA, 2003). In cases where an extended family member is unable or unavailable to care for a woman's minor child(ren), social services will place them in foster care. When a woman faces a long term of incarceration, the Adoption and Safe Families Act of 1997 terminates the parental rights in cases where children have been in foster care for

15 months (out of the previous 22 months). Given the increases in strict sentencing practices, the effects of this law mean that the majority of incarcerated women will lose their children if a family member is unable to care for them while the mother serves her sentence (Belknap, 2007).

For women who are able to have family members care for their children while incarcerated, how do they maintain a relationship with their children? The geographical location of most prisons (in many cases, far away from their families) and the financial challenges of traveling to these facilities mean that the majority of women do not have regular physical visitations with their children, while 35% of women correspond with their children via the telephone and 49% communicate via letters (Stringer & Barnes, 2012). Some facilities have developed specialized programs to help facilitate additional contact between parents and their children. Such contact not only helps mothers but can also provide an important support for the emotional health of the children (Snyder, 2009). These physical and emotional connections also allow incarcerated mothers to maintain an authoritative parental role. The development of this parent-child bond allows women to believe that they will be able to successfully return to their primary parenting role upon their release (Stringer & Barnes, 2012). In these cases, extended family members play a crucial role in maintaining the connection between incarcerated women and their children.

Given the number of women that will be reunited with their children following their incarceration, some prisons have implemented programming to help inmates develop effective parenting skills. Strengthening these parental skills can also serve as a method to prevent recidivism. Research by Sandifer (2008) investigated a parenting program that included an educational component as well as visitations with the inmates' children, which allowed inmates to put these new skills to use. The findings of this study indicate that participation in a parenting program increased mothers' knowledge about childhood development, altered their attitudes about physical discipline, and allowed them to develop an understanding about the needs and well-being of their children. Based on these findings, it appears that participating in parenting courses behind bars is an effective tool both for mothers and their children.

Case Study

Girl Scouts Beyond Bars Program

The first Girls Scouts Beyond Bars (GSBB) program was implemented at the Maryland Correctional Institution for Women in November 1992 as part of a National Institute of Justice project. By 2008, there were over 37 programs nationwide (Girl Scouts of America [GSA], 2008). The project began as a way to help meet the needs of girls whose mothers are incarcerated. Mothers meet with their daughters twice a month on prison grounds to work on troop projects, which focus on educational endeavors such as math and science as well as creative activities that highlight topics such as self-esteem, relationships, and teen development/pregnancy prevention. By allowing children to visit with their mothers on a regular basis, these women can have an active role in childrearing and strengthen the mother-child bond despite their incarceration (Moses, 1995). In addition, the caregivers of these children indicated that the youths' behavior at home and educational involvement improved as a result of their participation in the program (Block & Potthast, 1998). In a study of 16 different GSBB programs involving girls age 9–17 across the United States, researchers noted several positive benefits.

For example, 85% of the girls indicated that they had a closer bond with their mother as a result of the program. Additionally, a majority of the girls indicated that they learned a variety of prosocial behaviors, such as respect and leadership, and developed a positive attitude about their personal futures (GSA, 2008). While the GSBB programs offer significant benefits to both the incarcerated woman and her children, such programs require significant emotional and physical investment by its supporters. Like traditional Girl Scouts (GS) programs, GSBB programs are run primarily by volunteers. Whereas traditional GS programs are run by parents of the participants (troop leaders), GSBB programs require an investment by community members and caregivers to help facilitate these programs (Block, 1999). While many of the sites receive funding by the Office of Juvenile Justice and Delinquency Prevention, others seek out private donations and private grants to help subsidize the costs. Despite these challenges, the evaluations of the Girl Scouts Beyond Bars programs demonstrate positive effects for both the mother and her daughter, effects that have potential long-term implications on breaking the cycle of intergenerational recidivism.

Gender-Responsive Programming for Women in Prison

The needs of women have been significantly neglected by the prison system throughout history. In an effort to remedy the disparities in treatment, several court cases began to challenge the practices in women's prisons. The case of ***Barefield v. Leach* (1974)** was particularly important for women, as it set the standard through which the courts could measure whether women received a lower standard of treatment compared to men. Since *Barefield*, the courts have ruled that a number of policies that were biased against women were unconstitutional. For example, the case of ***Glover v. Johnson* (1979)** held that the state must provide the same opportunities for education, rehabilitation, and vocational training for female offender as provided for male offenders. ***Todaro v. Ward*** (1977) declared that the failure to provide access to health care for incarcerated women was a violation of the Eighth Amendment protection against cruel and unusual punishment. Cases such ***Cooper v. Morin* (1980)** held that the equal protection clause prevents prison administrators from justifying the disparate treatment of women on the grounds that providing such services for women is inconvenient. Ultimately, the courts held that "males and females must be treated equally unless there is a substantial reason which requires a distinction be made" (***Canterino v. Wilson,* 1982**).

While these cases began to establish a conversation on the accessibility of programming for women, these early discussions focused on the issue of **parity** between male and female prisoners. At the time, women comprised only about 5% of the total number of incarcerated offenders. During the 1970s, prison advocates worked toward providing women with the same opportunities for programming and treatment as men. Their efforts were relatively successful in that many gender-based policies were abolished, and new policies were put into place mandating that men and women be treated similarly (Zaitzow & Thomas, 2003). However, feminist criminologists soon discovered that parity and equality for female offenders does not necessarily mean that women benefit from the same treatment as men (Bloom, Owen, & Covington, 2003, 2004). Indeed, research has documented that programs designed for men fail the needs of women (Belknap, 2007).

These findings led to the emergence of a new philosophy of parity for women—gender-responsive programming. Much of the push for gender-specific and gender-responsive programming stemmed from the Office of Juvenile Justice and Delinquency Prevention. As you learned earlier in this book, the emphasis on developing programming and policies that center on the unique risk factors and needs of girls came as a result of the dramatic increase in the number of girls that were coming to the attention of the juvenile court. In response to these issues, the 1992 reauthorization of the Juvenile Justice and Delinquency Prevention Act acknowledged the need for juvenile agencies to provide gender-specific services to address the unique needs of female offenders and to provide funding to states to assess the needs of girls and develop appropriate options. These efforts toward girls in the juvenile court have led to similar discussions for the adult female offending population. As a result, scholars and practitioners were left with the important question of what it means to be gender responsive in our prison environments. Research by Bloom et al. (2003, 2004) highlights how six key principles can change the way in which programs and institutions design and manage programs, develop policies, train staff, and supervise offenders. These six principles are (1) gender, (2) environment, (3) relationships, (4) services and supervision, (5) socioeconomic status, and (6) community. Together, these six principles provide guidance for the effective management of female offenders.

The first principle, gender, discusses the importance for criminal justice systems and agents to recognize the role that gender plays in the offending of women and the unique treatment needs of women. As you learned earlier in this book, the pathways of women to crime are dramatically different from the pathways of men. Even though they may be incarcerated for similar crimes, their lives related to these offenses are dramatically different. As a result, men and women respond to treatment in different ways and have different issues to face within the context of rehabilitation. To offer the same programs to men and women may not adequately address the unique needs for both populations. Given that the majority of programs have been developed about male criminality and are used for male offenders, these programs often fail to meet the unique needs of women.

The second principle, environment, focuses on the need for officials to create a place where staff and inmates engage in practices of mutual respect and dignity. Given that many women involved in the criminal justice system come from a background of violence and abuse, it is critical that women feel safe and supported in their journey toward rehabilitation and recovery. Historically, the criminal justice system has emphasized a model of power and control, a model that limits the ability for nurturing, trust, and compassion. Rehabilitative programs for women need to create a safe environment where women can share about the intimate details of their lives (Covington, 1999).

The third element, relationships, refers to developing an understanding of why women commit crimes; the context of their lives prior to, during, and following incarceration; and the relationships that women build while they are incarcerated. In addition, the majority of incarcerated women attempt to sustain their relationships with family members outside the prison walls, particularly with their minor children. Given that the majority of incarcerated women present a low safety risk to the community, women should be placed in settings that are minimally restrictive, offer opportunities for programs and services, and reside in locations within reasonable proximity to their families and minor children. The concept of relationships also involves how program providers interact with and relate to their clients. Group participants need to feel supported by their treatment providers, and the providers need to be able to empower women to make positive choices about their lives (Covington, 1999).

The fourth principle identifies the need for gender-responsive programming to address the traumas that women have experienced throughout the context of their lives. As indicated throughout this text, the cycle to offending for women often begins with the experience of victimization. In addition, these victim experiences continue throughout their lives and often inform their criminal actions. Historically, treatment providers for substance abuse issues, trauma, and mental health issues have dealt with offenders on an individualized basis. Gender-responsive approaches highlight the need for program providers and institutions to address these issues as co-occurring disorders. Here, providers need to be cross-trained in these three issues in order to develop and implement effective programming options for women. In addition, community correctional settings need to acknowledge how these issues translate into challenges and barriers to success in the reentry process. This awareness can help support women in their return to the community.

The fifth principle focuses on the socioeconomic status of the majority of women in prison. Most women in prison turn to criminal activity as a survival mechanism. Earlier in this chapter, you learned that women in the system lack adequate educational and vocational resources to develop a sustainable life for themselves and their families and struggle with poverty, homelessness, and limited public assistance resources, particularly for drug-convicted offenders. In order to enhance the possibilities for success following their incarceration, women need to have access to opportunities to break the cycle of abuse and create positive options for their future. Without these skills and opportunities, many women will fall back into the criminal lifestyle out of economic necessity. Given that many women will reunite with their children following their release, these opportunities will help women make a better life not only for themselves but for their children as well.

The sixth principle, community, focuses on the need to develop collaborative relationships among providers in order to assist women in their transition toward independent living. Bloom et al. (2003) call for the need to develop wraparound services for women. Wraparound services refer to "a holistic and culturally sensitive plan for each woman that draws on a coordinated range of services within her community" (p. 82). Examples of these services include public and mental health systems, addiction recovery, welfare, emergency shelter organizations, and educational and vocational services. Certainly, wraparound services require a high degree of coordination between agencies and program providers. Given the multiple challenges that women face throughout their reentry process, the development of comprehensive services will help support women toward a successful transition. In addition, by having one case manager to address multiple issues, agencies can be more effective in meeting the needs of women and supervising them in the community while reducing the levels of bureaucracy and red tape in the delivery of resources.

Table 12.3 illustrates how the principles of gender, environment, relationships, services and supervision, socioeconomic status, and community can be utilized when developing gender-responsive policies and programming. These questions can assist institutional administrators and program providers in developing policies and procedures that represent the realities of women's lives and reflect ways in which rehabilitation efforts can be most effective for women. Within each of these topical considerations, correctional agencies should be reminded that the majority of female offenders are nonviolent in nature, are more likely to be at risk for personal injury versus injuring others, and are in need of services.

| Table 12.3 | Questions to Ask in Developing a Systemic Approach for Women Offenders |

Operational Practices

- Are the specifics of women's behavior and circumstances addressed in written planning, policy, programs, and operational practices? For example, are policies regarding classification, property, programs, and services appropriate to the actual behavior and composition of the female population?
- Does the staff reflect the offender population in terms of gender, race/ethnicity, sexual orientation, language (bilingual), ex-offender, and recovery status? Are female role models and mentors employed to reflect the racial/ethnic and cultural backgrounds of the clients?
- Does staff training prepare workers for the importance of relationships in the lives of women offenders? Does the training provide information on the nature of women's relational context, boundaries and setting limits, communication, and child-related issues? Are staff prepared to relate to women offenders in an empathetic and professional manner?
- Are staff training in appropriate gender-communication skills and in recognizing and dealing with the effects of trauma and post-traumatic stress disorder?

Services

- Is training on women offenders provided? Is this training available in initial academy or orientation sessions? Is the training provided on an ongoing basis? Is this training mandatory for executive-level staff?
- Does the organization see women's issues as a priority? Are women's issues important enough to warrant an agency-level position to manage women's services?
- Do resource allocation, staffing, training, and budgeting consider the facts of managing women offenders?

Review of Standard Procedures

- Do classification and other assessments consider gender in classification instruments, assessment tools, and individualized treatment plans? Has the existing classification system been validated on a sample of women? Does the database system allow for separate analysis of female characteristics?
- Is information about women offenders collected, coded, monitored, and analyzed in the agency?
- Are protocols established for reporting and investigating claims of staff misconduct, with protection from retaliation ensured? Are the concepts of privacy and personal safety incorporated in daily operations and architectural design, where applicable?
- How does policy address the issue of cross-gender strip searches and pat-downs?
- Does the policy include the concept of zero tolerance for inappropriate language, touching, and other inappropriate behavior and staff sexual misconduct?

Children and Families

- How do existing programs support connections between the female offender and her children and family? How are these connections undermined by current practice? In institutional environments, what provisions are made for visiting and for other opportunities for contact with children and family?
- Are there programs and services that enhance female offenders' parenting skills and their ability to support their children following release? In community supervision settings and community treatment programs, are parenting responsibilities acknowledged through education? Through child care?

SOURCE: Bloom, Owen & Covington (2004).

Community

- Are criminal justice services delivered in a manner that builds community trust, confidence, and partnerships?
- Do classification systems and housing configurations allow community custody placements? Are transitional programs in place that help women build long-term community support networks?
- Are professionals, providers, and community volunteer positions used to facilitate community connections? Are they used to develop partnerships between correctional agencies and community providers?

The Supervision of Women in the Community

In 2010, 4,055,514 adults were supervised in the community through probation services. According to the Bureau of Justice Statistics, 712,084 (24%) of these adults were women (Glaze & Bonczar, 2011).[2] *Probation* refers to a criminal sanction that allows offenders to remain in the community so long as they follow specific directives by the court. These can include rules about curfew, maintaining a job, attending drug and alcohol treatment or other therapeutic programs, and completing community service hours. Failure to comply with these regulations can result in an offender having their sentence revoked by the court and being resentenced to a term of incarceration in either prison or jail.

Like prisons, community-based services have struggled in providing gender-responsive services for women in the community, an issue that is linked with the recidivism rates for women. An example of an effective gender-responsive program for female probationers is the Moving On program, a curriculum designed to help women focus on building resiliency in their personal lives and generating support and resources in the community. Each session of the 26-unit program focuses on increasing the self-awareness of women's challenges and triggers that might lead to reoffending. The curriculum provides women with options to address these challenges and remain focused on their recovery and reintegration. A comparison between women involved in the Moving On program with women involved in traditional probationary supervision indicated that the women involved with the Moving On program had lower rates of recidivism in terms of new offenses but were more likely to receive a technical violation of probation compared to women under traditional probationary supervision. However, additional analyses revealed that these technical violations occurred in cases where the women failed to complete the program. These findings indicate that the completion of gender-responsive curriculum as part of a probationary sentence is an effective tool in reducing the recidivism rates of women (Gehring, Van Voorhis, & Bell, 2010).

A sentence of probation is all about reducing the levels of risk in the community—can an offender remain in the community without compromising the safety of the public? In their quest to assess the needs and risks for women on probation, many departments utilize actuarial assessment instruments designed to provide probation departments with estimates of risk to the public while identifying the needs of the offender. While these assessments are presented as gender neutral, scholars have suggested that they may not adequately reflect the needs of women (Davidson, 2011). As a result, many of these assessments have either failed to identify the needs of women or have misidentified these needs as risks to the community, which can lead to an increase in punitive supervision tactics.

Perhaps the most common assessment tool used for correctional populations is the **Level of Service Inventory-Revised (LSI-R)**. While the LSI-R has been validated as an effective tool in assessing risk, the majority of validation studies involved male offenders. Research on whether the LSI-R is an appropriate tool for female offenders is still ongoing, and findings have been somewhat mixed on whether this tool accurately portrays the gender-specific issues of female offenders. Another concern is whether these measures lead to overclassification, which can lead to experiences where additional security requirements are put into place that are not necessarily warranted by the needs of the women. Research by Davidson (2011) highlights that while the LSI-R may be an effective tool in identifying risks for recidivism, the measures don't necessarily highlight the context of these risks, an important dimension for rehabilitative purposes. In addition, the LSI-R fails to adequately capture some of the most significant needs of women, such as their abuse histories, health issues, and motherhood. Instead, these issues are hidden within the context of other risk factors, limiting the ability for programs to effectively address these needs.

To improve on the limited abilities of the LSI-R and other assessment tools, the National Institute of Corrections has partnered together with the University of Cincinnati to develop new assessment measures that will reflect gender-responsive perspectives. This project has yielded two new instruments. The first instrument is shorter in length and is designed to supplement existing assessments that are not gender specific, while the second instrument is designed to replace existing measures and should be used as a stand-alone tool in evaluating risk and identifying needs for female offenders. By embodying gender-responsive principles, these new assessment tools allow for probation and other correctional departments to indicate that many women on probation are low risk yet illustrate a high number of needs that can impact their ability to be successful on probation. In addition, these tools help highlight how the needs of women are not one dimensional and require agencies to respond to these interrelated issues (Salisbury, Van Voorhis, Wright, & Bauman, 2009). While these new instruments can be utilized in a variety of different correctional settings, they have specific uses within community supervision agencies. For example, probation departments can alter their supervision strategies for female-only caseloads and smaller caseloads and develop partnerships with other community agencies in an effort to devise wraparound services that will help increase the success levels of women on probation (Van Voorhis, Salisbury, Wright, & Bauman, 2008).

▲ **Photo 12.4** As the only all-female chain gang in the United States, women housed at the Estrella Jail in Phoenix, Arizona are transported to neighborhoods in the community to perform their community service hours as part of their jail sentences.

Another option for community-based services includes **alternative to incarceration programs (ATI)**. The philosophy behind ATI programs is to divert offenders from incarceration sentences, such as prison or jail, and provide supervision in the community. Many of these programs focus on the philosophies of rehabilitation and restorative justice and aim to improve the lives of participants in an effort to reduce recidivism rates. Research on ATI programs in New York indicates that substance abuse is a primary issue for women in the criminal justice system. As you learned in Chapter 9, not only are women addicted to different substances, but their motivations for using these substances vary significantly from those of male addicts. In addition, ATI participants referenced a number of barriers in accessing services. For women, the most prevalent of these barriers included the difficulties of meeting with service providers given the other demands on their time, such as school or work schedules, as well as the inability to access the providers via available public transportation or the costs of such transport. It is crucial for programs to consider these challenges when providing services for women. Failure to do so can jeopardize the successes of women involved in the criminal justice system (Wu et al., 2012).

Reentry Issues for Incarcerated Women

Like probation, parole also involves a period of supervision of offenders in the community. Unlike a probation sentence, which is typically used in lieu of an incarceration sentence, *parole* is a correctional strategy that is applied following an offender's release from prison. In 2010, 103,374 women were supervised on parole nationwide (Glaze & Bonczar, 2011). These numbers represent only 12% of all parolees and increase the challenges to provide gender-responsive programming due to the smaller number of women on parole compared to men. However, the needs of these women returning to their communities are great. Historically, the majority of research on parole and reentry issues has focused on whether offenders will reoffend and return to prison (*recidivism*). Recent scholars have shifted the focus on reentry to discussions on how to successfully transition offenders back into their communities. This process can be quite traumatic, and for women, a number of issues emerge in creating a successful reentry experience.

Consider the basic needs of a woman who has just left prison. She needs housing, clothing, and food. She may be eager to reestablish relationships with friends, family members, and her children. In addition, she has obligations as part of her release—appointments with her parole officer and treatment requirements. While once designed to provide services to support offenders in their exit from prison, today's parole systems serve to monitor offenders in to community, ready to catch an offender when they violate the conditions of their release. Due to high caseloads, parole officers have limited opportunities to provide individualized care to their clients. One woman shares the struggles in meeting these demands, expressing fear of the unknown in her new life and of her ability to be successful in her reentry process:

> I start my day running to drop my urine [drug testing]. Then I go see my children, show up for my training program, look for a job, go to a meeting [Alcoholics Anonymous], and show up at my part-time job. I have to take the bus everywhere, sometimes eight buses for 4 hours a day. I don't have the proper outer clothes, I don't have the money to buy lunch along the way, and everyone who works with me keeps me waiting so that I am late to my next appointment. If I fail any one of these things and my PO [probation officer] finds out, [probation is revoked]. I am so tired that I sometimes fall asleep on my way home from work at 2:00 A.M. and that's dangerous given where I live. And then the next day I have to start over again. I don't mind being busy and working hard. . . . That's part of my recovery. But this is a situation that is setting me up to fail. I just can't keep up and I don't know where to start. (Ritchie, 2001, p. 381)

Upon release, the majority of women find themselves returning to the same communities in which they lived prior to their incarceration, where they face the same problems of poverty, addiction, and dysfunction. For those few women who were able to receive some therapeutic treatment in prison, most acknowledge that these prison-based intervention programs provided few, if any, legitimate coping skills to deal with the realities of the life stressors that awaited them upon their release. In addition, they face an additional challenge—the label of an ex-offender, which can lead to experiences of discrimination and labeling and have greater consequences for women than men. This provides support for the evil woman hypothesis that was discussed in Chapter 11: Women can be judged for violating both the law as well as the socially prescribed gender roles. Research by LeBel (2012) highlights that while a woman's status as an ex-con presents the greatest source of discrimination, race/ethnicity, substance abuse, poverty, mental health, and sexual orientation all serve to complicate her return to society. Several of these barriers also have a negative effect on her self-esteem, which can further impact her ability to be successful.

In addition to the challenges of returning home from prison, many women continue to battle the demons that led them to criminal activity in the first place. Unfortunately, the limited treatment options behind bars mean that these issues continue to threaten the freedom of women once they are released and ultimately can impact recidivism rates. Research by Huebner, DeJong, and Cobbina (2010) indicates that drug addiction remains a significant issue for women and is a primary factor for women who reoffend following release, particularly for women of color. Drug addiction has a multiplying effect in the lives of women—not only can addiction threaten a woman's status on parole, but it impacts her ability to maintain stable employment, secure housing, and reunite with her children. Even when the need for drug treatment is documented, the majority of women fail to receive treatment, further jeopardizing their future success (Schram, Koons-Witt, Williams, & McShane, 2006).

Without continuing community-based resources, many women will return to the addictions and lifestyles in which they engaged prior to their incarceration. In addition, women have limited access to health care on the outside, often due to a lack of community resources, an inability to pay, or lack of knowledge about where to go to obtain assistance. Given the status of mental and physical health needs of incarcerated women, the management (or lack thereof) of chronic health problems can impede a woman's successful reentry process (Ritchie, 2001). Like the mental health care system in prisons, the mental health treatment options in the community continue to overemphasize the use of prescription psychotropic medications with a limited availability of therapeutic interventions (Kitty, 2012). In addition, women with children acknowledge that not only will they need therapeutic support to ensure an effective transition, but their children could benefit from counseling services as well (Snyder, 2009).

While women may turn to public assistance to help support their reentry transition, many come to find that these resources are either unavailable or are significantly limited. For example, the Welfare Reform Bill, signed by President Bill Clinton in 1996, has not only imposed time limits on the aid that women can receive but has significantly affected the road to success by denying services and resources for women with a criminal record, particularly in cases of women convicted of a felony drug-related charge (Hirsch, 2001). Section 115 of the **Welfare Reform Act** calls for a lifetime ban on benefits such as Temporary Assistance for Needy Families (TANF) and food stamps to offenders convicted in the state or federal courts for a felony drug offense. In addition, women convicted of a drug offense are barred from living in public housing developments, and in some areas, a criminal record can limit the availability of Section 8 housing options[3] (Jacobs, 2000). Drug charges are the only offense type subjected to this ban—even convicted murderers can apply for and receive government benefits following their release (Sentencing Project, 2006). In her research on drug-convicted women and their struggles with reentry, Hirsch (2001) found that the majority of women with drug convictions were incarcerated on charges involving low levels of substances designed for personal use, not distribution. Most of these women struggled with use and addiction since adolescence and early adulthood, often in response to significant experiences with abuse and victimization, but rarely had access to treatment to address their issues. They had relatively limited educational and vocational training and faced a variety of issues such as homelessness, mental health issues, and poverty. While many of them had children whom they cared for deeply, these relationships were often strained as a result of their issues with addiction and subsequent incarceration, making their family reunification efforts a challenge. Indeed, the limits of this ban jeopardize the very efforts toward sustainable and safe housing, education, and drug treatment that are needed in order for women to successfully transition from prison. Table 12.4 presents state-level data on the implementation of the ban on welfare benefits for felony drug convictions.

How many women are affected by the lifetime bans on assistance under Section 115? Research by the Sentencing Project indicates that as of 2006, more than 92,000 women were affected by the lifetime welfare ban. They also estimated that the denial of benefits placed more than 135,000 children of these mothers at risk for future contact with the criminal justice system due to economic struggles. The ban also disproportionately affects women of color, with approximately 35,000 Black women and 10,000 Hispanic women dealing with a loss of benefits. Since its enactment in 1996, 39 states have rescinded the lifetime ban on resources, either in its entirety or in part. However, 11 states have retained this ban on assistance, placing family reunification efforts between women and their children in jeopardy (Sentencing Project, 2006).

Even women without a drug conviction still face significant issues in obtaining public assistance. Federal welfare law prohibits states from providing assistance under programs such as TANF, SSI (Supplementary Security Income), housing assistance, or food stamps in cases where a woman has violated a condition of her probation or parole. In many cases, this can be as simple as failing to report for a meeting with a probation officer when she has a sick child. In addition, TANF carries a five-year lifetime limit for assistance. This lifetime limit applies to all women, not just those under the criminal justice system. In addition, the delay for receiving these services ranges from 45 days to several months, a delay that significantly affects the ability of women to put a roof over their children's heads, clothes on their bodies, and food in their bellies (Jacobs, 2000). Ultimately, these reforms are a reflection of budgetary decisions that often result in the slashing of social service and government aid programs, while the budgets for criminal justice agendas such as incarceration remain supported by state and government officials. These limits not only affect the women who are in the greatest need of services but their children as well, who will suffer physically, mentally, and emotionally throughout these economic struggles (Danner, 2012).

Despite the social stigma that comes with receiving welfare benefits, women in one study indicated that the receipt of welfare benefits represented progress toward a successful recovery and independence from reliance on friends, family, or a significant other for assistance. A failure to receive benefits could send these women into a downward spiral toward homelessness, abusive relationships, and relapse. As one woman reported to Hirsch (2001),

> We still need welfare until we are strong enough to get on our feet. [We're] trying to stay clean, trying to be responsible parents and take care of our families. We need welfare right now. If we lose it, we might be back out there selling drugs. We're trying to change our lives. Trying to stop doing wrong things. Some of us need help. Welfare helps us stay in touch with society. [We're] trying to do what's right for us. (p. 278)

Table 12.4   State Implementation of Lifetime Welfare Ban

State	Denies Benefits Entirely	Denies Benefits to Drug Manufacturers and Traffickers Only (Not Those Charged With Possession)	Benefits Dependent on Drug Treatment/ Drug Test Compliance	Benefits Dependent on Court Compliance	Restores Benefits After Time	Opted Out of Welfare Ban
Alabama	X					
Alaska	X					
Arizona				X		
Arkansas		X				
California			X			
Colorado				X		
Connecticut				X		
Delaware	X					
District of Columbia				X		
Florida		X				
Georgia	X					
Hawaii			X			
Idaho				X		
Illinois	X					
Indiana				X		
Iowa			X			
Kansas						X
Kentucky			X			
Louisiana					X (1 year)	
Maine						X
Maryland			X			
Massachusetts				X		
Michigan						X

State	Denies Benefits Entirely	Denies Benefits to Drug Manufacturers and Traffickers Only (Not Those Charged With Possession)	Benefits Dependent on Drug Treatment/ Drug Test Compliance	Benefits Dependent on Court Compliance	Restores Benefits After Time	Opted Out of Welfare Ban
Minnesota			X			
Mississippi	X					
Missouri	X					
Montana				X		
Nebraska	X					
Nevada			X			
New Hampshire						X
New Jersey						X
New Mexico						X
New York						X
North Carolina					X (6 months)	
North Dakota		X				
Ohio						X
Oklahoma						X
Oregon			X			
Pennsylvania						X
Rhode Island						X
South Carolina	X					
South Dakota	X					
Tennessee			X			
Texas	X					
Utah			X			
Vermont						X

(Continued)

Table 12.4 (Continued)						
State	Denies Benefits Entirely	Denies Benefits to Drug Manufacturers and Traffickers Only (Not Those Charged With Possession)	Benefits Dependent on Drug Treatment/ Drug Test Compliance	Benefits Dependent on Court Compliance	Restores Benefits After Time	Opted Out of Welfare Ban
Virginia			X			
Washington				X		
West Virginia	X					
Wisconsin			X			
Wyoming						X
U.S. total	12	3	12	9	2	13

SOURCE: Legal Action Center. (2011). *State TANF options drug felon ban*. Retrieved from http://www.lac.org/doc_library/lac/publications/HIRE_Network_State_TANF_Options_Drug_Felony_Ban.pdf

Throughout the reentry process, women also struggle with gaining access to services such as drug treatment and mental health treatment. Without these referrals by probation and parole officers, most women are denied access to treatment due to the limited availability of services or an inability to pay for such resources on their own. Here, women are actually at risk for recidivism, as their needs continue to be unmet. In addition, many of the therapeutic resources that are available to women fail to work within the context of their lives. For example, the majority of inpatient drug treatment programs do not provide the option for women to reside with and care for their children. These programs promote sobriety first and rarely create the opportunity for family reunification until women have successfully transitioned from treatment, have obtained a job, and can provide a sustainable environment for themselves. For many women, the desire to reunite with their children is their primary focus, and the inability for women to maintain connection with their children can threaten their path toward sobriety (Jacobs, 2000).

Clearly, women who make the transition from prison or jail back to their communities must achieve stability in their lives. With multiple demands on them (compliance with the terms and conditions of their release; dealing with long-term issues such as addiction, mental health, and physical health concerns; and the need for food, clothing, and shelter), this transition is anything but easy. Here, the influence of a positive mentor can provide significant support for women as they navigate this journey.

While it is true a woman in reentry has many tangible needs (housing, employment, family reunification, formal education), attention to intangible needs (empowerment, a sense of belonging, someone to talk to) can promote personal growth through positive reinforcement of progress, encouragement and support in the face of defeat and temptation, and a place to feel like a regular person. (WPA, 2008, p. 3)

Several key pieces of legislation have focused on the need for support and mentorship throughout the reentry process and have provided federal funding to support these networks. For example, the Ready4Work Initiative (2003), the Prisoner Reentry Initiative (2005), and the Second Chance Act (2007) all acknowledged the challenges that ex-offenders face when they exit the prison environment. These initiatives help support community organizations that provide comprehensive services for ex-offenders, including case management, mentoring, and other transitional services (WPA, 2008). Given the struggles that women face as part of their journey back from incarceration, it is clear that these initiatives can provide valuable resources to assist with the reentry process.

SUMMARY

- The first prison for women was opened in 1839 in response to the growing concerns of abuse of women in male prison facilities.
- The reformatory prison was designed to rehabilitate women from their immoral ways.
- The custodial institution offered very little in terms of rehabilitative programming for incarcerated women.
- Much of the early programming in women's prisons focused on gendered-normative values.
- Women of color are overrepresented in women's prisons.
- The rise of female incarceration has led to prison overcrowding, which has significant implications for women in custody.
- While in prison, women develop acquaintances, friendships, pseudo-families, and romantic relationships to provide emotional support.
- Women in custody face a variety of unique issues, many of which the prison is ill equipped to deal with.
- Many facilities rely on prescription medications rather than therapeutic treatment to manage the mental health needs of women in custody.
- Women who participate in drug treatment programs have lower recidivism rates compared to those who don't participate in drug treatment.
- Some facilities have prison nursery programs, which allow mothers to remain with their infant children while incarcerated.
- Programs such as Girl Scouts Beyond Bars help to provide the parent-child bond while mothers are incarcerated.
- Gender-responsive programming is designed to address the unique needs of female offenders.
- Probation allows women to receive correctional supervision while remaining in the community.
- Upon release, many women return to the communities in which they lived prior to their incarceration, where they face issues of addiction and dysfunction in their lives.

KEY TERMS

Alternative to incarceration programs (ATI)

Barefield v. Leach (1974)

Canterino v. Wilson (1982)

Cooper v. Morin (1980)

Custodial institutions

Fry, Elizabeth

Gender-responsive programming

Glover v. Johnson (1979)	Level of Service Inventory-Revised (LSI-R)	Pseudo-families
		Todaro v. Ward (1977)
Incarcerated mothers	Parity	Welfare Reform Act of 1996

DISCUSSION QUESTIONS

1. If you were to build a woman's prison that reflected gender-responsive principles, what key features would you integrate into your facility?

2. Discuss the profile for women who are incarcerated in our prison facilities. In what ways are incarcerated women different from incarcerated men?

3. What challenges do women face during their reentry process? How does the Welfare Reform Bill limit access to resources for some women following their incarceration?

4. How do traditional risk assessment instruments fail female offenders? What are the implications of these findings?

WEB RESOURCES

Hour Children http://www.hourchildren.org

Our Place DC http://www.ourplacedc.org

The Sentencing Project http://www.sentencingproject.org

Women's Prison Association http://www.wpaonline.org

REFERENCES

Anderson, T. L. (2006). Issues facing women prisoners in the early twenty-first century. In C. Renzetti, L. Goodstein, & S. L. Miller (Eds.), *Rethinking gender, crime and justice* (pp. 200–212). Los Angeles, CA: Roxbury.

Belknap, J. (2007). *The invisible woman: Gender, crime and justice* (3rd ed.). Belmont, CA: Thomson.

Berg, A. (2011, September 4). Stop shackling pregnant prisoners. *The Daily Beast*. Retrieved from http://www.thedailybeast.com/articles/2011/09/04/stop-shackling-pregnant-prisoners-new-push-to-ban-controversial-practice.html

Block, K. J. (1999). Bringing scouting to prison: Programs and challenges. *The Prison Journal, 79*(2), 269–283.

Block, K. J., & Potthast, M. J. (1998). Girl Scouts Beyond Bars: Facilitating parent-child contact in correctional settings. *Child Welfare, 77*(5), 561–579.

Bloom, B., Owen, B., & Covington, S. (2003). *Gender responsive strategies: Research, practice and guiding principles for women offenders*. Washington, DC: National Institute of Corrections, U.S. Department of Justice. Retrieved from http://nicic.gov/pubs/2003/018017.pdf

Bloom, B., Owen, B., & Covington, S. (2004). Gender-responsive strategies: Research, practice and guiding principles for women offenders. National Institute of Corrections. Retrieved at: http://www.nicic.org/Library/018017

Bloom, B., Owen, B., & Covington, S. (2004). Women offenders and the gendered effects of public policy. *Policy Research, 21*(1), 31–48.

Bush-Baskette, S. (1998). The War on Drugs as a war on Black women. In S. Miller (Ed.), *Crime control and women* (pp. 113–129). Thousand Oaks, CA: SAGE.

Clements-Nolle, K., Wolden, M., & Bargmann-Losche, J. (2009). Childhood trauma and risk for past and future suicide attempts among women in prison. *Women's Health Issues, 19*, 185–192.

Covington, S. (1999). *Helping women recover: A program for treating substance abuse.* San Francisco, CA: Jossey-Bass.

Danner, M. J. E. (2012). Three strikes and it's women who are out: The hidden consequences for women of criminal justice policy reforms. In R. Muraskin (Ed.), *It's a crime: Women and justice* (5th ed., pp. 344–353). Upper Saddle River, NJ: Prentice Hall.

Davidson, J. T. (2011). Managing risk in the community: How gender matters. In R. Sheehan, G. McIvor, & C. Trotter (Eds.) *Working with women offenders in the community* (pp. 216–240). New York, NY: Willan.

Freedman, E. B. (1984). *Their sisters' keepers: Women prison report in America, 1830–1930.* Ann Arbor, MI: University of Michigan Press.

Gartner, R., & Kruttschnitt, C. (2004). A brief history of doing time: The California Institution for Women in the 1960s and the 1990s. *Law and Society Review, 38*(2), 267–304.

Gehring, K., Van Voorhis, P., & Bell, V. (2010). "What works" for female probationers? An evaluation of the Moving On program. *Women, Girls and Criminal Justice, 11*(1), 6–10.

General Accounting Office. (1999). *Women in prison: Issues and challenges confronting U.S. correctional systems.* Washington, DC: U.S. Department of Justice.

Girl Scouts of America (GSA). (2008). *Third-year evaluation of Girl Scouts Beyond Bars final report.* Retrieved from http://www.girlscouts.org/research.pdf/gsbb_report.pdf

Glaze, L. E., & Bonczar, T. P. (2011). Probation and Parole in the United States, 2010. *Bureau of Justice Statistics.* Washington, DC: U.S. Department of Justice, Office of Justice Programs. Retrieved from http://bjs.ojp.usdoj.gov/content/pub/pdf/ppus10.pdf

Grella, C. E., & Rodriguez, L. (2011). Motivation for treatment among women offenders in prison-based treatment and longitudinal outcomes among those who participate in community aftercare. *Journal of Psychoactive Drugs, 43*(1), 58–67.

Guerino, P., Harrison, P. M., & Sabol, W. J. (2011). Prisoners in 2010. *Bureau of Justice Statistics.* Washington, DC: U.S. Department of Justice. Retrieved from http://bjs.ojp.usdoj.gov/content/pub/pdf/p10.pdf

Hirsch, A. E. (2001). Bringing back shame: Women, welfare reform and criminal justice. In P. J. Schram & B. Koons-Witt (Eds.), *Gendered (in)justice: Theory and practice in feminist criminology* (pp. 270–286). Long Grove, IL: Waveland Press.

Huebner, B. M., DeJong, C., & Cobbina, J. (2010). Women coming home: Long-term patterns of recidivism. *Justice Quarterly, 27*(2), 225–254.

Jacobs, A. (2000). *Give 'em a fighting chance: The challenges for women offenders trying to succeed in the community.* New York, NY: Women's Prison Association and Home, Inc. Retrieved from http://www.wpaonline.org/pdf/WPA_FightingChance.pdf

Kitty, J. M. (2012). "It's like they don't want you to get better": Psy control of women in the carceral context. *Feminism & Psychology, 22*(2), 162–182.

Kruttschnitt, C., Gartner, R., & Miller, A. (2000). Doing her own time? Women's responses to prison in the context of the old and the new penology. *Criminology, 38*(3), 681–717.

Kurshan, N. (2000). *Women and imprisonment in the United States: History and current reality.* Retrieved from http://www.prisonactivist.org/archive/women/women-and-imprisonment.html

LeBel, T. P. (2012). "If one doesn't get you another one will": Formerly incarcerated persons' perceptions of discrimination. *The Prison Journal, 92*(1), 63–87.

Legal Action Center. (2011). State TANF options drug felon ban. Retrieved from http://www.lac.org/doc_library/lac/publications/HIRE_Network_State_TANF_options_Drug_Felony_Ban.pdf

Lopez, A. (2012, April 9). Scott signs "historic" anti-shackling bill for incarcerated pregnant women. *Florida Independent.* Retrieved from http://floridaindependent.com/74661/rick-scott-anti-shackling-bill

Lord, E. A. (2008). The challenges of mentally ill female offenders in prison. *Criminal Justice and Behavior, 35*(8), 928–942.

Mastony, C. (2012, May 23). $4.1 million settlement set for pregnant inmates who said they were shackled before giving birth. *Chicago Tribune.* Retrieved from http://articles.chicagotribune.com/2012–05–23/news/ct-met-shackled-pregnant-women-20120523_1_pregnant-women-pregnant-inmates-shackles-and-belly-chains

Messina, N., Grella, C. E., Cartier, J., & Torres, S. (2010). A randomized experimental study of gender-responsive substance abuse treatment for women in prison. *Journal of Substance Abuse Treatment, 39,* 97–107.

Moses, M. (1995, December). A synergistic solution for children of incarcerated parents. *Corrections Today, 57*(7), 124–126.

Rafter, N. H. (1990). *Partial justice: Women in state prisons 1800–1935.* (2nd ed.). Boston, MA: New England University Press.

Rathbone, C. (2005). *A world apart: Women, prison and life behind bars.* New York, NY: Random House.

Ritchie, B. E. (2001). Challenges incarcerated women face as they return to their communities: Findings from life history interviews. *Crime and Delinquency, 47*(3), 368–389.

Salisbury, E. J., Van Voorhis, P., Wright, E. M., & Bauman, A. (2009). Changing probation experiences for female offenders based on women's needs and risk assessment project findings. *Women, Girls and Criminal Justice, 10*(6), 83–84, 92–95.

Sandifer, J. L. (2008). Evaluating the efficacy of a parenting program for incarcerated mothers. *The Prison Journal, 88*(3), 423–445.

Schadee, J. (2003). Passport to healthy families. *Corrections Today, 65*(3), 64.

Schram, P., Koons-Witt, B. A., Williams, F. P., III, & McShane, M. D. (2006). Supervision strategies and approaches for female parolees: Examining the link between unmet needs and parolee outcomes. *Crime and Delinquency, 52*(3), 450–471.

Sentencing Project. (2006). *Life sentences: Denying welfare benefits to women convicted of drug offenses.* Retrieved from http://www.sentencingproject.org/doc/publications/women_smy_lifesentences.pdf

Severance, T. A. (2005). "You know who you can go to": Cooperation and exchange between incarcerated women. *The Prison Journal, 85*(3), 343–367.

Sharkey, L. (2010). Does overcrowding in prisons exacerbate the risk of suicide among women prisoners? *The Howard Journal, 49*(2), 111–124.

Snyder, Z. K. (2009). Keeping families together: The importance of maintaining mother-child contact for incarcerated women. *Women & Criminal Justice, 19,* 37–59.

Stringer, E. C., & Barnes, S. L. (2012). Mothering while imprisoned: The effects of family and child dynamics on mothering attitudes. *Family Relations, 61,* 313–326.

Van Voorhis, P., Salisbury, E., Wright, E., & Bauman, A. (2008). *Achieving accurate pictures of risk and identifying gender responsive needs: Two new assessments for women offenders.* Washington, DC: United States Department of Justice, National Institute of Corrections.

Van Wormer, K. S., & Bartollas, C. (2010). *Women and the criminal justice system.* Boston, MA: Allyn and Bacon.

Wismont, J. M. (2000). The lived pregnancy experience of women in prison. *Journal of Midwifery and Women's Health, 45*(4), 292–300.

Women's Prison Association (WPA). (2003). *WPA focus on women and justice: A portrait of women in prison.* Retrieved from http://www.wpaonline.org/pdf/Focus_December 2003.pdf

Women's Prison Association (WPA). (2008). *Mentoring women in reentry.* Retrieved from http://66.29.139.159/pdf/Mentoring%20Women%20in%20Reentry%20WPA%20Practice%20Brief.pdf

Women's Prison Association (WPA). (2009a). *Quick facts: Women and criminal justice 2009.* Retrieved from http://www.wpaonline.org/pdf/Quick%20Facts%20Women%20and%20CJ_Sept09.pdf

Women's Prison Association (WPA). (2009b). *Mothers, infants and imprisonment: A national look at prison nurseries and community-based alternatives.* Retrieved from http://www.wpaonline.org/pdf/Mothers%20Infants%20 and%20Imprisonment%202009.pdf

Women's Prison Association (WPA). (n.d.). Laws banning shackling during childbirth gaining momentum nationwide. *Institute on Women and Criminal Justice.* Retrieved from www.wpaonline.org/pdf/Shackling%20Brief_ final.pdf

Wu, E., El-Bassel, N., Gilbert, L., Hess, L., Lee, H., & Rowell, T. L. (2012). Prior incarceration and barriers to receipt of services among entrants to alternative to incarceration programs: A gender-based disparity. *Journal of Urban Health: Bulletin of the New York Academy of Medicine, 89*(2), 384–396.

Zaitzow, B. H., & Thomas, J. (2003). *Women in prison: Gender and social control.* Boulder, CO: Lynne Rienner Publishers.

Zlotnick, C. (1997). Posttraumatic stress disorder (PTSD), PTSD comorbidity, and childhood abuse among incarcerated women. *Journal of Nervous and Mental Disease, 185,* 761–763.

NOTES

1. The manufacturer of Seroquel indicates that "Seroquel is an anti-psychotic medication, useful as a mono-drug therapy or as an adjunct to the drugs lithium or divalproex for the treatment of schizophrenia and the acute manic and depressive episodes in bipolar disorder" (Kitty, 2012, p. 168).

2. This number may be somewhat inaccurate, as data on gender were not reported by some states. 1,096,223 individuals were listed as "unknown or nor reported" on gender.

3. Section 8 housing provides government subsidies for housing in nonpublic housing developments. Here, private landlords are paid the difference between the amount of rent that a tenant can afford, based on his or her available income, and the fair market value of the residence.

PART IV

Women Professionals and the Criminal Justice System

CHAPTER

13

Women and Work in the Criminal Justice System

Police, Corrections, and Offender Services

Diana fought for acceptance in her police department throughout her entire career. After five years in patrol, she spent four years ignoring male colleagues' comments about her appearance as a hot under-cover decoy in vice. She tolerated her continual assignment to crimes involving children, families, and community nuisances, which weren't considered real police work. In robbery-homicide, she took undesirable cases for seven years, finally gaining acceptance when she solved three cold-case homicides in a single summer. While she garnered some professional respect, she was not really accepted as part of the inside group. So she spent her time training and sparring in martial arts. She even competed in hand-to-hand combat trials, winning nearly every match in which she competed, maintaining an unprecedented six-year state title. Despite these accomplishments, Diana was repeatedly passed over for promotion.

In her tenth year as a senior robbery-homicide detective, the Police Chief (a charter member of the good ol' boys club) announced his retirement. An abuse-of-force scandal derailed the chances for his handpicked successor, and a progressive candidate from an outside agency was hired as Chief. Within six months, he asked Diana to apply for a promotion to Captain, a position she was eager to pursue.

Diana's colleagues balked at her chances for promotion, and they were stunned when she was offered the position ahead of a male Lieutenant who was well connected with the old guard in the department. Rumors began to spread like wildfire: She must be sleeping with the Chief.

The presence of women in criminal justice professions is a relatively new phenomenon. Traditionally, criminal justice jobs were held by men, as the tough work of apprehending, supervising, or managing dangerous felons was believed to be beyond the scope of what women could—or should—do. Women first began to appear in criminal justice fields as police department employees (although not generally sworn) in the early 20th century, and their ranks have risen considerably at the time of this writing. However, their early presence within the academy was significantly limited, as many believed that policing (and later, corrections, probation, and parole) was a man's job and, therefore, unsuitable as an occupation for women. Research on criminal justice as man's work focused on traditional masculine traits such as aggression, physical skill, and being tough—traits that many argued were lacking for women, making them inherently less capable of doing the job (Appier, 1998).

Most members of the public assume that criminal justice work is characterized predominantly by incidents involving danger, excitement, and high levels of violence. These themes are echoed and reinforced in examples of popular culture, such as television, film, and news outlets laden with stories of dangerous offenders wreaking havoc on peaceful communities (Lersch & Bazley, 2012). While criminal justice officers can and do face such dangers during the course of their careers, such extreme examples misrepresent the reality of criminal justice work, which often involves hours of waiting, piles of paperwork, and frequent communication with community members. More often than the adrenaline rush depicted in the media, criminal justice personnel are faced with situations requiring empathy, compassion, and nurturing: traits that are stereotypically classified as *feminine* characteristics. Typical duties of an officer are not limited to the pursuit and capturing of the bad guys and more often include responding to victims of a crime; dealing with the welfare of children and the elderly; and addressing issues of addiction, housing, and mental health. Given the varying skills and traits required in criminal justice professions, particularly among law enforcement, jail, prison, probation, and parole personnel, has a place for women been established? Are there so-called *male traits* and *female traits*, and to what extent do such gendered traits contribute to criminal justice professions? Are there other differences in how women are hired, do their jobs, experience stressors, are promoted, and establish careers in criminal justice? These issues are discussed in this chapter.

Women in Policing

An examination of the early history of women in policing indicates that the work of moral reformers was instrumental in the emergence of policewomen. During the late 19th century, women's advocacy groups were heavily involved in social issues. Examples of their efforts include the creation of a separate court for juvenile offenders as well as crime prevention outreach related to the protection of young women from immoral sexual influences. However, women were not a formal part of the justice system and served instead as moral compass, informal advocates, and, when employed, as paid social workers. That changed at the start of the 20th century, when women entered the police force as bona fide sworn officers.

There are three claims as to the first female police officer. One recent report provides some evidence that the first female police officer was **Marie Owens**, a Chicago factory inspector who transferred to the police department in 1891 (Mastony, 2010). However, no mention of her police career was

▲ **Photo 13.1**   Captain Edyth Totten and the Women Police Reserve, New York City, 1918.

included in her obituary, despite an allegedly 32-year career in law enforcement. A second claim is for **Lola Baldwin**, reportedly hired in 1908 by the police department in Portland, Oregon, to supervise a group of social workers (Corsianos, 2009; Oregon Experience, 2012). Although she was a police department employee, there is some debate as to whether or not she was actually a sworn officer or a social worker employed by the police department (Los Angeles Almanac, 2012). In 1910, the Los Angeles Police Department (LAPD) hired **Alice Stebbins Wells**, who most scholars agree was the first sworn female police officer in the United States (Corsianos, 2009; Los Angeles Almanac, 2012; Women Police Officer's Association of America, 2007). At the time of her hiring, Ms. Wells was assigned to work with young female offenders, although she was also responsible for adult female offenders. Her philosophy as a female police officer reinforced the ideal of feminine traits of policing, echoed in her assertion that "I don't want to make arrests. I want to keep people from needing to be arrested, especially young people" (Appier, 1998, p. 9). As a result of the national and international attention of her hiring, she traveled the country promoting the benefits of hiring women in municipal policing agencies.

As an officer with the LAPD, Wells advocated for the protection of children and women, particularly when it came to sexual education. As part of her duties, she inspected dance halls, movie theaters, and locations for public recreation throughout the city, often addressing billboards with "unwholesome" messages or content. When she came into contact with girls of questionable moral status, she would lecture the girls on the dangers of premarital sex and advocate for the importance of purity. Her longstanding legacy was to promote the idea that policewomen were an asset to previously all-male departments, as women were uniquely suited to address the specific needs of female and juvenile offenders.

Following in the footsteps of Alice Stebbins Wells, many women sought out positions as police officers. The hiring of women by police agencies throughout the early 20th century did not mean that these women were assigned the same duties as male police officers. Rather, policewomen were essentially social workers armed with a badge. Their duties focused on preventing crime rather than responding to criminal activity. While hundreds of women joined the ranks of local law enforcement agencies between 1910–1920, they were a minority within most departments. Their tasks were typically relegated to the supervision of juvenile and female offenders, and their presence was often resented by their male colleagues. In an effort to distinguish the work of policewomen, many cities created separate branches within their respective police organizations. These women's bureaus were tasked with servicing the needs of women and girls in the community. Many of these bureaus were housed outside of the walls of the city police department in an attempt to create a more welcoming environment for citizens in need. Some scholars suggest that by making women's bureaus look more like a home, rather than a bureaucratic institution, women and children would be more comfortable and therefore more likely to seek out the services and advice of policewomen.

The mid-20th century saw significant growth in the number of women in policing. In 1922, there were approximately 500 policewomen in the United States—by 1960, more than 5,600 women were employed as officers (Schulz, 1995). Throughout this time, the majority of these policewomen remained limited in their duties, due in large part to a traditional policing (i.e., male) model. Policewomen were not permitted to engage in the same duties as policemen out of fear that these duties were too dangerous and that women would not be able to adequately serve in these positions. Most importantly, the "all-boys club" that existed in most departments simply did not want or welcome women intruding on their territory.

Despite these issues, women occasionally found themselves receiving expanded duties, particularly during times of war. With the decrease in manpower during World Wars I and II, many women found themselves placed in positions normally reserved for male officers, such as traffic control. In an effort to maintain adequate staffing levels during this period, the number of women hired within police agencies increased. However, the end of these wars saw the return of men to their policing posts and the displacement of women back to their gendered roles within their respective departments (Snow, 2010).

As in many other fields during the 1960s, the civil rights and women's movements had a tremendous effect on the presence of women in policing. Legal challenges paved the way toward gendered equality in policing by opening doors to allow women to serve in more active police capacities, such as patrol. In 1964, **Liz Coffal** and **Betty Blankenship** of the Indianapolis Police Department became the first women in the United States to serve as patrol officers, an assignment that was previously restricted to male officers throughout the country. As policewomen, Coffal and Blankenship were resented by their male colleagues, who believed that the work of a police officer was too dangerous for women. Coffal and Blankenship received little training for their new positions and often had to learn things on their own. They were ostracized by colleagues and administrators and found that dispatch often gave them the mundane and undesirable tasks, such as hospital transports. It soon became clear to Blankenship and Coffal that the likelihood of being requested for any sort of pursuit or arrest cases was slim. In an effort to gain increased experience in their position, they began to respond to calls at their own discretion. Armed with their police radio, they learned to interpret radio codes and began to respond to cases in their vicinity. They successfully navigated calls that most male officers believed they couldn't handle. As a result of their positive performances in often-tense situations, Coffal and Blankenship began to gain some respect from their male colleagues. However, they knew that any accolades could be short lived—one mistake and they ran the risk of being removed from their patrol status, and the traditional philosophy of "police work isn't for women" would be justified. While they eventually returned to some of the traditional feminine roles for women in policing, their experiences in patrol set the stage for significant changes for the futures of policewomen (Snow, 2010).

In addition to the differences in their duties, policewomen were historically subjected to different qualification standards for their positions. At the 1922 annual conference of the International Association of the Chiefs of Police, members suggested that policewomen should have completed college or nursing school (Snow, 2010). This standard is particularly ironic, given that male officers were not required to have even a high school diploma in most jurisdictions until the 1950s and 1960s. As a result, the career path of policewomen attracted women of higher educational and intellectual standing.

Not only were policewomen limited by their roles and duties within the department, they faced significant barriers in terms of the benefits and conditions of their employment. Like many other fields, policewomen were paid less for their work compared to policemen, in spite of the fact that most policewomen were more highly educated than their male colleagues. In addition, the advancement and promotional opportunities for women were significantly limited, as most departments did not allow women to participate in the exam process that would allow them to access opportunities for promotion. Generally speaking, the highest position that a policewoman could hold during this time was the commander of the women's bureau. Still, many agencies disagreed with that level of leadership, suggesting that women did not have the necessary skills or abilities to supervise officers or run a division. In some jurisdictions, women were forced to quit their positions when they got married, as many felt that women did not have enough time to care for a home, care for their husband, and fulfill their job duties. As one male officer explained it, "when they marry, they have to resign. You see, we might want them for some job or other when they have to be home cooking their husband's dinner. That would not be much use to us, would it?" (Snow, 2010, p. 23).

In 1967, the President's Commission on Law Enforcement (1967) and the Administration of Justice advocated for expanding the number of policewomen and diversifying their duties beyond the traditional female roles to which they were generally relegated. The commission wrote, "the value should not be considered as limited to staff functions or police work with juveniles; women should also serve regularly in patrol, vice, and investigative functions" (p. 125). Despite these assertions, few departments followed these recommendations, arguing that as members of a uniformed police patrol, officers required significant levels of upper-body strength in order to detain resistant offenders; women simply lacked the requisite upper-body strength to perform real police duties. In addition, many agency administrators argued that the job was simply too dangerous for women.

Until the 1970s, women represented only 1% of all sworn officers in the United States (Appier, 1998). However, new legislation and legal challenges in the 1960s and 1970s led to further changes involving the presence and role of policewomen. While the **Civil Rights Bill of 1964** was generally focused on eliminating racial discrimination, the word *sex* was added to the bill during the eleventh hour by House members, who hoped that this inclusion would raise objections among legislators and prohibit its passing. To the dismay of these dissenters, the bill was signed into law. In 1969, President Richard Nixon signed legislation that prohibited the use of sex as a requirement for hiring—meaning that jobs could not be restricted to men only (or women only). In addition, the Law Enforcement Assistance Administration (LEAA) mandated that agencies with federal funding (and police departments fell under this category) were prohibited from engaging in discriminatory hiring practices based on sex. While sex was now a protected category in terms of employment discrimination, the bill did little on its face to increase the presence of women in sworn policing roles, since most policewomen were employed by municipal departments, and the act exempted municipal government agencies from compliance. Further, the act prohibited discriminatory hiring practices but did little to curb a **gendered assignment** of duties once hired. This did little to change the nature of police assignments afforded women.

However, the passage of the Civil Rights Bill began a trend within departments to introduce women into ranks that were previously reserved exclusively for men. While several departments took the initiative to place women into patrol positions, many men in these departments issued strong objections against the practice. Thus, women in these positions often found themselves ostracized, with little support from their colleagues. Eight years later, in 1972, the Civil Rights Act was amended to extend employment protections to state and municipal government agencies, which opened the door to allow women to apply to all law enforcement jurisdictions as sworn officers without restrictions. While these changes increased the number of positions available to women (and to minorities), they also shifted the roles of policing away from the social service orientation that had been historically characteristic for women in policing. Their jobs now included the duties of crime fighting and the maintenance of order and public safety, just like their male counterparts (Schulz, 1995).

In every decade since, the numbers of women employed in sworn law enforcement positions made small but significant gains. Despite the continued informal resistance (or downright antagonism) toward female officers in many jurisdictions, the rates of women in sworn positions has risen steadily. By the late 1960s, approximately 1.1% of all sworn officers were women. By 1978, that figure rose to about 4.2%, and by 1986, approximately 8.8% of municipal officers were women (Rabe-Hemp, 2008). Women represented about 14% of all sworn officers in the U.S. in 1998, and 15.2% by 2008. However, women are far more present in large jurisdictions (roughly 22%) and federal agencies (roughly 24%) than in jurisdictions with fewer than 500 officers, where women represent roughly 8% of sworn officers (Langton, 2010). Not only are there fewer sworn women in small, rural agencies; in these cases, the rare sworn woman typically occupies lower positions and experience greater isolation and discrimination than her urban-employed contemporaries (Rabe-Hemp, 2008).

Women in sworn positions today experience a variety of responses by their male counterparts. Some male officers still refuse to accept female officers while others are indifferent to the presence of women on the force. Still others embrace the presence of female officers, a phenomenon that seems to be predicated on age and race, with younger male officers and male officers of color having greater levels of tolerance and acceptance of female officers (Renzetti, Goodstein, & Miller, 2006).

▲ **Photo 13.2** Beyond the struggles of early patrolwomen, women have battled for equal opportunities in work assignments and promotions. Here, two female detectives work at a crime scene.

Sadly, few female law enforcement officers achieve the higher ranks afforded their male counterparts. While court rulings in the 1970s opened the possibilities for promotion for policewomen, few women have successfully navigated their way to the top position of police chief. In 2009, there were 212 women serving in the top-ranking position in their departments nationwide (O'Connor, 2012). Most of these women served in small communities or led agencies with a specific focus, such as university police divisions or transit authorities (Schulz, 2003). Within metropolitan agencies (more than 100 sworn officers), only 7.3% of the top-level positions and 9.6% of supervisory positions are held by women. Additionally, women of color make up only 4.8% of sworn officers, and minority women are even less likely to appear in upper-level management positions, with only 1.6% of top-level positions and 3.1%

of supervisory roles filled by a woman of color. The situation is even bleaker for small and rural agencies, where only 3.4% of the top-level positions are staffed by women (Lonsway, Carrington et al., 2002).

Case Study

On the Beat: Chief Sheila Coley, Newark, NJ, Police Department

Sheila Coley is tough. *The Star-Ledger*, a New Jersey–based newspaper, reports that prior to taking her role as the first female chief of Newark Police Department, she fought the worst of the worst (Queally, 2011). Starting as one of only 15 women in the department in 1989, she slowly worked her way to the top. Taking on a variety of assignments, Coley proved she could handle whatever was thrown at her. She cleaned up the department's Sexual Assault Unit, notorious for mishandling evidence, losing track of sex offenders, and letting victims slip through the cracks. From there, she was asked to supervise the department's South Ward, a position known among insiders as "the city's bloodiest command" (Queally, 2011, para. 8). Working with community leaders, Coley actively increased citizen involvement in crime suppression, resulting in several police–community initiatives.

Coley's "can do" attitude, lauded by many of her peers, came from a background riddled with setbacks. She spent most of her childhood bouncing between relatives after her mother's passing when Coley was four. Though born in the South Bronx, she relocated many times, including a short stint with a family member in North Carolina. At 17, Coley joined the Air Force and served for three years before getting a college education.

Coley's appointment as the city's first female chief came as no surprise to anyone in the department; her reputation for hard work and dedication to her job made her the ideal candidate. This has also been reflected in other police departments. The *New York Times* (Mroz, 2008) reports that women are increasingly being promoted to higher positions within law enforcement agencies. In New Jersey alone, women have taken the helm of several large, urban police departments. Though a promising trend, it is a slow one; the "brass ceiling" is still intact for many agencies, and progress needs to be made to allow for more women to ascend to positions of authority (Lonsway, 2007).

For her part, Coley is taking steps to ensure that police work is a more attractive career choice for women. Breaking through the invisible wall holding women from command, Coley hopes that her appointment will empower other women to do the same. Other New Jersey departments have begun implementing maternity leave policies and more flexible hours in an effort to chip away at the family barriers once shying women away from policing's rigorous schedule.

Why is the representation of women so low in the field of policing? While legal challenges have mandated equal access to employment and promotion opportunities for women in policing, research indicates that the overemphasis on the physical fitness skills component of the hiring process excludes a number of qualified women from employment (Lonsway, Carrington et al., 2002). Physical fitness tests typical of law enforcement positions have been criticized as a tool to effectively exclude women from policing, despite evidence that it is not the physical abilities of officers that are most desirable.

Rather, it is their communication skills that are the best asset for the job requirements. The number of pushups that a woman can complete compared to a man says little about how well each will complete their job duties. Yet, standards such as these are used as evidence to suggest that women are inferior to their male colleagues. Women who are able to achieve the male standard of physical fitness are viewed more favorably by male colleagues compared to women who satisfy only the basic requirements for their gender (Schulze, 2012).

While historical perspectives have suggested that women lacked the physical prowess to manage the job duties of an officer, Rabe-Hemp (2009) suggests that these physical differences actually helped maintain peace when dealing with offenders. She writes,

> a man, whether they don't want to hurt you or they have that innate respect that they can't hit a woman or something, I don't know what it is, or that motherly instinct, I don't know. But generally, men for the most part don't want to fight with females. (Rabe-Hemp, 2009, p. 121)

While women have been subtly maligned in sworn positions, a few trends in policing have emphasized characteristics that are traditionally female. One such example is the emergence of **community policing** philosophies in the 1990s, which provided a shift in police culture that increased the number of women working in the field. The values of community policing emphasize relationships, care, and communication between officers and citizens. It allows officers to develop rapport with members of their community and respond to their concerns. Effective community policing strategies have led to improved relationships and respect of officers by residents. Research indicates that policewomen have been particularly successful within models of community policing due to their enhanced problem-solving skills through communication (Lersch & Bazley, 2012). As jurisdictions continue to grapple with community relations and community-oriented and problem-oriented policing, those traits traditionally maligned as *female* may continue to be valued, particularly in large, metropolitan jurisdictions.

Given the historical context of women in policing, it is not surprising that attributes such as compassion, fear, or anything else that is considered feminine are historically maligned, particularly by male officers. Given this masculine subculture that exists in policing, how does this affect women who are employed within the agency? What does it mean to be a woman in law enforcement? Are female police officers viewed as **POLICEwomen or policeWOMEN**?

While women today can and do serve in the same positions within a department as their male colleagues, research indicates that women in policing employ different tools and tactics in their daily experiences as an officer compared to their male counterparts. The National Center for Women and Policing indicates that women officers are typically not involved in cases of police brutality and corruption. In contrast, male officers are more than 8.5 times more likely than female officers to be accused of excessive force. Research also indicates that women are more likely to be successful at verbally diffusing difficult situations and have significantly fewer citizen complaints than men (Lonsway, Wood et al., 2002). The effective communication skills often associated with women come in handy, as female officers appear to be able to connect more easily with citizens in the community than male officers (Harrington & Lonsway, 2004).

Cara Rabe-Hemp (2009) explores the issue of gender identity for women in policing and finds that female officers do believe that their gender affects the way in which they function as officers. As similar research suggests, policewomen agree that they are more likely to rely on their interpersonal and communication skills within the context of their daily work and are less likely to jump to physical interventions than their male counterparts. They acknowledge that their gender is an asset when dealing with certain populations, such as children and women who have been victimized.

While research indicates that the use of gender is interwoven through the identities of women as police officers, policewomen sometimes acknowledge that they balance their skills of communication and care in such a way as to protect the masculine identity of their law enforcement peers (Rabe-Hemp, 2009). In other words, women not only use certain gendered traits in doing their job well, they are aware of their tenuous gender relations and roles in law enforcement, and they are mindful to protect the egos of their male colleagues. We know of no research that indicates that male officers are similarly cognizant of their female counterparts' egos or identities; in fact, research historically identified ostracizing of female officers by male officers as well as many informal social barriers for female officers, often constructed and maintained by their male peers.

Women continue to face a number of barriers in policing. One area that has revealed some interesting findings related to the issues of gender and job performance in policing is the topic of pregnancy. Indeed, given the physical challenges of their job duties, women in advanced stages of pregnancy may be physically unable to fulfill the contemporary job duties of policing, which could potentially present a danger to not only their own life but also the life of their unborn child. While laws such as the Pregnancy Discrimination Act prohibit the discrimination of women during pregnancy and have improved the conditions of employment for gestational women, they do not solve the issues for expectant women within law enforcement. In addition, laws such as the Family Medical Leave Act protect the employment status of women while on leave for up to 12 weeks (without compensation), a feature that often requires women to exhaust their sick and vacation reserves in order to maintain financial support for their family. However, these laws do little to respond to the needs of women who are able to work in a reduced capacity prior to the birth of their child. Given that many women may choose to have children, policies need to be constructed that not only reflect the needs of officers during pregnancy but also accommodate the needs of families for both male and female officers.

A review of 203 departments in the United States found that very few departments have written policies on family leave for its officers. Only 11% of departments had any sort of clear policy on family leave, and 5.4% of departments had a policy that specifies the availability of limited-duty assignments for gestational women. While a lack of policy does not indicate that there is a negative belief system by the agencies against motherhood, it does mean that there may be little consistency on how cases are handled. Most departments focus on family-based policies, which allow for the equal treatment of mothers and fathers, rather than focus specifically on the needs of pregnant women and postpartum motherhood (Schulze, 2008). While it is important that departments accommodate the needs of pregnant officers, this can be a delicate issue. Many women express frustration that, upon informing their superiors that they are expecting, they run the risk of being removed from their position, even though they remain (depending on the stage of their pregnancy) able to adequately fulfill the requirements of their job (Kruger, 2006). (For more on pregnancy issues for criminal justice staff, see box on page 314.)

Despite the significant advances that women in policing have made over the past century, research is mixed on whether the contemporary situation is improving for women in law enforcement. While legal challenges have required equal access to employment and promotion within law enforcement, research indicates that many women continue to be passed over for positions that were ultimately filled by a male officer. In many cases, women felt that they continually had to prove themselves to their male colleagues, regardless of the number of years that they spent within an organization. This experience was particularly prevalent when women moved to a new position (Rabe-Hemp, 2012). And while women report the same level of stress as their male counterparts, women may face other disadvantages in sworn policing. Griffin (2006) suggests that female officers have greater concerns about safety and organizational support for employees than men, while male officers more frequently perceive the organization to support equal treatment policies, at least in theory.

While women in policing report experiences of discrimination and harassment within their agencies, they also acknowledge that the culture of policing has become more accepting to women throughout their careers. However, these ideals of peace were not easily won and required daily support and maintenance by the women. For example, Harrison (2012) suggests that female officers reduce the stress of sexual harassment with strong social bonds on the job. While this may require greater effort by women to engage in conversations and activities to build social bonds in their given departments, strong social bonds can mitigate the stress of harassment experienced by many women, although this approach may not reduce the harassment itself.

Research by Rabe-Hemp (2008) identifies three additional ways in which policewomen gain acceptance within the **masculine culture** of policing: (1) experiences in violent confrontations requiring the use of force, (2) achieving a high rank within the department structure, and (3) distinguishing themselves as different from their male counterparts in terms of their skills and experience. Female police officers acknowledge that acceptance in the male-dominated police culture often comes with significant cost to their personal life and ideals. In many cases, policewomen talk about putting up with disrespect and harassment in order to achieve their goals. For others, they renegotiate their original goals and settle for second best.

Women in Corrections

Correctional officers are a central component of the criminal justice system. Responsible for the security of the correctional institution and the safety of the inmates housed within its walls, correctional officers are involved with every aspect of the inmate life. Indeed, correctional officers play an important part in the lives of the inmates as a result of their constant interaction. Contrary to other work assignments within the criminal justice field, the position of the correctional officer is integrated into every aspect of the daily life of prisoners. Duties of the correctional officer range from enforcing the rules and regulations of the facility to responding to inmate needs to diffusing inmate conflicts and supervising the daily movement and activities of the inmate (Britton, 2003).

Historically, the workforce of corrections has been largely male and White, regardless of the race or gender of the offender. As discussed earlier, the treatment of female offenders by male guards during the early days of the prison led to significant acts of neglect and abuse of female inmates. These acts of abuse resulted in the hiring of female matrons to supervise the incarcerated female population. However, these early positions differed significantly from the duties of male officers assigned to supervise male inmates, and opportunities for female staff to work outside this population of female-only inmates were rare. For those women who were successful in gaining employment in a male institution, their job duties were significantly limited compared to the responsibilities afforded their male counterparts. In particular, prison policies did not allow female correctional officers to work in direct supervision roles with male offenders. As in the realm of policing, correctional culture was masculine, and administrators believed it was too dangerous to assign a woman to supervise male inmates. In male facilities, female guards were restricted to positions that had little to no inmate contact, such as administrative positions, entry and control booths, and general surveillance (Britton, 2003).

Through most of the 20th century, women made significant gains in correctional employment. Female correctional officers, while largely relegated to contact positions with female and juvenile wards or noncontact positions in male institutions, were largely well-educated and well-informed reformers who advocated for rehabilitation of offenders in their care. Since institutions were governed by same-sex practices, these women rose to the ranks of head matrons and superintendents in female prisons decades before women found similar acceptance in private fields, policing, or male institutions (Feinman, 1994; Kim, Devalve, Devalve, & Johnson, 2003; Tewksbury & Collins, 2006).

Despite the increased access to employment opportunities for women through the 1970s, however, many female guards resented these restrictions on their job duties and filed suit with the courts, alleging that the restriction of duties based on gender constituted sex discrimination. While many cases alleged that the restriction of female guards from male units was done to maintain issues of privacy for the offenders, the courts rejected the majority of these arguments. In *Griffin v. Michigan Department of Corrections* (654 F. Supp. 690, 1982), the Court held that inmates do not possess any rights to be protected against being viewed in stages of undress or naked by a correctional officer, regardless of gender. In addition, the Court held that the positive aspects of offender rehabilitation outweighed any potential risks of assault for female correctional officers, and therefore, they should not be barred from working with a male incarcerated population. Other cases, such as *Grummett v. Rushen* (779 F2d 491, 1985), have concluded that the pat-down search of a male inmate (including their groin area) does not violate the Fourth Amendment protection against unreasonable search and seizure. However, the Courts have held that the inverse gender relationship can be considered offensive. In *Jordan v. Gardner* (986 F.2d 1137, 1992), the Court found that pat-down policies designed to control the introduction of contraband into a facility could be viewed as unconstitutional if conducted by male staff members against female inmates. Here, the court held that a cross-sex search could amount to a deliberate indifference with the potential for psychological pain (under the Eighth Amendment), given the high likelihood of a female offender's history of physical and sexual abuse.

Sexual Relationships Between Guards and Inmates

Despite the fact that most jurisdictions prohibit sex behind bars, sexual relationships do indeed occur in correctional institutions. When the public thinks about sex in correctional institutions, forcible rape undoubtedly comes to mind. Indeed, the crime of rape often occurs behind bars and can include inmate-on-inmate rape, rape perpetrated by correctional officers against inmates, or rape committed by inmates against correctional officers. The most common form of sexual victimization experienced by male inmates is coerced or forced sexual contact by another male inmate; the sexual assault of female inmates most commonly involves perpetration by male guards. Although rare, one current issue garnering public attention in light of recent highly publicized cases is the issue of sex between female guards and male inmates (Associated Press, 2010).

In January of 2010, Rachel Hoerner, a guard at Camp Hill State Prison in Pennsylvania, pled guilty to charges of institutional sexual assault for having sex with a male inmate (Boyer, 2010; Miller, 2010). In October of 2010, Danette Skelton was accused of custodial misconduct because of her sexual relationship

(Continued)

(Continued)

with an inmate at the Washington State Reformatory. She was also accused of bringing the inmate a cell phone—contraband in state prisons—so they could keep in touch when she was not on duty. In January of 2012, Renee Gutierrez, a guard at Lompoc's Federal Correctional Complex in Lompoc, California, plead guilty to charges of sexual abuse with a male ward (L. A. Now, 2012). In February of 2012, Orange County Sheriff's Deputy Jennifer McClain was arrested and charged for engaging in sexual activities with an inmate at the Men's Central Jail (Hernandez, 2012). The inmate reported the relationship but insisted the sexual activity was consensual.

Each of these women faced considerable jail/prison time for their crimes, ranging from one year in jail to 15 years in prison. So far, only Skelton has been sentenced to jail time; she received six months in jail for her offense, and she is also required to register as a sex offender for 10 years (Kaminsky, 2011). Hoerner is also required to register as a Megan's Law sex offender and will serve 23 months of probation in lieu of jail time. Gutierrez received a sentence of probation and community service for her crime (Mooradin, 2012). As of this writing, McClain's case is still under investigation.

The law clearly holds the correctional officer responsible in such crimes. However, in some cases, the female staff attributes these incidents to sexual coercion by an inmate. Such was the explanation given by five female staff members in a Montana prison, including a therapist, who engaged in sex with a male inmate. The female officers blamed the sexual encounters on the inmate, saying that once they provided small favors to him, he blackmailed them into sex. All five female staff members were fired for their sexual misconduct.

It is possible that female guards are easy prey for manipulative inmates. Alternately, it is possible that predatory female guards prey against male inmates under their supervision, coercing the confined to engage in sex in much the same way male guards victimize female inmates under their supervision. However, most of the female guards discussed here, as well as the inmates with whom they were involved, claimed that their relationships were consensual. Do you think sexual relationships can be consensual when they involve one party with tremendous power over the life and liberty on another? Most scholars and psychologists agree: When one person holds authority over another, as is the case between a guard and inmate, a consensual relationship cannot occur.

Although the prevalence is relatively low compared to other types of sexual assault behind bars, these examples of female guards having sex with male inmates illustrate the importance of gendered expectations in sexual misconduct. The public is often perplexed at such cases, which are counter-examples of the expected; these do not involve men in a position of power taking sexual advantage of subordinate women. On the contrary, these involve women with authority engaging in sex with men in subordinate positions. We are often more comfortable labeling the former as a sexual offense, as it conforms to the gendered expectation of male sex offender and female victim. With the latter, notions of consent and relationship often influence our interpretation of such events; the media often minimize such charges with innuendo (e.g., "prisoner of love" or "convict Casanova"), which serves to reduce criminal responsibility from this uncommon class of female offenders.

As a result of equal employment opportunity legislation, the doors of prison employment have been opened for women to serve as correctional officers. Today, women are increasingly involved in all areas of supervision of both male and female offenders and all ranks and positions today. Many women choose corrections as a career out of interest in the rehabilitation services as well as a perception that such a career provides job security (Hurst & Hurst, 1997). According to the 2007 Directory of Adult and Juvenile Correctional Departments, Institutions, and Agencies and Probation and Parole Authorities, women made up 37% of correctional officers in state adult facilities and 51% of juvenile correctional officers (American Correctional Association, 2007). Pastore and Maguire (2008) estimate that nearly 30% of all correctional staff today are women, including both correctional officers and ancillary positions within the institutions. Within these facilities, both men and women are assigned to same-sex as well as cross-sex supervisory positions. In addition, more women are working as correctional officers in exclusively male facilities, where they constitute 24.5% of the correctional personnel in these institutions (DiMarino, 2009).

Research indicates that gender can affect how officers approach their position, regardless of the inmate's sex. For women involved in the supervision of male inmates, their philosophies often differ significantly from that of male officers. For example, Britton (2003) found that while male officers functioned within a paramilitary role and were ready to use force if necessary, women saw their role as mentors and mothers, and they focused on the rehabilitation of the inmates.

Despite significant backlash and criticism against women in corrections, research indicates that the integration of women into the correctional field has significant benefits for prison culture. First, female correctional officers are less likely than male officers to be victimized by inmates. This finding contradicts traditional concerns that women would be at risk for harm if they were responsible for the direct supervision of male offenders. Second, women officers are more likely than male officers to use communication skills, rather than physical acts of force, to obtain compliance from inmates. While this is consistent with traditional concerns and stereotypes—that female officers won't respond with the same level of force as male officers—the effectiveness of the verbal approach suggests that perhaps the typical physical response isn't the only way to manage volatile inmates. Finally, female officers indicate a greater level of satisfaction from their work compared to male officers. Thus, perhaps the addition of female officers could raise staff morale and improve conditions for staff in correctional settings (Tewksbury & Collins, 2006).

While women have made significant career gains as correctional officers, women still struggle in this masculine, male-dominated environment. Research indicates that female correctional officers are frequent targets of sexual harassment (Chapman, 2009). The **good ol' boy network** remains quite pervasive in many facilities. Many women in leadership positions face significant challenges navigating this culture. For example, as one female officer puts it,

> men will perceive being assertive as a good quality in a guy, [but for women] they will still say, "Oh she's such a bitch." So you need to couch what you're saying a little differently so as not to offend these poor guys over here. (Greer, 2008, p. 5)

Like correctional officers, inmates also have conflicting perceptions about women working in the correctional field. Studies indicate that upon their first interactions, male inmates draw on stereotypical assumptions regarding female officers. Yet women in these positions possess the unique opportunity to offer a positive image of women (Cheeseman & Worley, 2006). Despite these gains, women who work in this field indicate that they experience persistent occurrences of sexual harassment by inmates. Despite this, studies suggest that these experiences do not affect female officers' job satisfaction—indeed, many accept that incidents of sexual harassment come with the territory of being a woman working in a male-dominated arena (Chapman, 2009).

How does gender affect the perceptions of work in a correctional setting? Like other criminal justice occupations, how do female correctional officers "do" gender in the context of their job duties? Many female correctional officers are hyperaware of their status as women and how gender affects their interactions with both fellow staff and inmates. In some cases, female officers utilize skills and techniques that many scholars identify as *feminine traits*—communication and care for the inmates, mutual respect between inmates and staff, and so on. Female staff members often become very aware of their physical status as a woman, particularly when working with male offenders, and respond by dressing down, wearing baggier clothing, and donning understated hairstyles and makeup to limit physical displays of gender in the workplace (Mallicoat, 2011).

Research on women in corrections echoes these themes. Women working in the correctional field are more likely to emphasize the social worker aspects of the job compared to their male counterparts (Stohr, Mays, Lovrich, & Gallegos, 1996). Here, women use their gender to their advantage—by drawing upon their communication skills, they are able to diffuse potentially dangerous situations before violence ensues. However, it is important to find balance between the feminine traits and masculine traits—too much communication between staff and inmates can be viewed negatively out of fear that staff will grow too close to an inmate and risk being taken advantage of (Britton, 2003). Given the increase of the prison population and the opportunities for employment, it is important for facilities to recognize the strengths and weaknesses for women who work in this field and their relationships with the incarcerated population.

Much of the research on women working in corrections deals with the issues of job satisfaction, stress, and **burnout**. While several scholars have indicated that women in corrections experience

▲ **Photo 13.3**   In the early history of prisons, women were only hired to work with female inmates. In response to equal opportunity policies and lawsuits by women in correctional fields, women today are now assigned to all types of supervision duties within the prison. Here, a female correctional officer engages in a pat-down search of an inmate to look for weapons or other contraband items.

higher degrees of stress than male officers, not all scholars have come to this conclusion. While certainly the correctional setting is a high-stress work environment, research by Griffin (2006) indicates that the levels of stress do not differ by gender. In contrast, Tewksbury and Collins (2006) find evidence that female correctional officers do indicate higher levels of job-related stress than male correctional officers. Griffin (2006) identifies two major themes of stress for female correctional officers: concern over issues of safety and of "bringing their work home." In addition, research by Lambert, Altheimer, and Hogan (2010) indicates that conflicts between work and family had a significant effect on the levels of job-related stress and job satisfaction for women, while conflict and ambiguity in the role played by an officer changed the levels of job satisfaction for men. Of particular interest are the findings reported by Tewksbury and Collins (2006): The major source of female officers' job-related stress comes from interactions with their coworkers, whereas male officers report that their job stress comes from working with inmates. In addition, men and women deal with their stress differently. While women are more likely to seek out social support as a mechanism for dealing with stress, men are more likely to engage in problem-solving skills to resolve their sources of stress (Hurst & Hurst, 1997).

Another major theme within the literature involves gender differences in inmate supervision preferences. Many correctional officers express disdain when they are assigned to work the female unit and articulate that women are much more difficult to work with than men, that women are more dramatic, manipulative, needy, emotional, and time consuming. Research by Pollock (1986, p. 174) provides details on why male and female correctional officers believe that working with women is less desirable than supervising men. While both male and female staff members believe that female inmates are more demanding, defiant, and complaining, male officers also express concerns about being accused of inappropriate behaviors against female inmates. Female officers express that they would prefer to work with male inmates, because they feel that they are more likely to be respected and appreciated by the male inmates than female inmates. Belief systems such as these have a significant impact on perceptions of working with female offenders and translate into a belief that working with women is an undesirable assignment (Rasche, 2012). Research indicates that among both male and female correctional officers (and regardless of rank), there appears to be a **male inmate preference**, despite the increased risks for violence associate with this population. However, Rasche (2012) found that the only population that does not express a preference for assignments working with male inmates are experienced female line staff members employed at all-female facilities.

Staff members who are assigned to work with women against their preference can do a significant disservice to programs that employ a gender-responsive approach. Interestingly, while correctional officers indicated that female offenders were more needy than male offenders, they attributed these differences to the differences between men and women generally. Indeed, as previous sections of this book have indicated, incarcerated women do have a variety of unique needs to which the correctional system must respond, including gynecological health needs, increased likelihood of mental health issues, and the strain of being separated from their children. Gaarder and Belknap (2004) found that detention workers received little to no training on how to work with female offenders and on how, as a population, they present a variety of needs that differ from those of the male population. This lack of specialized training led to the (mis)perceptions that women were more difficult to work with than men. Just as programming needs to be gender responsive, so does the training of officers who supervise female offenders.

As discussed earlier, women employed in corrections have attained the highest ranks, perhaps in part because they have historically served as matrons and wardens of all-female institutions. This is but one area in which the history of women in police diverges from the history of women in corrections; women, including women of color, can reasonably hope to attain high ranks within correctional settings, including that of warden. Kim et al. (2003) found many similarities between male and female wardens, suggesting greater gender neutrality among correctional officers than previously thought. Likewise, Lambert, Hogan, Altheimer, and Wareham (2010) found few differences between the attitudes of male and female correctional officers once on the job for a period of time, suggesting that the work environment shapes their views, not necessarily their gender. And although male colleagues presented a primary stressor and source of resistance to women in corrections, current research suggests that resistance toward female correctional officers may come from a surprising source today: other female officers. In her qualitative study of female correctional officers, Rader (2007) found that female correctional officers view other female officers more negatively than previously thought and believe that other female correctional officers make their own jobs more difficult.

Pregnant Behind Bars . . . at Work

In the United States, employment laws protect employees from discrimination based on race, sex, religion, and medical condition. This includes the medical condition of pregnancy, and it applies to persons employed as law enforcement officers in sworn positions, including jails and prisons.

It is well established that pregnant police officers can continue to perform their duties as long as medically able but that their duties may be modified according to medical limitations. Thus, a female police officer would likely be assigned to light or administrative duty during her final weeks before maternity leave. A 2001 lawsuit against Suffolk County Police Department in New York affirmed that pregnant officers were entitled to **light duty**/desk jobs when they were medically unable to perform active police duty on the streets (McDonough, 2006). At the time, light duty assignments were available only for officers who were injured on the job or who faced disciplinary action; it was not available for pregnant officers. The court found that this violated the Pregnancy Discrimination Act, emphasizing that the law requires equal treatment, not preferential treatment, for pregnant employees (Baker, 2008). Given that light duty was available for officers injured on the job, pregnant officers should similarly be afforded light duty; this is equal treatment. While most jurisdictions do allow light duty for sworn personnel for a variety of reasons (including pregnancy), the courts have established that such accommodations are not the inherent right of an employee or fetus, but light duty accommodations must apply to pregnant employees if it is available to any class of employee. But, what about those who are employed as sworn officers in a custodial setting—a jail or prison? Does light duty ever apply to a custodial setting? Are there inherent dangers in these settings, and should specific accommodations be given to pregnant officers working in jails or prisons?

Bach (2010) interviewed 67 pregnant women employed in various positions, including custodial settings. Notably, the pregnant women in his study who were working in custodial settings had more than twice the number of absences than pregnant women working elsewhere. Surprisingly, some scholars suggest pregnant correctional officers had far more frequent experiences of violence at work (17%) than most other groups, including women employed in other settings (about 4%), sworn officers in the United States overall (11.9%), and those assigned to custody (12.8%; Bach 2010; Federal Bureau of Investigation, 2005). One the other hand, recent research suggests that female correctional officers are underrepresented in prison assaults, representing nearly 40% of correctional staff but experiencing only a quarter of all reported correctional violence against staff (Sorensen, Cunningham, Vigen, & Woods, 2011).

These trends raise several important questions. Should pregnant custodial staff be required to accept light duty assignments? The courts would likely interpret this mandate as preferential treatment, a violation of the Pregnancy Discrimination Act. Does the fetus have rights, and if so, would these rights require light duty of a mother employed in a correctional setting?

Consider one final aspect of this issue. As of this writing, the L. A. County Men's Central Jail precludes pregnant women from touring or working in this facility (Men's Central Jail Tour Guidelines/Information, 2011). This prohibition is specific to this one location and does not apply to pregnant women who wish to work or tour any other county jail. This restriction for pregnant employees and visitors is due in large part to the conditions of violence and communicable disease, which plague this particular institution to a greater extent than comparable facilities. Do you think the institution should be allowed to bar a particular class of employees—pregnant ones—from a specific job site? If so, based on the high risk of violence and communicable disease in this facility, what might be the implications for non-pregnant employees working at this jail, for pregnant visitors of jail inmates, or for the inmates themselves?

Clearly, the issue of pregnant officers working behind bars is a complex one, and the courts will be sorting out these issues for years to come.

Community Corrections: Female Probation and Parole Officers

To date, there has been very little research in the area of female probation and parole officers. There seems to be an assumption that the issues facing women in correctional fields transcends assignments—issues for women in police departments, prisons, and probation/parole are the same regardless of the placement of such sworn female personnel in corrections. To some extent, this assumption is probably correct: Both police and corrections are traditionally male-dominated fields in which the hiring of women was discouraged through most of the 20th century. Further, the emergence of women in all such policing and correctional environments has been plagued with resistance and harassment, and many initially questioned the ability of women to do a man's job. These issues are discussed at length earlier in this chapter. But is this all there is to say about women working in community corrections, namely probation and parole? Certainly, probation and parole represent a unique correctional environment, as officers in such assignments are sworn and work in the community (similar to police), yet they manage a convicted population (similar to prison guards). While there is scant research to date on issues facing female probation officers/parole agents, this section hopes to outline what is known.

Schoonmaker and Brooks (1975) published one of the earliest articles on female parole agents at a time when their presence was emerging in the ranks of sworn agents. In their nationwide survey of state parole agencies, the authors found a dramatic shift in supervision paradigms, with states overwhelmingly using same-sex caseloads in 1970 but allowing opposite-sex caseloads by 1974. This is interesting, as the shift suggests both the incorporation of the Civil Rights Act as well as some recognition that gender-segregated caseloads were inefficient, perhaps in part because there were so few female parole agents in the U.S. at the time. In this era, female parole agents were a rarity, and they often supervised all-female units with special needs, such as custody of minor children. In some instances, female agents were not permitted to carry a weapon and were limited in duties compared to their male counterparts; however, court rulings and the growing awareness that women could perform the duties of parole agents led to this monumental paradigm shift. Simply put, there was a growing awareness that women might be able to do a man's job.

Ireland and Berg (2007) discussed these issues with a small sample of female parole agents who pioneered the entry of women into the man's domain of parole supervision and were promoted to high rank during their careers. Many of the subjects, hired in the 1960s and 1970s, experienced discrimination and harassment similar to their pioneering sisters in police departments. These instances included subtle forms of discrimination, including gossip, being denied promotion, being given an undesirable schedule, and comments from male peers about not being able to perform specific tasks such as firearms qualification, arrest, or supervision as well as male agents. These also included more egregious forms of harassment, including defamation, accusations of sexual impropriety with supervisors or inmates, and subterfuges, such as sending female staff to the wrong location at the wrong time for required meetings or training. How then did these women not only survive the harassment but excel in their careers and gain high-ranking appointments?

Several gender-adaptive styles were identified to explain women's survival in the hostile settings of early parole. The first of these is overcompensation, in which some female parole agents exerted far more effort than was needed to demonstrate competence according to the male standard. This could be achieved, for example, by becoming a sharpshooter, physical combat trainer, or gang expert and by expressing a disdain for working with women, juveniles, and the "softer" side of parole. In this way, these women demonstrated their competence to doubtful male colleagues by exceeding the male ideal to gain acceptance, and ultimately success, in their career. Others compensated by reinforcing female stereotypes, such as emphasizing communication and care of female parolees with children. They shied away from more masculine tasks such as arrest and field activities, focusing instead on traditionally female traits. In this way, some women did not challenge the male-female stereotypes but reinforced them by filling a void within the department (Ireland & Berg, 2007). Despite these coping styles, many female parole agents did not find a suitable working environment; turnover rates in parole remained high in the 1970s and 1980s, and women were grossly underrepresented among the ranks of parole agents.

Today, women represent nearly 30% of all parole agents in the United States, and many have achieved high-ranking positions. These numbers are slightly higher than the representation of women in sworn law enforcement (police) positions, perhaps because most parole agents work for state parole agencies, which are by definition larger than most municipal police departments. Thus, a better comparison might be sworn female officers in large agencies (over 500), with women representing roughly 22% of sworn officers, or federal agencies, with women representing about 24% of sworn agents (Langton, 2010).

Since women appear to have a relative stronghold in parole, how do they do their jobs? Do they conduct their supervision tasks in a similar manner to male police officers? Is this different than their male colleagues employed in parole? Ireland and Berg (2008) found that while parole agencies continue to emphasize male law enforcement traits such as "physical presence, authoritative commands, and demonstrative control," female parole agents differ in their approach. Instead, female parole agents appear to use stereotypical female traits of intuition, communication, and relationships with both parolees and community members to exact supervision and achieve compliance and public safety. Even in supervising the most high-risk or volatile sex offender caseloads, female parole agents were consistently grounded in paradigms of mutual respect and rapport with parolees. As one female parole agent who supervised high-risk sex offender caseloads put it, "I never had a fight with a parolee unless they were somebody else's—[whisper] usually the guys' [the male parole agents']" (p. 483).

Females have established themselves as competent parole agents. Indeed, this career path seems to be favorable for women, as more women are employed in parole than any other police or correctional environment. While female parole agents have come a long way to achieving equality, however, they still face issues of harassment and discrimination in the workplace. The box on Rebecca Hernandez exemplifies this issue, below.

Case Study

Rebecca R. Hernandez v. California Department of Corrections and Rehabilitation (2006)

In 2006, Parole Agent Supervisor Becky Hernandez filed suit against the California Department of Corrections and Rehabilitation and several parole division colleagues for gender discrimination, harassment, retaliation, defamation, and intentional infliction of emotional distress. Hernandez, a career parole agent who was both a marksman and firearms instructor, was highly decorated and well respected for her innovative work with addicted, gang-involved, repeat offenders in a high-risk parole unit in Huntington Park, CA. She was instrumental in developing a Parolee Day Treatment program for parolees who were at high risk for recidivism but who did not qualify for other services because of the high-risk factors in their histories. When the administrator of her division was promoted, the working conditions at her assigned office deteriorated rapidly, prompting Hernandez's lawsuit.

In her 2006 complaint, Hernandez outlines what appears to be an unbelievable story of harassment, degradation, personal attack, and abuse at work. Her allegations are even more jaw-dropping when one considers the context: Her workplace was a parole office, and both she and her coworkers (four of whom were named as codefendants) were armed, sworn, law enforcement personnel employed by the State of California. This becomes even more atrocious when one considers the catalyst for the harassment: internal competition for a promotion.

What were the allegations? Hernandez's complaint includes a myriad of sordid details, including a barrage of slanderous comments made by parole staff (including false claims that she mismanaged funds), insubordination, continual harassment to derail her career and promotional opportunities, and veiled threats against her family. In one egregious example of these unfathomable working conditions, Hernandez came into her office after one parole officer left hurriedly, snickering with another staff member in the hall. Upon entering her office, Hernandez was confronted with a distinct smell of ammonia, and she found her chair soaked in urine.

Unbelievable? On its face, these allegations are so far-fetched, one would be hard pressed to believe these could occur in current times. Likewise, a jury was so outraged when the case was presented at trial, they unanimously held the state liable and recommended a $1.5 million award for Hernandez, although some reports indicate the actual award was slightly lower, at around $900,000 (Binder, 2009; Pacovilla, 2007).

As atrocious as these circumstances are, they illustrate an extreme example of the kinds of discrimination and harassment events women have experienced in the workplace, especially in workplaces that are entrenched in male dominance and stereotypes, such as law enforcement settings and particularly parole. The behavior of the male codefendants in Hernandez's suit, while egregious, are poignant examples of the "good ol boys" historical treatment of women in such settings. However, the primary codefendant believed to have slandered Hernandez and instigated much of the other atrocities that ensued was a woman. This raises additional questions about discrimination and harassment of women in such male-dominated settings as corrections and criminal justice. As female

(Continued)

(Continued)

staff members become increasingly present in historically male-dominated assignments, will gender discrimination come at the hands of men or women? Can we expect different types of harassment by women compared to the harassment typically inflicted by men? When one staff member entices a group to harass a single member, is this a new kind of harassment? If a female staff member harasses another female because she's a woman, is this gender discrimination? The court believed so in *Hernandez v. California Department of Corrections and Rehabilitation* and awarded close to one million dollars as compensation (California Department of Corrections and Rehabilitation, 2009).

Conclusion

Despite the gains of women in criminal justice occupations, they continue to confront a glass ceiling in terms of equal representation, compensation, and opportunity within the field, particularly policing. Women who work in these fields become a symbol for all things gender related in these male-dominated settings. At the heart of the research for each of these fields, two major themes emerge: (1) how gender can affect the way in which women who work in these fields satisfy the demands of their positions and (2) how gender affects the experiences that women have within their jobs. These factors are multiplied for women of color, whereby race serves as yet another variable through which discrimination can occur. For some of the most masculine positions, such as policing and corrections, women must fight against firmly held beliefs that such jobs are inappropriate for women. While equal employment opportunity legislation has opened the doors for access for women in these traditionally male-dominated fields, women still face an uphill battle, as they have been denied opportunities for opportunity and promotion throughout history. Despite these struggles, women remain an important presence in these fields with significant contributions that need to be encouraged and acknowledged, particularly for future generations of women in these fields.

SUMMARY

- Traditionally male occupations such as policing and corrections have historically excluded employment options for women on the grounds that the work was too dangerous.
- Early policewomen were involved in crime prevention efforts, primarily with juvenile and female populations.
- While equal opportunity legislation may have opened access for women in policing and corrections, institutional cultures and standards continue to create barriers for women in these occupations for entry and advancement.
- Women police and correctional officers use different tools and techniques in their daily experiences in their positions compared to male officers.
- Few women have successfully navigated to the top levels of their fields in law enforcement and corrections.
- As correctional officers, women are subjected to issues with job satisfaction, stress, and burnout.

- Many correctional officers prefer not to work with female inmates, as they assume that women are more difficult to work with than male inmates.
- There are more women employed in parole than any other law enforcement or correctional environment.
- Female parole agents face many of the same barriers, discrimination, and harassment as their female counterparts in policing.
- Female parole agents may overcompensate for gender stressors by achieving benchmarks of male competence, such as martial arts or firearms expertise, but female parole agents generally rely on female traits such as communication to affect the duties of their job.

KEY TERMS

Baldwin, Lola

Blankenship, Betty

Burnout

Civil Rights Bill of 1964

Coffal, Liz

Community policing

Gendered assignment

Good ol' boy network

Griffin v. Michigan Department of Corrections

Grummett v. Rushen

Jordan v. Gardner

Light duty

Male inmate preference

Masculine culture

Owens, Marie

POLICEwomen or policeWOMEN

Wells, Alice Stebbins

DISCUSSION QUESTIONS

1. Based on the research, how do women "do" gender within traditional male-dominated criminal justice occupations?

2. What challenges do women who work in criminal justice occupations face that their male counterparts do not?

3. What suggestions can be made to improve the status of women within criminal justice occupations?

WEB RESOURCES

American Correctional Association http://www.aca.org

Association of Women Executives in Corrections http://www.awec.us

National Center for Women & Policing http://www.womenandpolicing.org

REFERENCES

American Correctional Association. (2007). *Directory of adult and juvenile correctional departments, institutions and agencies and probation and parole authorities.* Alexandria, VA: Author.

Appier, J. (1998). *Policing women: The sexual politics of law enforcement and the LAPD.* Philadelphia, PA: Temple University Press.

Associated Press. (2010, March 15). Female prison guards often behind sex misconduct. *FoxNews*. Retrieved from http://www.foxnews.com/story/0,2933,589222,00.html

Bach, H. B. (2010). Pregnancy and working as a prison officer. *SFI: Danish National Centre for Social Research*. Retrieved from http://www.sfi.dk/publications-4844.aspx?Action=1&NewsId=2820&PID=10056

Baker, L. A. (2008, March). Pregnancy Discrimination Act: Guarantee of equal treatment, not preferential treatment. *FBI Law Enforcement Bulletin*, 26–34. Retrieved from http://web.ebscohost.com.mcc1.library.csulb.edu/ehost/pdfviewer/pdfviewer?sid=7cae86f0–74aa-4e54–9c24-c0e578e31899%40sessionmgr12&vid=4&hid=12

Binder, R. (2009). Parole agent settlement reaches $900,000. *Legal Pad LA*. Retrieved from http://www.uslaw.com/library/Legal_News/Parole_agent_settlement_reaches_900000.php?item=492858

Boyer, L. (2010, May 04). Former female guard at Camp Hill State Prison gets probation for having sex with inmate. *The Patriot News*. Retrieved from http://www.pennlive.com/midstate/index.ssf/2010/05/former_female_guard_at_camp_hi.html

Britton, D. M. (2003). *At work in the iron cage: The prison as a gendered organization*. New York, NY: New York University Press.

California Department of Corrections and Rehabilitation. (2009). Parole agent wins $900,000 in corrections suit. *CDCR Star—Corrections Clips*. Retrieved from http://cdcr-star.blogspot.com/2009/06/cdcr-star-corrections-clips_02.html

Chapman, S. B. (2009). *Inmate-perpetrated harassment: Exploring the gender-specific experience of female correctional officers*. (Dissertation). New York, NY: City University of New York.

Cheeseman, K. A., & Worley, R. M. (2006). A "captive" audience: Legal responses and remedies to the sexual abuse of female inmates. *Criminal Law Bulletin–Boston*, *42*(4), 439.

Corsianos, M. (2009). *Policing and gendered justice: Examining the possibilities*. Toronto, Canada: UTP Higher Education.

DiMarino, F. (2009). Women as corrections professionals. *Corrections.com*. Retrieved from http://www.corrections.com/articles/21703-women-as-corrections-professionals

Federal Bureau of Investigation. (2005). *Law enforcement officers assaulted*. Retrieved from http://www2.fbi.gov/ucr/killed/2005/assaulted.htm

Feinman, C. (1994). *Women in the criminal justice system*. New York, NY: Praeger Pub Text.

Gaarder, E., & Belknap, J. (2004). Little women. *Women & Criminal Justice*, *15*(2), 51–80.

Greer, K. (2008). When women hold the keys: Gender, leadership and correctional policy. *Management and Training Institute*. Retrieved from http://nicic.gov/Library/023347

Griffin, M. L. (2006). Gender and stress: A comparative assessment of sources of stress among correctional officers. *Journal of Contemporary Criminal Justice*, *22*(1), 4–25.

Griffin v. Michigan Department of Corrections. (1982). 654 F. Supp. 690

Grummett v. Rushen. (1985). 779 F2d 491

Harrington, P., & Lonsway, K. A. (2004). Current barriers and future promise for women in policing. In B. R. Price & N. J. Sokoloff (Eds.). *The criminal justice system and women: Offenders, prisoners, victims and workers* (3rd ed.; pp. 495–510). Boston, MA: McGraw-Hill.

Harrison, J. (2012). Women in law enforcement: Subverting sexual harassment with social bonds. *Women & Criminal Justice*, *22*(3), 226–238. doi: 10.1080/08974454.2012.687964

Hernandez, S. (2012, February 20). Deputy suspected of sexual acts with inmate. *Orange County Register*. Retrieved from http://www.ocregister.com/articles/deputy-339767-sexual-county-html

Hurst, T. E., & Hurst, M. M. (1997). Gender differences in mediation of severe occupational stress among correctional officers. *American Journal of Criminal Justice*, *22*(1), 121–137.

Ireland, C., & Berg, B. (2007). Women in parole: Gendered adaptations of female parole agents in California. *Women & Criminal Justice*, *18*(1–2), 131–150.

Ireland, C., & Berg, B. (2008). Women in parole: Respect and rapport. *International Journal of Offender Therapy and Comparative Criminology*, *52*(4), 474–491.

Jordan v. Gardner (1992). 986 F.2d 1137

Kaminsky, J. (2011, September 16). Former prison guard sentenced to six months in jail—and 10 years in the sex offender registry—for sex with inmate. *Seattle Weekly.* Retrieved from http://blogs.seattleweekly.com/daily weekly/2011/09/former_prison_guard_sentenced

Kim, A., Devalve, M., Devalve, E. Q., & Johnson, W. W. (2003). Female wardens: Results from a National Survey of State Correctional Executives. *The Prison Journal, 83*, 406–425. doi: 10.1177/0032885503260176

Kruger, K. J. (2006). Pregnancy and policing: Are they compatible? *bePress Legal Series.* Paper 1357. Retrieved from http://law.bepress.com/cgi/viewcontent.cgi?article=6262&context=expresso

L. A. Now. (2012, January 19). Female prison guard pleads guilty to sex with inmate. *Los Angeles Times.* Retrieved from http://latimesblog.latimes.com/lanow/2012/01/prison-guard-sex-inmate-guilty.html

Lambert, E., Altheimer, I., & Hogan, N. L. (2010). An exploratory examination of a gendered model of the effects of role stressors. *Women and Criminal Justice, 20*(3), 193–217.

Lambert, E., Hogan, N. L., Altheimer, I., & Wareham, J. (2010). The effects of different aspects of supervision among female and male correctional staff: A preliminary study. *Criminal Justice Review, 35*, 492–513. doi: 10.1177/0734016810372068

Langton, L. (2010). Crime data brief: Women in law enforcement. *Bureau of Justice Statistics.* Retrieved from http://bjs.ojp.usdoj.gov/content/pub/pdf/wle8708.pdf

Lersch, K. M., & Bazley, T. (2012). A paler shade of blue? Women and the police subculture. In R. Muraskin (Ed.), *Women and justice: It's a crime* (5th ed., pp. 514–526). Upper Saddle River, NJ: Prentice Hall.

Lonsway, K. (2007). Are we there yet? The progress of women in one large law enforcement agency. *Women & Criminal Justice, 18*(1–2), 1–48.

Lonsway, K., Carrington, S., Aguirre, P., Wood, M., Moore, M., Harrington, P., . . . Spillar, K. (2002). Equality denied: The status of women in policing: 2001. *The National Center for Women and Policing.* Retrieved from http://www.womenandpolicing.org/PDF/2002_Status_Report.pdf

Lonsway, K., Wood, M., Fickling, M., De Leon, A., Moore, M., Harrington, P., . . . Spillar, K. (2002). Men, women and police excessive force: A tale of two genders: A content analysis of civil liability cases, sustained allegations and citizen complaints. *The National Center for Women and Policing.* Retrieved from http://www.womenand policing.org/PDF/2002_Excessive_Force.pdf

Los Angeles Almanac. (2012). *LAPD had the nation's first police woman.* [Website.] Retrieved from http://www .laalmanac.com/crime/cr73b.htm

Mallicoat, S. (2011). *Women and crime: A text reader.* Thousand Oaks, CA: SAGE.

Mastony, C. (2010). Was Chicago home to the country's 1st female cop? Researcher uncovers the story of Sgt. Marie Owens. *Chicago Tribune.* Retrieved from http://articles.chicagotribune.com/2010–09–01/news/ct-met-first-police-woman-20100901_1_female-officer-police-officer-female-cop

McDonough, M. (2006). Pregnant pause. *ABA Journal, 92*(8). Retrieved from http://www.abajournal.com/maga zine/article/pregnant_pause/

Men's Central Jail Tour Guidelines/Information. (2011). *Los Angeles County Sheriff's Department.* Retrieved from http://www.lasdhq.org/divisions/custody/mcj/graphics/MCJTourGuidelines_May2011.pdf

Miller, M. (2010, January 14). Female prison guard pleads guilty to having sex with state inmate. *The Patriot News.* Retrieved from http://www.pennlive.com/midstate/index.ssf/2010/01/female_prison_guard_pleads_gui .html

Mooradin, N. (2012, March 26). Correctional officer gets probation for sex with prisoner. *Redondo Beach Patch.* Retrieved from http://redondobeach.patch.com/topics/Renee+Gutierrez

Mroz, J. (2008, April 6). Female police chiefs, a novelty no more. *New York Times.* Retrieved from http://www .nytimes.com/2008/04/06/nyregion/nyregionspecia12/06Rpolice.html?_r=1&pagewanted=all

O'Connor, M. L. (2012). Early policing in the United States: "Help wanted—women need not apply!" In R. Muraskin (Ed.), *Women and justice: It's a crime* (5th ed., pp. 487–499). Upper Saddle River, NJ: Prentice Hall.

Oregon Experience. (2012). *Lola G. Baldwin.* Portland: Oregon Public Broadcasting. Retrieved from http://www.opb.org/programs/oregonexperiencearchive/baldwin/index.php

Pacovilla. (2007). Agent prevails in post "sex offender shuffle" lawsuit! Retrieved from http://www.pacovilla.com/?p=31713

Pastore, A., & Maguire, K. (Eds.). (2008). *Sourcebook of criminal justice statistics.* University at Albany. Retrieved from http://www.albany.edu/sourcebook/

Pollock, J. M. (1986). *Sex and supervision: Guarding male and female inmates.* New York, NY: Greenwood Press.

President's Commission on Law Enforcement and the Administration of Justice. (1967). *The challenge of crime in a free society.* Washington DC: U.S. Government Printing Office.

Queally, J. (2011, September 2). Newark's first female police chief brings no-nonsense approach to city police force. *The Star-Ledger.* Retrieved from http://www.nj.com/news/index.ssf/2011/09 /newarks_first_female_police_ch.html

Rabe-Hemp, C. E. (2008). Survival in an "all boys club": Policewomen and their fight for acceptance. *Policing: An International Journal of Police Strategies and Management, 31*(2), 251–270.

Rabe-Hemp, C. E. (2009). POLICEwomen or PoliceWOMEN? Doing gender and police work. *Feminist Criminology, 4*(2), 114–129.

Rabe-Hemp, C. E. (2012). The career trajectories of female police executives. In R. Muraskin (Ed.), *Women and justice: It's a crime* (5th ed., pp. 527–543). Upper Saddle River, NJ: Prentice Hall.

Rader, N. E. (2007). Surrendering solidarity. *Women & Criminal Justice, 16*(3), 27–42. doi: 10.1300/J012v16n03_02

Rasche, C. E. (2012). The dislike of female offenders among correctional officers: A need for specialized training. In R. Muraskin (Ed.), *Women and justice: It's a crime* (5th ed., pp. 544–562). Upper Saddle River, NJ: Prentice Hall.

Renzetti, C. M., Goodstein, L., & Miller, S. E. (2006). *Rethinking gender, crime, and justice: Feminist readings.* New York, NY: Oxford University Press.

Schoonmaker, M. H., & Brooks, J. S. (1975). Women in probation and parole, 1974. *Crime & Delinquency, 21*(2), 109–115.

Schulz, D. M. (1995). *From social worker to crime fighter: Women in United States municipal policing.* Westport, CT: Praeger.

Schulz, D. M. (2003). Women police chiefs: A statistical profile. *Police Quarterly, 6*(3), 330–345.

Schulze, C. (2008). *Maternity leave policy in U.S. police departments and school districts: The impact of descriptive and social group representation in a context of gendered institutions.* (Unpublished doctoral dissertation) University of New Orleans, New Orleans, LA.

Schulze, C. (2012). The policies of United States police departments: Equal access, equal treatment. In R. Muraskin (Ed.), *Women and justice: It's a crime* (5th ed., pp. 500–513). Upper Saddle River, NJ: Prentice Hall.

Snow, R. L. (2010). *Policewomen who made history: Breaking through the ranks.* Lanham, MD: Rowman and Littlefield.

Sorensen, J. R., Cunningham, M. D., Vigen, M. P., & Woods, S.O. (2011). Serious assaults on prison staff: A descriptive analysis. *Journal of Criminal Justice, 39*, 143–150. doi:10.1016/j.jcrimjus.2011.01.002

Stohr, M. K., Mays, G. L., Lovrich, N. P., & Gallegos, A. M. (1996). *Partial perceptions: Gender, job enrichment and job satisfaction among correctional officers in women's jails.* Paper presented at the Annual Meeting of the Academy of Criminal Justice Sciences, Las Vegas, Nevada.

Tewksbury, R., & Collins, S. C. (2006). Aggression levels among correctional officers. *The Prison Journal, 86*(3), 327–343.

Women Police Officer's Association of America. (2007). *The first women police officer in the U.S.* Retrieved from http://www.wpoaca.com/archives/wells.htm

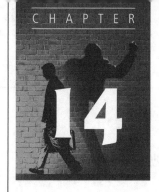

Women and Work in the Criminal Justice System

Courts and Victim Services

Tired of fighting for respect, Diana realized that her promotion to Captain would be her highest promotion within the department. She tolerated the rumors that she was sleeping with the Chief for eight months, until he took a position as Chief with a bigger department. She was left in a position as the highest-ranking woman in her medium-sized police department, which hired its next Chief from within: the male Lieutenant who was passed over for the Captain's position Diana took. She decided a change was in order; she began looking for other opportunities and took a senior investigative position at the County District Attorney's office, with a moderate raise in pay.

After successfully completing her fourth drug treatment episode, Karla maintained sobriety for five years. She earned a certificate in drug and alcohol counseling and found employment as a drug and alcohol counselor at a nonprofit treatment facility adjacent to, and contracted with, the county jail.

As both of their positions required regular visits to the county jail to interview inmates, it was inevitable that Diana and Karla would eventually meet again. For two years, they missed each another by minutes while interviewing inmates in the county jail. In her seventh year of sobriety, Karla found herself face-to-face with Diana, her childhood friend, in the official visitor section of the county jail. The two caught up over lunch, and Diana began helping Karla search for her oldest daughter, Angel, who had been adopted when Karla was just 13 years old.

> **Chapter Highlights**
>
> - The gendered experience of women employed in the legal field
> - Future directions for women working in courts and the law
> - The role of victims' advocates in rape-crisis and domestic violence agencies

 ## Women and the Law

The Feminization of the Legal Field

Historically, legal work has been a man's domain. In the 1800s, several women, all of whom graduated from prestigious law schools and passed state bar exams, petitioned the courts for the right to be admitted to the bar and practice law; most were denied. In 1869, Belle Mansfield became the first woman admitted to a state bar in the United States, in the state of Iowa (Morello, 1986; Robinson, 1890). In 1872, Charlotte E. Ray became the first Black woman admitted to the bar for the District of Columbia; she replaced her first name with her initials, "C. E.," on her application, leading the bar committee to assume the application was from a man (Law Library of Congress, n.d.; Robinson, 1890). Shortly thereafter, Belva Ann Lockwood lobbied for an antidiscrimination bill to allow qualified attorneys, men or women, to practice law in any federal court. Passed by Congress and signed by President Hays in 1879, Lockwood became the first woman to practice law before the United States Supreme Court in 1879 (Cook, 1997; Law Library of Congress, n.d.; Smith, 1998). Over the next few decades, an occasional woman would be admitted into a state bar and be permitted to practice law, with Mary Florence Lathrop as the first woman admitted to the American Bar Association (ABA) in 1918 (ABA, 2012). However, these were rare occurrences, and in practice, many female pioneers were relegated to the fringes of the profession and lacked the respectability and prestige afforded their male colleagues (Drachman, 1998). More commonly, women who made a career of law faced decades of discrimination by colleagues, the community, and the courts. For example, one Supreme Court decision upholding state rights to refuse bar admission for women read: "the natural and proper timidity and delicacy which belongs to the female sex evidently unfits it for many of the occupations of civil life," including the practice of law (*Bradwell vs. Illinois*, 1873). As Robinson (1890, p. 10) wrote,

> the novelty of her very existence has scarcely begun to wear off, and the newspapers publish and republish little floating items about women lawyers along with those of the latest sea-serpent, the popular idea seeming to be that the one is about as real as the other.

While times have improved significantly for women in this field, they still endure several challenges based on gender.

Today, women have reached near parity in terms of law school enrollment and faculty positions. Women make up almost half of all students enrolled in law school (47.1% in 2009–2010; ABA, 2009, 2012), and the majority of law clerks (51%) nationwide (National Association for Legal Career Professionals, 2010). Several high-ranking law schools have clinics and journals relating to gender issues, including Columbia's Sexuality and Gender Law Clinic and the *Duke Journal of Gender, Law, and*

Policy. Women also make up a significant presence among law school faculty. According to the ABA (2010), women make up 54.6% of the tenured, tenure-track, or visiting full-time faculty at law schools across the nation. In addition, more women are finding their way into the top administrative positions within these schools. While women are less likely than men to hold the highest office (26.9% of dean positions are staffed by women), they are more likely than men to hold the offices of associate or vice dean (60.6%) and assistant dean/director (69.7%).

Despite the increased presence of women within the legal academy, the number of male attorneys dwarfs female attorneys in the United States. According to the ABA (2012), 31% of practicing attorneys in the United States are women, with the

▲ **Photo 14.1**   A female attorney questions a witness in the courtroom.

remaining 69% of attorneys being men. Among large corporations, female attorneys are rare, with only 18% of the Fortune 500 General Counsel being women and 87% of these being Caucasian women (ABA, 2011). Research further indicates that women employed in the legal field continue to face challenges and adversity based on their gender, such as differences in pay, denial for promotion and partnership, and the challenges of balancing family life with the demands of a legal career. For example, women continue to earn less than their male counterparts, as the Bureau of Labor Statistics (2009; ABA, 2011) indicates that women in the legal field earn approximately 75% of male salaries, a drop from 80% in 2008. Contributing to this pay gap is the finding that women are less likely to make partner than men (Noonan, Corcoran, & Courant, 2008). Both the National Association for Law Placement (2010) and the National Association of Women Lawyers (2009, 2010) note this trend, identifying women as only 2% of the managing partners in the 200 largest law firms in the United States. Women are also rare among partners in general, with 80% of partners being men. Women approach parity, however, at the level of associate (45%; ABA, 2011). It is not surprising that the one area in law in which the number of women exceeds the number of men is judicial clerking, where women represented 51% of law clerks nationwide, 54% of state clerkships, and 45% of federal clerkships in 2009 (National Association for Legal Career Professionals, 2010).

Like many of the fields within the criminal justice system, women in the legal profession also face challenges in balancing the needs of their career with the demands of motherhood and family life. Within the corporate model of the legal system, the emphasis on billable hours requires attorneys to work long hours, both during the week and on weekends. The demands of this type of position often conflict with family responsibilities. For many women, this conflict results in either delaying the start of a family or choosing their career over motherhood entirely. Others choose to leave their legal positions prior to making partner or leave their positions for ones that are less stressful and afford greater flexibility.

While firms may offer opportunities for part-time work, research indicates that few women avail themselves of these opportunities for fear that doing so would damage their potential for career advancement. For those women who choose these career trajectories, research indicates that these positions do not necessarily involve compensatory reductions in workload, forcing many to bring their work home with them, work for which they do not receive compensation. Thus, these women work as much as their full-time colleagues but at fractional pay. In addition, these women often believed that a reduction in time spent in the office could ultimately affect their chances for promotion and earning potential and also fostered negative assumptions regarding their work ethic and level of commitment among their colleagues (Bacik & Drew, 2006).

As women in private law practice become discouraged regarding their likelihood of achieving partner status, many make the decision to leave their positions. Indeed, men are two to three times more likely to become partners than women and also earn significantly higher salaries (ABA, 2011). While the decisions to get married, have children, and take time away from their jobs or reduce their employment status to part-time do not have a significant effect for men or women in their likelihood to leave private practice, these variables are associated with levels of satisfaction surrounding the balance of work and family needs. Here, satisfaction is the key, not their decisions regarding family status (Noonan & Corcoran, 2004).

The majority of research on women in the legal profession lacks any discussion of how race and ethnicity interact with gender for women of color. Indeed, 67% of lawyers are White men, 25% are White women, and 8% are people of color. Research by Garcia-Lopez (2008) finds that race and ethnicity have significant effects on the gendered nature of legal work. Generally speaking, men were more likely to be assigned high-profile cases, whereas women were assigned cases related to education and other social issues. In addition, one respondent indicated that White women and women of other minority groups were more likely to be viewed as "good attorneys," while Hispanic women were less likely to be viewed as valuable professionals in their field. Here, women of color are put in a position wherein they need to constantly prove themselves to their colleagues. As one woman of color commented, "they just didn't appreciate me; [they] didn't think I was capable" (Garcia-Lopez, 2008, p. 598). In addition, Hispanic women were more likely than White women to be overburdened with larger, lower-profile caseloads. They also felt as though they were the key representatives and spokespersons for their racial/ethnic group. As another individual observed, "It's like they expect you to answer for the entire Latino population; like you should know everything there is to know about Latinos" (p. 601). Unlike other racial/ethnic and gender groups, Hispanic female attorneys did not define their success by financial achievements. Rather, social justice and helping people in their community play a key function in their concept of success and happiness with their lives and careers (Garcia-Lopez, 2008).

Scholars debate whether or not women can achieve equality in the legal profession. Some suggest that as older (and mostly male) partners retire, younger attorneys will be more likely to include a greater representation of women, given the increase in the number of women who attend and graduate from law school (French, 2000). Others argue that this theory neglects the fact that any change in the culture of the law firm will be slow in coming, due to the small numbers of women who choose to work within these types of positions and are successful on the partnership track (Reichman & Sterling, 2001). The economy undoubtedly plays a part in this parity, especially given the rash of unemployed attorneys and the outsourcing of attorneys overseas, as widely discussed in the media since 2011 (Cotts & Kufchock, 2007; Segal, 2011). Perhaps this trend, combined with the other challenges facing female attorneys today, also partially explains the drop in salaries for female attorneys from 80% of men's salaries in 2008 to 74% of men's salaries in 2009 (ABA, 2011; Bureau of Labor Statistics, 2009).

Women and the Judiciary

In the judiciary, the representation of women has grown substantially over the last several decades. Sandra Day O'Connor was the first woman appointed to the U.S. Supreme Court in 1981. At that time, there were few women in high-ranking judicial positions at the state and federal level. O'Connor began her tenure on the court as a conservative voice, and she voted with her conservative colleagues in the overwhelming majority of her decisions ("Nine Justices, Ten Years: A Statistical Retrospective," 2004). However, she was not always aligned with the political right and became the swing vote alongside more liberal justices in some high-profile cases before the court. For example, while she voted to uphold state bans against second-trimester abortions in *Webster v. Reproductive Health Services* (1989), she refused to overrule *Roe v. Wade* in this case. Likewise, in *Lawrence v. Texas* (2003), she ruled with her liberal colleagues that laws banning sodomy for homosexuals but not heterosexuals was unconstitutional. O'Connor remained the lone

▲ **Photo 14.2**   The four women of the U.S. Supreme Court. From left to right: Sandra Day O'Connor, Sonia Sotomayor, Ruth Bader Ginsburg, and Elena Kagan.

woman on the court until 1993, when Clinton appointed a second woman to the court (Ruth Bader Ginsburg). While O'Connor retired in 2005 to spend time with her ailing husband, Ginsburg remains on the court today. Recently, Ginsberg has been joined by two additional female justices: Sonia Sotomayor (2009) and Elena Kagan (2010). Their appointments mark a shift in the judiciary of the highest court in the land. Sotomayor is the first woman of color, a Latina, to serve on the Supreme Court, and the inclusion of Kagan creates a historical first, as this is the first time in history that three women have served simultaneously on the Court.

Although many scholars focus on the primacy of female appointment to the U.S. Supreme Court, judicial appointments of women at all levels of court, including both the state and federal levels, have been noteworthy. The judicial appointments made by President Bill Clinton in the 1990s made a significant impact on the judiciary, as he appointed more women to judicial positions at the federal appellate level than any other president before or after him (Goldman, 1995, in Palmer, 2001). By 2000, 25% of state Supreme Court justices were women; by 2010, this figure rose to 31% (National Association of Women Judges, 2010). Historically, the majority of female judges served in courts of general jurisdiction, not the upper-ranking positions of appeals courts. For example, in 2005 in California, 92% of women judges served in courts at the trial level, with only 8% serving at higher levels of appointment (Williams, 2007). By 2010, the National Association of Women Judges reported that 84% of women judges served in trial courts. However, this is somewhat misleading, as women represent only 28% of California state judges and 3 of 7 state Supreme Court justices, a whopping 43% (see Table 14.1). Although the proportion of male judges pales female judges at the state level, with women making up only about 26% of all state court judges, female judges across the United States are disproportionately found in higher courts today compared to just a few years ago (ABA, 2011; National Association of Women Judges, 2010; Refki & Long, 2010). Specifically, while women represent 24% of state general jurisdiction courts nationwide, they represent 31% of the judges at final state courts of appeal (National Association of Women Judges, 2010). Clearly, women are more frequently represented at higher levels of judiciary than ever before.

At the federal level, women represent about 22% of all federal judges (Refki & Long, 2010). Again, however, female judges have a greater proportion of judges at higher levels than lower levels in courts

Table 14.1	2010 Representation of California State Court Women Judges		
	Women	**Total**	**Percentage of Women**
All Judges in California	502	1774	28%
State Final Appellate Jurisdiction Courts: California State Supreme Court	3	7	43%
State Intermediate Appellate Courts: California Courts of Appeal	28	95	29%
State General Jurisdiction Courts: Superior Courts of California	423	1498	28%

SOURCE: National Association of Women Judges. (2010). *2010 Representation of United States state court women judges: California*. Retrieved from http://www.nawj.org/us_state_court_statistics_2010.asp

federal jurisdiction. For example, women hold 48 of the 179 seats as judges for Circuit Courts of Appeals or roughly 30% (ABA, 2011). As previously discussed, three of the nine United States Supreme Court Justices are women or 33% (ABA; Refki & Long, 2010). However, some research indicates that despite these increases, women may still serve as the token females on these courts, limiting the future possibilities of more women on the bench in some regions.

What factors affect the appointment of women to the judiciary? Williams (2007) suggests that more women receive a judicial appointment as a result of a nonpartisan election compared to partisan elections. Liberal states are more likely to have women in judicial positions compared to conservative states. In addition, the presence of female attorneys in the state also increases the representation of women as judges in the trial courts. At the appellate level, three variables affect the representation of women in these positions: (1) as more seats are generally available on the appellate bench, the representation of women at this level increases; (2) as the number of female attorneys in a state increases, so does the number of women judges at the appellate level; (3) states that use the merit selection process to fill seats have an increased number of women on the bench compared to those states that rely on a partisan election to fill these positions.

Does being female affect the way in which judges make decisions? In a study involving hypothetical vignettes, the findings indicated several areas where gender differences existed among judges who participated in the survey. In most of the scenarios, the female judges imposed longer sentences in cases of simple assault and were less likely to award civil damages for these cases. However, when damages were to be awarded, female judges awarded significantly higher monetary levels compared to male judges (Coontz, 2000). When reviewing outcomes in real-life cases, research by Steffensmeier and Hebert (1999) finds that women judges tend to be harsher in their sentencing decisions compared to their male counterparts. Controlling for offender characteristics, the presence of a woman on the bench increases both the likelihood of prison time for offenders (10%) and the length of their sentences (+5 months longer). In addition, property offenders and repeat offenders are the ones most likely to bear the brunt of this increased severity when facing a female judge. Similar research on gender differences in sentencing by Songer, Davis, and Haire (1994) indicates that male and female judges do not differ in judicial decision making in federal cases involving obscenity charges or criminal search and seizure cases, but female judges were significantly more likely to decide in favor of the victim in cases of employment discrimination. At the state Supreme Court level, research indicates that not only do women tend to vote more liberally in death penalty and obscenity cases, but the presence of a woman on the court increases the likelihood that the male judges will vote in a liberal fashion (Songer & Crews-Meyer, 2000).

Women in Law: Justice Sonia Sotomayor, Supreme Court of the United States

What is the formula for a fair and balanced mind? It seems that until the 1980s, the answer to that question was White, Protestant, and male. Presidents, politicians, and Supreme Court justices have primarily followed this model since our nation's earliest days. The Supreme Court, with its slow turn-over of vacancies, has lagged in introducing diversity to its ranks. It took until 1981 for the first female to be appointed to the Court, and it was not until 2009, upon Sonia Sotomayor's appointment, that an individual of a racial minority finally broke the monochromatic spell. But Sotomayor's victory was not just one for Hispanics; her journey to the highest court in the land is the embodiment of the American Dream.

The White House (2009) reports that Sotomayor was born in 1954 to Puerto Rican immigrants. Sotomayor's father died when she was only nine years old, a year before she was further diagnosed with diabetes. Her mother, now a single parent working for a meager salary, was left as the sole provider for Sotomayor and her brother. However, Sotomayor never let these events hold her back. By the age of 30, she had graduated *summa cum laude* from Princeton University, finished her legal education from Yale Law (where she served as an editor for both the *Yale Law Review* and *Yale Studies in World Public Order*), and landed a position as a successful prosecutor in the city of New York. Moving into the private sector, Sotomayor began litigating international and intellectual property cases. In addition to holding a post as a professor at New York University Law School until 2007, she served first as a district judge, then as a federal appellate judge, for a total of 11 years prior to her appointment as a Supreme Court Justice in 2009.

The *New York Times* ("Sonia Sotomayor," 2012) writes that she is most famous, perhaps, for her ruling in 1995 against Major League Baseball administrators, ending an eight-month strike. Some hailed her as the hero who saved baseball. Sotomayor also made waves as the federal appellate judge who ruled against several Connecticut firefighters, claiming that their objection to the discarded results of a promotional exam, due to a lack of minority applicants who would have qualified for the position, held no water. The case was eventually heard by the Supreme Court, who decided in a close 5-to-4 ruling that the fire department was wrong to disregard the exam results.

As a Supreme Court Justice, Sotomayor now holds the job for life. Not only that, but she is only the third woman (behind Sandra Day O'Connor and Ruth Bader Ginsburg) and the first individual of Hispanic descent to occupy the role. In her short tenure, Sotomayor has already helped decide the fate of nation-wide healthcare reform, several issues surrounding freedom of speech, and contentious immigration laws.

(Continued)

(Continued)

Holding a more liberal position in the Court, Sotomayor is viewed as a champion for the rights of the downtrodden (Savage, 2009). Women are slowly being properly included in our nation's highest court. However, due to the tenured, slow-turning nature of the position, it could be years before more progress is seen.

Women and Work in Victim Services

In the majority of criminal cases, there is a victim that has been wronged by the actions of an offender. Unfortunately, victims have historically played a minor role throughout the criminal justice process. Generally speaking, victims were not entitled to information about the case nor were they invited to take an active role in the process. During the 1970s, the fight for victims' rights began to emerge. These efforts were generally community-based grassroots efforts. One of the first programs to offer assistance to victims was a rape-crisis center located in San Francisco, California. The creation of the National Organization for Victim Assistance (NOVA) in 1975 served to bring together victims' rights groups across the nation and provide a voice to the needs of victims of crime (Young & Stein, 2004).

As the political steam for victims' rights grew, so did the agencies to provide services for victims. The organization of these agencies ranges from nonprofit organizations to programs housed within local and state government bureaus. For example, many of the victim services programs in California are housed within the California Emergency Management Agency (Cal EMA) and are divided into four topical areas: child abuse, domestic violence, rape and sexual assault, and victim/witness programs. While many of these programs receive state and federal funds, they also rely on grants and private subsidies to sustain their efforts (Cal EMA, 2011). California also has a number of private nonprofit agencies in the community whose mission is to provide support and services for victims of crime.

While women are the victims of all different types of crimes, Chapters 5 and 6 stated that women are disproportionately represented as victims of rape, sexual assault, and intimate partner violence. Given that many of the workers in these fields identify as survivors of these crimes, it is not surprising that the staffing of these organizations tends to be predominantly female. This gender dynamic brings a unique perspective to these agencies where traits such as compassion, care, and support are a critical part of their daily work environment. Given the highly sensitive nature of victimization, workers in these fields are often faced with high exposures to emotion within the context of their work. The following sections highlight the challenges that victim advocates face in the workplace with agencies that provide services for victims of intimate partner abuse and sexual assault.

Advocates for Intimate Partner Abuse

One example of a victims' services agency includes organizations focused on issues of intimate partner abuse. The decision to seek out assistance in cases of intimate partner abuse can be a difficult one. In an effort to provide increased services to victims, some jurisdictions have created specialty courts for cases involving intimate partner abuse. Here, the actors of the courtroom (attorneys, judges, and court advocates) receive specific training in domestic violence so that they can adequately respond to the needs of victims in these cases. However, specialty courts are not found in all jurisdictions, meaning that cases of intimate partner abuse are handled in a traditional courtroom setting. The criminal justice system can be very intimidating to individuals. The duties of a domestic violence advocate can include helping victims throughout the court process and providing them with referrals for counseling and shelter or other types of care (Camacho & Alarid, 2008). They may also be involved in helping victims develop plans for their immediate safety for the future (Slattery & Goodman, 2009).

On a daily basis, advocates hear about acts of physical, sexual, and psychological abuse from their clients. This emotional context means that the work of an advocate in this field can be filled with high-pressure crisis situations. Given that many victims do

▲ **Photo 14.3** Many women are drawn to work in the field of victim's services. Here, a counselor provides support to a young girl at a domestic violence center.

not seek out services at the first sign of intimate partner abuse and wait until an event of violence or high stress occurs for them, the advocate needs to be prepared for anything. These experiences of high emotional stress can lead to burnout amongst the workers. The literature on burnout for domestic violence advocates is characterized by three stages: (1) emotional exhaustion due to the high levels of stress on the job, (2) depersonalization whereby advocates can become less connected to their clients and their work, and (3) reduced personal accomplishment, which can occur when advocates question their efficacy and value of their work (Babin, Palazzolo, & Rivera, 2012).

The risk of burnout is particularly high when an advocate feels that they are unable to help their victims. In Chapter 6, you learned that victims of intimate partner abuse often leave their abusers several times before they are able to completely sever their relationship. For advocates, this can translate to feelings of frustration about their lack of efficacy in their clients. In some cases, advocates can become disillusioned with their clients and question whether their clients indeed want help. Over time, these types of experiences can impact the level of sympathy that an advocate feels for her client. This emotional contradiction can impact an advocate's ability to effectively deliver services. In cases such as these, "an absence of sympathy could jeopardize not only their moral identity, but their claims to feminity as well" (Kolb, 2011, p. 106)

Given the challenges of exiting a battering relationship, advocates often find themselves in a moral dilemma when it comes to garnering support for their clients. On one hand, they see their work as empowering their clients to make choices in their lives. However, when these choices lead the victim to return to their batterers, advocates can feel as though they have failed in their task. In an effort to continue support for their client, advocates will often excuse or justify their clients' actions in an effort to not take their decision as a personal rejection. One advocate expressed this experience in the following way: "It takes the heat off (the client) and it makes it easier, especially with abusers, to say that we made them do it, we made them take out the charges. It's frustrating but that's what an advocate does" (Kolb 2011, p. 110).

While workers and volunteers who work with victims of intimate partner abuse fight to change the social perceptions of blame in a violent relationship, even they are not immune to assigning responsibility to the victims. Research by Thapar-Bjorkert and Morgan (2010) indicates that volunteers in these agencies struggle with placing the all of the responsibility for the violence on the perpetrator. While these advocates don't place specific blame on victims, they do appear to show support for gender-normative values within a patriarchal society. In the words of one volunteer: "So I—you know—I'm not subscribed to the view that women do bring it on themselves, although sometimes I think people don't know when to stop and they don't know when to shut up" (Thapar-Bjorkert & Morgan, p. 41). Here, it appears that even the training provided by these agencies may not completely erase the effects of a culture that perpetuates victim blaming. This loss of compassion for their clients has significant effects not only for advocates in the field, but for society in general: "If clients cannot elicit sympathy from staff members at DV [domestic violence] and SA [sexual assault] agencies, they are even less likely to do so among the wider public" (Kolb, 2011, p. 103).

As a result of the emotional contexts of their work, advocates may experience their own psychological strain, or **secondary trauma stress (STS).** Similar to post-traumatic stress disorder (PTSD), STS is defined as "stress resulting from helping or wanting to help a traumatized or suffering person" (Figley, 1995, p. 7). While research by Slattery and Goodman (2009) hypothesized that exposure to trauma from clients would predict STS, results indicate that a personal experiences as a survivor of intimate partner abuse is the only significant factor for domestic violence advocates. Given that many advocates in the field have a personal history of victimization by an intimate partner, this is an important result to consider. However, research indicates that organizational support structures within the workplace can serve as a protective factor against STS. Here, the ability to be able to contribute to the structural organization of the agency decreased the likelihood that advocates would experiences trauma in the workplace (Slattery & Goodman, 2009).

Rape-Crisis Workers

Like many other victim services, rape-crisis organization emerged across the United States in the 1970s in response to the high needs of victims of sexual assault. These organizations began as community-based grassroots agencies. Initially, these organizations were run primarily by a volunteer work force, the majority of whom were women. Like advocates in the field of domestic violence, many of these female volunteers were also once victims of rape and sexual assault (Mallicoat, Marquez, & Rosenbaum, 2007). In addition to fighting for the rights of sexual assault victims, these early centers also worked toward influencing legislative actions in cases of violence against women (Maier, 2011). During the 1980s and 1990s, rape-crisis organizations began to link up with local hospitals, police departments, and other community-based services. These efforts transformed the rape-crisis agency into one with a professional identity, which changed the way that these organizations functioned. Much of this was driven by budgetary concerns and funding requirements (Mallicoat et al., 2007). In addition, state governments began to take an interest in ensuring that services were available for the victims of these crimes (Maier, 2011). Today, rape-crisis organizations vary significantly from providing crisis hotlines (many of which are staffed 24 hours a day) to crisis counseling and advocacy for dealing with the legal and medical fields that a victim may encounter (Ullman & Townsend, 2007). As organizations have increased in size and expanded their resources, they can provide a greater diversity of services for their clients, including services for non-English speakers, training opportunities for affiliated organizations, and proactive education on rape prevention (Maier, 2011). While rape-crisis work has become a full-time professional occupation for many in the field, organizations continue to rely on the role of volunteers to help serve the needs of the community (Mallicoat et al., 2007). Rape-crisis centers today are also less focused on the political activism that was a core component of early rape-crisis centers in the 1970s (Maier, 2011).

While rape-crisis workers share a common ground in helping victims of sexual assault, their job duties can vary depending on the organizational structure of their agency. Some organizations focus on crisis intervention, while others focus on the larger community goal of educating people about rape and sexual assault. The duties of an advocate can include accompanying victims to the hospital for medical services or to the police agency to file a report. They may also provide direct therapeutic care or referrals for counseling services in the community. Other advocates may help prepare clients for the legal process of having charges filed against an offender and testifying in court (Parkinson, 2010).

In addition to the variety of services they provide, rape-crisis organizations vary significantly in terms of the populations they serve (rural vs. urban, multicultural populations), types of services provided (direct services vs. community outreach), their connection to other community agencies, and staff composition (Gornick, Burt, & Pitman, 1985). Despite these differences, rape-crisis agencies tend to have a similar guiding philosophy that places victim advocacy as a central priority (Mallicoat et al., 2007).

While some agencies have utilized male advocates within their ranks, most agencies tend to present a female-centered workforce. In their interviews of 95 rape-crisis advocates from 12 agencies across California, Marquez and Rosenbaum (1997) found that 96% of the work staff was female. Here, gender was seen as an asset that created a supportive workplace. In addition, half of the women indicated that they were survivors of sexual victimization, a rate significantly higher than that found in the general community. There are several reasons why survivors of this type of victimization may be drawn to this work. Many volunteers may see working in a rape-crisis organization as a way of giving back to a community that assisted them with their own victimization experience. Others may see the work as a way to continue to work through their own victim experience (Mallicoat et al., 2007). Regardless of any personal history with rape and sexual assault, rape-crisis workers generally see their role as one whose purpose is to empower their clients. Central to this theme is the ability to create opportunities for the victim to be in control of her life—something that was taken away during her assault. Other examples of empowerment include teaching survivors how to create safe environments and how to create social support for themselves (Ullman & Townsend, 2008).

Rape-crisis workers play an important role in limiting or preventing *secondary victimization*. Secondary victimization occurs when victims of sexual assault have a negative experience with the interventions, which can further traumatize them. Examples of this include psychological distress from legal, medical, and police organizations. How does this revictimization occur? Due to the nature of police investigations, victims may experience further trauma due to the inquisitive nature of being questioned (often by different officers, which requires the victim to share the details of the experience multiple times). While the intent of this process is to document the assault in detail, it can often lead to the victim to feel as if the police are blaming them for their assault. Medical professionals can also exacerbate further trauma to the victim. The collection of data for the rape kit is an extensive process that requires significant time to collect data. Given the violating manner in which many sexual assaults occur, the process of collecting evidence from these regions can be particularly emotional.[1] In addition, this process requires specific training of professionals collecting the data. If a sexual assault nurse examiner is not available, not only could the collection of the evidence be compromised but the experience could lead to additional emotional trauma for the victim (Maier, 2008a). Many victims also express frustration with the criminal justice system in general. Sexual assault cases can be particularly traumatizing—not only do victims relive the assault when testifying as a witness, but they are often left with limited information about the case as it moves through the various stages of the criminal justice process (Kelleher & McGilloway, 2009). However, the presence of an advocate appears to positively impact these difficult events, as victims indicate that they encounter less distress as a result of their interactions with the police and medical professionals. Victims also receive an enhanced standard of care by hospital staff when a crisis counselor was present (Campbell, 2006).

Despite the value that rape-crisis centers bring for victims and the community, rape-crisis workers face a number of barriers in their attempts to deliver services. Research by Ullman and Townsend (2007) acknowledge that the misperceptions about rape by society often make it difficult to provide support for the victim, particularly given social biases about race, gender, class, and sexual orientation. In addition, the availability of resources and general disorganization of an agency can reduce the ability of rape-crisis workers to provide services to victims. Here, the first line of defense is the need to raise awareness in the community regarding the availability of services for victims as well as to provide public education about the realities of rape and sexual assault (Kelleher & McGilloway, 2009).

Rape-crisis organizations can vary significantly based on location. Unfortunately, rape and sexual assaults are not limited to larger urban areas, where increased services might be more accessible. Here, working as a rape-crisis worker in a rural community presents its own set of unique challenges. First, many rural communities tend to be tight-knit, where everyone knows everybody (and their business). The effect of this limited privacy is that issues of confidentiality can be compromised. The small community experience can also impact reporting practices, particularly when cases involve a family member or when community members engage in victim blaming (Annan, 2011). The practice of victim blaming is heavily influenced by cultural factors in rural communities. These include issues such as traditional notions about gender roles or conservative religious values (McGrath, Johnson, & Miller, 2012). Rural community agencies also have greater struggles in meeting the needs of victims due to a limited availability of resources or reduced accessibility to resources. Research indicates that a lack of available transportation is one of the greatest challenges in delivering services to survivors. Poverty also serves to limit the availability of resources for some communities (McGrath et al., 2012). Despite these challenges, rape-crisis workers in rural communities believe that their small size allows them to provide personalized attention to their clients. Not only does this individualized care allow for advocates to provide consistent care throughout the system, it can also be less intimidating to know that there are fewer players involved, which may reduce the likelihood of the case getting lost within the system. In addition, the tight-knit community allows advocates to develop close relationships with related practitioners, which improves the continuum of care for victims (Annan, 2011).

In Chapter 5, you learned about how women of color have different experiences of sexual assault. These differences are demonstrated in a variety of ways, including prevalence rates, reporting behaviors, disclosure practices, help-seeking behaviors, and responses by the justice system. Given these differences, it is not surprising that women of color have different needs when it comes to rape-crisis support services. Research by Maier (2008b) investigates the efficacy of rape-crisis workers in responding to the cultural differences of rape-crisis needs for women of color. Her findings indicate that most advocates perceive that race and ethnicity have a significant effect on the experience of sexual assault.[2] Several themes emerged from this study. First, race, ethnicity, and culture play an important role in reporting cases of sexual assault. Here, victims believed that their victimization could potentially create feelings of shame for their family members. For example, victims in Indian cultures believed that to be victimized meant that they were no longer *pure*, a high status symbol within the community. Rather than disgrace their family, the women chose to remain silent. Second, advocates noted the lack of support system for victims of sexual assault in communities of color. Here, the presence of victim blaming is significant, both from a community stance as well as self-blame by the individual. In addition, many advocates expressed almost a sense of acceptance within the community, as if to say that sexual assault has become normalized, and it isn't necessary to make a big deal about it. Finally, some advocates believed that the presence of racism in society led to differential treatment of victims of color by the criminal justice system, particularly for cases of interracial victimization. In the words of one advocate

> If a woman of color is assaulted by a White man there is almost a guarantee of hopelessness—nothing is going to happen. If a White woman is assaulted by a person of color, the whole thing changes. It is going to be on the front page of the news. (Maier, 2008b, p. 311)

Another challenge for rape-crisis workers involves dealing with issues of job satisfaction and burnout. While many acknowledge that they have high levels of job satisfaction in their work with victims (despite comparatively low salaries), they also face high levels of burnout due to the physical and emotional burdens of their work. Earlier in this chapter, you learned about issues of burnout and secondary trauma for domestic violence advocates, and rape-crisis counselors deal with many of the same issues in the context of their work environments. As a result, it is important that workers balance the demands of work with healthy physical and emotional outlets outside of the workplace (Mallicoat et al., 2007).

Women and the Academy

The criminal justice academy—including research and academic positions—has historically been a male-dominated profession. Yet the number of women has grown significantly over the past four decades. While the American Society of Criminology (ASC) roots date back to 1941, the founding members of the organization were all men (ASC, n.d.). It wasn't until 1975 that the annual conference showcased an entire panel on women and crime. While the majority of the association members questioned whether gender was a worthwhile variable to study, a small group of female scholars came together to lobby for more panels on the study of women and crime. After a few years of informal meetings and attempts to be recognized as an official division of the ASC, the Division on Women and Crime was instituted as an official branch of the ASC in 1984. Today, the Division is the largest division of the ASC, with 384 members in 2012.

As a result of the efforts of early female criminologists, the representation of gender and crime research at the annual meeting of the ASC has grown substantially. Today, hundreds of scholarly papers are presented each year on issues related to gender and crime, including panels on offending, rehabilitation, victimization, and services as well as those centered on the criminal justice academy, including such topics as hiring, promotion, and employment issues for women within the criminal justice system as well as the challenges of balancing career and family responsibilities. A review of conference presentations at the American Society of Criminology between 1999 and 2008 indicates that themes related to women and crime research represent 16.13% of the 18,911 presentations.

(Continued)

(Continued)

The top five topic areas of these presentations include (1) domestic violence/intimate partner abuse, (2) gender-specific programming and policies, (3) gender differences in criminal behavior, (4) victimization of women, and (5) international perspectives on women and crime. Other topics of discussion, such as offense-specific presentations (drugs, prostitution, etc.) and racial differences in crime were also common themes within the conference programs (Kim & Merlo, 2012).

While the number of men in senior faculty positions outnumbers women, the presence of women entering the academy is growing. In 2007, 57% of doctoral students in criminology and criminal justice programs were women. This marks a significant trend for a field (practitioners and the criminal justice academy) that has been historically dominated by men (Frost & Clear, 2007). The increases in the number of women in faculty and research positions and the proportion of presentations on issues of women and crime have led some to ponder: How does the productivity of female scholars compare to that of male scholars? Men do appear to publish more than women. However, the gender gap on publishing is reduced when we consider the length of time in the academy, as the men in this study reported a longer career history than women (Snell, Sorenson, Rodriguez, & Kuanliang, 2009). In terms of the top-tier journals in the field, men are more likely than women to be the lead author (Tewksbury, DeMichele, & Miller, 2005). However, the number of publications with women as the lead authors is growing at a rapid pace. A review of early career academics whose research is published in the top-tier criminology and criminal justice journals indicates that women make up 27% of these individuals, leading the authors of this study to comment that the future of the "most productive and influential scholars will have a more markedly feminine quality" (Rice, Terry, Miller, & Ackerman, 2007, p. 379).

Leadership by women in these academic organizations is also shifting—what was once a "boys club" now reflects an increase in the participation of women on executive boards as well as officer positions within the organization. Indeed, the recent election of Joanne Belknap and Karen Heimer as President and Vice President of the American Society of Criminology illustrates just how far women in criminology have come, as this is the first time in the 74-year history of the organization where the top positions of the association were both held by women (and only the seventh time that the Presidential role has been filled by a woman). While significant gains have been made in terms of women in these leadership positions, the representation of women of color in these roles is still limited.

As the Division on Women and Crime of the American Society of Criminology (one of two academic national organizations) approaches its 30-year anniversary in 2014, it is evident that feminist scholars have made a significant impact on the study of crime throughout the 20th and 21st century and will continue to do so.

Conclusion

Despite the gains of women in traditionally male-dominated criminal justice occupations, they continue to confront a glass ceiling in terms of equal representation, compensation, and opportunity within the field. Women who work in these fields become a symbol for all things gender. In many cases, the organization itself becomes gendered in response to its feminist foundations. At the heart of the research for each of these fields, two major themes emerge: (1) gender can affect the way in which women who work in these fields satisfy the demands of their positions, and (2) gender affects the experiences that they have within their jobs. These factors are multiplied for women of color, whereby race serves as yet another variable through which discrimination and other challenges can persist. While equal employment opportunity legislation has opened the doors for access for women in these traditionally male-dominated fields, women still face an uphill battle, as they have been denied opportunities for opportunity and promotion throughout history. In occupations such as attorneys and judges, the proportion of women in these fields has significantly increased in recent decades. While woman are represented at both upper and lower levels of the judiciary, their presence may still be as token females. In the case of victims' services agencies, the majority of these organizations are female-dominated, creating a unique environment. However, many advocates in these fields suffer from emotional burdens and challenges to gender-normative values that can impact their ability to deliver services to victims. Despite these struggles, women remain an important presence in these fields with significant contributions that need to be encouraged and acknowledged, particularly for future generations of women in these fields.

SUMMARY

- Women in the legal field struggle with balancing work demands with family life. These struggles can affect the advancement of women in their field.
- While the number of women in the judiciary has increased, the majority of these positions are at the lower levels.
- Many rape-crisis and intimate partner abuse organizations are predominately staffed by women.
- Many women who serve as victims' advocates have their own personal experience with victimization.
- Victim advocates face issues of burnout and secondary trauma that can affect not only their levels of job satisfaction but also their abilities to offer care to victims and survivors of these crimes.
- Advocates working with victims of color need to consider the cultural issues in these communities when providing services and outreach.
- Rural communities face unique considerations in providing services and support for victims of crime.

KEY TERMS

Secondary Trauma   Victim advocate   Work-family balance
Stress (STS)

DISCUSSION QUESTIONS

1. Based on the research, how do women "do" gender within the traditional male-dominated legal occupations?

2. What challenges do women who work in law-related occupations face that their male counterparts do not?

3. What suggestions can be made to improve the status of women within law-related occupations?

4. How can organizations help support women in these occupations in improving job satisfaction and limiting burnout?

5. How do the challenges for specialized populations (race/ethnicity, culture, and rural/urban environments) impact the delivery of services for victims?

WEB RESOURCES

International Association of Women Judges http://www.iawj.org

National Association of Women Judges http://www.nawj.org

National Association of Women Lawyers http://www.nawl.org

REFERENCES

American Bar Association (ABA). (2009). *Enrollment and degrees awarded 1963–2009 academic years.* Retrieved from http://www.americanbar.org/content/dam/aba/migrated/legaled/statistics/charts/stats_1.authcheck dam.pdf

American Bar Association (ABA). (2010). *Law school staff by gender and ethnicity.* Retrieved from http://www .americanbar.org/content/dam/aba/migrated/legaled/statistics/charts/facultyinformationbygender.auth checkdam.pdf

American Bar Association (ABA). (2011). A current glance at women in the law, 2011. *Commission on Women in the Profession, American Bar Association.* Retrieved from http://www.americanbar.org/content/dam/aba/ marketing/women/current_glance_statistics_2011.authcheckdam.pdf

American Bar Association (ABA). (2012). *Goal III Report: An annual report on women's advancement into leadership positions in the American Bar Association.* Retrieved from http://www.americanbar.org/content/dam/aba/ administrative/women/2012_goa13_women.authcheckdam.pdf

American Society of Criminology (ASC). (n.d.) [Website.] Retrieved from http://www.asc41.com

Annan, S. L. (2011). "It's not just a job. This is where we live. This is our backyard": The experiences of expert legal and advocate providers with sexually assaulted women in rural areas. *Journal of the American Psychiatric Nurses Association, 17*(2), 139–147.

Babin, E. A., Palazzolo, K. E., & Rivera, K. D. (2012). Communication skills, social support and burnout among advocates in a domestic violence agency. *Journal of Applied Communication Research, 40*(2), 147–166.

Bacik, I., & Drew, E. (2006). Struggling with juggling: Gender and work/life balance in the legal professions. *Women's Studies International Forum, 29,* 136–146.

Bradwell v. Illinois. (1873). 84 U. S. (16 *Wall.*) 130

Bureau of Labor Statistics. (2009). *Median weekly earnings of full-time wage and salary workers by detailed occupation and sex.* Retrieved from http://www.bls.gov/cps/cpsaat39.pdf

California Emergency Management Agency (Cal EMA). (2011). *Victim services programs.* Retrieved from http:// www.calema.ca.gov/PublicSafetyandVictimServices/Pages/Victim-Services-Programs.aspx

Camacho, C. M., & Alarid, L. F. (2008). The significance of the victim advocate for domestic violence victims in Municipal Court. *Violence and Victims, 23*(3), 288–300.

Campbell, R. (2006). Rape survivors' experiences with the legal and medical systems: Do rape victim advocates make a difference? *Violence Against Women, 12*(1), 30–45.

Cook, F. A. (1997). Belva Ann Lockwood: For peace, justice, and president. *Women's Legal History Biography Project,* Robert Crown Law Library, Stanford Law School.

Coontz, P. (2000). Gender and judicial decisions: Do female judges decide cases differently than male judges? *Gender Issues, 18*(4), 59–73.

Cotts, C., & Kufchock, L. (2007). U.S. firms outsource legal services to India. *New York Times.* Retrieved from http://www.nytimes.com/2007/08/21/business/worldbusiness/21iht-law.4.7199252.html

Drachman, V. G. (1998). *Sisters in law: Women lawyers in modern American history.* Cambridge, MA: Harvard University Press.

Figley, C. R. (1995). *Compassion fatigue: Coping with secondary traumatic stress disorder in those who treat the traumatized.* New York, NY: Burnner/Mazel.

French, S. (2000). Of problems, pitfalls and possibilities: A comprehensive look at female attorneys and law firm partnership. *Women's Rights Law Reporter, 21*(3), 189–216.

Frost, N. A., & Clear, T. R. (2007). Doctoral education in criminology and criminal justice. *Journal of Criminal Justice Education, 18*, 35–52.

Garcia-Lopez, G. (2008). Nunca te toman en cuenta (They never take you into account): The challenges of inclusion and strategies for success of Chicana attorneys. *Gender and Society, 22*(5), 590–612.

Gornick, J., Burt, M. J., & Pitman, P. J. (1985). Structures and activities of rape crisis centers in the early 1980s. *Crime and Delinquency, 31*, 247–268.

Kelleher, C., & McGilloway, S. (2009). "Nobody every chooses this . . .": A qualitative study of service providers working in the sexual violence sector—key issues and challenges. *Health and Social Care in the Community, 17*(3), 295–303.

Kim, B., & Merlo, A. V. (2012). In her own voice: Presentations on women, crime and criminal justice at American Society of Criminology meetings from 1999–2008. *Women & Criminal Justice, 22*, 68–88.

Kolb, K. H. (2011). Sympathy work: Identity and emotion management among victim-advocates and counselors. *Qualitative Sociology, 34*, 101–119.

Law Library of Congress. (n.d.). Women lawyers and state bar admission. *The Library of Congress.* Retrieved from http://memory.loc.gov/ammem/awhhtml/awlaw3/women_lawyers.html

Lawrence v. Texas. (2003). 539 U.S. 558

Maier, S. L. (2008a). "I have heard terrible stories . . .": Rape victim advocates' perceptions of the revictimization of rape victims by the police and medical system. *Violence Against Women, 14*(7), 786–808.

Maier, S. L. (2008b). Rape victim advocates' perception of the influence of race and ethnicity on victims' responses to rape. *Journal of Ethnicity and Criminal Justice, 6*(4), 295–326.

Maier, S. L. (2011). "We belong to them": The costs of funding for rape crisis centers. *Violence Against Women, 17*(11), 1383–1408.

Mallicoat, S. L., Marquez, S. A., & Rosenbaum, J. L. (2007). Guiding philosophies for rape crisis centers. In R. Muraskin (Ed.) *It's a crime: Women and criminal justice* (4th ed., p. 217–225). Upper Saddle River, NJ: Prentice Hall.

Marquez, S., & Rosenbaum, J. (1997). *Transition to outcomes-based evaluation rape crisis intervention.* Sacramento: California Office of Criminal Justice Planning.

McGrath, S. A., Johnson, M., & Miller, M. H. (2012). The social ecological challenges of rural victim advocacy: An exploratory study. *Journal of Community Psychology, 40*(5), 588–606.

Morello, K. (1986). *The invisible bar: The woman lawyer in America 1638 to the present.* New York, NY: Random House.

National Association for Law Placement. (2010). *Law firm diversity among associates erodes in 2010.* Washington, DC: National Association for Law Placement. Retrieved from www.nalp.org/uploads/PressReleases/10NALP WomenMinoritiesPressRel.pdf

National Association for Legal Career Professionals. (2010). A Demographic Profile of Judicial Clerks—Patterns of Disproportionality. *NALP Bulletin.* Retrieved from http://www.nalp.org/nov2010_demog_clerkships

National Association of Women Judges. (2010). *The American bench: Judges of the nation, 2010 edition.* Sacramento, CA: Forster-Long, Inc. Retrieved from http://www.nawj.org/us_state_court_statistics_2010.asp

National Association of Women Lawyers and The NAWL Foundation. (2009). *Report of the fourth annual national survey on retention and promotion of women in law firms.* Retrieved from http://nawl.timberlakepublishing .com/files/2009%20Survey%20Report%20FINAL.pdf

National Association of Women Lawyers and The NAWL Foundation. (2010). *Report of the fifth annual national survey on retention and promotion of women in law firms.* Retrieved from http://nawl.timberlakepublishing .com/files/NAWL%202010%20Final(1).pdf

Nine justices, ten years: A statistical retrospective. (2004). *Harvard Law Review, 118*(1), 521. Retrieved from http://web.archive.org/web/20060327053526/http://www.harvardlawreview.org/issues/118/Nov04/Nine_ Justices_Ten_YearsFTX.pdf

Noonan, M. C., & Corcoran, M. E. (2004). The mommy track and partnership: Temporary delay or dead end? *Annals of the American Academy of Political and Social Science, 596,* 130–150.

Noonan, M. C., Corcoran, M. E., & Courant, P. N. (2008). Is the partnership gap closing for women? Cohort differences in the sex gap in partnership chances. *Social Science Research, 37,* 156–179.

Palmer, B. (2001). Women in the American judiciary: Their influence and impact. *Women and Politics, 23*(3), 91–101.

Parkinson, D. (2010) Supporting victims through the legal process: The role of sexual assault service providers. *Australian Centre for the Study of Sexual Assault, 8.* Retrieved from http://192.135.208.240/acssa/pubs/wrap/ wrap8/w8.pdf

Refki, D., & Long, C. (2010, Spring). *Women in federal and state-level judgeships.* A Report of the Center for Women in Government & Civil Society, Rockefeller College of Public Affairs & Policy, University at Albany, State University of New York. Retrieved from http://www.albany.edu/womeningov/judgeships_report_final_ web.pdf

Reichman, N. J., & Sterling, J. S. (2001). Recasting the brass ring: Deconstructing and reconstructing workplace opportunities for women lawyers. *Capital University Law Review, 29,* 923–977.

Rice, S. K., Terry, K. J., Miller, H. V., & Ackerman, A. R. (2007). Research trajectories of female scholars in criminology and criminal justice. *Journal of Criminal Justice Education, 18,* 360–384.

Robinson, L. (1890). Woman lawyers in the United States. *The Green Bag, 2*(10).

Savage, D. G. (2009). Sotomayor takes her seat. *American Bar Association Journals, 95*(10), 24–25.

Segal, D. (2011). Is law school a losing game? *New York Times.* Retrieved from http://www.nytimes.com/2011/01/09/ business/091aw.html

Slattery, S. M., & Goodman, L. A. (2009). Secondary traumatic stress among domestic violence advocates: Workplace risk and protective factors. *Violence Against Women, 15*(11), 1358–1379.

Smith, J. C. (1998). *Rebels in law: Voices in history of Black women lawyers.* Ann Arbor: University of Michigan. (KF299.A35 R43 1998).

Snell, C., Sorenson, J., Rodriguez, J. J., & Kuanliang, A. (2009). Gender differences in research productivity among criminal justice and criminology scholars. *Journal of Criminal Justice, 37,* 288–295.

Songer, D. R., & Crews-Meyer, K. A. (2000). Does judge gender matter? Decision making in state Supreme Courts. *Social Science Quarterly, 8*(3), 750–762.

Songer, D. R., Davis, S., & Haire, S. (1994). A reappraisal of diversification in the federal courts: Gender effects in the court of appeals. *Journal of Politics, 56*(2), 425–439.

Sonia Sotomayor. (2012). *New York Times.* Retrieved from http://topics.nytimes.com/top/reference/timestopics/ people/s/sonia_sotomayor/index.html?8qa

Steffensmeier, D., & Hebert, C. (1999). Women and men policymakers: Does the judge's gender affect the sentencing of criminal defendants? *Social Forces, 77*(3), 1163–1196.

Tewksbury, R., DeMichele, M. T., & Miller, J. M. (2005). Methodological orientations of articles appearing in criminal justice's top journals: Who publishes what and where? *Journal of Criminal Justice Education, 16,* 265–382.

Thapar-Bjorkert, S., & Morgan, K. J. (2010). "But sometimes I think . . . they put themselves in the situation.": Exploring blame and responsibility in interpersonal violence. *Violence Against Women, 16*(1), 32–59.

Ullman, S. E., & Townsend, S. M. (2007). Barriers to working with sexual assault providers. *Violence Against Women, 13*(4), 412–443.

Ullman, S. E., & Townsend, S. M. (2008). What is an empowerment approach to working with sexual assault survivors? *Journal of Community Psychology, 36*(3), 299–312.

Webster v. Reproductive Health Services. (1989). 492 U.S. 490

The White House. (2009). *Judge Sonia Sotomayor* [Press release]. Retrieved from http://www.whitehouse.gov/the_press_office/Background-on-Judge-Sonia-Sotomayor/

Williams, M. (2007). Women's representation on state trial and appellate courts. *Social Science Quarterly, 88*(5), 1192–1204.

Young, M., & Stein, J. (2004). *The history of the crime victims' movement in the United States: A component of the Office for Victims of Crime Oral History Project.* Washington, DC: U.S. Department of Justice. Retrieved from https://www.ncjrs.gov/ovc_archives/ncvrw/2005/pdf/historyofcrime.pdf

NOTES

1. The rape kit involves collecting data from a variety of different places in search of DNA that may have been left from the offender and includes a pelvic exam, scraping under the fingernails, combing for hairs in the pubic region, and oral swabbing.

2. What makes these findings particularly unique in the field is that it involved a number of respondents who identified as a member of a minority group. Of the 18 women of color in her sample (n = 58), 44% of them were survivors of sexual abuse, providing an additional level in understanding the cultural needs of sexual assault survivors.

Epilogue

In the two years since Karla and Diana met again, Karla has learned that her mother was deported home to Honduras and lived with cousins there before her death, three years before Karla became sober. Karla's older brother is currently serving a life sentence for double homicide, and she visits him at holidays. Her younger brother died of a drug overdose when he was 17. With drug-impaired memory on the details of her second delivery, she was unable to reconstruct either the timing or location where she delivered her premature baby; she has come to accept that she will probably never find this child. Despite these painful discoveries, Karla has maintained sobriety for nine years and still hopes to find her first child, the daughter she named Angel, one day.

Meanwhile, Diana began taking law classes at night and completed her JD. She plans to take the bar exam in the coming cycle and hopes to transition from investigative to legal work at the District Attorney's office, where she remains employed today.

Glossary

1992 Reauthorization of the Juvenile Justice and Delinquency Prevention (JJDP) Act: acknowledged the need to provide gender-specific services to address the unique needs of female offenders.

Abusive incident: the second phase of Lenore Walker's cycle of violence in which the batterer becomes highly abusive and engages in physical and/or sexual violence to control his victim.

Acquaintance rape: the victim knows the perpetrator; it usually accounts for the majority of rape and sexual assault cases.

Adler, Freda: her works were inspired by the emancipation of women that resulted from the effects of the second wave of feminism. Adler suggested that women's rates of violent crime would increase.

Affiliate: a person who has a direct or indirect role within the gang; for example, a female who married a gang member but is no longer active in criminal activity.

Age-gap exceptions: also known as *Romeo and Juliet clauses*; prohibit prosecution for statutory rape in cases where the parties' ages are within a specified range, as stated in the statute.

Age-of-consent campaign: designed to protect young women from men who preyed on the innocence of girls by raising the age of sexual consent to 16 or 18 in all states by 1920.

Agnew, Robert: focused on revitalizing and continuing the development of strain theory. Agnew's modern adaptation of strain theory became known as general strain theory (GST).

Alternative to incarceration programs (ATI): a community-based service that is used to divert offenders from incarceration sentences, such as prison or jail, and provide supervision in the community.

Altruistic filicide: the mother believes that it is in the best interest of her child to be dead and that the mother is doing a good thing by killing her child.

Attachment: the bond that people have with the values of society as a result of their relationships with family, friends, and social institutions.

Baldwin, Lola: hired in 1908 by the Portland, Oregon, police department to provide supervisory assistance to a group of social workers. Her employment sparked debates as to whether she was a sworn officer or a social worker.

Barefield v. Leach **(1974):** set the standard through which the courts could measure whether women received a lower standard of treatment compared to men.

Battered women's movement: shelters and counseling programs were established throughout the United States to help women in need as a result of the feminist movements in the 1960s and 1970s. It led to systemic changes in how the police and courts handled cases of domestic violence.

Battered women's syndrome (BWS): developed by Lenore Walker (1979); the most recognized explanation of the consequences of intimate partner abuse for victims; has been introduced as evidence to explain the actions of women on trial for killing their abusers.

Belief: a general acceptance of society's rules.

Blankenship, Betty: one of the first women in the United States to serve as a patrol officer; worked for the Indianapolis Police Department in 1964; helped set the stage for significant changes for the futures of policewomen.

Bootstrapping: modern-day practice of institutionalizing girls for status offenses.

Brothel: a legal business where people go to engage in sexual acts for money with prostitutes.

Burnout: the feeling of being under high levels emotional and physical duress. This feeling is often categorized into three stages: (1) emotional exhaustion due to stress, (2) depersonalization, and (3) reduced personal accomplishment.

Canterino v. Wilson (1982): held that males and females must all be treated equally unless there is a substantial reason that requires a distinction to be made.

Child rape: also known as *child sexual assault*; refers to sexual activity between an adult or adolescent and a child. The perpetrator is generally close to the child, and the victims of this crime tend to have a higher risk of long-term physical and emotional harm.

Child sexual abuse: also known as *child sexual victimization*; is the unlawful sexual assault of a child. The perpetrators have been known to be predominantly male but can also include female offenders.

Chivalry: instances in which women receive preferential treatment by the justice system.

Civil Rights Bill of 1964: focused on eliminating racial discrimination; however, the word *sex* was added to the bill, prohibiting the use of sex as a requirement for hiring.

Coffal, Liz: one of the first women in the United States to serve as a patrol officer, for the Indianapolis Police Department in 1964; helped set the stage for significant changes for the future of policewomen.

Commitment: the investment that an individual has to the normative values of society.

Community policing: a policing strategy that is based on the idea that the community is extremely important in achieving shared goals; emphasizes community support from its members, which can help reduce crime and fear.

Cooper v. Morin (1980): the equal protection clause prevents prison administrators from justifying the disparate treatment of women on the grounds that providing such services for women is inconvenient for the institution.

Core rights of victims: vary by jurisdiction; however, the following core rights have been found in many state constitutions: Right to Attend, Right to Compensation, Right to Be Heard, Right to Be Informed, Right to Protection, Right to Restitution, Right to Return of Property, Right to a Speedy Trial, and Right to Enforcement.

Corrective rape: a South African rape myth, which holds that rape of a female by a male will correct the female's misbehavior. This crime often involves the rape of a female by her father or male caretaker.

Crimes Against Humanity: crimes that are usually directed toward groups based on their gender, race, ethnicity, or religion. Examples include human trafficking, war rape, genocide, and ethnic cleansing.

Custodial institutions: similar to male institutions, women are warehoused and little programming or treatment is offered to the inmates.

Cyberstalking: incidents that create fear in the lives of its victims; the anonymity that is involved creates opportunities for offenders to control, dominate, and manipulate their victims.

Cycle of victimization and offending: explains how young girls often run away from home in an attempt to escape from an abusive situation, usually ending up as offenders themselves.

Cycle of violence: conceptualized by Lenore Walker in 1979 to help explain how perpetrators of intimate partner abuse maintain control over their victims over time. The cycle is made up of three distinct time frames: tension building, the abusive incident, and the honeymoon period.

Dark figure of crime: the amount of crime that is unreported by victims and/or police officers.

Dating violence: violence that occurs between two people who are unmarried; teenagers are seen as the most at-risk population.

Decriminalization: allowed brothel owners to have legal sites of business, which created a tax base and revenue for the government as well as enabled labor laws to be enacted to provide safe working conditions for prostitutes.

Deportation fear: refers to the fears held by undocumented workers who are at risk of deportation; undocumented workers seek (and find) work with employers who prey on this vulnerability.

Differential association theory: focuses on the influence that one's social relationships may have in encouraging delinquent behavior. This theory also incorporated various characteristics of the social learning theory, suggesting that criminality is a learned behavior.

Discretionary arrest: police officers have the option to arrest or not arrest the offender based on their free choice within the context of their professional judgment.

Drug-facilitated sexual assault: an unwanted sexual act following the deliberate intoxication of a victim.

Emancipation/Liberation theories: lead to an increased participation of women in criminal activities; however true these theories may be, they may not indicate that women are more compelled to actually engage in crime.

Emotional battering/abuse: one of the most damaging types of abuse. It robs the victim of self-esteem. The perpetrator seeks to control the victim by derogatory name calling; limiting the victim from being social, whether in the workplace, in school, or with family and friends; controlling all the finances; and limiting access to information regarding money.

Ethnic cleansing: the killing or removal of groups based on their race, ethnicity, or religion; the tactics used to remove certain groups from their region often include the rape of women.

Evil woman hypothesis: women are punished not only for violating the law but also for breaking the socialized norms of gender-role expectations.

Extralegal factors: can include the type of attorney (private or public defender), which can significantly affect the likelihood of pretrial release for women.

Fear of victimization: a gendered experience where women experience higher rates of fear of crime compared to males. This idea is based on the distorted portrayal of the criminal justice system by the media.

Federal Interstate Stalking Law: passed in 1996 and amended in 2000; restricted the use of mail or electronic communications for the purposes of stalking and harassments.

Femicide: the killing of women based on gender discrimination. The murders often involve sexual torture and body mutilation.

Feminism: a series of social and political movements (also referred to as the *three waves of feminism*) that advocated for women's rights and gender equality.

Feminist criminology: developed as a reaction against traditional criminology, which failed to address women and girls in research. It reflects several of the themes of gender roles and socialization that resulted from the second wave of feminism.

Feminist pathways perspective: provides some of the best understanding of how women find themselves stuck in a cycle that begins with victimization and leads to offending.

Feminist research methods: largely qualitative in nature and allow for emotions and values to be present as part of the research process.

Filicide: the homicide of children older than one year of age by their parent.

Forcible rape: a sexual offense in which the victim does not give consent; the crime is usually committed by force or threat of force. The perpetrators are predominantly male but can also include female offenders.

Formal processing: a petition is filed requesting a court hearing, which can initiate the designation of being labeled as a delinquent.

Fry, Elizabeth: a key figure in the crusade to improve the conditions of incarcerated women in the United Kingdom and an inspiration for the American women's prison reform movement.

Gender gap: refers to the differences in male and female offending for different types of offenses.

Gendered assignment: job duties that were usually assigned to officers based on their gender; female officers were more inclined to receive social service positions rather than patrol and crime-fighting positions.

Gendered justice: also referred to as *injustice*; the discrimination of individuals based on their gender. This idea is often seen in the criminal justice system where females' needs and unique experiences go unmet due to the fact that the theories of offending have come from the male perspective.

Gender entrapment: refers to the ways in which women can be led into criminal activities as a result of culturally expected gender roles, intimate partner violence and patriarchal social systems.

Gender-neutral laws: have significantly increased the number of women serving time in U.S. prisons, because they assume that men and women have an equal position in society, and women's needs are not considered when making sentencing decisions.

Gender-responsive programming: designed to address the unique needs of the female offender; includes six key principles that provide guidance for effective management: gender, environment, relationships, services and supervision, socioeconomic status, and community.

Gender-specific programming: must be able to address the wide variety of needs of the delinquent girl. Efforts by Congress have been made to allocate the resources necessary for analyzing, planning, and implementing these services.

General strain theory (GST): Agnew's adaptation of strain theory; this theory expanded into individualized psychological sources of strain: failure in achieving positive goals, the loss of positive influences, and the arrival of negative influences.

Genocide: the intention to kill or destroy a specific ethnic group. This crime often times involves sexual violence.

Glass ceiling: a barrier that prevents females and/or minorities from gaining equal representation, compensation, and opportunity within their respective fields.

Glover v. Johnson (1979): holds that the state must provide the same opportunities for education, rehabilitation, and vocational training for female offenders as those provided for male offenders.

Good ol' boy network: a social network of people who provide access and grant favors to each other. It is usually made up of elite White males, and they tend to exclude other members of their community.

Griffin v. Michigan Department of Corrections (1982): held that inmates do not possess any rights to be protected against being viewed in stages of undress or naked by a correctional officer, regardless of gender.

Grummett v. Rushen (1985): the pat-down search of a male inmate (including the groin area) does not violate one's Fourth Amendment protection against unreasonable search and seizure.

Hagan, John: developed the power control theory; his research focused on the roles within the family unit, especially that of patriarchy.

Harassment: acts which are indicative of stalking behaviors but do not ignite feelings of fear in the victim.

Hirschi, Travis: proposed the social bonds theory; his research focused primarily on delinquency and the reasons why people may not become involved in criminal activity.

Hollywood stalkers: the stalking offender experiences delusions of love toward the celebrity victim.

Honeymoon period: the third phase of Lenore Walker's cycle of violence; the batterer becomes very apologetic and is often loving and promises to change. This phase has a tendency to not last and can sometimes become nonexistent.

Honor-based violence (HBV): murders that are executed by a male family member and are a response to a belief that the woman has offended a family's honor and has brought shame to the family.

Human trafficking: the exploitation and forced labor of individuals for the purposes of prostitution, domestic servitude, and other forms of involuntary servitude in agricultural and factory industries.

Immigrant victims of intimate partner abuse: do not report abuse or crimes nor do they seek out assistance for fear that they will be deported. In many cultural settings, these victims have come to accept the abuse.

Incapacitated rape: an unwanted sexual act that occurs after a victim voluntarily consumes drugs or alcohol.

Incarcerated mothers: have a significant effect on children. The geographical location of the prison and length of sentencing determine whether mothers can have ties with their children; in many cases, the children are either cared for by family members or are placed in foster care.

Independent female gang: the absence of a male gang hierarchy; this type of gang tends to experience high levels of violence as a result of selling drugs and their interactions on the streets with other girls.

Infanticide: an act in which a parent kills his or her child within the first year.

Informal processing: sanctions that the youth participates in on a voluntary basis; these include community service, victim restitution, mediation, and voluntary supervision.

Intimate partner abuse (IPA): any form of abuse between individuals who have or have had an intimate relationship.

Involvement: one's level of participation in conventional activities (studying, playing sports, or participating in extracurricular activities).

***Jail the offender* and *protect the victim* models:** prioritization is given to the prosecution of offenders over the needs of the victims; however, these models are widely criticized due to their limitations and inability to deter individuals from participating in the offenses.

***Jordan v. Gardner* (1992):** the pat-down policy designed to control the introduction of contraband into the facility could be viewed as unconstitutional if conducted by male staff members against female inmates.

Jumped in: also known as *walking the line*; a gang initiation process for girls in which they are subjected to assault by their fellow gang members.

Just world hypothesis: society has a need to believe that people deserve whatever comes to them; this paradigm is linked to patterns of victim blaming.

Juvenile delinquency: the repeated committing of crimes by young children and adolescents.

Juvenile Justice and Delinquency Prevention (JJDP) Act of 1974: provides funding for state and local governments to help decrease the number of juvenile delinquents and to help provide community and rehabilitative programs to offenders.

Karo-kari: literally "Black man/Black woman"; this is a form of premeditated killing of both male and female adulterers and is a part of Pakistan's cultural tradition.

Las muertas de Juarez/Dead women of Juarez: the group of women who are killed and tortured in Ciudad Juarez.

Laub, John: codeveloped the life course theory; his research has primarily focused on the following criminological and sociological topics: deviance, the life course, and juvenile delinquency and justice.

Learned helplessness: victims may believe that their batterer is exempt from laws against battering and that their status as a victim is unworthy.

Legal factors: have an impact on the decision-making process for both males and females in different ways. They vary from jurisdiction to jurisdiction and they can range from criminal history to offense severity.

Legalization: by allowing brothels to register as businesses, authorities are also able to gain control of the industry by mandating public health and safety screenings for sex workers.

Level of Service Inventory-Revised (LSI-R): a risk assessment tool used for correctional populations.

Liberation hypothesis: posits that female participation in gangs is increasing, which is related to an increase in opportunities to participate in traditionally male domains of crime.

Life course theory: examines how adverse life events impact criminality over time and can provide insight on both female and male offending patterns.

Lifestyle theory: developed to explore the risks of victimization from personal crimes and seeks to relate the patterns of one's everyday activities to the potential for victimization.

Light duty: also known as *desk jobs*; were often assigned to officers who were injured on the job or who faced disciplinary action. They were not available for pregnant officers until the 2001 lawsuit against Suffolk County Police Department ruled that pregnant officers were in fact entitled to light duty/desk jobs.

Lombroso, Cesare, and William Ferrero: the first criminologists to investigate the nature of the female offender, they worked together to publish *The Female Offender* in 1985.

Machista: also referred to as *chauvinistic*; a belief in which masculinity is praised and seen as superior.

Male inmate preference: women inmates are perceived as more demanding, defiant, and harder to work with, so male and female officers would much rather work with male inmates.

Mandatory arrest: surfaced during the 1980s and 1990s with the intention to stop domestic violence by deterring offenders. It clarified the roles of police officers when dealing with domestic violence calls and removed the responsibility of arrest from the victim.

Maquiladoras: assembly plants or factories that reside in another country; they are responsible for manufacturing and assembling parts and then shipping the products to the originating country.

Masculine culture: also known as the *male-dominated police culture*; while attempting to gain acceptance into this culture, females are often disrespected and harassed by their male counterparts.

Masked criminality of women: Otto Pollak's theory that suggested that women gain power by deceiving men through sexual playacting, faked sexual responses, and menstruation.

Mendelsohn's six categories of victims: distinguished categories of victims based on the responsibility of the victim and the degree to which the victim had the power to make decisions that could alter his or her likelihood of victimization.

Minneapolis Domestic Violence Experiment: helped show the decrease in recidivism rates when an actual arrest was made in misdemeanor domestic violence incidents, in comparison to when a police officer just counseled the aggressor.

Missing White woman syndrome: refers to the disproportionate media coverage associated with the reporting of missing persons; missing persons who are young, White, middle-class girls or women tend to get more coverage than missing persons who are male or of a minority race.

Mixed-gender gangs: gangs comprising both male and female members. For girls, it can often serve as a protective factor, but it also places the girls at risk of rape and sexual assault by their male counterparts.

National Crime Victimization Survey (NCVS): gathers additional data about crimes to help fill in the gap between reported and unreported crime (also known as the dark figure of crime).

National Incident Based Reporting System (NIBRS): an incident-based reporting system that was created to provide a more comprehensive understanding of crime in the United States.

National Intimate Partner and Sexual Violence Survey (NISVS): conducted in November of 1995 and May of 1996; gathered data on a variety of crimes, including sexual assault, intimate partner violence, and stalking.

National Violence Against Women Survey (NVAWS): one of the first comprehensive data assessments of violence against women by acts of intimate partner abuse, stalking, and sexual assault.

Neonaticide: an act of homicide of an infant during the first 24 hours after the birth of the child.

Net widening: alternatives are provided as a means to deter the offenders from the system, but in reality, the number of offenders in the courts increases.

No-drop policies: developed in response to a victim's lack of participation in the prosecution of her batterer; these policies have led to the disempowering of victims.

Owens, Marie: a contender for the title of first female police officer; worked as a Chicago factory inspector, transferred to the police department in 1891, and allegedly served on the force for 32 years.

Parens patriae: originated in the English Chancery Courts; gives the state custody of children in cases where the child has no parents or the parents are deemed unfit care providers.

Parity: providing the same opportunities for programming and treatment to men and women.

Parole: a correctional strategy that is applied following an offender's release from prison; involves a period of supervision of offenders in the community.

Pathways to addiction: refers to the ways in which women find themselves in the cycle of drug use. Understanding these pathways is important in designing interventions for women who abuse substances such as illicit drugs, prescription medication and alcohol.

Physical battery/abuse: can sometimes lead to murder; it is very hard to research and measure, because it tends to happen behind closed doors, and the victims are usually too afraid to report it.

POLICEwomen or policeWOMEN: the gender identity debate in which female officers believe that their gender may or may not affect the way in which they function as officers.

Pollak, Otto: wrote *The Criminality of Women* in 1961 to further explain his belief that crime data sources failed to reflect the true extent of female crime.

Postpartum syndrome: a severe case of mental illness; makes the mother unaware of her actions or unable to appreciate the wrongfulness of her behaviors.

Post-traumatic stress disorder (PTSD): having high levels of stress or anxiety that are related to traumatizing events.

Power control theory: looks at the effects of patriarchy within the family unit as a tool of socialization for gender roles.

Probation: a criminal sanction that allows offenders to remain in the community as long as they follow specific directives by the court. These directives include a curfew, maintaining a job, attending drug and alcohol treatment or other therapeutic programs, and completing community service hours.

Property crimes: a series of nonviolent crimes, such as larceny-theft, shoplifting, burglary, and dealing in stolen goods; these crimes are usually committed by both men and women.

Prostitution recovery program: a program that helps recovering prostitutes by building their self-esteem and addressing the issues that have caused drug addictions and led to their overall lifestyle.

Protocol to Prevent, Suppress and Punish Trafficking in Persons, especially Women and Children: a multinational legal agreement developed by the United Nations in order to facilitate international cooperation in detecting and prosecuting persons responsible for human trafficking.

Pseudo-families: the relationship among individuals who are not related; these relationships are common in the prison system and are often created as a means to provide emotional support to one another during their imprisonment.

Pulling a train: also known as *sexed in*; example of the gang initiation process that requires sexual assault by multiple male members.

Rape myth acceptance: the acceptance of the false beliefs held within the rape myths; this acceptance is often a contributing factor in the practice of victim blaming.

Rape myths: false beliefs that are seen as justifiable causes for sexual aggression against women.

Rape shield law: a series of statutes that vary by jurisdiction; these laws offer protections to the victims in sexual assault cases, with the understanding that female rape victims experience secondary victimization during trial.

Rape: the act of forced sexual intercourse, which involves penile-vaginal penetration; the laws regarding this act tend to vary from state to state.

Reentry: the transition from an incarcerated setting to the community; usually involves meetings with parole officers who provide referrals to receive treatment; unsuccessful reentry often leads to recidivism.

Reformatory: a new concept that saw incarceration as an institution designed with the intent to rehabilitate women from their immoral ways.

Resiliency: also known as *protective factors*; these can enable female victims and female offenders to succeed.

Restraining order: available in every jurisdiction, designed to provide the victim with the opportunity to separate from the batterer and prohibit the batterer from contacting the victim.

Risk factors for female delinquency: include a poor family relationship, a history of abuse, poor school performance, negative peer relationships, and issues with substance abuse.

Romeo and Juliet clauses: see *age-gap exceptions.*

Routine activities theory: created to discuss the risk of victimization in property crimes. It suggests that the likelihood of a criminal act or the likelihood of victimization occurs when an offender, a potential victim, and the absence of a guardian that would deter said offender from making contact with the victim are combined.

Same-sex sexual assault: oftentimes refers to male-on-male assault, due to the limited research on woman-on-woman sexual violence.

Sampson, Robert: codeveloped the *life course theory*; his research has focused on a variety of topics within the fields of criminology and sociology.

Secondary Trauma Stress (STS): high levels of stress that result from the need and/or want to help a victim; victim advocates are often affected by this type of stress.

Secondary victimization: the idea that victims become more traumatized after the primary victimization. It can stem from victim blaming or from the process of collecting evidence (physical or testimonial).

Sentencing guidelines: created in conjunction with the Sentencing Reform Act of 1984; the only factors to be considered in imposing a sentence were offense committed, the presence of aggravating or mitigating circumstances, and the criminal history of the offender.

Serial killer: a perpetrator who murders three or more people within a short period of time. Perpetrators are predominantly male, but there have been instances where a female has fallen within this category.

Sexed in: see *pulling a train.*

Sexual assault: used to identify forms of sexual victimization that are not included under the definition of rape. Laws expanded the definitions to include sodomy, forced oral copulation, and unwanted touching of a sexual nature.

Sexual harassment: a social problem that can be presented in many ways, such as verbal comment with a sexual reference, inappropriate physical touching, derogatory looks or gestures, sharing of sexually based jokes or stories, displaying of sexually graphic pictures or writings, or even comments about a person's clothing. It tends to happen in the workplace, educational location, house, and public spaces.

Sexual slavery: the use of lies, deceit, and kidnapping tactics to force people to participate in sexual acts.

Shadow of sexual assault: women experience a greater fear of crime because they believe that any crime could ultimately become sexually based; thus this theory is linked to causes of rape or sexual assault.

Simon, Rita: hypothesized that women would make up a greater proportion of property crimes as a result of their "liberation" from traditional gender roles and restrictions.

Social bond theory: focused on four criteria, or bonds, which prevent people from acting on potential criminological impulses or desires. Travis Hirschi identified these bonds as attachment, commitment, involvement, and belief.

Social injury hypothesis: posits that girls in gangs experience higher levels of risk, danger, and injury compared to their male counterparts.

Spousal rape: involves emotional coercion or physical force against a spouse to achieve nonconsensual sexual intercourse; it can often lead to domestic violence.

Stalking: a course of conduct directed at a specific person that would cause a reasonable person to feel fear.

Status offenses: acts that are only illegal if committed by juveniles, such as underage consumption of alcohol, running away from home, truancy, and curfew violations.

Statutory rape: sexual activity that is unlawful because it is prohibited by stature or code; generally involves someone who is not of legal age to give consent.

Stranger rape: the perpetrator is unknown to the victim and is usually associated with a lack of safety, such as walking home at night or not locking the doors.

Street prostitution: an illegal form of prostitution that takes place in public places.

Sutherland, Edwin: proposed the differential association theory; his research focused on one's social relationships and their influence on delinquent behavior.

Symbolic assailant: a perpetrator, often of minority ethnicity, who hides in dark shadows awaiting the abduction, rape, or murder of unknown innocents. He/she attacks at random, is unprovoked, and is difficult to apprehend.

Tension building: the first phase of Lenore Walker's cycle of violence; the batterer increases control over a victim. It is usually characterized by poor communication skills between the partners.

Todaro v. Ward (1977): mandated reforms to provide health care in prisons; failure to do so was a violation of the Eighth Amendment protection against cruel and unusual punishment.

Trafficking Victims Protection Act (TVPA): designed to punish traffickers, protect victims, and facilitate prevention efforts in the community to fight against human trafficking.

T-visa and U-visa: visas issued by the United States for victims; the T-visa is issued for human trafficking victims and the U-visa for noncitizen victims of crime.

Uniform Crime Reports (UCR): crime statistics that are compiled and then published in an annual report by the Federal Bureau of Investigation (FBI).

Vice Queens: a female auxiliary gang that was an affiliate of the Vice Lords (a Black conflict gang in Chicago during the 1960s); they lacked cohesion within the group and had no formal leadership structure.

Victim advocate: a worker who provides services to victims; advocates hear about acts of physical, sexual, and psychological abuse from their clients on a daily basis.

Victim blaming: shifting the blame of rape from the offender to the victim; by doing so, the confrontation of the realities of rape and sexual assault in society are avoided.

Violence Against Women Act (VAWA): passed in 1994; provided funding for battered women's shelters and outreach education, funding for domestic violence training for police and court personnel, and the opportunity for victims to sue for civil damages as a result of violent acts perpetuated against them.

Violent offenses: a series of violent crimes, such as sexually based offenses (forcible rape, child sexual victimization), homicide, assault, and kidnapping.

Virgin rape myth: a South African myth that holds that rape of a virgin cures HIV/AIDS; it has led to a plague of child rape by HIV/AIDS-infected men who seek to cure their status.

von Hentig's 13 categories of victims: focuses on how personal factors such as biological, social, and psychological characteristics influence risk factors for victimization.

Walking the line: see *jumped in.*

War rape: the sexual assault of women by invading male soldiers, officials, and men in authority. This act is unlawful under the Fourth Geneva Convention of 1949 and Protocol 1 for the Protection of Victims of International Armed Conflicts of 1977.

Welfare Reform Act of 1996: signed by President Bill Clinton in 1996; imposed time limits on the aid that women can receive and denies services and resources to women with a criminal record.

Wells, Alice Stebbins: the first female police officer hired in the United States by the Los Angeles Police Department in 1920; she advocated for the protection of children and women, especially when it came to sexual education.

Westernized: participating in modern-day activities such as wearing jeans, listening to music, and developing friendships.

White-collar crime: a series of nonviolent crimes, such as forgery/counterfeiting, embezzlement, and fraud; these crimes are committed by both men and women.

Work-family balance: a challenge that affects women in every profession, especially in careers that require the work to be done at home or on the weekends. The stress and issues regarding this often put females on the "mommy track" or in some cases, the females decide to not start a family.

Wraparound services: holistic and culturally sensitive plans for each woman that draw on a coordinated range of services within her community, such as public and mental health systems, addiction recovery, welfare, emergency shelter organizations, and educational and vocational services.

Zero-tolerance policies: used as a deterrent. These policies prevent women with felony drug convictions from receiving assistance such as public housing and federal financial aid to attend college.

Photo Credits

Part I. Foundations of Feminist Criminology

Photo 1.1, p. 5: Stacy L. Mallicoat. Printed with permission.

Photo 1.2, p. 6: The National Museum of American History, Smithsonian Institution.

Photo 2.1, p. 14: © ThinkstockImages/Comstock/Thinkstock

Photo 3.1, p. 32: Stacy L. Mallicoat. Printed with permission.

Photo 4.1, p. 58: © Stockbyte/Thinkstock Images

Part II. Women as Victims

Photo 5.1, p. 76: © R. Jeanette Martin/Demotix/Corbis

Photo 5.2: p. 87: © Ron Haviv/VII/Corbis

Photo 6.1, p. 106: © Photodisc/ ThinkStock images 200301578-001

Photo 6.2, p. 116: © Viviane Moos/CORBIS

Photo 6.3, p. 121: © Comstock/Thinkstock 78480043

Photo 7.1, p.139: © epa/Corbis 42-16849683

Photo 7.2, p.143: © Katie Orlinsky/Corbis

Part III. Women as Offenders

Photo 8.1, p. 178: © Comstock/Thinkstock Images

Photo 9.1, p. 196: © BananaStock/Thinkstock 79166773

Photo 9.2, p. 208: © BananaStock/Thinkstock 79166538

Photo 10.1, p. 226: © Marc Asnin/CORBIS SABA

Photo 12.1, p. 273: © Getty Images/

Photo 12.2, p. 276: © Viviane Moos/CORBIS

Photo 12.3, p. 277: © Can Stock Photo Inc

Photo 12.4, p. 284: © JIM LO SCALZO/epa/Corbis

Part IV. Women Professionals and the Criminal Justice System

Photo 13.1, p. 301: Library of Congress

Photo 13.2, p. 304: © Can Stock Photo Inc

Photo 13.3, p. 312: © Comstock/Thinkstock Images

Photo 14.1, p. 325: © iStockphoto/Thinkstock

Photo 14.2, p. 327: © Steve Petteway, photographer for the Supreme Court of the United States.

Photo 14.3, p. 331: © Lynn Johnson/National Geographic Society/ Corbis

Index

Letters following pages indicate figure/chart (f), table (t), photo (p) and note (n).

About the Authors

Stacy Mallicoat is currently an Associate Professor of Criminal Justice and has served as the Acting Chair for the Division of Politics, Administration and Justice at California State University, Fullerton. She earned her BA in Legal Studies and Sociology, with a concentration in Crime and Deviance from Pacific Lutheran University (Tacoma, WA) in 1997 and received her PhD from the University of Colorado at Boulder in Sociology in 2003. Her primary research interests include feminist criminology and public opinion on the death penalty. She is the author of three books, including *Women and Crime: A Text/Reader* (SAGE) and *California's Criminal Justice System* (with Christine L. Gardiner, Carolina Academic Press). Her fourth book (with Christine L. Gardiner), *Criminal Justice Policy* (SAGE), is in progress. Her work also appears in a number of journals such as *Feminist Criminology, Journal of Criminal Justice, Journal of Ethnicity and Criminal Justice*, and *Southwestern Journal of Criminal Justice*, as well as a number of edited volumes. She is an active member of the American Society of Criminology, the ASC's Division on Women and Crime (where she currently serves as an Executive Counselor), Western Society of Criminology, and the Academy of Criminal Justice Sciences.

Connie Estrada Ireland earned her BA in Psychology and Social Behavior in 1996, followed by a second B.A. in Criminology, Law and Society in 1997 from the University of California, Irvine (UCI). She earned her MA in Social Ecology in 2001 and PhD in Criminology, Law & Society in 2003, also from UCI. Dr. Ireland began her position in the Department of Criminal Justice at California State University, Long Beach in 2003, where she is currently an Associate Professor and Graduate Advisor. Her primary research interests are in corrections, especially parolee reintegration and service delivery, as well as the operations of correctional agencies, with an emphasis on drug treatment and gender. She is a member of the Western Society of Criminology, for which she was a board member between 2004-2007, the Academy of Criminal Justice Sciences, and the American Society of Criminology, where she is active in the divisions on Corrections and Women & Crime. Dr. Ireland received official recognition from the United States House of Representatives for her research on Women in Parole, which was exhibited at the T. H. Pendergast Parole Museum in 2005. Since her appointment at CSULB, she has published three books and fifteen peer-reviewed articles and delivered more than fifty conference presentations. Her fourth book, *Sex, Law and (In)justice*, is in progress.